INNOVATION, SPACE AND ECONOMIC DEVELOPMENT

Innovation, Space and Economic Development

Selected Essays of Peter Nijkamp
Volume 1

Peter Nijkamp

*Professor in Regional, Urban and Environmental Economics, Free
University, Amsterdam, The Netherlands*

Edward Elgar

Cheltenham, UK • Northampton, MA, USA

Published by
Edward Elgar Publishing Limited
Glensanda House
Montpellier Parade
Cheltenham
Glos GL50 1UA
UK

Edward Elgar Publishing, Inc.
136 West Street
Suite 202
Northampton
Massachusetts 01060
USA

A catalogue record for this book
is available from the British Library

ISBN 1 84376 269 2

Printed and bound in Great Britain by MPG Books Ltd, Bodmin, Cornwall

Contents

PART III   MICRO STUDIES

PART IV   POLICY

Acknowledgements

The author and publisher wish to thank the following who have kindly given permission for the use of copyright material.

Ashgate Publishing for 'Local Opportunities and Innovative Behaviour: A Meta-Analytic Study of European Cities', with A. Kangasharju and M. van Geenhuizen, in *Regional Development in an Age of Structural Economic Change*, P. Rietveld and D. Shefer (eds), 1999, 15–34.

Blackwell Publishers for 'Comparative Regional Policy Impact Analysis: Ex post Evaluation of the Performance of the European Regional Development Fund', with E. Blaas, *Journal of Regional Science*, **35** (4), 1995, 579–97.

Elsevier b.v. for 'Information Use and Company Performance: An Application to the Retail Electrical Appliances Sector', with H. Ouwersloot and P. Rietveld, *Journal of Retailing and Consumer Services*, **2** (4), 1995, 229–40; 'Information-Communications Technologies (ICT) and Transport: Does Knowledge Underpin Policy?', with G. Cohen and I. Salomon, *Telecommunications Policy*, **26**, 2002, 31–52.

Growth and Change for 'Growth Effects of Governmental Policies: A Comparative Analysis in a Multi-Country Context', with M.R.E. Brons and H.L.F. de Groot, **31** (4), 2000, 547–72.

Kluwer Academic Publishers for 'Endogenous Production of R&D and Stable Economic Development', with J. Rouwendal, *De Economist*, **137** (2), 1989, 202–16; 'Resilience: An Evolutionary Approach to Spatial Economic Systems', with A. Reggiani and T. de Graaff, *Networks and Spatial Economics*, **2**, 2002, 211–29.

Royal Dutch Geographical Society for 'A Flow Approach to Industrial Sites, Firm Dynamics and Regional Employment Growth: A Case Study of Amsterdam-North', with C. Gorter and F. Bruinsma, *Journal of Economic and Social Geography* (TESG), **92** (2), 2001, 119–38; 'A Comparative Industrial Profile Analysis of Urban Regions in Western Europe: An Application of Rough Set Classification', with F. Bruinsma and R. Vreeker, *Journal of Economic and Social Geography* (TESG), **93** (4), 2002, 454–63.

Springer-Verlag for 'Spatial Perspectives on New Theories of Economic Growth', with J. Poot, *Annals of Regional Science*, **32** (1), 1998, 7–37; 'Spatial Dispersion of Technological Innovation: A Review', with E.J. Davelaar, in *Innovative Behaviour in Space and Time*, C.S. Bertuglia, S. Lombardo and P. Nijkamp (eds), 1997, 17–40; 'Spatial Dynamics and Government Policy: An Artificial Intelligence Approach to Comparing Complex Systems', with J. Poot and G. Vindigni, in *Knowledge Complexity* *and Innovation Systems*, M.M. Fischer and J. Fröhlich (eds), 2001, 369–401; 'Industrial Dynamics and Rational Expectations in a Spatial Setting', with M.A. van der Ende, *Technological Change, Economic Development and Space*, C.S. Bertuglia, M.M. Fischer and G. Preto (eds), 1995, 238–53; 'Entrepreneurship and Innovation in the SME Sector', with E. Masurel and K. van Montfort, in *The Emergence of the Knowledge Economy: A Regional Perspective*, Z.J. Acs, H.L.F. de Groot and P. Nijkamp (eds), 2002, 47–63.

Taylor and Francis Ltd for 'Entrepreneurship in a Modern Network Economy', *Regional Studies*, **37** (4), 2003, 395–405; 'Regional Variations in Production Network Externalities', with R. Capello, *Regional Studies*, **30** (3), 1996, 225–37.

Urban Studies for 'A Meta-analytical Evaluation of Sustainable City Initiatives', with G. Pepping, **35** (9), 1998, 1481–500.

Every effort has been made to trace all the copyright holders but if any have been inadvertently overlooked the publishers will be pleased to make the necessary arrangements at the first opportunity.

Preface

The genesis of this book on *Innovation, Space and Economic Development* was inspired by intellectual challenges in the complex domain of human behaviour at the interface of the space-economy and economic dynamics. This volume seeks to offer a collection of novel contributions to the spatial-economic analysis of innovation, entrepreneurship and urban and regional development. It is being published simultaneously with three other volumes, which include *Transport Systems and Policy: Selected Essays of Peter Nijkamp, Volume 2, Location, Travel and Information Technology: Selected Essays of Peter Nijkamp, Volume 3* and *Environmental Economics and Evaluation: Selected Essays of Peter Nijkamp, Volume 4*.

The age of innovation has drastic implications for economic development in time and space. Innovation forms the cornerstone of entrepreneurship and hence of spatial-economic dynamics. The modern information and communication technology creates an additional opportunity to contemporary entrepreneurship.

This book brings together a collection of studies on innovation and spatial-economic development. These studies address the micro-economic foundations of spatial-economic growth as well as industrial development and policy issues. The various contributions cover both theoretical ground and applied meso- and macro-economic analyses of spatial dynamics, against the background of technological progress and recent urban and regional policies.

Innovation, Space and Economic Development is essentially a multi-product undertaking, in the sense that the various contributions are largely multi-authored publications. All these co-authors deserve the full credit for this volume, as they have been the scientific source of the research contributions included in the present book. Hence, this book forms an intellectual tribute to a new generation which has the task to carry research on the dynamics of the space-economy further. This volume demonstrates their great talents and offers unprecedented hopes for a promising research future in this fascinating field.

Peter Nijkamp
Amsterdam, September 2004

Innovation and Spatial-Economic Development: Introduction
Peter Nijkamp

Innovative behaviour and entrepreneurship

We live at present in the age of innovation. In a competitive and liberalized market, economic and technological dynamics has become a prominent feature of our modern world.

Innovation and entrepreneurship are regarded as key factors for a high economic performance in a competitive economy (see Acs 2002 and Suarez-Villa 2000). The unprecedented and accelerated economic growth in the past decades has to a large extent taken place in and was spurred on by the information and telecommunications sector (see Roller and Waverman 2001), through which the advanced knowledge economy could materialize. However, the fruits of the modern knowledge economy are not equally spread over all regions, but exhibit a clear regional and local differentiation (see Acs et al. 2002, Nijkamp and Poot 1997, Porter 2003, Roper 2001). The spatial dimension of innovation, production and knowledge dissemination has become an important field of study (Fischer and Varga 2003). The innovation literature shows that different analytical frameworks appear to offer different explanatory findings, such as the new economic geography, the new growth theory and the new economics of innovation (see Acs 2002). Such differences in empirical findings emerge inter alia from the role and seedbed conditions of knowledge production, the apppropriability of knowledge in a broader spatial network, as well as the filters and barriers in knowledge spillovers. Knowledge creation and acquisition have nowadays also become part of modern industry and of advanced entrepreneurship (Capello 2002, Shane and Venkataraman 2000). Not surprisingly, the impact of policy on innovation and entrepreneurship in a regional setting has recently received broad attention in the scientific literature.

Structural change and economic development is usually seen as the outgrowth of new and creative combinations of economic activity. The dynamics in this development process can largely be ascribed to innovative behaviour of risk-taking entrepreneurs. It is noteworthy that studies on entrepreneurship have shown in the course of economic history a fluctuating pattern of interest among economists. Illuminating examples can be found in the works of Schumpeter (1934) and Galbraith (1967). An interesting overview can inter alia be found in Hébert and Link (1988), who address the motives and economic backgrounds of entrepreneurship; in their rather comprehensive study they distinguish the German, Chicago and Austrian schools of thought. In general, there appears to be a broad consensus that the entrepreneurial act is pursued by a risk-taking rational businessman in a small-scale setting, who dares to choose new, potentially beneficial directions and to explore less travelled pathways. Innovative acts are not generated by formal policies, but by challenging stress situations in a competitive environment that may bring about high revenues but also unexpected losses. From an evolutionary perspective, the 'animal spirit' is the driving force in a real entrepreneurial climate.

Innovation and entrepreneurship is not equally distributed among sectors and regions. In the past two decades we have witnessed a renewed interest in the seedbed conditions for small- and medium-sized enterprises (SMEs), as it was recognized that the innovative potential of the SME sector was very high (Acs 2002, Acs and Audretsch 1990). Many start-ups appear to be small-scale in nature and hence it is no surprise that new entrepreneurship is often found in the SME sector. The current economic conditions reflect also new types of industrial organization among commercial firms (for example, network constellations) in which entrepreneurship plays a key role. It is therefore conceivable that in recent years the action-oriented concept of entrepreneurship is back on the stage with a particular view to the regional and network conditions for the emergence of innovative and competitive entrepreneurship (Danson 1995, Davidsson 1995, Deakins 1999, Foss and Klein 2002, Nijkamp 2003, Pineder 2001, Preissl and Solimene 2003, Stain 2003). Entrepreneurship means a sailing tour under very uncertain and changeable weather conditions, driven by survival strategies in a competitive and sometimes antagonistic world (see Mehlum et al. 2003, Stough et al. 2002). In such evolutionary economic developments due attention is to be given to incubation conditions and technogenesis processes which drive regional growth.

Modern economic and technological systems are indeed in a state of flux. Consequently, recent years have witnessed an avalanche of interest in entrepreneurship, in particular the critical success factors of the modern 'entrepreneurial hero' and the wider urban and regional development implications of emerging entrepreneurship in favourable seedbed areas. It goes without saying that in the recent past also the conditions that facilitate proper entrepreneurship policy or the opportunities of public–private partnership constellations have received increasing attention. Research in this field has focused in particular on fact finding, on theory development and on modelling contributions and has aimed to get a better understanding of this complex multi-actor force field. Contributions have been made by representatives from different disciplines, in particular economics, regional science, industrial organization or behavioural psychology. And in this context, the critical importance of knowledge and information in our ICT-driven world is increasingly recognized and has become an important field of study.

In both science and policy circles, it is nowadays widely accepted that knowledge is the key to success, and that explains why with the advent of the ICT revolution so much emphasis is placed on the promises offered by our modern knowledge society (see Audretsch and Thurik 1999, Nijkamp and Stough 2002). The ICT sector, in combination with drastic changes in the industrial organization, will exert profound influences on modern spatial-economic systems. These dynamic developments will undoubtedly create a new urban and regional scene dominated by the digital economy (see Cairncross 1997). The ICT sector may in principle create the conditions for a dispersal of economic activity, but the network constellations of a modern industrial system will call at the same time for close interactions favouring agglomeration forces. What we actually observe in recent years is a reinforced position of urban nodes in global networks (see Castells 1996, Preissl and Solimene 2003, Scott and Storper 2003). Furthermore, the ICT orientation of urban areas induces also a clear emphasis on knowledge infrastructure and knowledge transfer in urban agglomerations, a development which induces both centripetal and centrifugal urban development (see Kolko 2002, Smith 2001). Learning and training mechanisms in a modern urban and entrepreneurial setting are apparently the key conditions for economic performance. In a recent book, Drennan (2002) demonstrates clearly that the ICT sector flourishes best in large urban concentrations, as this favours scale advantages and human interaction. In conclusion, our world is showing an unprecedented techno-economic dynamics, with far-reaching implications for the space-economy.

The spatial dynamics of industrial organization

In the traditional regional economics literature we find already that space offers discriminating economic conditions. And also nowadays we realize that, despite the ICT sector, knowledge and entrepreneurship are not ubiquitous goods that are freely available everywhere, but have clearly geographical and institutional backgrounds. There is a recent avalanche of studies on the geography of innovation and economic progress (see for example, Boekema et al. 2000, Brons and Pellenbarg 2003, Gallup et al. 1999, Van Oort 2004). Notwithstanding the 'death of distance', physical geography is nowadays still a major determinant of competitive economic conditions, such as access to main transport and communication arteries.

Clearly, geographical space is not able to create sufficient conditions for innovative developments or novel institutional arrangements, but it is important in that it may embody necessary or desirable conditions for new forms of behaviour in both the private and the public domain. The urban incubation theory is a nice illustration of this argument. The recent interest in the new economic geography has clearly pointed out the critical importance of spatial accessibility in regard to the emergence of innovative attitudes and of institutional support mechanisms (see Acemoglu et al. 2001, Hall and Jones 1999). Such institutional ramifications are not only related to regulatory systems such as property rights or stable political regimes, but also to self-organized modes of cooperation and competition in the private sector. The main challenge from a research perspective is the identification of promising human capital conditions from a regional–institutional perspective, while taking account of the self-organizing potential of business life in a given area (see Lundvall 1999, Norton 2001, Oakey 1996). The concept of a 'learning economy' has to be mentioned in this context as well, as this notion indicates that evolution is not a rectilinear development, but is dependent on deliberate choices and cognitive feedback decisions of humans in an uncertain environment, who respond endogenously to new challenges and to creative opportunities offered by social and economic interaction. This new mode of producing and interacting is a major departure from Fordist mass production methods in the past.

Mass production in large-scale concentrations has been a prominent success factor in the age of industrialization. Labour specialization and – later on – capital specialization was a *sine qua non* for a productivity rise that was needed to survive in a competitive economy or to become a winner in a growing market. Mass production, however, creates also a high degree of path dependency, lock-in behaviour and hence inertia in large-scale enterprises, with the consequence of a low degree of flexibility and adaptability to new circumstances. In the course of history we have learned that mass production is not the only mode of industrial organization, but is also accompanied and sometimes even facilitated by SMEs which have often demonstrated a surprising ability to adopt new production possibilities, including distribution and logistics (see Marsili 2001, Suarez-Villa 1989). The fact that 'big size' is not always the optimal level of a firm has been thoroughly analysed by You (1995), who offers four explanatory frameworks:

1. *Technological:* the optimal scale of a firm is determined by economies of scale and scope as well as by the span of control, so that the optimal firm size is the result of scale economies and diseconomies.
2. *Institutional:* according to the transaction cost theory (see Coase 1937 and Williamson 1985), the governance of a complex undertaking with many activities may cause high internal transaction costs, so that it may be more beneficial to resort to the market for specific activities (for example, non-core activities).
3. *Organizational:* the type of industrial organization (for example, monopoly, oligopoly or monopolistic competition) is reflected in the market share of a firm, which is in turn determined by the price, the product uniformity (or speciality) and the managerial structure.
4. *Dynamic:* due to path dependency, lock-in behaviour, cultural environment, age of the firm and other determinants, the past situation of the firm may impact on its future size.

Although the Industrial Revolution has created the seedbed conditions for large-scale industries, the importance of small-scale activities has to be mentioned here. The existence – and sometimes resurrection – of a strong SME sector in various regions or urban districts was already noted by Marshall (1910) and later on by many industrial economists, who observed that innovative behaviour of existing or new firms does not necessarily increase their firm size. Examples may be found in many industrial districts (for example, Lyon, Solingen, Sheffield, Rhode Island), where differentiated market orientation, flexible modes of production, and regional governing institutions controlling a balance between competition and cooperation were the most prominent features. This model was called *flexible specialization* (see for details Piore and Sabel 1984 and Sabel and Zeitlin 1985) and was based on networks of partly competing, partly cooperating firms involved in production and/or distribution of goods in a given region. Innovation was the driving force of these networks, which were subject to permanent change, depending on market conditions and competition. The strong feature of flexible specialization was the high degree of craftmanship and skills of all actors involved in a clearly visible regional profile. When market conditions were changing, new networks could spontaneously emerge, so that the market positions could be kept. This industrial constellation could only be maintained under conditions of flexibility and mutual support of all actors involved.

Nowadays, with the advent of the ICT sector favouring network formation, such constellations based on flexible specialization are usually coined *virtual organizations* or *virtual enterprises* (see Cooke and Morgan 1992). They refer to organization networks that have a flexible structure, that are governed by trust and innovative spirit, and that appear to the outer world as one unambiguously identifiable and complete organization. The control and command structure is not always very clear and may be flexible as well. According to Hale and Whitlam (1997) 'The virtual organisation is the name given to any organisation which is continually evolving, redefining and reinventing itself for practical business purposes'. Virtual enterprises may have different appearance forms. Examples of this organizational model are (see Noorman 2002):

- *internal virtual organization:* an organization comprising relatively autonomous teams which can be flexibly employed (Campbell 1997); illustrations can be found in virtual offices and lean offices.
- *stable virtual organization:* an industrial model based on an outsourcing of non-core activities to a relatively small and fixed number of intermediaries.
- *dynamic virtual organization:* large-scale but flexible cooperation between industrial organizations based on ad hoc opportunistic market motives (see Upton and McAfee 1996).
- *web-enterprise:* an organization centred around a (temporary) network of experts in a given field, sharing knowledge management and information for dedicated purposes.

The advances in the ICT sector have of course induced the transition to virtual network activity. It is clear that a wide variety of virtual enterprises is emerging nowadays. Their common feature is the trend to shorten the product life-cycles, to be subject to permanent innovation pressure, to be information-oriented, to be driven by high quality targets (*zero defect*), to operate in non-hierarchical modes, to be market-oriented through learning-by-using interactions and to take care of the entire value chain (see Morgan 1991).

The governance of such a complex network organization is fraught with many problems, as innovative behaviour cannot so much be steered by policy. But policy can create support mechanisms through which self-reliance, self-esteem and confidence may be shaped. This requires in particular proper administrative support systems that favour business trust via non-bureaucratic, flexible and tailor-made governance initiatives.

Despite much variety, we observe in almost all cases a decentralized mechanism for governing cooperative relationships. Cooperation becomes volatile, but needs rules and trust. Consequently, the principle of trust has become a popular concept; it is less based on emotion but rather on economic rationality which may be more transaction-specific (Dasgupta 1988, Granovetter 1985, Linders et al. 2004). Consequently, there may be a need for more institutional support systems or various forms of institutional embeddedness in order to prevent destruction of human capital for ad hoc purposes (see Hagen and Choe 1998). This brings us to a major issue for public policy: is a non-formal public–private governance mechanism feasible that ensures the public interest (for example, a stable regional development) and enhances private performance (for example, innovative behaviour)? Availability of resources, smart infrastructure and proper education and training systems, accompanied by close interactions between the business world and the public sector are critical success factors in this context (see Stough 2003). It goes without saying that the spatial context of innovation and entrepreneurship needs an intensive research effort in order to understand the complex mechanism of regional and urban economic development.

A cross-sectional overview

The present volume brings together a collection of studies in the area of business innovation, entrepreneurial climate, micro-economic growth theory and public policy. The various contributions in this book are the result of joint research undertaken with many creative young scholars, who were fascinated by the scientific challenges inherent in the dynamics of our complex space-economy.

The first part of this volume comprises publications which are more theoretical in nature. They address issues like the micro-economic foundation of spatial development (in particular, in the context of endogenous growth theory), the relevance of spatial innovation and urban incubation theory (including the modern infrastructural perspective), the role of networks and new spatial policy constellations for entrepreneurial behaviour, and the importance of novel evolutionary perspectives (for example, spatial resilience) for understanding regional economic dynamics.

The second part of this book focuses the attention on empirical macro and meso (in particular, regional) dimensions of economic development. This part deals inter alia with the economic growth impact of public policy seen from a comparative perspective, the identification of local critical success factors for innovations, the importance of network externalities for regional growth and the implications of the rational expectations paradigm for industrial dynamics.

In the third part of this volume the focus is put on empirical micro-economic studies of economic performance. This part contains amongst others studies on the effect of information use for business performance, the role of innovation and entrepreneurship for the economic potential of the SME sector, the reliability of accurate sectoral forecasts for business performance, and the importance of local facilitating conditions such as industrial sites for local dynamics.

The final part of the present volume puts the emphasis on the scope and effect of public policy for spatial-economic performance. The following issues are dealt with in particular: the role of ICT policy in a spatial setting, the importance of regional industrial policy in a competitive international environment, the new potential of urban sustainability policy, the impact of European regional development policy on the growth of regions, and the relevance of policies favouring the learning capabilities of regions.

All these studies illustrate the wealth of a thorough economic analysis in the innovation and growth field, and set the stage for novel, promising and more sophisticated applied research in this fascinating scientific domain.

References

Acemoglu, D., S. Johnson and J.A. Robinson (2001), 'The Colonial Origins of Comparative Development', *American Economic Review*, **91** (5), pp. 1369–401.

Acs, Z.J. and D.B. Audretsch (1990), *Innovation and Small Firms*, Cambridge, MA: MIT Press.

Acs, Z.J., F.R. FitzRoy and I. Smith (2002), 'High-Technology Employment and R&D in Cities: Heterogeneity vs. Specialization', *Annals of Regional Science*, **36** (3), pp. 373–96.

Acs, Z.J. (2002), *Innovation and the Growth of Cities*, Cheltenham: Edward Elgar.

Audretsch, D.B. and A.R. Thurik (eds) (1999), *Innovation, Industry Evolution and Employment*, Cambridge: Cambridge University Press.

Boekema, F., K. Morgan, S. Bakkers and R. Rutten (eds) (2000), *Knowledge, Innovation and Economic Growth*, Cheltenham: Edward Elgar.

Brons, M. and P.H. Pellenbarg (2003), 'Economy, Culture and Entrepreneurship in a Spatial Context', *Spatial Aspects of Entrepreneurship*, T. Marszal (ed.), Warsaw: Polish Academy of Sciences, pp. 11–36.

Cairncross, F. (1997), *The Death of Distance*, Boston, MA: Harvard Business School Press.
Campbell, A. (1997), *Knowledge Management in the Virtual Enterprise, Proceedings of the Second International Workshop on Telework*, J. Jackson and J.V.D. van der Wielen (eds), pp. 15–25.
Capello, R. (2002), 'Entrepreneurship and Spatial Externalities: Theory and Measurement', *Annals of Regional Science*, **36** (3), pp. 387–402.
Castells, M. (1996), *The Rise of the Network Society*, Oxford: Blackwell.
Coase, R.H. (1937), 'Some Notes on Monopoly Price', *Review of Economic Studies*, **5** (1), pp. 17–31.
Cooke and Morgan (1993), 'The Network Paradigm: New Departures in Corporate and Regional Development', *Environment and Planning D: Society and Space*, **11**, pp. 543–64.
Danson, M.W. (1995), 'New Firm Formation and Regional Economic Development', *Small Business Economics*, **7**, pp. 81–7.
Dasgupta, P. (1988), 'Trust as a Commodity', *Trust; Making and Breaking Cooperative Relations*, D. Gambetta (ed.), pp. 49–72.
Davidsson, P. (1995), 'Culture Structure and Regional Levels of Entrepreneurship', *Entrepreneurship and Regional Development*, **7**, pp. 41–62.
Deakins, D. (1999), *Entrepreneurship and Small Firms*, London: McGraw Hill.
Drennan, M.P. (2002), *The Information Economy and American Cities*, Baltimore: Johns Hopkins University Press.
Fischer, M.M. and A. Varga (2003), 'Spatial Knowledge Spillovers and University Research', *Annals of Regional Science*, **37** (2), pp. 303–22.
Foss, N.J. and P.G. Klein (eds) (2002), *Entrepreneurship and the Firm*, Cheltenham: Edward Elgar.
Galbraith, J.K. (1967), *The New Industrial State*, London: Routledge.
Gallup, J.L., J.D. Sachs and A.D. Mellinger (1999), *Geography and Economic Development*, Washington, DC: National Bureau of Economic Research, Working Paper no. 6849.
Granovetter, M.S. (1985), 'Economic Action and Social Structure, The Problem of Embeddedness', *American Journal of Sociology*, no. 91, pp. 481–510.
Hagen, J.M. and S. Choe (1998), 'Trust in Japanese Interfirm Relations: Institutional Sanctions Matter', *Academy of Management Review*, no. 23, pp. 589–600.
Hale, R. and P. Whitlam (1997), *Towards the Virtual Organization*, London: McGraw-Hill.
Hall, R.E. and C. Jones (1999), 'Why Do Some Countries Produce So Much More Output per Head than Others?', *Quarterly Journal of Economics*, **10**, pp. 463–83.
Hébert, R.F. and A.N. Link (1988), *The Entrepreneur, Mainstream Views and Radical Critiques*, New York: Praeger.
Kolko, J. (2002), 'Silicon Mountains, Silicon Molehills: Geographic Concentration and Convergence of Internet Industries in the US', *Information Economics and Policy*, **14**, pp. 211–32.
Linders, G.J., H. de Groot and P. Nijkamp (2004), 'Economic Development, Institutions and Trust', *Festschrift in Honour of Jan Lambooy*, Dordrecht: Kluwer (forthcoming).
Lundvall, B.-A. (1999), 'Technology Policy in the Learning Economy', *Innovation Policy in a Global Economy*, D. Archibugi, J. Howells and J. Michie (eds), Cambridge: Cambridge University Press, pp. 19–34.
Marshall, A. (1910), *Principles of Economics*, London: Macmillan.
Marsili, O. (2001), *The Anatomy and Evolution of Industries*, Cheltenham: Edward Elgar.
Mehlum, H., K. Moene and R. Torvik (2003), 'Predator or Prey? Parasitic Enterprises in Economic Development', *European Economic Review*, **47** (2), pp. 275–94..
Morgan, K. (1991), 'Competition and Collaboration in Electronics: What are the Prospects for Britain?', *Environment and Planning A*, no. 23, pp. 1459–82.
Nijkamp, P. and J. Poot (1997), 'Endogenous Technological Change, Long Run Growth and Spatial Interdependence: a Survey', *Innovative Behavior in Time and Space*, C. Bertuglia, S. Lombardi and P. Nijkamp (eds), Heidelberg: Springer, pp. 213–38.
Nijkamp, P. and R. Stough (eds) (2002), 'Entrepreneurship and Regional Economic Development', *Special Issue, Annals of Regional Science*, **36** (3).
Nijkamp, P. (2003), 'Entrepreneurship in a Modern Network Economy', *Regional Studies*, **37** (4), pp. 395–405.
Noorman, J. (2002), *Flexibele Specialisatie en Virtuele Organisaties*, MA Thesis, Amsterdam: Free University.
Norton, R.D. (2001), *Creating the New Economy*, Cheltenham: Edward Elgar.
Oakey, R. (ed.) (1996), *New Technology-Based Firms in the 1990s*, London: Paul Chapman.
Oort, F.G. van (2004), *Urban Growth and Innovation*, Aldershot, UK: Ashgate.
Pineder, M. (2001), *Entrepreneurial Competition and Industrial Location*, Cheltenham: Edward Elgar.
Piore, M.J. and C.F. Sabel (1984), *The Second Industrial Divide: Possibilities for Prosperity*, New York: Basic Books.
Porter, M. (2003), 'The Economic Performance of Regions', *Regional Studies*, **37** (6/7), pp. 549–78.

Preissl, B. and L. Solimene (2003), *The Dynamics of Clusters and Innovation*, Berlin: Springer-Verlag.

Roller, L. and L. Waverman (2001), 'Telecommunications Infrastructure and Economic Development: a Simultaneous Approach', *American Economic Review*, **91**, pp. 909–23.

Roper, S. (2001), 'Innovation, Networks and Plant Location: Some Evidence for Ireland', *Regional Studies*, **36** (3), pp. 373–86.

Sabel, C.F. and J. Zeitlin (1985), 'Historical Alternatives to Mass Production: Politics, Markets and Technology in Nineteenth Century Industrialization', *Past and Present*, no. 108, pp. 133–76.

Schumpeter, J.A. (1934), *The Theory of Economic Development*, Cambridge, MA: Harvard University Press.

Scott, A.J. and M. Storper (2003), 'Regions, Globalization, Development', *Regional Studies*, **37** (6/7), pp. 579–94.

Shane S. and A. Venkataraman (2000), 'The Promise of Entrepreneurship as a Field of Research', *Academy of Management Review*, **25**, pp. 217–26.

Smith, M.P. (2001), *Transnational Urbanism: Locating Globalization*, Oxford: Blackwell.

Stam, E. (2003), *Why Butterflies Don't Leave*, PhD Thesis, University of Utrecht.

Stough, R., R. Kukkarni and J. Paelinck (2002), 'ICT and Knowledge Challenges for Entrepreneurs in Regional Economic Development', *The Emergence of the Knowledge Economy. A Regional Perspective*, Z.J. Acs, H.L.F. de Groot and P. Nijkamp (eds), Berlin: Springer-Verlag, pp. 195–214.

Stough, R. (2003), 'Strategic Management of Places and Policy', *Annals of Regional Science*, **37** (2), pp. 179–202.

Suarez-Villa, L. (2000), *Invention and the Rise of Technocapitalism*, New York: Rowman & Littlefield.

Suarez-Villa, L. (1989), *The Evolution of Regional Economies*, New York: Praeger.

Upton, D.M. and A. McAfee (1996), 'The Real Virtual Factory', *Harvard Business Review*, July–August, p. 199.

Williamson, O. (1985), *The Economic Institutions of Capitalism*, New York: The Free Press.

You, J. (1995), 'Critical Survey: Small Firms in Economic Theory', *Cambridge Journal of Economics*, **20**, pp. 441–62.

PART I

THEORY

Ann Reg Sci (1998) 32:7–37

—— The Annals of ——
Regional Science
© Springer-Verlag 1998

Spatial perspectives on new theories of economic growth *

Peter Nijkamp[1], Jacques Poot[2]

[1] Department of Spatial Economics, Free University Amsterdam, De Boelelaan 1105,
1081 HV Amsterdam, The Netherlands
(Tel.: +31-20-4 44 60 94; Fax: +31-20-4 44 60 04; e-mail: pnijkamp@econ.vu.nl)
[2] School of Economics and Finance, Victoria University of Wellington, P.O. Box 600,
Wellington, New Zealand
(Tel.: +64-4-4 72 10 00; Fax: +64-4-4 95 50 14; e-mail: jacques.poot@vuw.ac.nz)

Abstract. A new wave of interest in long-run economic growth emerged since the late 1980s. This paper uses a simple model to illustrate how technological change can be endogenised in macroeconomic theories of growth and then surveys how – through factor mobility, the diffusion of innovations and trade – spatial interdependence in a system of regions can influence technological change and growth. Endogenous technological change generates in our illustrative model long-run steady-state growth in a closed economy. However, it turns out that the dynamic impact of spatial interdependence depends on the specification of the model. Spatial convergence, a steady state with persisting spatial differences in growth rates and unstable growth are all theoretically possible. Issues relating to the role of aggregate demand and policy also receive attention. There is much scope for further theoretical and empirical work on endogenous growth in a spatial-economic context, while a better integration of micro and macro level approaches is also desirable.

1. Introduction

The spatial-economic landscape exhibits a panorama of changing hills and valleys of welfare levels. Why growth rates differ between nations, or regions, is a fundamental question which has intrigued economists ever since Adam Smith's (1776) "Inquiry into the nature and causes of the wealth of nations". Research on the subject, however, has not been at a steady pace during the past two centuries. Instead, there have been several waves of in-

---

* This is a revised version of a paper presented at the international seminar on Endogenous Growth and the Space Economy, 19–20 December 1996. Tinbergen Institute, Amsterdam. This paper was written while Poot was Visiting Professor at the Institute of Policy and Planning Sciences of the University of Tsukuba, Japan. The hospitality of the Institute is gratefully acknowledged.

terest. Temporal and spatial differences in the standard of living were important issues for classical economists such as Adam Smith, Malthus (1798) and Ricardo (1817). Except for Marx's (1867) alternative interpretation of the driving forces in long-term capitalist accumulation, further major theorising did not occur until the 20th century. During the first half of this century, Schumpeter (1934) laid the foundations for recent insights into the role of technological change and entrepreneurial competition in long-run development, while Harrod (1939) and, independently, Domar (1946) studied the growth of a Keynesian economy. In their model, the long run growth path would be likely to exhibit either growing unemployment or accelerating inflation.

The second half of this century has seen two major waves of interest in the macroeconomics of growth. The first of these commenced with the seminal articles by Solow (1956) and Swan (1956), whose neoclassical growth model provided a more plausible description of the long-term path of the economy than the Harrod-Domar model. Yet the major weakness of the standard neoclassical model, and of the wave of theoretical contributions which built upon it, was that it did not provide an explanation for the actual "engines" of long-run growth in income per worker, although its predictions were consistent with several stylised facts of economic development.

The reason for this deficiency was not that economists were ignorant about the causes of spatial or temporal differences in long-run growth rates but, instead, that causes of productivity improvements such as innovation, economies of scale and learning-by-doing had effects on the economy which violated the assumptions of perfect competition and constant returns to scale. As Krugman (1995) argued, the theoretical tools were not yet available in the 1950s to study such phenomena of increasing returns and imperfect competition within the accepted axiomatic neoclassical framework. Consequently, policy makers requiring advice on how to improve national and regional growth rates needed to look elsewhere and the fields of development economics and regional economics emerged respectively as more pragmatic responses to fill this vacuum. Thus, theoretical and empirical models of regional growth could build upon the idea of growth poles (Perroux 1955) or cumulative causation (Myrdal 1957; Kaldor 1970).

When several North-American macroeconomists returned to the issue of long-run growth in the mid 1980s, now with new tools to formulate equilibrium models with increasing returns and imperfectly competitive sectors, a revival of the field emerged starting with the influential articles by Paul Romer (1986) and Robert Lucas (1988). This literature describes macroeconomic outcomes in terms of microfoundations such as an intertemporal optimisation of consumption by rational and forward-looking households. However, the essence of this idea itself goes back to Ramsey (1928) and was earlier applied to growth modelling by Cass (1965) and Koopmans (1965).

Parallel to the development of the new theoretical explanations, a vast literature on the empirics of growth emerged, commencing with the contribution of Kormendi and Meguire (1985). Here the objective was not only to identify causes of growth, but also to find out whether growth rates across countries or regions converge or diverge over time.

The importance of increasing returns, externalities and imperfect competition for an understanding of the dynamics of economic development by means of the "New Growth Theories" has also led to two related research paradigms. One of these is the "New International Economics", which provides a reformulation of the theories of trade and trade policy (see e.g. Krugman 1988). The other is the "New Economic Geography", which attempts to explain the spatial distribution of economic activity, both in terms of urban systems and in terms of regional development (see e.g. Krugman 1991; Fujita et al. 1995).

The wave of "New Growth Theories" and its empirical counterpart has now reached a stage of maturity whose substantive contribution has already been assessed in special issues of major journals and general surveys (e.g. Ehrlich 1990; Stern 1991; Jones and Stokey 1992; Verspagen 1992; Romer 1994; Mankiw 1995; Jones and Manuelli 1997). There is also some dissent, e.g. Scott (1989) provides an alternative approach which rejects the use of the neoclassical production function. The empirical work on growth has benefited from new comparative data bases for a wide range of countries in the world (e.g. Summers and Heston 1991; International Monetary Fund, various years; World Bank, various years). However, some of the conclusions regarding the determinants of growth drawn from such data appear as yet rather fragile (Levine and Renelt 1992; Mankiw 1995). Theory and empirics are brought together skillfully in the textbook by Barro and Sala-i-Martin (1995) which provides an advanced, but accessible, treatment of all the major issues in theoretical models of economic growth and the related empirical investigations.

Thus, the present paper does not purport to provide yet another broad survey. Instead, we will focus only on the spatial aspects of the neoclassical and the new growth models. A distinction is made between differences in growth rates due to spatial variations in parameters which influence growth in closed economies and causes of differences in growth rates between open economies. The predictions of the models are also compared with the main conclusions of the well-established literature on regional economic development. Finally, implications for regional policies are identified briefly.

Many of the neoclassical and new growth models describe accumulation in closed economies. Explanations for spatial differences in growth rates between such economies must necessarily derive from differences in parameters, initial conditions or other exogenous variables. Closed economy explanations of differences in growth rates are discussed in Sect. 2.

At the regional level, there is spatial interaction in terms of trade, capital flows, migration, diffusion of technological innovation and information exchanges. Thus, the closed economy models can provide at best a very limited understanding of regional growth. Section 3 considers the implications of introducing factor mobility, trade, economic integration and innovation diffusion into models of growth. It will become clear that the extension of the new growth models to the case of open economies is not yet fully satisfactory, and much work remains to be done in this area (Barro and Sala-i-Martin 1995, p. 128).

Section 4 focuses on the transitional dynamics in closed or open economies. An understanding of the transitional dynamics will enable predictions to be made about convergence or divergence. An assessment of the sometimes contradictory empirical evidence on this matter is provided.

Section 5 compares the new theories of growth with the conventional theories of regional development. While some of these have built upon neoclassical theories (as surveyed in e.g. McCombie 1988a), the post-Keynesian perspective which puts more emphasis on the role of demand in the economy and Kaldor's formulation of technical change (Kaldor 1957), had tended to be more popular (McCombie 1988b). The contribution, and potential, of evolutionary economics for an understanding of the regional growth process is also briefly addressed in this context. The final section provides some general conclusions and suggestions for further research in the field of spatial modelling of economic growth.

2. Why growth rates differ between closed economies

The process of economic growth, by which we mean the growth in real income per person in an economy, can be described in a simple way by the neoclassical model formulated by Robert Solow (1956) and independently by Trevor Swan (1956). Their work remains important because many of the new growth models can generate steady-state long-run growth paths which resemble those of the Solow-Swan model, with the only difference being that the new models now provide endogenous explanations for aspects of the Solow-Swan model which were assumed to be constant and given, such as the production function, the rate of technological change, the propensity to save and the population growth rate. Moreover, some of the stylised facts of development of economies are consistent with the predictions of the Solow-Swan model, provided capital accumulation in the model is interpreted as including human capital accumulation through education and training (e.g. Mankiw 1995; Bal and Nijkamp 1997).

Thus, it is useful to commence with reviewing briefly the key features of the Solow-Swan model. Consider a closed economy with competitive markets and a constant returns technology. At date t, labour supply is $L(t)$. The exogenously given rate of growth of $L(t)$ is n. Real production $Y(t)$ is assumed to result from combining inputs according to

$$Y(t) = F(K(t), L(t)e^{vt}) \tag{1}$$

where $K(t)$ is the stock of capital at time t and e^{vt} represents the effect of exogenous labour-augmenting technical progress. The model neglects labour-leisure choices and assumes full employment. Population and labour force are therefore equivalent concepts and both grow at rate n. Equation (1) can be rewritten as

$$\hat{y} = f(\hat{k}) \tag{2}$$

where the symbol $\wedge$ denotes a quantity per effective unit of labour $L(t)e^{xt}$. We shall assume that $f(.)$ has the usual "well-behaved" properties, formalised in the Inada (1963) conditions. If the rate of depreciation of capital is a fraction δ of the stock, net investment is given by

$$\dot{K} = Y - C - \delta K \tag{3}$$

where $\cdot$ denotes a derivative with respect to time and C is the level of consumption. Under these assumptions, we can derive the following equation of motion for the amount of capital per effective unit of labour $\hat{k}$:

$$\dot{\hat{k}} = f(\hat{k}) - \hat{c} - (n + x + \delta)\hat{k} . \tag{4}$$

In the Solow-Swan model, the tradeoff between current and future consumption is not explicitly considered. Households simply consume a constant fraction of income, which implies that there is a constant savings rate

$$s = \frac{f(\hat{k}) - \hat{c}}{f(\hat{k})} . \tag{5}$$

Substituting (5) into (4) gives the fundamental growth equation:

$$\dot{\hat{k}} = sf(\hat{k}) - (n + x + \delta)\hat{k} . \tag{6}$$

It is straightforward to show that given the assumptions made, any initial resources $K(0)$ and $L(0)$ and the dynamics described by (6), the economy will converge to a balanced, or steady-state, path asymptotically. In the steady state, the quantities $\hat{y}$, $\hat{k}$ and $\hat{c}$ do not change and the steady-state value of $\hat{k}$. $\hat{k}^*$ is found by setting the left-hand side of (6) equal to zero. Income, capital and consumption per capita each grow in the steady state at the rate of technological progress, x. The absolute quantities Y. K and C grow at the rate $x + n$.

This simple model suggests that if countries or regions have access to the same technology (the same production function and the same rate of technical change x), income per head must in the long run grow in each one at the same rate. During the transition to the steady state, the less capital endowed economy will have a lower income per head and grow faster. In the steady state, income per head will be higher in the economies with lower population growth and lower depreciation of capital.

The model as outlined above is only consistent with some of the stylised facts about the growth of nations and regions. Mankiw (1995, p. 277) summarises the predictions of the model as follows:

1. In the long run, the economy approaches a steady state that is independent of initial conditions.
2. The steady-state level of income depends on the rate of saving and population growth.
3. The steady-state rate of growth of income per head depends only on the rate of technological progress.
4. In the steady state, the capital-to-income ratio is constant.
5. In the steady state, the marginal product of capital is constant and the marginal product of labour grows at the rate of technological change.

Predictions 2, 4 and 5 among these are broadly supported by the empirical evidence. However, predictions 1 and 3 are more contentious and have led to a large empirical literature, which we review in Sect. 4.

The oldest way to endogenise one of the aspects of the Solow-Swan model is to make savings behaviour endogenous. Following Barro and Sala-i-Martin (1995), we refer to this model as the Ramsey model since the original idea of optimal savings behaviour was developed by Ramsey (1928). Cass (1965) showed that from any starting-point optimal capital accumulation converges to the balanced Solow-Swan growth path. The advantage of the Ramsey approach is that it permits a description of the economy in terms of the rational optimising behaviour of individual households and firms, which is now the cornerstone of modern macroeconomics. It can be shown that the Solow-Swan model predictions are consistent with those of a model with intertemporal optimisation in an Arrow-Debreu competitive equilibrium framework (e.g. Romer 1989).

In the Ramsey model, households seek to maximise lifetime utility[1] given by

$$W = \int_{t=0}^{\infty} u(c)e^{nt}e^{-\rho t}dt \tag{7}$$

where $c = C/L$ and ρ is the constant rate of time preference. Note that household utility rather than individual utility is in the welfare criterion since the utility of each person's consumption is multiplied by household membership which grows at rate n. Assuming that the utility function has the form

$$u(c) = \frac{c^{1-\theta} - 1}{1 - \theta} . \tag{8}$$

---

[1] Note that the usual "infinite horizon" assumption has been introduced for simplicity. Alternatively, economic growth models can use the overlapping generations approach, first formulated by Maurice Allais (1947) and subsequently in the seminal paper by Paul Samuelson (1958).

marginal utility $u'(c)$ has the constant elasticity $-\theta$ with respect to c.[2] To find the consumption path $c(t)$ which maximises (7) subject to (6) is a standard dynamic optimisation problem, which can be solved by Pontryagin's maximum principle of optimal control (Pontryagin et al. 1962). It can be shown that on the optimal time path for consumption

$$\tilde{c} = [f'(\hat{k}) - \delta - \rho]/\theta \tag{9}$$

where $^-$ refers to a rate of growth, i.e. $\dot{c}/c = .\tilde{c}$ (see e.g. Barro and Sala-i-Martin 1995, chapter 2). The long-run rate of return to capital is $f'(\hat{k}^*)$ where $\hat{k}^*$ is the steady-state effective capital intensity found by setting the rate of growth in per capita consumption in (9) equal to x. Hence,

$$f'(\hat{k}^*) = \delta + \rho + \theta x . \tag{10}$$

Some explicit formulae for the level and growth rate of income and the optimal propensity to save can be easily derived with the use of a Cobb-Douglas production function. If a denotes the share of profits in income, this production function is given by

$$f(\hat{k}) = A\hat{k}^a . \tag{11}$$

It is then straightforward to derive an equation for the time path of real income per capita once the steady-state has been reached:

$$y(t) = A^{\frac{1}{1-a}} \left[\frac{a}{\delta + \rho + \theta x} \right]^{\frac{a}{1-a}} e^{xt} . \tag{12}$$

The optimal propensity to save in the steady-state is again constant, as in the Solow-Swan model, and is equal to

$$s^* = \frac{(n + x + \delta)\hat{k}^*}{f(\hat{k}^*)} = \frac{a(n + x + \delta)}{(\delta + \rho + \theta x)} . \tag{13}$$

It can be seen from (13) that a low rate of time preference ρ and a high intertemporal elasticity of substitution (i.e. small θ) increase s^*. This demonstrates the well-known prediction of the neoclassical model that a thrifty society will in the long run be wealthier than an impatient one, but does not grow faster. Note also that population growth no longer affects real income per head in Eq. (12). A faster growing population will simply find it optimal to save more (see Eq. (13)).

---

[2] The reciprocal of θ is called the intertemporal elasticity of substitution σ. A special case occurs when the intertemporal elasticity of substitution is one. In this case $\theta = \sigma = 1$ and $u(c) = \ln c$. Consequently, a 1% postponement of consumption from now until later raises marginal utility in the current period by 1%.

Both the Solow-Swan and the Ramsey model provide only two reasons for differences in growth rates between regions or countries. The first is that the rate of technological change x differs between economies. Reasons for such differences are not explained. Secondly, economies may not yet be on the steady-state growth path. In this case, poor economies with a low quantity of capital per head would grow faster than rich economies. This is referred to as the *absolute convergence* property of the model.

Barro and Sala-i-Martin (1995) suggest parameter values which will make the Ramsey model generate both a plausible long-run growth rate, but also a slow convergence to this growth rate which is consistent with empirical observations (see also Sect. 4). The slow convergence can only be explained with an interpretation of capital as a broad concept which also includes human capital accumulation. With this interpretation, the share of capital in income (combined with returns to education) is perhaps 0.75. Thus, $a = 0.75$. Other plausible parameter values for developed economies are: the natural growth rate $n = 0.01$, the rate of technical change $x = 0.02$; the rate of depreciation $\delta = 0.05$, the rate of time preference $\rho = 0.02$ and the elasticity of marginal utility $\theta = 3$. Substituting these values in (12) suggests an optimal propensity to save of 45% (including investments in education and training).

The purpose of many of the models of growth which have been developed during the last decade is to provide an endogenous explanation for the natural growth rate n, or the rate of technical change x, or both.[3] We will focus here primarily on the latter issue, but we refer to Barro and Becker (1989) for a model which explains the natural growth rate n in a closed economy with exogenous technical change. In such an economy, the population growth rate and the rate of technical change are inversely related. Their model is an extension of the Ramsey model, namely through the introduction of a dynastic utility function: parents care about the utility attained by their children when reaching adulthood and by subsequent generations.

Becker et al. (1990) describe a closed-economy model in which technical change and population growth are both endogenous (with productivity growth driven by education). In this case, multiple equilibria emerge with the possibility of an economy becoming trapped in a "low income growth with high fertility" steady state. This is an example of a growth model in which the steady state is sensitive to initial conditions, which is a general feature of increasing returns and other "positive-feedback loop" models (see also Arthur 1994). Thus, historical endowments and "luck" may be critical determinants of differentials in growth which we may observe between countries or regions in such models.

A "poverty trap" can also be generated by the original Solow-Swan model by simply assuming that the average product of capital $f(k)/k$ is initially declining, then increasing and finally again declining with increasing

---

[3] Another possibility is to make the internal rate of time preference, i.e. the discount rate, endogenous. See Drugeon (1996) for the impact of growing impatience on long-run growth.

values of k (see Barro and Sala-i-Martin 1995, pp. 49–52). The possibility of a poverty trap is a popular idea in the development literature, see for example the "Big Push" model of Lewis (1954).

The process of labour-augmenting technological change, which proceeds at a constant rate x in the Solow-Swan model, is the simplest formalization of many phenomena which may lead to long-run productivity improvements. In macroeconomic models with only one good, technological change represents a growth of knowledge. There are four ways of accumulating knowledge: research, schooling, learning-by-doing and training. Alternatively, if a model permits more than one good, technological change may be due to an increase in the variety of intermediate inputs or consumer goods. Furthermore, the quality of goods may improve for a given variety. Finally, increasing returns may result from economies of scale.

Endogenous growth models have been formulated for each of these situations. For example, Lucas (1988) describes one model in which education generates external benefits and another model in which productivity improves through learning by doing. The idea that experience spills over to other producers goes back to Arrow (1962) and is also the engine of growth in Romer's (1986) model.

Other papers explicitly describe the activities of the R&D sector which generates new knowhow, see e.g. Romer (1990) and Aghion and Howitt (1992). Osano (1992) points out that basic research may have a stronger impact on the growth rate than applied research. He proceeds therefore to formulate a growth model with two research sectors. Schmitz (1989) points to the importance of entrepreneurial imitation, while Stokey (1988) studies the effects of the introduction of new goods on long-run growth. In this context, Jovanovic (1995) notes that the emphasis on generating new knowledge is overemphasised in the new growth models. A significant proportion of resources in an economy is devoted to adopting existing recent technologies rather than inventing new ones and firms frequently adopt "dominated" technologies. Thus, new growth models which explicitly consider the adoption decision are warranted. A recent issue in this context is also the optimal timing of adoption of a new technology (Choi 1994). Early adoption may create a competitive edge, but may be costly. Late adoption may be less risky, but may also generate less benefits (see also Koski and Nijkamp 1996).

A key issue is that technological inputs create spillovers due to the fact that they are non-rival goods. New inventions are produced at a high cost for the first unit but subsequent units (e.g. photocopies) can be produced at virtually zero cost. This generates nonconvexities in production, even if such goods are partially excludable (i.e. appropriable) through patents and if adoption is costly. The technological spillover phenomenon is better captured by human capital accumulation or the introduction of new goods rather than by physical capital accumulation.

In many of the models with endogenous technological change, the characteristics of the dynamic competitive equilibrium can be traced by setting up an optimal control problem similar to the Ramsey model. Where a steady-state exists, the presence of an externality, e.g. through R&D, creates a divergence between the private and social rates of return and the competitive equilibrium may not be Pareto-optimal.

To highlight some common features of many endogenous growth models we will now formulate a simple model of endogenous technological change in which the existence and properties of the steady-state are readily established without having to explicitly solve the underlying dynamic optimisation problem.[4] This will also simplify the discussion of growth in the open economy in the next section.

As noted earlier, technological change is most conveniently interpreted as a labour-augmenting process. Thus, if N measures the effective labour input. $N = LT$, where L is the quantity of workers and T is an index of the average quality of labour input, which depends on the stock of knowledge and practices. In the Solow-Swan model, T grows at the exogenous rate x. Here we relax this assumption. Central to the current view about the process of technological innovation is that a change in T requires a production process with real resource inputs, a multi-product output, its own technology, market structure, spatial differentiation and, indeed, its own changing technology (e.g. Dosi 1988). Hence we shall assume that a change in T is generated by the following process of knowledge creation:

$$\dot{T} = H\left(\frac{R}{L}, T\right) \tag{14}$$

where R/L is expenditure per worker on activities such as education, training. R&D etc.[5] Thus, the change in T is positively related to the intensity of the effort devoted to the enhancement of labour quality as well as the current level of labour quality. This function is assumed to be homogeneous of degree one, twice differentiable and concave. Both the public sector and private sector in the economy carry out knowledge-creating activities, funded through taxes and retained profits respectively. For simplicity, we lump these activities here together and assume that a fraction τ of national income is allocated to this process of technical change. Hence,

$$R = \tau Y. \tag{15}$$

As in the case of the accumulation of physical capital, a trade-off arises in that a large value of τ reduces current consumption, but yields a higher level of output in the future. Using (14) and (15) we can derive that

$$\dot{T} = H\left(\frac{R}{LT}, 1\right) = H(\tau \hat{y}, 1) \equiv h(\tau f(\hat{k})) \tag{16}$$

---

[4] Solow (1994, p. 49) has in fact argued that the intertemporally-optimising representative agent formulation in itself has had little to add to the insights of the New Growth literature.
[5] This equation is a generalisation of a model of endogenous technical change proposed by Conlisk (1967), who assumed that dT/dt would be a linear function of Y/L and T.

Households now maximise lifetime utility according to Eq. (7) as before, but consumption per capita c at any time cannot exceed $f(k) - \dot{k} - \tau f(k) - \delta k$. There are now two decision variables, the propensity to save and the propensity to allocate resources to technical change, and if a steady-state growth path exists these propensities will both be constant on the steady-state path. Consequently, income per head will still grow at a constant rate in the steady state, as in the standard neoclassical model, but (16) shows that this rate is now a function of both τ (the proportion of resources devoted to education, innovation etc.), and $\hat{k}$ (the effective capital intensity). If we assume that the labour input L again grows at an exogenous rate, n, we can derive a "fundamental growth" equation similar to Eq. (6) for the Solow-Swan model. For given s and τ, the path of the effective capital intensity $\hat{k}$ is given by

$$\dot{\hat{k}} = sf(\hat{k}) - [n + h(\tau f(\hat{k})) + \delta]\hat{k} . \qquad (17)$$

The long-run equilibrium level of the effective capital intensity is given by $\hat{k}^*$ for which $\dot{\hat{k}} = 0$. Under the specified conditions, such an equilibrium exists and is stable (see Nijkamp and Poot 1993a).

The merit of this simple model of endogenous technical change is that, in contrast with the Solow-Swan or Ramsey model, it identifies various sources of differences in growth rates between countries and regions. Firstly, the model shows that thriftiness is good for an economy: if, e.g., a removal of tax distortions raises the propensity to save, the per capita growth rate becomes permanently higher.[6] Similarly, if capital is depreciated faster or the labour force grows faster, the rate of growth of output per capita decreases. Finally, if the proportion of income devoted to the production of technical change increases, the rate of growth of output per capita increases. These results can be readily derived from considering the effect on the per capita growth rate $h(\tau f(\hat{k}^*))$ when changing a parameter in (17) and setting $\dot{\hat{k}} = 0$.

If government can influence the parameters of the growth model (savings behaviour, R&D, population growth), the endogenous growth model also points to ways in which government could permanently raise the long-run growth rate. It is also possible to formulate endogenous growth models in which the activities of government become explicit in the form of provision of infrastructure, pure public goods, the protection of property rights and taxation policies. For example, Barro (1990) considers a model in which the total of government purchases becomes an additional production factor (external effect) in the production function of private firms.

---

[6] One issue. which we do not address in this paper, is the effect of savings behaviour in models of heterogeneous capital. The introduction of heterogeneous capital may lead to paradoxical results, see e.g. Garegnani (1970) and Hatta (1976). The issue was raised in the context of the "Cambridge-Cambridge" debate regarding the meaning of the concept of capital and the notion of an aggregate production function (see e.g. Jones 1975 for an introduction into this debate).

The above model generates constant long-run growth, but endogenous growth models may also generate ever-increasing growth rates due to increasing returns. An example can be found in Romer (1986), who justifies such a model by the observation that in the very long run (over several centuries) worldwide labour-productivity growth has been accelerating (see also Kremer 1993), although it is equally true that during the last forty years productivity growth exhibited a downward trend among developed countries (Romer, 1989). Nijkamp and Poot (1993b) formulate a model of increasing returns in which such ever-increasing growth is eventually checked by technological, social and economic capacity constraints.

Another plausible break on ever-increasing growth is a deterioration of the natural environment. On the one hand we may find that damage to the environment or an increasing scarcity of natural resources restricts the economy's ability to generate innovations which drive the growth in income per head (Barbier 1996). On the other hand, it is likely that a society becomes more interested in environmental preservation at higher incomes. A growing preference for a clean environment may then become incompatible with growth when the production technology exhibits increasing returns to scale (Yoshida 1995). However, if pollution abatement technologies themselves benefit from endogenous technological change, more resources devoted to such activities may lower output growth in the short run, but increase it in the long run (Bovenberg and Smulders 1996). This phenomenon is also referred to as the environmental Kutznets curve.

3. Long-run growth tendencies in open economies

Our analysis has been so far confined to the case of the closed economy. The growing importance of trade, capital flows, a diffusion of product and process innovations, and migration at the interregional and international levels, suggests that spatial interactions need to be explicitly considered, both in terms of their direct effects on growth and their effects on technological change. In this section we address these issues by considering, in this order: factor mobility, diffusion and trade.

3.1 Factor mobility

If interregional differences in preferences, factor endowments or technology generate interregional differences in returns to production factors, a reallocation of production factors may be expected. The impact of this reallocation depends on the assumed characteristics of the model of the interacting economies. In standard neoclassical analyses in which spatial factor price differentials are due to differences in factor endowments, factor movements have an equilibrating effect. However, with differences in preferences or technology, factor movements may lead to divergence in which all mobile resources are eventually attracted to one region (see e.g. Nana and Poot 1996).

This contrast is also evident in the attempts to date to formulate the neoclassical growth model in an open economy setting. For example, it is often considered plausible to assume perfect capital mobility and immobile labour. Barro and Sala-i-Martin (1995, chapter 3) find that in these circumstances a multi-country Ramsey model generates several paradoxical conclusions. Firstly, the speed of convergence to the steady state is infinite. Secondly, consumption in all but the most patient country tends to zero and assets in these countries become negative. Finally, the most patient country eventually owns all resources and consumes all output.

In practice, capital is far from being perfectly mobile and, specifically, capital does not seem to flow from rich to poor countries to the extent that neoclassical models would predict. Similarly, human capital may migrate from places where it is scarce to places where it is abundant (a process sometimes referred to as the "braindrain"), rather than vice versa (Lucas 1988). These observations may be explained by asymmetric information, imperfect credit markets or labour markets, or adjustment costs for investment (Barro and Sala-i-Martin 1995; Gordon and Bovenberg 1996). Alternatively, the incentives for capital mobility may be exaggerated, because spatial real risk-adjusted rate of return differentials may in fact be small due to significant differences between countries in human capital accumulation, the external benefits of human capital, capital market imperfections and political uncertainties (Lucas 1990; Mankiw 1995).

However, as long as a production factor moves in the "right" direction (i.e. to where its price is higher) it has in the neoclassical growth models the tendency to speed up convergence to the steady-state. As an example, we illustrate the role of factor mobility in the endogenous growth models by explicitly considering labour migration.

Separating the effect of "natural" growth and migration, the change in labour supply is given

$$\dot{L} = nL + M \tag{18}$$

in which net migration M may be assumed to be given positively related to the effective capital intensity $\hat{k}$ since the real wage is $f(\hat{k}) - \hat{k}f'(\hat{k})$, which increases with higher values of $\hat{k}$ (see also Barro and Sala-i-Martin 1995, p. 288). Hence

$$M = m(\hat{k})L \tag{19}$$

in which $m(\hat{k})$ is the migration rate, which is an increasing function of $\hat{k}$. Migrants can also bring capital with them, so that the change in the domestic capital stock is now given by:

$$\dot{K} = sF(K, \hat{L}) - \delta K + \phi M \tag{20}$$

where ϕ is the value of capital per migrant (which could be human capital when K is interpreted in a broad sense). When we combine (18)–(20) with our earlier model of endogenous technical change, the following dynamic equation for the effective capital intensity emerges:

$$\dot{k} = sf(\hat{k}) - [h(\tau f(\hat{k})) + \delta + n + m(\hat{k})]\hat{k} + m(\hat{k})\hat{\phi} . \tag{21}$$

As in the previous models, Eq. (21) can be used to identify which factors influence the long-run growth rate. It is clear that in addition to policies with influence R&D, immigration policies can now also affect the long-run growth rate. For example, if immigration controls are relaxed, the $m(\hat{k})$ function may shift upward. This would lead to a lower steady-state effective capital intensity $\hat{k}^*$ and it would also lower the long-run growth rate in per capita income.

The conclusion that immigration lowers the growth rate requires the assumption that there is no change in the amount of capital which immigrants bring with them. If a new immigration policy targets specifically highly skilled workers, this raises $\hat{\phi}$ and leads to an increase in $\hat{k}^*$, so that in this case the long-run growth rate will increase.

In addition, migrants may directly influence productivity growth in various ways. If migrants provide new ideas and encourage investment which embodies new technologies, there are dynamic gains from inward migration not captured in (21). The empirical literature suggests that there are indeed dynamic gains from migration, at least in the traditional immigrant receiving countries of North America and Australasia (see also Gorter et al. forthcoming). This literature suggests that net immigration in these developed countries has raised per capita incomes. The regional literature also suggests that migrants on balance move in the "right" direction, but that this reallocation does not reduce interregional disparities (e.g. Van Dijk et al. 1989). These observations would be consistent with a "cumulative causation" process rather than neoclassical convergence. However, recent work by Persson (1994) and Cashin and Loayza (1995) finds empirical evidence for migration aiding convergence among Swedish regions and between South Pacific countries respectively.

A final point to note with respect to growth models with endogenous migration is that the migration function in Eq. (19) is a macro function, which does not explicitly consider the micro-level behaviour of individual households. For example, migration will be a function of the gain from migration in terms of wages or amenities, but this gain may depend on interregional differences in the rate of technical change rather than just the amount of capital per worker. Moreover, if the productivity growth rate between regions or countries differs, mobile labour may have the same effect as mobile capital which we discussed earlier, namely the final equilibrium may be a corner solution in which all population is concentrated in one region. To avoid such an extreme, it is plausible to introduce some capacity constraint either in terms of technological bottlenecks or congestion of a natural resource (see also Nijkamp and Poot 1993b). Braun (1993) formulates several growth models with endogenous migration.

3.2 Diffusion

Diffusion analysis has become an important field of research in industrial economics. At the micro level, it does not only focus on the distribution and adoption of new technologies (see Brown 1981; Soete and Turner 1984), but also on business services and networks related to technological transformations (Cappellin 1989; Bertuglia et al. 1997). In most diffusion studies the S-shaped (or logistic) curve forms a central component (Davies 1979; Morrill et al. 1988). Both the adoption time and the adoption rate can be pictured in this curve. The precise shape of the S-curve can then be explained from firm size, market structure, profitability of innovations etc. (Kamien and Schwartz 1982).

An important negative role can be played in this context by barriers to information transfer in a multi-region system (Giaoutzi and Nijkamp 1988). Without the right local conditions, the adoption of diffused technological innovations may also not be effective. For example when adoption requires a skilled work force, a low level of human capital accumulation will slow down technological change. Kubo and Kim (1996) find evidence of a strong complementarity between imported technology and human capital in a study of growth in Japan and Korea.

Several authors have proposed long-run growth models which incorporate the diffusion of technological change, for example Krugman (1979), Grossman and Helpman (1991) and Barro and Sala-i-Martin (1995, chapter 8).

For simplicity, we do not consider logistic diffusion here. The simplest way to investigate the effect of diffusion in our dynamical system is to replace the equation for productivity growth (16) by

$$\tilde{T} = h(\tau f(\hat{k})) + dh(\tau^f f(\hat{k}^f)) \qquad (22)$$

where d is a diffusion parameter and the superscript f refers to a second country or region. This parameter is likely to vary over time and space. In the general case, the dynamics of a multi-regional system with endogenous technological change and innovation diffusion can be quite complex, but the properties of the system can be studied by means of simulation results (see Nijkamp et al. 1991).

When d is taken to be a constant parameter, it is straightforward to show that diffusion is compatible with a steady state in which both regions could grow at different rates. This result is obtained by substituting the endogenous rate of technical change (22) into (17) or (21) and by writing down a similar equation for the second country. The equilibrium effective capital intensities $\hat{k}^*$ and $\hat{k}^{f*}$ can then be found as the steady-state solution to the resulting two simultaneous differential equations (see Nijkamp and Poot 1993a).

As $\hat{k}^*$ and $\hat{k}^{f*}$ need not be identical, there can be in this model of technological change and diffusion a difference in steady-state growth rates between regions. Regions will then diverge in terms of a growing absolute difference in real income per head. If the steady-state growth rates differ, because the equilibrium capital intensities differ, there will be a persistent, and constant, difference in the rate of return on capital and an increasing real wage gap unless migration and capital movements (in opposite directions) are significant enough to reduce the factor price gaps.

If the diffusion parameter is very large, "overshooting" may take place and the system would then be characterized by saddle-path stability (see Nijkamp and Poot 1993a). Thus, ever increasing growth rates or growth rates reducing to zero are then a possibility. [7]

In conclusion, factor mobility and a plausible rate of diffusion have in this model the usual equilibrating effect of bringing capital intensities closer. In the circumstances in which a steady state exists, it is easy to identify the benefits of diffusion: compared with the situation of autarky, the equilibrium effective capital intensity is lower, the rate of return to capital is higher and income per capita grows at a faster rate.

The model discussed above treats both countries identically, i.e. diffusion takes place in both directions. As the adoption of imported technology usually also requires resources, firms must compare at the margin the cost of adopting imported technology with the cost of their own R&D activities. Barro and Sala-i-Martin (1995, p. 276) show that it is likely that a leader-follower situation will emerge in which one country eventually allocates its entire product and process development budget to imitation of foreign ideas while the R&D sector in the other generates all new ideas. Switches of roles may take place in the long run (see also Choi 1994).

Similar results regarding the choice between imported technology and R&D activity along the optimal growth path were obtained by Nijkamp and Poot (1993b). During the "take off" phase of the growth path – when real incomes are still low – productivity growth is driven by importing new technology. At the second stage, a domestic R&D sector may develop, which leads to increasing returns in the economy. However, the R&D sector eventually matures when growth becomes limited by natural resource constraints or other bottlenecks. The issue of an absorptive capacity for technological change in a growth model is also addressed by Keller (1996).

3.3 Trade

The Solow-Swan model, Ramsey model and the endogenous growth models referred to so far focus only on the supply side of the economy, i.e. the production factors and the level of technology. Within the standard neoclassical framework, trade has in fact no role to play beyond speeding up convergence (through Heckscher-Ohlin resource reallocation effects) and determining the steady-state world prices. The long-run growth rate itself remains purely a function of technological change and this process is not influenced by trade in the standard models.

---

[7] This was confirmed by simulations with a three-region model of endogenous technical change and spatial diffusion. A wide range of outcomes could emerge (see Nijkamp et al. 1991).

For example, the traditional neoclassical trade-and-growth model (Oniki and Uzawa 1965), suggests that two trading regions (with an identical rate of growth of labour supply) would, under standard conditions, move towards a long-run balanced growth path. The two regions grow on this path at identical rates and the pattern of specialisation is determined by the equilibrium factor intensities, i.e. the regions would produce relatively more of the good which uses the abundant production factor more intensively.

The restrictive assumptions of equal labour force growth and identical technological change are in fact required to ensure a stable long-run steady state in which relative prices (and therefore the terms of trade) are constant. Nijkamp and Poot (1993a) show that when the Oniki and Uzawa trade model is extended to include the model of technological change described in the previous section, a steady state is unlikely to exist and the terms of trade will continue to change. A qualitatively similar result is obtained by Lucas (1988) in a model of learning by doing and trade.

The description of technological change as a process of imperfect competition and increasing returns through increases in the variety of goods or improvements in product quality lead naturally to the question what the impact of trade would be under these more realistic assumptions of the new growth models. Grossman and Helpman (1991) provide an extensive discussion of the links between innovation, trade and growth in the open economy. Several new "trade and growth" models have been formulated. Rivera-Batiz and Romer (1991) show that when R&D activity is driven by the monopoly rights of producers to sell new intermediate goods, economic integration of these types of economies (assuming they are structurally identical) can raise the world growth rate. Thus there are both static and dynamic gains from trade in this type of model. However, Rivera-Batiz and Xie (1993) show that when the countries have different sizes and diverging resource endowments, economic integration will lower the growth rate of a country with a high (autarky) growth rate, while it will raise the growth rate of a country with a low (autarky) growth rate. Devereux and Lapham (1993) find that the post-integration equilibria in these types of trade and growth models may be unstable. Moreover, a specialisation based on comparative advantage leads to a sub-optimal investment in R&D activities by resource-rich economies (Grossman and Helpman 1994).

The Oniki and Uzawa trade- and growth-model assumed that the labour-augmenting technical change affects both the consumption and the investment goods sectors equally. In contrast, the new growth models describe how labour productivity improvements can vary between sectors, or how a trade advantage is generated by product innovations such as is described in the product cycle theory (Vernon 1966; Krugman 1979). Alternatively, it may be the level of activity in specific sectors which provides a "learning by doing" spillover benefit for the whole economy. In this case it is straightforward to show that an increase in the supply of the resource used intensively in the knowledge-generating sector speeds up growth (Grossman and Helpman 1990a). Similarly, the market allocation of resources to this sector is suboptimal because firms do not take a spillover benefit into account. Not surprisingly, the presence of a positive externality implies that subsidising the R&D sector improves welfare.

In a multi-regional context, the capture of spillover benefits from other regions increases growth, but what matters now from the policy perspective is which of the regions has a comparative advantage in the R&D sector. If subsidies are given to regions which are better at manufacturing rather than innovating, the overall growth rate may decline.

A typical model of comparative advantage and long-run growth is described by Grossman and Helpman (1990b). In their model, there are three sectors: an R&D sector, which produces blueprints for new products and also generates increases in the stock of knowledge, an intermediate goods sector and a final consumption goods sector. Resources devoted to R&D raise the number of available varieties of differentiated inputs in final production and this in turn raises total factor productivity. If this model is applied to two regions, each which fixed primary resources, a steady-state growth rate can be computed and its sensitivity to policies analysed. For example, a small R&D subsidy in both regions increases in this model the rate of growth, while a national trade policy that switches spending toward the consumer good produced by the region with a comparative advantage in R&D will cause long-run growth rates to decline. Diffusion can also have a significant effect on the long-run growth rate in this type of model. Moreover, it is also possible to study environmental externalities and environmental policies in this context (Elbasha and Roe 1996).

The increasing returns due to economies of scale or technical change in many of these models generates a sensitivity to initial conditions. It is intuitively clear that "uneven development" is a necessary outcome of such a situation: an initial discrepancy in capital-labour ratios between regions will be reinforced over time. Trade specialisation may also generate such uneven development. Kugman (1981) provides a well known example of this situation. Krugman assumed that two products, an agricultural good and a manufactured good, can be produced by means of Ricardian production techniques, with increasing external economies of scale. Such external economies are of course often empirically indistinguishable from technical change. In either case, the technical coefficients representing the input requirements per unit of output decline as the capital stock increases. In this situation the region with the larger initial capital stock has the higher profit rate and, if all profits are saved, generates the fastest capital accumulation. The result is an ever-increasing divergence between the regions, which only ends when a boundary of some kind has been reached. Krugman assumed this to be a limit to labour supply. Kubo (1995) formulated an extension of Krugman's model in which there is an interregional externality in the form of spillovers of knowledge or other benefits of regional agglomeration. In this case, a range of stable or unstable development patterns may emerge with the actual outcome dependent on the values of the parameters.

Production factor growth and commodity trade may also reinforce each other through technical change. Lucas (1988) suggested that a difference in human capital accumulation is one of the main causes of a difference in growth rates between regions or countries. Different goods have different potentials for human capital growth through on-the-job training or through learning-by-doing. Consequently, the comparative advantage which determines which goods get produced also determines the rate of growth in human capital (and therefore technical change). Lucas' (1988) model of trade and growth has features similar to Krugman's (1981) model, although the increase in the efficiency of the Ricardian production technology in the former is due to human capital accumulation through learning by doing, rather than economies of scale through physical capital accumulation. Nonetheless, if two goods are produced which are "good" substitutes (i.e. they have a substitution elasticity greater than one), there will be a tendency for complete specialisation with the direction of specialisation determined by the initial conditions.

Many of the "new growth theory", "new economic geography" and "new international economics" models have in common a possibility of multiple stable or unstable equilibria and a sensitivity to initial conditions. Consequently, they point to a role for policy to ensure that initial conditions on the growth path are generated which take the possibility of a technological comparative advantage into account. For example, to ensure that more resources are devoted to the good with a high learning-by-doing propensity, an industrial policy of "picking winners" would appear helpful in the Lucas (1988) model. The introduction of trade in this framework also generates complete specialisation. Over time, the terms of trade change continuously to reinforce the pattern of comparative advantage. Provided the goods are good substitutes, regions which produce the good which enjoys a faster technical change will continue to have a higher growth rate, resulting in a persisting change in the terms of trade. Thus, this dynamic trade model suggests again a persistent pattern of uneven development. Markusen (1996) recently emphasised that industrial policy consequently favours the highly urbanised high-income regions and that a top-down regional policy continues to be desirable to avoid increasing inequities between regions.

There is of course a fairly long tradition of emphasising uneven development in the regional growth literature, such as expounded, for example, in Myrdal's (1957) cumulative causation theory. For a recent contribution of the link between cumulative causation and trade, see Venables (1996).

A challenge in modelling regional growth with cumulative causation effects is to be able to endogenise changes in the position of individual regions in this growth continuum. Possibilities for such growth switches would include – on the demand side – the introduction of different income elasticities for different classes of goods; and on the supply side the continuing introduction of new goods, with learning potentials declining with the amount produced. Such factors could continuously shake up the existing pattern of specialisation and explain why, for example, the rapid growth in Newly Industrialised Economies has been associated with a growth of exports in products initially not produced in these countries.

4. Transitional dynamics: convergence or divergence

Parallel to the development of the new models of growth which we discussed in the previous two sections, a related empirical literature has burgeoned. However, this literature has not attempted as yet to verify empirically whether the new sophisticated models provide an adequate description of cross-section or intertemporal differences in growth rates. It is often difficult to derive from the new theories estimable equations, for example because the behaviour away from the steady state is theoretically uncertain. Also, some of the variables of the new models such as knowledge are hard to measure (Mankiw 1995).

Because it is possible to describe exactly in the Solow-Swan model how an economy develops over time from any initial position, and therefore how the transition to the steady state will be made, much of the literature on transitional dynamics and convergence is based on this traditional model (e.g. King and Rebelo 1993). Indeed, some research suggests that the empirical evidence on convergence is not consistent with theories in which trend growth rates differ across economies endogenously (Evans and Karras 1996).

There are two notions of convergence. *Weak* convergence, also called β-convergence, takes place when low income regions or countries grow faster than high-income ones, all else being equal. *Strong* convergence, also called σ-convergence, takes place when the standard deviation of the distribution of income across regions or countries declines. β-Convergence is a necessary but not sufficient condition for σ-convergence (Sala-i-Martin 1996). In simple terms, β is the slope coefficient from a regression of the growth of real income on the logarithm of its level. Convergence to the steady state would imply a negative coefficient. This type of regression can be carried out both with time-series data or with cross-section data. In the former case, the specification would be

$$\log\left(y_t/y_{t-1}\right) = a - (1 - e^{-\beta})\log\left(y_{t-1}\right) + u_t \tag{23}$$

for a time series of observations $t = 1, 2. ..., T$ while in the case of a cross section of regions or countries $i = 1, 2, ... I$ the regression equation is

$$(1/T)\log\left(y_{iT}/y_{i0}\right) = a - [(1 - e^{-\beta T})/T]\log\left(y_{i0}\right) + u_{i0,T} \tag{24}$$

where 0 and T now refer to two points in time over which growth is computed. When the estimated Eqs. (23) and (24) provide a good fit, this would suggest so-called absolute convergence. In practice, there are many structural differences between countries or regions which would influence a cross-section equation or shocks to the growth process which would affect the time series equation. Consequently, research in this area usually proceeds to estimate (23) and (24) with a range of additional variables added and a significant β in this situation is referred to as conditional β convergence. Some data sets may in fact permit estimation with pooling of cross-section and time-series data (e.g. Knight et al. 1993).

Barro and Sala-i-Martin (1995) show how the value of β is related to the parameters of the Solow-Swan model with a Cobb-Douglas production function for a growth process that is actually described by this model. They find that $\beta = (1 - a)(x + n + \delta)$. Using the parameter values given in Sect. 2, we get $\beta = (1 - 0.75)(0.02 + 0.01 + 0.05) = 0.02$. This suggests that 2% of the gap between the current income and the steady state is reduced each year.

There is indeed some evidence of convergence at this rate. This evidence is stronger for regions than for countries and, within a cross section of countries, stronger for similar nations than for a broader cross section. For example, Barro and Sala-i-Martin (1992) and Sala-i-Martin (1996) find convergence across the states of the USA, prefectures of Japan and five European countries. Similarly, Andres et al. (1996) find convergence among OECD countries. Persson (1994) finds convergence across Swedish counties. Even Quah (1996), who is generally sceptical of claims of strong convergence in economic growth, finds evidence of such convergence across US states. Ben-David (1996) finds that convergence is stronger among countries that have strong trading relationships.

The speed of convergence is similar in many empirical studies, namely about 2% per year and therefore only consistent with the Solow-Swan model when capital is interpreted as including human capital (so that the share of capital in income is as high as 75%). Using more conventional parameter values, Mankiw (1995) finds that the Solow model suggests convergence at a speed of 4% per year, i.e. faster than is actually the case, although Cashin and Loayza (1995) find a speed of convergence at this rate after controlling for the effect of net international migration in a sample of nine South Pacific countries.

A by-product of the regression equations specified above is that the additional explanatory variables may lead to some insight into the causes of differences in growth rates. For example, Barro and Sala-i-Martin (1992) explain the persisting differences in steady-state growth rates in rather ad hoc fashion by school enrolment rates and government consumption expenditure (excluding education and defence). A cross-section of countries shows in their research a lesser tendency to convergence. Similarly, Mankiw et al. (1992) show that the textbook Solow-Swan model needs to be augmented to make the model useful in explaining differences in income per capita across countries. They find that introducing human capital accumulation explicitly (measured by secondary school enrolment rates) has the same type of positive effect on income per head as the savings ratio s^* in the standard Solow model. The augmented model provides some evidence of inter-country convergence, although again at a slow rate.

Regional openness and interconnectedness may of course be responsible for the somewhat more convincing patterns of convergence observed at the regional level than in cross-country comparisons. For example, Barro and Sala-i-Martin (1992) point to diffusion of technological change having the potential of generating convergence even if the marginal product of capital is not declining. Nonetheless, despite well known historical evidence of convergence of incomes across states of the USA (e.g. Easterlin 1960), there are fairly lengthy periods during which one can observe divergence[8] and the evidence that factor mobility operates as an equilibrating process is also rather inconclusive.[9] Richer models are needed to explain such observations.

A vast literature has emerged during the last decade on which factors, in addition to the convergence effect, explain differences in growth rates between regions or countries. A review of this literature is beyond the scope of the present paper, but see inter alia Kormendi and Meguire (1985), Baumol (1986), De Long (1988), Dowrick and Nguyen (1989), Barro (1991) and Barro and Sala-i-Martin (1992). However, Levine and Renelt (1992) find that many of the regression models may suffer from specification errors and the results are not very robust. Moreover, Evans (1995) shows that the usual approach of estimation with OLS is in this context inappropriate.

In recent years, several studies have also attempted to focus on specific variables which are often considered to be important from the growth perspective. For example, De Long and Summers (1991) find that equipment investment can raise growth rates, and more strongly than investment in structures. Perroti (1996) finds that a lower income inequality raises growth rates, while Barro (1996) finds that political freedom has a positive effect on growth. Finally, Devarajan et al. (1996) show that the composition of public expenditure can have an important effect on growth. Specifically, governments of developing countries appear to have allocated relatively too many funds to public capital expenditures, at the expense of current expenditures.

5. Alternative approaches

Although the Solow-Swan model was also extensively used for the purpose of studying the growth of regions, of which Borts and Stein (1964) is a well-known example, dissatisfaction with this model led to a search for alternatives. This dissatisfaction was due to several reasons. Firstly, the neoclassical model predicted convergence, which contradicted with many case studies of uneven development. Secondly, the theory did not provide any guidance regarding policy instruments which could help to raise the growth rate. Thirdly, the macro focus of the neoclassical model is inadequate to explain any regional differences in growth rates which may be due to significant differences in sectoral composition. In this context it is useful to note that Bernard and Jones (1996) found recently, using data on 14 OECD countries, that there is a lack of convergence in manufacturing while aggre-

---

[8] The periods 1840–1880, 1920–1940 and 1970–1980 are periods of interregional divergence in the USA. See also Carlino and Mills (1996).

[9] See for example the discussion in Armstrong and Taylor (1985, pp. 118–121).

gate convergence results may be driven by services. Fourthly, the neoclassical model in a regional setting only permits the study of regions as point economies, with a possible interaction through factor flows, but it does not address the distribution of economic activity over continuous space.

Consequently, many alternative approaches were proposed during the 1960s and 1970s, such as the export base model, econometric models, (multi-regional) input-output and computable general equilibrium models; multisector development planning models, cumulative causation dynamic models etc. (see e.g. Richardson 1973). Some of the current endeavours to obtain a precise micro-level description of all sectors and the requirements for general equilibrium could already be found in the optimal space-time development models of regional science literature (e.g. Isard et al. 1979). However, the questions of the existence, uniqueness and stability of optimal solutions could not yet be addressed at the time.

The rather secondary role of trade in the neoclassical model led to a significant popularity of Keynesian modelling with a heavy emphasis on demand considerations. For example, output growth in a region is driven in the well-known Kaldor-Dixon-Thirlwall model by relative competitiveness and income growth outside the region (Dixon and Thirlwall 1975). Supply-side factors play in such an export-led growth model only a role in terms of the effects of cost inflation and productivity on relative competitiveness, with the latter effect being generated by means of Verdoorn's law (Verdoorn 1949). This model explains differences in equilibrium growth rates between regions in terms of differences in price and income elasticities in the demand for exports and differences in rates of autonomous productivity growth.

In more formal terms, output growth is assumed to be export-led:

$$\tilde{Y} = \omega \tilde{X} \tag{25}$$

where $\tilde{}$ refers again to a rate of growth and X to the volume of exports. The export demand function has constant price and income elasticities

$$\tilde{X} = -\eta \tilde{p} + \xi \tilde{p}^f + \pi \tilde{Y}^f . \tag{26}$$

Price inflation results from fixed mark-up pricing on production costs, which in turn depend on unit wage costs w and labour productivity. Thus, in rate of change terms

$$\tilde{p} = \tilde{w} - \tilde{y} . \tag{27}$$

Central to this growth model is that labour productivity is partly dependent on growth of output itself, i.e. Verdoorn's Law:

$$\tilde{y} = \kappa + \lambda \tilde{Y} . \tag{28}$$

This equation is the result of inductive macroeconomic research and increasing returns may be the driving force behind it. However, the key weakness of this approach is that it does not explain which processes at the micro-level cause the positive feedback effect from output growth on productivity growth. Nonetheless, an extensive literature exists regarding the empirical evidence for the Verdoorn equation (reviewed in e.g. Bairam 1987). This literature suggests that the observed relationship may be the result of simultaneous responses in output and labour markets to changes in demand, combined with the effects of economies of scale and technical progress. Naturally, a simultaneous equation approach is required for empirical estimation of the parameters in (28). By and large, the empirical evidence suggests that λ is positive.

The reduced form of the model (25)–(28) is readily computed and suggests a constant rate of growth of income per worker:

$$\tilde{y} = \kappa + \frac{\lambda\omega[-\eta(\tilde{w} - \kappa) + \xi\tilde{p}^f + \pi\tilde{Y}^f]}{1 - \lambda\omega\eta}. \tag{29}$$

This model has unrealistic implications if it is considered in an explicit two region situation in which income growth in either region affects growth in the other region through trade between them. It is fairly straightforward to compute the reduced form for the per capita income growth rates in both regions, but dependent on the choice of parameters, these growth rates could obviously differ and would suggest a persisting trade imbalance (Nijkamp and Poot 1993a). Krugman (1989) noted that long-run balance of payments equilibrium in such a regional growth-and-trade framework necessitates a strict relationship between differences in growth rates between regions on the one hand and income elasticities of the demand for exports and imports on the other.[10] The Kaldor-Dixon-Thirlwall model is itself not informative about the processes which would ensure that the growth rates which this model generates would be consistent with long-run balance of payments equilibrium.

For example, if technical change proceeds at a different pace in two regions, growth in the more innovative region could be hampered by lower demand for its output from the less innovative, and less competitive, region. Indeed, if the Verdoorn effect is strong enough, a situation of "immiserising" growth may be generated in which a detrimental shock in the trading partner's economy (e.g. a rapid growth in nominal wages) is more than compensated by an, on balance, negative effect on the local economy.

The model discussed above does not take into account explicitly the possibility of factor flows between the regions, nor the diffusion and adoption of technological advances. These phenomena cannot be readily introduced here. For example, net migration would respond to the difference in

---

[10] Interestingly, the latter condition appears indeed consistent with international trade data, i.e. countries which grow fast tend to experience a high income elasticity of the demand for their exports, while the income elasticity of their demand for imports is low.

growth rates in per capita incomes, but the latter are again likely to be themselves affected by net migration. Moreover, production capacity limits are assumed unimportant here. In essence, the model describes the properties of a demand-driven steady-state growth path rather than full dynamics.[11] Yet it does make explicit that an exogenous shock to trade can have a long-term impact on the equilibrium growth rate, although our discussion suggests that the introduction of simple explicit feedback effects (here aggregate demand and relative competitiveness) can strongly modify the behaviour which may be expected in the absence of such effects.[12] Recently, Targetti and Foti (1997) showed that a blending of the ideas of neoclassical conditional convergence, Kaldorian technological progress and export-led demand growth can be fruitful for cross-section econometric explanations of country growth rates, although their results are quite sensitive to the choice of groups of countries.

The various approaches discussed in this paper have in common the interpretation of economic growth as a moving macroeconomic equilibrium in which the underlying processes can be described in rather mechanical terms. An alternative approach is to consider regional growth as the result of (un)stable evolution in a system of competing regions. Evolutionary economics has tried to examine the space-time trajectories of dynamic complex systems on the basis of biological metaphors (see for an excellent overview Nelson 1995). Notions like predator-prey, resilience, fragility and shocks are used to map out the various types of dynamics that may emerge once a system of open economies with indigenous externalities is described by nonlinear complex (synergetic) dynamics (see Nijkamp and Reggiani 1997). In such cases, a wide spectrum of dynamic behaviour may emerge, in particular if the parameters defining the architecture of a system are also becoming time-dependent in the long-run. Evolutionary theories of economic growth have already existed for some time (see, for example, the overview of Nelson and Winter 1974). Yet there is still a great potential for further in-depth study of economic growth and dynamics in a multiregional system by means of evolutionary economics.

6. Conclusions

In this paper we have surveyed the literature on the new models of economic growth which have been developed during the last decade. We have contrasted these with the earlier theories and with the common alternative approaches of studying regional development. Despite their macro-level orientation, the strength of the new models is that they give better insight into

---

[11] It is possible to introduce lags in the behavioural equations. Dixon and Thirlwall (1975) showed that the introduction of one-period lags in the export demand function still generates convergence to the equilibrium growth rate for plausible values of the elasticities.

[12] This is a general conclusion for models of interdependent regions. See also, for example, the models which have been developed by Frenkel and Razin (1987) to describe the effects of fiscal policies and monetary conditions on equilibrium output in a "two-region world".

the economic dynamics in an open system, specifically with respect to spatial interdependencies in the form of trade, factor mobility and innovation diffusion.

Many new models have been proposed in the literature. Such models capture one or more of the important features of development: sectoral composition, human and physical capital accumulation, natural endowments, economies of scale, trade, technological innovation and diffusion, factor mobility, government policies and market imperfections. However, the design of a coherent and unified framework appears to be far from easy. Moreover, most of the new theories require further extensive empirical scrutiny. In such empirical work it will be important to distinguish between transitional dynamics and long-run steady-state tendencies.

Much of the current literature adopts a macro perspective, albeit with carefully specified micro foundations. A common problem in empirical macroeconomics is that the macro data are sometimes unable to permit the researcher to conclusively choose between competing theories. For example, this problem has reduced what we can learn for policy formulation from the large literature on cross-country and cross-region growth regressions (see also e.g. Mankiw 1995).

Both the export-led growth model and the general equilibrium models considered in this paper had the ability to generate persisting differences in long-run growth rates in the presence of some spatial interdependency, provided there were barriers to other types of flows. Moreover, some models with increasing returns due to endogenous technical change suggest that there is a tendency for a highly interdependent system to be unstable, with a likelihood of "uneven development". While the new growth models offer interesting and appropriate foundation stones for a thorough analysis of the evolutionary patterns of a multi-regional system, it is obvious that much work in this area remains to be done. In particular, a better integration of micro- and macro-level approaches is required.

For example, the locational aspects of R&D creation, diffusion and adoption deserves much closer attention. To some extent, this issue is comparable to the infrastructure debate as presented, among others, in Biehl et al. (1986) and Nijkamp (1986). Production theories may be used to assess the implications of a favourable infrastructure in particular regions with respect to differential competitiveness. Endogenous growth initiatives may also be relevant in this context. The lumpiness of infrastructure means that the regional benefits may only be expected in the long run, while investments are to be made in the short run. Thus, financial resources have to be set aside which may have an uncertain future return, in particular since the demand responses to supply of public infrastructure are difficult to gauge. The same applies to unforeseen impacts of economic integration (the European market, NAFTA, etc.). Therefore, issues on the demand side, such as household behaviour, impediments to trade and the institutional structure, should not be ignored either.

In our context, a regional dynamisation of a production function, accompanied by a technological diffusion function with parameters dependent on information barriers on the one hand and competitive behaviour on the other, would provide a promising starting-point. Changing trade patterns, factor flows and public policies can then be incorporated to identify the long-run growth tendencies of the regions in the system.

References

Aghion P, Howitt P (1992) A model of growth through creative destruction. Econometrica 60(2):323–351

Allais M (1947) Économie et interêt. Imprimerie National, Paris

Andres J, Domenech R, Molinas C (1996) Macroeconomic performance and convergence in OECD countries. European Economic Review 40(9):1683–1704

Armstrong H, Taylor J (1985) Regional economics and policy. Philip Allen, Oxford

Arrow KJ (1962) The economic implications of learning by doing. Review of Economic Studies 29 (June):155–173

Arthur WB (1994) Increasing returns and path dependence in the economy. University of Michigan Press, Ann Arbor

Bairam EI (1987) The Verdoorn law, returns to scale and industrial growth: a review of the literature. Australian Economic Papers 26 (June):20–42

Bal F, Nijkamp P (1997) Exogenous and endogenous spatial growth models. TI Discussion Paper 97-022/3, Tinbergen Institute, Amsterdam

Barbier EB (1996) Endogenous growth and natural resource scarcity. Working Paper 45.96. Fondazione Eni Enrico Mattei, Milano, Italy

Barro RJ (1990) Government spending in a simple model of endogenous growth. Journal of Political Economy 98(5.2):S103–125

Barro RJ (1991) Economic growth in a cross section of countries. Quarterly Journal of Economics 106:407–443

Barro RJ (1996) Determinants of growth: a cross-country empirical study. NBER Working Paper No. 5698

Barro RJ, Becker GS (1989) Fertility choice in a model of economic growth. Econometrica 57(2):481–501

Barro RJ, Sala-i-Martin X (1992) Convergence. Journal of Political Economy 100(2):223–251

Barro RJ, Sala-i-Martin X (1995) Economic growth. McGraw-Hill, New York

Baumol WJ (1986) Productivity growth, convergence, and welfare: what the long run data show. American Economic Review 76(5):1072–1085

Becker GS, Murphy KM, Tamura RF (1990) Human capital, fertility, and economic growth. Journal of Political Economy 98(5.2):S12–S37

Ben-David D (1996) Trade and convergence among countries. Journal of International Economics 40:279–298

Bernard AB, Jones CI (1997) Comparing apples to oranges: productivity convergence and measurement across industries and countries. American Economic Review 86(5):1216–1238

Bertuglia CS, Lombardo S, Nijkamp P (eds) (1997) Innovation behaviour in space and time. Springer, Berlin Heidelberg New York

Biehl D et al. (1986) The contribution of infrastructure to regional development. Commission of European Communities, Brussels

Borts GH, Stein JL (1964) Economic growth in a free market. Columbia University Press, New York

Bovenberg AL, Smulders SA (1996) Transitional impacts of environmental policy in an endogenous growth model. International Economic Review 37(4):861–893

Braun J (1993) Essays on economic growth and migration. PhD Dissertation. Harvard University

Brown LA (1981) Innovation diffusion. Methuen, London

Cappellin R (1989) The diffusion of producer services in the urban system. In: Cappellin R, Nijkamp P (eds) Theories and policies of technological development at the local level. Gower, Aldershot

Carlino G, Mills L (1996) Convergence and the U.S. states: a time-series analysis. Journal of Regional Science 36(4):597–616

Cashin P, Loayza N (1995) Paradise lost? Growth, convergence and migration in the South Pacific. IMF Staff Papers 42(3):608–641

Cass D (1965) Optimum growth in an aggregative model of capital accumulation. Review of Economic Studies 32(3):233–240

Choi JP (1994) Irreversible choice of uncertain technologies with network externalities. Rand Journal of Economics 25:382–400

Conlisk J (1967) A modified neo-classical growth model with endogenous technical change. Southern Economic Journal 34(October):199–208

Davies S (1979) The diffusion of process innovations. Cambridge University Press, Cambridge

De Long JB (1988) Productivity growth, convergence, and welfare: comment. American Economic Review 78(5):1138–1154

De Long JB, Summers LH (1991) Equipment investment and economic growth. Quarterly Journal of Economics 106(2):445–502

Devarajan S, Swaroop V, Zou H (1996) The composition of public expenditure and economic growth. Journal of Monetary Economics 37(2):313–344

Devereux MB, Lapham BJ (1993) The stability of economic integration and endogenous growth. Discussion Paper No. 878, Institute for Economic Research, Queen's University, Canada

Dixon R, Thirlwall AP (1975) A model of regional growth-rate differences on Kaldorian lines. Oxford Economic Papers 27:201–214

Domar ED (1946) Capital expansion, rate of growth, and employment. Econometrica 14(April):137–147

Dosi G (1988) Sources, procedures, and microeconomic effects of innovation. Journal of Economic Literature 88(3):1120–1171

Dowrick S, Nguyen D (1989) OECD comparative economic growth 1950–85: catch-up and convergence. American Economic Review 79(5):1010–1030

Drugeon JP (1996) Impatience and long-run growth. Journal of Economic Dynamics and Control 20:281–313

Easterlin RA (1960) Interregional differences in per capita income, population, and total income, 1840-1950. In: Conference on Research in Income and Wealth, NBER Studies in Income and Wealth, vol 24

Ehrlich I (1990) The problem of development: introduction. Journal of Political Economy 98(5.2):S1–S11

Elbasha EH, Roe TL (1996) On endogenous growth: the implications of environmental externalities. Journal of Environmental Economics and Management 31:240–268

Evans P (1995) How to estimate growth regressions consistently. Department of Economics, Ohio State University, mimeo

Evans P, Karras G (1996) Convergence revisited. Journal of Monetary Economics 37:249–265

Frenkel JA, Razin A (1987) Fiscal policies and the world economy: an intertemporal approach. MIT Press, Cambridge, Mass.

Fujita M, Krugman P, Mori T (1995) On the evolution of hierarchical urban systems. Discussion Paper No. 419, Institute of Economic Research, Kyoto University

Garegnani P (1970) Heterogeneous capital, the production function and the theory of capital. Review of Economic Studies 37:407–436

Giaoutzi M, Nijkamp P (eds) (1988) Informatics and regional development. Gower, Aldershot

Gordon RH, Bovenberg AL (1996) Why is capital so immobile internationally? Possible explanations and implications for capital income taxation. American Economic Review 86(5):1057–1075

Gorter C, Nijkamp P, Poot J (forthcoming) Crossing borders: regional and urban perspectives on international migration. Avebury, Aldershot

Grossman GM, Helpman E (1990a) Trade, innovation and growth. American Economic Review 80(2):86–91

Grossman GM, Helpman E (1990b) Comparative advantage and long-run growth. American Economic Review 80(4):796–815

Grossman GM, Helpman E (1991) Innovation and growth in the global economy. MIT Press, Cambridge, Mass

Grossman GM, Helpman E (1994) Endogenous innovation in the theory of growth. Journal of Economic Perspectives 8(1):23–44

Harrod RF (1939) An essay in dynamic theory. Economic Journal 49 (June):14–33

Hatta T (1976) The paradox in capital theory and complementarity of inputs. Review of Economic Studies 43:127–142

Inada K (1963) On a two-sector model of economic growth: comments and a generalization. Review of Economic Studies 30(June):119–127

International Monetary Fund (various years) International Financial Statistics. International Monetary Fund, Washington, DC

Isard W, Liossatos P, Kanemoto Y, Kaniss PC (1979) Spatial dynamics and optimal space-time development. North-Holland Publishing Company, Amsterdam

Jones H (1975) An introduction to modern theories of economic growth. Nelson, London

Jones LE, Manuelli RE (1997) Endogenous growth theory: an introduction. Journal of Economic Dynamics and Control 21(1):11–22

Jones LE, Stokey NL (1992) Introduction: symposium on economic growth, theory and computations. Journal of Economic Theory 58:117–134

Jovanovic B (1995) Research, schooling, training and learning by doing in the theory of growth. Department of Economics, University of Pennsylvania, mimeo

Kaldor N (1957) A model of economic growth. Economic Journal 67:591–624

Kaldor N (1970) The case for regional policies. Scottish Journal of Political Economy 17(3):337–348

Kamien MI, Schwartz NL (1982) Market structure and innovation. Cambridge University Press, Cambridge

Keller W (1996) Absorptive capacity: on the creation and acquisition of technology in development. Journal of Development Economics 49(1):199–227

King RG, Rebelo ST (1993) Transitional dynamics and economic growth in the neoclassical model. American Economic Review 83(4):908–931

Knight M, Loayza N, Villanueva D (1993) Testing the neoclassical theory of economic growth. IMF Staff Papers 40(3):512–541

Koopmans TC (1965) On the concept of optimal economic growth. In: The econometric approach to development planning. North-Holland, Amsterdam

Kormendi R, Meguire P (1985) Macroeconomic determinants of growth: cross-country evidence. Journal of Monetary Economics 16:141–163

Koski H, Nijkamp P (1996) Timing of adoption of new communication technology. TI Discussion Paper 96-61/5, Tinbergen Institute, Amsterdam

Kremer M (1993) Population growth and technological change: one million B.C. to 1990. Quarterly Journal of Economics 108(3):681–716

Krugman P (1979) A model of innovation, technology transfer, and the world distribution of income. Journal of Political Economy 87:253–266

Krugman P (1981) Trade, accumulation and uneven development. Journal of Development Economics 8:149–161

Krugman P (ed) (1988) Strategic trade policy and the new international economics. MIT Press, Cambridge, Mass

Krugman P (1989) Income elasticities and real exchange rates. European Economic Review 33:1031–1054

Krugman P (1991) Geography and trade. MIT Press, Cambridge, Mass

Krugman P (1995) Development, geography and economic theory. MIT Press, Cambridge, Mass

Kubo Y (1995) Scale economies, regional externalities, and the possibility of uneven regional development. Journal of Regional Science 35(1):29–42

Kubo Y, Kim H (1996) Human capital, imported technology and economic growth: a comparative study of Korea and Japan. Discussion Paper 695, Institute of Policy and Planning Sciences, University of Tsukuba

Levine R, Renelt D (1992) A sensitivity analysis of cross-country growth regressions. American Economic Review 82(4):942–963

Lewis WA (1954) Economic development with unlimited supplies of labor. Manchester School of Economics and Social Studies 22 (May):139–191

Lucas RE (1988) On the mechanics of economic development. Journal of Monetary Economics 22(1):3–42

Lucas RE (1990) Why doesn't capital flow from rich to poor countries? American Economic Review 80(2):92–96

Malthus TR (1798) An essay on the principle of population, 1986 edition. W. Pickering, London

Mankiw NG (1995) The growth of nations. Brookings Papers on Economic Activity 1:275–310

Mankiw NG, Romer D, Weil DN (1992) A contribution to the empirics of economic growth. Quarterly Journal of Economics 107 (May):407–438

Markusen A (1996) Interaction between regional and industrial policies. International Regional Science Review 19(1&2):49–78

Marx K (1867) Capital Vol I, 1967 edition. International Publishers, New York

McCombie JSL (1988a) A synoptic view of regional growth and unemployment: I – the neoclassical theory. Urban Studies 25(4):267–281

McCombie JSL (1988b) A synoptic view of regional growth and unemployment: II – the post-Keynesian theory. Urban Studies 25(5):399–417

Morrill R, Gaile GL, Thrall GI (1988) Spatial diffusion. Sage, Beverley Hills

Myrdal G (1957) Economic theory and underdeveloped regions. Duckworth, London

Nana G, Poot J (1996) A study of trade liberalisation and factor mobility with a CGE model of Australia and New Zealand. Studies in Regional Science 26(2):27–52

Nelson R (1995) Recent evolutionary theorizing about economic change. Journal of Economic Literature 33(1):48–90

Nelson R, Winter S (1974) Neoclassical vs. evolutionary theories of economic growth: critique and prospectus. Economic Journal 84(336):886–905

Nijkamp P (1986) Infrastructure and regional development: a multidimensional policy analysis. Empirical Economics 11:1–21

Nijkamp P, Poot J (1993a) Technological progress and spatial dynamics: a theoretical reflection. In: Kohno H, Nijkamp P (eds) Potentials and bottlenecks of spatial economic development. Springer, Berlin Heidelberg New York

Nijkamp P, Poot J (1993b) Endogenous technological change, innovation diffusion and transitional dynamics in a nonlinear growth model. Australian Economic Papers 32(4):191–213

Nijkamp P, Poot J, Rouwendal J (1991) A nonlinear dynamic model of spatial development and R&D policy. Annals of Regional Science 25:287–302

Nijkamp P, Reggiani A (1997) The economics of complex spatial systems. Elsevier, Amsterdam

Oniki H, Uzawa H (1965) Patterns of trade and investment in a dynamic model of international trade. Review of Economic Studies 32:15–38

Osano H (1992) Basic research and applied R&D in a model of endogenous economic growth. Osaka Economic Papers 42(1/2):144–167

Perroti R (1996) Growth, income distribution and democracy; what the data say. Journal of Economic Growth (June)

Perroux F (1955) Note sur la notion de pôle de croissance'. Cahiers de l'Institut de Science Economique Appliquée. Series D No. 8

Perrson J (1994) Convergence in per capita income and migration across the Swedish counties 1906–1990. Institute for International Economic Studies, Stockholm University, mimeo

Pontryagin LS et al. (1962) The mathematical theory of optimal processes. Interscience Publishers, New York

Quah DT (1996) Empirics for economic growth and convergence. European Economic Review 40:1353–1375

Ramsey F (1928) A mathematical theory of saving. Economic Journal 38(December):543-559

Ricardo D (1817) On the principles of political economy and taxation, 1951 edition. Cambridge University Press, Cambridge, Mass

Richardson HW (1973) Regional growth theory. Macmillan, London

Rivera-Batiz LA, Xie Danyang (1993) Integration among unequals. Regional Science and Urban Economics 23(3):337–354

Rivera-Batiz LA, Romer PM (1991) Economic integration and endogenous growth. Quarterly Journal of Economics 106(2):531–556

Romer PM (1986) Increasing returns and long-run growth. Journal of Political Economy 94(5):1002–1037

Romer PM (1989) Capital accumulation in the theory of long-run growth. In: Barro RJ (ed) Modern business cycle theory. Harvard University Press, Cambridge, Mass

Romer PM (1990) Endogenous technological change. Journal of Political Economy 98(5.2): S71–S102

Romer PM (1994) The origins of endogenous growth. Journal of Economic Perspectives 8(1):3–22

Sala-i-Martin X (1996) Regional cohesion: evidence and theories of regional growth and convergence. European Economic Review 40:1325–1352

Samuelson PA (1958) An exact consumption-loan model of interest with or without the social contrivance of money. Journal of Political Economy 66(6):467–482

Schmitz JA (1989) Imitation, entrepreneurship, and long-run growth. Journal of Political Economy 97(3):721–739

Schumpeter JA (1934) The theory of economic development. Harvard University Press, Cambridge, Mass

Scott M (1989) A new view of economic growth. Oxford University Press, Oxford

Smith A (1776) An inquiry into the nature and causes of the wealth of nations. 1937 edition, Random House, New York

Soete L, Turner R (1984) Technology diffusion and the rate of technical change. Economic Journal 94:612–623

Solow RM (1956) A contribution to the theory of economic growth. Quarterly Journal of Economics 70:65–94

Solow RM (1994) Perspectives on growth theory. Journal of Economic Perspectives 8(1):45–54

Stern N (1991) The determinants of growth. Economic Journal 101 (January):122–133

Stokey NL (1988) Learning by doing and the introduction of new goods. Journal of Political Economy 96:701–717

Summers R, Heston A (1991) The Penn World Table (Mark 5): an expanded set of international comparisons, 1950–1988. Quarterly Journal of Economics 106(2):327–368

Swan TW (1956) Economic growth and capital accumulation. Economic Record 32(November):334–361

Targetti F, Foti A (1997) Growth and productivity: a model of cumulative growth and catching up. Cambridge Journal of Economics 21(1):27–43

Van Dijk J, Folmer H, Herzog Jr HW, Schlottmann AM (1989) Migration and labour market adjustment. Kluwer, Dordrecht

Venables AJ (1996) Trade policy, cumulative causation, and industrial development. Journal of Development Economics 49(1):179–197

Verdoorn PJ (1949) Fattori che regolano la sviluppo della produttivita del lavoro [Factors governing the growth of labour productivity]. L'Industria 1:3–10 [English translation: Thirlwall AP, Thirlwall G, Research in Population and Economics, 1979]

Vernon R (1966) International investment and international trade in the product cycle. Quarterly Journal of Economics 80:190–207

Verspagen B (1992) Endogenous innovation in neo-classical growth models: a survey. Journal of Macroeconomics 14(4):631–662

World Bank (various years) World Bank national accounts. World Bank, Washington. DC

Yoshida M (1995) Compatibility between growth and environmental preservation: threshold effects of the environment on health risks. Institute of Policy and Planning Sciences, University of Tsukuba

[2]

DE ECONOMIST 137, NR. 2, 1989

ENDOGENOUS PRODUCTION OF R&D
AND
STABLE ECONOMIC DEVELOPMENT

BY

JAN ROUWENDAL AND PETER NIJKAMP*

1 THE MODEL

Awareness has grown that technological change is not external to the economic system ('manna from heaven'), but is to a large extent governed by specific creative investments in the form of R&D. The implications of endogenizing technological progress in an economic system therefore deserve closer attention. This is the subject of this paper.

We assume the existence of two sectors, one concerned with the production of a commodity that is used for consumption and investment, the other with technology creation. The first is called sector 1, the second sector 2. The existence of a neo-classical production function is·assumed for both sectors (see also for earlier discussions Gomulka, 1970, Phelps, 1966, Shell, 1967).

Production in sector 1 is denoted as P_1:

$$P_1 = F_1(\alpha L_1, K_1) \tag{1}$$

In this equation F_1 represents the production function, α is an index of (labour augmenting) technological change, L_1 is the volume of labour used in sector 1, and K_1 the volume of capital.

The production function is assumed to be homogeneous of degree 1 in labour and capital to be twice differentiable with positive first-order derivatives and diminishing returns for each factor (see e.g. Hacche, 1979). Moreover, both inputs are assumed to be essential for the production process (i.e., $L_1 = 0$ or $K_1 = 0$ implies $P_1 = 0$). The commodity produced in sector 1 serves as the numéraire in the model.

Capital and labour will be paid the value of their marginal products. The wage rate, w, and the rate of return on capital, r, can thus be determined as:

$$w = \partial F_1(\alpha L_1, K_1)/\partial L_1 \tag{2}$$

$$r = \partial F_1(\alpha L_1, K_1)/\partial K_1 \tag{3}$$

* Free University of Amsterdam, Department of Economics, Amsterdam, The Netherlands.

This ensures, in combination with the homogeneity of F_1, that P_1 is equal to the total amount of real income (measured in units of the commodity produced) generated in sector 1:

$$Y_1 = wL_1 + rK_1 \tag{4}$$

$$Y_1 = P_1 \tag{5}$$

The creation of new technology results in increases of the parameter α. The following relation is assumed:

$$\dot{\alpha} = F_2(L_2, K_2, \alpha) \tag{6}$$

where $\dot{\alpha} = d\alpha/dt$, F_2 is a neo-classical production function which is assumed to be homogeneous in L_2 and K_2, respectively the amounts of labour and capital used for the production of R&D. This function is also assumed to be twice differentiable with positive first-order derivatives and diminishing returns for each factor. The value of α is included as an argument in F_2 in order to be able to deal with the effects of the stock of already available technological knowledge on the possibilities to increase it (*i.e.*, self-generating knowledge). The direction of these effects is *a priori* ambiguous: increases in the stock of knowledge may favour a rapid development of new inventions but, beyond a critical level, a 'decreasing returns to scale' phenomenon may also occur which may make it difficult to increase the existing stock of knowledge when it has already become large.

It is assumed throughout the paper that in sector 2 the same wage and rate of return on capital will be paid as in sector 1. The wage and the rate of return are in this case not necessarily equal to the marginal products $\partial F_2/\partial L_2$ and $\partial F_2/\partial K_2$, however (see section 3). Total income generated by sector 2 is of course equal to the total budget available for R&D, Y_2:

$$Y_2 = wL_2 + rK_2 \tag{7}$$

There is no reason for Y_2 to be equal to $\dot{\alpha}$. It is assumed that R&D expenditures, in a way similar to conventional investments, have to be financed from the total amount of savings S:

$$S = \dot{K}_1 + \dot{K}_2 + Y_2 \tag{8}$$

where $\dot{K}_1 = dK_1/dt$ and $\dot{K}_2 = dK_2/dt$. We have abstracted here from depreciation. Clearly equation (8) implies equilibrium on the market for capital.

To complete the model, total labour force, capital stock and income are defined as:

$$L = L_1 + L_2 \tag{9}$$

$$K = K_1 + K_2 \tag{10}$$

$$Y = Y_1 + Y_2 \tag{11}$$

Having now presented the basic structure of our endogenous R&D expenditures model, we will examine its most important properties in the next section.

2 TOTAL INCOME AND SAVINGS FOR R&D

In the present model, R&D differs from capital in that it is a derived input: conventional production factors have to be devoted to R&D which could otherwise have been used for commodity production. On the other hand, the fact that these production factors are paid the same wages and rents as those used for commodity production indicates that total income in an economy with R&D expenditures is not lower than that in the same economy without R&D (*i.e.*, when all available labour and capital are used for goods production). It can even be demonstrated that in the present model total income in an economy with R&D will usually be higher than that in a comparable economy without R&D. It should be noted that the comparison refers to a situation where α is the same in both economies. This is the subject of proposition 1.

Proposition 1 – The following condition is valid: $Y \geq F_1(\alpha L, K)$, with the equality holding only if $K_1/\alpha L_1 = K/\alpha L$.

Proof – Because of the homogeneity of F_1 we can say:

$$F_1(\alpha L_1, K_1) = \alpha L_1 f_1(k_1)$$

where $k_1 = K_1/\alpha L_1$ and $f_1(k_1)$ is defined as $f_1(k_1) = F_1(1, K_1/\alpha L_1)$. From this equation it can be derived, by using (2) and (3), that (see *e.g.* Hacche, 1979):

$$w = \alpha f_1(k_1) - \alpha k_1 f_1'(k_1) \tag{12}$$

$$r = f_1'(k_1) \tag{13}$$

where $f_1'(k_1) = d f_1(k_1)/dk_1$. It follows from equations (4), (7) and (9) – (11) that:

$$Y = wL + rK \tag{14}$$

Substitution of (12) and (13) gives:

$$Y = [\alpha f_1(k_1) - \alpha k_1 f'(k_1)]L + f'(k_1)K \tag{15}$$

In this equation Y has been written as a function of k_1 and the exogenous variables α, L and K only. In order to examine the relationship between Y and K, we determine the first derivative:

$$\frac{dY}{dk_1} = f''(k_1)\{K - \alpha L k_1\} \tag{16}$$

where $f''(k_1) = d^2 f_1(k_1)/dk_1^2$, which is negative. Writing $K/\alpha L$ as k we conclude that Y is a decreasing function of k_1 when $k_1 < k$, reaches a minimum when $k_1 = k$, and is an increasing function of k_1 when $k_1 > k$.

When $k_1 = k$, it is easily seen that the values of the first partial derivatives of F_1 are equal at the points (L_1, K_1) and (L, K). The proof follows from the homogeneity of degree 1 of F_1. This implies that in this case

$$wL + rK = F_1(\alpha L, K) \tag{17}$$

It may be concluded therefore that $Y > F_1(\alpha L, K)$ when $k_1 \neq k$ and that $Y = F_1(\alpha L, K)$ if $k_1 = k$. This completes the proof of proposition 1.

Proposition 1 is also illustrated in Fig. 1. The point (L_1, K_1) denotes the actual amounts of production factors devoted to the commodity production. In

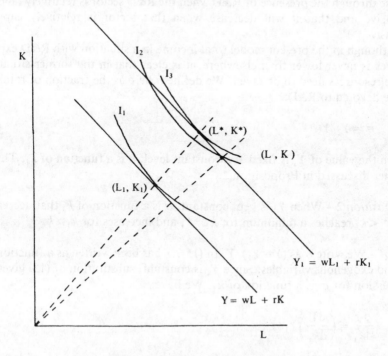

Figure 1 – Isoquants and income lines

this point the slope of the isoquant I_1 corresponding to a production volume P_1 is equal to that of the line $wL_1 + rK_1 = Y_1$. The isoquant I_2 refers to the production volume and touches the line $wL + rK = Y$ in point (L^*, K^*). The income Y that has actually been reached in the presence of R&D corresponds therefore to the one that could have been reached when the total volumes of production factors would have been equal to L^* and K^* and would have been used completely in sector 1.

In the presence of R&D, total income will in general be higher than in the situation without R&D. This higher income will be distributed somewhat differently over the two production factors. In the configuration shown in Fig. 1, the conventional sector will have a capital-labour ratio K_1/L_1 that is higher than K/L. Marginal productivity theory implies then that in the presence of R&D the wage-rent ratio w/r will also be higher than in a situation without R&D. Since the total amounts of both production factors are the same in the two situations that are compared, this means that labour will receive a greater share in total income in the presence of R&D.

The situation would of course be different when the ratio K_1/L_1 would be lower than K/L. In that case the share of labour would be lower compared to the situation without R&D.

In general we may conclude that the share of labour in total income will increase through the presence of R&D when the R&D sector is relatively labour-intensive and that it will decrease when that sector is relatively capital-intensive.

Although in the present model total income in a situation with R&D expenditures is never lower than elsewhere, it is clear that in the former situation more resources need to be saved. We define σ here as the fraction of total income devoted to R&D:

$$\sigma = Y_2/Y \tag{18}$$

When the value of Y_1 is fixed at a constant level, σ is a function of k_1. This is further discussed in Proposition 2.

Proposition 2 – When Y_1 is kept constant, σ is a function of k_1 that decreases for $k_1 < k$, reaches a minimum for $k_1 = k$, and increases for $k_1 > k$.

Proof – We write σ as $(Y - Y_1)/Y$. In (15), Y has been written as a function of k_1 and exogenous variables. Since Y_1 is constant, substitution of (15) gives an expression for σ as a function of k_1. We have:

$$\frac{d\sigma}{dk_1} = \left(\frac{dY}{dk_1}\right)Y_1/Y^2$$

and conclude that $d\sigma/dk_1$ has the same sign as dY_t/dk_1. This completes the proof of this proposition.

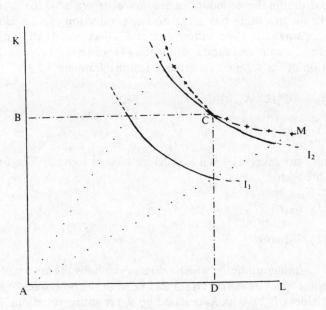

Figure 2 – Total income and savings for R&D

Proposition 2 is illustrated in Fig. 2. In this figure, I_1 is the isoquant corresponding to an (arbitrarily selected) level of income generated in sector 1. I_2 is the isoquant passing through the point (L, K), which is denoted as C in Fig. 2. The line M connects the points corresponding to the maximum income that can be reached. For example, point (L^*, K^*) from Fig. 1 is located on this line. Proposition 2 implies essentially that M is more convex than I_2.

In Fig. 2 the square with corner points $ABCD$ gives all feasible combinations of L_1 and K_1. It is clear from the figure that at the particular income level selected only a relatively small part of all nonnegative values K_1 can actually be chosen. If a lower level of Y_1 were selected, more values of k_1 would have been feasible.

It is noteworthy that, for a given value for k_1, the same amount of total income Y would be generated, independently of the value of Y_1. Of course a lower level of Y_1 would require a higher rate of savings σ for R&D, but total immediate income would not be influenced.

Having now shown the validity of two interesting propositions, we will turn in the next section to the allocation problem of R&D expenditures.

3 ALLOCATION OF PRODUCTION FACTORS TO R&D

The rate of technical progress in the economy described in section 1 is determined by the amount of income Y_2 spent on R&D, by the prices for labour and capital, and by the allocation of Y_2 over both production factors.

We assume that in this economy an amount Y_2 is available for R&D expenditures and that this budget is spent on the production factors labour and capital in such a way that the resulting output $\dot{\alpha}$ is maximized. This implies that the demand for labour and capital originating from sector 2 can be described as the solution of the following mathematical programme:

Max. $\dot{\alpha} = F_2(L_2, K_2, \alpha)$

s.t. $Y_2 = wL_2 + rK_2$

where w and r are taken as given and determined in sector 1. The first order conditions are then:

$$\partial F_2(L_2, K_2, \alpha)/\partial L_2 = \theta w \tag{19}$$

$$\partial F_2(L_2, K_2, \alpha)/\partial K_2 = \theta r \tag{20}$$

where θ is a Lagrange multiplier which reflects essentially the (average) productivity of income spent on R&D. To see this we multiply both sides of (19) with L_2 and both sides of (20) with K_2 and add up the resulting equations. Then we find:

$$(\partial F_2/\partial L_2)L_2 + (\partial F_2/\partial K_2)K_2 = \theta(wL_2 + rK_2) \tag{21}$$

The left-hand-side of this equation is equal to α, given the homogeneity of F_2. The term in brackets at the right-hand-side is equal to Y_2. Therefore we may conclude:

$$\dot{\alpha} = \theta Y_2 \tag{22}$$

The value of θ can be interpreted as the productivity of the income spent on R&D (*i.e.*, the increase in α associated with one unit of income spent on R&D) or, equivalently, as the inverse of the shadow price of R&D.

Taking the ratio of (19) and (20) we find:

$$\frac{\partial F_2(L_2, K_2, \alpha)/\partial L_2}{\partial F_2(L_2, K_2, \alpha)/\partial K_2} = \frac{w}{r} \tag{23}$$

From this it can be seen that w and r are equal to the marginal products of F_1 at point (L_1, K_1). Since the marginal products or both production functions can be written in terms of k_1 resp. K_2, we may now formulate a proposition on the efficient allocation for R&D.

Proposition 3 – When a given amount Y_2 of income is devoted to R&D and is to be allocated efficiently, the following condition holds:

$$h_1(k_1) = h_2(k_2, \alpha) \tag{24}$$

where

$$h_1(k_1) = \frac{1}{\alpha} \frac{\partial F_1(\alpha L_1, K_1)/\partial L_1}{\partial F_1(\alpha L_1, K_1)/\partial K_1} \tag{25}$$

and

$$h_2(k_2) = \frac{1}{\alpha} \frac{\partial F_2(L_2, K_2, \alpha)/\partial L_2}{\partial F_2(L_2, K_2, \alpha)/\partial K_2} \tag{26}$$

Proof – By using (23) and (2) and (3), it is easy to verify that the ratios of the marginal products with respect to labour and capital of both production functions should be equal. It remains to be shown that these ratios can be written in terms of k_1 and α only. Using (12) and (13) we find:

$$\frac{\partial F_1/\partial L_1}{\partial F_1/\partial K_1} = \alpha \left\{ \frac{f_1(k_1)}{f_1'(k_1)} - k_1 \right\}$$

Now $h_1(k_1)$ is defined as the expression within curley brackets.

Because of its homogeneity in L_2 and K_2, $F_2(L_2, K_2\alpha)$ can be written as $\alpha L_2 F_2(1/\alpha, k_2, \alpha)$ where k_2 is defined as $K_2/\alpha L_2$. Defining $f_2(k_2, \alpha)$ as $F_2(1/\alpha, k_2, \alpha)$ we can derive:

$$\frac{\partial F_2/\partial L_2}{\partial F_2/\partial K_2} = \alpha \left\{ \frac{f_2(k_2, \alpha)}{f_2'(k_2, \alpha)} - k_2 \right\}$$

Defining $h_2(k_2, \alpha)$ as the expression between curley brackets in this equation, we can verify the validity of eq. (24). This completes the proof.

The function $h_1(k_1)$ has a value 0 for $k_1 = 0$ and has a positive first derivative. Its value increases without upper bound as k_1 does so. Analogously $h_2(k_2, \alpha)$ has a value zero for $k_2 = 0$, has a positive first derivative $\partial h_2(k_2, \alpha)/\partial k_2$, and increases without an upper bound when k_2 does so.

The optimal allocation defined by (24) can be represented as the contract curve in the Edgeworth box *ABCD* of Fig. 3. The points for which equation (24) is satisfied are those for which the slopes of the isoquants of F_1 and F_2 are equal. It can be shown that, under the assumptions made with respect to F_1 and F_2, the contract curve is indeed a continuously increasing function starting in the south-west corner of the Edgeworth box and ending up in its north-east corner.

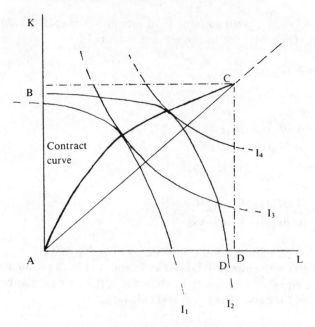

Figure 3 – Edgeworth box

One important fact in the present context is that the contract curve is entirely located at one side of the main diagonal of the Edgeworth box (*i.e.* the line *AC*), or coincides with it. To show this, we suppose that one point of the main diagonal lies on the contract curve. Then the marginal rates of substitution of both production functions are equal at that point. It follows by the homogeneity of the production function that the same must be true for all points on the line *AC*. Thus the contract curve will never intersect the main diagonal of the Edgeworth box.

4 STEADY STATES

Until now we have essentially been concerned with the analysis of the allocation of production factors in the economy described by our model at one point in time. In this section we will focus attention on steady states. A steady state can be regarded as a form of dynamic equilibrium. It is defined as a situation in which both capital and income grow at the same rate (say g), while the labour force grows at another (lower) rate (say λ) and k remains constant:

$$\dot{L}/L = \lambda$$
$$\dot{K}/K = g$$
$$\dot{Y}/Y = g \quad\quad\quad (27)$$
$$\dot{k} = 0$$

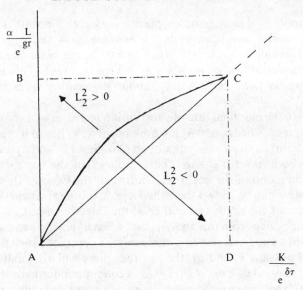

Figure 4 – Development of the contract curve over time.

In these equations a dot denotes (as above) the time derivative of a variable.
Because the following condition holds:

$$\dot{k}/k = \dot{K}/K - \dot{L}/L - \dot{\alpha}/\alpha$$

(27) implies that α should grow at a constant rate $g - \lambda$ in the steady state.

One may study the implications of a steady state growth in the present model by using a variant of Fig. 3, where αL instead of L is pictured on the horizontal axis and where the units in which K and h are measured change over time in such a way that the point $(L(\tau), K(\tau))$ remains at the same place over time. Then the curvature of the isoquants of F_1 do not change over time, although of course the 'same' isoquant corresponds to an ever increasing production volume.

It is easy to see that in the resulting picture (see Fig. 4) the contract curve will remain at the same place when the isoquant of F_2 will not change over time. This will, however, only happen when technological change influences F_2 in the same way as it does F_1. In other words, technological progress should be purely labour-augmenting in the R&D sector, just as it is in the goods-producing sector.

To see how the contract curve will change over time we analyze the effects of small changes in α on condition (24). We have:

$$h_1'(k_1)dk_1 = h_2^1(k_2,\alpha)dk_2 + h_2^2(k_2,\alpha)d\alpha \tag{28}$$

where $h_1'(K_1) = dh_1/dk_1$, $h_2^1(k_2,\alpha) = \partial h_2/\partial k_2$, and $h_2^2(k_2,\alpha) = \partial h_2/\partial \alpha$.

When technological progress takes place it is clear that $d\alpha > 0$. The contract curve remains at the same place when it is possible for k_1 and k_2 to remain unchanged. This requires that $h_2^2 = 0$. When $h_2^2 = 0$, the marginal rate of substitution of F_2 is independent of α, when k_2 is kept constant. This implies that technical progress takes on a purely labour-augmenting form in the R&D sector.

When $h_2^2 > 0$, the marginal rate of substitution increases as a consequence of technical progress. Since h_1' and h_2^1 are both positive, k_1 has to increase or k_1 to decrease (or both) to ensure the equality in (28). Since k_1 and k_2 are related to each other,[1] both have to change. This implies that the contract curve will move in the direction of the north-west corner of the Edgeworth box.

Analogously it can be shown that when $h_2^2 < 0$, the contract curve will move in the direction of the south-east corner of the Edgeworth box.

It can be concluded from this analysis that when h_2^2 always has the same sign and is bounded away from zero (*i.e.* there exists a constant ε such that $|f_2^2(k_2, \alpha)| > \varepsilon$ for all possible k_2 and α), the contract curve will eventually approach one of the lines *ABC* or *ADC*. The economic interpretation of this phenomenon is that, when technical progress works out differently in both sectors (and therefore the isoquants of F_1 and F_2 change in a different way), ultimately a situation will be approached in which each of the sectors uses only one production factor.

This gives some reason to conjecture that a non-zero value for f_2^2 is not compatible with steady-state growth as defined in (27).

Proposition 4 – Steady-state growth is possible only when $\partial h_2(k_2, \alpha)/\partial\alpha = 0$.

Proof – We use equation (15). Both sides of the equation should grow at the same rate g. Since Y, αL and K grow at this rate, given the definition of the steady-state, it follows that both $f'(k_1)$ and $f_1(k) - k_1 f'(k_1)$ have to be constant. This implies that k_1 has to remain constant on the steady-state growth path. It was already shown above that this is possible only when h_2^2 equals zero.

The only case left for the existence of steady growth is the one in which h_2^2 equals zero. It turns out that, when this is the case, some specific statements on the properties of the production function F_2 can be made (see Proposition 5).

Proposition 5 – When $\partial h_2(k_2, \alpha)/\partial\alpha = 0$, the production function of sector 2 can be written as:

$$F_2(L_2, K_2, \alpha) = G(\alpha L_2, K_2)\alpha^{-\delta} \tag{29}$$

where G is again a neo-classical production function.

---

[1] We have:

$$k = \frac{L_1}{L}k_1 + \frac{L_2}{L} \cdot k_2$$

Proof - We can write: $F_2(L_2, K_2, \alpha)$ as $\alpha L_2 f_2(k_2, \alpha)$. It follows that we should have:

$$\frac{\dot{\alpha}}{\alpha} = L_2 f_2(k_2, \alpha)$$

On the steady-state growth path the left-hand side of this equation is equal to $g - \lambda$. From the discussion above it follows that when $h_2^2 = 0$, k_2 will be constant on the steady-state growth path. This implies that L_2 should grow at a rate λ (as does L), and therefore $f_2(k_2 \alpha)$ should grow at a rate $-\lambda$. It follows that:

$$f_2(k_2, \alpha_0 e^{(g-\lambda)\tau}) = e^{-\lambda\tau} f_2(k_2, a_0)$$

which implies that $f_2(k_2, \alpha)$ is homogeneous of degree $-\lambda/(g-\lambda)$ in α.

From this we conclude:

$$\alpha f_2'(k_2, \alpha) = [-\lambda/(g-\lambda)] f_2(k_2, \alpha)$$

where $f_2'(k_2, \alpha) = \partial f_2(k_2, \alpha)/\partial\alpha$. The solution of this differential equation is:

$$f_2(k_2, \alpha) = g(k_2) a^{-\lambda/(g-\lambda)}$$

where the result has been used that each neo-classical production function $G(\alpha L_2, K_2)$ can be written as $\alpha L_2 g(k_2)$; this gives us the latter expression after defining δ as $\lambda/(g-\lambda)$.

Proposition 5 establishes that F_2 should incorporate technological change in essentially the same way as F_1 does since it is equal to the product of a neo-classical production function G with purely labour augmenting technological change and a term $\alpha^{-\delta}$ that reflects decreasing returns associated with technical progress.

The growth rate g depends on the natural rate of growth λ and on the decreasing returns parameter δ as follows:

$$g = \lambda(1+\delta)/\delta \tag{30}$$

A smaller value of δ thus implies a higher value of g. This plausible result confirms our intuition according to which a higher growth rate is possible as it is easier to invent new production techniques. It is also noteworthy that g always exceeds λ, but approaches it for high values of δ.

5 DISCUSSION

In the foregoing model with endogenous technical progress it was shown that steady-state growth is possible only when two conditions are fulfilled: (i) technical progress should be of the same (purely labour augmenting) form in both sectors and (ii) an increase in the stock of knowledge should make it more difficult to invent still newer production techniques. These conditions will be discussed shortly.

Purely labour augmenting technical progress was postulated in F_1 because it is well-known that in the standard neo-classical model (with exogenous technical progress) this is the only form compatible with steady-state growth (see e.g. Hacche, 1979). There seems to be no reason, however, to expect that technical progress has the same consequences for labour productivity in goods production as it has for labour productivity in R&D. Thus, in the framework of the present model we may conclude that a steady state is not very plausible. When technical progress is not of the same labour augmenting form in both sectors, sustained (non steady-state) growth leads eventually to a situation in which one production factor is almost completely used in one sector (that is: the contract curve approaches the north-west or south-east corner of the Edgeworth box of Fig. 4).

An increase in technological knowledge has two effects on the R&D sector: on the one hand the productivity of labour improves, which makes it easier to improve knowledge still further; on the other hand the decreasing results to scale tend to make it more difficult to increase the stock of knowledge. To investigate which of these effects is most important, we compute $\partial F_2(L_2, K_2, \alpha)/\partial\alpha$:

$$\frac{\partial F_2(L_2, K_2, \alpha)}{\partial\alpha} = \alpha^{-\delta-1}\left\{\alpha\frac{\partial G(\alpha L_2, K_2)}{\partial\alpha} - \delta G(\alpha L_2, K_2)\right\} \tag{31}$$

This can – after some manipulations[2] – be rewritten as:

$$\frac{\partial F_2(L_2, K_2, \alpha)}{\partial\alpha} = \alpha^{-\delta-1}\{(1-\delta)G(\alpha L_2, K_2) - K_2 g'(k_2)\} \tag{32}$$

which is certainly negative when $\delta \geq 1$. It may be concluded therefore that the net effect of an increase in technical knowledge on R&D production can only be positive when the decreasing returns associated with this knowledge are very modest in size.

A further point of interest is the development of the production of income spent on R&D. From (22) it can be inferred that in a steady state θ will grow at a rate $-\lambda$ (since $\dot\alpha$ grows at the same rate as α). This implies that, as time goes by, more and more income needs to be spent on R&D in order to achieve the same increase in α. Technical progress thus becomes more expensive.

---

[2]   We used the fact that $\partial G/\partial L_2 = (\alpha/L_2)\partial G/\partial\alpha$ and wrote G as $\alpha L_2 g(K_2)$.

One parameter of the R&D production function that was not made explicit so far is the stock of pure scientific knowledge. A scientific breakthrough may stimulate the invention of a great many new production possibilities (a 'radical change' à la Mensch, 1979). For instance, one may imagine that the value of δ depends on the stock of pure scientific knowledge that has not been applied in production techniques so far, but which is of potential interest for R&D. A scientific breakthrough may then cause a temporarily lower value of δ and a higher rate of growth. These science policy speculations do of course take us outside the realm of steady-state analysis.

Finally, also the spatial implications of a dynamic economic system are worth mentioning (see Nijkamp, 1986). The development potential or the incubator profile of a specific region may favour specific technological innovations and may also cause spatial discrepancies in the competetive positions of regions. Such spatially varying developments are also influenced by distance barriers and diffusion mechanisms (*cf.* Brown, 1981, and Soete and Turner, 1984). In this context we may also imagine a steady-state of a whole system of regions in which technology is first produced in the leading region and afterwards diffused over and adapted by the others. This diffusion path may depend on a hierarchical system of cities in the economy concerned (*cf.* Nijkamp, 1981, Pred, 1977). Clearly it may also be assumed that the rate of adopting a technical change realized elsewhere in a certain region is co-determined by its 'distance' (not measured necessarily in physical terms), but may also be linked to psychological attitudes toward innovation or to accessibility of the communication network.

REFERENCES

Brown, L.A., *Innovation Diffusion*, London, 1981.

Gomulka, S., 'Extensions of "The Golden Rule of Research" of Phelps,' *Review of Economic Studies*, January 1970, pp. 73–93.

Hacche, G., *The Theory of Economic Growth: An Introduction*, 1979.

Mensch, G., *Stalemate in Technology*, Cambridge, 1976.

Nijkamp, P., 'Perspectives for Urban Analyses and Policies,' in: P. Nijkamp and P. Rietveld (eds.), *Cities in Transition*, Dordrecht, 1981, pp. 67–98.

Nijkamp, P. (ed.), *Technological Change, Employment and Spatial Dynamics*, Berlin, 1986.

Phelps, E.S., 'Models of Technical Progress and the Golden Rule of Research,' *Review of Economic Studies*, April 1966, pp. 133–145.

Pred, A., *City Systems in Advanced Economies*, Hutchinson, 1977.

Rouwendal, J., 'On the Production and Diffusion of Technological Change,' in: P. Nijkamp (ed.), *Technological Change, Employment and Spatial Dynamics*, Berlin, 1986, pp. 371–381.

Shell, K., 'A Model of Inventive Activity and Capital Accumulation,' in: K. Schell (ed.), *Essays on the Theory of Optimal Economic Growth*, Cambridge, Mass., 1967, pp. 67–85.

Shephard, *Cost and Production Functions*, Princeton, 1953.

Soete, L. and R. Turner, 'Technology Diffusion and the Rate of Technical Change,' *Economic Journal*, 94 (1984), pp. 612–623.

Stoneman, P., *The Economic Analysis of Technological Change*, Oxford, 1983.

Summary

ENDOGENOUS PRODUCTION OF R&D AND STABLE ECONOMIC DEVELOPMENT

Changes in production technology are usually a result of R&D efforts. In this paper a model is presented in which technological change emanates from production factors used for R&D. The model consists of two production sectors, one concerned with the production of consumption and investment goods, the other with that of new technologies. By means of this model we analyse the impact of R&D on the level of immediate income and the efficient allocation of production factors over both sectors. Furthermore, the existence of a steady state in this model is examined. It turns out that such a state is only possible under restrictive conditions.

[3]
Spatial Dispersion of Technological Innovation: A Review

Evert Jan Davelaar and Peter Nijkamp

2.1 Introduction

In recent years there has been growing interest in the dynamics of existing firms and the formation of new firms. World-wide economic stagnation has called for a thorough analysis of the conditions that favour the offspring of new economic activities (see also Cuadrado-Roura et al. 1994 and Suarez-Villa and Cuadrado-Roura 1994). In this context, much emphasis has been placed on the growth potential of the high-technology industry. Although this sector, through the diffusion and widespread application of high-technology products, may indirectly account for a large share in total employment change, the direct employment base of this sector is relatively small (ranging from 3 to 13 percent of total national employment). Consequently, the broader process of technological progress, the diffusion of technological innovations and the birth of new firms deserves much more attention than the high-technology sector per se.

It is also worth noting that excessive attention to the high-technology sector carries the risk of neglecting the growth potential of other new - sometimes small-scale - activities outside the high-technology sector which might also significantly contribute to a further economic growth.

The geographical location of new firms (both inside and outside the high-technology sector) does not have a uniform pattern. Both concentration and dispersion may occur simultaneously. High-technology industries (such as micro-electronics and computer-based firms) can be found in large geographical concentrations like California's Silicon Valley or Massachusetts' Route 128. Other non directly high-technology based new activities are often found in older districts of larger cities, as these provide seedbeds for the emergence of new - often semi-informal - firms in a dynamic and often uncertain development climate. Consequently, a more thorough analysis of the geographical dimensions of industrial dynamics is warranted (cf. Capello 1994).

In general, innovation is considered as one of the key elements in the dynamics of the industry. Especially in recent years a wide variety of studies have pointed out the close links between (often basic) innovations and the long-term performance of an economy. In this context, structural economic changes and long-run fluctuations (e.g., Kondratieff cycles) have to be given particular mention (see, among others, Bianchi et al. 1985; Davelaar 1992; Kleinknecht 1985; Mensch 1979). Such dynamic processes have a clear impact on regional and urban economic development, as the latter phenomenon is co-determined by the production, diffusion and adoption of innovations (see Nijkamp 1986).

Various investigations have taken place on the employment effects of industrial innovations. If one takes a microscopic view on the individual firm level, it is indeed in many cases difficult to assert the existence of a clearly positive relationship (see Gunning et al. 1986). On the other hand, if one takes a macroscopic viewpoint, it is no doubt true that innovations increase the competitive position of a country or region. It can be claimed that without innovations the country or region would be worse off (see OECD 1984). Industrial innovation can therefore be considered at worst inevitable and at best beneficial. This dilemma is closely related to the well-known technology-push demand-pull discussion in industrial and spatial dynamics.

In this context, it is useful to make a distinction between the *production and the diffusion* of innovative activities (see also Stoneman 1983). The production of innovations has an impact on the competitive position of a region, while the diffusion influences the spatial distribution of the performance or potential of a spatial system. Thus both the production and the diffusion of innovations are complementary processes in the development path of regions.

In recent years, the potential and the success of local or regional initiatives in encouraging innovative firm behaviour has led to increased interest in the so-called urban incubator hypothesis. The main focus of the present paper will be on this hypothesis, which states that urban centres provide the seedbed for the emergence of new - often small-scale - firms. It suggests that older districts in such cities provide the breeding place for the creation of new activities due to their less structured, more flexible and often informal economy (see Hoover and Vernon 1959; Vernon 1960). Later on this hypothesis was broadened, and it was assumed that large-scale agglomerations provided favourable conditions for the start of a range of entrepreneurial activities (Davelaar 1992; Fagg 1980; Davelaar and Nijkamp 1986). More recently, it has also been hypothesized, that urban areas specifically provide the seedbed for new innovative firms.

In the literature it is often stated that certain cities or even parts of cities are particularly fertile environments for the creation of new firms. The term *incubation milieu* is often used to describe such areas (cf. De Ruijter 1983; Steed 1976; Fagg 1980; etc.). This concept can also be related to the *innovation potential* of cities (cf. De Ruijter 1978; Nijkamp 1985). The essence of the innovation incubation hypothesis is that certain cities are especially favourable for the production and adoption of innovations. It is useful at this point to make a clear distinction between the use of this hypothesis for the *production* and the *diffusion* process of innovations. A fertile production environment of innovations does not necessarily imply a fertile adoption environment. The central question in this context is: Which regions are especially favourable for the production (adoption) of innovations? The problem one encounters in trying to answer this question is then: *when* is a region *especially* fertile?

This paper is organized as follows. After a general discussion on the location and formation or new activities (Section 2.2), a concise presentation is given of the main aspects of the innovation production process (Section 2.3) and of the innovation diffusion process (Section 2.4) in the framework of the incubator hypothesis. This concept is then linked to agglomeration economies and social overhead capital, and followed by a discussion of impact assessment of incubation phenomena.

2.2 Formation and Location of New Activities

Firms seek to locate in a certain place for a wide variety of complex reasons. The needs and expectations of a firm (the 'demand profile') on the one hand, and the potential and quality of a certain area (the 'supply profile') on the other jointly determine the locational pattern of new economic activities. From a US study it has become evident that the factors considered important by high-technology and non high-technology firms are very similar, although apparently weighted differently (see Office of Technology Assessment 1984).

The geographical pattern of new economic activities can be analyzed from two different viewpoints, viz. the *macro-economic oriented regional growth theory* and the *micro-oriented industrial location theory*. The following examples of conventional regional *macro* growth theory can be mentioned:

- **export base theory**: this theory presupposes that regional growth rates are dependent on the region's interregional or international export performance. Multiplier effects are thus decisive for the growth potential of a region. In this framework, the main locational question is therefore the selection of appropriate new activities in a given region.
- **factor price equalization theory**: this theory (based on international trade theory) takes for granted that mobility of production factors depends on their regional return. Spatial equilibrium is hence determined by a combination of factor substitution and spatial substitution. Consequently, technological efficiency is decisive for the locational pattern of new activities.
- **unbalanced growth theory**: this theory focuses on spatial divergence as a mechanism of economic growth. Regional stress factors, cumulative causation, and backwash and/or spread effects determine the locational picture of a country, and thus the type of new activities determines the spatial development pattern.
- **growth pole theory**: this theory is based on the notion of centrifugal polarization effects from a central region outwards. The success of a growth pole strategy thus depends on the degree of propulsiveness of new activities (including both the generation and diffusion of promising growth effects).
- **product life cycle theory**: this theory recognizes that economic activities have different locational requirements at different stages in their development (innovations need a different seedbed from mass produced goods, for instance). Consequently, the locational profile of a firm is determined by the type of new activity at some place (including the development stage).

- **diffusion theory**: this theory states that it is the speed and spatial trajectory of new (innovative) activities which determine the performance of entrepreneurial initiatives.

Various alternative approaches can be identified, such as the adoption-adaption model, the hierarchical diffusion model, the interindustry diffusion model and the institutional-management diffusion model. In all these cases, attention is focused on new activities that have maximum performance in terms of diffusion potential.

Examples of *micro*-based industrial location theory cannot easily be classified according to major dynamic growth forces. However, it is possible to make a distinction according to the main determinants of individual location decisions of firms, such as labour costs, transportation and communication costs, capital costs, availability or land, market access, access to information and research centres, quality of life and amenities, taxes, access to venture capital and so forth. This micro-oriented approach has gained much popularity in recent years.

The theoretical contributions to the study of the location of new activities mentioned above are fairly general in nature and do not offer any specific insight into the urban-regional dimensions of new activities (either inside or outside the high- technology sector). Therefore, it is understandable that in recent years a search for more satisfactory explanatory paradigms has started. One of the main paradigms investigated has been the incubation hypothesis. In order to provide a proper context for discussion of this hypothesis, we will briefly discuss the locational dimensions of innovation production and innovation diffusion.

2.3 Spatial Aspects of Innovation Production

In this paper we define as *local* determinants of the production of innovations those factors which are *external* to the firm, which are expected to have an important influence on its *production* decisions and which are characterized (among other things) by a specific *spatial* orientation. It is evident that such firm-specific factors have a more or less heterogeneous pattern in space. We will ignore here factors which are internal to the firm (e.g. if a new permanent communication structure or interaction between various functional divisions in a firm has an important influence on the production of innovations, we consider this as a factor internal to the firm). So the question to be treated here is: what are the major locational determinants of the production process of innovations? Or otherwise: why are certain regions particularly fertile concerning the production of innovations? As empirical evidence is scarce, our discussion on this issue will mainly be theoretical in nature.

Now the most intriguing question is which external factors can be considered locational determinants of the innovations produced?

In our key factor analysis we will identify four clusters or major driving forces that - according to an extensive literature survey - may be assumed to exert a significant impact on the production or innovations in a certain place, i.e. (1) the composition and spatial size distribution of sectors, (2) the demography and population structure or an area, (3) the information infrastructure, and (4) the physical and institutional infrastructure. These four clusters will now briefly be discussed.

1 Composition and spatial size distribution of economic sectors

In the first place, the most straightforward factor in this context is of course the *number and type of firms* belonging to sector s in region r. The regional sectoral composition is clearly of decisive importance, so in testing the fertility of certain regions concerning the production of innovations we have to be aware of the spatial distribution of the various sectors. The mere occurrence of a large number of innovations produced in a region may to a large extent be explained by a relatively high concentration of innovative sectors within this region (cf. Andersson and Johansson, 1984).

Next, the spatial concentration of *similar* firms may play a role, as this may result in lower costs (a joint sharing of certain overhead costs, for example), but also in a higher awareness of the actions of the competitors or a greater need to innovate in order to attain a share of the market (cf. Mouwen 1984; Hansen 1980). As a result of these incentives to innovate, more innovations may be produced in regions with a higher concentration of similar firms.

On the other hand, the spatial clustering of *dissimilar* firms may also have a positive influence on the production of innovations because of a diversity of buyers and suppliers close at hand (cf. Thwaites 1981; Carlino 1978; Hoover and Vernon 1959; Vernon 1960). As innovations often have to be modified during the 'introduction phase', the 'producer' of the innovation frequently has to change his product more or less drastically. A higher diversity of suppliers may reduce the risks involved in this process of change and consequently increase the number of innovations being produced. In this context one can also consider the spatial clustering of R&D departments of *different* firms and public R&D institutions (e.g. Silicon Valley) and the resulting positive effects (cross-fertilization of ideas, good opportunities to start new innovative firms because of subcontracting, spin-off effects and so on; cf. Aydalot 1985 and Stohr 1985). It should be added however, that according to some authors there may also be certain limits with regard to spatial scale advantages (cf. Mouwen, 1984, Nijkamp and Schubert 1983; Camagni and Diappi 1985). The implication of this argument is that certain *diseconomies* may come to the fore when the spatial concentration of firms (and population) becomes too large with respect to the existing capacity of the area. With regard to the important centres of R&D just mentioned, Malecki (1979c) has indeed found some evidence concerning these hypotheses (implying deconcentration of R&D divisions of firms away from the largest urban areas).

Furthermore, the *spatial distribution of the various size categories of firms* may be relevant for the spatial distribution of innovations produced. It is important to note in this context that large firms seem to spend more on R&D (as a percentage of sales) than small firms (cf. Cappellin 1983; Hoogteijling 1984; Malecki 1979a; Dasgupta 1982). Large firms also produce the highest number of innovations (cf. Kok et al. 1985; Thomas 1981). Small firms, however, seem to have a higher productivity concerning the production of innovations (cf. Cappellin 1983; Hoogteijling 1984 and Malecki 1979a). Cappellin (1983, p. 464) states: "It seems, moreover, that the productivity of R&D expenditure is highest for small firms in terms of patent or output growth". It is interesting to observe in this context that Rothwell and Zegveld (1982) claim that small and large firms are complementary. This is best illustrated by means of the following citation: "Thus we see a certain complementary interaction between the large and the small, the nature of the relationship being based on their relative strengths (e.g. the small firm's entrepreneurship; the large firm's access to resources)" (p.247). In their opinion there exists an 'optimal mix' between the number of small and large firms. At first sight, we are tempted to infer that large firms may be more favourable to the production of innovations than small firms. But, if the argument of Rothwell and Zegveld holds true, the 'mix effect' may be more important. In that case, we may state that the spatial size distribution is of considerable importance.

In the current literature on regions a considerable amount of attention is being paid to multi-locational firms (cf. Pred 1977). The spread of *multi-plant firms* is expected to influence the spatial production of innovations. So the location of the various types of R&D may be determined by the spatial distribution of the various 'components' of these firms. Basic research could be attracted to the head offices, and development and 'applied' research to the of branch plants (cf. Howells 1984; Thwaites 1981).

2 Demography and population structure

An important factor often mentioned in the literature is the total number of people living in a region (or city). Malecki (1979, p. 226), for example, remarks: 'There is an increasing relationship between R&D activity and city size, suggesting increasing economies of urban size for R&D". In this context one should be aware of the fact that R&D can be considered as an input to the production process of innovations. The relationship between R&D input and output (innovations) is certainly not independent (cf. Mansfield 1968).

Often a particular subgroup of the total population is considered to be especially important: such as the number of technical, managerial or R&D personnel (cf. Andersson and Johansson 1984; Mouwen and Nijkamp 1985; De Jong and Lambooy 1985; Johansson and Nijkamp 1986; Bushwell et al. 1983; Malecki 1979b; Oakey 1983; Thwaites 1981). As R&D personnel can be considered a labour input in the production process of innovations, it is logical to include this variable in group (2).

From a *demographic* viewpoint, the existence of minority groups in a region is sometimes assumed to influence the production of innovations positively (cf. De Ruijter 1983; Pred 1977). This can be 'explained' by the fact that such groups have nothing to lose, so that they have a lower risk aversion and a higher propensity to try something new. It may also be the case that those people start to introduce products or services which are familiar in their native country but not in their new home country. So the influence of a segmented population composition in a region on the production of innovations is expected to be positive.

Another important key factor is the influence of *agglomeration size* on the production of innovations. Malecki and Varaiya (1986, p. 7) for example remark: "Agglomeration economies play a multiple role: they promote technical progress and higher productivity." It is convenient to distinguish these economies into *localization* and *urbanization economies* (cf. Carlino 1978; Hansen 1980). By localization economies we mean advantages in a system that result from the spatial concentration of firms in the same sector, while urbanization economies refer to advantages which result from the spatial concentration of firms in different sectors. To a certain extent these advantages are related to the 'locational determinants' discussed above (for example, information exchange). In Biehl et al. (1986) it is stated that agglomeration economies refer to 'external economies' which are related to *size* and *concentration*.

3 Information infrastructure

Information availability is generally regarded as a major determinant of innovation. The term itself incorporates several diverse components of knowledge transfer. Various components may be distinguished by discriminating between the different 'senders' of the information (the 'receivers' being in each case the innovation producing firms). We will distinguish three different sources of information.

Inter-firm contact patterns deal with a mutual private information exchange between firms. As Pred (1977) has already noted, every exchange of goods and services between firms is accompanied by information exchange. Thus the flow of goods and services between regions can be seen as a 'proxy' for this kind of information exchange. In this way Pred shows that these kinds of information flows are highly spatially biased (i.e. urban based) (see also Norton 1979; Andersson and Johansson 1984). The production of innovations may be stimulated by means of this kind of information exchange, mainly because firms in the centre of these information flows are aware of market opportunities, market imperfections, and so on (cf. Nijkamp 1982; Pred 1977). So we may expect that a higher intensity of goods and services exchange results in a more intensive information exchange and, consequently, in more innovations being produced.

Public research institutes, universities, institutes of technology and knowledge transfer centres are expected to influence the innovation potential of the regions in which they are located in a positive way (cf. Malecki 1979b; Gibbs and Thwaites 1985; De Jong and Lambooy 1985; Feldman 1984; Mouwen 1985). Firms may consult these organizations if they have technical and marketing problems. Also the spin-off implications need to be mentioned in this context (cf. Van Tilburg and Van der Meer 1983; Rothwell and Zegveld 1982). Oakey (1983) even remarks: "However, the importance of local American universities may be in their role of providers of 'spin-off' entrepreneurs and skilled workers rather than in terms of interactive collaboration with existing firms' (see p. 244). People working in research institutions may also begin the production of a new commodity by establishing a new innovative firm. Often this firm will be located near the parent institution because of subcontracting with this institution, or because a founder locates his new firm near his place of residence (cf. Gudgin 1978; Aydalot 1985). It is thus expected that a higher concentration of such

institutions will influence the innovation production potential of a region in a positive way.
Demographic and spatial interaction patterns exert in general a positive influence on the innovation potential of a region (cf. Vernon 1960; Pred 1977). For example, an intensive flow of customers to a certain region (or city) means that firms located in this region have the advantage of a permanent and intensive information exchange with their customers. In this way they can keep abreast of certain developments in consumer tastes and may adjust their innovation strategy accordingly. So a higher intensity of personal interaction is likely to have a positive influence on the total number of innovations produced. In this context we may also mention the importance of 'face to face' contacts for innovation production (cf. Lambooy 1984; Pred 1977; Batten 1981 Kok et al. 1985; Moss 1985; Nijkamp and Schubert 1983). Clearly, with regard to this communication factor, metropolitan regions are normally in a favourable position.

4 Physical and institutional infrastructure

Cultural and educational *amenities* (theatres, cinemas, libraries, art galleries and so on) may influence the production of innovation in a positive way. This can be explained as follows. Highly educated R&D personnel can be considered a scarce input in relation to innovation (cf. Malecki and Varaiya 1986), so R&D institutions of private firms cannot be considered as footloose. In order to attract adequate research personnel they often have to locate where their personnel wants to live in order to attract adequate research personnel (cf. Feldman 1984, Bushwell et al. 1983). Those people seem to be attracted to cities with many cultural and educational amenities (cf. Aydalot 1984; Cappellin 1983; Malecki and Varaiya 1986; Howells 1984). Malecki and Varaiya (1986) remark: "These workers favour attractive urban regions where cultural, educational and alternative employment opportunities are abundant". The locational preferences of R&D personnel may have a significant influence on the location of R&D activity and in this way on the production of innovations in amenity-rich regions.

Physical climate and environmental qualities may also influence the production of innovations in a positive way by means of the mechanism outlined above: the attraction of highly skilled R&D personnel. Malecki and Varaiya (1986) explain the rise of certain Sunbelt states in the U.S. by means of such a mechanism. Also in France some evidence concerning this hypothesis can be found (cf. Aydalot 1984).

Moreover, it is also worth noting that the *availability of public (physical) infrastructure* is sometimes considered a necessity to the production of innovations. "In conclusion, the availability or a satisfactory infrastructure capital stock (in its broadest sense) shapes the necessary conditions for innovative capacities in an area" (Nijkamp 1982, p. 6). In this context Feldman (1984) points to the need of many firms in bio-technology to be located in the vicinity of an airport.

The financing of innovative products or services is often problematic (cf. Feldman 1984). Therefore, the spatial pattern of institutions offering *venture capital* can be considered an important 'explanatory' variable to the regional distribution of the innovations produced (cf. Bushwell et al. 1983; Thwaites 1981; Lambooy 1978; Stöhr 1985; Oakey 1983; Mouwen 1984; Rothwell and Zegveld

1982). Stöhr for example emphasizes the role of venture capital in his discussion on the Mondragon project in Spain.

A last factor in this context concerns *institutional arrangements* (cf. Aydalot 1984; Rothwell and Zegveld 1982; Brown 1981). It is possible to identify a number of regulations which may stimulate or demotivate the production of innovations. There has been, however, a lack of serious investigation into the precise effects of such institutional measures.

In conclusion, one can derive from the literature many factors which many influence the total number of innovations produced. The empirical evidence concerning the individual relevance of each factor, however, is rather scarce. The overall impacts are summarized in Figure 2.1. Clearly, the explanatory variables may be interdependent. In this scheme we have not drawn all these links, but in the following section more attention will be paid to this issue in relation to the diffusion of innovation.

In Figure 2.1 the dependent variable is the total number of innovations produced in a region. So in comparing and explaining the innovativeness of different regions we should compare the different intensities ('values') of each of these explanatory (locational) factors. Thus, region A may produce more innovations than region B simply because region A has ceteris paribus a larger number of innovative firms within its boundaries. If one is not interested in this scale effect, one has to compare the total number of innovations produced per firm (in a certain sector) in each region.

2.4 Diffusion of Innovations in a Spatial Context

Both the theoretical and empirical literature on innovation diffusion is quite extensive. In this section we will concentrate in particular on the diffusion of technical-economic innovations. As stated before, the diffusion process may be more important than the pure effects of production of innovations. Consequently, a region or country may even attain a strong position in the world market just by importing innovations that have been produced elsewhere (cf. Rothwell and Zegveld 1985). This does not imply, however, that the production of innovations is irrelevant. In the first place, firms located in the producing region may have easier access to the innovations produced. Secondly, exporting innovations may be quite profitable.

The question to be raised in this section is: What are the locational determinants of the innovation diffusion process? Or stated in another way: Why are certain regions so attractive regarding the adoption or innovations? In the following we will again focus attention on the external determinants of the diffusion of innovations. In some cases a few remarks in relation to the explanatory factors will be sufficient, because they have already been discussed in the previous section. It will be useful to distinguish between supply and demand side factors (cf. Brown 1981).

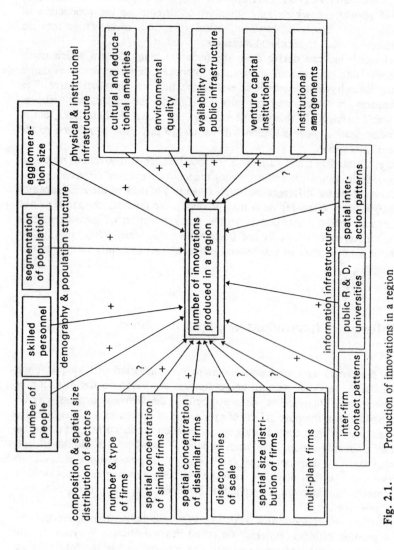

Fig. 2.1.   Production of innovations in a region

We will start with some *supply side factors*. Brown (1981) stated that although innovation diffusion research has tended to concentrate on demand side factors (cf. the adoption perspective of Hagerstrand 1967), supply side factors may be (equally) important. The essence of the supply side approach is that the strategy pursued by a supplier of an innovation may have important locational implications. This strategy may of course in part be determined by factors internal to the firm (profit rate, market perception and so on), but these factors will not be discussed here, as they are to a large extent be firm-specific. We will only concentrate on those locational factors which may influence the choices made by firms concerning the distribution of produced innovations. The literature concerning the supply side factors is rather scarce, as only recently has attention been paid to this issue.

Three main classes of determinants will be discussed here, viz. (1) sectoral composition, (2) information network, and (3) agglomeration economies.

1 Sectoral composition

To a certain extent we can expect that the *total number of (innovative) firms in a region* will influence the supply of the various innovations positively. *The role of multi-locational firms* should also be stressed in this context (cf. Pred 1977). In fact, innovations are sometimes only diffused *within* a (multi-plant) firm. So in this case the spatial organization of the multi-locational firm will determine the spatial supply pattern of innovations.

2 Information network

The *spatial concentration of information flows* is a second factor which needs to be mentioned in this context. It is noteworthy that information between (dis-)similar firms may result in imitative behaviour. When a firm recognizes that a competitor offers a certain innovation, it may 'follow the leader' (cf. Brown 1981; Nijkamp and Schubert 1983). An adequate communication infrastructure may reduce the costs of supplying the innovation or it may even occur that the availability of certain infrastructural components is a necessity for offering the innovation (cf. Brown 1981).

3 Agglomeration economies

Agglomeration economies may stimulate the number of innovations supplied since the supplier can expect a higher demand potential and fewer risks in improving the innovation (because of the diversity of input supplies and an intensive contact with potential customers) (cf. Andersson and Johansson 1984; Mouwen 1984; Heinemeyer 1978). The introduction of a new product or service often requires a minimum 'threshold' concerning the number of firms and/or the size of population (cf. Koerhuis and Cnossen 1982; Andersson and Johansson 1984; Lambooy 1978).

Next, we will discuss *demand side factors*. Four different categories will be considered here: (1) sectoral structure, (2) communication network, (3) agglomeration advantages, and (4) physical infrastructure.

1 Sectoral structure

The *number and size of firms* will in general exert a positive influence upon the number of innovations demanded in a region (cf. Cappellin 1983; Howells 1984). As the influence of this variable is again straightforward, it will not be discussed any further in this section.

The *spatial distribution of the various size categories of firms* is also expected to influence the innovation demand potential of a region (cf. Davies 1979). In Davies' model, for example, the most significant explanatory variable of innovation adoption is the size of the firm. Large firms may be in a favourable position concerning the adoption of innovations because of larger (internal) resources.

In regional research there is a tendency to stress the role of *multi-locational organizations* in explaining regional economic phenomena (cf. Holland 1979). This phenomenon can also be observed in the study of innovation diffusion. Pred (1977); Malecki (1979a) for example stress the role of multi-plant firms, although it is very difficult to identify this factor. One can often observe a reasonably integrated production and diffusion process. By this we mean that the R&D departments of these firms 'produce' certain innovations which are then diffused to the various branch plants of the firm (there is only limited information, goods and service exchange between establishments of a multi-locational firm). Although it is difficult to hypothesize the expected influence, the role of these firms in relation to innovation diffusion may be quite surprising and even cause peripheral regions to have a relatively high degree of innovation adoption (the branch plants of these firms may be located in peripheral regions simply because of relatively low wages and low congestion; cf. Thwaites 1981; Oakey 1983).

2 Communication network

Not everybody seems to be equally receptive to the *adoption* of innovations. In this context the term 'opinion leaders' is sometimes used for first adopters of an innovation (cf. Brown 1981; Malecki 1982). These opinion leaders are essential for the further diffusion of innovations, because informal communication between adopters and potential adopters seems to be essential to the adoption of the innovation among the great mass of people (cf. Rogers 1983; Pred 1977; Batten 1981; Kok et al. 1985). So the spatial distribution (and number) of 'opinion leaders' may be an essential component of the demand for innovations.

Information availability will influence the demand for innovations positively (cf. Brown 1981; Hagerstrand 1967; Nijkamp 1982; Malecki and Varaiya 1985; Batten 1981; Pred 1977). In the first place one can expect a greater awareness among potential adopters when the information availability increases. Secondly, greater information availability may increase imitative behaviour of the potential adopters (cf. Pred 1977; Hagerstrand 1967; Brown 1981). Brown (1981) even states that in accordance with the 'adoption perspective' (cf. Hagerstrand 1967) information flows are fundamental.

3 Agglomeration advantages

Some authors are of the opinion that *agglomeration economies* will stimulate the number of innovations adopted in a region (by households and firms). To a certain extent these agglomeration economies are related to the other variables mentioned in this section. These mutual relations will be studied later on in this paper. Now some more attention will be paid to the reason why agglomeration economies will influence the innovations adoption positively. In the first place one can point to the positive influence of *spatial clustering on the information exchange between firms and people* (cf. Mouwen 1984; Heinemeyer 1978; Lambooy 1978). Secondly, it may be less costly to supply the innovations because of *lower transportation and communication costs* (cf. Brown 1981). Thirdly, the number of *face to face contacts* will increase in large agglomerations. These contacts can of course be considered as a special subgroup of information exchange, but according to many authors this element is of such importance that it needs to be mentioned separately (cf. Lambooy 1973; Heinemeyer 1978; Pred 1977; Nijkamp and Schubert 1983; Norton 1979; Batten 1981). Batten (1981), for example, states that the social dimension of innovation adoption is of paramount importance.

4 Physical infrastructure

A last factor to be mentioned in this section is the *influence of physical infrastructure* (cf. Brown 1981; Mouwen 1984; Nijkamp and Schubert 1983). Brown for example states: "Thus the characteristics of the relevant public and private infrastructures - such as service, delivery, information, transportation - also have an important influence upon the rate and spatial patterning of diffusion" (p. 9). Brown also shows that some innovations (computers) can only be adopted when physical infrastructure is close at hand. The availability of physical infrastructure will of course also increase the agglomeration economies to be gained in a certain region and, consequently, the intensity of information exchange between firms and people.

In this section we have discussed several locational factors influencing the diffusion of innovations, and indicated how and why the innovation diffusion process may be spatially biased. Schematically the above arguments can be summarized by means of a key factor analysis (see Figure 2.2). In this figure, it is shown how the perception of innovation supply vis-à-vis potential demand in the various regions influences the probability that certain innovation distribution centres will be located in the region. The more such centres a region has, the more innovations will be supplied in this region. It is also shown how several demand side factors may influence the total numbers of innovations demanded in this region. The actual number of innovations adopted (over a certain period of time) will depend on the interaction between total demand and supply.

In the present paper, we are especially interested in the effects of *agglomeration economies* and *social overhead capital* on the innovation potential of firms in a region (i.e. the potential of firms to produce and adopt innovations), in the framework of the *urban incubation hypothesis*. These issues will be taken up in the next section.

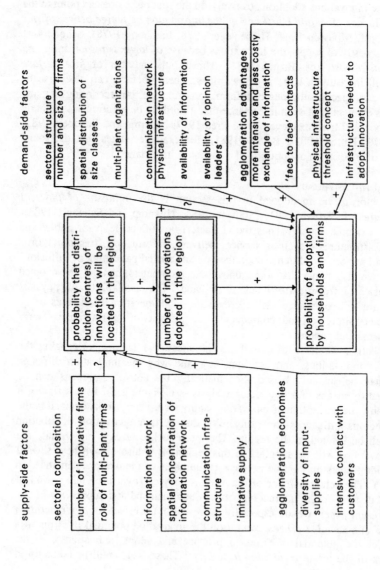

demand-side factors

sectoral structure
number and size of firms
spatial distribution of size classes
multi-plant organizations

communication network
physical infrastructure
availability of information
availability of 'opinion leaders'

agglomeration advantages
more intensive and less costly exchange of information
'face to face' contacts

physical infrastructure
threshold concept
infrastructure needed to adopt innovation

probability that distribution (centres) of innovations will be located in the region

number of innovations adopted in the region

probability of adoption by households and firms

supply-side factors

sectoral composition
number of innovative firms
role of multi-plant firms

information network
spatial concentration of information network
communication infrastructure
'imitative supply'

agglomeration economies
diversity of input-supplies
intensive contact with customers

Fig. 2.2.   Spatial diffusion of innovations

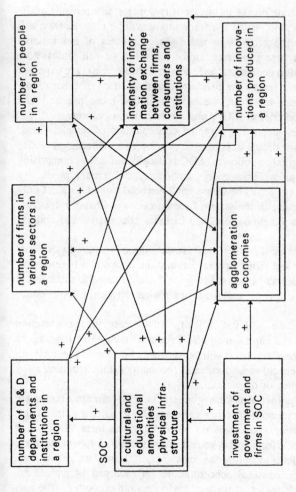

Fig. 2.3. Determinants of agglomeration economies and social overhead capital and their influence on the production of innovations

2.5 The Concepts of Agglomeration Economies and Social Overhead Capital Reconsidered

In this section we concentrate on the influence of two major determinants of the innovation potential of a region. From the foregoing it will be clear that we will again distinguish between the *production* and *diffusion* process of innovations. Figures 2.1 and 2.2 depict these processes. In the following we will discuss how the elements of agglomeration economies and social overhead capital are expected to influence (in a theoretical sense) the *production* and *diffusion* of innovations. Before turning to this issue however, we have to define more precisely the concepts of *social overhead capital* (SOC) and *agglomeration economies*.

Agglomeration economies mean that a spatial concentration of people, firms, institutions and so on, is favourable to economic development. Hirschman (1958) defines social overhead capital as follows: "SOC is usually defined as comprising those basic services without which primary, secondary, and tertiary productive activities cannot function" (p. 83). The term social overhead capital does not only refer to physical infrastructure in the sense of roads, railways ('band' infrastructure according to Biehl et al. 1986), but also includes educational and cultural amenities.

Agglomeration economies on the other hand are determined by two dimensions, i.e. the *number* of people and firms in a region and the *distance* between them. Thus, various locational factors sketched in Figure 2.1 are related to this concept (for example, the number of people and firms in a region, physical infrastructure, and so on).

In the following figures we will indicate how an increase in agglomeration economies or social overhead capital may affect the total number of innovations produced in a region. In these figures it will be assumed, for ease of presentation, that there is no limit (bottleneck) to agglomeration economies (thus assuming away for the moment the existence of diseconomies).

In Figure 2.3 we have supposed that the agglomeration economies in a region are independent of the characteristics of other regions. The important point in this context is that agglomeration economies do not refer to the mere *existence* of firms, but to the positive effects to be gained from *spatial clustering* of these firms. Although it is difficult to define the term *spatial cluster*, we will assume that the distances between industrial concentrations for each pair of regions are large enough to allow each region to possess agglomeration economies (the only exception being the case in which a certain industrial concentration crosses several boundaries). In the following we will assume, however, that the size and shape of the regions concerned (no agglomerations crossing regional boundaries) have been composed in such a way that any increase in the number of firms (or people) - or decrease in the distances between them - can be classified as agglomeration economies in only one region. Figure 2.3 shows that the term agglomeration economies comprises several factors concerning the location of innovation production. Up to a certain point (beyond which diseconomies might start), we expect the influence of agglomeration economies on the production of innovations to be positive. The same can be said concerning the influence of social overhead capital, which is to a large extent an instrument of government policy. In the first, place the effect of physical infrastructure on agglomeration economies will be positive (by reducing the average distance between producers and consumers). Secondly, the effect of cultural and educational amenities (both being part of social overhead capital) on the production innovations in a region is expected to be positive, because this will increase the attractiveness of the region for highly educated R&D personnel (and as a consequence attract R&D departments and institutions).

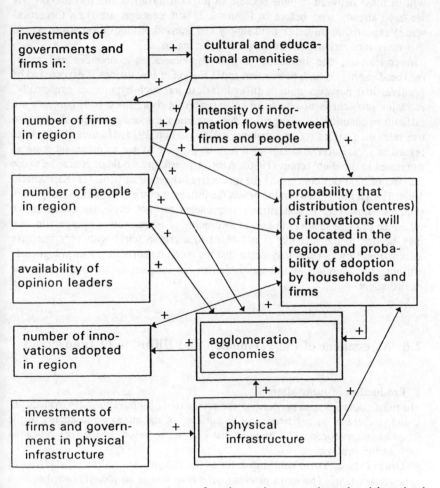

Fig. 2.4. The effects (and determinants of) agglomeration economies and social overhead capital on innovation diffusion

We will now turn to the expected influence of agglomeration economies and social overhead capital on the adoption (diffusion) process of innovations in a region. Figure 2.4 shows which factors of Figure 2.2 determine the extent of agglomeration economies and social overhead capital. This figure indicates how agglomeration economies and social overhead capital may influence the diffusion of innovations. As in Figure 2.3 we can see that the two concepts are not independent. An increase in physical infrastructure will diminish the relative distances between firms and consumers and consequently result in increasing agglomeration economies.

A certain part of these agglomeration economies will consist of intensified information flows in the specific region. It may also be the case that these flows will increase between regions because of physical infrastructure investments. As we have already seen before in Figure 2.2, both concepts are (in a theoretical sense) expected to influence both supply and demand of innovation positively, so that more innovations will be adopted in the region.

In conclusion, the influence of both agglomeration economies and social overhead capital on both production and diffusion of innovations is expected to be positive. It is however quite a difficult task to test such hypotheses empirically. A major problem is of course to collect relevant data, since both concepts are difficult to quantify. With regard to *agglomeration economies* one possibility is to use relevant proxies (cf. Kawashima 1974; Carlino 1978; Hansen 1983). With regard to *social overhead capital* it may be possible to use a compound score as suggested in the Biehl report (1986). Another possibility would of course be to use the data of inquiries concerning the innovative behaviour of firms (cf. Kleinknecht 1984; Hoogteijling 1984) and to assess the influence of these stimuli. An important problem, however, is that firms/entrepreneurs are not explicitly aware of the influence of these factors. The mere *awareness* of an innovation by a certain firm may be due to the fact that it is located in a region (city) with very intensive information flows. Yet it may occur that the entrepreneur will not unambiguously attribute his adoption of the innovation to his location in an information-rich environment.

2.6   Assessment of the Production and Diffusion of Innovations

1   Production of innovations
In most countries data concerning the production of innovations are inadequate. Usually, there is no registration or monitoring of the number and quality of the innovations produced. This implies that one has to resort to indirect indicators such as the following:

* **Output data.** These data may refer to the rise in sales and/or productivity of a certain firm. The main problem here is of course to identify whether such changes in economic performance can be ascribed to innovations or to general labour or capital productivity rises, market changes, etc.
* **Licence or patent data.** The use of these indicators has the disadvantage that not all firms will apply for licences or patents because this often does not prevent imitative behaviour by rivals. Nor does licence or patent data usually

give any information about the quality of the innovation. In addition, patent statistics are biased as larger companies are usually over-represented. One can make a distinction between important and less important innovations, the important innovations being those for which the producer will apply for licences or patents more than once.

- **The volume of inputs** being used in the production process of innovations. In this case one may think of the percentage of non-manual workers in the total workforce of a region or firm (cf. Oakey 1983), R&D as a percentage of total sales of a firm, the number of R&D personnel working in a firm or region, or related measures. The idea behind this approach is essentially based on a production function of innovations which relates output (number and quality of innovations) to certain inputs (R&D personnel, R&D costs, and so on). Although the existence of a relationship between R&D inputs and outputs cannot be denied (cf. Mansfield 1968), it is not at all clear how such a production function should be specified. One may even question the production function approach in this context (cf. Nelson and Winter 1982).
- **The number of awards** regarding innovations that have been produced. The fact that not all innovations will be rewarded is, however, is an important disadvantage of this approach.
- Design of firm-oriented **inquiries** (cf. Hoogteijling 1984; Kleinknecht 1984). One can try to establish whether a certain innovation in a firm has been produced within a given firm or has been adopted from outside. An important weakness of this approach, however, is the non-uniformity of the interpretation of the innovation concept from the side of the entrepreneurs.

Given the above complications it is clear that the measurement of the production of innovations can be considered a difficult task. One can only try to use proxies which map out the production of innovations as reliably as possible.

2 Diffusion of innovations

In regard to the diffusion process one should be aware of the fact that diffusion is a dynamic phenomenon. In general however, it is only possible to measure the degree Oof diffusion (of a certain innovation) at *a certain moment in time*.

When the objective is to try to study the whole diffusion path through time, this will require a high standard of reliability and completeness in the innovation diffusion data (cf. Hagerstrand 1967). This will be possible for a limited number of innovations however: for example, when the 'seller' of the innovation has complete records concerning the buyers of the innovation (cf. Pred 1977; Hagerstrand 1967).

As already noted, complete data will only be available for a very limited number of innovations, and as a consequence one has to rely on an 'approximation' method, for example, by means of inquiries (cf. Hoogteijling 1984; Kleinknecht 1984) or licence data. These approximations have the same disadvantages already discussed under the heading of the production process of innovations.

2.7 Influence of Agglomeration Economies and Social Overhead Capital on the Innovation Potential of a Region: Retrospect

In this concluding section we will summarize our findings in the form of a series of concise propositions.

- Innovations are often considered to be of paramount importance for the economic well-being of a country, region or firm. Due to this (supposed) importance, innovation studies are at present enjoying much popularity. Further *behavioural* analyses of the production and 'adoption of innovation are no doubt warranted.
- The innovation potential of a region should be divided into the potential of a region to *produce* innovations and the potential to *adopt* innovations. To a certain extent, both processes are complementary.
- Innovations are produced and adopted in a certain spatial context, so that a central issue is the *locational determinant(s)* of innovation production and adoption in these regions.
- According to these determinants some regions may be more fertile concerning the innovation potential. In this context, one may use the term *'incubation milieu'* analogous to the incubation hypothesis of cities with regard to the generation of new firms (cf. Hoover and Vernon 1959; Jacobs 1961).
- *Agglomeration economies* and *social overhead capital* are two elements of the incubation milieu of a region. They are generally expected to have a positive influence.
- Given the importance of these factors for the innovation potential of a region, a *key factor analysis* which studies the (expected) influences of these concepts on the production and diffusion of innovations is needed.
- In general, it is plausible to assume that agglomeration economies are not transferable across regional boundaries, because the central element of this concept is the synergy to be gained from *spatial* clustering.
- With regard to social overhead capital it is meaningful to follow the *multidimensional profile* approach, as *inter alia* adopted in the Biehl report (1986). In this case, however, we should stress those elements of social overhead capital which are expected to be of special relevance to innovation production and diffusion.
- The *subdivision of agglomeration economies* into different constituents, proposed among others by Hansen (1980); Carlino (1978); Kawashima (1974), may be useful for measuring the extent of agglomeration economies to be gained in the various regions.

- It is of paramount importance to test whether the influence of agglomeration economies and social overhead capital on innovation production and diffusion is *significantly different* in the various regions of a given spatial system.

References

Andersson A E and B Johansson (1994) Knowledge Intensity and Product Cycles in Metropolitan Regions, Contributions to the Metropolitan Study: 8. IIASA. Laxenburg

Aydalot P (1984) Reversals of Spatial Trends In French Industry since 1974. In: Lambooy J G (Ed) New Spatial Dynamics and Economic Crisis. Tampere 41-61

Aydalot P (1985) Some Comments on the Location of New Firm Creation. Paper presented at the Sixth Italian Conference of the RSA Genova (mimeographed)

Batten D F (1981) On the Dynamics of Industrial Evolution. Umea Economic Studies 97 Umea

Bianchi G, Bruckmann G, Delbeke J and T Vasko (Eds) (1985) Long Waves, Depression, and Innovation. International Institute for Applied Systems Analysis Laxenburg

Biehl D et al (Ed) (1986) The Contribution of Infrastructure to Regional Development. Directorate-General Regional Policy. Commission of European Communities Brussels

Boer N A de and W F Heinemeyer (Eds) (1978) Het Grootstedelijk Milieu. Van Gorcum Assen

Brown L A (1981) Innovation Diffusion, A New Perspective. Methuen London

Bushwell R J (1983) Research and Development and Regional Development: A Review. In: Gillespie A (Ed) Technological Change and Regional Development. London 9-22

Camagni R and L Diappi (1985) Urban Growth and Decline in a Hierarchical System: A Supply-Side Dynamic Approach. Paper presented at the IIASA Workshop on Dynamics Or Metropolitan Areas Rotterdam

Capello R (1994) Spatial Economic Analysis of Telecommunication Network Externalities. Avebury Aldershot UK

Cappellin R (1983) Productivity Growth and Technological Change in a Regional Perspective. Giornale degli Economisti e Analisi Economia 459-482

Carlino G A (1978) Economies of Scale in Manufacturing Location. Martinus Nijhoff Leiden

Cuadrado-Roura J R, Nijkamp P and P Salva (Eds) (1994) Moving Frontiers. Avebury Aldershot UK

Dasgupta P (1982) The Theory of Technological Competition. London School of Economics London

Davelaar E J (1992) Regional Economic Analysis of Innovation and Incubation. Avebury Aldershot UK

Davelaar E J and P Nijkamp (1986) De Stad als Broedplaats van Nieuwe Activiteiten: Theorie en Onderzoek. Stedebouw en Volkshuisvesting 2:61-66

Gudgin G (1978) Industrial Location Processes and Regional Employment Growth. Saxon House Farnborough

Gunning J W, Hoogteijling E and P Nijkamp (1986) Spatial Dimensions of Innovation and Employment: Some Dutch Results. In: Nijkamp P (Ed) Technological Change, Employment and Spatial Dynamics. Springer Verlag Berlin

Hagerstrand T (1967) Innovation Diffusion as a Spatial Process. University of Chicago Press Chicago

Hansen E R (1983) Why Do Firms Locate Where They Do?, World Bank Discussion Paper Wudd 25. Washington DC

Hirschman A O (1958) The Strategy of Economic Development. Yale University Press Connecticut

Holland S (1979) Capital Versus the Regions. The MacMillan Press London

Hoogteijling E M J (1984) Innovatie en Arbeidsmarkt (ESI VU) Amsterdam

Hoover E M and R Vernon (1959) Anatomy of a Metropolis. Harvard University Press Cambridge

Howells J R L (1984) The Location of Research and Development: Some Observations and Evidence from Britain. Regional Studies 18:13-29

Jacobs J (1961) The Life and Death of Great American Cities. Vintage Books London

Jansen A C M (1981) "Inkubatie-milieu": Analyse van een Geografisch Begrip. KNAC Geografisch Tijdschrift XY 1981. 4:306-314

Johannson B and P Nijkamp (1984) Analysis of Episodes in Urban Event Histories. In Burns L and L K Klaassen (Eds) Spatial Cycles. Gower Aldershot 133-151

Jong M W de and J G Lambooy (1984) De Informatica-sector Centraal. Perspectieven voor de Amsterdamse Binnenstad. EGI University of Amsterdam

Kawashima T (1975) Urban Agglomeration Economies in Manufacturing Industries. Papers of the RSA 157-175

Kleinknecht A (1986) Crisis and Prosperity in Schumpeterian Innovation Patterns. MacMillan London

Koerhuis H and W Gnossen (1982) De Software- en Computerservice-bedrijven. Sociaal Geografische Reeks 23 Groningen

Kok J A A M, Offerman G J D and P H Pellenbarg (1985) Innovatie in het Midden- en Kleinbedrijf. In Molle WTM (Ed) Innovatie en Regio. The Hague 143-165

Lambooy J G (1973) Economic and Geonomic Space: Some Theoretical Considerations in the Case of Urban Core Symbiosis. Papers of the RSA 145-158

Lambooy J G (1978) Het Grootstedelijk Milieu. In: Boer N A de and W F Heinemeyer (1978) (op cit)

Lambooy J G (Ed) (1984) New Spatial Dynamics and Economic Crisis. Jyvaakyla

Leone R A and R Struyk (1976) The Incubator Hypothesis: Evidence from Five SMSAs. Urban Studies 13:325-331

Malecki E J (1979a) Corporate Organization of R&D and the Location of Technological Activities. Regional Studies 14:219-234

Malecki E J (1979b) Agglomeration and Intra-firm Linkage in R&D Locations in the United States. Tijdschrift voor Economische en Sociale Geografie 70 6

Malecki E J (1979c) Locational Trends in R&D by Large U.S. Corporations. Economic Geography 5:309-323

Malecki E J (1979d) Corporate Organizations of R and D and the Location of Technological Activities. Regional Studies 14:219-234

Malecki E J (1982) Technology and Regional Development: A Survey. International Regional Science Review 122-148

Malecki E J and P Varaiya (1985) Innovation and Changes in Regional Structure. In Nijkamp P O (Ed) Handbook Regional Economics. North-Holland Publishing Company Amsterdam 484-515

Mansfield E (1968) Industrial Research and Technological Innovation. Longman New York

Meer J D van der and J J Tilburg van (1983) Spin-offs uit de Nederlandse Kenniscentra. Projekt Technologiebeleid/Ministerie van Economische Zaken

Mensch G (1979) The Stalemate Technology. Ballinger Cambridge Massachusetts

Molle W T M (Ed) (1985) Innovatie en Regio. Staatsuitgevertij Den Haag

Moss M L 1985) Telecommunications and the Future of Cities. Paper presented at the Conference of Landtronics London

Mouwen A (1984) Theorie en Praktijk van Lange-termijn Stedelijke Ontwikkelingen. Discussion Paper 1984-7. Free University Amsterdam

Mouwen A (1985) Transfercentra en Stedelijke Herstructurering. Discussion Paper. Free University Amsterdam

Mouwen A and P Nijkamp (1985) Knowledge Centres as Strategic Tools in Regional Policy. Research Memorandum. Dept of Economics. Free University Amsterdam

Nelson R R and S G Winter (1982) An Evolutionary Theory of Economic Change. Harvard University Press Cambridge

Norton R D (1979) City Life Cycles and American Urban Policy. Academic Press New York

Nijkamp P (1982) Technological Change, Policy Response and Spatial Dynamics. In: Griffith D A (Ed) Evolving Geographical Structure. The Hague 269-291

Nijkamp P and U Schubert (1983) Structural Change in Urban Systems. Contributions to the Metropolitan study: 5. IIASA Laxenburg

Nijkamp P et al (1985) Innovatie en Regionale Omgeving: een Test van enkele Hypotheses. In: Molle W T M (Ed) Innovatie en Regio. Den Haag 221-223

Nijkamp P (Ed) (1986) Technological Change, Employment and Spatial Dynamics, Springer-Verlag Berlin

Oakey R P (1981) High Technology Industry and Industrial Location. Gower Aldershot

Oakey R P (1983) Innovation and Regional Growth in Small High Technology Firms: Evidence from Britain and the USA. Regional Studies. 18.3:237-251

OECD (1984) Changing Market Structures in Telecommunications. Ergers H and J Okayama (Eds) North-Holland Amsterdam

Office of Technology Assessment (1984) Technology, Innovation and Regional Economic Development. US Congress OTA-SII-238. Washington DC

Pred A (1977) City Systems in Advanced Economies. Hutchinson London

Rogers E M (1962) Diffusion of Innovations. The Free Press of Glencoe New York

Rothwell R and W Zegveld (1982) Innovation and the Small and Medium Sized Firm. Pinter London

Rothwell R and W Zegveld (1985) Reindustrialization and Technology. Longman Somerset

Ruijter P A (1983) De Bruikbaarheid van het Begrip "Incubatiemilieu". KNAC Geografisch Tijdschrift XVII 2:106-110

40

Steed G P F (1976) Standardizations Scale, Incubation and Inertia: Montreal and Toronto Clothing Industries. Canadian Geographer 20:298-309

Stohr W B (1985) Industrial Structural Change and Regional Development Strategies, Towards a Conceptual Framework. IIR Discussion 21. Vienna

Stoneman P (1983) The Economic Analysis of Technological Change. Oxford University Press Oxford

Suarez-Villa L and J R Cuadrado-Roura (1994) Regional Economic Integration and the Evolution of Disparities. Papers in Regional Science 4:369-387

Thomas M D (1981) Growth and Change In Innovative Manufacturing Industries and Firms. Discussion Paper. IIASA Laxenburg

Thwaites A T (1982) Some Evidence on Regional Variations in the Introduction and Differentiation of Industrial Products within British Industry. Regional Studies, vol. 16 5:357-81

Vernon R (1960) Metropolis 1985. Harvard University Press Cambridge

[4]

ional Studies, Vol. 37.4, pp. 395–405, 2003

Carfax Publishing
Taylor & Francis Group

Debates and Surveys

Edited by M. W. DANSON

Entrepreneurship in a Modern Network Economy

PETER NIJKAMP

*Department of Regional Economics, Free University, De Boelelaan 1105, 1081 HV Amsterdam, The Netherlands.
Email: pnijkamp@feweb.vu.nl*

(Received March 2001; in revised form October 2001)

NIJKAMP P. (2003) Entrepreneurship in a modern network economy, *Reg. Studies* **37**, 395–405. In this survey paper the literature on entrepreneurship is summarized from the perspective of geographical seedbed conditions and network constellations. We argue that in many cases urban areas offer favourable incubator conditions for innovative entrepreneurship, as a result of economies of density and the opportunities created by the city as a nucleus of a broader network, both local and global. Clearly, network participation by creative entrepreneurs does not necessarily need an urban base, although informal spatial networks among specific business segments (e.g. ethnic niches) may be favourable for economic performance. We conclude that a modern entrepreneur tends to become increasingly a creative network operator and manager.

| Entrepreneurship | Innovation | Network | Incubation | Ethnic business |

NIJKAMP P. (2003) L'esprit d'entreprise dans une économie de réseau moderne, *Reg. Studies* **37**, 395–405. Cet article cherche à résumer la documentation sur l'esprit d'entreprise du point de vue des conditions géographiques propices aux pépinières d'entreprise et des constellations de réseaux. On affirme que souvent les agglomérations urbaines fournissent aux pépinières des conditions qui sont favorables à l'esprit d'entreprise innovateur à cause des économies d'agglomération et des possibilités engendrées par la ville en tant que noyau d'un réseau encore plus grand, au niveau local ainsi que sur le plan mondial. Il est évident que la participation des entrepreneurs innovateurs dans des réseaux ne nécessite pas forcément une base urbaine, quoique des réseaux géographiques informels dans des secteurs commerciaux particuliers (p.e. créneaux éthniques) puissent s'avérer favorables à la performance économique. En guise de conclusion, on affirme qu'un entrepreneur moderne a tendance à devenir de plus en plus un opérateur de réseau et un manager créateurs.

| Esprit d'entreprise | Innovation | Réseau | Pépinière |
| Commerce éthnique |

NIJKAMP P. (2003) Unternehmertum in einer modernen Netzwerkwirtschaft, *Reg. Studies* **37**, 395–405. In dieser Untersuchung wird die Literatur über Unternehmertum aus der Perspektive geographischer Brutstättenbedingungen und Netzwerk-konstellationen zusammengefaßt. Es wird der Standpunkt vertreten, daß in vielen Fällen Stadtgebiete günstige Brutkastenbedingungen für innovatives Unternehmertum bieten, die auf Wirtschaftlichkeit der Dichte und den Gelegenheiten beruhen, welche die Großstadt als Kern eines allgemeinen, sowohl örtlichen als auch globale, Netzwerks darstellt. Es ist klar, daß für schöpferische Unternehmer Teilnahme am Netzwerk nicht unbedingt eine Stadtbasis voraussetzt, obschon informale räumliche Netzwerke in spezifischen Geschäftssparten (z.B.) ethnischen Nischen) wirtschaftliche Leistung begünstigen mögen. Es wird der Schluß gezogen, daß ein moderner Unternehmer zunehmend dahin tendiert, ein schöpferischer Netzwerkoperator und -manager zu werden.

| Unternehmertum | Innovation | Netzwerk |
| Brutkasten | Ethnischer Betrieb |

0034-3404 print/1360-0591 online/03/040395-11 ©2003 Regional Studies Association
http://www.regional-studies-assoc.ac.uk

DOI: 10.1080/0034340032000074424

ENTREPRENEURSHIP IN PERSPECTIVE

Competition is the seedbed of the entrepreneurial spirit and the driving force of modern economies. It is based on the striving for survival by individual firms who have to operate as efficiently as possible. Since the early history of economics (Adam Smith, Ricardo) good entrepreneurship has been regarded as the critical success factor for economic performance. The notion of entrepreneurial competition was developed more fully a century ago by Marshall. A really path-breaking contribution to the analysis of entrepreneurship from a broad historical perspective was offered by Joseph Schumpeter in his book *The Theory of Economic Development* (SCHUMPETER, 1934). Starting from a circular flow of goods and money of a given size in a static context, he argues that without growth or economic progress, there is no scope for entrepreneurship; history will then repeat itself. However, if the exogenous circumstances are changing, the circular equilibrium will also change. This disturbance of an equilibrium towards a new position is called 'creative destruction'. One of the driving forces for a change towards a new equilibrium is formed by innovation, which means a breakthrough of existing patterns of production and productivity. Innovation is thus a creative *modus operandi* of an entrepreneur and induces a process of economic growth. Clearly, flexibility and vitality of the economic system is a *sine qua non* for an adjustment ('resilience') after a disturbance in the original equilibrium position. Since the 1980s, economic research has witnessed an avalanche of interest in the innovative behaviour of firms, in particular in the context of regional competitive conditions (for a review, see BERTUGLIA *et al.*, 1998, and FISCHER and FRÖHLICH, 2001). Regions (including cities) are increasingly regarded as important nodes of production, consumption, trade and decision making and play a critical role in global modes of production and transportation. Locality and globality are two sides of the same medal in an open network. The conventional comparative advantage perspective on regions is not sufficient anymore to explain the relative economic performance of regions in a global economy, as participation in ICT networks, educational systems and business culture are also important economic success factors. This awareness has had important implications for regional growth theory culminating in the popularity of the 'new' growth theory (for an overview, see also NIJKAMP and POOT, 1998).

A new phenomenon in modern economies is the emergence of interwoven global networks (see CASTELLS, 1996) which allow for global interaction and communications, a process through which market areas may obtain a worldwide coverage (for example, through the Internet). Consequently, interaction costs, transaction costs and transportation costs form an interconnected portfolio of new market opportunities (and

impediments) for modern business firms. Against this background, it is plausible that communication potential and knowledge are nowadays seen as critical success factors for the 'global entrepreneur'. The pathway towards global business is not easy to find; there is no single recipe, so that learning strategies are of great importance here. To reduce the risk of 'misinvestments', there is much scope for collective learning strategies which manifest themselves in two configurations, viz. network participation and geographical agglomeration. At present, both forces are at work simultaneously and create the new geographic landscape at the beginning of the new millennium (see also VAN GEENHUIZEN and RATTI, 2001).

The focus on knowledge as a factor *par excellence* for business performance ties in with the present emphasis on endogenous growth theory which takes for granted that economic growth is not automatically emerging from technological innovation as 'manna from heaven', but is the result of deliberate actions and choices of various stakeholders, including the government. Government policy in a modern society is, however, no longer a controlling strategy, but a facilitating strategy through which, by means of investments in R&D, education, training and knowledge centres etc., the seedbed conditions may be created for successful entrepreneurial performance.

The entrepreneur is thus back on the scene. But these strategies may be entirely different from those in the past, as the institutional and technological environment of entrepreneurship has drastically changed. To put these modern strategies more in perspective, in the next section we will offer a concise historical overview of the position of the entrepreneur in economic-historical thinking.

THE ENTREPRENEUR IN ECONOMIC HISTORY

In a recent textbook on economics (STIGLITZ and DRIFFILL, 2000), the entrepreneur is defined as a person who creates new businesses, brings new products to market, or develops new processes of production. This concise and simplified description does not do full justice to the wealth of literature on the history of economic thinking where the vibrant role of the entrepreneur has been extensively discussed.

The role of the entrepreneur in economic development has been a source of much scientific inspiration and research since the early history of economics. Important features of entrepreneurship were *inter alia* the degree of risk-taking by a firm, the innovative attitude of a firm, the degree of profit orientation by a firm and the long-range spin-off of business activities. In their standard work, *The Entrepreneur*, HÉBERT and LINK, 1982, offer the following typological classification of the 'species' of the entrepreneur:

1. The entrepreneur is the person who assumes the risk associated with uncertainty (e.g. Cantillon, Von Thünen, Mill, Hawley, Knight, Von Mises, Cole, Shackle)
2. The entrepreneur is the person who supplies financial capital (e.g. Smith, Böhm-Bawerk, Pigou, Von Mises)
3. The entrepreneur is an innovator (e.g. Bentham, Von Thünen, Schmoller, Sombart, Weber, Schumpeter, Shackle)
4. The entrepreneur is a decision maker (e.g. Cantillon, Menger, Marshall, Wieser, Amasa Walker, Francis Walker, Keynes, Von Mises, Cole, Schultz)
5. The entrepreneur is an industrial leader (e.g. Say, Saint-Simon, Amasa Walker, Francis Walker, Marshall, Wieser, Sombart, Weber, Schumpeter)
6. The entrepreneur is a manager or superintendent (e.g. Say, Mill, Marshall, Menger)
7. The entrepreneur is an organizer and coordinator of economic resources (e.g. Say, Wieser, Sombart, Weber, Clark, Davenport, Schumpeter, Coase)
8. The entrepreneur is the owner of an enterprise (e.g. Quesnay, Wieser, Pigou, Hawley)
9. The entrepreneur is an employer of factors of production (e.g. Amasa Walker, Francis Walker, Wieser, Keynes)
10. The entrepreneur is a contractor (e.g. Bentham)
11. The entrepreneur is an 'arbitrageur' (e.g. Cantillon, Walras, Kirzner)
12. The entrepreneur is an allocator of resources among alternative uses (e.g. Cantillon, Schultz).

Apparently, entrepreneurship is a multi-faceted phenomenon that can be viewed from different angles. Based on this long list of possible characteristics of the entrepreneur, one may argue that in the literature the following four main issues centring around entrepreneurship come generally to the fore (see also HÉBERT and LINK, 1982; VAN PRAAG, 1996, 1998; and VAN DIJK and THURIK, 1998):

• the position of the entrepreneur both in the surrounding economic system and within his/her own corporate organization
• the identification of the economic tasks of the entrepreneur
• the financial remuneration of the entrepreneur for his/her risk-taking activities, based on his/her economic motives
• the dynamics in (local and global) markets, seen from the perspective of the entrepreneur.

These four attributes of an entrepreneur show up with varying intensities in the literature on the essence of entrepreneurship. By way of illustration we will address concisely here the scientific contributions on entrepreneurship offered by Cantillon, Say, Marshall, Schumpeter, Knight and Kirzner, respectively.

The pioneering study of CANTILLON, 1931, on the role of entrepreneurship made a main distinction between the following economic agents: (1) *land owners* who were financially independent; (2) *arbitrageurs (entrepreneurs)* who were involved in risk-taking activities with a view to profit-making; and (3) *servants* who were ensured of a fairly stable income by means of a labour contract. In Cantillon's view, the market economy was a 'self-regulating network of reciprocal exchange arrangements' which were able to produce equilibrium prices through free entry and exit of business firms. In Cantillon's perception of entrepreneurship, the mediating role of the economic actor, who needs to anticipate uncertain future events and to see uncertainty as an economic opportunity, is more important than his innovative attitude. The 'survival of the fittest' would be best guaranteed by those entrepreneurs who know how to handle risk situations properly.

A more modern view on entrepreneurship was advocated by SAY, 1803, who identified the entrepreneur as a coordinating manager in the production and distribution process of goods, through which welfare for society was created. The degree of welfare creation by the entrepreneur (be it in agriculture, industrial production or trade) was dependent on three factors: (1) the generation of theoretical knowledge on production and distribution; (2) the application of this knowledge to real-world practices; and (3) the implementation of production and distribution processes. In Say's view: 'The application of knowledge to the creation of a product for human consumption is the entrepreneur's occupation' (*ibid.*, p. 330). Clearly, this knowledge was not of a generic nature, but had to be focused on the creation of welfare by means of entrepreneurial activity. Interestingly enough, risk-taking behaviour is, in Say's view, less important for entrepreneurship than the application of proper knowledge leading to good business judgement. Such qualities are rare, and hence 'the survival of the fittest' means that only a limited number of successful entrepreneurs are left in the market. This scarcity situation may also explain the high financial remuneration for good entrepreneurs. It is noteworthy that the restructuring role of an entrepreneur in a dynamic economy was much less recognized by Say.

Based on a neoclassical perspective, MARSHALL, 1890, focused due attention on the specific properties of entrepreneurship, more than other neoclassical economists in whose view perfect information, free competition and similar economic objectives would apply to all business behaviour. In Marshall's view the entrepreneur is a 'superintendent': the main task of the entrepreneur is to offer good products, while he may also focus on innovative strategies and economic progress. The entrepreneur is responsible for the proper functioning of his business. For that purpose he should have general abilities (such as a good memory, reliability, flexibility, etc.) and specialized abilities (such as good foresight, proper judgement and leadership). In Marshall's conception of the economic world, the business enterprise is mainly functioning in a static context; the 'survival of the fittest' is mainly determined by the remuneration for entrepreneurship relative to the financial rewards from other occupations.

A radically new perspective was offered by Schumpeter. Changes in economic systems in his view were not only the result of external (contextual) changes, but also of endogenous forces. The intrinsic dynamics of an economic system are caused by the entrepreneur (RIPSAS, 1998). Based on his 'circular economy' concept, he argues that growth and progress will be hampered in a static economic system. A breakthrough will be created by innovative entrepreneurship, through which – by a process of 'creative destruction' – static conditions will be changed, leading to a new equilibrium. The entrepreneur is not a manager, but an innovator. Successful innovative behaviour is essentially based on entrepreneurial spirit and intelligence. To quote Schumpeter: 'Everyone is an entrepreneur only when he actually "carries out new combinations" and loses that character as soon as he has built up his business, when he settles down to running it as other people run their business' (SCHUMPETER, 1934, p. 78). It is interesting to observe that risk-taking is an explicit attribute of entrepreneurship is not explicitly emphasized by Schumpeter, perhaps because in his view risk is more limited to financial risks than to a broader set of entrepreneurial challenges to be faced by the company.

More emphasis on risk behaviour was laid by KNIGHT, 1921. He made a distinction between risks that could be insured and those that could not. In his view the main mission of the entrepreneur is to decide *what* has to be done and *how* things have to be done, without having perfect information on future situations. The lack of insight may thus relate to *risk* situations (which may be analysed by standard statistical procedures) and *uncertainties* (which often have a unique character). Knight states in this context: 'In the first place, goods are produced for a market, on the basis of an entirely impersonal prediction of wants, not for the satisfaction of the wants of the producers themselves. The producer takes the responsibility for forecasting the consumers' wants' (*ibid.*, p. 268). The proper management of 'real' uncertainty is in the core business of the entrepreneur. In addition, the entrepreneur needs to have sufficient financial resources, courage, self-confidence, creativeness and foresight. Whether or not someone would decide to become an entrepreneur would be dependent on the relative financial revenues for this task compared to those originating from other tasks.

In his study *Competition and Entrepreneurship*, KIRZNER, 1973, offers a sharp criticism on the neo-classical world by questioning the assumptions of perfect information and equilibrium prices. He emphasizes the presence of asymmetric information leading to various forms of market disequilibrium. Good entrepreneurship is based on the ability to deal with these 'anomalies' adequately. To be successful, however, it is necessary to have a specific type of entrepreneurial knowledge: 'knowing where to look for knowledge'. He called this 'the highest order of knowledge'. The entrepreneur need not be rich, but has to be alert, viz. to have the ability to recognize profit opportunities under uncertain conditions.

Since the 1980s we have witnessed an almost explosive interest in entrepreneurship, in particular from the perspective of innovative behaviour (see, for a review, CUNNINGHAM and LISCHERON, 1991). It is noteworthy that especially the small and medium sized enterprise sector (SME) has received much attention in the 'entrepreneurial age', as a result of vertical integration of large firms, the shift from manufacturing to service industries, the strategic downsizing of large corporations and the flexible adjustment potential of small size firms (HARRISON, 1994). Even though empirical facts on the glory of entrepreneurialism were subject to criticism (NODOUSHANI and NODOUSHANI, 1999), the idea of the creative entrepreneur – or the 'entrepreneurial hero' – has been pervasive in the SME literature (REICH, 1987). In recent years we have seen very dynamic patterns of firm behaviour as a result of technological innovation and globalization, reflected *inter alia* in flexible specialization, corporate restructuring and new worldwide industrial networks (HARRISON and KELLEY, 1993). As a result the industrial organization has changed drastically, for instance, with an orientation towards industrial districts and specialized geographical clusters (e.g. the Third Italy). Networking and flexible specialization have become closely interwoven phenomena, but these phenomena take place in a geographic force field of regions or cities. The intricate embeddedness of modern enterprises in global networks has also challenged the position of the 'entrepreneurial hero'. Modern entrepreneurship is increasingly focused on organizing a complex force field influenced by many (internal and external) stakeholders (see ACKOFF, 1990). In a way one might even speak of a democratization of entrepreneurship.

In conclusion, entrepreneurship is a multi-faceted phenomenon that plays a central role in a market economy. The risks of entrepreneurship can be mitigated by an orientation towards a support system offered by the urbanization economies in geographical space.

DRIVERS OF MODERN ENTREPRENEURSHIP

After the discussion of the essential features and peculiarities of the 'entrepreneurial animal', we will now turn to the question of the drivers of entrepreneurship. The popularity of the 'new pioneer' (PETZINGER, 1999) or entrepreneurial hero' prompts an investigation into the determinants of creative entrepreneurship (see TAS-TAN, 2000). The literature does not offer an unambiguous explanation, but suggests at least three complementary factors which may be used in an explanatory framework. These factors are: personal motivation; social environment; and external business culture. They will now be discussed concisely.

Personal motivation

What are the driving forces for an individual to become an entrepreneur? In a survey article, HORNADAY and VESPER, 1982, identified several characteristics which may be seen as the determining psychological factors for entrepreneurship. These are:

● *need for achievement:* this is a traditional argument already dealt with by MCCLELLAND, 1961, in his book *The Achieving Society*. This attitude is found among people who want to be personally responsible for the resolution of problems, for the implementation of strategies and for the formulation of goals. It should be added that such a strong motivation does not always lead to successful entrepreneurship.

● *locus of control:* the degree to which an individual thinks they are able to influence the outcomes of business activities is another determining factor. The management control may relate to both internal and external factors (see SHAPERO, 1984).

● *risk taking:* entrepreneurship means risk taking. There is of course always a trade-off between profitability and financial risk, but this is not a simple relationship. Risks form a multi-faceted portfolio of financial, socio-economic, personal and managerial uncertainties, so that 'calculated risks' may be difficult to identify.

Clearly, the above-discussed psychological approach has also been severely criticized, as empirical research has demonstrated that the relative presence of these motivational factors can also be found among non-entrepreneurs or unsuccessful entrepreneurs. STEVENSON and SAHLMAN, 1985, p. 102, conclude therefore: 'Finally, while many have purported to find statistically significant common characteristics of entrepreneurs, the ability to attribute causality to these factors is seriously in doubt'. Therefore, a broader set of explanatory factors has to be envisaged.

Social environment

The social 'milieu' appears to be another determining factor for entrepreneurship. SHAPERO, 1984, has distinguished four factors in this context:

● *displacement:* examples of the displacement motive are loss of job, dissatisfaction with present job, discrimination, migration or social unrest (see NIJOEN,

2000). These are mainly push factors. Also, in the case of displacement with choice options, various pull factors may play a prominent role for the individual (such as new market opportunities, completion of a study, etc.)

● *disposition to act:* this motive originates from the wish to change one's position in order to be independent, to develop one's own career pattern, etc.

● *credibility:* this factor may be important as a start-up motive, which may be related to the need to receive recognition in a business environment

● *availability of resources:* this driving force is essentially more a prerequisite for a start-up, in terms of financial support, tax exemptions, subsidies, etc.

The above 'milieu' factors in many cases play a significant role, but they appear to be neither necessary nor sufficient for successful entrepreneurship. Thus this model is not able to offer a complete or unambiguous specification of a complicated entrepreneurial choice process (CHOENNI, 1997).

External business culture

Entrepreneurship is historically also determined by cultural and political factors (BAUMOL, 1990). If financial rewards or power are the ultimate goal of an individual, then it might count to enter, for instance, politics rather than industry (like in the ancient Chinese or Roman period). A low societal appreciation for entrepreneurship may lead to a low entry rate of start-up firms. If the recognition profile of successful entrepreneurs is high, we may see a huge interest in entering the business sector.

Also other external factors may play a decisive role, e.g. technological changes. This can be illustrated by the share of ICT business start-ups in recent years. Similarly, structural changes in industrial composition and organization, shifts in the labour market, changes in institutional and governmental structures or socio-demographic changes may encourage entrepreneurship as well (see, for example, ACS, 1994; BAUMOL, 1990; BROCK and EVANS, 1989; and EVANS and LEIGHTON, 1989).

The step towards creative entrepreneurship is certainly a complicated and multi-dimensional phenomenon. There are apparently necessary conditions, desirable conditions and facilitating conditions. This complex array calls for further empirical research.

In retrospect, the above concise descriptions of the role of and motives for entrepreneurship have brought to light that in general the role of the entrepreneur is concerned with a proper treatment of uncertainty and with the need to explore new endeavours, to initiate creative and innovative strategies, and to collect and deploy new knowledge. Spatially discriminating opportunities and impediments, however, have mainly been overlooked in these considerations. This also holds for the role of spatial public policy. It is surprising to observe that the geography of entrepreneurship has indeed received far less attention. Therefore, in the next section a few observations on the spatial aspects of entrepreneurship will be offered.

ENTREPRENEURSHIP IN SPATIO-TEMPORAL CONTEXT

The birth, growth, contraction and death process of enterprises has become an important field of research in so-called firm demographics (see VAN WISSEN, 2000). This new field of research is concerned with the analysis of the spatial-temporal change pattern of firms from a behavioural-analytical perspective (see NELSON and WINTER, 1982). Recent interesting studies in this field can be found *inter alia* in BRÜDERL and SCHUSSERL, 1990; CARROLL and HANNAN, 2000; and SIEGFRIED and EVANS, 1994. Many studies on growth processes of firms originate from industrial economics or organization and management disciplines, often complemented with notions from geography, demography, or psychology (e.g. CAVES, 1998; EVANS, 1987; GERTLER, 1988; HAYTER, 1997; or STINCHCOMBE *et al.*, 1968).

The roots of this new approach can be found in the 1980s when in a period of economic recession much attention was given to the birth of new firms. From a regional economic perspective much research was undertaken on the geographical differentiation in the birth and growth process of new firms (see, for example, KEEBLE and WEVER, 1986; OAKEY, 1993; STOREY, 1994; SUAREZ-VILLA, 1996; and SUTTON, 1998).

The predominant focus on new firm formation tended to neglect the spatio-temporal dynamics of incumbent firms, in particular the way they survive, grow or decline. From that perspective also the role of the adoption of new technology had to receive due attention (see, for example, ABERNATHY *et al.*, 1983; STORPER and SCOTT, 1989; DAVELAAR, 1991; PETTIGREW and WHIPP, 1991; and NOOTEBOOM, 1993). This has also prompted several studies on the life cycles of firms (in particular, competitive performance, product differentiation, spatial relocation, organizational restructuring, etc). There are various reasons why of all types of firm dynamics, new firm formation has attracted much concern (see VAN GEENHUIZEN and NIJKAMP, 1995). Perhaps most significant is the fact that new firms provide new jobs. A second reason is that new firms are often involved in the introduction of new products and processes in the market. Accordingly, they may provide a major challenge to established firms and encourage them to improve their product quality and service or to reduce prices. On the other hand, it ought to be recognized that newly established firms face relatively large risks, due to lack of organizational experience and cohesion. As a consequence, the

death rate among start-ups is relatively high and tends to decrease over time. Many 'entrepreneurial heroes' appear to die at a young age. It is clear that successful new enterprises in a geographical area contribute significantly to the economy and employment in the region concerned. There is, however, usually a large sectoral and geographical variation among the success or survival rates of new entrepreneurs (see ACS, 1994).

Empirical research has shown that in most cases enterprises change their strategies (products, markets, etc.) in an incremental way. From historical research it appears that radical adjustments do take place, but occur infrequently (MINTZBERG, 1978). In evolutionary economics it is emphasized that organizations develop, stabilize and follow routines. These routines may change over time, but in the short run they function as stable carriers for knowledge and experience. This causes a certain degree of 'inertia'. Related to the latter point is the core concept of search behaviour. Organizations are not invariant, but change as a result of a search for new solutions when older ones fail to work. Search behaviour follows routines, for example, based upon perceptions 'coloured' by the previous situation and biases in information processing (see also VAN GEENHUIZEN and NIJKAMP, 1995). The study of the development trajectories of individual firms from a spatio-temporal perspective is sometimes called 'company life history analysis' (see VAN GEEN-HUIZEN, 1993). It mainly uses a case study approach and aims to trace and explain the evolution of firms over a longer period. Particular attention is then given to entrepreneurial motives for corporate change at the micro level. Factors to be considered are *inter alia* the business environment, leadership, links between strategic and operational change, human resource management and coherence in management (see also PETTIGREW and WHIPP, 1991). Information acquisition, e.g. through participation in networks of industries, is of course also an important element to be considered. In this context, also the local 'milieu' (e.g. through *filières*) may play an important role.

It is a widely held belief that a metropolitan environment offers favourable incubator conditions for creative entrepreneurship, as in this setting the conditions for proper human resource management (e.g. by means of specialized training and educational institutes) and labour recruitment are most favourable (see, for example, THOMPSON, 1968; LEONE and STRUYCK, 1976; PRED, 1977; or DAVELAAR, 1991). But it ought to be recognized that various non-metropolitan areas also do offer favourable seedbed conditions to the management of corporate change. The reason is that in many non-metropolitan areas the information needs are met in localized learning mechanisms, based on a dynamic territorial interplay between actors in a coherent production system, local culture, tradition and experiences (see CAMAGNI, 1991; RATTI, 1992; STORPER, 1992, 1993). This view comes close to the one which puts a strong emphasis on the trend for localization in less central areas where doing business is a final resort or a survival strategy. Advocates of the latter idea adhere to a vertically disintegrated and locationally fixed production, based on a shift to flexible specialization. Some empirical evidence on non-urban seedbeds is found in high technology regions such as Silicon Valley, Boston, the M4 Corridor, and in semi-rural areas such as the Third Italy. Although the success of economic restructuring in these regions – as a result of many high-tech start-up firms – is, without doubt, the pervasiveness of the trend for flexible specialization, concomitant localization is not sufficiently proven (see GERTLER, 1988; VAN GEENHUIZEN and VAN DER KNAAP, 1994). Aside from a trend towards localization there is a trend towards globalization, associated with the growing influence of multinational corporations and their global networking with smaller firms (see AMIN, 1993).

In the light of the previous observations it may plausibly be argued that modern entrepreneurship is based on associated skills of a varied nature. An entrepreneur is certainly an opportunity seeker, but in so doing he needs to have an open eye on a rapidly changing external environment. As a consequence, firm demography is a multidimensional field of research in which psychology, sociology, marketing, political science, economics, finance and management come together. A demographic approach to entrepreneurship may unravel various components of the spatio-temporal dynamics of both existing and new firms. In-depth case study research as advocated in company life history analysis is certainly necessary to identify motives and barriers concerning successful entrepreneurship, but there is also a clear need for more analytical comparative research leading to research synthesis and transferable lessons. An interesting example of the latter type of research approach can be found in a recent study by BRESCHI, 2000, who conducted a cross-sector analysis of the geography of innovative activities. Using the evolutionary concept of a technological regime he was able to identify the background factors of variations in spatial patterns of innovations, viz. knowledge base, technological opportunities, appropriability conditions and cumulativeness of technical advances. Undertaking more of such studies might advance the idea that geography counts in a modern entrepreneurial age. Cities offer important seedbed conditions for modern entrepreneurship in an open network economy, but this role is by no means exclusive. We observe at the same time local niches or shells in isolated areas which offer due protection or incubation for creative entrepreneurial abilities. Important stimulating factors may be: the presence of training and educational facilities; an open business culture; venture capital; public support; local suppliers and subcontractors; and so forth. Consequently, the geographic landscape of modern

entrepreneurship is varied and calls for intensified research efforts aimed at more synthesis.

ENTREPRENEURSHIP AND NETWORKS

Entrepreneurship means also the management of business network constellations. An interesting and rather comprehensive review of the relationship between entrepreneurship and network involvement has been given by MALECKI, 1997. The local environment (including its culture, knowledge base and business attitude) appears to act often as a critical success factor for new forms of entrepreneurship, a finding also obtained by CAMAGNI, 1991. Apparently, the local 'milieu' offers various types of networks which tend to encourage the 'entrepreneurial act' (see SHAPERO, 1984).

In the Schumpeterian view the entrepreneur is seeking for new combinations while destroying in a creative way existing constellations. This highly risk-taking behaviour, however, can be ameliorated by externalizing some of the risks through participation or involvement in local or broader industrial networks. In general, the urban climate offers many possibilities for strategic network involvement, either material or virtual. In this way, the real entrepreneur tends to become an organizer of change. The early urban economics literature (HOOVER and VERNON, 1959) has already spelt out the great potential of urban industrial districts for creative entrepreneurship (for a review of the incubation literature, see DAVELAAR, 1991). Also in the sociologically-oriented writings of JACOBS, 1961, we observe similar arguments. Apparently, urban modes of life create scale economies which favour the rise of new enterprises. To some extent, this idea was already propagated by MARSHALL, 1890, who introduced the concept of industrial districts which generated an enormous economic growth potential (see also AMIN and THRIFT, 1992; MARKUSEN, 1996; and PACI and USAI, 2000). In general, vertical disintegration in combination with network strategies at a local level may induce a resurgence of Marshallian districts as self-contained local networks of creative economic development.

It seems as though the modern entrepreneurial 'hero' is largely a 'network hero'. But it ought to be recognized that networking as a business strategy is not falling from heaven, but requires investments in social communication, informal bonds, training and education. To build up and to operate effectively in networks requires time and effort. Furthermore, networking may be a desirable or necessary condition, but it is by no means sufficient to ensure good entrepreneurship. And last but not least, network behaviour may also stimulate uniformity, which may contradict the entrepreneurial spirit.

Networks may, in general, relate to physical configurations (such as aviation networks, road networks, railway networks or telecommunication networks) or to virtual networks (such as industrial clubs, knowledge networks or information networks). Many networks may have a local character, but may also extend towards global levels. Such networks may favour industrial diversity, entrepreneurial spirit and resource mobilization (see also ANDERSSON, 1985; and VAN DE VEN, 1993). In general, local inter-firm networks may be seen as supporting mechanisms for new forms of creative entrepreneurship (especially among high-tech start-up firms), as such networks are a blend of openness (necessary for competition) and protection (needed for an 'infant industry'). It may be interesting to quote here the final conclusions of MALECKI, 1997, p. 98: 'Thus, it is difficult for any "recipe" from one place to work when transplanted into another place, with its unique culture, traditions, capabilities, and networks'.

In the context of endogenous growth theory an intense debate has started on the way regions and governments can stimulate local economic growth. Following the seminal contributions by ROMER, 1986, and LUCAS, 1988, a wide interest has emerged in the critical conditions for modern economic growth (see, for example, DIXIT and STIGLITZ 1977; HELPMAN, 1992; BARRO and SALA-I-MARTIN, 1995; KIRZNER, 1997; AGHION and HOWITT, 1998; NIJKAMP and POOT, 1998; BLUESTONE and HARRISON, 2000).

An important element in the discussion on endogenous growth concerned the role of knowledge and knowledge networks. The foundation for the theory of knowledge use was essentially laid several decades back by SOLOW, 1956, 1957, and ARROW, 1962, who advocated the significance of learning mechanisms for increasing productivity.

From the perspective of a business environment, information and knowledge is a *sine qua non* for entrepreneurial success, not only for large-scale companies but also for SMEs. MALECKI and POEHLING, 1999, have given a very valuable review of the literature on this issue; learning-by-doing, supported by inter-firm network collaboration, enhances the competitive potential of new firm initiatives. They observe a variety of network configurations, such as suppliers or customers networks, local networks of neighbouring firms, professional networks and knowledge networks, which all may contribute to a better entrepreneurial performance. Empirical research in this area, however, is still scarce and there would be scope for more systematic comparative investigations into the knowledge drivers of modern entrepreneurship. It is certainly true that information and knowledge is an important asset in an enterprise, but the economic evaluation of such knowledge (e.g. as a private good or a public good with a non-rivalry character) needs to be studied more thoroughly (see SHANE and VENKATARAMAN, 2000).

The potential benefits of up-to-date information may be high, but knowledge acquisition also has its costs. As SOETE, 2000, p. 89, argues:

> But of course there are costs in acquiring knowledge. It explains why markets for exchange of knowledge are rare and why firms prefer in principle to carry out Research and Development in-house rather than have it contracted out or licensed. It also provides a rationale for policies focusing on the importance of investment in knowledge accumulation. Such investments are likely to have high so-called 'social' rates of return, often much higher than the private rate of return. Investment in knowledge cannot be simply left to the market.

An interesting illustration of the importance of local networks for new firm formation can be found in the literature on ethnic entrepreneurship (see WALDINGER 1996). Many cities in a modern industrialized world are confronted with a large influx of foreign migrants (see, for example, MCMANUS, 1990, BORJAS, 1992, 1995; BREZIS and TEMIN, 1997; YAP, 1997; and GORTER et al., 1998). The socioeconomic problems involved have created an enormous tension and have prompted many policy initiatives on housing, job creation, education, etc. But the successes of such policies have not yet been impressive. The seedbed conditions for active economic participation are often weak, as a result of low levels of skill, language deficiencies, cultural gaps and stigmatization. One of the more recent promising efforts has been to favour ethnic entrepreneurship, so that through a system of self-employment socio-cultural minorities might be able to improve their less favoured position. Ethnic entrepreneurship has different appearances, e.g. production for the indigenous ethnic market or low skilled activities, but increasingly we see also an upgrading of the ethnic production sector (e.g. shops, software firms, consultancy).

In a recent survey study, VAN DELFT et al., 2000, have demonstrated that the access to and use of local support networks is a critical success factor for various urban policy programmes addressing the new immigrants. Such networks may relate to socio-economic support, provision of venture capital or access to the urban community at large. The importance of social bonds and kinship relationships has also been emphasized by several other authors (for instance, BOYD, 1989; CHISWICK and MILLER, 1996; BOROOAH and HART, 1999; and NDOEN, 2000). In general, such networks appear to create various externalities in terms of entrepreneurial spirit, search for opportunities, self-organization and self-education, and business information and access to local markets.

But it is noteworthy that such network connections are geared toward the geographical space in which ethnic entrepreneurs operate. It should be added that in most cities ethnic networks are not uniform, but reflect local cultures from the country of origin. Many ethnic entrepreneurs operate in volatile markets and, although network participation is needed to cope with many market uncertainties, business or social networks are usually not sufficient to survive in a competitive environment (see BARRETT *et al.* 1996). There is a need for more thorough empirical research on the motives and performance of ethnic entrepreneurs (see also MASUREL *et al.*, 2002). The ethnic entrepreneur as a network manager is still a concept that has not become deeply rooted in the ethnic business environment.

CONCLUDING REMARKS

The history of economic thinking has demonstrated a fluctuating interest in entrepreneurship. In the past decades we have seen much emphasis on the innovative role of the entrepreneur, while more recently a trend can be observed in which the entrepreneur is conceived of as a network operator or manager. Clearly, changing patterns of economic life have had a decisive influence on views on entrepreneurship.

The 'network entrepreneur' needs specific skills in terms of information processing, international access, alertness to world market developments and search for partnership. Metropolitan environments appear to offer sometimes fruitful conditions for network behaviour, as a result of economies of density, suitable communication modes and associative cultures (including a scientific environment). Large-scale companies are usually able to manage complex worldwide interactions, but

for firms in the SME sector quite a few hurdles have to be taken in terms of training, network access, marketing channel choice, e-commerce opportunities, and inter-firm cooperation. An urban environment with an abundance of formal and informal contacts may then offer a protective shell for new ventures. It seems therefore plausible that the rise of the network society will (continue to) favour urban modes of operation for creative entrepreneurship. The entrepreneurial role model seems to find promising seedbeds in urban cultures, as is witnessed by ethnic business cultures. But a word of caution is in order here. The urban incubation potential is a desirable condition for new start-ups, but it may also lead to a social trap that prevents real entrepreneurial creativeness. Networks are instrumental, but require a proper management by a change agent, i.e. the modern entrepreneur.

The above review of entrepreneurship in a modern network economy has brought to light promising ventures for applied research to be undertaken in order to understand fully the changing landscape of the 'entrepreneurial hero'. Important elements on a research agenda are: the critical success and failure factors of entrepreneurial activities in an open economic system; the impact of uncertainty on business decisions of both starting and incumbent firms and the role of (material and virtual) networks in uncertainty management; and the geographic network conditions (including urban incubator phenomena) that shape a favourable business environment. It may be concluded that modern entrepreneurship in a spatial network constellation offers fascinating new research challenges.

REFERENCES

ABERNATHY W. J., CLARK K. B. and KANTROW A. M. (1983) *Industrial Renaissance: Producing a Competitive Future for America.* Basic Books, New York.
ACKOFF R. L. (1990) The management of change and the change it requires of management, *Systems Practice* 3(5), 427–40.
ACS Z. (Ed) (1994) *Regional Innovation, Knowledge and Global Change.* Frances Pinter, London.
AGHION P. and HOWITT P. (1998) *Endogenous Growth Theory.* MIT Press, Cambridge, MA.
AMIN A. (1993) The globalization of the economy: an erosion of regional networks?, in GRABHER G. (Ed) *The Embedded Firm: On the Socio-economics of Industrial Networks,* pp. 278–95. Routledge, London.
AMIN A. and THRIFT N. (1992) Neo-Marshallian nodes in global networks, *Int. J. Urban & Reg. Res.* 16(4), 571–87.
ANDERSSON A. (1985) Creativity on regional development, *Pap. Reg. Sci. Ass.* 56, 5–20
ARROW K. (1962) The economic implications of learning by doing, *Rev. Econ. Studies* 29, 155–73.
BARRETT G., JONES T. and MCEVOY D. (1996) Ethnic minority business: theoretical discourse in Britain and North America. *Urban Studies* 33(4/5), 783–809.
BARRO R. and SALA-I-MARTIN X. (1995) *Economic Growth.* McGraw-Hill, New York.
BAUMOL W. J. (1990) Entrepreneurship, *J. Pol. Econ.* 98(5), 893–921.
BERTUGLIA C. S., LOMBARDO S. and NIJKAMP P. (Eds) (1998) *Innovative Behaviour in Space and Time.* Springer-Verlag, Berlin.
BLUESTONE B. and HARRISON B. (2000) *Growing Prosperity.* Houghton Mifflin, New York.
BORJAS G. (1992) Ethnic capital and intergenerational mobility, *Quart. J. Econ.* 107(1), 123–50.
BORJAS G. (1995) Ethnicity, neighbourhoods and human capital externalities, *Am. Econ. Rev.* 85(3), 365–90.
BOROOAH V. K. and HART M. (1999) Factors affecting self-employment among Indian and Caribbean men in Britain, *Small Bus. Econ.* 13, 111–29.
BOYD M. (1989) Family and personal networks in international migration: recent developments and new agendas, *Int. Migration Rev.* 23(3), 638–70.
BRESCHI S. (2000) The geography of innovation: a cross-sector analysis, *Reg. Studies* 34(3), 111–34.
BREZIS E. S. and TEMIN P. (Eds) (1997) *Elites, Minorities and Economic Growth.* North-Holland, Amsterdam.

BROCK W. A. and EVANS D. S. (1989) Small business economics, *Small Bus. Econ.* 1, 7–20.
BRÜDERL J. and SCHUSSLER R. (1990) Organizational mortality, *Admin. Sci. Quart.* 35, 530–37.
CAMAGNI R. (1991) *Innovation Networks: Spatial Perspectives.* Belhaven Press, London.
CANTILLON R. (1931) *Essai sur la Nature du Commerce en Général.* Macmillan, London.
CARROLL G. R. and HANNAN M. T. (2000) *The Demography of Corporations and Industries.* Princeton University Press, Princeton, NJ.
CASTELLS M. (1996) *The Rise of the Network Society.* Blackwell, London.
CAVES R. E. (1998) Industrial organisation and new findings on the turnover and mobility of firms, *J. Econ. Lit.* 36, 1,947–82.
CHISWICK B. R. and MILLER P.W. (1996) Ethnic networks and language proficiency among immigrants, *J. Pop. Econ.* 9(1), 19–35.
CHOENNI A. (1997) *Veelsoortig Assortiment.* Het Spinhuis, Amsterdam.
CUNNINGHAM J. B. and LISCHERON J. (1991) Defining entrepreneurship, *J. Small Bus. Mgt.* 29(1), 45–61.
CURRAN J. and BLACKBURN R. A. (1993) *Ethnic Enterprise and the High Street Bank.* Small Business Research Centre, Kingston University, London.
DAVELAAR E. J (1991) *Incubation and Innovation: A Spatial Perspective.* Ashgate, Aldershot.
DIXIT A. and STIGLITZ J. (1977) Monopolistic competition and optimum product diversity, *Am. Econ. Rev.* 67, 297–308.
EVANS D. (1987) The relationship between firm growth, size and age, *J. Ind. Econ.* 35, 567–81.
EVANS D. S. and LEIGHTON L. S. (1989) The determinants of changes in US self-employment, *Small Bus. Econ.* 1, 111–19.
FISCHER M. M. and FRÖHLICH J. (Eds) (2001) *Knowledge, Complexity and Innovation Systems.* Springer-Verlag, Berlin.
GERTLER M. (1988) The limits of flexibility: comments on the Post-Fordist vision of production and its geography, *Trans. Inst. Brit. Geogr.* 17, 410–32.
GORTER C., NIJKAMP P. and POOT J. (Eds) (1998) *Crossing Borders.* Ashgate, Aldershot.
HAYTER R. (1997) *The Dynamics of Industrial Location.* John Wiley, Chichester.
HARRISON B. (1994) The myth of small firms as the predominant job generators, *Econ. Develop. Quart.* 8(1), 3–18.
HARRISON B. and KELLY M. R. (1993) Outsourcing and the search for flexibility, *Work, Employment & Society* 7(2), 213–35.
HÉBERT R. M. and LINK A. N. (1982) *The Entrepreneur.* Praeger, New York.
HELPMAN E. (1992) Endogenous macroeconomic growth theory, *Europ. Econ. Rev.* 36, 237–67.
HORNADAY J. A. and VESPER K. H. (1982) Frontiers of entrepreneurship research, Proceedings of the 1982 Babson College Entrepreneurship Research Conference, pp. 526–39, Center for Entrepreneurial Studies, Babson College, Wellesley, MA.
HOOVER E. M. and VERNON R. (1959) *Anatomy of a Metropolis.* Harvard University Press, Cambridge, MA.
JACOBS J. (1961) *The Death and Life of Great American Cities.* Cape, London.
KEEBLE D. and WEVER E. (Eds) (1986) *New Firms and Regional Development in Europe.* Croom Helm, London.
KIRZNER I. M. D. (1973) *Competition and Entrepreneurship.* University of Chicago Press, Chicago.
KIRZNER I. M. D. (1997) Entrepreneurial discovery and the competitive market process, *J. Econ. Lit.* 35(1), 60–85.
KNIGHT F. H. (1921) *Risk, Uncertainty and Profit.* Houghton Mifflin, New York.
LEONE R. A. and STRUYCK R. (1976) The incubator hypothesis: evidence from five SMSAs, *Urban Studies* 13, 325–31.
LUCAS R. (1988) On the mechanics of economic development, *J. Monetary Econ.* 22, 3–42.
MACCLELLAND D. C. (1961) *The Achieving Society.* Free Press, New York.
MALECKI E. J. (1997) Entrepreneurs, networks, and economic development, *Advances in Entrepreneurship, Firm Emergence & Growth* 3, 57–118.
MALECKI E. J. and POEHLING R. M. (1999) Extroverts and introverts: small manufactures and their information sources, *Entrepreneurship & Reg. Develop.* 11, 247–68.
MARKUSEN A. (1996) Sticky places in slippery space: a typology of industrial districts, *Econ. Geogr.* 72(3), 293–313.
MARSHALL A. (1890) *Principles of Economics.* Macmillan, London.
MASUREL E., NIJKAMP P., TASTAN M. and VINDIGNI G. (2002) Motivations and performance conditions for ethnic entrepreneurship, *Growth & Change* 33(2), 238–60.
MCMANUS W. S. (1990) Labour market effects of language enclaves, *J. Hum. Resources* 25(2), 228–52.
MINTZBERG H. (1978) Patterns of strategy formation, *Mgt. Science* 36, 934–48.
NDOEN M. (2000) *Migrants and Entrepreneurial Activities in Peripheral Indonesia.* Thesis Publishers, Amsterdam.
NELSON R. R. and WINTER S.G. (1982) *An Evolutionary Theory of Economic Changes.* Harvard University Press, Cambridge, MA.
NIJKAMP P. and POOT J. (1998) Spatial perspectives on new theories of economic growth, *Ann. Reg. Sci.* 32, 7–37.
NODOUSHANI O. and NODOUSHANI P. A. (1999) Entrepreneurship in an age of flexibility, *J. Bus. & Society* 12(2), 144–58.
NOOTEBOOM B. (1993) Networks and transactions: do they connect?, in GROENEWEGEN J. (Ed) *Dynamics of the Firm: Strategies of Pricing and Organisation*, pp. 9–26. Edward Elgar, Aldershot.
OAKEY R. (1993) High technology small firms: a more realistic evaluation of their growth potential, in KARLSSON C., JOHANNISSON B. and STOREY D. (Eds) *Small Business Dynamics: International, National and Regional Perspectives*, pp. 224–42. Routledge, London.
PACI R. and USAI S. (2000) Technological enclaves and industrial districts, *Reg. Studies* 34(2), 97–114.
PETTIGREW A. and WHIPP R. (1991) *Managing Change for Competitive Success.* Blackwell, Oxford.
PETZINGER T. JR. (1999) *The New Pioneers.* Simon & Schuster, New York.
PRED A. (1977) *City-Systems in Advanced Economies.* Hutchinson, London.
RATTI R. (1992) *Innovation Technologies et Development Regional.* IRE-Meta Editions, Bellinzona.

EICH R. B. (1987) Entrepreneurship reconsidered: the team as hero, *Harv. Bus. Rev.* **65**(3), 77–83.

IPSAS S. (1998) Towards an interdisciplinary theory of entrepreneurship, *Small Bus. Econ.* **10**(2). 103–15.

OMER P. (1986) Increasing returns and long-run growth, *J. Pol. Econ.* **94**, 1,002–37

AY J. B. (1803) *A Treatise on Political Economy* (translated by C. R. PRINSEP). Grigg & Elliot, Philadelphia.

IANE S. and VENKATARAMAN S. (2000) The promise of entrepreneurship as a field of research. *Acad. Mgt. Rev.* **96**, 98–121.

CHUMPETER J. (1934) *The Theory of Economic Development*. Harvard University Press, Cambridge. MA.

HAPERO A. (1984) The entrepreneurial event. in KENT C. A. (Ed) *The Environment for Entrepreneurship*, pp. 21–40. Lexington Books, Lexington, MA.

IEGFRIED J. J. and EVANS L. B. (1994) Empirical studies of entry and exit, *Rev. Ind. Organisation* **9**. 121–55.

DETE L. (2000) The new economy: a European perspective, in ARCHIBUGI D. and LUNDVALL B. A. (Eds) *The Globalizing Learning Economy*. Oxford University Press, Oxford.

OLOW R. (1956) A contribution to the theory of economic growth, *Quart. J. Econ.* **70**, 65–94.

OLOW R. (1957) Technical change in an aggregative model of economic growth, *Int. Econ. Rev.* **6**, 18–31.

TEVENSON H. H. and SAHLMAN W. A. (1985) Capital market myopia, in HORNADAY J. A. *et al.* (Eds) *Frontiers of Entrepreneurship Research*, Proceedings of the Fifth Annual Babson College Entrepreneurship Research conference, pp. 85–104. Center for Entrepreneurial Studies, Babson College, Wellesley, MA.

TIGLITZ J. E. and DRIFFILL J. (2000) *Economics*. W. W. Norton, New York.

TINCHCOMBE A. L., MACDILL M. S. and WALKER D. (1968) Demography of organisations, *Am. J. Sociol.* **74**, 221–29.

TOREY D. J. (1994) *Understanding the Small Business Sector*. Routledge, London.

TORPER M. (1992) The limits to globalization: technology district and international trade, *Econ. Geogr.* **68**, 60–93.

TORPER M. (1993) Regional 'worlds' of production: learning and innovation in the technology districts of France, Italy and the USA, *Reg. Studies* **27**, 433–55.

TORPER M. and SCOTT A. J. (1989) The geographical foundations and social regulation of flexible production complexes, in WOLCH J. and DEAR M. (Eds) *The Power of Geography: How Territory Shapes Social Life*. Unwin Hyman, Boston, MA.

UAREZ-VILLA L. (1996) Innovative capacity. infrastructure and regional policy, in BATTEN D. F. and KARLSSON C. Eds) *Infrastructure and the Complexity of Economic Development*, pp. 251–70. Springer-Verlag, Berlin.

UTTON J. (1998) *Market Structure and Innovation.*, MIT Press, Cambridge, MA.

ASTAN M. (2000) Determinanten van Succesvol Allochtoon Ondernemerschap, M.Sc. thesis, Department of Economics, Free University, Amsterdam.

HOMPSON W. R. (1968) Internal and external factors in the development of urban economies, in PERLOFF H. S. and WINGO L. (Eds) *Issues in Urban Economics*, pp. 43–62. The Johns Hopkins University Press, Baltimore, MD.

VALDINGER R. (1996) *Still the Promised City?* Harvard University Press, Cambridge, MA.

AN DELFT H., GORTER C. and NIJKAMP P. (2000) In search of ethnic entrepreneurship opportunities in the city; a comparative study, *Environ. Plann. C* **18**(4), 429–51.

AN DIJK B. and THURIK A. R. (1998) Entrepreneurship: Visies en Benaderingen, in SCHERJON D. P. and THURIK A. R. (Eds) *Handboek Ondernemers en Adviseurs in het MKB*, pp. 127–47. Kluwer, Deventer.

AN GEENHUIZEN M. (1993) A longitudinal analysis of the growth of firms, PhD thesis, Erasmus University, Rotterdam.

AN GEENHUIZEN M. and NIJKAMP P. (1995) A demographic approach to firm dynamics, Research Paper. Department of Economics, Free University, Amsterdam.

AN GEENHUIZEN M. and RATTI R. (Eds) (2001) *Gaining Advantage from Open Borders*. Ashgate. Aldershot.

AN GEENHUIZEN M. and VAN DER KNAAP G. A. (1994) Dutch textile industry in a global economy, *Reg. Studies* **28**, 695–711.

AN PRAAG C. M. (1996) *Determinants of Successful Entrepreneurship*. Thesis Publishers, Amsterdam.

AN PRAAG C. M. (1998) Succesvolle Ondernemingen, De Rol van de Ondernemer, in SCHARJON D. P. and THURIK A. R. (Eds) *Handboek Ondernemers en Adviseurs in het MKB*, pp. 103–26. Kluwer, Deventer.

AN DE VEN A. (1993) The development of an infrastructure for entrepreneurship, *J. Bus. Venturing* **8**, 211–30.

AN WISSEN L. J. G. (2000) A micro-simulation model of firms: applications of the concept of the demography of firms, *Pap. Reg. Sci.* **79**, 111–34.

AP L. (1977) The attraction of cities: a review of the migration literature, *J. Development Econ.* **4**, 239–302.

[5]

Networks and Spatial Economics, 2: (2002) 211–229
© 2002 Kluwer Academic Publishers, Manufactured in the Netherlands.

Resilience: An Evolutionary Approach to Spatial Economic Systems

AURA REGGIANI
*Department of Economics, Faculty of Statistics, University of Bologna, Piazza Scaravilli 2,
40126 Bologna, Italy*
e-mail: reggiani@economia.unibo.it

THOMAS DE GRAAFF AND PETER NIJKAMP
*Department of Economics, Faculty of Economics, Free University of Amsterdam, De Boelelaan 1105,
1085 HV Amsterdam, The Netherlands*
e-mail: tgraaff@feweb, pnijkamp@feweb.vu.nl

Abstract

The concept of resilience has received a great deal of attention in the past decades. Starting from the first fundamental definitions offered by Holling, Pimms and Perrings in an economic-ecological modeling context, the present paper explores the 'evolution' of the resilience concept—as well as related different measures—in both a continuous and discrete time setting.

From this perspective, the paper explores the relevance of the resilience concept in socio-economic systems, by focussing the attention on the relationships among resilience, transition dynamics and lock-in effects, in particular in the light of the dynamics of technological innovation diffusion and adaptive behaviour of firms. In this framework we will describe an empirical application, in which the resilience and dynamics of the West-German labour market will be investigated. This empirical illustration is offered by making use of an algorithm constructed for detecting Lyapunov exponents, so as to classify the resilience among employment sectors in our case study.

Keywords: resilience, dynamics, labour market

1. Setting the Scene

The analysis of dynamic systems has become a fashionable research topic in the past decade. Several disciplines, such as biology, ecology, sociology, and increasingly also economics, have drawn particular attention to behavioural aspects of non-linear dynamic models, with reference to positive and negative feedback relations, synergetic responses and adaptive behaviour. The methodology of the social sciences has recently increasingly directed its attention to the analysis of complex systems, often characterised by non-linear dynamics and unpredictable time-paths and outcomes.

Furthermore, many dynamic systems are increasingly examined from a multi-layer and multi-actor perspective, and address issues like evolutionary behaviour, endogenous growth, resilience and the like. Particularly the concept of resilience is at present the subject of interesting and controversial debates, as is witnessed by the following statement:

"The modern study of stability in ecology can be said to have begun with the appearance of 'Fluctuations of Animal Populations and a Measure of Community Stability'. by R.H. MacArthur in 1955. Since the publication of this influential paper, ecologists have investigated the properties of a number of different stability and stability-related concepts; the concepts of persistence, resilience, resistance, and variability readily come to mind. Of these various concepts, the concept of resilience itself appears to have been rather resilient. Indeed, as Neubert and Caswell (1997) and others have noted, today there is a vast literature on resilience" (Batabyal, 1998, p. 235).

In addition, recently several authors have argued that the concept of resilience is not only applicable to ecosystems, but also to socio-economic systems. Consequently, it seems worthwhile to create a perspective on the state of the art in this context (e.g., definitions and measurements of resilience) as well as on recent advances concerning the potential applications in the space-economy.

This paper is organised as follows. We will first offer in the next Section an introduction to the different definitions of resilience in the scientific literature (Section 2). Then, in Section 3—after offering some methodological reflections on resilience, particularly by analysing the two interpretations of engineering and ecological resilience—we will give a concise description of the possibility to employ the resilience concept in spatial-economic systems. Next, in Section 4 we will show an empirical illustration concerning the application of the (engineering) resilience concept in the context of regional employment in West-Germany. Finally, in Section 5 we will offer some retrospective and prospective remarks.

2. The Concept of Resilience: Definitions and Measurements

The concept of resilience is heavily based on the hypothesis that different states of a system involve different equilibria. In other words, it is assumed that the evolution of ecological, economic, etc.) systems is formed by the 'switch' of these systems from one equilibrium-state (or stability domain) to another one. For example, ecologists believe that "change in most territorial systems is not continuous and gradual, but is punctuated by the sudden reorganisation of the stock resources. This often occurs after long period of apparent stability, and often after some 'exogenous' perturbation of the systems" Perrings, 1994, p. 36).

In this context we may distinguish two different ways of defining resilience (see Perrings, 1998, p. 505): "One refers to the properties of the system near some stable equilibrium (i.e., in the neighbourhood of a stable focus or node). This definition, due to Pimm (1984), takes the resilience of a system to be a measure of the speed to its return to equilibrium. The second definition refers to the perturbation that can be absorbed before the system is displaced from one state to another. This definition, due to Holling (1973, 1986, 1992), does not depend on whether a system is at or near some equilibrium. It assumes that ecological systems are characterised by multiple locally stable equilibria, and the measure of a system's resilience in any local stability domain is the extent of the shocks it can absorb before being displaced into some other local stability domain. Perturbation may induce the system to change from one attractor (stability domain) to another, or not. If not, the system may be resilient with respect to that perturbation."

From these conceptual description it is clear that both definitions are based on the following assumptions:

(a) the existence of local stability for these equilibria;
(b) the existence of sudden 'exogenous' perturbations.

Given these hypotheses, *resilience* in both cases refers to the "capacity of a systems to retain its organisational structure following perturbation of some state variable from a given value" (Perrings, 1994, p. 30).

Clearly, these definitions have some intrinsic limitations, as nothing is said on the question whether:

(a) the system is conceived of in continuous or discrete terms;
(b) the system is deterministic or stochastic;
(c) these definitions can be assumed also for systems with more than two state variables.

The *first definition* by Pimm, more 'traditional', focuses on the property of the systems near some stable equilibrium point. Perrings (1994) identifies this equilibrium point with a stable focus or nodus, which clearly belongs to a continuous system of two dimensions, as demonstrated by the Poincare'-Bendixon theorem (see Nijkamp and Reggiani, 1992).

Consequently, while on the one hand the measurement of Pimm resilience is certainly easier—from an empirical viewpoint—than Holling resilience, on the other hand it appears to be more 'restrictive', since it regards only the equilibrium points, rather than the stability domains or basins of attraction.

The *second definition* by Holling focusses on the property of the systems further away from the stable state (i.e., the size of the stability domain). The measure of resilience by this definition is the perturbation that can be absorbed before the system converges on another equilibrium state, by crossing an unstable manifold (Perrings, 1994).

A clear representation of the measure of resilience according to Holling definition is again given by Perrings (1994), as displayed in figure 1.

In concise terms, in figure 1 $k_p(t)$, $k_n(t)$, are the state variables, while $\mathbf{k}^*$ represents the equilibrium point surrounded by its attraction basin with coordinates α_i, α_j, etc. From this figure we can immediately derive an interesting element, which differentiates the resilience definition from the usual stability definition, i.e., *that the resilience measure can be different in the same system, by varying according to the direction of the perturbation.*

Let us consider the formal definition given by Perrings here (1994, p. 37):

"The resilience of a system at some point in the basin of a locally stable equilibrium, $\mathbf{k}^*$, with respect to change in any of the state variables of that system, is the maximum perturbation that can be sustained in those variables without causing the system to leave the α_j-neighbourhood of $\mathbf{k}^*$."

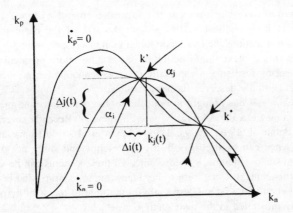

Figure 1. The measure of system resilience according to Holling. Source: Perrings (1994, p. 35).

The measure of the system's resilience in direction i or j is simply $\alpha_i - k_i(t)$ or $\alpha_j - k_j(t)$. It then follows that:

(a) a point in the system close to the boundary of the attraction basin is less resilient than one near the equilibrium point;

(b) the resilience is different for different directions of the perturbation;

(c) if the system loses resilience with respect to some perturbation (e.g., $\alpha_i - k_i(t)$ is negative), then the system switches from one basin to another one (k' in figure 1), via the manifold α_j.

From this analysis, it is then evident that the possibility of the system to remain in the unstable manifold is not considered by Perrings, at least not in the short run. This point has been also addressed by Batabyal (2000a) who has derived a measure of *short run or transient resilience*. This is undoubtedly an intriguing issue worth further exploration.

In conclusion, from a *methodological viewpoint* both definitions are interesting and complementary. Particularly, we observe that on the one side (Pimm) resilience depends on the *strength of the perturbation*; on the other side (Holling) on the *size of the attractor/ stability domain*. Clearly, a formulation of resilience integrating these two aspects is extremely important. A first interesting contribution in this respect has been given by Dalmazzone (1998), who integrates both these two definitions by considering the system no longer as deterministic, but as stochastic, subject to continuous disturbances of a Brownian motion type. Consequently, this author identifies as a measure of resilience the potential (the Hamiltonian equation) associated with the dynamic system involved.

In this context it should be noted that also various stochastic measures of resilience have been proposed in the literature as outlined by Batabyal (1998). This author also provides a theoretical and operational probability characterisation of ecological resilience (Batabyal, 1999a).

From an *empirical viewpoint* it is clear that difficulties emerge when we want to measure empirically the Holling resilience. How should the size of the basin of attraction be measured? Perrings mentions the Lyapunov function in this respect; this is however, quite a critical issue. In this context Pimm definition is certainly more practical. However, the problem of measuring resilience—especially in socio-economic terms—remains a rather difficult one and certainly deserves further attention.

The previous analysis has brought to light the formal definitions and measurements of resilience, stemming from an ecologically-based framework. Recently several authors (see among others, Batabyal, 1998, 1999a, 1999b; Levin et al., 1998) have argued that the concept of resilience can be used to effectively describe and study not only ecological systems, but also socio-economic systems, since all these systems can be viewed as only one system. In this context it may turn to be interesting to explore what resilience means for socio-spatial-economic systems, especially in the light of the stability paradigm. This will be concisely illustrated in the next section.

3. Resilience: A New Concept Beyond Stability?

3.1. A new perspective

In the previous sections resilience has been interpreted as a 'measure' of the system stability in the presence of external shocks, mainly related to the size of the basin of attraction surrounding the equilibrium point.

In the present section we will explore a different interpretation of resilience, viz., how resilience could transcend the 'myth' of stability, by addressing a new concept, i.e., the 'myth' of multiple stability. As a consequence, following Holling (1986), we will pinpoint—in this first step of our research—a 'dynamic' view of a system by considering:

1. a multiplicity of resting points instead of one (multi-equilibrium structures);
2. the evolution conceived of as the movement of the variables from one domain to another (and this behaviour may be discontinuous);
3. the irrelevance of the kind of equilibrium;
4. variability patterns in space and time which may change the systems parameters.

Clearly, a joint dynamic-stochastic perspective is more suitable for analysing the resilience notion. However, in this paper we will focus our attention on a dynamic-deterministic view, given also the deterministic character of our empirical experiments.

In the light of the four mentioned aspects, *resilience* points out the *'possibility to change'*, while *stability* emphasises the *'impossibility to change'*. An idea, which was also put forward by Timmerman (1986, p. 444): "Equilibrium myths are way of picturing nature as *natura naturata*—i.e., nature as object, fixed or fixable. The myth of resilience, on the other hand, sees nature as *natura naturans*—nature naturing—i.e., nature actively altering and responding in various ways to predictable or unpredictable stresses." We may also refer here to Holling (1986, p. 297) for a similar view: "Stability, as here defined, emphasises equilibrium, low variability, and resistance to and absorption of change. In sharp contrast, resilience emphasises the boundary of a stability domain and events far from equilibrium, high variability, and adaptation to change."

By using the above two definitions as a starting point, it is then clear that the structures with multiple equilibria, that are able to maintain their structural features in the presence of parameters changes, become more relevant than the ones with only one steady-point.

In this context an interesting interpretation of resilience is underlined by Peterson et al. 1998).

a) *Engineering Resilience*: Rate at which a system returns to a single steady or cyclic state following perturbation (Holling, 1986). This interpretation is clearly according to Pimm's definition.

b) *Ecological Resilience*: The amount of disturbance that can be sustained before the system changes its structure by changing the variables and processes that control behavior (see also Gunderson and Holling. 2001).

If we then consider resilience in the light of these two above perspectives, we obtain a *clearer* view of the resilience concept and the related measurement in a deterministic system.

An interesting example in this respect may be offered by the *two-dimensional prey-predator system*—in a continuous setting—in its oscillating form (displaying in the phase-port the so-called neutral stability). This system shows a multiplicity of limit cycles, without changing its 'organisational structure', by varying the parameter values of the model. In this case ecological resilience is possible, but also engineering resilience can be identified here, since the system will return—in the short or long run—to the limit cycle attractor. In other words, both engineering and ecological resilience legitimate structures ending up with cycles, which have been always considered as a 'transition-phase' between stable and chaotic domains.

More ambiguous is the situation in which a system displays chaos. In this case the engineering resilience definition is not fulfilled (the system is far from the equilibrium steady-state), while the ecological resilience can occur here (instabilities can flip the system into another regime behaviour). Also recently Gunderson and Holling (2001, p. 21) emphasised this distinction between engineering and ecological resilience by underlining the two related contrasting aspects of stability:

"One focuses on maintaining *efficiency* of function (engineering resilience). In contrast, the other focuses on maintaining *existence* of function (ecosystem resilience)."

Let us consider, for example, the well-known (Verhulst) logistic equation in discrete terms:

$$y(t + 1) = ry(t)(1 - y(t))$$

by performing the related phase-space analysis (y vs. r). It is well-known that for the values $3 < r < 3.824 \ldots$ the logistic equation gives rise to cycles, before starting the chaotic

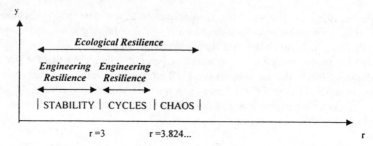

Figure 2. The engineering and ecological resilience for the logistic equation in discrete terms.

period for $r = 3.824\dots$ The engineering resilience, defined above, can be then identified with the stability period as well as with the period of cycles for the logistic equation under analysis. In addition, the ecological resilience can reflect, also in the chaotic period, the property of a system to persist, i.e., its capability of absorbing extreme waves of fluctuations.

We can now summarise the interpretation of the resilience concept, by using the discrete logistic equation as a concrete example (see figure 2).

But how to measure the capacity of a system of displaying and/or facing this multi-equilibria region (resilience domain) before changing its structure? Clearly, difficulties in analysing resilience may emerge for high-dimensional dynamic systems or networks with a consequential number of parameters (the so-called 'complex' systems), and mostly on empirical studies.

3.2. Resilience in spatial economic systems

It becomes clear from the previous considerations that both the engineering and ecological resilience concepts are extremely appealing for spatial economic systems, and useful for exploring the characteristics of their evolutionary stages.

In an interesting article, Levin et al. (1998) indicate that socio-economic and spatial systems have to be adequate on addressing new challenges and sudden qualitative shifts, while it is usually difficult to detect strong signals of change early enough to motivate and induce effective solutions. The authors state: "To deal with such problems, one needs a response system that is flexible and adaptive" (Levin et al., 1998, p. 224), and also:

> "In ecological and socioeconomic systems alike, human activities can lead to qualitative shifts in structure and function, evidence that the system concerned has lost resilience: that is no longer capable of absorbing the stresses and shocks imposed by human activity without undergoing a fundamental change involving loss of function and, often, loss of productivity. Resilience, the ability to experience change and disturbances without catastrophic qualitative change in the basic functional organisation, is a measure of the system's integrity (Holling, 1973)" (Levin et al., 1998, p. 224).

Perrings (1998) explores the relevance of resilience in joint economic-environmental systems, by emphasising the necessity of carrying out research in the area of *stochastic evolutionary theory*, by adopting renewal theory and/or Markov theory. This is undoubtedly a significant step forward, since, in this way, one focuses the attention also on the *transition dynamics* of stochastic multiple equilibrium systems, by overcoming the implicit drawbacks emerging from the Pimm and Holling definitions (see the previous section). In this context Perrings also makes a distinction between *absorbing states and transient states*:

" ... the greater the probability that the system in one state will change to some other state, the less resilient is the system in the first state. ... Absorbing states are more resilient than transient states. It also follows that the system will evolve from less resilient transient groups of states to more resilient absorbing groups of states, and that their transition will be irreversible. Another way of describing the same things is that the system will get locked-in to a particular group of absorbing states. In its future evolution will then involve only transition between states in the group" (Perrings, 1998, p. 510).

It should be noted that a theoretical characterisation of resilience—based on renewal theory—has also been proposed by Batabyal (1999c), for the study of the optimal management of ecological-economic systems.

From the above considerations the following question clearly emerges: How much is resilience desirable for a socio-economic and spatial system? On the one hand, 'too much stability' or 'too strong absorbing states' could lock-in people or actors in pattern behaviours precluding any positive evolution, by reducing also their resilience (i.e., their capacity to absorb shocks). Firms, companies, group styles, who are subject to small continuous changes and have to fight for survival, probably develop a 'better' resilience than very stable groups. On the other hand, 'very low resilience' may lead the system towards unstable states, likely irreversible.

In other words, it might be worth to analyse not only resilience, but also the '*optimum*' *resilience* for a certain group, company, or state of the system. In this respect, the Holling measure could certainly be useful in understanding 'how much' the system is able to absorb shocks. In addition, the conceptualisation of resilience as stationary probability—identified by Batabyal (2000b)—may offer optimal measures of resilience. Another way could be, by following Perrings (1998), to reduce the probability of transition into undesirable states or to increase the probability of transition into desirable states. Certainly, the measure of the 'optimum' resilience should deserve further attention. An interesting direction in this perspective, worth to be explored, is the concept of *entropy*, as indicated by Dalmazzone (1998). Here the author refers entropy to dynamic stochastic continuous systems. The following step in this respect could be then the 'search' for optimum entropy, by means of stochastic optimal control. Consequently, the use of 'entropy' for measuring resilience should be thoroughly investigated in future scientific work.

A still ongoing debate also concerns the relationships between resilience, density dependence, field effects and diversity, in order to evaluate the adaptive behaviour of a system. Mainly, *density dependence* and *field effects* are based, respectively, on the growth dynamics of distinct populations (depending on their size) and on the interdependence of people's preferences (concentration of activities). Both these two factors—at a high dimensional level—seem to lock-in the system into a particular technology or market choice, by reducing then the related resilience. Concerning *diversity*, one view sees complex systems less resilient than simple systems; the second view gives more attention to the number of 'alternative' populations which can take over a particular function when a system is perturbated (the so-called 'passenger species' which can take the role of 'drivers or keystone species'). The presence of these species insures then the resilience of systems, that is, their ability to adapt to new conditions (see van den Bergh and Gowdy, 2000; Perrings, 1998). It then follows that:

"Evolving economic systems may also be described as being more or less resilient, in terms of being adaptable to economic changes as well as environmental changes, due to some redundancy of capacity and information present in them" (van den Bergh and Gowdy, 2000, p. 20).

Finally, it may be worthwhile to explore the link of the resilience concept with other concepts currently appearing in spatial economics, like the concept of 'consilience' (Wilson, 1998), 'persistence' (Batabyal, 2000c), 'adaptive learning', 'learning behaviour', 'path dependence', 'emergence' (see, e.g., Arthur, 1994a, 1994b; Batten, 2000; van Geenhuizen and Nijkamp, 1998; Holland, 1998; Kaufmann, 1995; Wilson, 2000), 'survival of the fittest' (Holland, 1975; Nijkamp and Reggiani, 1998; Reggiani et al., 2000), 'small-world phenomena' (Schintler and Kulkarni, 2000; Watts and Strogatz, 1998). In conclusion, more research is certainly needed, *theoretically* and *methodologically*, on the resilience concept, as well as on its integration with all the above mentioned approaches adopted in spatial economics. *Empirically*, applications of resilience measures to real case studies in economic science are still missing to our knowledge. In this context, given the feasibility of measuring the engineering resilience, empirical applications in this perspective are a first step towards the measurement of ecological resilience. An attempt in this respect is offered in the next section, showing an empirical illustration related to the dynamics of regional labour markets in West-Germany. Particularly, we use the method of Lyapunov exponents in order to identify non-resilient (unstable) trends in the context of engineering resilience. The remaining trends are then further considered by us in order to extract some 'typology' of 'resilience', by looking—empirically—at their return time to stability in the face of external shocks (Pimm's approach).

Before discussing our empirical illustration, we will then briefly depict the method of Lyapunov exponents used for identifying (non)resilient systems (in the engineering sense).

4. An Empirical Illustration: The Labour Market in West-Germany

4.1. Introduction

In this section we will adopt the technique of finding Lyapunov exponents in order to identify—among eleven sectors of employment in West-Germany—the ones more able to absorb shocks, i.e. the more resilient ones. In this contest a first screening will be carried out by the method of Lyapunov exponents, since this method may be used to classify and help determining the type of stability of an attractor.[1] In the previous section we argue that the occurrence of chaotic dynamics precludes a system from being resilient in the engineering sense. Measuring Lyapunov exponents in a system was one of the first methods to detect chaotic dynamics, first in physics (see e.g. Wolf et al., 1985; Holzfuss and Lauterbom, 1988) and later on in the social sciences (see e.g. Brock, 1986). The largest Lyapunov exponent being positive indicates the presence of a strange attractor, and, thus, chaos. Therefore, we use Lyapunov exponents to identify whether a system is resilient in the engineering sense.

4.2. Measuring 'engineering resilience' by Lyapunov exponents

4.2.1. Measuring Lyapunov exponents from a time series
Though it is relatively easy to compute Lyapunov exponents out of a known map, computing Lyapunov exponents out of empirical (time series) data may be somewhat more difficult and trickier. This subsection will briefly discuss an evolutionary algorithm (see Wolf et al., 1985), which is used to obtain the largest Lyapunov exponent from a time series. The next subsection will apply this algorithm in order to extract the largest Lyapunov exponents from German regional employment data.

First, for each embedding dimension m the time-series w_i will be used to form the residual-series $\{w_i^m\}$ or the so-called m-histories, for $i = 1, \ldots, (T-m+1)$, where:

$$w_i^m = \{w_i, w_{i+1}, \ldots, w_{i+m-1}\}. \tag{1}$$

We will now concisely describe the computational algorithm. Start the algorithm to locate the nearest neighbour $w_j^m \neq w_1^m$, for $j = 2, \ldots, (T-m+1)$, to the initial m-history w_1^m. Now let $d_1^{(1)}$ be the smallest positive distance, set t_1 equal to j and let, for a positive integer q, $d_2^{(1)}$ be:

$$d_2^{(1)} = \left\| w_{t_1}^m - w_1^m \right\|$$

and

$$d_2^{(1)} = \left\| w_{t_1+q}^m - w_{1-q}^m \right\| \tag{2}$$

Now store $g_1(q) = d_2^{(1)}/d_1^{(1)}$ and define q as the evolution time. This ends the first iteration. For finding the new m-history $w_{t_2}^m$ near $w_{t_1+q}^m$, we have to construct a penalty function, which should minimise the angle between the new m-history and the last founded

m-history, compared with the m-history of the status of the evolutionary process. So, in formal equations, we store for iteration k,

$$d_1^{(k)} = \left\| w_{t_k}^m - w_{1+(k-1)q}^m \right\|, \quad d_1^{(k)} = \left\| w_{t_k}^m - w_{1+kq}^m \right\|$$

and

$$g_k(q) = \frac{d_2^k}{d_1^k}. \tag{3}$$

The point t_k in (3) may then be found by minimising the following penalty function:

$$p_{k.m.q.\hat{w}} \equiv \left\| w_{t_k}^m - w_{1+(k-1)q}^m \right\| + \hat{w} |\theta(w_{t_k}^m - w_{1+(k-1)q}^m, w_{t_{k-1}+q}^m - w_{1+(k-1)q}^m)|,$$

where $\hat{w}$ is a chosen penalty weight on the deviation of the angle θ from zero, and where t_k is subject to $w_{t_k}^m \neq w_{1+(k-1)q}^m$. Just continue this procedure until $k = K$, where K solves max $\{k | 1 + kq \leq T - m + 1\}$. Finally, to calculate the empirical Lyapunov exponent $\hat{\lambda}_q$, we set:

$$\hat{\lambda}_q = \frac{1}{K} \sum_{k=1}^{K} \frac{\ln(g_k(q))}{q}. \tag{4}$$

Wolf et al. have shown in 1985 that the empirical $\hat{\lambda}_q$ will converge to the real largest Lyapunov exponent, when $T \to \infty$ and $m \to \infty$. Numerical experiments have confirmed that this algorithm indeed identifies the largest Lyapunov exponent. However, we note that these experiments usually consisted of more than 10,000 replications, whereas empirical socio-economic applications usually deal with less than 1,000 observations.

We can make the algorithms described above clear by using figure 3.

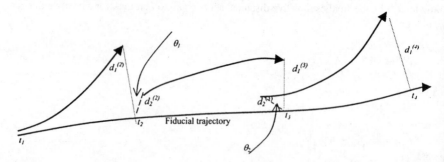

Figure 3. A schematic representation of the evolution and replacement procedure for estimating the largest Lyapunov exponent. The largest Lyapunov exponent is computed here from the growth of length elements. When the length of the vector between two points becomes large, a new point is chosen near the reference trajectory, minimising both the replacement length $d^{(k)}$ and the orientation angle θ (see Grassberger and Procaccia, 1984).

In figure 3 one can see the working of the algorithm schematically. Note that figure 3 resembles both discrete and continuous cases. The length of a vector between two points in time is determined by the evolution time, and the angle θ should keep the successive vectors as close to the fiducial trajectory as possible.

4.2.2. Empirical illustration: the labour market in West-Germany In order to illustrate the algorithm above we will apply the concept of engineering resilience to the case of the German labour market. We have a rich data set, which consists of the absolute number of employment in the 327 regions (the so-called Kreisen) in the former BRD. We have information over these regions for 11 years (1987–1997) and these employment figures are subdivided in 11 sectors (see for a list of sectors table 1).

Figure 4 gives the time paths of the absolute figures of employment in Germany for the 11 sectors.

Figure 4 shows us that the main characteristic of the German labour market between 1987 and 1997 is that it is rather stable across the industrial sectors. This could be expected because of the nature of the German labour market. According to most scales the German labour market is rather corporatistic, has a centralised union wage bargaining and has an inflexible and protected labour force (see, for a characterisation of the German labour market from a corporatistic perspective, Teulings and Hartog, 1998).

On the other hand, one may expect to find some dynamics on the German labour market, not merely because of the wide-scale introduction of new technologies in the 90s, but mainly because of German unification in 1990 and especially the subsequent mass migration from former East-Germany to West-Germany. Nevertheless small changes are found in figure 4 and the only sectors that grew in the observed 11 years are distributive services, financial services and services for society.

Table 1. Lyapunov exponents of employment trajectories of the different industrial sectors in Germany (1987–1997)

Industrial sectors	M-histories		
	$m=2$	$m=3$	$m=4$
Primary sector	0.03	0.02	0.04
Energy/mining	−0.09	−0.02	0.00
Goods−producing industry	0.12	0.15	0.16
Capital goods	0.02	−0.03	0.03
Consumer goods	0.10	0.08	0.08
Manufacture of food products	0.07	0.02	−0.04
Construction	0.09	0.07	0.06
Distributive services	0.06	0.05	0.03
Financial services	−0.02	−0.05	−0.12
Household services	0.03	0.00	−0.04
Services for society	0.01	−0.04	−0.09

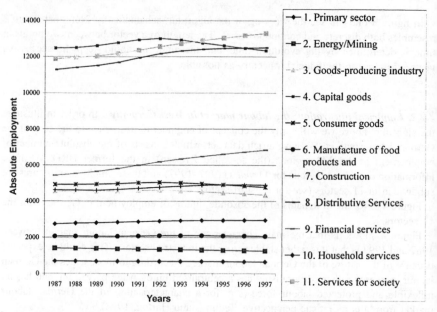

Figure 4. The time paths of German employment in the various industrial sectors between 1987 and 1997.

Even though it seems that the German labour market is rather stable, employment changes on the regional scale may be more fluctuating. Therefore, we have calculated the Lyapunov exponents for all 11 sectors. where each w_i represents a vector of regional employment for each sector. The distance between w_i and w_j is then easily calculated as:

$$\|w_i - w_j\| = \sqrt{(w_{i1} - w_{j1})^2 + \cdots + (w_{ir} - w_{jr})^2 + \cdots + (w_{iR} - w_{jR})^2},$$

for each $i, j \in \{1, \ldots, T - m + 1\}$ and $r \in \{1, \ldots, R\}$. The lack of temporal observations is made up by the large amount of regional observations. If we consider our data as an extended panel data set,[2] then we may even say that the amount of data is rather sizeable. Unfortunately, we cannot say much about the absolute value of the Lyapunov exponent, because we are not able to compute standard errors and because of the small size of the data set compared to the controlled experiments in physics.[3] Nonetheless, comparing between sectors could be valuable and may give additional insights into the dynamics of the German labour market. In Table 1 we present the empirical Lyapunov exponents for different m-histories for the various sectors.

From table 1 we observe that the Lyapunov exponents seem to depend heavily on the chosen m-history, a feature which is known from the literature. Ideally, m should converge to ∞, however, at a much slower rate than T. Therefore we will set m at 2.

As mentioned before, we cannot say much about the absolute value of the Lyapunov xponents, especially with the low numbers of m and T, but we are able to compare the elative values. From table 1 it seems that the goods-producing industry, the consumer goods, and to a lower extent construction are the less stable sectors, whereas financial ervices, household services, services for society and energy/mining seem to be the more table or resilient (in the engineering sense) sectors across time. Not surprisingly, the ormer group of sectors is more dependent on the business cycle, whereas the latter group s not. Note that stable behaviour could also contain continually up- or downward move-nents, as is the case for financial services and energy/mining respectively.

To gain a better understanding in what table 1 actually displays, we have drawn the growth rates of the West-German employment in the various sectors in figures 5 and 6. In igure 6 we see that the more unstable sectors have all experienced growth rates that are both positive and negative. In figure 5 this is only true for capital goods and manufacture

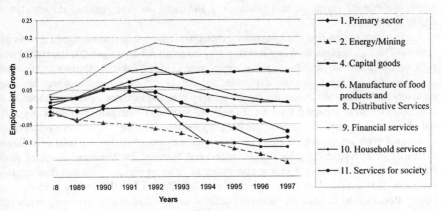

growth rates of employment in selected sectors in Germany (1987–1997).

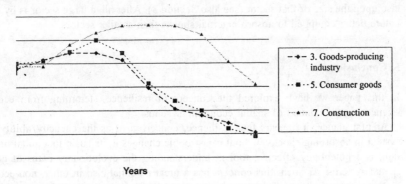

growth rates of employment in selected sectors in Germany (1987–1997).

of food products. The other sectors have all more or less steady growth paths, or are at leas only positive or negative. Furthermore, note that there is a break in all growth paths from the fourth or fifth observation; this is around the year of the German unification. This is probably the shock that the resilient systems have absorbed, since they returned to stability after a certain period; on the contrary, the same shock seems to have led the non-resilient systems to instability.

Also notable is the large similarity in growth paths between consumer goods and the goods producing industry, reflecting the complementary nature of these two industries. The absolute value of employment decline for especially consumer goods and the goods-producing industry is rather high and equals even that of the energy/mining sector, an industry which is rapidly fading away in the last three decades in Western Europe.

Based on this scarce evidence, we may say that the consumer goods and the goods-producing industry (and to a lesser account construction) seem to be less resilient (in the engineering sense, as underlined in Section 3.1) than the other sectors, but we must emphasise that the result are still preliminary and, until we have standard errors, statistically not precise.

Another way to compare the Lyapunov exponents, is the comparison between groups of regions. The 327 regions in West Germany may be subdivided into groups, depending on their urbanisation rate and the type of cities they contain. Table 2 displays a regional decomposition of the Lyapunov exponents for the 11 different sectors. Again we see relatively high Lyapunov exponents for the goods producing industry, consumer goods and construction, but in the same time we see regional instability emerging. Normally, we will not observe these patterns, because the large majority of German employment is working in regions with urban agglomerations. However, we can now observe relatively large dynamics of energy/mining in regions with rural features. Furthermore, it seems that employment in the primary sector is also rather unstable in regions with an urban agglomeration. That both sectors are in a decline is widely known, but the decline is likely not linear. Remarkable is also the relative stability of the distributive services, financial services, household services and services for society, also because these sectors are the largest employers in West-Germany (figure 4). This may raise the question whether stability or resilience is not only dependent of the intrinsic nature of a certain sector, but also upon the size of that sector (see also Section 3). After all, a large sector is by its very nature better equipped to absorb external shocks than smaller sectors.

5. Conclusions

In this paper we have explored the concept of resilience, stemming from ecological sciences, in the context of spatial economic systems.

At first glance, it appears that resilience, conceived of as the capacity/ability of the system in absorbing shocks without catastrophic changes in its basic functional organisation, is a potentially effective tool in understanding the evolutionary paths of complex spatial systems. As such, this concept has a great potential also in other, non-ecological systems, in particular socio-economic systems. Moreover resilience seems to offer a new

Table 2. Lyapunov exponents (m = 2) for different types of regions, for the 11 industrial sectors. The numbers in the heading represent the industrial sectors below

		1	2	3	4	5	6	7	8	9	10	11
A. Regions with urban agglomeration	1. Central cities	0.09	-0.17	0.17	0.05	0.08	0.11	0.12	0.10	-0.05	0.02	0.04
	2. Highly urbanized districts	0.03	0.08	0.15	0.01	0.20	0.19	0.07	0.02	0.09	0.04	0.01
	3. Urbanized districts	0.03	-0.05	0.13	0.01	0.12	0.11	0.14	0.00	0.05	0.01	-0.01
	4. Rural districts	0.12	0.10	0.07	-0.05	0.13	0.14	0.04	0.00	0.07	-0.01	-0.02
	5. Central cities	0.04	0.22	0.40	0.06	0.11	0.12	0.13	0.06	0.03	-0.08	0.02
B. Regions with tendencies towards agglomeration	6. Highly urbanized districts	0.07	0.03	0.09	0.01	0.07	0.03	0.03	0.00	-0.04	0.07	0.01
	7. Rural districts	-0.02	0.07	0.21	-0.02	0.06	0.07	0.10	0.00	0.08	0.05	0.03
C. Regions with rural features	8. Urbanized districts	0.06	0.25	0.08	-0.05	0.08	0.12	0.10	0.01	-0.01	0.04	0.02
	9. Rural districts	0.06	0.20	0.12	0.04	0.07	0.04	0.07	0.03	0.02	-0.02	0.03

1. Primary sector, 2. Energy/Mining, 3. Goods-producing industry, 4. Capital goods, 5. Consumer goods, 6. Manufacture of food products, 7. Construction, 8. Distributive services, 9. Financial services, 10. Household services, 11. Services for society.

approach to evolutionary networks, where systems able to shift—in the presence of external shocks—to new equilibria become relevant. But there also limitations in terms of operationalisation and measurement. And therefore, an integration of this concept with other recently developed, novel concepts in economics, like emergence, consilience, adaptive behaviour, path analysis, selection behaviour, small world phenomenon, might certainly be fruitful in this respect.

Empirically, the measure of resilience is still a rather critical issue. Several measures have been proposed in the literature (e.g., time of recovering from shocks, size of the stability domain absorbing the shocks, potential, entropy, transition probabilities, etc.); however, they still remain at a formal-theoretical level. In this framework we conclude that the two different interpretations (engineering and ecological resilience) advocated in the literature are certainly useful for grasping and deepening the resilience concept.

In the context of measuring resilience we have investigated the possibility of using the method of Lyapunov exponents in order to identify whether (non-)resilience exists in employment concerning the regional labour market in West-Germany.

Our preliminary findings, although satisfying in detecting the more resilient sectors, underline the difficulties in implementing, in practice, a resilience measure. More research would have to be done to explore this issue. Particularly the relationships—and related measures—between resilience and sustainability, in both a deterministic and a stochastic perspective, are worth to be further investigated, also in the light of institutional and policy landscapes.

Notes

[1] "In order for an attractor to exists the sum of the exponents must be negative, and for attractors other than an equilibrium point, at least one exponent must be zero. For non-chaotic attractors, all exponents must be negative for an asymptotically stable equilibrium point, while for an asymptotically stable k-torus, k exponents must be zero and the remainder negative." (Donaghy, 2000, p. 251)

[2] Panel data usually is two-dimensional (temporal and another dimension), while our data set is three-dimensional (temporal, sectoral and regional).

[3] An even more troublesome feature of this method is the fact that we do not know its power against *other* kinds of dependencies. From Monte-Carlo simulations performed on other tests designed to detect non-linearities and chaotics we know that these are sensitive to almost all kinds of dependencies. However, if we assume that all sectors are affected equally by other forms of inter-temporal and inter-sectoral dependencies, then relative comparisons are still allowed.

Acknowledgements

The authors wish to acknowledge the Institute for Employment Research of the Federal Employment Services (IAB) in Nürnberg (Germany), in particular Dr. Uwe Blien, Dr. Erich Maierhofer and Dr Alexandros Tassinopoulos, for providing the data set used in the empirical analysis. In addition they wish to thank three referees for providing useful comments and suggestions.

References

Arthur, W.B. (1994a). *Increasing Returns and Path Dependence in the Economy.* Ann Arbor: University of Michigan Press.

Arthur, W.B. (1994b). "Inductive Behaviour and Bounded Rationality." *American Economic Review* 84, 406–411.

Batabyal, A.A. (1998). "The Concept of Resilience: Retrospect and Prospect." *Environment and Development Economics* 3, 235–239.

Batabyal, A.A. (1999a). "The Stability of Stochastic Systems: The Case of Persistence and Resilience." *Mathematical and Computer Modelling* 30, 27–34.

Batabyal, A.A. (1999b). "Contemporary Research in Ecological Economics: Five Outstanding Issues." *International Journal of Ecology and Environmental Sciences* 25, 143–154.

Batabyal, A.A. (1999c). "Species, Substitutability, Resilience, and the Optimal Management of Ecological-Economic Systems." *Mathematical and Computer Modelling* 29, 35–43.

Batabyal, A.A. (2000a). "Quantifying the Transient Response of Ecological-Economic Systems to Perturbations." *Environmental Impact Assessment Review* 20, 125–133.

Batabyal, A.A. (2000b). "An Analysis of Persistence, Resilience, and the Conservation of Keystone Species." *International Journal of Ecology and Environmental Sciences* 26, 1–10.

Batabyal, A.A. (2000c). "Aspects of Ecosystem Persistence and the Optimal Conservation of Species." *International Review of Economics and Finance* 1.9, 69–77.

Batten, D. (2000). "Complex Landscapes of Spatial Interaction." In A. Reggiani (ed.), *Spatial Economic Science: New Frontiers in Theory and Methodology.* Berlin: Springer-Verlag, 51–74.

Bergh, J.C.J.M. van den and J.M. Gowdy. (2000). "Evolutionary Theories in Environmental and Resource Economics: Approaches and Applications." *Environmental and Resource Economics* 17, 37–57.

Brock, W.A. (1986). "Distinguishing Random and Deterministic Systems. Abridged Version." *Journal of Economic Theory* 40, 168–195.

Dalmazzone, S. (1998). "Economic Activities and the Resilience of Ecological Systems: A Stochastic Approach." Working Paper, N. 55, CEIS (Center for International Studies and Economic Growth), University of "Tor Vergata", Rome.

Donaghy, K.P. (2000). "Generalized Stability Analysis of a Non-Linear Dynamic Model." In A. Reggiani (ed.), *Spatial Economic Science: New Frontiers in Theory and Methodology.* Berlin: Springer-Verlag, 243–257.

Geenhuizen, M. van and P. Nijkamp. (1998). "The Learning Capability of Regions: Patterns and Policies." Department of Spatial Economics, Amsterdam: Free University.

Grassberger, P. and I. Procaccia. (1983). "Measuring the Strangeness of Strange Attractors." *Physica* 9D, 189–208.

Gunderson, L. and C.S. Holling (eds.) (2001). *Panarchy: Understanding Transformations in Systems of Human and Nature.* Covelo: CA, Island Press.

Holland, J.H. (1975). *Adaptation in Natural and Artificial Systems.* Ann Arbor: University of Michigan Press.

Holland, J.H. (1998). *Emergence: From Chaos to Order.* Reading, Mass: Addison-Wesley.

Holling, C.S. (1973). "Resilience and Stability of Ecological Systems." *Annual Review of Ecological Systems* 4, 1–24.

Holling, C.S. (1986). "The Resilience of Terrestrial Ecosystems: Local Surprise and Global Change." In W.C. Clarck and R.E. Munn (eds.), *Sustainable Development of the Biosphere.* Cambridge: Cambridge University Press, 292–317.

Holling, C.S. (1992). "Cross-Scale Morphology Geometry and Dynamics of Ecosystems." *Ecological Monographs* 62, 447–502.

Holzfuss, J. and W. Lauterborn. (1988). "Liapunov Exponents From a Time Series of Acoustic Chaos." *Physical Review A* 39, 2146–2147.

Kauffman, S.A. (1995). *At Home in the Universe: The Search for the Laws of Complexity.* London: Viking.

Levin, S.A., S. Barrett, S. Aniyar, W. Baumol, C. Bliss, B. Bolin, P. Dasgupta, P. Ehrlich, C. Folke, I.-M. Gren, C.S. Holling, A. Jansson, K.-G. Mäler, D. Martin, C. Perrings. and E. Sheshinski. (1998). "Resilience in Natural and Socioeconomic Systems." *Environment and Development Economics* 3, 222–235.

MacArthur, R.H. (1955). "Fluctuations of Animal Populations and a Measure of Community Stability." *Ecology* 36, 533–536.

Neubert, M.G. and H. Caswell. (1997). "Alternatives to Resilience for Measuring the Responses of Ecological Systems to Perturbations." *Ecology* 78, 653–665.

Nijkamp, P. and A. Reggiani. (1992). *Interaction, Evolution and Chaos in Space.* Berlin: Springer-Verlag.

Nijkamp, P. and A. Reggiani. (1998). *The Economics of Complex Spatial Systems.* Amsterdam: Elsevier.

Perrings, C. (1994). "Ecological Resilience in the Sustainability of Economic Development" International Symposium on "Models of Sustainable Development", Paris, Vol. II, 27–41.

Perrings, C. (1998). "Resilience in the Dynamics of Economy-Environment Systems." *Environmental and Resource Economics* 11, 503–520.

Peterson, G., C.R. Allen. and C.S. Holling. (1998). "Ecological Resilience, Biodiversity, and Scale." *Ecosystems* 1, 6–18.

Pimm, S.L. (1984). "The Complexity and Stability of Ecosystems." *Nature* 307, 321–326.

Reggiani, A., P. Nijkamp, and E. Sabella. (2000). "A Comparative Analysis of the Performance of Evolutionary Algorithms and Logit Models in Spatial Networks." In A. Reggiani (ed.), *Spatial Economic Science: New Frontiers in Theory and Methodology.* Berlin: Springer-Verlag, 331–354.

Schintler, L.A. and R. Kulkarni. (2000). "The Emergence of Small World Phenomenon in Urban Transportation Networks: An Exploratory Analysis." In A. Reggiani (ed.), *Spatial Economic Science: New Frontiers in Theory and Methodology.* Berlin: Springer-Verlag, 419–434.

Teulings, C. and J. Hartog. (1998). *Corporatism and Competition? Labour Contracts, Institutions an Wage Structures in International Comparison.* Cambridge: Cambridge University Press.

Timmerman, P. (1986). "Mythology and Surprise in the Sustainable Development of the Biosphere." In W.C. Clarck and R.E. Munn (eds.), *Sustainable Development of the Biosphere.* Cambridge: Cambridge University Press, 435–453.

Watts, D.J. and S.H. Strogatz. (1998). "Collective Dynamics of Small-World Networks." *Nature* 393, 440–442.

Wilson, A. (2000). "Spatial Modelling: Conceptual, Mathematical and Computational Challenges." In A. Reggiani (ed.), *Spatial Economic Science: New Frontiers in Theory and Methodology.* Berlin: Springer-Verlag, 15–29.

Wilson, E.O. (1998). *Consilience: The Unit of Knowledge.* New York: Alfred A. Knoff.

Wolf, A., J. Swift, H. Swinney. and J. Vastano. (1985). "Determination of Lyapunov Exponents from Time-series." *Physica D* 16, 285–317.

PART II

MACRO AND REGIONAL STUDIES

[6]

Growth and Change
Vol. 31 (Fall 2000), pp. 547-572

Growth Effects of Governmental Policies: A Comparative Analysis in a Multi-Country Context

MARTIJN R.E. BRONS, HENRI L.F. DE GROOT AND PETER NIJKAMP

ABSTRACT   The potential interactions among governmental policies, investments and economic growth are complex and manifold. This paper will perform a systematic comparative analysis of the various economic insights that are currently available on these complex relationships, both theoretically (by a selective literature review) and empirically (by reviewing the empirically obtained insights). Despite the wide variety of potential theoretical relationships between government expenditures, taxation and growth, most empirical analyses are restricted to simple linear regressions of growth on some measure of government expenditures. We will indicate directions for future empirical research that may enrich our knowledge about the complex relationship between fiscal policies and economic growth, not only nationally but also regionally.

Introduction

G rowth theory is a focal point of modern economics. It addresses not only the causes of economic growth, but also the implications of growth for the relative wealth of nations (as is illustrated by, for example, the convergence debate and discussions on poverty traps). There are at least two central issues in this debate. First, several authors (e.g., Arrow 1962, and Arthur 1994) have emphasized the critical importance of learning-by-doing mechanisms through which an economic system might be stimulated to achieve self-sustaining growth. But do learning mechanisms emerge as an automatic 'manna from heaven' or should there be an explicit act of government to induce such a mechanism (e.g., through training facilities, R&D etc.)? Against this background, the discussion on endogenous growth mechanisms, the central role of knowledge and the possibilities

Martijn Brons was a student assistant during the writing of the paper, Henri de Groot a post-doc researcher and Peter Nijkamp a professor of regional economics at the Department of Spatial Economics of the Vrije Universiteit, Amsterdam. They would like to thank two anonymous referees of this journal for useful comments on an earlier version of the paper.

Submitted Sep. 1999, revised Mar. 2000.
© 2000 Gatton College of Business and Economics, University of Kentucky.
Published by Blackwell Publishers, 350 Main Street, Malden MA 02148 US, and 108 Cowley Road, Oxford, OX4 1JF, UK.

for fostering knowledge accumulation and dissemination is of great importance. Secondly, endogenous growth theory is relevant since it may provide answers to questions on the phenomenon of winners and losers and on the role the public sector has to play (e.g., by providing education and infrastructure) in a competitive system of different—territorially demarcated—economies. Also the role of institutions (e.g., labor unions) comes increasingly into play. An important question here is whether increasing returns and free factor mobility in an open economic system leads to automatic spatial-economic convergence, or whether spatial-economic disparities tend to become more pronounced and need to be tackled by explicit policy initiatives of governments and institutions (*cf.* Fujita and Mori 1998). This issue has gained special importance with the advent of unification in Europe.

Thus, the ultimate 'drivers' of economic growth and the associated spatial-economic disparities need to be given due analytical attention (*cf.* Nijkamp and Poot 1998). The integration of temporal and spatial dynamics in economics is, however, fraught with many difficulties and often requires the use of non-linear dynamic models for complex spatial systems (see for a review and illustrations Nijkamp and Reggiani 1998). Since the path-breaking contributions of Romer (1986) and Lucas (1988) a wealth of scientific contributions has emerged on the integration of increasing returns and imperfect competition in general equilibrium models. First attempts have also been made to investigate the spatial openness and interactive feedbacks of such systems and the role of governments and institutions. The relevance of this kind of investigations has been (re-)emphasized in the 'new economic geography' (see e.g., Krugman 1991). Good illustrations of solid growth theory in both spatial and non-spatial contexts can be found in Barro and Sala-i-Martin (1995) and Aghion and Howitt (1998).

However, a quick glance at the current literature on modern growth theory also reveals severe weaknesses. First, although the availability of rich data sets like those of Summers and Heston (1991), Maddison (1982 and 1995) and Barro and Lee (1994) has spurred research on the empirics of economic growth, the empirical nature and quality of the analyses are in most cases feeble (see Temple 1999 for an excellent overview of what has been achieved as well as for a research agenda for the coming decades). Second, many theoretical and empirical contributions assume an essentially space-less economy, so that transactions and flows of goods and ideas across regions are neglected. And finally, the steering role of government bodies and institutions (e.g., unions, employers' associations) is mostly left out of consideration. This paper tries to fill at least some of the above-mentioned gaps. It emphasizes in particular the impact of governmental agencies on growth and seeks to pinpoint the associated opportunities for public intervention in development policy. Finally, by means of illustration, some empirical evidence is offered on the role of governments by a comparative study on the growth performance of several countries.

This paper proceeds as follows. First, the available theoretical insights on the relationship between the fiscal and non-fiscal activities and behavior of governments and economic growth will be briefly reviewed. It will be argued that this literature has not yielded many clear, testable implications. Despite the lack of clear testable implications following from economic theory, much empirical research has tried to shed some light on the relationships between fiscal policy and economic growth, which will be subsequently reviewed.[1] These studies try to explain average growth rates over long periods by explanatory variables like initial income (to test the convergence hypothesis; see, for example, Barro and Sala-i-Martin 1995), investment ratios (to test for the effect of capital accumulation) and various kinds of policy variables like government expenditure, taxation, black market premiums on foreign exchange, tariff rates and schooling variables (see, e.g., Barro and Sala-i-Martin 1995). These types of regression equations have become popular due to Barro (1991) and are by now known as 'Barro-regressions'. Some evidence will be presented on the role of fiscal policy that has resulted from these studies, and also some attention paid to the problems that they face. Next, some empirical findings resulting from an applied analysis executed within the framework of this paper will be presented, and the conclusion will discuss some possible ways for improving empirical knowledge on the complex relationship between growth and the role of governments.

Government Spending, Taxation and Economic Growth: The Theory

In neo-classical growth models (as developed independently by Solow 1956 and Swan 1956), growth in income per capita in the steady state is exogenously given and depends only on the exogenous rate of technological progress that falls like 'manna from heaven'. Economic growth is invariant to any kind of policy (although policy will affect the steady state *level* at which the economy operates). Only during the transition of economies to their steady state can·economic policy have an effect on *rates* of growth. For decades, this model was the standard reference and formed the basis for policy views on government spending and taxation. It is therefore not surprising that most research on the role of the government focused on the 'division and stabilization of the cake' instead of its 'enlargement'. With the advent of the new, endogenous, growth theory that was initiated by the pioneering work of Romer (1986) and Lucas (1988), the perspective on the role of the government has drastically changed. In this class of model, not only transitional growth rates are endogenous, but also the steady-state growth rates. Factors that have been proposed as being important for determining long-run growth are, among others, preferences, trade intensity (for example, Grossman and Helpman 1991), Research and Development (for example, Grossman and Helpman 1991), income inequality (Persson and Tabellini 1991) and fiscal policies (Barro 1990 and Glomm and Ravikumar 1994 and 1997). In all endogenous growth models that have been developed in the past decade, the government can influence growth, either directly or indirectly. Thereby, it can have major effects on the standards of living. A crucial distinguishing characteristic of the endogenous growth theory is its perception of the nature of knowledge. In contrast to the neo-classical theory of growth, knowledge is not considered to be a public good and need not be characterized by diminishing returns to scale. The former characteristic implies that the government may have to play an active role in providing subsidies to overcome under-investment due to non-appropriability, or in defining property rights. The latter characteristic implies that a once and for all increase in investments in, for example, education may permanently foster economic growth (which is in contrast with the neo-classical growth theory). In this section, the potential (theoretical) effects of government spending and taxation on economic growth will be described. Afterwards, attention will be shifted towards other government 'activities' and their relationship with economic growth. Subsequently, the available empirical evidence will be reviewed.

As a first step toward studying the relationship between government spending, taxation and economic growth, it is of crucial importance to divide government activities in several categories. The broadest division is into spending and revenue raising. Spending can be subdivided into government consumption (which includes government subsidies) and investments. These investments may further be divided into investments in infrastructure, education, defense, etc. Also the ways in which revenues are being raised need further classification. The first distinction is between distortionary and non-distortionary (lump-sum) taxation. Distortionary taxation can further be classified along capital- and labor-income taxation, their degree of progressivity, etc. Finally, government spending and revenue raising cannot be considered in isolation. The difference between the two is the government deficit, which accumulates into government debt.

The *partial* effects of these variables on economic growth have been well investigated in the literature. Stated generally, government investments have a growth enhancing effect, as have, for example, subsidies aimed at enhancing private investments (in physical, human, and knowledge capital). Government consumption can, as far as economic growth is concerned, be considered as 'throwing money in the sea' and will thus have no direct effect on economic growth. It has even been argued (Barro 1990) that government services entering only into utility unambiguously decrease savings and consequently the growth rate. A first issue that needs to be addressed in the context of revenue raising is concerned with the question whether the government finances its expenditures by issuing debt or by levying lump-sum taxes. According to the Ricardian Equivalence Theorem (RET), the government's financing decisions should be irrelevant. In this view, in order to establish the growth effects of government activities, the only concern is the size and composition of government spending. There are however, several flaws to this argument (see, for example, Romer 1996 for a discussion). Among these are that (i) the logic of the RET only applies for infinite-lived households (for finitely lived households the issuing of debts represents net wealth for people living at the time the debt is issued and will thus affect their behavior), (ii) liquidity constraints may affect the borrowing capacity of people (issuing debts instead of levying taxes then relieves this constraint and may again affect people's behavior) and (iii) taxes may be distortionary. Distortionary taxation may reduce incentives to save and/or invest and will thereby have a depressing effect on economic growth. As to the effects of the stock of government debt, there is no accordance in the literature on its effects on growth. It is, however, likely that a huge debt will tend to have a growth-depressing effect as expectations on profitability of investments and savings will tend to be lower.

Although these partial effects can relatively easily be (and have been) demonstrated, the fact that government spending will have to be backed with revenues is likely to result in complex and non-linear relationships between government spending and growth. This has neatly been demonstrated in the seminal theoretical work on endogenous growth and the role of the government by Barro (1990). In his basic model, he assumes that services provided by the government are of productive use in the private sector (think of, for example, investments in infrastructure). However, government expenditures should be financed and this is done by a proportional tax on income (which is assumed to be such that the government runs a balanced budget). It turns out that in this fairly simple model of endogenous growth, the effect of increased government spending on economic growth is non-monotonic. With a small size of the government, the productivity effect dominates and there is a positive relationship between growth and the size of the government. As the government becomes larger, the distortionary effect of the taxes that have to be raised to finance the expenditures becomes more important and beyond a certain size of the government, the relationship between growth and the size of the government turns into a negative one. There is, in other words, a hump-shaped relationship between the size of the government and the rate of economic growth, implying some optimal size of the government. Clearly, it is not obvious beforehand from this model whether one should empirically expect a positive or negative relationship between growth and taxes. The answer on this question depends on whether governments in the countries under consideration are on, below, or above their optimal size. The finding of no effect of government spending (or taxation) on growth may be interpreted as indicating that all countries are close to a situation with an optimally sized government.

This basic result has been reestablished in various other studies in some way or another. For example, Glomm and Ravikumar (1994 and 1997) consider the relationship between government spending on infrastructure or education and economic growth. The implications their models yield depend, in general, on how the expenditures are being conceived (i.e., being productive or just as throwing money into the sea), and how they look at the effects of taxes that have to be raised in order to finance the expenditures. The general empirical implications that follow from these models are that one expects a positive (partial) correlation of growth with productive expenditures (on, for example, education and infrastructure) and a negative (partial) correlation with government consumption and distortionary taxes. However, it is important to note that there is no uniformity in these models and that there are not many clear, testable implications that follow from the literature. Most agreement probably exists on the fact that the relationship between fiscal policy and economic growth is non-linear and depends on various partial effects that are difficult to disentangle.[2] Despite this fact, much empirical work has been done in the field of the relationship between fiscal policy and economic growth and the next section will discuss some of the evidence that follows from this work.

In conclusion, theoretical studies have described various channels through which fiscal policy might affect economic growth. The relationship turns out to be a complex one and to depend on various partial effects, implying many complex tradeoffs between the potentially beneficial effects of government services and the negative effects of distortionary taxes on economic growth and development.

Systemic Governmental Effects on Economic Growth

So far, attention has been restricted to the government as an economic agent that collects money via taxation and spends it on education, provision of subsidies, infrastructure, government consumption, etc. These activities were shown to affect economic growth along various channels. One may, however, also identify other mechanisms through which governments can directly or indirectly influence economic growth. These may be referred to as non-financial conditions or prevailing domestic, political, or institutional arrangements (see, for example, the work by North 1991 and Olson 1982 for rich and extensive discussions on these issues). In a way, these conditions with flanking policies to match them can be regarded as public goods in that they have indivisible consequences for whole nations. As far as policy is concerned, an important issue appears to be not only that of a possibly positive outcome in quantitative terms of expenditures and fiscal policies, but also that of a possible outweigh of efficiency-reducing government intervention (due to, e.g., the presence of public sector enterprises and price and quantitative controls) by efficiency-enhancing government intervention (by, for example, addressing market failures, providing social and economic infrastructure), resulting in a net positive impact on overall economic performance and hence on growth. The remainder of this section will briefly describe some of the channels that have attained a distinct position in the literature on economic growth.

Although possible distortionary effects of taxation have been pointed out in the previous section, they were not yet dealt with exhaustively. Government taxation is not only a means of raising revenues to back up expenditures, but it is also an instrument through which income inequality and labor markets can be affected. An obvious result of an increase in effective taxes on labor would be that of an increase in labor costs. According to Daveri and Tabellini (1997), an excessively high cost of labor is the main cause of an increasing rate of unemployment as well as the slowdown in economic growth in Europe nowadays. Given a non-competitive nature of labor markets, an exogenous and permanent increase of labor costs will force firms to substitute capital for labor. This results in a decrease of the marginal product of capital over long periods of time; this in turn will diminish the incentive to accumulate and thus to grow.

Governments also play an important role in influencing the distribution of income over various agents in the economy. The importance of income distribution has, for example, been underlined by Persson and Tabellini (1991). They show that inequality is harmful to growth. The reason for this is that a society with more inequality where distributional conflicts are important is characterized by political decisions that allow private individuals to appropriate less of the returns on accumulation of physical and human capital. These societies are consequently faced with lower rates of capital accumulation, resulting in lower growth rates. In an indirect way, fiscal policies aimed at reducing inequality can thus be said to be favorable to growth. On the other hand, by providing generous social benefits, governments may foster unemployment which in turn may be bad for economic growth (e.g., Daveri and Tabellini 1997 and de Groot 2000).[3]

Governments are also important in providing a stable and legal framework in which property rights are clearly defined (now and in the future), and also a monetary environment with stable prices. An interesting point of view in this context is given by Olson (1982). He argues that the longer a society enjoys political stability, the more likely it is to develop powerful special-interest organizations that in turn make it economically less efficient. They will have both an incentive to make the society in which they operate more prosperous, and an incentive to redistribute income to their members with the lowest possible excess burden. In practice, these distributional organizations are bound to slow down a society's capacity to adopt new technologies and to reallocate resources in response to changing conditions, and thereby will reduce the rate of economic growth (see also Canton et al. 1999). The accumulation of distributional institutions and agencies will, due to an increasing complexity of regulation, bureaucracy, and political intervention in markets, cause an increasing importance of an active role of the government.

Immaterial effects of governmental policies may also derive from the degree to which people have (political) freedom within a political system. Friedman (1962) and Hayek (1944) among others, have argued that freedom should facilitate economic performance and hence growth. Proponents of planned economies have argued that a country requires autocratic control and reduced freedom in order to grow rapidly. Olson (1982), for example, argues that countries that have had democratic freedom of organization without any upheaval or invasion for relatively long periods will suffer most from growth-repressing organizations. Moreover, countries whose distributional coalitions, emerged as described above, have been emasculated or abolished by totalitarian government or foreign occupation should grow relatively quickly after a free and stable legal order has been established.

Finally, a factor in which government involvement meets regional perspectives is the degree of openness of an economic system. With respect to economic growth, attention may be focused on the manner in which openness affects convergence across countries (*cf.* Puga 1999). The importance of trade, capital flows, the diffusion of product and process innovations and net migration at the interregional and international levels suggests that spatial interactions need to be considered, both in terms of their direct effects on growth and their effects on technological change. In the neo-classical growth model, trade is not necessary for income convergence to take place, though a free flow of capital may speed up the process (*cf.* Barro et al. 1995). In its essence, endogenous growth theory predicts—in the absence of cross-country knowledge spillovers—divergence, by relaxing the assumption of diminishing returns to capital, due to which the ratio of saving or investment to GDP also matters for long-run growth (Baldwin 1999). The introduction of endogenous technological change may be a dis-equilibrating factor in a trade model. Although Rivera-Batiz and Romer (1991) showed an increased average growth rate resulting from an integration of regional economies, it is possible that a specialization based on comparative advantage leads to sub-optimal investment in R&D activities by resource rich economies (Grossman and Helpman 1991). From a policy perspective, the question which region has a comparative advantage in the R&D sector is relevant since it may be the level of activity in this specific sector that provides a learning by doing spill-over benefit for all regions. Hence, an increase in the supply of the resource used intensively in the knowledge-generating sector will obviously speed up growth. Despite all this, the disequilibrium issue here comes down to the fact that the regions that produce the good which enjoys a faster technological change will, in the absence of knowledge spillovers (!), continue to have a higher growth rate, resulting in a continuing change in the terms of trade.

The Empirical Evidence: A Comparative Review

Inspired by the theoretical studies on the relationship between fiscal policies and economic growth and the appearance of data sets from, for example, Summers and Heston (Penn World Table; 1991) and Barro and Lee (1994), in recent years much research has been performed, trying to find evidence for such relationships. Refer to Temple (1999) for an excellent overview of this 'new growth evidence', as well as for an overview of the problems of this literature and the resulting research agenda which will probably occupy researchers for the next decades. In this section, attention will be restricted to a discussion of cross-section evidence on the relationship between government activities and economic growth.[4] This empirical literature was initiated by Barro (1991).[5] His study covers 98 countries over the period 1960-1985. It considers the relationships (in a cross section of countries) between the growth rate of real GDP per capita and proxies for human capital, initial real GDP, investment in physical capital, measures of political stability, proxies for market distortions, the share of government consumption in GDP and the share of public investment. A distinction is made between government consumption (excluding spending on education and defense, as these spending categories are more likely to add to private sector productivity) and public investment. As one would expect theoretically, a negative correlation between growth and government consumption is found. The argument being that government consumption has no direct effect on private sector productivity, but lowers savings and growth through the distorting effects of taxes (as previously discussed). No significant relationship was found between public investment and growth Especially regarding endogenous growth however, it is important to bear in mind that, given its underlying assumptions on the absence of diminishing returns to capital, public investment may affect growth in an indirect, rather than in a direct manner. This holds for human capital as well as for physical capital. This kind of study has been done and redone in various, slightly different, ways. Most extensive in this were Easterly and Rebelo (1993) and Levine and Renelt (1992). The most important findings derived from Easterly and Rebelo's study are that: (i) measures of fiscal policies tend to be insignificantly related with growth, (ii) these measures often cause the coefficient on initial income to become insignificant, pointing at a strong correlation between initial income and fiscal policy measures,[6] (iii) growth and public investments in transport and communication are consistently positively related, while investments in transport and communication are not related with the investment rate. This last finding implies that the effect of public investment does not run via capital accumulation but via the efficiency of resource allocation.

In an extensive overview of the empirical growth literature, Levine and Renelt (1992) address the question of the robustness of the relationships that have been found. They do so by employing the Extreme Bounds Analysis (EBA), developed by Leamer (1983 and 1985).[7] They call a relationship between economic growth and a particular variable robust, if (i) it remains statistically significant, and (ii) it remains of the theoretically predicted sign, when the conditioning set of variables in the regression equation changes. The main conclusion of their study is that there is a positive and robust relationship between economic growth and the investment share of GDP. Furthermore, the investment share is robustly correlated with the share of trade in GDP. Finally, they find qualified support for the hypothesis of conditional convergence: including a measure of human capital, there is a robust negative correlation between growth and initial income. As far as government activities are concerned, they show that there are no robust relationships between growth and government consumption expenditures, total government expenditures, government expenditures net of spending on education and defense, central government surpluses,[8] government capital formation as a ratio of GDP, government education expenditure as a ratio of GDP, government defense expenditure as a ratio of GDP, and various tax measures.[9] Also, there turns out to be no robust relation of the above mentioned variables with the investment share in GDP. A final remark on this robustness analysis is that fiscal indicators enter with the predicted sign for many specifications when investment is included, while the indicators are insignificantly correlated with the investment ratio itself. The general conclusion should thus be that, if there is any relationship between growth and fiscal policy at all, it runs via efficiency of resource allocation and not via the accumulation of physical capital as implied by many of the existing theories.

Another source that casts some doubt on the potential of policy variables to explain variations in economic growth is a study by Easterly et al. (1993). They start with the notion that much of the existing growth literature explains differences in growth performances by focusing on differences in country characteristics such as savings rates, education levels, and also various kinds of policy measures (this characteristic applies to all studies described previously). Starting from this notion, it is convincingly shown in the paper that growth rates show little persistence over time. This conclusion holds independent of whether one determines persistence by means of simple or rank correlations or a cross plot of growth rates in two different periods for various countries. It also holds independent of the length of the period that is chosen. Therefore, the persistence of country characteristics should be low as well in case these characteristics should be able to explain the differences in growth performance of countries over time. It is shown, however, that the persistence over time of various country characteristics like inflation, government consumption, assassinations, the trade share, the black market premium, initial income, enrolment rates, investment shares, etc. is large relative to the persistence of growth rates. The implication of this result is clear. Country characteristics are not well suited to explain the observed differences in growth performance of countries over time. In the remainder of the paper, it is shown that shock variables like terms of trade, external transfers, the change in the number of war-related casualties per capita on the national territory, and the presence of a debt crisis can explain much of the low persistence in growth rates over time. Especially the importance of the terms of trade is stressed. The effect of these shocks is partly direct but also partly indirect, as the shocks influence policy variables. Fiscal policies are thus probably partly endogenous. The conclusion of the paper is, therefore, that given the high persistence of country characteristics (among which are policy characteristics) and the low persistence of growth rates over time, one should be cautious in concluding that good growth performances can be attributed to good policy. This casts some doubt on the importance of fiscal policy for explaining growth performance.

Another driving force for growth that can be influenced by governmental policy is trade (see, for example, Thirlwall 1999). Although theoretical discussions frequently focus on the relationship between international trade, knowledge spillovers and growth, empirical research has typically examined the relationship between just exports or openness and growth. As already mentioned in the previous section, endogenous growth theory differs from neo-classical growth theory by the fact that it predicts—in the absence of knowledge spill-overs—divergence (or only conditional convergence) among countries. One of the first convergence studies regressing per capita income growth on the initial level of per capita income was Barro (1991). The sign on the initial per capita income only turned negative after adding school-enrolment rates in the equation. This kind of result has been a typical feature in subsequent large sample studies by Mankiw et al. (1992), Knight et al. (1993) and Barro and Lee (1994). All these studies showed no evidence of unconditional convergence, but evidence of conditional convergence when other factors affecting the growth of income per capita are allowed for, such as political instability, government activity, market distortions and trade variables (Thirlwall and Sanna 1996). One of the best examples where free trade and factor mobility is associated with a narrowing down of regional differences in economic welfare can be found in the United States. Here, a regional per capita income convergence process is, according to Barro and Sala-i-Martin (1992), taking place over the last hundred years.

An important empirical issue is that, while traditional trade theory tends to emphasize that it is increased openness—and not necessarily the actual volume of trade—that should lead to an equalization of incomes, the evidence from that earlier work points to a very strong relationship between the two (e.g. Ben-David 1996). A conclusion might be then that the level of trade is an appropriate proxy for the degree of openness of a country. Indeed, a variety of empirical studies has provided evidence that income convergence among countries is a prevailing feature among countries that trade extensively with one another. Some (weak) evidence for the hypothesis that countries that become increasingly open experience higher economic growth (rather than 'just' convergence) was found by Kormendi and Meguire (1985). More recently, Hansen (1994) found an insignificant relationship between exports and economic growth for individual country estimates.[10] For the pooled sample the coefficient was positive and highly significant when using gross investment data, but insignificant when utilized net capital stock data were used. One of Hansen's conclusions is that the results reported in the literature regarding the positive effect of exports on economic growth are not robust.

This issue of lack of robustness once again leads to the 'Levine and Renelt critique'. They examined the robustness of export indicators used in past studies, while in addition they examined the relationship between growth and import indicators, total-trade indicators, and more direct estimates of trade policy and the distortion between domestic and international prices. In their extreme bound analysis Levine and Renelt hardly found a regression in which the ratio of exports to GDP enters positively and significantly when investment is used as a conditioning variable (see the earlier discussion above on the EBA-method). However, as soon as investment is dropped from the list of conditioning variables the ratio of export proves to be robustly positively related with economic growth. Also, a robustly positive correlation between the share of trade in GDP and the share of investment in GDP was found. These results suggest an important two-link chain between trade and growth through investment and were taken by Levine and Renelt as an indication that, in contrast to standard theory, the relationship between trade and growth may be based on enhanced resource accumulation and not necessarily on the improved allocation of resources.[11]

From the above discussion, it will be evident that the empirical literature on the effects of government spending, taxation, trade, and openness is fraught with problems. The problems increase further when attention is shifted to the effects of non-financial conditions and prevalent political circumstances. In the literature concerned with these issues, the discrepancy between theoretical coverage and their respective empirical implementations are even wider. The main problem is often to find a variable which can be taken as an appropriate proxy for the political circumstance under consideration and which can also be represented by a quantifiable measure. The discussion that has enrolled on these issues is extensive.

Take, as an example, the measurement of the degree of stability of the political system. In order to define this degree, Barro (1991) included two variables from Bank's (1979) data set, namely the number of revolutions and coups per year and the number of political assassinations per million inhabitants per year.[12] Barro empirically tested his predictions and found a negative relationship between his proxies for political instability and economic growth, though the coefficients still proved to be negative when the investment/income ratio was held constant (see the previous discussion on these issues). Barro's approach has been criticized by, for example, Knack and Keefer (1995). First, Barro's proxies for political instability are restricted to non-constitutional political disturbances. This limits the coverage of his predictions, since the actions of political leaders facing a higher risk of losing power in a constitutional way are not captured by these proxies. Second, the proxy itself may be a misleading one. The correlation between revolutions, coups, and assassinations on the one hand and the security of property rights on the other might be lower than expected. For example, Germany and France score at least as poorly on Barro's measures of political violence as Malawi and Zambia. Evidently, this by no means points to an equal security of property rights. Third, the ways in which governments and institutions affect property rights are not restricted to political instability. The latter is only a crude indicator and is not covering much of the relevant influences. Fourth, there is a simultaneity problem. Economic performance in its turn is likely to have an effect on the appearance of political violence (Barro already mentioned this possibility in an attempt to explain high correlation in the absence of decreasing investment ratios).

Another example of measurement problems occurs with the measurement of political rights and civil liberties. Gastil (1979) has constructed indices of these indicators for most countries in the world.[13] Empirically, Gastil's contribution has been used and interpreted in different ways. Authors like Kormendi and Meguire (1985) treat the index of civil liberties as an additional explanatory variable for economic growth (finding a positive relationship between the degree of civil liberty and economic growth, while the effect on growth operates mainly through the investment channel). In a more recent paper, Guseh (1997) uses Gastil's classifications to transform them into dummy variables to compensate for extreme capitalist and socialist economies. Again, Knack and Keefer have adopted a more skeptic attitude to the explanatory value of the indices. They argue that these are aggregate measures, which have been compiled without the explicit aim of measuring the security of property rights. For many purposes, these variables are of great importance. However, many of the dimensions are not closely related to property rights. Knack and Keefer also emphasize the problem of considerable measurement error in evaluating the institutions that are thought to affect property rights, contracting rights, and the efficiency with which public goods are allocated. A major problem is that these indices are not disaggregated and the implicit weights attached to the various dimensions will vary over time and between countries.

As a means to resolve the problems with measuring 'political circumstances', Knack and Keefer (1995) come up with an alternative set of institutional indicators compiled by two private international investment risk services, viz. International Country Risk Guide (ICRG) and Business Environment Risk Intelligence (BERI). The ICRG variables consist of expropriation risk, rule of law, repudiation of contracts by government, corruption in government, and quality of bureaucracy. Expropriation risk, rule of law, and repudiation are interpreted by Knack and Keefer as proxies for the security of property and contract rights.[14] Corruption in government and quality of bureaucracy are taken as proxies for the general efficiency with which government services are provided, and for the extent and damage of rent-seeking behavior.[15] The BERI variables used by Knack and Keefer consist of contract enforceability, infrastructure quality, nationalization potential, and bureaucratic delays, with the latter two paralleling the ICRG variables expropriation risk and quality of bureaucracy. Contract enforceability could be taken as a proxy for the security of contract rights with consequences for investments as already mentioned above. The variable of infrastructure quality reflects the efficiency with which governments allocate public goods. One of the conclusions of Knack and Keefer is that the correlation between the ICRG and BERI variables on the one hand and Barro's political violence variables and Gastil's political and civil liberties indices on the other hand are relatively low. This indicates that the ICRG and BERI variables contain a substantial amount of information not being present in the other variables.

This section has reviewed some of the central studies yielding insights into the empirical relationships between fiscal policy, trade, institutions, and economic growth. Some general remarks on this type of cross-sectional empirical studies are in place. First, all studies face serious measurement problems. There are neither data available on *marginal* tax rates and subsidies, nor are there reliable data on the levels of public investment and (quality of) institutions.[16] Second, the studies face a potential problem of reverse causation. The correlation between initial income and fiscal policy measures, as implied by the Barro-type of equations, has already been noted. More extensive studies indeed show a statistically significant relationship between initial income (as a measure for the level of development) and fiscal policy measures (e.g., Easterly and Rebelo 1993). Third, as has already been emphasized in this paper, the relationship between government activities and economic growth is complex and likely to be non-linear. The finding of no significant relationship between growth and government spending might therefore have to do with the specific (non-linear) form of the relationship. One way to test for this could be to add taxes in a non-linear fashion to the regression equation, in order to be able to grasp the complex relationships between growth and fiscal policies[17]. Fourth, the paper by Levine and Renelt (1992) shows rather convincingly that none of the results on the relation between fiscal policy, trade, institutions, and economic growth is robust. If any general conclusion can be drawn from the previously described studies, it should be that there is no unanimity on the relationship between governmental policies and economic growth. Maybe this should not be surprising in a research area where so few testable implications follow from the underlying theories, in which non-linearities and complex trade-offs seem to be especially important, and in which good and reliable data are scarce. A fifth problem is that hardly any evidence exists on the efficiency of government spending. Finally, it should be mentioned that many of the results that have been obtained are not easily interpretable. It was mentioned, for example, that the black-market premium on foreign exchange has been used as a variable by Barro (see, e.g., Barro and Sala-i-Martin 1995) to measure the effects of economic policy. It is, however, not at all clear how to interpret the negative relation between growth and the black-market premium that has been found, not to speak about formulating policy recommendations on the basis of this type of evidence. Drawing policy lessons from cross-country regression evidence should in other words be done with the utmost caution and recommendations should be treated with sound and fair skepticism.

Empirical Experiments

In this section, some empirical experiments will be offered to illustrate some of the above mentioned conclusions on the determinants of economic growth, as well as to illustrate the problems with the empirical research on economic growth. After a concise introduction to the methodology, the data set will be described and some results offered and interpreted.

Methodology. In this section, a simple regression analysis considering the explanatory power of various governmental and other variables with respect to economic growth, as dealt with in this paper, will be carried out. The regression study has a pooled time-series cross-section character. Hence, results can be derived on the relevance of country-specific economic, political or other situational conditions in explaining growth, as well as on the relevance of changing economic, political or other situational aspects within a country in explaining changes in growth over time. Data have been gathered for fourteen countries and six time periods, resulting in a total number of 84 observations for each variable in the data set. The countries included are Australia, Belgium, Canada, Finland, France, Germany, Italy, Japan, Norway, the Netherlands, Spain, Sweden, United Kingdom and the United States. The time periods considered are six five-year spans in the period 1960-1990.

The regression methodology used here is the strategy of "sequential elimination by reducing the set of explanatory variables" as described in Theil (1971)[18]. This method basically consists of running regressions on a given large set of possibly relevant variables and removing in each run the variable which according to significance tests proves to be least appropriate from the set until all remaining variables show statistical significance.[19] This approach is particularly useful if there is no unambiguous theoretical framework that would lead to a clear choice for the identification of explanatory variables (a case of a semantically insufficient model). Additionally, various tests of robustness were performed by applying a (slightly modified) version of Leamer's Extreme Bound Analysis.

Variables employed in the analysis. For a complete overview and explanation of all variables used, refer to the Appendix. In particular the focus is on fiscal expenditures as well as taxation variables. The fiscal expenditure variables used are the GDP-ratios of expenditure on education, expenditure on defense, and consumption expenditure net of spending on education and defense. Also, public investments are considered. The taxation variables used are the effective tax rates on labor income and capital income. Also, a number of variables capturing the political situation have been accounted for. For this, the number of assassinations and revolutions, and indices of political rights and civil liberties were used. Educational aspects and human capital stocks are reflected in the number of years of education, gross enrolment ratios, pupil to teacher ratios and the percentage of people with no schooling in the total population. Finally, a set of variables capturing openness and trade has been incorporated in the data-set. These variables are the average import and export share, a measure of free trade openness, distance to major markets, a tariff restriction variable, and a trade shock variable. Dummy variables are used for all countries (except for the United States which serves as the reference country) and for all periods (except for the last period, i.e. 1985-1990, which serves as the reference period) to detect any country or period specific growth effects.

The results. The results derived by applying Theil's elimination procedure are given in Table 1. Regression coefficients and corresponding t-values have been given in the last two columns. The percentage in parentheses behind the estimated coefficient corresponds to the percentage of regression equations in which the regression coefficient remained of the initial sign when adding all other potentially explanatory variables (see Appendix) in all possible combinations of groups of, at most, three to the regression equation reported in Table 1. Similarly, the percentage in parentheses behind the t-value corresponds to the percentage of regression equations in which the t-value remained significant when adding all other potentially explanatory variables (see Appendix) in all possible combinations of groups of three to the regression equation reported in Table 1. For this analysis, 2626 regressions were run.

Applying Theil's procedure, both the initial income level and the share of private investment turn out to be statistically significant as well as of the theoretically predicted sign in the final equation. The positive effect of the private investment share on economic growth can be interpreted as some supporting evidence for endogenous growth type of models. The negative sign of the coefficient of initial income level upholds the case for the conditional convergence hypothesis. The robustness analysis reveals that most variables are robust in the sense of Leamer; they are always of the same sign and always significant, independent of the set of conditioning variables.[20]

Concerning the influence of human capital it is noteworthy that it is not education expenditures (a flow), but rather the accumulated stock, represented

COMPARATIVE EFFECTS OF POLICIES 563

TABLE 1. REGRESSION RESULTS FOR ECONOMIC GROWTH (pooled cross-section analysis); $R^2=0.84$.

	coefficient	t-value
Intercept	-0.021	-2.64
Rate of initial GDP per capita to USA	-0.177	-8.62
	(100 %)	(100 %)
Ratio of real private investment to real GDP	0.119	4.81
	(100 %)	(100 %)
Effective tax rates on labor income	-0.063	-5.60
	(100 %)	(100 %)
Terms of trade shock	0.189	3.99
	(100 %)	(100 %)
Index of political rights	0.009	3.42
	(100 %)	(99 %)
Percentage of total population with 'no schooling'	-0.002	-7.72
	(100 %)	(100 %)
Total gross enrolment ratio for higher education	0.059	4.58
	(100 %)	(97 %)
Dummy Finland	-0.024	-4.96
	(100 %)	(100 %)
Dummy Japan	-0.012	-2.42
	(100 %)	(59 %)
Dummy Sweden	0.013	3.28
	(100 %)	(90 %)
Dummy period 1970-1974	-0.008	-3.45
	100 %)	(100 %)
Dummy period 1980-1984	-0.012	-4.82
	(100 %)	(100 %)

by high-school enrolment rate and the share of population lacking education, which strongest affects economic growth. The high-school enrolment rates are positively related with economic growth, while the 'no-school' variable negatively affects economic growth. The two variables may be regarded as sufficiently complementary since they show a weak mutual correlation.

The negative sign of the coefficient of taxes on labor income suggests a considerable relevance of disturbances on the labor market. An explanation may be that the increased labor costs resulting from higher labor taxes lead to a process of substitution of labor for capital, causing the marginal product of capital to fall and hence negatively affecting incentives to accumulate physical capital (see Daveri and Tabellini 1997).

Rather surprising is the fact that the index for political rights shows up with a positive coefficient, signifying that economic growth is higher when political rights are less respected. This does, however, coincide with Olson's theory concerning growth-depressing distributional coalitions arising in economies with democratic freedom of organization as described in this paper. The 'trade-shock' variable, constructed as the growth rate of export prices minus the growth rates of import prices positively affects economic growth, which may be caused by relative price elasticities of export to import being lower than one.

The period dummies of the early seventies and eighties indicate a less than average performance in these periods, reflecting the poor worldwide economic performance in this period of crisis. Finally, there are some country dummies showing up as significant in the regression results. These are the dummies for Finland, Japan, and Sweden, of whom the coefficients of the first two are negative while the last one has a positive coefficient. The fact that Japan is performing poorly is somewhat surprising. With respect to Finland's negative dummy coefficient, it may be concluded that the geographical peripheral location plays to some degree a role in its growth pattern. The positive coefficient of the dummy for Sweden may perhaps be taken as evidence for a relatively well-performing Swedish model.

Conclusions and Future Research

The interest in endogenous growth policy is rapidly rising, not only from the perspective of international trade developments and related comparative advantages, but also from the perspective of local or regional development efforts. In a more open and globalizing economy, localities and regions have the need to create a more distinct profile through territorial competition (see also Cheshire and Gordon 1998). This is exemplified by current efforts of many areas to attract foreign direct investments (see, e.g., Van Geenhuizen and Nijkamp 1998). The main idea is to develop and promote the territory as a competitive place for industrial growth and related spin-offs. This view prompts also an interest in public policy as an endogenous response to the needs and opportunities of business life (e.g., by means of tax exemptions, local incentives, etc.). The exploitation of the strong economic-geographical aspects of a given area may increase economic efficiency, although it may also increase regional-economic disparities. Thus, the open character of many regional economies has induced more competition, which may put more stress on interregional convergence often aimed at in regional economic policies.

Profit-seeking behavior of firms may cause imbalances in a multi-regional system, if the location and competitive conditions are not equal. In this context, R&D policies may become an important endogenous policy tool. This R&D policy is not only related to innovative behavior of firms, but also to human capital development. The latter is usually more a competence of governments, and hence public policy plays a critical role in an endogenous growth context, not only as a generator but also as a disseminator of scientific knowledge (*cf.* Acs et al. 1994). In this context, regional authorities have to become alert actors with a non-bureaucratic mind (the so-called 'learning regions' concept). Knowledge spillovers do not only use conventional channels (such as academic research institutes, scientific publications etc.), but increasingly also the entire modern information and communication technology (ICT) sector (e.g., Internet), as well as physical mobility of people. Consequently, the role of the government may also cover the infrastructure of knowledge transfer and the dissemination of technological competence, so as to encourage local innovative performance. Another element that is of pivotal importance for the relevance of endogenous growth mechanisms in a multi-regional setting is the multi-layer structure of institutional governance (e.g., fiscal federalism). The way governments and institutions impact on regional growth is contingent on the ramifications of formal and informal decision-making systems, so that the impacts of endogenous regional development strategies are co-determined by institutional configurations.

The richness of these ideas and this theorizing about the complex and intriguing potential relationships and trade-offs at the interface of policy and economic growth (see also previous sections) is in sharp contrast with the ways in which the effects of governmental policies have empirically been tested. This has been shown in this paper. From the available empirical evidence on the role of governmental policies, as reviewed in the previous section, it is concluded that there are only few clear and robust conclusions to be drawn from the empirical research on government spending, taxation, trade, openness, the prevailing political situation, and economic growth. This should not come as a surprise, given the fact that the relationship shows various complex causal mechanisms according to the theory. Furthermore, it is concluded that the literature meets various econometric problems like a lack of good and reliable data, possibilities of measurement errors, reverse causation, and endogeneity biases. It has been argued that a serious problem from which almost all the evidence suffers is the 'Levine and Renelt critique'; only few of the results that have been obtained seem to stand the scrutiny of an extensive robustness analysis. One can consider the Levine and Renelt critique is almost a 'deathblow' for all cross-section regression studies that have been performed in the last decade. See, however, Sala-i-Martin (1997) for a less skeptical conclusion about what can be learned from cross-sectional growth regressions. An interesting potential way out would be to perform an extensive meta-analytical study on the variety of insights that have been gained in the literature in order to put some testable structure to the obtained evidence. Such a meta-analytical experiment might have various constituents, namely (i) a comparative analysis of the strengths and weaknesses of the various theoretical paradigms involved, (ii) a review and cross-comparison of various methods used to test the validity of endogenous growth approaches and (iii) a statistical meta-analytical experiment to test the commonality and transferability of the various study findings. Anyway, for the time being, one has to be aware of the problems that the empirical literature faces and one has to treat the results and conclusions with fair skepticism. The results obtained should at most be viewed as empirical regularities, and not as stylized facts or behavioral relationships on which future policies should be designed!

NOTES

1. We deliberately restrict our attention to cross-section studies. Note however, that also time-series evidence has been obtained (e.g., Easterly and Rebelo 1993, and Persson and Tabellini 1991). Furthermore, there is some evidence from growth accounting studies (see, e.g., Maddison 1982), as well as evidence from the estimation of production functions including some kind of public capital (see Glomm and Ravikumar 1997 for an overview).

2. This point is forcefully made by Levine and Renelt (1992) when they discuss the problems that arise when performing *linear* cross-section growth regressions (as is done in most of the empirical studies, see section 3).

3. This brings us to the scale effects that characterize many of the models developed in endogenous growth theory of which Daveri and Tabellini (1998) and de Groot (2000), provide examples. Characteristic for these models is that the endogenously determined rate of growth depends on some measure of the scale of the economy, like effective labor supply or population size. Jones (1995) has criticized models of endogenous growth since the scale effects have not been found convincingly in empirical studies. Recent studies have shown that this problem of scale effects can relatively easily be circumvented without altering most of the essential insights that have been derived from endogenous growth theories. We refer here to, among others, de Groot (2000), Smulders and van de Klundert (1995) and Young (1998) for extensive discussions on the issue of scale effects and ways to circumvent them in models of endogenous growth.

4. For some time-series evidence we refer to, for example, Easterly and Rebelo (1993) and Persson and Tabellini (1991). In the context of growth accounting studies, some material on the effect of fiscal policy can be found in, for example, Maddison (1982). Another type of evidence comes from studies, aiming at estimating aggregate production functions that include some measures of public capital (see Glomm and Ravikumar 1997 for a review).

5. An update and extension of these results can be found in Barro and Sala-i-Martin (1995). The general conclusions in these two studies are not essentially different.

6. Another troublesome conclusion is that the significance of relations of the 'standard' variables like assassinations, revolutions and war casualties with growth depends on the type of tax measure that is included. This points to robustness problems in these results.

7. For an intuitive overview of the EBA-methodology we refer to Levine and Renelt (1992). The essence of the methodology is that one tests whether a certain relationship between two variables remains significant and is of the theoretically predicted sign, if one changes the conditioning set of variables that is employed in the regression. Note that there has been some discussion on the usefulness of the EBA-methodology (e.g., McAleer 1994, and McAleer and Veall 1989, Sala-i-Martin 1997). Nevertheless, Levine and Renelt make an important point in their study and it is important to refer to their results in the context of the subject under consideration in the present paper.

8. Several studies investigated the relationship between central government surpluses and economic growth. Thornton (1990), for example, found the relationships between the rate of economic growth on the one hand and government deficit, inflation, the price level,

interest rates and private savings on the other hand to be statistically insignificant. Miller and Russek (1997) distinguished between developed and developing countries while analyzing the relationship between governmental policy and economic growth. They found the method of financing government expenditure to play an important role in determining the effect of that expenditure on economic growth. This result indicates a lack of general validity of the Ricardian Equivalence theorem. Specific results they found were that for developing countries, debt-financed increases in government expenditure retard economic growth and tax-financed increases lead to higher growth, while for developed countries, debt-financed increases in government expenditure do not affect economic growth and tax-financed increases lead to lower growth. The study thereby clearly demonstrates the major dependency of support for a theoretical concept like the Ricardian Equivalence on the concept's specific empirical implementation.

9. An update of this part of the analysis by Levine and Renelt is found in Levine and Zervos (1993). In this study, the initial analysis is extended by using, for example, data from Easterly and Rebelo (1993). The conclusion of no robust relation between growth and fiscal policies remains to stand upright, however.

10. Hansen used a rather small country set consisting of Canada, West Germany, Japan, United Kingdom and United States.

11. Levine and Renelt also examined more direct measures like the measure of openness, constructed by Leamer (1988) by using the Hekscher-Ohlin-Vanek trade model. This index represents the difference between the actual and predicted level of trade, a higher value of this index representing more openness. Levine and Renelt did not find this index to be robustly correlated with GDP per capita growth. They did, however, find a robust, positive correlation between the index and the investment share.

12. The idea behind the inclusion of these variables is evident. Given an increase in the chance of being replaced within a sufficiently small period of time, a political leader is likely to be more inclined to carry on expropriationary actions, since the costs can be passed over to successors. Bearing in mind that mechanisms for protecting property and contractual rights are already fragile in a period of political instability–especially when instability is cause by non-constitutional events–it is evident that high numbers of revolutions, coups and assassinations will cause a reduction and reallocation of investments and will thus have a negative effect on economic growth.

13. These indices are ordinal measures which range from 1 (most free) to 7 (least free). Political rights are rights to participate meaningfully in the political process. In a democracy this means the right of all adults to vote and compete for public office, and for elected representatives to have a decisive vote on public policies. Civil liberties are rights to free expression, to organize or demonstrate, as well as a degree of autonomy such as provided by freedom of religion, education, travel, and other personal rights. From these two indices Gastil derives the status of political freedom for a country as either free, partially free, or not free.

14. A low score on one or more of these variables means that countries are likely to suffer a reduction in the quantity and efficiency of physical and perhaps human capital investment.

15. A low score on these variables implies a situation in which criteria other than efficiency are likely to prevail with respect to the determination of government policies and the allocation of public goods. Moreover, the fact that a corrupt government and a low

quality bureaucracy will negatively affect security of property rights may result in a diminishing quantity and efficiency of capital investment.

16. Easterly and Rebelo (1993) try to overcome this problem by constructing the marginal tax rates in four different ways. For the problems with each of these measures, see Easterly and Rebelo (1993). Also for public investment, various measures are constructed.

17. Levine and Renelt (1992) make this point forcefully. Nevertheless, they do not extend their analysis to deal with the non-linearities (which could be done by adding, for example, quadratic terms to the regression equation).

18. This methodology turned out to be somewhat unstable in the sense that only slightly different data sets yielded different outcomes. For that reason, an Extreme Bound Analysis has also been performed to test for the robustness of the significant relationships found by applying Theil's procedure.

19. In all our experiments, we will control for the initial income per capita relative to the USA and the private investment ratio (the variables that have been found to be robust by Levine and Renelt in their extensive study).

20. Among the group of conditioning variables, the coefficients of the following variables had the same sign in more than 95% of the cases: education expenditures (negative), defense expenditures (positive), capital taxation (positive), export share (positive), primary enrolment (positive), secondary enrolment (negative), pupil-teacher ratio in primary and secondary schools (positive), liquid liabilities (positive), free trade (negative), revolutions (negative) and participation (negative); see Sala-i-Martin (1997) for a similar kind of analysis.

REFERENCES

Acs, Z.J., D.B. Audretsch, and M.P. Feldman. 1994. R&D Spillovers and recipient firm size, *Review of Economics and Statistics* 76: 336-340.

Aghion, P., and P. Howitt. 1998. *Endogenous growth theory*. Cambridge MA: MIT Press.

Arrow, K.J. 1962. The economic implications of learning by doing, *Review of Economic Studies* 29: 155-173.

Arthur, W.B. 1994. *Increasing returns and path dependence in the economy*. Ann Arbor: University of Michigan Press.

Baldwin, R.E. 1999. Agglomeration and endogenous capital, *European Economic Review* 43: 253-280.

Barro, R.J. 1990. Government spending in a simple model of endogenous growth, *Journal of Political Economy* 98: 103-125.

———. 1991. Economic growth in a cross section of countries, *Quarterly Journal of Economics* 104: 407-443.

Barro, R.J., and J.W. Lee. 1994. *Data set for a panel of 138 countries*.

Barro, R.J., N.G. Mankiw, and X. Sala-i-Martin. 1995. Capital mobility in neoclassical models of growth, *American Economic Review* 85: 103-115.

Barro, R.J., and X. Sala-i-Martin. 1992. Convergence, *Journal of Political Economy* 100: 223-251.

———. 1995. *Economic growth*. New York: McGraw-Hill.

Ben-David, D. 1996. Trade and convergence among countries, *Journal of International Economics* 40: 279-298.

Canton, E.J.F., H.L.F. de Groot, and R. Nahuis. 1999. *Vested interests and resistance to technology adoption*. Center Discussion Paper 99106, Tilburg.

Cheshire, P.C., and I.R. Gordon. 1998. Territorial competition: Some lessons for policy, *Annals of Regional Science* 32: 321-346.

Daveri, F., and G. Tabellini. 1997. *Unemployment, growth and taxation in industrial countries*. Discussion Papers del Dipartimento di Scienze Economische 9706, Brescia.

de Groot, H.L.F. 2000. *Growth, unemployment and deindustrialization*. Cheltenham: Edward Elgar.

Devarajan, S., V. Swaroop, and H. Zou. 1996. The composition of public expenditure and economic growth, *Journal of Monetary Economics* 37:313-344.

Easterly W., and S. Rebelo. 1993. Fiscal policy and economic growth: An empirical investigation, *Journal of Monetary Economics* 32: 417-458.

Easterly W., M. Kremer, L. Pritchett, and L.H. Summers. 1993. Good policy or good luck? Country growth performance and temporary shocks, *Journal of Monetary Economics* 32: 459-483.

Friedman, M. 1962. *Capitalism and freedom*. Chicago: University of Chicago Press.

Fujita, M., and T. Mori. 1998. On the dynamics of frontier economies: Endogenous growth or the self-organisation of a dissipative system? *Annals of Regional Science* 32: 39-62.

Gastil, R.D. 1997. *Freedom in the world*. New Brunswick: Transaction Books.

Glomm, G., and B. Ravikumar. 1994. *Growth effects of government spending on education*, mimeo.

———. 1997. Productive government expenditures and long run growth, *Journal of Economic Dynamics and Control* 21: 183-204.

Grossman, G., and Helpman, E. 1991. *Innovation and growth in the global economy*. Cambridge MA: MIT Press.

Guseh, J.S. 1997. Government size and economic growth in developing countries: A political-economy framework, *Journal of Macroeconomics* 19: 175-192.

Hansen, P. 1994. Investment data and the empirical relationship between exporters, government and economic growth, *Applied Economic Letters* 1: 107-110.

Hayek, F.A. 1944. *The road to serfdom*. Chicago: University of Chicago Press.

Jones, C.I. 1995. Time series tests of endogenous growth models, *Quarterly Journal of Economics* 110: 495-525.

Knack, S., and P. Keefer. 1995. Institutions and economic performance: Cross-country tests using alternative institutional measures, *Economics and Politics* 7: 207-227.

Knight, M., N. Loyaza, and D. Villanueva. 1993. *Testing the neoclassical theory of economic growth*, IMF Staff Papers. Washington: IMF.

Kormendi, R.C., and P.G. Meguire. 1985. Macroeconomic determinants of growth, *Journal of Monetary Economics* 16: 141-163.

Krugman, P.R. 1991. *Geography and trade*. Cambridge MA: MIT Press.

———. 1993. On the relationship between trade theory and location theory, *Review of International Economics* 1: 110-122.

Leamer, E.E. 1983. Let's take the con out of econometrics, *American Economic Review* 73: 31-43.

———. 1985. Sensitivity analysis would help, *American Economic Review* 75: 308-313.

Levine, R., and D. Renelt. 1992. A sensitivity analysis of cross-country growth regressions, *American Economic Review* 82: 942-963.

Levine, R., and S. Zervos. 1993. *Looking at the facts; what we know about policy and growth from cross-country analysis*, World Bank Policy Research Working Papers, 1115, Washington.

Lucas, R.E. 1988. On the mechanics of economic development, *Journal of Monetary Economics* 22: 3-42.

Maddison, A. 1982. *Phases of capitalist development*. Oxford: Oxford University Press.

———. 1995. *Monitoring the world economy, 1820-1992*. Washington DC: Organization for Economic Cooperation and Development.

Magrini, S. 1999. The evolution of income disparities among the regions of the European Union, *Regional Science and Urban Economics* 29: 257-281.

Mankiw, N.G., D. Romer, and D.N. Weil. 1992. A contribution to the empirics of economic growth, *Quarterly Journal of Economics* 107: 407-437.

McAleer, M. 1994. Sherlock Holmes and the search for truth: A diagnostic tale, *Journal of Economic Surveys* 8: 327-351.

McAleer, M., and M.R. Veall. 1989. How fragile are fragile inferences? A re-evaluation of the deterrent effect of capital punishment. *The Review of Economics and Statistics* 71: 99-106.

Miller, S.M., and F.S. Russek. 1997. Fiscal structures and economic growth: International evidence, *Economic Inquiry* 35:603-613.

North, D.C. 1991. *Institutions, institutional change and economic performance.* Cambridge: Cambridge University Press.

Nijkamp, P., and A. Reggiani, 1998. *The economics of complex spatial systems.* Amsterdam: Elsevier.

Nijkamp, P., and J. Poot. 1998. Spatial perspectives on new theories of economic growth, *Annals of Regional Science* 32: 7-38.

Olson, M. 1982. *The rise and decline of nations*. New Haven: Yale University Press.

Persson, T., and G. Tabellini. 1991. *Is inequality harmful for growth?* Theory and Evidence, CEPR Discussion Paper 581, London.

Puga, D. 1999. The rise and fall of regional inequalities, *European Economic Review* 43: 303-334.

Rivera-Batiz, L.A., and P.M. Romer. 1991. Economic integration and endogenous growth, *Quarterly Journal of Economics* 106: 531-555.

Romer, D. 1996. *Advanced macroeconomics*. New York: McGraw-Hill.

Romer, P.M. 1986. Increasing returns and long-run growth, *Journal of Political Economy* 94: 1002-1037.

Sala-i-Martin, X. 1997. I just ran two million regressions, *American Economic Review* 87: 178-183.

Sattar, Z. 1993. Government control and economic growth in Asia: Evidence from time series data, *The Pakistan Development Review* 32: 179-197.

Smulders, S., and Th. van de Klundert. 1995. Imperfect competition, concentration and growth with firm-specific R&D, *European Economic Review* 39: 139-160.

Solow, R.M. 1956. A contribution to the theory of economic growth, *Quarterly Journal of Economics* 70: 65-94.

Swan, T. 1956. Economic growth and capital accumulation, *Economic Record* 32: 334-361.

Summers, R., and A. Heston. 1991. The Penn World Table (Mark 5): An expanded set of international comparisons, 1950-1988, *Quarterly Journal of Economics* 106: 327-368.

Temple, J. 1999. The new growth evidence, *Journal of Economic Literature* 37: 112-156.

Theil, H. 1971. *Principles of econometrics*. New York: Wiley.

Thirlwall, A.P. 1999. *Factor mobility, trade and 'regional' economic differences in the European Union: What story should we tell our children?*, paper presented in Lecture at the Technical University of Lisboa.

Thirlwall, A.P., and G. Sanna. 1996. The macrodeterminants of growth and 'new' growth theory: An evaluation and further evidence, in: *Employment, economic growth and the tyranny of the market: Essays in honour of Paul Davidson*, edited by P. Arretis, Cheltenham: Edward Elgar.

Thornton, D.L. 1990. Do government deficits matter?, *Federal Reserve Bank of St. Louis Review* 72: 25-39.

Van Geenhuizen, M.S., and P. Nijkamp. 1998. Potentials for East-West integration: The case of foreign direct investment, *Environment & Planning C* 16: 105-120.

Young, A. 1998. Growth without scale effects, *Journal of Political Economy* 106: 41-63.

APPENDIX. LIST OF DEPLOYED VARIABLES.

Independent variable: Growth rate of real GDP per capita[1]

General:	Natural log of initial GDP relative to GDP in the USA[*]
	Population growth[1*]
	Share of workers in total population (participation rate)
Government expenditure:	Share of nominal government expenditures on education in nominal GDP
	Share of nominal government expenditures on defense in nominal GDP
	Share of real government consumption expenditure net of spending on defense and education in real GDP
Investment:	Share of real public domestic investment in real GDP
	Share of real private investment in real GDP
Taxation:	Effective tax rate on labor income[2**]
	Effective tax rate on capital income[2**]
Political variables:	Index of political rights (1=most rights, 7=least rights)
	Index of civil liberties (1=most free, 7=least free)
	Number of assassinations per million inhabitants per year
	Number of revolutions per year
Trade and openness:	Share of exports in GDP
	Share of imports in GDP

Human capital:

Terms of trade shock[3]
Distance[4]
Measure of free trade openness[5]
Measure of tariff restriction[6]
Total gross enrolment for higher education
Total gross enrolment for primary education
Total gross enrolment for secondary education
Average schooling years of total population older than 25

All variables were taken from the Barro-Lee data set except the indexed ones. Single starred variables are derived from the latest version of the Penn World Table (1995); Double starred variables were taken from Daveri and Tabellini (1997).

APPENDIX NOTES

1. Growth rates are average annual growth rates for the corresponding five year periods;
2. Tax data are derived by "shifting" the five year periods used by Daveri and Tabellini one year backwards. Shifting of a period is done by first assuming tax rates in each year within a Daveri and Tabellini period to equal the period average after which the yearly tax rates are averaged for the appropriate five year periods used in this paper;
3. Terms of trade shock is constructed as growth rate of export prices minus growth rate of import prices;
4. Distance is the average distance to capitals of the world's 20 major exporters, weighted by values of bilateral imports in thousand kilometres;
5. The measure of free trade openness employed is constructed as .528 - .026 log (AREA) -.095 log (DIST), in which AREA is the size of land in million square miles and DIST is equal to the distance variable used;
6. The measure of tariff restriction is constructed as (free trade openness) = log (1+OWTI) in which OWTI is the own-import weighted tariff rate on intermediate inputs and capital goods.

[7]
Local Opportunities and Innovative Behaviour: A Meta-Analytic Study of European Cities

PETER NIJKAMP, ANDAKI KANGASHARJU AND
MARINA VAN GEENHUIZEN

2.1 The Critical Role of the Urban Milieu

Science and technology are often regarded as competitive weapons of cities or regions. Consequently, the interest in dedicated science and technology initiatives which aim to stimulate urban and regional economies is increasing. The growing role of knowledge in wealth creation at the urban and regional level is more and more recognized (see Van Geenhuizen and Nijkamp 1996a and 1996b; and Gibbons et al. 1994). There is, however, also an increasing awareness that knowledge creation needs specific urban or regional breeding place conditions, and – as a consequence – presently the critical role of urban and regional milieus and cultures in knowledge development is increasingly coming to the fore (see Florax 1992; Van Geenhuizen et al. 1996a and 1996b; and Lambooy 1996).

The above breeding place hypothesis presupposes that the process of knowledge development is not uniformly distributed over space, but is contingent on specific locational and local conditions, which may concern the availability of venture capital, access to advanced communications and transportation infrastructure, presence of research facilities and so forth. Many of these conditions are met in cities (or urban areas), which explains why such areas are prominent places for technological innovation and incubation (see Charles and Howells 1992; Davelaar 1991). In addition, there is the clear tendency that modern industries are becoming, on the one hand, more science-based and knowledge-intensive and, on the other hand, increasingly oriented towards urban areas regarding their management and research function. These areas are able to influence positively their future development, as many business activities in a post-industrial era tend to become sensitive to the urban milieu and urban quality of life. At one level globalization means a levelling of access to new knowledge and technology, such as through the spread of electronic networks and databases. Accordingly, urban areas are losing their advantage of knowledge producing localities. However, on another level particular uncertainties in

15

management and research can only be reduced in specific urban regions with excellent knowledge resources and learning capacity (Amin and Thrift 1994; Van Geenhuizen and Van der Knaap 1997; and Kanter 1995). This capacity is based on knowledge that is created and released locally but also on connectivity with sources of knowledge somewhere else in the world. The recent shift to knowledge- based and information-oriented urban areas takes place because of the network externalities, and the abundant knowledge resource and incubation potential of these areas. Thus, knowledge, science and technology are likely to become primary forces driving development towards and orientation to the urban milieu, which is marked by creativity, synergy and innovation (see Camagni 1991).

In a recent study by Van Geenhuizen et al. (1996b) it is argued that the urban knowledge capacity is a major asset in the economic competitive power of cities. This knowledge capacity comprises essential activities in the urban space, leading to several scale and scope advantages, notably (see FAST 1992):

- new research and development (R&D) results (including product innovation)
- new research methods (hardware and software) (including process innovation)
- new dissemination and marketing channels for research products (or innovations)
- new ways of organizing and managing R&D.

In the same FAST document it is argued – and empirically demonstrated on the basis of a large sample of European cities – that the local availability of a knowledge and information pool (e.g. skilled staff and scientists) is critical for the production of new R&D results, followed by availability of land and buildings, local suppliers of equipment, and presence of local financial institutions. A more detailed analysis of the local knowledge and information pool brought to light that several local factors are important here: skilled labour, training support for researchers, presence of libraries, presence of conference facilities, availability of local cooperation partners, local subcontractors and management links with local educational facilities.

In conclusion, modern cities have the opportunity to act as major islands of science-based innovations through the use of local networks offering local economic synergy and through the connectivity with (inter)national information and communication networks. Further empirical evidence on the relevance of the 'local milieu' for future innovations activities of European companies can be found in Traseler et al. (1994). Most notable is the overwhelming importance for European firms of labour market skills and training support regarding all four types of innovation. This is followed by local synergy from suppliers, subcontractors, customers, and universities for product innovations, and connectivity advantages (through telecommunication and transport) regarding other types of innovation.

16

Clearly, it is also evident that several cities have major deficiencies in the supply of the above success conditions. For example, several firms mention lack of office space as a major bottleneck. Also local support (e.g. contacts with the local public sector and the attitude of local politicians towards the R&D sector) are usually regarded as major impediments (see again FAST 1992). In general, access to local and international transport and telecommunication networks appears to be a top priority urban policy concern. The FAST dossier then concludes that there is need for action.

All cities in the New Europe will have to come to grips with the fact that economic welfare will depend on the establishment of an integrated system of creation and transfer of scientific knowledge as the knowledge content of goods and services is rising. Income opportunities of citizens and the public sector will critically depend on the innovation potential of cities. Enhancing the milieu as a necessary condition for such a potential to materialize becomes a top priority task. It will require a multilevel approach as the milieu is the result of actions by many decision-making units in the private and public sector.

Although it has to be recognized that in particular modern information and communication allow in principle for a rapid diffusion of scientific knowledge, in reality many innovative activities are rather centripetal as far as their invention, development and management is concerned. Consequently, we observe concentration and deconcentration tendencies at the same time. Clearly, improvement of knowledge networks at a wider scale than the metropolitan level would be needed to cope with the problems of peripherality and of the social-geographical exclusion.

2.2   Local Dynamics and Innovativeness

Regional and local dynamics depend to a large extent on entrepreneurial innovation. Besides, intrinsic regional features may affect innovativeness of firms within a given region, in addition to the different engagement of these firms in the development of new technologies and processes. Thus, on the one hand, the region's innovative activity is determined by R&D activity, size, market power, industry, and phase of the 'industry-technology' life-cycle of firms located in the region (see Ormrod 1996 and Love et al. 1996). On the other hand, regional characteristics affect the innovative activity of firms by enhancing or inhibiting the effects of innovative inputs of firms in the region. Davelaar (1991) coins these factors as production structure and 'production milieu' components, respectively. Consequently, firms which are located in different regions, but have identical innovative inputs, may have different innovative outputs resulting in differing innovativeness of regions (see Figure 2.1). According to Camagni

17

(1991), the local (innovative) milieu may enhance innovativeness and thus growth of firms, if it reduces the intrinsic uncertainty of the innovation process concerned. Clearly, there is a complex array of factors determining local economic dynamics.

A fairly comprehensive analysis of spatial aspects of innovation has been given by Davelaar (1991) who distinguishes four groups of local factors which affect local innovativeness: (A) agglomeration economies which include location economies accruing from the presence of the same industry, and urban economies accruing from the presence of different industries; (B) demography and population structure which refers to local resources of human capital, local customers and size of the local market area; (C) availability of specialized information and intensive communication networks (information infrastructure) also including educational institutes; and (D) social overhead capital (physical and institutional infrastructure) which responds faster to new demand for technological systems in central areas than in the periphery and which requires various local institutions and physical infrastructure (see also Davelaar and Nijkamp 1997). These force fields are mapped out in Figure 2.1. We will translate some of the major linkages from Figure 2.1 in four testable hypotheses in an empirical setting.

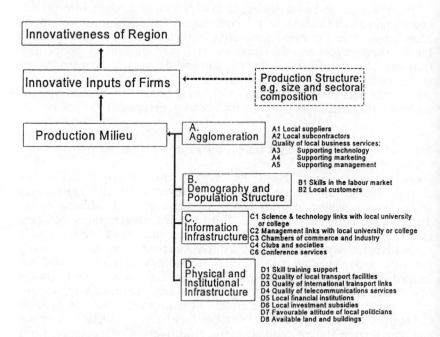

Figure 2.1   Operational variables for the four groups of explanatory local factors (A–D)

It needs to be mentioned that the critical role of the so-called 'production milieu' can also be interpreted in a different way. Advocates of the 'innovative milieu' school argue that, in addition to infrastructural factors, human capital, (mainly) informal linkages between firms in a region and synergy effects from a common cultural, psychological and political background are decisive (Camagni 1991). In other words, this school emphasizes more the synergy effects, which promote a collective learning process and reduce dynamic uncertainty, than Davelaar's static local factors, like infrastructure, which reduce transaction costs and produce external economies (see also Gertler 1996 and Harrison 1996).

The importance of local resources of human capital results from the fact that it tends to stimulate local collective learning processes, because labour is more mobile within a region than between regions. Boschma (1994) argues that local education and research facilities contribute to this local accumulation of skills and knowledge, because producers gain when at least part of the costs of job training as well as basic R&D are carried out by such institutions specialized in knowledge acquisition and transfer.

Furthermore, Camagni (1991) emphasizes the importance of informal linkages both between firms and within various economic actors such as firms, employees and institutions. Local formal and informal networks between firms, which are essential in the acquisition of the latest technology, will likely lead to lower information gathering costs. Local institutions are important parts of local networks, because they overcome market imperfections which inhibit innovative behaviour. The development of collective knowledge as well as formal and informal linkages between suppliers of labour, capital and institutions contribute to a regional identity and culture, which may result in a desire for cooperation. According to Camagni (1991), common cultural roots are important in the formation of tacit knowledge in order to understand and use complex messages, and in the formation of commonly accepted beliefs in new products and technologies in a given area.

Our previous observation on the role of uncertainty in innovative behaviour may lead to our first testable hypothesis. Because process innovations enhance the use of existing products, the uncertainty is lower here, and thus the role of local factors tends to be smaller. Therefore, the first hypothesis is:

H1: local factors are more important for product than for process innovations.

It should be noted that in the standard approach to the analysis of technological change, the innovation model has essentially three stages: (i) basic research produces a scientific or technological discovery; (ii) creative firms develop this invention towards a new product; (iii) and existing firms apply this product for commercial use. Through market reactions, successful commercial use has feedback effects on scientific basic research as well as on R&D efforts of firms (see e.g. Kline and Rosenberg 1987). Davelaar (1991) argues that such a change in science and technology leads to major inventions and basic innovations which, together with socio-institutional and economic forces, form a new technological system whose occurrence may be discontinuous in time. Dosi (1988) emphasizes the importance of basic research from the viewpoint that the progress in scientific knowledge widens the pool of potential technological paradigms (or technological systems) from which only a small set of paradigms is actually developed. New technological systems, which happen to emerge, give birth to new technological trajectories or sequences of innovations, along with a swarming process of (new Schumpeterian) firms producing further product and process innovations with a decreasing marginal product. A good example of such a technological regime (or system) is the microelectronics industry which has been built up around such major innovations as the transistor (Boschma 1994). These swarming processes along technological trajectories form life cycles for technologies and industries. In essence, this approach is closely related to the well known spatial product life cycle approach developed by Vernon (1966). When adjustments and innovations within existing systems become rare and marginal, new technological systems or regimes will eventually replace the old ones. Therefore, our second hypothesis is related to this life cycle approach so that economic dynamics is introduced.

At the beginning of an industrial life cycle firms produce numerous early (and often significant) innovations, which are mostly product innovations and which are encouraged by the technological push of a basic scientific invention. Products are then not yet standardized, which means that the uncertainty concerning market reactions is high. Innovations during this phase put specific demands on the surrounding business environment. Information concerning unstandardized products, market reactions and skills on the labour market in terms of producing and developing these new products are important conditions for a successful innovation. In a later stage, when main products within the new industry have been established and when they are becoming more standardized, the role of the business environment may decline. Therefore, our second hypothesis to be tested is:

H2: local factors are more important for a (more innovative) younger than for an (less innovative) older industry.

Clearly, this hypothesis is plausible, because younger industries tend to produce more product innovations than older ones. Local factors are more important for product than process innovations for the reasons mentioned above. In addition, new product innovations tend to become more marginal during the later phases of the industrial life cycle, while process innovations tend to become more wide spread. Product innovations lose importance over time, as they cannot be created endlessly within one and the same technological system. Process

20

innovations will then gradually take over, because when further product innovations are increasingly hard to create and when products become more standardized, firms try to develop better production processes to ensure or enhance their competitiveness. Thus, free market competition is a driving force.

It is of course true that local factors are not equally valuable. And therefore, we will also study more carefully the subset of local factors, which appear to act often as critical success conditions for entrepreneurial innovations. Such a more detailed analysis will be carried out in order to model the effects of this subset of local factors (production milieu) on innovativeness of firms. The impact of the 'production milieu' in empirical research is not always very significant. Davelaar (1991) argues that after controlling for the industrial structure, there is limited evidence for a positive impact of the urban 'milieu' on innovativeness of firms. This statement however, may be questioned and should at least be further investigated and tested. Therefore. the third testable hypothesis in our series is:

H3: the local 'production milieu' has a positive impact on innovativeness of firms in the area concerned.

Having specified three hypotheses to be tested in an applied context, we will now proceed by describing the data base for our empirical work.

2.3   The Data Set: Description and Exploratory Analysis

The hypotheses of our study require information on the micro level of firms. The data set used in our empirical work stems from the so-called URBINNO study[1] and has been compiled by extensively interviewing many manufacturing companies in the United Kingdom (208 firms), the Netherlands (33) and Italy (32). Interviews on a structured basis were held among firms in different manufacturing industries in different cities. For practical reasons, the empirical investigation in our study is mainly concentrated on those industries which have for the sector concerned a sufficient number of observations. These are: manufacturing of machinery and equipment (SIC 29); electrical machinery and apparatus (SIC 31); medical precision and optical instruments, watches and clocks (SIC 33); and motor vehicles, trailers and semitrailers (SIC 34). In addition to these sectors, our empirical investigation is also dealing with two other, aggregate sectors in order to have a sufficiently large data base, viz. textile, clothing and leather industries (SIC 17, 18 and 19 taken together), and basic materials and metal industries (SIC 27 and 28). This seems a plausible approach, because the latter industries are sufficiently close to one another to benefit from the same source of technological development, so that they are likely to live on the same technological trajectory. The urban background of innovative behaviour has been given due attention in the

21

interviews, in the sense that a systematic typology of cities in all the countries concerned is made.

We have adopted the most straightforward measure of innovativeness (see Harrison et al. 1996); innovativeness of industries in a city is measured by calculating the percentage of firms that has adopted an innovation during the past few years. The frequency of these firms is given in Figure 2.2. These results indicate that 39.9 percent of the total of 273 firms mentioned an innovation in the sense defined above. At a two-digit level, industry 34 turned out to be the most innovative, as 77.3 percent of the firms in that industry mentioned an innovation. In contrast, in the industries 27-28 together only 29.0 percent mentioned an innovation, while this figure was even down to 21.1 percent for the firms in the industries 17-19. There are thus quite some variations in outcomes, and it is therefore interesting to seek a spatial bias in these outcomes.

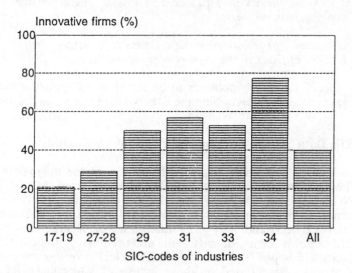

Figure 2.2   Innovativeness of firms by industry class

We will now first present some exploratory results from a descriptive analysis of our data set. To begin with, our two first hypotheses (H_1 and H_2) on the importance of the local 'milieu' will be tested by means of exploratory background variables derived from Davelaar's (1991) classification into four local factors (see for details Figure 2.1 above). The lists of specific local factors under the four headings are examples of factors whose presence will plausibly contribute to the innovativeness of firms in the region. The factors distinguished in Figure 2.1 are the ones included in above mentioned URBINNO questionnaire. Given a set of individual firm data, the importance of local factors for product and process innovations will be tested. Figure 2.3 shows the results for all

22

industries together. This figure includes only those 11 local factors which the respondents considered commonly as valuable factors in terms of either product or process innovations.

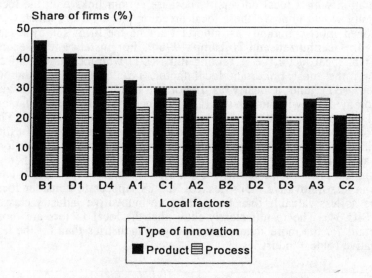

Figure 2.3 Percentage of firms which consider local factors important for innovation

According to the firms surveyed, local factors are more important for product than for process innovations. There are only two exceptions: 'Management links with local university or college' (C2) and 'Quality of local business services supporting technology' (A3) are more important from the point of view of process innovations than from that of product innovations. Hence, our overall results suggest that the firms in our sample behaved in accordance with our first hypothesis (H1). The results also indicate that local skills in the labour market (B1), and local skills training support (D1) are the most important local factors. It appears that 48.6 percent of firms consider skills in the labour market as of 'some importance' or of 'major importance' for product innovations, while 36.1 percent of firms do so for process innovations. The respective numbers concerning training support are 41.4 and 36.1 percent. From an indepth analysis among medium sized firms in the Netherlands it appeared that the strong labour market concern dealt with the following three types of attributes: (1) shortages of certain handicraft skills, (2) shortages in skills to apply modern technology in traditional fields, such as informatics in textile industry, and (3) a general shortage of practical skills of young people who complete vocational and academic training (Van Geenhuizen and Nijkamp 1996a). Clearly the latter two point to a potentially important role of local universities. The quality of telecommunications services (D4), local

23

suppliers (A1) and science and technology links with universities (C1) are the next important factors.

The above results imply that firms can apparently benefit from cooperation with a local university, because certain links with the local university would improve those local breeding place factors which were mentioned most commonly as important among the firms surveyed (see also Van Geenhuizen and Nijkamp 1996b). For instance, the second important local factor, i.e. 'Training links (D1) with local universities', supports the most important local factor, i.e. 'Skills in the labour market' (B1); and a nearly as important factor, viz. 'Science and technology links with university' (C1) enhances knowhow. Both factors would be possible candidates to promote innovativeness of firms. The role of university links of firms for innovativeness will be further examined by using a logit and rough set analysis below in Subsections 2.4.1 and 2.4.2, respectively.

Figure 2.4 presents the results for the selected industries, for example, firms in less innovative industries, SIC 27-28, appear to consider local factors as less valuable than firms in more innovative industry classes (e.g. SIC 34). The results clearly show that the local factors are more important for the more innovative (younger) industries than for the less innovative (older) industries.

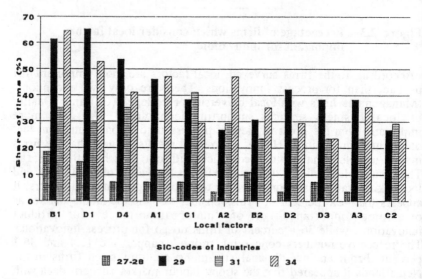

Figure 2.4   Percentage of firms in different industries which consider a local factor as important for innovation

Figure 2.5 presents the results for a classification of industries (this classification was made according to industrial innovative behaviour). The black bar represents highly innovative and the bar with streaks low innovative industries (57 percent of firms in the highly innovating industries mentioned an innovation in contrast to only 18 percent of firms in the low innovating industries). Local factors are clearly more often important for highly innovative than for low innovative industries. Therefore, these results indicate that – regardless of the classification used (high or low innovative industry, different industries) – there is a structural tendency that the more firms innovate the more important local factors are. Clearly, these results support our second hypothesis (H_2).

So far we have been investigating how firms in different industries value local factors in terms of innovations. The exploratory analysis did not reveal, however, whether or not local factors actually affect innovativeness of firms, i.e. so far we have not tested our third hypothesis. This is the subject of the next section.

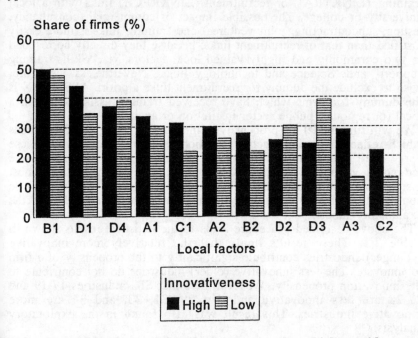

Figure 2.5   Percentage of firms in two categories which consider a local factor as important for innovation

2.4   Explanatory Analysis

2.4.1   *Logit Analysis*

We will now offer an explanatory analysis for the firm's innovative behaviour by applying a logit analysis. We will model innovativeness by industrial and production milieu variables in order to test our second and third hypotheses. Logit analysis cannot be applied to testing of our first hypothesis, because our dataset does not include separate measurable variables for product and process innovations.

In our data set on industrial attributes only 0–1 categorical variables are available. For various modelling purposes we have altogether 13 dummy variables in our data set. In the present context, the most interesting variables are of course industrial and urban 'milieu' variables. Variables which begin with IND... (e.g. IND1719DUM) are dummies for the 6 selected industries. The urban 'milieu' variables mainly represent those local factors, which were commonly found to be important among firms surveyed, viz. various links of firms with local institutions. A variable which begins with LINK... is one of the 3 dummies for the industries which have commercial (LINKCOMM), training (LINKTRAI) or recruitment (LINKRECR) links with a local university or college. The possible impact of commercial (consultancy, testing, subcontracting, joint ventures) and training links is more easily justified than that of recruitment links, because they directly correspond to two commonly and highly valued local factors, viz. 'Skills training support' and 'Science and technology links'. Nevertheless, we do not wish to exclude the dummy for recruitment links a priori. ASSTRAIN is the dummy for firms which have received training assistance from a local (or regional) public sector institution or agency.[2]

We will first model the propensity to innovate by using all 13 dummies which reflect industrial structure, location, or local factors. We will use here Theil's sequential elimination procedure, by discarding one redundant variable at a time from the equation beginning with the most insignificant variable (Theil 1971). This reduction procedure will be continued until only statistically significant regressors are left in the explanatory model.

The above described procedure leads to the statistical results shown in Table 2.1. These results imply that the relatively more innovative (younger) industries contribute significantly to the propensity of a firm to innovate. The less innovative (older) industries do not contribute to the innovation propensity. We recall here that SIC-industries 17-19 and 27-28 are less innovative and that 29, 31, 33, and 34 are more innovative industries. This result was also found in the exploratory analysis.

Training links appear to be positively related to innovativeness, but commercial or recruitment links are not (see Table 2.1). This indicates that at least such local factors as training links with a local university tend to contribute to innovations, a result which partially supports our third hypothesis (H₃). This also complies with the above obtained results that 'milieu' factors, which affect innovativeness of firms, are not equally important. In particular, this result is in line with the previous finding that firms regard skills training support more often as an important local factor inducing innovations than science and technology links (commercial links) or managerial links with the local university. It also turns out that training support from other local or regional institutions is not a statistically significant regressor either. This implies that skills training support offered by a university tends to be more important than that offered by other skills training institutions.

Table 2.1 Innovation as dependent variable in a logit analysis

-2 Log Likelihood: 367.30157 (restricted model)
-2 Log Likelihood: 323.413 (full model)

Variable	B	S.E.
IND29DUM	1.0613	.3427
IND31DUM	1.2892	.4229
IND33DUM	1.2720	.5115
IND34DUM	2.0964	.5507
LINKTRAI	.9312	.2799
Constant	-1.6011	.2635

Note: B=estimated coefficient and S.E.=standard error.

A related question is now for which industries the most important factor, viz. training links, contributes to innovativeness. Also, an important question whether is the other links (commercial and recruitment) contribute to innovativeness in any industry. In other words, we are interested in finding out a possible confirmation for our second hypothesis and further support for our third hypothesis. We can partially test these hypotheses by distinguishing the firms within each industry into two classes, viz. those with a link (LINKTRAIN, LINKCOMME and LINKRECR) and those without a link (LINKTRNO, LINKCONO and LINKRECNO). This subdivision is made for all three links, namely training, commercial and recruitment links. After the model reduction procedure described above the estimation results are given in Table 2.2. This table prompts us to make the following comments on the results.
The firms in the industries 29 and 33 with training links appear to innovate more often than the firms in the other industries with training links and the firms in the same industries without training links (see Table 2.2). This implies that training links are more important for the relatively more innovative (younger) than for less innovative (older) industries, and thus gives partial support to the second hypotheses. In addition, the firms in the industry 31 with commercial links tend to innovate more often than the firms in other industries or in the same industries without commercial links. On the one hand, firms in industry 34 with commercial links appear to be more innovative than firms in other industries with commercial links and firms in the same industry without commercial links. On the other hand, an opposite result is found: firms in industry 34 without commercial links turn out to be

27

more innovative. These results imply that commercial links would not play a decisive role in the motor vehicle industry (34), but would certainly play a role in the electronics industry (31). Nonetheless, this implies that commercial links are also more important for the relatively younger than for older industries, which also renders partial support to the second hypothesis. Also the third hypothesis is partly supported by these results, which indicate that such local factors as training and commercial links with a local university influence the innovativeness of firms.

Table 2.2 Innovation as dependent variable in a logit analysis

–2 Log Likelihood: 367.302 (restricted)		
–2 Log Likelihood: 310.698 (full)		
Variable	B	S.E.
IND33DUM*LINKTRAIN	3.0709	1.0717
IND29DUM*LINKTRAIN	2.4603	.5762
IND34DUM*LINKCOMM	2.1981	.6776
IND34DUM*LINKCOMNO	2.2469	.8177
IND31DUM*LINKCOMM	1.6873	.5708
IND29DUM*LINKRECRU	-1.7174	.8552
Constant	-.9942	.1608

Table 2.2 also shows that firms in industry 29 with recruitment links tend to innovate less often than firms in other industries with such links and firms in the same industry without recruitment links. This does not seem to be the case for other industries. These results tend to suggest that for one of the younger industrial sectors the recruitment links would even have a negative effect on innovativeness, a finding which implies a low importance of recruitment links for innovativeness. Despite the latter observation our statistical results seem to largely confirm our two hypotheses.

2.4.2   Rough Set Analysis

A limitation of the analysis in Subsection 2.4.1 is the large number of categorical (binary) variables. Now we will seek some further evidence for the importance of the production milieu for innovativeness of firms (H_3) by applying rough set analysis. Rough set analysis is a fairly recent classification method of an 'if-then' nature (see e.g. Pawlak 1991; and Slowinski 1993).[3] The analysis classifies objects into equivalence classes using available attributes which act as equivalence relationships for the objects considered. Objects in the same equivalence class are indiscernible (indistinguishable). A class which contains only indispensable equivalence relationships (attributes) is called a core. An attribute is indispensable if the classification of the objects becomes less precise when that attribute is left out. The values of the attributes of all objects may be subdivided into condition (background) and decision (response) attributes.

The aim of rough set analysis is usually first, to classify decision attributes on the basis of condition attributes and second, to form decision rules which are implication relationships between the description of the condition attributes and that of decision attributes. Decision rules can be seen as conditional statements of an 'if-then' nature. Rough set analysis basically evaluates the importance of attributes for a classification of objects, reduces all superfluous objects and attributes, discovers most significant relationships between condition attributes and objects' assignments to decision classes, and represents these relationships e.g. in the form of decision rules (Slowinski and Stefanowski 1993). Rough set analysis is clearly very appropriate in case of qualitative or categorical statements obtained in interviews. Therefore, we will apply rough set analysis for our empirical work on the background factors of innovative behaviour.

In our rough set analysis a total of 273 firms appear to act as indiscernible objects. The decision attribute (dependent variable) here is whether or not a firm has innovated. Our investigation will focus on those condition attributes (local milieu factors) which in the above exploration turned out to be the most important. The condition attributes (explanatory variables) are the following: 1) industry (SIC industries 17–19, 27–28, 29, 31, 33, 34, and the class 'rest'); 2) training links (yes, no); 3) commercial links (yes, no); 4) recruitment links (yes, no) with a local university; and 5) assistance (investment, training, or other) given by a local or regional institution.[4] Production milieu variables (2-5) represent important local factors, i.e., various links of firms with local institutions (see Figure 2.2).

As shown in the first row in Table 2.3, the condition attributes appear to allocate 69 firms to the class 'innovation' and 126 firms to the class 'no innovation' (lower approximations). This means that out of the total of 273 firms, 71.4 percent firms can be classified to either the innovative or the non-innovative category. An interesting rough set result is that all condition attributes turn out to belong to the core. In other words, there are no redundant attributes, which means that an exclusion of one of these features would reduce the accuracy of classification. This result tends to show that both the production milieu and structure are important attributes of innovativeness. With regard to production structure, however, we need to make a restriction. The production structure is only an important attribute when the industry sectors involved are significantly overrepresented in the urban areas under study.

The relative importance of the attributes can be investigated by removing, one at a time, the attributes from the core. The lower rows in Table 2.3 show the number of classifications and the quality (percentage) of classifications when each attribute is excluded in turn. The second row indicates that when the attribute 'Industry' is excluded, the quality of classification is the lowest; then, only 30.4 percent of the firms can be classified. The quality of the classification decreases the least when the attribute 'Recruitment links' is excluded. Then, even 65.6 percent of the firms can still be classified. Although link attributes (milieu variables), namely training, commercial, recruitment and assistance attributes, tend to be less important than the others for the proper classification of the firms in terms of innovativeness, they belong to the core and are necessary for a high quality classification. In other words, the above rough set results clearly indicate that production milieu tends to affect the innovativeness of firms in a region, a finding which supports our third hypothesis (H_3). Thus, we may conclude that also rough set results tend to confirm our prior expectations laid down in three hypotheses.

Table 2.3 Lower approximations for rough set classes

N=273	Innovation	Innovation	Quality of classification
Classification with core attributes			
	69	126	0.714
Classification with a temporarily reduced condition attribute			
Industry	26	57	0.304
Training links	60	104	0.601
Assistance	56	110	0.608
Commercial links	56	112	0.615
Recruitment links	61	118	0.656

2.5   Concluding Comments

Our industrial society is increasingly moving towards a knowledge-based society, characterized by close links with R&D and educational centres. The present study has investigated the importance of local factors on innovativeness. Empirical results on the importance of local factors supported the three main hypotheses specified. The exploratory analysis produced some evidence that local factors are considered as more important for product than for process innovations and that they are more important for more innovative, younger industries than for less innovative, older industries. We also saw that a possible cooperation of firms with a university may incorporate those factors, which were most commonly mentioned as important, viz. skills of the labour force by training links, and science and technology links. The logit analysis revealed that among those links with universities, especially training links tend to promote more innovativeness than commercial or recruitment links, a result which leads to a policy recommendation on the significance of increased schooling and training expenditures. Both rough set and logit analyses produced also some evidence that the production structure of regions is not insignificant, but does certainly not entirely govern the innovativeness of regions, as in particular cases distinct local factors appear to affect innovativeness of firms. This implies that the production 'milieu' component also clearly affects innovativeness of regions. In other words, this calls for actions by local and regional governments to improve the quality of the local business environment.

This analysis had a strong focus on links of firms in European cities with local universities, based upon specific labour market needs. Two factors which also appeared to influence the innovativeness of regions, i.e. local production networks (suppliers, subcontractors and customers) and local connectivity with larger (global) networks (telecommunication and transport links) have received much less attention. It is the interaction of the three factors from a knowledge perspective, which is an interesting field for further research, because it is largely open. The question then is whether the local labour market needs and production network needs are concerned with reduction of uncertainty using locally produced and released knowledge, or – via connectivity – using globally available knowledge (potentially in a specific niche). It would be interesting to scrutinize whether there is a difference between European cities in local self-containment of knowledge production, local conditions to insert global knowledge in the local economy, and the existence of a blend of local and global knowledge, and how this relates to the need of innovative firms for fast adjustment in view of risk and uncertainty. Thus, particularly the relationship between the local and global asks for attention, in terms of mutual dependency and cross-fertilization. In addition, it is increasingly realised that knowledge networks – regarding type and geographical scale – may be different between different (young) sectors and even between product groups within sectors (Storper 1996). Dependent on different demands for local knowledge and access to global knowledge, different urban policies need to be established in European cities.

Acknowledgements

This study was part of a research project funded by the Academy of Finland. The authors wish to thank Tomaso Pompili and Peter Townroe for their assistance in collecting the data.

References

Amin, A. and Thrift, N. (1994), 'Living in the Globe', in Amin, A. and Thrift, N. (eds), *Globalization, Institutions, and Regional Development in Europe*, Oxford University Press, Oxford, pp. 1–22.

31

Baaijens, S. and Nijkamp, P. (1997), 'Meta-Analytic Methods for Comparative and Exploratory Policy Research', *Journal of Policy Modelling* (forthcoming).

Bergh, van den J.C.J.M, Button, K. Nijkamp, P. and Pepping, G. (1997), *Meta-Analysis for Meso Environmental Policy*, Kluwer, Dordrecht.

Camagni, R. (1991), 'Local 'Milieu', Uncertainty and Innovation Networks: Towards a New Dynamic Theory of Economic Space', in Camagni, R. (ed.), *Innovation Networks: Spatial Perspectives*, Belhaven Press, London and New York, pp. 121–44.

Camagni, R. (1991), 'Local 'Milieu', Uncertainty and Innovation Networks: Towards a New Dynamic Theory of Economic Space', in Camagni, R. (ed.), *Innovation Networks: Spatial Perspectives*, Belhaven Press, London and New York, pp. 121–44.

Charles, D. and Howells, J. (1992), *Technology Transfer in Europe*, Belhaven, London.

Davelaar, E.J. (1991), *Regional Economic Analysis of Innovation and Incubation*, Avebury, Aldershot, UK.

Davelaar, E.J. and Nijkamp, P. (1997), 'Spatial Dispersion of Technological Innovation: A Review', in Bertuglia, C.S., Lombardo, S. and Nijkamp, P. (eds), *Innovative Behaviour in Space & Time*, Springer-Verlag, Berlin.

Dosi, G. (1988), 'The Nature of the Innovative Process', in Dosi, G. et al. (eds), *Technical Change and Economic Theory*, Printer Publishers, London and New York.

FAST (1992), 'The Future of European Cities; The Role of Science and Technology', Dossier no. 4, Commission of the European Communities, DG XII, Brussels.

Florax, R. (1992), *The University: A Regional Booster*, Avebury, Aldershot, UK.

Geenhuizen, M. van, Damman, M. and Nijkamp, P. (1996a), 'The Local Environment as a Supportive Operator in Innovation Diffusion', Research Memorandum 1996-15, Dept. of Economics, Free University, Amsterdam.

Geenhuizen, M. van, and van der Knaap, G.A. (1997), 'R&D and Regional Network Dynamics in the Dutch Pharmaceutical Industry', *Journal of Economic and Social Geography*, vol. 88, no. 4, pp. 307–70.

Geenhuizen, M. and Nijkamp, P. (1996a), 'What Makes the Local Environment Important for High Tech Small Firms', in Oakey, R. (ed.), *New Technology-Based Firms in the 1990s*, vol. II, Paul Chapman, London, pp. 141–51.

Geenhuizen, M. and Nijkamp, P. (1996b), 'Technology Transfer: How to Remove Obstacles in Advancing Employment Growth', in Kuklinski A. (ed.), *Production of Knowledge and the Dignity of Science*, Euroreg, Warsaw, pp. 79–96

Geenhuizen, M. van, Nijkamp, P. and Rijckenberg, H. (1996b), 'Universities as Key Actors in Knowledge-based Economic Growth,

Reserach Memorandum 1996–14', Dept. of Economics, Free University, Amsterdam.

Gertler, M.S. (1995), 'Being There: Proximity, Organization, and Culture in the Development and Adoption of Advanced Manufacturing Technologies', *Economic Geography*, vol. 71, no. 1, pp. 1–26.

Gibbons, M., Limoge, C., Nowotny, H.,Schwartzman, S., Scott, P. and Trow, M. (1994), *The Production of Knowledge: the Dynamics of Science and Research in Contemporary Societies*, Sage, London.

Harrison, B., Kelley, M.R. and Gant, J. (1996), 'Innovative Firm Behavior and Local Milieu: Exploring the Intersection of Agglomeration, Firm Effects, and Technological Change', *Economic Geography*, vol. 72, no. 3, pp. 233–58.

Kangasharju, A. and Nijkamp, P. (1997), 'Innovation Dynamics in Space: Local Actors and Local Factors', Discussion Paper, Tinbergen Institute, Free University of Amsterdam, (forthcoming).

Kanter, R.M. (1995), *World Class: Thriving Locally in a Global Market*, Simon and Schuster, New York.

Kline, S.J. and Rosenberg, N. (1987), 'An Overview of Innovation', in Landau, R. et al. (eds), *The Positive Sum Strategy*, National Academy Press, Washington, DC.

Lambooy, J.G. (1996), 'Knowledge Production Organization and Agglomeration Economies', Research Paper, Economic-Geographical Institute, University of Amsterdam.

Love, J.H., Ashcroft, B. and Dunlop, S. (1996), 'External Ownership, Corporate Structure and Product Innovation', Paper presented at 36th Congress of the European Regional Science Association.

Ormrod, R.O. (1990), 'Local Context and Innovation Diffusion in a Well-Connected World', *Economic Geography*, vol. 66, no. 2, pp. 109–22.

Ratti, R. (1991), 'Small and Medium-sized Enterprises, Local Synergies and Spatial Cycles of Innovation', in Camagni, R. (ed.), *Innovation Networks: Spatial Perspectives*, Belhaven Press, London and New York, pp. 71–88.

Storper, M. (1996), 'Innovation as Collective Action: Conventions, Products and Technologies', *Industrial and Corporate Change*, vol. 5, no. 3, pp. 731–90.

Theil, H. (1971), *Principles of Econometrics*, John Wiley, New York.

Traseler, J., Schubert, U. and Townroe, P.M. (1994), 'R&D Activities in Companies and Universities and their Role in Urban Development, Research Paper Vienna University of Economics and Business Administration.

Vernon, R. (1966), 'International Investment and Institutional Trade in the Product Cycle', *Quarterly Journal of Economics*, vol. 80, pp. 190–207.

Notes

1. The URBINNO group ('Urban Innovation') was a network of researchers in several European countries. The objective of the group was to study innovations in several urban areas from various points of view, viz. population, urban economy, institutions and infrastructure, and from a micro-urban (i.e. firm level) perspective.

2. Due to an incomplete dataset, our logit analysis had to exclude a few indicators on production structure which may be expected to affect the propensity to innovate (such as size, market power and growth rate of a firm).

3. Formally, a rough set is characterized by the feature that it is not possible to tell a priori which objects belong to a given set, although it is in principle possible to identify all objects which may belong to that set (see for details, Van den Bergh et al. 1997, and for several applications, e.g. Baaijens and Nijkamp 1997).

4. The analysis also included variables for areal categories (central, intermediate, and periphery) and competitive edge (innovativeness; cost-effectiveness; and marketing, financing, or other). The results for those variables are given in Kangasharju and Nijkamp (1997).

34

[8]

Spatial Dynamics and Government Policy: An Artificial Intelligence Approach to Comparing Complex Systems

Peter Nijkamp[*], Jacques Poot[**], and Gabriella Vindigni[***]
[*] Department of Spatial Economics, Free University Amsterdam
[**] Department of Economics, Victoria University of Wellington
[***] Department of Economics, University of Catania

18.1 Complexity in a Dynamic Spatial-Economic Context

Complexity is concerned with the unpredictable nature of non-linear and dynamic systems. Complexity can relate to a dynamic causal sequence of events at an object-specific micro-level [such as in the case of the weather, business performance, market impact of innovation, individual well-being, etc.], but it may also refer to the outcomes of repeated experiments in a semi-controlled setting. A comparison of the results of case studies is a good illustration of the latter interpretation of complexity. In this case, it is useful to see to what extent the outcome is shaped by the systemic background and the specific research methodologies used.

The rapidly changing and often unpredictable economic events of the past decades call for a thorough analysis of the behavioural and methodological foundations of contemporary economic systems. This applies not only to national economies, but also to industrial systems at both a regional and a global level. We are witnessing in modern economic research an increase of interest in the behaviour of actors and agents from a micro-economic perspective, with a view to deriving behavioural implications at a meso or macro-level [e.g. supranational economic policy, group decision-making, industrial concentration tendencies, institutional network developments, international mergers, functioning of spatial labour markets, etc.]. This multi-layer interlinked and inherently complex behaviour lies at the heart of modern theories on economic dynamics, such as endogenous growth theory, evolutionary theory, externality theory, game theory, models of search behaviour, network theory, location theory under monopolistic competition, or option theory. Complex economic behaviour appears in a wide range of forms in the space-time context, from slow dynamics [e.g. changes in trade and location patterns, the process of regulatory reforms or evolving technological trajectories] to fast dynamics [e.g. changes in financial markets, in transport patterns or in industrial growth]. Intermediate and hybrid forms of dynamics may emerge as well [e.g. in urban evolution or in the transformation of social security systems]. In this context, institutional configurations may play a mitigating role, but also have a retarding effect, as has been shown in recent studies on transaction costs in the private sector and in the public sector.

The development of economic systems in the industrialised world has in recent years exhibited various dynamic patterns, partly caused by drastic changes in international markets and relations [such as in Central and Eastern Europe, the Asian crisis, etc.], and partly by intrinsic changes in the way that economic systems themselves function [e.g. greater deregulation, outsourcing]. There have been drastic changes in market configurations not only at the local but also at the global level. The internationalisation of business life has led to a situation where local and global markets are, more than ever before, spatially-linked platforms of economic activity. The parallel development in institutional reform [e.g. privatisation of networks] has created enormous economic flexibility and adjustment potential which has had far-reaching implications for the behaviour of actors and agents.

Given these complex economic changes, it is not surprising that during the last decade there has been considerable scientific interest in the causes of economic growth, both local and global. The seminal contributions by Lucas (1988) and Romer (1986) have generated a wave of new research. Initially, the aim was to formulate dynamic general equilibrium models with precisely formulated microeconomic foundations that would enable a clearer understanding of processes such as physical and human capital accumulation, innovation, or knowledge and product differentiation in terms of their impact on long-run economic growth. The extension of the traditional Solow-Swan growth framework with various endogenous learning and technology mechanisms has led to a wealth of literature since the 1980s on endogenous growth (see Nijkamp and Poot 1998 for a survey which also addresses the spatial implications). These growth theories focus on the role of various externalities related to technological change: specialisation and trade, monopoly rents from innovation and 'creative destruction', human capital and government policy. There have also already been several attempts to endogenise technical progress within models designed to address environmental issues and sustainability (e.g. Gradus and Smulders 1993; den Butter, Delling and Hofkes 1995; van den Bergh and Nijkamp 1994; Bovenberg and Smulders 1995). Other treatments of the relationship between technology, growth and externalities have stressed its disequilibrium, uncertainty and evolutionary [or Schumpeterian] character (e.g. Dosi et al. 1988; Aghion and Howitt 1998; and in an environmental context; Faber and Proops 1990; Clark, Perez-Trejo and Allen 1995).

At the same time, an empirical research programme has emerged, setting out to explain the variation in long-run growth rates across regions or countries by means of cross section or panel data. Both the theoretical and the empirical research programmes have reached a stage of maturity at which graduate level text books have been published (Barro and Sala-i-Martin 1995; Aghion and Howitt 1998), providing an excellent overview of what has been accomplished to date. Yet, as the authors of recent books and other surveys of the recent literature have concluded, much research remains to be done. Firstly, the empirical work on growth accounting and convergence at the macro-level has rarely provided a direct verification of the micro-level behavioural mechanisms that drive the growth process in the theoretical models. Secondly, much of the theoretical literature has been concerned with models of single, closed economies. Thirdly, while the theoretical research points to why and how governments can influence the long-run growth rate, the empirical literature on this aspect appears rather fragmented and inconclusive.

Endogenous growth phenomena, as described above in the context of complexity, are also particularly relevant for the study of the interactive behaviour of actors in modern *evolutionary* economics. Recently much attention has been given to evolutionary and learning processes in the game-theoretic literature, see for example Maynard Smith and Price (1973), Kandori, Mailath and Rob (1993), Young (1993), Weibull (1995), Samuelson (1997) and the survey paper of Van der Laan and Tieman (1998). The main stance taken in this literature is that players react to the circumstances with a bounded rationality. They learn 'how to play the game' through time. In most studies of this kind, we begin with a population of players who, together, form a social network. It is often assumed that the players are randomly matched in pairs and play one stage of the game at each round of play. At any time, the players use learning rules to decide how to play. Such learning rules map the past history of play into what to do next. A closely related approach is to assume that the fraction of players using a certain strategy evolves over time through some replicator dynamics, see e.g. Crawford (1989), Björnerstedt and Weibull (1993), Ellison (1993) and Karandikar et al. (1998). The central question addressed in this literature is whether the resulting dynamic system converges and, if so, what is the outcome?

The strategies of researchers who build on the successes and failures of earlier endeavours may also be interpreted in an evolutionary game-theoretic context! Consequently, there is much scope for international comparative research [e.g. through meta-analysis, or value transfer] and it is not suprising, given our earlier observations, that this strand of research is gaining in importance in economics. *Meta-analysis* is a promising approach which has been employed in the present study. In Section 18.2 we offer a concise introduction to meta-analysis as a modern tool for research synthesis. Next, in Section 18.3, we introduce *rough set analysis* as a recently developed artificial intelligence tool, which is able to draw generally valid inferences from a series of classified studies. Then in Section 18.4 we examine some studies on government expenditure and economic growth in order to create a sample of studies on the role of governments in complex spatial systems which can be empirically tested. Rough set analysis will then be used in Section 18.5 as a method for extracting valid results. Section 18.concludes the chapter with some reflections on the findings and implications for public policy.

18.2 Research Synthesis and Meta-Analysis

In the field of economics research, we are seeing the emergence of a veritable 'knowledge economy', and an exponential growth in the number of research findings. In certain areas, such as studies of innovation or of government policy impact, an enormous number of publications exist. This suggests that there is an urgent need for a synthesis of such results. The question is whether a common knowledge pool can be identified from so many individual studies. Meta-analysis is one of the more promising quantitative research techniques for creating a synthesis from different studies on similar issues. While the approach has a relatively long pedigree in certain areas of research [e.g. medical science, physics, psychology], its use in economics is rather more recent (see e.g. Van den Bergh et al. 1997; Florax, Nijkamp and Willis 2000).

The introduction of meta-analysis as a formal analytical procedure has emerged from the need to be able to summarise and infer general results from scientific studies. Glass (1976, pp.3-8), who coined the term meta-analysis, provides a simple definition of this approach: 'Meta-analysis refers to the statistical analysis of a large collection of results from individual studies for the purpose of integrating the findings. It connotes a rigorous alternative to the casual, narrative discussions of research studies which typify our attempt to make sense of the rapidly expanding research literature'.

Meta-analysis is not a single technique, but a collection of quantitative methods that serve to derive additional [cumulated] knowledge from the *ex post* analysis of a well-defined set of independent [case] studies on similar issues. Clearly, case study research focuses essentially on the inference of general or transferable findings and thus also involves optimal experimentation (for further details see Yin 1994). However, a major problem inherent in social science research is the lack of controlled experimentation in empirical investigations. Case studies carried out in different countries rarely have a common design. This is clearly exemplified by the *ceteris paribus* conditions often assumed in such studies. At best, case studies addressing the same phenomenon, may use more or less the same research methodology or employ similar data. This of course makes a rigorous synthesis difficult, and also the degree of transferability may sometimes be questionable. It is a particular problem when case studies which were never meant to be integrated are pooled in a meta-analytical experiment.

The conditions for a correct application of conventional statistical meta-analysis are fairly stringent. After its genesis in medicine and the natural sciences, meta-analysis was introduced in social science research in the 1970s to overcome problems of common application, the lack of large data sets needed to derive general results, and the problem of uncertainty of information. The advantage of meta-analysis is that it provides a systematic framework for the synthesis and comparison of studies, and can also extend and re-examine the results in order to produce more general results than could previously be obtained, by focusing on a common kernel of research.

The meta-analysis approach thus offers a series of techniques permitting a quantitative aggregation of results across different studies. In so doing, it can serve to calculate more accurate numerical values from available data, for instance in studies of economic costs and benefits. When reviewing the usefulness of parameters derived from prior studies, it can also act as a supplement to more common literary-type approaches, and help direct new research to related areas. Finally, it may also be of help in establishing the robustness of certain findings by using the research synthesis as a kind of sensitivity analysis.

A related and commonly-used method in social science research is *meta-regression analysis*. This statistical technique has been widely and successfully applied in biometrics and sociometrics. The primary characteristics of a meta-regression analysis are similar to those used in standard regression analysis, i.e. the search for a statistical linkage between one of the variables [the dependent variable] and other variables [the independent variables]. Since a statistical tool is used, the input data must of course be quantitative. The main problem is of course the existence of variance in the original case study data.

The application of a meta-regression analysis, which identifies average parameter values, helps to generate meaningful comparative results from a survey of literature or a research synthesis. Having obtained the regression results, tests must be carried out to verify their correctness. Such tests will generally try to assess the magnitude of any effects being explored by the study. For instance, we can test the extent to which an elasticity, chosen to investigate certain effects, depends upon the design of the research study, or how different estimates can be combined into one.

A general guideline for deciding whether or not a particular study should be considered in a meta-analytical formulation is the existence of a basic similarity between the studies. A meta-regression analysis rests upon the following general rules: all studies included must focus on the same phenomenon, they must use similar measures of any given outcome and have the same population characteristics. Finally, they must have a similar underlying research objective. In order to identify relevant studies to be included in the analysis, it is essential to establish selection criteria. As already mentioned above, the available data needs to be of a quantitative nature. Moreover, it is necessary to verify uniformity in order to minimise possible errors in the calculation. It may be necessary to conduct further experiments or carry out new analyses of the data presented in the individual studies (see Van den Bergh et al. 1997).

In addition to meta-regression analysis, there is also a wide variety of other techniques for research synthesis of a sample of individual studies. These include content analysis, fuzzy set analysis, rough set analysis, multicriteria analysis, discriminant analysis and the like. Especially in case of categorical data [such as nominal or binary data], rough set analysis is a very promising tool for research synthesis. This method will be discussed in the next section.

In conclusion, meta-analysis has several interesting features as a method of research synthesis. First, while it deals predominantly with quantitative knowledge, it can also be used with qualitative knowledge under certain conditions. Second, meta-analytical techniques can isolate relevant knowledge from a well-defined collection of previous studies. Compared to other techniques, more knowledge is acquired and made available for value transfers. Third, in certain circumstances, key parameters can be quantified and corrected for bias (Hunter and Schmidt 1990). Fourth, meta-analysis reduces the context-dependency of research findings. In a value transfer context, there is greater transparency. Hence, meta-analysis encourages the building of a more objective body of knowledge. Not only are moderator variables present, they are also quantified to some degree. In contrast with the information contained in individual case studies, a more objective, relational structure becomes available for value transfer. Quantifying allows relationships to be ordered. This ordering process may have interesting features that facilitate the application of a value transfer. Moderator variables can be determined within a subset. A classification of constants and variables is also possible. In a practical context, such as the valuation of a recreational site, common variables can be distinguished from specific values.

18.3   Rough Set Analysis as an Artificial Intelligence Tool for Research Synthesis

Many empirical studies focus on 'what...if' questions, in particular in impact assessment and effect analysis. The empirical findings often show considerable variation, be it quantitative [e.g. in terms of elasticities] or qualitative. Rough set analysis provides a powerful tool for research synthesis based on multiple classification analysis. Rough set analysis belongs to the family of artificial intelligence approaches, and aims to identify which statements on cause-effect relationships [if...then] are consistent with a collection of empirical, cross-classified data. It seeks to compose 'decision rules' that – at least across the sample of individual study results – lead to an unambiguous mapping of empirically justified statements.

The aim of rough set analysis is to recognise possible cause-effect relationships in the available data, as well as to underline the importance and strategic role of certain data and irrelevance of other data (Pawlak 1986, 1991). The approach focuses on regularities in the data in order to draw aspects and relationships from them which are less evident immediately, but which amy be useful for further research and policy making.

Rough set analysis is one of the new mathematical tools designed to investigate the meaning of knowledge and its representation, i.e. to organise and classify data. It is evident that such a method is potentially very useful for the analysis of assessment problems. The data from which a decision-maker determines an evaluation are often disorganised, they contain useless details, or are incomplete and vague. This type of data does not represent structured and systematic knowledge.

Knowledge, according to the rough set philosophy, is generated when we are able to define a classification of relevant objects, e.g., states, processes, events. By doing this we divide and cluster objects within the same pattern classes. These classes are the building blocks [granules, atoms] of the knowledge we employ to define the basic concepts used in rough set analysis. But how can we tackle the problem of imprecision which occurs when the granules of knowledge can be expressed only vaguely?

'In the rough set theory each imprecise concept is replaced by a pair of precise concepts called its lower and upper approximation; the lower approximation of a concept consists of all objects which surely belong to the concept whereas the upper approximation of the concept consists of all objects which possibly belong to the concept in question' (Pawlak 1992, p.1).

By using the lower and upper approximation, we address the problem of vague information, and focus in particular on the problem of dependency and the relationships among attributes. A crucial aspect in the assessment process is the need to distinguish between the conditions through which we make a decision and the attributes that describe the various options. Rough set analysis can examine, on the one hand, the dependencies among attributes but, on the other hand, can also describe these objects in terms of available attributes in order to find essential differences between objects. This latter analysis, which represents the knowledge representation system [or dissimilarity analysis], assumes an important role in many decision-making processes in which it is necessary to indicate the differences among possible options, in order to eliminate superfluous information for a proper decision choice.

Let us consider a finite universe of *objects* which we would like to examine and classify. For each object we can define a number of *attributes* in order to create a sufficient basis for the required characterisation of the object. If the attribute is qualitative, the domain will consist of a discrete set of levels. If the attribute is quantitative, we divide its continous domain into discrete sub-intervals to obtain an categorical description of the object. We have classified our objects by means of the attributes, and thus we can assign to each object a vector of attributes. The table containing all this organised information is called the *information table*. From this table, we can immediately observe which objects share the same levels of each of the attributes. Two separate objects have an *indiscernibility* relation when they have the same descriptive attributes. Such a binary relation is reflexive, symmetric and transitive.

We can now introduce a fundamental concept in the rough set analysis procedure. Let us imagine that Q is the set of attributes that describe the set of objects U. Let P represent a sub-set of the set of attributes Q, and X represent a sub-set of the set of objects U. We define as a sub-set of X those objects which all have the attributes belonging to set P. Such a set is called the *P-lower approximation* of set X, and is denoted as P_LX. We then define as *P-upper approximation* of X, denoted as P_UX, the sub-set of U having as its elements all objects belonging to the P set of attributes and which has at least one element in common with set X.

The definition of the upper and lower approximation sets has an important role in the rough set methodology. Through these sets we can classify and examine the importance of any uncertain information that we have collected. Consequently, this approach could lead to an imprecise representation of reality by reducing the information-specific sets. This objection may be better understood if we recall that the capacity to manipulate uncertain information and consequent ability to reach conclusions is one of the most essential assets of the human mind in obtaining knowledge. Therefore, the representation of reality by means of rough set analysis is indeed a reduction of the perceived real phenomenon, but it is done in such a way as to enable us to classify, distinguish and express judgements about it.

So far we have focused on the classification of uncertain data. Let us now examine the case where we wish to study the conditions for making a choice among different alternatives; i.e. when we confront an assessment problem. In this case, we can distinguish two classes among the set of attributes in the information table: a class of *condition* attributes and a class of *decision* attributes. The class of condition attributes describe the object following the procedure described above. The class of decision attributes is defined by all the attributes the object must have in order to be selected as an acceptable alternative. For instance, a set of objects can be described by values of condition attributes, while expert judgements may be represented by values of decision attributes.

At this point we must define a *decision rule* as an implication relation between the description of a condition class and the description of a decision class. The decision rule can be *exact* or deterministic when the class of decision is contained in the set of conditions, i.e. all the decision attributes belong to the class of the condition attributes. We have an *approximate* rule when more than one value of the decision attributes corresponds to the same combination of values of the condition attributes. Therefore, an exact rule offers a sufficient condition for belonging to a decision class; an approximate rule only admits the possibility of this.

The decision rules and the information table are the basic elements needed to solve multi-attribute choice and ranking problems. The binary preference relations between the decision rules and the description of the objects by means of the condition attributes determine a set of potentially acceptable actions. In order to rank such alternatives, we need to conduct a final binary comparison among the potential actions. This procedure will define the most acceptable action or alternative.

The technique of rough set analysis is rather cumbersome, although at present some interesting and user-friendly software algorithms do exist. A basic question in all investigations is whether a *core* does exist. A core is a common explanatory factor that shows up in all decision rules. In case of a core, it is clear that we have found a situation where the core variables are the most critical explanatory factors. Several applications of rough set analysis to research synthesis can be found in Van den Bergh et al. (1998), Capello, Nijkamp and Pepping (1999) and Florax, Nijkamp and Willis (2000).

18.4   A Sample of Studies on Government and Growth

After the theoretical and methodological expositions above, we will now present the empirical basis for our applied meta-analysis. The basic question is whether conclusive regularities or explanatory factors can be identified from the great many historical studies on the relationship between the nature and intensity of government policy and coincident economic growth. Since the mid 1980s there have been many empirical analyses of the relationship between government and growth, either as a by-product of tests of conditional convergence between countries or regions, or to address the issue explicitly. Not all studies have a solid theoretical framework or an appropriate econometric methodology. From this vast literature of several hundred published and unpublished papers, a selection was made of 93 published articles from the period 1983-98. Features of each of the articles are reported in Appendix A-18.1 and further summaries of each article can be found in Poot (2000).

All the selected articles were published in refereed international journals in the English language. Being cited in later research was also a criterion for inclusion. However, by focusing specifically on relatively high-quality commonly cited papers, it was felt that useful generalisations could be made from this body of knowledge. The synthesis attempted here undoubtedly suffers from the so-called *publication bias* in that significant findings are likely to be more prominent in the papers summarised here than in the excluded papers (Begg 1994). However, the ultimate objective of the exercise is to assess the difference in robustness of the findings across different areas of government behaviour and it is not clear that publication bias would systematically differ across these different areas.

A coded summary of the information contained in each of the studies is provided in Appendix A-18.1. Following the terminology of rough set analysis described in the previous section, each individual study is referred to as an object, the features of the studies that are reported in Appendix A-18.1 are referred to as attributes [A1 to A9] and the conclusion is referred to as the decision variable [D]. Because several growth studies considered more than one policy area, the 93 articles yielded 123 objects for the information table in Appendix A-18.1.

With respect to fiscal policy, five policy areas were considered: general government consumption in relation to overall GDP [also referred to as government size], taxation policy, education levels, defence spending and infrastructure. These are coded as values one to five respectively of study attribute A1. Quantitative research characteristics that are included in Appendix A-18.1 are the variables: year of publication [A2], number of observations [A4], year of earliest observation [A5] and the year of the most recent observation [A6]. The qualitative [categorical] variables included in the table are the spatial level of the data [A3]; the level of development [A7], the method of research [A8] and the ranking of the journal in which the results were published [A9].

Before a detailed analysis of the data summarised in Appendix A-18.1 is undertaken in the next section, it is useful to point out some general features of this body of research. Firstly, the vast majority of studies have used standard regression techniques. Ordinary Least Squares [OLS] was the most commonly adopted technique [attribute A8 at level 1]. The suitability of this method was rarely tested by means of diagnostic statistics which could have signalled that the use of OLS was problematic for the data in hand.

Thirty five of the 123 observations relied on cross-section [CS] data, but there has been an increasing use of pooled cross-section time-series data [A8 at level 3], as the availability of such data has improved. Forty seven studies used pooled data. This is a welcome trend, as the pooled data studies show that region and period effects are important. In time series studies [A8 at level 2], we see in recent years a growing use of vector autoregressions, Granger causality tests and the co-integration framework (see also Anwar, Davies and Sampath 1996).

The dearth of studies adopting other methods [A8 at level 4], such as dynamic simulation modelling approaches is rather surprising. The sample of 93 articles included only two studies that adopted a calibration/simulation approach. There also appear to be few studies that have adopted a computable general equilibrium [CGE] model approach. A recent example of a dynamic CGE model of the impact of infrastructure on growth is Kim (1998). An additional weakness of many past regression studies is that these purport to provide information on long-run growth, but use observations over only a relative short time span of 5 to 30 years [attributes A4 and A5]. For example, it is possible that public infrastructure does raise the [local] long-run growth rate, *ceteris paribus*, but that the effect emerges only very gradually over time, for example because of a complementarity with certain types of private capital that may, for various reasons, only be undertaken at a slow rate. It this case, it may be very hard to detect the effect of an additional amount of public investment compared with the [unobservable] counterfactual.

In an influential paper, Levine and Renelt (1992) use Extreme Bounds Analysis [EBA] to show that many of the results from CS regression analyses of the determinants of long-run growth are not robust. However, their conclusion does not appear to have discouraged others from continuing to carry out CS regression analyses, although time series and pooled data analyses have become far more prominent in recent years. Indeed, Sala-i-Martin (1997) argued that the EBA criterion of fragility is too strict to be of any use. Assessing instead the robustness of a variable by the probability that the coefficient is on one side of zero in the cumulative distribution function of the regressions which include this variable, Sala-i-Martin finds that 22 out of 59 possible determinants of growth are 'significant'. Interestingly, no measure of government spending [including investment] is among these 22 variables. Moreover, Evans (1996) finds by means of long-run data (1870-1989) for thirteen countries, that there is much evidence that these countries converge to a common trend, i.e. that policies and other shocks influence the growth rate only temporarily.

With respect to the publication outlet, four categories are considered. These are based on the Towe and Wright (1995) classification. These authors distinguish four groups: the top 12 journals in terms of citations, a second group of 23 journals, a third-ranked group of 36 journals and a fourth group of all other journals. The relative frequencies of these journals in our sample of articles are 17 percent, 16 percent, 24 percent and 43 percent respectively.

Virtually all studies of government and growth are *primary* analyses (Glass 1976). Each study has rather unique features in terms of the specification of the model, the sample of countries or regions considered, the time period of observation and the range and definitions of the variables used. Few authors have carried out replications or extensions of earlier research [so-called *secondary* analysis], although *tertiary analysis* in the form of a survey is more common. Among the articles included in our sample, there is only one example of *meta-regression* analysis – a study by Button (1998) on infrastructure and growth.

A final general finding from our sample of publications is that most of the studies on the relationship between government and growth have focused on government at the national level [attribute A3 at level 0] and have consequently used country data. Only about one fifth of the studies use regional data. This sample will now be exposed to the 'meta-scope' in the form of rough set analysis.

18.5   The Generalised Rough Set Method: A Multilevel Strategy Learning Approach

This section proposes and evaluates a multilevel strategy learning approach, based on rough set analysis, that seeks to retain most of the knowledge gains of multiple data set classification. This is done by dividing the full database into different subsets composed of the number of growth studies grouped according to the various levels of each attribute, while the original sample of studies is of course still also considered in its entirety. Given the discretisation which we apply to continuous attributes [see below], this yields a total of 31 benchmark data sets for rough set analysis [30 subsets plus the original dataset with 123 objects]. For the sake of brevity, we will present here only the results related to the type of government policy and the level of the development in different countries.

The sample database of studies is first treated as a general information system (Appendix A-18.1). The articles from which the information was derived are listed in Appendix A-18.2. Each pattern [object, study] consists of the same set of multiple attributes [study features] described in the previous section, and each pattern has a known *class identity* associated with it. The class identity is equal to the conclusion of the study, i.e. a negative, none/inconclusive or positive impact of government policy on growth.

The first phase of our analysis deals with the application of rough set theory to the full sample of studies concerning economic growth with the aim of finding robust relationships between variables incorporated in the modern endogenous growth literature and the impacts found in the studies. For example, we distinguish between cross section, time series and pooled analyses. This will enable us to identify the importance of path dependencies for persistent differences in growth performance. Meta-variables such as the year of the publication and level of the journal in which the articles have been published are also included to understand better the evolution of scientific inquiry in this literature during the last twenty years.

The collected data set is characterised by a certain number of continuous variables, namely the attributes A2, A4, A5, A6. Due to the fact that the learning algorithms used in this paper accept exclusively discrete data as input, those attributes in the decision table which are continuous variables in the real domain have been transformed into discrete attributes [for an overview on such data pre-processing, see Famili et al. 1997). This transformation requires the specification of so-called cutting points [cuts]. The cutting points, defined over the domains of the continuous attributes, divide these into consecutive intervals. The real values of the attributes are converted into discrete ones by assigning each value to the number of the interval to which it belongs (Susmaga 1997).

Numerous algorithms have been developed for this discretisation. These utilise different methods of searching for appropriate cutting points. Discretisations featuring intervals defined by cutting points are called *hard discretisations*. Because such a 'knife-edge' approach may be viewed as too categorical in some situations, new ideas have emerged in which some additional 'softening' thresholds were introduced. More recent approaches employ other types of discretisations, the so-called *fuzzy discretisations*, in which the hard intervals defined by the cutting points are replaced with fuzzy intervals defined by fuzzy numbers with overlapping bounds. However, there is still some ambiguity in methodology and terminology (see Dougherty, Kohavi and Sahami 1995; Fayyad and Irany 1993, Kerber 1992). For example, besides hard versus fuzzy discretisation, a distinction is also made between supervised versus unsupervised, local versus global, and parametrized versus non-parametrised discretisation.

Supervised methods take into consideration the reported values of the decision attribute [or attributes] when producing the discretisation, the unsupervised methods are, on the other hand, information blind [or class-blind]. Local methods discretise only one condition attribute at a time, while the global ones attempt simulaneous discretisation of all attributes. Parametrised methods are those for which the maximal number of intervals generated for a given feature is specified in advance, while the non-parametrised methods determine this value algorithmically.

In spite of all these extensions, hard discretisation still remains the most commonly used form. It is also the form most frequently adopted in existing discretisation algorithms. Consequently, it has been adopted here also and the discretisation has been implemented in the following way:

- A2 : [before 1985 = 0; from 1985-1996 = 1; after 1996 = 2],
- A4 : [up to 7 = 0 ; from 7- 49 = 1 ; more than 49 =2],
- A5 : [before 1959 = 0; from 1959-1969 = 1; after 1969 = 2],
- A6 : [before 1984 = 0; from 1984-1993 = 1; after 1993 = 2].

As noted in the previous section, Appendix A-18.1 constitutes an information system in which the rows represent the case studies and the columns the attributes considered. Thus, two central questions are important in the process of knowledge representation and acquisition: how the knowledge is organised and how it can be increased. The first relates to the classification ability of the constructed system, i.e. how well it is suited to a meta-analytical perspective, also in the sense that it can be used to classify newly published case studies on economic growth. Classification, which involves the process of finding rules to partition a given data set into disjoint groups, is one class of data-mining problems. It is the process that finds the common properties among a set of objects in a database and divides them into different classes, according to a classification model. The performance of the system as a classifier is measured by the classification accuracy, which can be viewed as the main evaluation criterion.

The second aspect regarding the application of rough set analysis concerns the accumulation of knowledge acquired through learning from case studies or examples. Knowledge is usually represented here in form of *rules*. The generation of rules aims to create a symbolic representation of the knowledge contained in the data; it consists of the process of creating valid generalisations or detecting data patterns.

Hence three approaches were used to evaluate the system. These are considered in the following order: (i) classification accuracy and quality, (ii) core of the attributes, and (iii) rules. The results from carrying out rough set analysis applied to the full database are presented in Table 18.1, which gives the lower and upper approximations, the accuracy and the quality of the classification, and the core of the attributes. Table 18.1 shows that 32 case studies concluded that the impact of government policy on growth was negative, 44 studies were inconclusive and 47 suggested that the impact was positive.

The accuracy of the classification is 0.84. All attributes, except the geographic unit of measurement [countries or regions] and the year of the earliest observation, form the core of the attributes; these are the attributes that cannot be eliminated without disturbing the quality of classification.

Table 18.1   Classification and core of the attributes

Class	Lower Approximation	Upper Approximation	Accuracy
Class 1 – 32 objects	31	34	0.9118
Class 2 – 44 objects	38	49	0.7755
Class 3 – 47 objects	43	51	0.8431
Quality of the Classification:		0.9106	
Accuracy of the Classification:		0.8358	
Core A1, A2, A4, A5, A7, A8, A9			

In the next step, the induction of decision rules was performed. Rules are generated by repeated application of an algorithm to the data. The quality of the rules, and hence the knowledge discovered, is heavily dependent on the algorithm used to analyse the data. Thus, the central problem in knowledge extraction is the choice of techniques to generate such rules. In our experiment we adopted an approach that uses two learning systems for knowledge representation: first in the form of decision rules corresponding to the so-called minimal covering, secondly in the form of generating general knowledge. The rule induction algorithm called 'learning from examples' [LEM2] was used first. This search technique has the technical advantage that it is a 'depth-first' simpler equivalent of the search technique used in the algorithm *Explore* (for details see Stefanoski and Wilk 1999).

The output of LEM2 is a set of rules that is minimal and provides a description of all classes defined only by the examples supporting it [positive examples]. The large number of rules generated [56 exact rules and four approximate ones] and their low quality, expressed in terms of support found by the numerical computation, showed a high level of fragmentation of the data system. The average strength is only three observations per rule (see Table 18.2). It can be shown that for studies reporting a negative or inconclusive impact on growth the highest level of support is represented by only ten percent of these studies.

Table 18.2   Results of applying the LEM 2 algorithm to induce rules

Number of Exact Rules	Number of Approximate Rules	Average Strength	Discrimination Level
56	4	3	100 %

However, the main aim of the LEM2 algorithm is to derive the so-called minimal set of rules covering – ideally, all learning examples. However, it is also useful to consider an induction algorithm that generates rules which cover the most general examples (Stefanoski 1998). This led us to choose another rule induction algorithm. The algorithm *Explore*, originally proposed by Stefanowski and Vanderpoten (see Mienko *et al.* 1996) was chosen as a tool for inducing general rules. This algorithm generates all short and sufficiently 'strong' general rules for a given data set. Examples uncovered by these rules can be used to identify exceptions and atypical cases. The adjective 'strong' means here that the rules are satisfied by a relatively large number of learning examples.

The *Explore* algorithm induces all decision rules which satisfy predefined requirements with respect to the rule strength [that is, the relative number of learning examples that support the rule], the length of the conditioning part [i.e. 'if <conditioning part>, then...'], the level of confidence in the rule, as well as requirements to the syntax of conditions. As argues by Mienko et al. (1996), focusing mainly on the strength of rules will result in obtaining a limited number of rules which cover only a certain subset of the learning examples that represent general information patterns in the data, while leaving uncovered some more difficult and specific examples.

The search for rules in the algorithm *Explore* is controlled by parameters called *stopping conditions SC* that reflect the user's requirements. As our main selection criterion will be the strength of the rules, the definition of *SC* is connected with determining the threshold value for the minimal strength of the conjunction being candidate for the conditioning part of the rule. If its strength is lower than *SC*, it is discarded, otherwise it can be evaluated further. Additionally, one can define a threshold d that expresses the minimum value of the level of discrimination $D(R)$ of the rules to be generated. The algorithm *Explore* is based on the *breadth-first* strategy, which generates rules of increasing size starting from the shortest ones (Stefanoski and Wilk 1999).

In general, *Explore* is an algorithm that incorporates searching strategies to adapt the discovery processes to the characteristics of the applications. Knowledge discovery is evaluated locally in the form of the filtering of redundant rules, that is by finding something that is useful to the user (Deogun et al. 1996). In fact, *Explore* is specifically designed to work with data that changes regularly. This is helpful in our context, as new studies on economic growth are continually emerging and it will be useful to be able to assess whether these new findings are consistent with the knowledge discovered in the past.

In our experiment, we used the following procedure of parameter tuning. Firstly, initial values of threshold were calculated on the basis of the strength of rules generated by the LEM2 algorithm because, as noted above, it is an efficient algorithm to derive the minimal number of rules with a good classification ability. Thus, the following threshold values were adopted: discrimination level = 100 percent, minimal strength of support within the class = 15 percent, maximum length of the conditioning items = five.

Table 18.3   Set of decision rules generated using *Explore* algorithm

---

rule 1. (A1 = 2) & (A2 = 0) => (D1=1); [5, 5, 15.63%, 100.00%] [5, 0, 0]
   [{ 1, 5, 7, 8, 9 }, {}, {}]
rule 2. (A4 = 2) & (A5 = 0) & (A6 = 0) => (D1=1); [5, 5, 15.63%, 100.00%] [5, 0, 0]
   [{ 8, 12, 13, 20, 27 }, {}, {}]
rule 3. (A5 = 0) & (A6 = 0) & (A8 = 3) => (D1=1); [5, 5, 15.63%, 100.00%] [5, 0, 0]
   [{ 8, 12, 13, 20, 27 }, {}, {}]
rule 4. (A1 = 4) & (A8 = 2) => (D1=3); [12, 12, 25.53%, 100.00%] [0, 0, 12]
   [{}, {}, { 6, 25, 26, 37, 51, 53, 60, 97, 100, 103, 112, 114 }]
rule 5. (A1 = 4) & (A2 = 1) & (A5 = 0) => (D1=3); [10, 10, 21.28%, 100.00%] [0, 0, 10]
   [{}, {}, { 25, 26, 37, 47, 51, 59, 60, 97, 100, 103 }]
rule 6. (A1 = 4) & (A3 = 0) & (A4 = 1) => (D1=3); [11, 11, 23.40%, 100.00%] [0, 0, 11]
   [{}, {}, { 6, 25, 26, 37, 51, 53, 60, 97, 103, 109, 122 }]
rule 7. (A1 = 4) & (A3 = 0) & (A9 = 1) => (D1=3); [8, 8, 17.02%, 100.00%] [0, 0, 8]
   [{}, {}, { 24, 37, 53, 97, 109, 115, 121, 122 }]
rule 8. (A1 = 4) & (A4 = 1) & (A5 = 0) => (D1=3); [9, 9, 19.15%, 100.00%] [0, 0, 9]
   [{}, {}, { 6, 25, 26, 37, 47, 51, 60, 97, 103 }]
rule 9. (A1 = 4) & (A4 = 1) & (A6 = 1) => (D1=3); [12, 12, 25.53%, 100.00%] [0, 0, 12]
   [{}, {}, { 25, 26, 37, 38, 43, 51, 52, 53, 60, 97, 103, 122 }]
rule 10. (A1 = 4) & (A4 = 1) & (A9 = 1) => (D1=3); [8, 8, 17.02%, 100.00%] [0, 0, 8]
   [{}, {}, { 37, 38, 43, 53, 97, 109, 119, 122 }]
rule 11. (A1 = 4) & (A5 = 0) & (A6 = 1) => (D1=3); [11, 11, 23.40%, 100.00%] [0, 0, 11]
   [{}, {}, { 25, 26, 37, 51, 59, 60, 97, 100, 103, 112, 114 }]

Table 18.3 shows that the resulting output consists of eleven rules. Given that LEM2 generated 60 rules, we can conclude that significant progress has been made towards knowledge reduction. Interestingly, no rules were found for the class of inconclusive studies regarding the impact of public policy on economic growth. Regarding a negative impact of policy on growth, only three rules were obtained, all of which are supported by five examples [studies] and hence with a support of 5/32 [15.63 percent]. Specifically, we observe that:

- *If* the study focuses on defence expenditure and the year of publication is before 1985 then negative impact (Table 18.3 rule 1);
- *If* the number of observations is more than 49 and the year of the earliest observation is before 1959 and the year of the most recent observation is before 1984 then negative impact (Table 18.3, rule 2);
- *If* the year of the earliest observation is before 1959 and the year of the most recent *observation* is before 1984 and the method adopted is pooled cross section time series analysis then negative impact (Table 18.3, rule 3).

Furthermore, we obtained a significant of rules with respect to the class of a positive policy impact on economic growth. The support ranged from 8 to 12 examples while the relative support consequently ranged from 17.02 percent to 25.53 percent. All eight rules referred to studies of the impact on growth of public investment in infrastructure. In particular, we have:

- *If* the study focuses on infrastructure expenditure and the method adopted is time series analysis then positive impact (Table 18.3, rule 4);
- *If* the study focuses on infrastructure expenditure and year of the publication is between 1985 and 1996 and year of the earliest observation is before 1959 then positive impact (Table 18.3, rule 5);
- *If* the study focuses on infrastructure expenditure and study data are at country level and number of observations are between 7 and 49 then positive impact (Table 18.3, rule 6);
- *If* the study focuses on infrastructure expenditure and study data are at the country level and published at the unclassified journal level then positive impact (Table 18.3, rule 7);
- *If* the study focuses on infrastructure expenditure and the number of observations is between 7 and 49 and year of the earliest observation is before 1959 then positive impact (Table 18.3, rule 8);
- *If* the study focuses on infrastructure expenditure and number of observations is between 7 and 49 and year of the most recent observation is between 1984 and 1993 then positive impact (Table 18.3, rule 9);
- *If* the study focuses on infrastructure expenditure and number of observations is between 7 and 49 and published in the unclassified journal level then positive impact (Table 18.3, rule 10);
- *If* the study focuses on infrastructure expenditure and year of the earliest observation is before 1959 and year of the most recent observation is between 1984 and 1993 then positive impact (Table 18.3, rule 11).

Such class descriptions have of course great potential and can be used to classify further studies in the field of economic growth research. Nevertheless, if this process is used to classify new additional knowledge, we are interested in verifying the possibility that additional information is likely to improve our knowledge. Because of this concern with knowledge, rather than simply looking for accurate prediction, a more in-depth analysis was sought. There are also practical reasons for doing this. Meta-analysis makes specific demands on rough set algorithms. Even when predictive decision rules are the sole goal, comprehensibility is an important condition because it facilitates the process of interactive refinement that is at the heart of most successful artificial intelligence applications.

Thus, the subset of studies concerning government spending was divided into five data sets: fiscal policy, defence expenditure, taxation policy, education policy and infrastructure policy. As in the previous rule generation experiment on the overall data set, we used a parametric fine-tuning procedure. Here we chose the same *SC* as for the full data set, but with the difference that an absolute strength equal to five was adopted. However, an absolute class strength of three was used in the case of taxation studies due to the limited number of examples [10] present in the data set.

Table 18.4 shows that in the case of studies of pure fiscal policy [i.e. government expenditure as a proportion of GDP], the attributes 'year of the publication', 'year of the earliest observation', 'level of development', 'method' and 'journal level' make up the core of the attributes. The algorithm generated the following rules:

- *If* the year of publication is between 1985 and 1996 *and* the number of observations is more than 49 *and* the year of the first observation is between 1959-1969 and low journal level *then* the impact is inconclusive (Table 18.5, rule 1);
- *If* year of the publication is between 1985 and 1996 *and* the year of the recent observation is between 1959-1969 *and* year of the most recent observation is between 1984 and 1993 *and* low journal level *then* the impact is inconclusive (Table 18.5, rule 2);
- *If* country level data *and* year of the most recent observation is between 1984 and 1993 *and* data on developed countries *and* low journal level *then* the impact is inconclusive (Table 18.5, rule 3).

Table 18.4 Subset of fiscal policy studies (A1=1): Approximation, quality and accuracy of the classification and core of the attributes

Class: 1	Class: 2	Class: 3
Objects: 12	Objects: 22	Objects: 7
Lower: 11 ; Upper: 14	Lower: 18;Upper: 25	Lower: 5;Upper: 9
Accuracy: 0.7857	Accuracy: 0.7200	Accuracy: 0.5556
Quality: 0.8293; Accuracy: 0.7083		
Core: 0.7805; Attributes: A2, A5,A7,A8,A9		

Table 18.5 Subset of fiscal policy studies (A1=1): Rules

Parameters: Class: *General* -> SC1 (absolute) = 5 SC2 = 5 D = 100
rule 1. (A2 = 1) & (A4 = 2) & (A5 = 1) & (A9 = 1) => (D1=2); [5, 5, 22.73%, 100.00%] [0, 5, 0]
rule 2. (A2 = 1) & (A5 = 1) & (A6 = 1) & (A9 = 1) => (D1=2); [6, 6, 27.27%, 100.00%] [0, 6, 0]
rule 3. (A3 = 0) & (A6 = 1) & (A7 = 3) & (A9 = 1) => (D1=2); [5, 5, 22.73%, 100.00%] [0, 5, 0]

Table 18.6 shows that the subset of 22 defence expenditure studies has the following core attributes: 'year of publication', 'number of observations', 'year of

the earliest observation', 'level of development' and 'method used'. Table 18.7 shows that only one rule was generated:

- *If* data at *country* level *then* negative impact (Table 18.7, rule 1).

Table 18.6 Subset of defence policy studies (A1=2): Approximation, quality and accuracy of the classification and core of the attributes

Class: 1	Class: 2	Class: 3
Objects: 12	Objects: 9	Objects: 1
Lower: 12; Upper: 12	Lower: 9;Upper: 9	Lower: 1; Upper: 1
Accuracy: 1.0000	Accuracy: 1.0000	Accuracy: 1.0000
Quality: 1.0000; Accuracy: 1.0000		
Core: 1.0000; Attributes :A2, A4,A5,A7,A8		

Table 18.7   Subset of defence policy studies (A1=2): Rules

Parameters: Class: *General* ->   SC1 (absolute) = 5   SC2 = 5   D = 100
rule 1. (A2 = 0) => (D1=1); [5, 5, 41.67%, 100.00%] [5, 0, 0]

Table 18.8 shows that the subset of 10 tax policy studies has an empty core. The rules found are given in Table 18.9:

- *If* data at regional level *then* negative impact (Table 18.9, rule 1);
- *If* low journal level *then* negative impact (Table 18.9, rule 2);
- *If* year of the publication between 1985 and 1996 and high journal level *then* inconclusive impact (Table 18.9, rule 3).

Table 18.8   Subset of tax policy studies (A1=3): Approximation, quality and accuracy of the classification and core of the attributes

Class: 1	Class: 2
Objects: 6	Objects: 4
Lower: 6; Upper: 6	Lower: 4; Upper: 4
Accuracy: 1.0000	Accuracy: 1.0000
Quality: 1.0000; Accuracy: 1.0000	
Core: 0.0000	

Table 18.9   Subset of tax policy studies (A1=3): Rules

Parameters: Class: *General* -> SC1 (absolute) = 3   SC2 = 5   D = 100
rule 1. (A3 = 1) => (D1=1); [3, 3, 50.00%, 100.00%] [3, 0]
rule 2. (A9 = 1) => (D1=1); [3, 3, 50.00%, 100.00%] [3, 0]
rule 3. (A2 = 1) & (A9 = 3) => (D1=2); [3, 3, 75.00%, 100.00%] [0, 3]

In the subset of 38 infrastructure studies, the core is composed of 'number of observations', 'the year of the earliest observation' and 'journal level' (see Table 18.10). The algorithm generated twelve rules for a positive impact. These are fully reported in Table 18.11. For example, rule 10 states that:

- *If* the year of the earliest observation is before 1959 *and* the year of the most recent *observation* is between 1984 and 1993 *then* positive impact (Table 18.11, rule 10).

Table 18.10 Subset of infrastructure policy studies (A1=4): Approximation, quality and accuracy of the classification and core of the attributes

Class: 1	Class: 2	Class: 3
Objects: 2	Objects: 8	Objects: 28
Lower: 2; Upper: 2	Lower: 7; Upper: 9	Lower: 27; Upper: 29
Accuracy: 1.0000	Accuracy: 0.7778	Accuracy: 0.9310
Quality: 0.9474; Accuracy: 0.9000		
Core: 0.7895; Attributes A4; A5,A9		

Table 18.11 Subset of infrastructure policy studies (A1=4): Rules

Parameters: Class: *General* -> SC1 (absolute) = 5   SC2 = 5   D = 100
rule 1. (A2 = 2) => (D1=3); [7, 7, 25.00%, 100.00%] [0, 0, 7]
rule 2. (A8 = 2) => (D1=3); [12, 12, 42.86%, 100.00%] [0, 0, 12]
rule 3. (A2 = 1) & (A5 = 0) => (D1=3); [10, 10, 35.71%, 100.00%] [0, 0, 10]
rule 4. (A3 = 0) & (A4 = 1) => (D1=3); [11, 11, 39.29%, 100.00%] [0, 0, 11]
rule 5. (A3 = 0) & (A9 = 1) => (D1=3); [8, 8, 28.57%, 100.00%] [0, 0, 8]
rule 6. (A4 = 1) & (A5 = 0) => (D1=3); [9, 9, 32.14%, 100.00%] [0, 0, 9]
rule 7. (A4 = 1) & (A5 = 2) => (D1=3); [7, 7, 25.00%, 100.00%] [0, 0, 7]
rule 8. (A4 = 1) & (A6 = 1) => (D1=3); [12, 12, 42.86%, 100.00%] [0, 0, 12]
rule 9. (A4 = 1) & (A9 = 1) => (D1=3); [8, 8, 28.57%, 100.00%] [0, 0, 8]
rule 10. (A5 = 0) & (A6 = 1) => (D1=3); [11, 11, 39.29%, 100.00%] [0, 0, 11]
rule 11. (A5 = 0) & (A9 = 3) => (D1=3); [6, 6, 21.43%, 100.00%] [0, 0, 6]
rule 12. (A7 = 3) & (A9 = 3) => (D1=3); [6, 6, 21.43%, 100.00%] [0, 0, 6]

For the sake of brevity, we will not describe the others in sentence form. Table 18.12 shows that the subset of education expenditure studies has an empty core. Table 18.13 shows that two rules were generated by the algorithm:

- *If* year of publication is after 1996 *then* positive impact (Table 18.13, rule 1);
- *If* the number of observations is between 7 and 49 *then* positive impact (Table 18.13, rule 2).

As noted earlier, we also divided the original data set into three subsets with respect to the level of development of the countries concerned. The three subsets relate to: less developed countries, mixed countries and developed countries. Due to the different sizes of these subsets, a new parameter tuning procedure was adopted. Specifically, the following *SC* have been used: absolute strength = 3 for the less developed and mixed countries subsets; absolute strength = 8 for the developed countries subset, and maximum conditioning length = 5, discrimination level = 100 percent for all three subsets.

Table 18.12   Subset of education policy studies (A1=5): Approximation, quality and accuracy of the classification and core of the attributes

Class: 2	Class: 3
Objects: 1	Objects: 11
Lower: 0; Upper: 2	Lower: 10; Upper: 12
Accuracy: 0.0000	Accuracy: 0.8333
Quality: 0.8333; Accuracy: 0.7143	
Core: 0.0000	

Table 18.13   Subset of education policy studies (A1=5): Rules

Parameters: Class: *General*   ->   SC1 (absolute) = 5   SC2 = 5   D = 100
rule 1. (A2 = 2) => (D1=3); [5, 5, 45.45%, 100.00%] [0, 5]
rule 2. (A4 = 1) => (D1=3); [5, 5, 45.45%, 100.00%] [0, 5]

A very significant result is that the type of government policy [government size, taxation policy, etc.] is part of the core for all three subsets. Table 18.14 shows that in the subset of less developed countries the attributes of the core are 'government spending', 'year of the publication', 'number of observations', 'year of the earliest observation' and 'method'. The principal rule in this subset is:

- *If* year of the publication between 1985-1996 *and* year of the earliest observation is between 1959 and 1969 *and* year of the most recent observation is between 1984 and 1993 *then* inconclusive impact (Table 18.15, rule 3).

Table 18.14   Subset of less developed countries (A7=1): Approximation, quality and accuracy of the classification and core of the attributes

Class: 1	Class: 2	Class: 3
Objects: 11	Objects: 10	Objects: 7
Lower: 11;Upper: 11	Lower: 10; Upper: 10	Lower: 7; Upper: 7
Accuracy: 1.0000	Accuracy: 1.0000	Accuracy: 1.0000
Quality: 1.0000; Accuracy: 1.0000		
Core A1, A2, A4, A5, A8		

Table 18.15 Subset of less developed countries (A7=1): Rules

Parameters: Class: *General* -> SC1 (absolute) = 3 SC2 = 5 D = 100

rule 1. (A1 = 2) & (A8 = 2) => (D1=2); [3, 3, 30.00%, 100.00%] [0, 3, 0]
rule 2. (A1 = 2) & (A2 = 1) & (A5 = 1) => (D1=2); [3, 3, 30.00%, 100.00%] [0, 3, 0]
rule 3. (A2 = 1) & (A5 = 1) & (A6 = 1) => (D1=2); [4, 4, 40.00%, 100.00%] [0, 4, 0]
rule 4. (A2 = 1) & (A5 = 1) & (A8 = 3) => (D1=2); [3, 3, 30.00%, 100.00%] [0, 3, 0]
rule 5. (A2 = 1) & (A3 = 0) & (A4 = 2) & (A5 = 1) => (D1=2); [3, 3, 30.00%, 100.00%] [0, 3, 0]

In the subset of mixed countries, the core is made up of the attributes 'government spending', 'year of the publication', 'method' and 'journal level' (Table 18.16). Two strong rules were generated:

- *If* year of the publication is after 1996 *and* year of the earliest observation is after 1969 *then* positive impact (Table 18.17, rule 3);
- *If* year of the earliest observation is after 1969 *and* lowest journal level *then* positive impact (Table 18.17, rule 5).

Table 18.16 Subset of mixed countries (A7=2): Approximation, quality and accuracy of the classification and core of the attributes

Class: 1	Class: 2	Class: 3
Objects: 8	Objects: 15	Objects: 12
Lower: 7; Upper: 10	Lower: 10; Upper: 19	Lower: 9;Upper: 15
Accuracy: 0.7000	Accuracy: 0.5263	Accuracy: 0.6000
Quality: 0.7429; Accuracy: 0.5909		
Core attributes A1, A2, A8, A9		

Table 18.17 Subset of mixed countries (A7=2): Rules

Parameters: Class: *General* -> SC1 (absolute) = 3 SC2 = 5 D = 100

rule 1. (A1 = 4) & (A5 = 2) => (D1=3); [3, 3, 25.00%, 100.00%] [0, 0, 3]
rule 2. (A2 = 2) & (A4 = 1) => (D1=3); [3, 3, 25.00%, 100.00%] [0, 0, 3]
rule 3. (A2 = 2) & (A5 = 2) => (D1=3); [5, 5, 41.67%, 100.00%] [0, 0, 5]
rule 4. (A2 = 2) & (A8 = 1) => (D1=3); [3, 3, 25.00%, 100.00%] [0, 0, 3]
rule 5. (A5 = 2) & (A9 = 1) => (D1=3); [4, 4, 33.33%, 100.00%] [0, 0, 4]

In the subset of developed countries, the core consists of the attributes 'government spending', 'number of observations', 'year of the earliest observation' and 'journal level' (Table 18.18). Six strong rules were generated which reconfirmed the results obtained in the full set of studies. For example, rule 1 in Table 18.19 is the same as rule 4 in Table 18.3, rule 2 in Table 18.19 is the same as rule 5 in Table 18.3, etc.

Table 18.18   Subset of developed countries (A7=3): Approximation, quality and accuracy of the classification and core of the attributes

Class: 1	Class: 2	Class: 3
Objects: 13	Objects: 19	Objects: 28
Lower: 13; Upper: 13	Lower: 18; Upper: 20	Lower: 27; Upper: 29
Accuracy: 1.0000	Accuracy: 0.9000	Accuracy: 0.9310
Quality: 0.9667; Accuracy: 0.9355		
Core attributes: A1, A4, A5, A9		

Table 18.19   Subset of developed countries (A7=3): Rules

Parameters: Class: *General*   ->   SC1 (absolute) = 8   SC2 = 5   D = 100

rule 1. $(A1 = 4)$ & $(A8 = 2)$ => $(D1=3)$; [12, 12, 42.86%, 100.00%] [0, 0, 12]
rule 2. $(A1 = 4)$ & $(A2 = 1)$ & $(A5 = 0)$ => $(D1=3)$; [10, 10, 35.71%, 100.00%] [0, 0, 10]
rule 3. $(A1 = 4)$ & $(A3 = 0)$ & $(A4 = 1)$ => $(D1=3)$; [9, 9, 32.14%, 100.00%] [0, 0, 9]
rule 4. $(A1 = 4)$ & $(A4 = 1)$ & $(A5 = 0)$ => $(D1=3)$; [9, 9, 32.14%, 100.00%] [0, 0, 9]
rule 5. $(A1 = 4)$ & $(A4 = 1)$ & $(A6 = 1)$ => $(D1=3)$; [11, 11, 39.29%, 100.00%] [0, 0, 11]
rule 6. $(A1 = 4)$ & $(A5 = 0)$ & $(A6 = 1)$ => $(D1=3)$; [11, 11, 39.29%, 100.00%] [0, 0, 11]

18.6   Conclusions

After the computations of the previous section, we may conclude that significant progress has been made towards achieving the goals of accuracy, stability and comprehensibility of the meta-analysis of growth studies. It turned out in our empirical analysis that the classification showed a stable result from the point of view of accuracy, but the overarching goal of output comprehensibility remains elusive. The present study has aimed to move closer to this ideal by having proposed a learning method combining some of the accuracy and stability gains of a multiple data set with the comprehensibility of a single overall data set.

Of course, the results by themselves do not explain the uneven distribution of growth among different countries and regions. Output comprehensibility is more difficult to measure than accuracy, since it is ultimately subjective. The flexibility of the approach, while essential to improving our knowledge in the field, has the disadvantage of allowing data mining algorithms to be overly responsive to the full data set, producing models that can change dramatically with small changes in the data. Of course there is an analogy with classical regression analysis that model over-fitting leads to excellent goodness of fit statistics but bad forecasts. In the same way, instability undermines the claim of artificial intelligence systems to be efficient in the production of knowledge. However, the rough set approach has shown a great potential for knowledge reduction, which is the main focus of this line of research (Famili et al. 1997).

In this contribution we have attempted to identify a robust set of predictive statements regarding the impact of government on long-run growth. In conventional econometric analyses, this type of endeavour would have involved the collection of a range of characteristics for a sample of constituencies and the statistical inference of causal relationships from such characteristics to the economic growth rates of the constituencies. However, the impossibility of carrying out such causal analyses in controlled experimental settings have in the past thwarted our ability to derive strong predictive statements. Missing relevant variables and a space-time dependency of the causal relationships have contributed to this failure, and are partly responsible for the 'dismal science' label of our discipline.

However, the prospects for empirical verification of the body of current theories are becoming brighter. There are at least four reasons. Firstly, the information and communication technology [ICT] revolution has contributed to making the findings of empirical research a greater availability far more rapidly and readily. Working papers can be easily downloaded from the Internet and published results that would traditionally have only been available from a few local libraries can now be accessed throughout the world. Secondly, ICT developments have also decreased the cost of data collection in the form of surveys. The growing number of purpose-designed surveys is providing large new micro-level data sets, often of a panel nature. Thirdly, modern ICT generates vast amounts of data as the by-product of financial and administrative transactions. Although privacy issues are of increasing concern, there is no doubt that there has been a great improvement in the availability of rich information on many socio-economic phenomena [although special features of information, such as monopoly supply and near zero marginal costs of distribution create special pricing problems]. Fourthly, new methods have become available for the analysis of such data. These include neural network analysis, non-linear dynamics and chaos theory, logit models, GIS systems, multi criteria analysis, rough set analysis and other methods for the study of soft or qualitative data.

In this contribution we have adopted the method of rough set analysis to identify specific predictive patterns in a sample of 123 empirical studies of the impact of fiscal policies on the long-run growth rate. The vast majority of these studies were conventional cross-section or panel data regression models. Our results reconfirm other recent evidence, provided for instance by Kneller, Bleaney and Gemmell (1999), that productive government expenditure [education and infrastructure] enhance growth while non-productive expenditure [public services, administration, transfer payments] do not. However, the results are sensitive to various characteristics of the studies. For example, early studies were more supportive of a 'peace dividend' than more recent ones.. Also, we find that the impact of infrastructural investment cannot be detected in the short-run: the positive impact of infrastructure on growth can only be detected in time-series analyses, not in cross section analyses. Furthermore, the impact of government expenditure on growth appears to depend on whether the studies are concerned with developed or less developed countries. Recently, Obersteiner and Wilk (1999) also showed by means of rough set analysis of the growth experience of a cross section of countries that a partitioning into industrialised and non-industrialised countries is essential.

While rough set analysis has enabled us to identify a few firm conclusions from a large body of empirical literature, the method has also some limitations. One problem is that there is a trade-off between sample size and the range of attributes. Large samples may be considered more representative of the available literature than small samples, but they are also more heterogeneous and the range of attributes that are common to all studies is correspondingly rather small. A much wider range of attributes may be available for a small range of more narrowly focussed studies, e.g. all studies concerned with the impact on growth of an increase in R&D subsidies. In this case meta-regression analysis may also become feasible, but the value transfer of the findings from a few location, time and method-specific studies may then be in doubt.

A weakness that rough set analysis has in common with some other meta-analytic techniques is the potential sensitivity of the results to publication bias. If it is true that it is easier to get results that report significant findings published than insignificant ones, then the proportion of studies in our sample revealing a conclusive positive or negative fiscal impact, 64 percent, may be overestimated. One indication of publication bias is the absence of a link between the number of observations and the levels of the decision variable. Statistical theory would suggest that conclusive results [positive or negative] are less common among data sets with a large number of observations, but our sample does not appear to support this prediction. Future research will investigate to what extent pre-testing and specification searches have affected published findings in this literature.

While our rough set analysis highlights the importance of education and infrastructure expenditure, the available information is unfortunately not specific enough to translate the findings into policy recommendations. Moreover, much of the literature ignores the budget constraints under which governments must operate. Another issue is the potential endogeneity of the fiscal variables. Wagner's law suggests that the share of government expenditure in total income is positively related to per capita income. This may explain the growth in the public sector in developed economies in the second half of the 20th century, although Olekalns (1999) recently showed that some of this correlation was due the changing age distribution of the population. However, without substituting suitable instruments for the fiscal variables in the growth regression models, the results may again be biased, and this would also affect our rough set analysis. Indeed, there appears to be scope for investigating causality and endogeneity issues in rough set analysis by assessing the implications of switching condition and decision attributes.

Finally, the present analysis is too narrowly focussed to inform policy. Much of government expenditure is concerned with equity considerations rather than efficiency. The issue of whether government faces a trade-off in its pursuit of long-run economic growth and an equitable distribution of income has not yet been resolved (see Aghion, Caroli and Garcia-Penalosa 1999 for a recent survey). Nonetheless, there would be merit in extending the rough set analysis of the impact of fiscal variables to one with multiple decision variables, in which each variable measures one of a range of public policy objectives.

Appendix A-18.1: The Information Table

Objects / Authors [see Appendix A-18.2]	Observation Number	A1 Type of Government Spending C=1, D=2, T=3, I=4, E=5	A2 Year of Publication	A3 Countries (0) or Regions (1)	A4 Number of Observations	A5 Year of Earliest Observation	A6 Year of Most Recent Observation	A7 Level of Development 1=LDC 2=mixed 3=DC	A8 Method CS=1 TS=2 CSTS=3 Other=4	A9 Journal Level 1=low to 4=top journal	Decision D1 Fiscal Impact 1=negative 2=inconclusive 3=positive
Deger and Smith	1	2	1983	0	50	1965	1973	2		1	1
Gemmell	2	1	1983	0	54	1960	1970	2	3	2	2
Landau	3	5	1983	0	96	1960	1977	2		2	3
Landau	4	1	1983	0	96	1960	1977	2	1	2	1
Lim	5	2	1983	0	54	1965	1973	1		2	3
Ratner	6	4	1983	0	24	1949	1973	3	2	3	3
Cappelen, Gledisch and Bjerkholt	7	2	1984	0	85	1960	1980	3	3	3	1
Faini, Annez and Taylor	8	2	1984	0	1,242	1952	1970	2	3	1	1
Lindgren	9	2	1984	0	41	1968	1984	3	4	2	1
Helms	10	3	1985	1	672	1965	1979	3	3	4	1
Kormendi and Meguire	11	1	1985	0	47	1950	1977	2	3	3	2
Landau	12	4	1985	0	384	1952	1976	3	3	2	1
Landau	13	1	1985	0	384	1952	1976	3	3	2	2
Saunders	14	2	1985	0	46	1960	1981	3	3	1	2
Biswas and Ram	15	2	1986	0	116	1960	1977	1	3	2	2
Landau	16	4	1986	0	1,152	1960	1980	2	3	2	2
Landau	17	1	1986	0	1,152	1960	1980	2	3	2	2
Ram	18	1	1986	0	230	1960	1980	2	3	4	3
Ram	19	1	1986	0	2,300	1960	1980	2	3	4	3
Canto and Webb	20	3	1987	1	960	1957	1977	1	1	2	3
da Silva Costa, Ellson and Martin	21	1	1987	1	48	1972	1972	3	3	2	3
Bairam	22	1	1988	0	20	1960	1980	3	2		3
Grossman	23	1	1988	0	34	1949	1984	3	2	2	2
Aschauer - a	24	4	1989	0	133	1966	1985	3	3	1	3
Aschauer - b	25	4	1989	0	36	1949	1985	3	2	3	3
Aschauer - c	26	4	1989	0	33	1953	1986	3	2	3	3
Grier and Tullock	27	1	1989	0	565	1950	1981	2	3	3	1

(*continued overleaf*)

No.	Author	N	Year	F	Value	Start	End				ctd.
29	Gyimah-Brempong	2	1989	0	390	1973	1983	1	1	3	1
28	Grobar and Porter	2	1989	0	29	1972	1988	-	4	4	-
30	Koester and Kormendi	3	1989	0	63	1970	1979	2	3	3	2
31	Rao	1	1989	0	230	1960	1980	2	4	3	2
32	Rao	1	1989	0	2,300	1960	1980	2	4	-	2
33	Scully	1	1989	0	115	1960	1985	1	2	3	1
34	Bairam	1	1990	0	300	1960	1983	-	-	-	2
35	Grossman	4	1990	1	48	1970	1966	2	2	2	2
36	Mullen and Williams	4	1990	0	29	1963	1987	3	2	-	3
37	Munnell - a	4	1990	1	38	1949	1986	3	-	1	3
38	Munnell - b	5	1990	0	48	1970	1985	2	4	-	3
39	Barro	1	1991	0	98	1960	1985	2	4	1	2
40	Barro	4	1991	0	98	1960	1985	1	1	2	2
41	Barro	2	1991	0	98	1960	1987	3	-	3	3
42	Chowdhury	4	1991	1	1,430	1961	1986	3	2	4	3
43	Eisner	4	1991	1	48	1970	1986	4	2	1	2
44	Hulten and Schwab	4	1991	1	144	1970	1986	3	2	3	2
45	Hulten and Schwab	5	1991	1	144	1970	1976	3	2	1	3
46	Moomaw and Williams	4	1991	1	48	1954	1976	3	2	-	1
47	Moomaw and Williams	3	1991	1	48	1954	1985	3	1	2	2
48	Yu, Wallace and Nardinelli	5	1992	0	336	1929	1989	3	4	4	2
49	Levine and Renelt	1	1992	0	103	1960	1989	2	4	4	3
50	Levine and Renelt	4	1992	0	103	1960	1989	2	4	3	3
51	Lynde and Richmond	4	1992	0	32	1958	1989	3	4	1	2
52	Munnell	4	1992	1	38	1973	1992	3	2	1	4
53	Bajo-Rubio and Sosvilla-Rivero	4	1993	0	25	1964	1988	3	1	1	2
54	Binswanger et al	1	1993	1	85	1960	1981	3	-	-	1
55	Durden and Elledge	3	1993	1	48	1982	1993	2	1	3	1
56	Easterly and Rebelo	4	1993	0	100	1970	1988	2	3	3	2
57	Easterly and Rebelo	4	1993	0	100	1970	1988	3	3	3	2
58	Easterly and Rebelo	3	1993	0	3,304	1870	1988	3	3	3	3
59	Easterly and Rebelo	4	1993	0	3,304	1870	1988	3	3	3	3
60	Lynde and Richmond	4	1993	0	32	1958	1989	2	4	3	3

													ctd
Mohammed	61	2	1993	0	390	1973	1983	1	1	4	—	1	2
Park	62	2	1993	0	25	1963	1987	1	1	2	—	1	2
Sattar	63	1	1993	0	560	1950	1985	3	3	3	1	3	3
Sattar	64	1	1993	0	280	1950	1985	2	1	1	1	2	2
Sheehey	65	3	1993	0	102	1985	1980	3	4	4	1	3	1
van Sinderen	66	1	1993	0	1	1970	1985	3	3	3	—	1	1
Assane and Pourgerami	67	5	1994	1	46	1970	1990	3	4	3	4	3	3
Evans and Karras	68	1	1994	1	768	1970	1986	3	4	3	4	3	1
Evans and Karras	69	4	1994	1	768	1970	1986	3	4	3	4	3	2
Evans and Karras	70	1	1994	1	768	1970	1986	3	1	3	4	3	2
Hansen - a	71	1	1994	0	242	1966	1988	3	2	3	1	3	2
Hansen - b	72	5	1994	0	92	1968	1991	3	2	2	2	3	3
Hansson and Henrekson	73	4	1994	0	153	1970	1987	3	1	1	—	3	2
Hansson and Henrekson	74	4	1994	0	153	1970	1987	3	1	1	2	3	2
Hansson and Henrekson	75	4	1994	0	153	1970	1987	3	1	1	—	3	2
Holtz-Eakin	76	4	1994	1	816	1969	1986	3	3	3	4	3	2
Hsieh and Lai	77	2	1994	0	714	1885	1987	3	2	2	2	3	2
Kusi	78	1	1994	0	1,386	1971	1989	1	—	1	—	1	2
Lee and Lin	79	1	1994	0	114	1960	1985	3	2	4	4	2	2
Lin	80	1	1994	0	20	1960	1985	1	1	1	—	2	3
Lin	81	1	1994	0	42	1960	1985	1	2	3	1	2	3
Sala-i-Martin	82	1	1994	0	12	1986	1993	2	4	4	2	3	3
Sala-i-Martin	83	5	1994	0	12	1986	1993	3	3	3	3	3	3
Andrews and Swanson	84	4	1995	1	768	1970	1986	3	4	3	—	3	3
Berthelemy, Herrera and Sen	85	2	1995	0	2	1972	1972	1	4	4	1	1	1
Chletsos and Kollias	86	2	1995	0	17	1974	1990	3	2	2	—	2	2
Garrison and Lee	87	2	1995	0	67	1960	1987	2	1	1	—	1	1
Garrison and Lee	88	3	1995	0	67	1960	1987	2	1	—	—	1	1
Holtz-Eakin and Schwartz	89	4	1995	1	720	1971	1986	3	3	3	2	2	2
Karikari	90	1	1995	0	21	1963	1984	1	2	2	1	1	—
Macnair et al.	91	2	1995	0	370	1951	1988	3	3	3	2	3	3
Macnair et al.	92	—	1995	0	370	1951	1988	3	3	3	2	3	3
Andres, Domenech and Molinas	93	1	1996	0	720	1960	1990	3	3	3	3	3	2

(*continued overleaf*)

											ctd
Devarajan, Swaroop and Zou	94	1	1996	0	860	1970	1990	1	3	3	3
Devarajan, Swaroop and Zou	95	4	1996	0	860	1970	1990	1	3	3	1
Dunne	96	2	1996	0	54	1973	1996	3	4	1	2
Harmatuck	97	4	1996	0	36	1949	1985	3	2	4	3
Kocherlakota and Yi	98	3	1996	0	71	1917	1988	3	2	4	2
Kocherlakota and Yi	99	2	1996	0	71	1917	1988	3	2	4	2
Kocherlakota and Yi	100	4	1996	1	71	1917	1988	3	2	4	3
Morrison and Schwartz	101	2	1996	0	816	1970	1987	3	2	2	1
Roux	102	4	1996	0	30	1960	1990	3	2	2	3
Wylie	103	4	1996	0	45	1946	1991	3	2	3	3
Ansari and Singh	104	5	1997	0	36	1951	1987	2	2	3	1
Barro	105	5	1997	0	3,000	1960	1990	2	3	1	3
Barro	106	1	1997	0	3,000	1960	1990	2	3	1	3
Brumm	107	2	1997	0	88	1974	1989	2	1	4	3
Glomm and Ravikumar	108	5	1997	0	31	1983	1994	2	4	4	1
Glomm and Ravikumar	109	4	1997	0	31	1983	1994	2	4	4	3
Guseh	110	1	1997	0	1,475	1960	1985	1	3	3	3
Kocherlakota and Yi	111	3	1997	0	320	1831	1991	3	2	2	1
Kocherlakota and Yi	112	4	1997	0	320	1831	1991	3	2	2	3
Kollias and Makrydakis	113	2	1997	0	39	1954	1993	3	2	1	2
Lau and Sin	114	4	1997	0	64	1925	1989	3	2	2	3
Odedokun	115	4	1997	0	960	1970	1990	1	3	1	3
Singh and Weber	116	5	1997	0	44	1950	1994	3	2	2	3
Baffes and Shah	117	2	1998	0	420	1965	1984	1	3	2	1
Baffes and Shah	118	5	1998	0	420	1965	1984	1	3	2	3
Button	119	4	1998	1	28	1973	1994	3	4	1	3
Cronovich	120	1	1998	0	30	1970	1990	2	1	2	3
Sanchez-Robles	121	4	1998	0	57	1970	1992	2	1	1	3
Sanchez-Robles	122	4	1998	0	19	1970	1985	2	1	1	3
Zhang and Zou	123	1	1998	0	420	1978	1992	1	3	3	2

Appendix A-18.2:
The 93 articles used in compiling Appendix A-18.1

Andrés J., Doménech R. and Molinas C. (1996): Macroeconomic Performance and Convergence in OECD Countries, *European Economic Review* 40, 1683-1704

Andrews K. and Swanson J. (1995): Does Public Infrastructure Affect Regional Performance? *Growth and Change* 26 (2), 204-216

Ansari M.I. and Singh S.K. (1997): Public Spending on Education and Economic Growth in India: Evidence From VAR Modelling, *Indian Journal of Applied Economics* 6 (2), 43-64

Aschauer D.A. (1989a): Public Investment and Productivity Growth in the Group of Seven, *Economic Perspectives* 13 (5), 17-25

Aschauer D.A. (1989b): Is Public Expenditure Productive? *Journal of Monetary Economics* 23 (2), 177-200

Aschauer D.A. (1989c): Does Public Capital Crowd Out Private Capital? *Journal of Monetary Economics* 24, 171-188

Assane D. and Pourgerami A. (1994): Monetary Co-operation and Economic Growth in Africa: Comparative Evidence From the CFA-Zone Countries, *Journal of Development Studies* 30 (2), 423-442

Baffes J. and Shah A. (1998): Productivity of Public Spending, Sectorial Allocation Choices and Economic Growth, *Economic Development and Cultural Change* 46 (2), 291-303

Bairam E. (1988): Government Expenditure and Economic Growth: Some Evidence From New Zealand Time Series Data, *Keio Economic Studies* 25 (1), 59-66

Bairam E. (1990): Government Size and Economic Growth: The African Experience, 1960-1985, *Applied Economics* 22 (10), 1427-1435

Bajo-Rubio O. and Sosvilla-Rivero S. (1993): Does Public Capital Affect Private Sector Performance? An Analysis of the Spanish Case, 1964-88, *Economic Modelling* 10, 179-185

Barro R.J. (1991): Economic Growth in a Cross-Section of Countries, *Quarterly Journal of Economics* (May), 407-443

Barro R.J. (1997): *Determinants of Economic Growth: A Cross-Country Empirical Study*, MIT Press, Cambridge [MA]

Berthélemy J.C., Herrera R. and Sen S. (1995): Military Expenditure and Economic Development: An Endogenous Growth Perspective, *Economics of Planning* 28 (2-3), 205-233

Binswanger H.P., Khandker S.R. and Rosenzweig M.R. (1993): How Infrastructure and Financial Institutions Affect Agricultural Output and Investment in India, *Journal of Development Economics* 41, 337-366

Biswas B. and Ram R. (1986): Military Expenditures and Economic Growth in Less Developed Countries: An Augmented Model and Further Evidence, *Economic Development and Cultural Change* 34, 361-372

Brumm H. (1997): Military Spending, Government Disarray, and Economic Growth: A Cross-Country Empirical Analysis, *Journal of Macroeconomics* 19 (4), 827-838

Button K. (1998): Infrastructure Investment, Endogenous Growth and Economic Convergence, *The Annals of Regional Science* 32 (1), 145-162

Canto V. and Webb R.I. (1987): The Effect of State Fiscal Policy on State Relative Economic Performance, *Southern Economic Journal* 54 (July), 186-202

Cappelen A., Gleditsch N.P. and Bjerkholt O. (1984): Military Spending and Economic Growth in OECD Countries, *Journal of Peace Research* 21(4), 361-373

Chletsos M. and Kollias C. (1995): Defence Spending and Growth in Greece 1974-1990: Some Preliminary Econometric Results, *Applied Economics* 27 (9), 883-890

Chowdhury AR (1991): A Causal Analysis of Defense Spending and Economic Growth, *Journal of Conflict Resolution* 35 (1), 80-97

Cronovich R. (1998): Measuring the Human Capital Intensity of Government Spending and its Impact on Economic Growth in a Cross Section of Countries, *Scottish Journal of Political Economy* 45 (1), 48-77

da Silva Costa J., Ellson R.W. and Martin R.C. (1987): Public Capital, Regional Output, and Development: Some Empirical Evidence, *Journal of Regional Science* 27 (3), 419-437

Deger S. and Smith R. (1983): Military Expenditure and Growth in Less Developed Countries, *Journal of Conflict Resolution* 27 (2), 335-353

Devarajan S., Swaroop V. and Zou H. (1996): The Composition of Public Expenditure and Economic Growth, *Journal of Monetary Economics* 37 (2), 313-344

Dunne J.P. (1996): Economic Effects of Military Expenditure in Developing Countries: A survey. In: Gleditsch N.P., Bjerkholt O., Cappelen A., Smith R.P., Dunne J.P. (eds.), *The Peace Dividend*, Elsevier Science, Amsterdam, pp. 195-211

Durden G. and Elledge B. (1993): The Effect of Government Size on Economic Growth: Evidence From Gross State Product Data, *Review of Regional Studies* 23 (2), 183-190

Easterly W. and Rebelo S. (1993): Fiscal Policy and Economic Growth: An Empirical Investigation, *Journal of Monetary Economics* 32 (3), 417-458

Eisner R. (1991): Infrastructure and Regional Economic Performance: Comment, *New England Economic Review* 74 (Sep/Oct), 47-58

Evans P. and Karras G. (1994): Are Government Activities Productive? Evidence From a Panel of U.S. States, *Review of Economics and Statistics* 76 (1), 1-11

Faini R., Annez P. and Taylor L (1984): Defense Spending, Economic Structure, and Growth: Evidence Among Countries and Over Time, *Economic Development and Cultural Change* 32 (3), 487-498

Garrison C.B. and Lee F.Y. (1995): The Effect of Macroeconomic Variables on Economic Growth Rates: A Cross-Country Study, *Journal of Macroeconomic* 17 (2), 303-317

Gemmell N. (1983): International Comparison of the Effects of Non-Market Sector Growth, *Journal of Comparative Economics* 7, 368-381

Glomm G. and Ravikumar B. (1997): Productive Government Expenditures and Long-Run Growth, *Journal of Economic Dynamics and Control* 21 (1), 183-204

Grier K.B. and Tullock G. (1989): An Empirical Analysis of Cross-National Economic Growth, 1951-80, *Journal of Monetary Economics* 24, 259-276

Grobar L.M. and Porter R.C. (1989): Benoit Revisited: Defense Spending and Economic Growth in LDCs, *Journal of Conflict Resolution* 33 (2), 318-345

Grossman P.J. (1988): Growth in Government and Economic Growth: The Australian Experience, *Australian Economic Papers* 27 (50), 33-43

Grossman P.J. (1990): Government and Growth: Cross-Sectional Evidence, *Public Choice* 65 (3), 217-227

Guseh J.S. (1997): Government Size and Economic Growth in Developing Countries: A Political-Economy Framework, *Journal of Macroeconomic* 19 (1), 175-192

Gyimah-Brempong K. (1989): Defense Spending and Economic Growth in Subsaharan Afria: An Econometric Investigation, *Journal of Peace Research* 26 (1), 79-90

Hansen P. (1994a): Investment Data and the Empirical Relationship Between Exporters, Government and Economic Growth, *Applied Economics Letters* 1994 (1), 107-110

Hansen P. (1994b): The Government, Exporters and Economic Growth in New Zealand, *New Zealand Economic Papers* 28 (2), 133-142

Hansson P. and Henrekson M. (1994): A New Framework for Testing the Effect of Government Spending on Growth and Productivity, *Public Choice* 81 (3-4), 381-401

Harmatuck D.J. (1996): The Influence of Transportation Infrastructure on Economic Development, *Logistics and Transportation Review* 32 (1), 63-76

Helms L.J. (1985): The Effects of State and Local Taxes on Economic Growth: A Time Series-Cross Section Approach, *Review of Economics and Statistics* 67 (Nov.), 574-582

Holtz-Eakin D. (1994): Public Sector Capital and the Productivity Puzzle, *Review of Economics and Statistics* 76 (1), 12-21

Holtz-Eakin D. and Schwartz A.E. (1995): Infrastructure in a Structural Model of Economic Growth, *Regional Science and Urban Economics* 25 (2), 131-151

Hsieh E. and Lai K.S. (1994): Government Spending and Economic Growth: The G-7 Experience, *Applied Economics* 26 (5), 535-542

Hulten C. and Schwab R. (1991): Public Capital Formation and the Growth of Regional Manufacturing Industries, *National Tax Journal* 44 (4), 121-134

Karikari J.A. (1995): Government and Economic Growth in a Developing Nation: The Case of Ghana, *Journal of Economic Development* 20 (2), 85-97

Kocherlakota N. and Yi K.M. (1996): A Simple Time Series Test of Endogenous versus Exogenous Growth Models: An Application to the United States, *Review of Economics and Statistics* 78, 126-134

Kocherlakota N. and Yi K.M. (1997): Is There Endogenous Long-Run Growth? Evidence from the United States and the United Kingdom, *Journal of Money, Credit and Banking* 29 (2), 235-262

Koester R.B. and Kormendi R.C. (1989): Taxation, Aggregate Activity and Economic Growth: Cross-Country Evidence on Some Supply-Side Hypotheses, *Economic Inquiry* 27, 367-386

Kollias C. and Makrydakis S. (1997): Defence Spending and Growth in Turkey 1954-1993: A Causal Analysis, *Defence and Peace Economics* 8 (2), 189-204

Kormendi R.C. and Meguire P.G. (1985): Macroeconomic Determinants of Growth: Cross-Country Evidence, *Journal of Monetary Economics* 16 (2), 141-163

Kusi N.K. (1994): Economic Growth and Defense Spending in Developing Countries: A Causal Analysis, *Journal of Conflict Resolution* 38 (1), 152-159

Landau D.L. (1983): Government Expenditure and Economic Growth: A Cross-Country Study, *Southern Economic Journal* 49 (3), 783-792

Landau D.L. (1985): Government Expenditure and Economic Growth in the Developed Countries: 1952-76, *Public Choice* 47, 459-477

Landau D.L. (1986): Government and Economic Growth in the Less Developed Countries: An Empirical Study for 1960-1980, *Economic Development and Cultural Change* 35 (1), 34-75

Lau S.H.P. and Sin C.Y. (1997): Public Infrastructure and Economic Growth: Time-Series Properties and Evidence, *Economic Record* 73 (221), 125-135

Lee B.S. and Lin S. (1994): Government Size, Demographic Changes, and Economic growth, *International Economic Journal* 8 (1), 91-108

Levine R. and Renelt D. (1992): A Sensitivity Analysis of Cross-Country Growth Regressions, *American Economic Review* 82 (4), 942-963

Lim D. (1983): Another Look at Growth and Defense in Less Developed Countries, *Economic Development and Cultural Change* 31 (January), 377-384

Lin S.A.Y. (1994): Government Spending and Economic Growth, *Applied Economics* 26 (1), 83-94

Lindgren G. (1984): Review Essay: Armaments and Economic Performance in Industrialized Market Economies, *Journal of Peace Research* 21 (4), 375-387

Lynde C. and Richmond J. (1992): The Role of Public Capital in Production, *Review of Economics and Statistics* 74, 37-44

Lynde C. and Richmond J. (1993): Public Capital and Total Factor Productivity, *International Economic Review*, 34 (2), 401-444

Macnair E.S., Murdoch J.C., Pi C.R. and Sandler T. (1995): Growth and Defense: Pooled Estimates for the NATO Alliance, 1951-1988, *Southern Economic Journal* 61 (3), 846-860

Mohammed N.A.L. (1993): Defense Spending and Economic Growth in Subsaharan Africa: Comment on Gyimah-Brempong, *Journal of Peace Research* 30 (1), 95-99

Moomaw R. and Williams, M. (1991) Total Factor Productivity Growth in Manufacturing: Further Evidence from the States, *Journal of Regional Science* 31 (1), 17-34

Morrison C.J. and Schwartz A.E. (1996): State Infrastructure and Productive Performance. *American Economic Review* 86 (5), 1095-1111

Mullen J. and Williams M. (1990): Explaining Total Factor Productivity Differentials in Urban Manufacturing, *Journal of Urban Economics* 28, 103-123

Munnell A.H. (1990a): Why Has Productivity Growth Declined? Productivity and Public Investment, *New England Economic Review* 30 (January/February), 3-22

Munnell A.H. (1990b): How Does Public Infrastructure Affect Regional Performance? *New England Economic Review* 30 (Sept/Oct), 11-32

Munnell A.H. (1992): Infrastructure Investment and Economic Growth, *Journal of Economic Perspectives* 6 (4), 189-198

Odedokun M.O. (1997): Relative Effects of Public Versus Private Investment Spending on Economic Efficiency and Growth in Developing Countries, *Applied Economics* 29 (10), 1325-1336

Park K.Y. (1993): Pouring New Wine into Fresh Wineskins: Defense Spending and Economic Growth in LDCs with Application to South Korea, *Journal of Peace Research* 30 (1), 79-93

Ram R. (1986): Government Size and Economic Growth: A New Framework and Some Evidence From Cross-Section and Time-Series Data, *American Economic Review* 76 (1), 191-203

Rao V.V.B. (1989): Government Size and Economic Growth: A New Framework and Some Evidence From Cross-Section and Time-Series Data. Comment, *American Economic Review* 79 (1), 272-280

Ratner J.B. (1983): Government Capital and the Production Function for U.S. Private Output, *Economics Letters* 13, 213-217

Roux A. (1996): Defense Expenditure and Economic Growth in South Africa, *Journal for Studies in Economics and Econometrics* 20 (1), 19-34

Sala-i-Martin X. (1994): Economic Growth: Cross-Sectional Regressions and the Empirics of Economic Growth, *European Economic Review* 38 (3-4), 739-747

Sanchez-Robles B. (1998): Infrastructure Investment and Growth: Some Empirical Evidence, *Contemporary Economic Policy* 16 (1), 98-108

Sattar Z. (1993): Government Control and Economic Growth in Asia: Evidence From Time Series Data, *The Pakistan Development Review* 32 (2), 179-197

Saunders P. (1985): Public Expenditure and Economic Performance in OECD Countries, *Journal of Public Policy* 5 (1), 1-21

Scully G.W. (1989): The Size of the State, Economic Growth and the Efficient Utilization of National Resources, *Public Choice* 63 (2), 149-164

Sheehey A.J. (1993): The Effect of Government Size on Economic Growth, *Eastern Economic Journal* 19 (3), 321-328

Singh R.J. and Weber R. (1997): The Composition of Public Expenditure and Economic Growth: Can Anything Be Learned From Swiss Data? *Schweizerische Zeitschrift fur Volkswirtschaft und Statistik/Swiss Journal of Economics and Statistics* 133 (3), 617-634

Van Sinderen J. (1993): Taxation and Economic Growth, *Economic Modelling* 10 (3), 285-300

Wylie P.J. (1996): Infrastructure and Canadian Economic Growth, 1946-1991, *Canadian Journal of Economics* 29 [Special Issue Part 1], 350-355

Yu W., Wallace M.S. and Nardinelli C. (1991): State Growth Rates: Taxes, Spending and Catching Up, *Public Finance Quarterly* 19 (1), 80-93

Zhang T. and Zou H.F. (1998): Fiscal Decentralization, Public Spending and Economic Growth in China, *Journal of Public Economics* 67 (2), 221-240

Regional Studies, Vol. 30.3, pp. 225–237

Regional Variations in Production Network Externalities

ROBERTA CAPELLO* and PETER NIJKAMP†

*Department of Economics and Production, Polytechnic of Milan, Piazza Leonardo da Vinci 32, 20133 Milano, Italy
†Department of Regional Economics, Free University, De Boelelaan 1105, 1081 HV – Amsterdam, the Netherlands

(Received March 1994; in revised form July 1995)

CAPELLO R. and NIJKAMP P. (1996) Regional variations in production network externalities, *Reg. Studies*, **30**, 225–237. In th present paper the main area of analysis is the concept of *network externalities* and its interpretation from a theoretical, conceptua and empirical point of view. A conceptual framework is built on the proposition that network externalities are one of the decisiv reasons for entering a telecommunication network. Since externality mechanisms arise at the user side and impact on the deman function, they can be labelled 'consumption network externalities'. However, this paper goes a step further than the recent literatur by claiming that telecommunication networks are not only governed by *consumption network externalities*, but also generate *productio network externalities*, since their advantages may be measured in terms of the performance of firms and regions. The paper presen a conceptual model on the role network externality plays on the performance of firms and regions, a methodology to measur these externalities at an empirical level and the results of the empirical analysis developed in Italy. Strong regional variations in th way network externalities are exploited emerge from the empirical analysis.

Network externalities   Regional disparities   Regional development   Telecommunications network and services
Technological exploitation

CAPELLO R. et NIJKAMP P. (1996). Variations régionales dans les effets externes de production en réseaux, *Reg. Studies* **30**, 225–237. Cet article cherche principalement à analyser la notion d'*effets externes en réseaux* et à l'interpréter du point de vue théorique, conceptuel et empirique. Un cadre conceptuel est établi à partir de la proposition que les effets externes en réseaux constituent l'un des facteurs décisifs qui expliquent la participation à un réseau de télécommunications. Vu que les mécanismes des effets externes se font sentir côté usager et influent sur la fonction de demande, on peut les cataloguer comme *effets externes de consommation en réseaux*. Néanmoins, cet article va plus loin par rapport à la documentation récente, prétendant que les réseaux de télécommunications sont contrôlés non seulement par des *effets externes de consommation en réseaux*, mais engendrent aussi des *effets externes de production en réseaux*, étant donné que leurs avantages peuvent être évalués en termes de la performance des entreprises et des régions. L'article présente un modèle conceptuel du rôle que joue les effets externes dans la performance des entreprises et des régions, une méthodologie afin d'évaluer ces effets externes au niveau empirique, et les résultats de l'analyse empirique développée en Italie. Il ressort de l'analyse empirique de fortes variations régionales dans l'exploitation des effets externes en réseaux.

Effets en réseaux   Ecarts régionaux   Aménagement
du territoire   Réseaux de télécommunications et services
Exploitation technologique

CAPELLO R. und NIJKAMP P. (1996). Regionale Abwei chungen bei Anbieternetzexternalisierungen, *Reg. Studies* **30** 225–237. In dem vorliegenden Aufsatz bezieht sich da Hauptgebiet der Analyse auf das Konzept der Netzexternali sierungen und seine Interpretation vom theoretischen konzeptuellen und empirischen Gesichtspunkt aus. Es wird ei konzeptueller Rahmen auf der Proposition errichtet, da Netzexternalisierungen einer der entscheidenden Gründe fü den Beitritt zum Telekommunikationsnetzsystem sind. Da Externalisationsmechanismen von Seiten des Benutzer entstehen, und sich auf die Nachfragefunktion auswirken können sie als Verbrauchernetzexternalisierung bezeichne werden. Dieser Aufsatz geht jedoch einen Schritt weiter als di kürzlich erschienene Literatur, indem er die Behauptun aufstellt, daß Telekommunikationsnetze nicht von Ver brauchernetzexternalisierung bestimmt werden, sondern auc Anbieternetzexternalisierung bewirken, da ihre Vorteile ver standen und gemessen werden können. Dieser Aufsatz stell ein konzeptuelles Modell der Rolle dar, die Netzexternali sierung bei der Leistung von Firmen und Regionen spielt sowie eine Methodik der Messung dieser Externalisierungen auf empirischer Ebene und die Ergebnisse der empirische Analyse, die in Italien entwickelt wurde. Sie weist bedeutend regionale Abweichungen in der Art und Weise der Nutzun der Netzexternalisierungen auf.

Netzexternalisierungen   Regionale Abweichungen
Regionale Entwicklung   Technologische Nutzung
Telekommunikationsnetz und -dienstleistungen

Roberta Capello and Peter Nijkamp

INTRODUCTION[1]

In the past few decades, the recognition of the importance of technological change in the telecommunications sector has acted as a catalyst for the emerging information economy. This has also induced many studies in industrial economics which aimed at identifying the economic regularities underlying the diffusion mechanisms of these technologies. The demand for telecommunication services has been widely analysed in this period within a conventional economic framework which stressed the importance of price and revenue elasticity. In recent years the attention has shifted to a new concept, viz. the concept of *network externalities*, which addresses the importance and impact of each adopter on the user-value of the network.[2] The associated mechanism of interdependent preferences of users provokes a 'bandwagon effect', i.e. a fast cumulative process in the diffusion and acceptance of these technologies. According to a growing body of literature, an extremely interesting feature of a telecommunication network is the *interrelation among decision-making processes of different users*. This direct interdependence explains the rhythm of adoption, since the user-value of these technologies is highly dependent on the number of existing subscribers (or actors connected to the network). In other words, in the diffusion mechanisms of these technologies, so-called *consumption externalities*[3] matter and define the diffusion rate of these technologies.

On the basis of the latter observation, many studies have been undertaken, at both a theoretical and an empirical level, which try to conceptualize the above phenomenon and to prove empirically the validity of this observation. The presence of network externalities has some important implications. First, when externalities matter and exist, markets may perform poorly, as then prices do not reflect all relevant information. Second, when externalities play a role, the co-ordination of diffusion processes among actors requires augmented signalling devices, such as information exchange based on an *ex ante* evaluation of firms, which complement the pricing system (ANTONELLI, 1992). If network externalities are the reason for entering a network, these implications have to be taken into consideration when infrastructural intervention policies are established in order to support the diffusion of these technologies among industrial and territorial systems. It is on this area of analysis that our work will focus, as we will explain in more detail in the next section.

In the present paper the main area of analysis is the concept of *network externalities* and its interpretation from a theoretical, conceptual and empirical point of view. In this study a conceptual framework is built on the proposition that network externalities are one of the decisive reasons for entering a telecommunication network. Since externality mechanisms arise at the user side and impact on the demand function, they can be labelled 'consumption network externalities'. However, this paper goes a step further than the recent literature, by claiming that telecommunication networks are not only governed by *consumption network externalities*, but also generate *production network externalities*, since their advantages may be measured in terms of the performance of firms and regions.

The positive effects generated by production network externalities on the performance of firms have little to do with the traditional effects on corporate performance generated by innovation processes or economies of scale. Although the effects of innovative processes and economies of scale are similar, the nature of production network externality effects is rather different, because their advantages stem from the difference between the marginal costs and benefits of being networked. This is not true for positive effects generated by innovative processes, or by economies of scale. The former stem from an increase in productivity of production processes, the latter from a decrease in costs resulting from large production operations.

In our view these 'network advantages', or network externalities, are rather difficult to exploit; while the adoption of new telecommunications technologies is similar to a 'public good' available to everybody at the same price, what is not at all a public good is the capacity to exploit these technologies in the most appropriate way. The exploitation of advanced computer networks requires organizational, managerial, technical and strategic knowledge, which is not present everywhere, and is not at all a 'public good'. For this reason it would be misleading to think that the impacts of these telecommunications technologies on the performance of firms and regions are similar everywhere. The paper tests this hypothesis from an empirical point of view, in the two contrasting regions of the North and the South of Italy.

The structure of the paper is as follows. In the next section we will briefly deal with the concept of network externality. In the third section attention is given to the development of a conceptual framework based on the idea that if network externalities are the main reason for adoption, better economic performance is the effect they produce. The fourth section then presents a methodology for network externality measurement, while the fifth section presents some results obtained by our empirical work from Italy. Some conclusions are drawn in the final section.

THE CONCEPT OF NETWORK EXTERNALITY

The term 'network externality' stems from the well-known economic concept of externality. In economic theory an externality is said to exist when an external person to a transaction is directly affected (positively or negatively) by the events of the transaction. The concept of 'network externality' is related to a simple but fundamental observation that the user-value of a network is highly dependent on the number of already existing subscribers or clients. This means that the choice for a potential user to become a member of the network is co-determined by the number of these participants. This basic but crucial statement has strong implications not only for the development trajectories of new networks, but also for some other important elements such as tariff structure, network interconnections, standardization processes, optimal dimensions of networks and inter-network competition. In other words, the existence of network externality has some far-reaching consequences for the actual operation and policy choices regarding networks. The notion of network externality is thus essentially related to the value of the network, expressed in terms of its subscriber base.

Recent studies have highlighted the vital role played by network externalities in understanding the economic and institutional environment required for the adoption of innovations and the new capital goods that interlock with them. However, it is still very difficult to give a definition of this concept, as it is subject to many interpretations and easily confused with other phenomena which have little to do with the original concept of external economies. To clarify the concept of network externalities it is useful to keep in mind the two important characteristics attributed to externalities in the economic literature. A first element is *interdependence*, which refers to an interaction between the decisions of economic agents. The second is *no compensation*, so that the one who creates costs (or enjoys benefits) is not obliged to pay for them (NIJKAMP, 1977). In the case of network externalities, the first element, inter-depenence, is easily identified. The decision of a person to join a network is highly dependent on the number of existing subscribers, i.e. on the number of people who have already made the same choice.

More complex is the identification of the second characteristic of externalities, i.e. no compensation. Useful for this purpose is the distinction between the notion of the cost of purchase and that of the adoption of these technologies. In the case of a telecommunications network, the profitability of these technologies depends only to a limited extent on the price of the equipment on the market (i.e. the price of fax machines, modems, personal computers to link to networks). Much more relevant are the costs of adoption, such as the learning process and the organizational changes firms have to cope with in order to use and exploit these technologies. The costs stem from the behaviour of other firms (which technology they adopt) and on the general level of penetration of the technology in the region (ANTONELLI, 1991). The higher the number of adopters, the higher the advantage obtained by the technology. This advantage is not (or hardly) incorporated in the cost of purchase of technical equipment, as the cost is not dependent on the number of already existing subscribers. In this case, the cost of adopting the technology does not reflect all benefits and advantages

generated by that technology, hence the 'no compensation' element is present. In other words, the actual economic value of telecommunication networks and services is only partially reflected in the benefits the individual consumers derive from telecommunication because (see SAUNDER *et al.*, 1983):

- subscribers may value the service higher than the amount that they are required to pay for it, that is there might be *consumer surplus* that is not quantified
- new telephone subscribers not only occur benefits for themselves, but also increase the benefits of being connected to the system for those who have already joined, that is, there are *subscriber network externalities*
- the willingness to pay a certain price for a given network use reflects only a minimum estimate of the benefits incurred by the caller and does not reflect the benefits received by the recipient of the call of those whom the caller or recipient of the call the contact, that is, there are *call-related externalities*.

As HAYASHI, 1992, argues, in the telephone network subscribers can benefit either from receiving telephone calls, usually on a free charge basis since the call is charged to the sender, or from enjoying a wide range of call opportunities due to the increasingly large number of subscribers. Both cases are examples of network externality. The former is often labelled 'call externality' and excluded from the narrower concept of network externality. The latter is often called 'subscriber externality' and viewed as the core of the network externality concept (NAMBU, 1986; WENDERS, 1987; HAYASHI, 1992). As explained before, the concept of network externality is related to the advantages which are not paid for once a subscriber joins a network; these advantages are higher the larger the network.

The concept of network externality is thus related to the value of the network. From this perspective network externalities are the *economic* reasons for the adoption of and entry to the network and therefore they are becoming the essential explanation for the diffusion of new interrelated technologies. Firms' decisions to join a new network depend clearly on the subscriber base of the network and the expectations that potential entrants have of the size of the subscriber base in the near future. Thus, the cost of purchasing the technology itself is not the single element in the decision-making process. Network externalities are thus the most significant mechanisms explaining the diffusion of interrelated technologies, such as telecommunications networks and network-based services. The basic idea – present in the literature – is that once the critical mass has been reached, the diffusion process proceeds to develop with ever higher diffusion rates among potential users. However, only a few attempts have been made to measure these mechanisms, while in particular no effort has been made to see whether network externalities are exploited by particular firms and are induced by particular seedbed areas. In fact, it may very well be that etwork externalities influence the industrial and spatial iffusion processes, reinforcing or hindering the raditional technological and spatial dynamics.

The effects that network externalities generate on the erformance of firms have so far largely been neglected. he present paper provides a conceptual analysis of the ffects that the existence of network externalities roduces on the industrial performance of firms which se these technologies. In the next section a conceptual ramework is developed and used to analyse the expected ndustrial and spatial performance due to advanced elecommunications technologies. The aim of the ramework is to make a first step towards the integration f the spatial aspects of technological changes and network externalities theories, the latter being con- idered as *the* main driving forces for the development of modern telecommunications technologies.

A CONCEPTUAL FRAMEWORK FOR PRODUCTION NETWORK EXTERNALITIES

The economic symbiosis concept

Our basic research questions are related to the linkage between network externalities and industrial and re- gional performance. In particular, our main aim is the analysis of the question whether or not network externalities may be measured in terms of industrial (i.e. micro-) and regional (i.e. macro-) performance. Such a research question is fraught with many empirical difficulties of a methodological nature, which will be dealt with in the empirical sections of this paper. At the purely conceptual level however, it is easier to envisage a positive relationship between network externalities and the corporate productivity.

The achievement of greater economic performance by exploiting benefits derived from joining a network is what we call an 'economic symbiosis' (ES) effect, an improvement in the economic performance based on non-paid-for synergies among firms. ES may be better defined on the basis of a set of firms strongly interrelated with each other via a physical network. This set of firms and its interdependent sectors have a relatively high productivity because of the achievement of strong advantages in comparison with the non-networked firms. These advantages may be classified in terms of direct and indirect advantages. The definition of direct advantages is related to the fact that the advantages a firm gets via a network directly affect (positively) the productivity of a firm. These can be classified as:

- *static advantages*, which may be summarized in synergies among actors operating in different economic environments
- *dynamic advantages*, represented by the possible achievement of network-based innovation, and of previously unknown markets

Other advantages may be achieved via a network, which indirectly affect the productivity of firms:

- *static advantages*, such as information provision induced via network interconnection
- *dynamic advantages*, such as complementary assets necessary to a firm involved in product or process innovations, which are in the hands of other firms and which are exchanges to the co-operation agreements and to computer network connections.

These advantages are generated by the existence of a physical linkage in the network, i.e. by what we call 'positive network externalities'. These advantages are expected to generate a positive effect on the performance of firms. As a result of more and better information, of more synergies with other sectors operating in different economic environments, of a higher degree of innova- tiveness in bureaucratic procedures and of more comple- mentary assets, these industries are more efficient (in terms of productivity) than others. The synergetic and 'symbiosis' effect generates a set of advantages the firm receives from being networked but does not pay a marginal price for. Thus, via a network, both pecuniary and technical externalities may be achieved and exploited.

The ES model may show many similarities with the 'growth pole' theory of PERROUX, 1955. In Perroux's approach, a set of firms, strongly interrelated to each other via input–output linkages around a leading industry (*l'industrie môtrice*), is able to generate strong cumulative and multiplier effects on the economy via spillover effects. The effects of a growth pole and of an economic symbiosis are very similar indeed. The positive and cumulative effects of a set of industries are the outcome, however, of two different phenomena. In the growth pole theory, the determinants of the strong dynamic effects are the existence of advanced techno- logical practices and high innovation rates in this set of industries. In the ES approach, the dynamics of these industries are explained by the physical linkage among firms, generating advantages such as more synergies among economic operators and more information. The access to a network and the non-paid-for advantages a firm gets by joining the network both play a crucial role in the performance of firms, primarily via an increase in productivity. This assumption is evident, since a firm may obtain advantages from being networked, without paying a marginal price for them. In other words, the (technical and pecuniary) network externalities gener- ated via the network are the intrinsic explanation of the ES phenomena.

Although there may be similarities in effects reflecting a better performance of firms, the causes or main reasons for this phenomenon may have completely different origins and a completely different nature. Without denying the existence of other major factors which improve the performance of firms (i.e. international market developments, better marketing strategies, etc.),

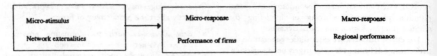

Fig. 1. Conceptual framework of network externality effects

the present framework aims at focusing only on one distinct cause of increased performance, viz. production network externalities. At the conceptual level, the framework thus rests on the assumption that the main micro-stimulus explaining adoption processes of advanced telecommunication technologies is the existence of network externalities (Fig. 1).

An interesting question at this time is whether the ES effects of a physical linkage are positive for every firm joining the network. The existing literature on this issue (see ANTONELLI, 1990; CAMAGNI and DE BLASIO, 1993) tends to attribute a positive effect to each new entrant in the network. The issue is however, rather complex and needs further investigation and discussion (see CAPELLO, 1994).

The spatial symbiosis concept

The existence and exploitation of network externalities are not confined to the firm level. The ES concept can in fact be translated into a spatial setting. This can be done, first, by the simple extension that the set of networked industries is spatially clustered and, secondly, by focusing on spillover effects not for the economy as a whole, but in the immediately surrounding hinterland.

In other words, a 'spatial symbiosis' (SS) effect takes place when a set of 'networked firms' are present in a specific region (Fig. 2). This leads to a non-zero sum of the positive effects on the firms' performance generated by the non-paid-for advantages of being networked. A set of spillover effects is in this way generated on the local (regional) economy, which can be measured in terms of better regional performance. This phenomenon can give rise to cumulative effects à la MYRDAL, 1959, and can guarantee a local sustainable development.

The SS concept is very similar to the 'growth centre' theory of BOUDEVILLE, 1968, who first provided a 'translation' of Perroux's growth role in geographical rather than economic space. Boudeville's theory emphasizes the importance of agglomeration and concentration of economic activities for local economic growth. The geographical clustering of a set of innovative industries produces strong backwash and spillover effects over space, which may lead, in the presence of some local prerequisites (i.e. a highly developed infrastructure, provision of centrally supplied public and social services, a demand for labour) to local economic growth.

The difference between the growth centre and the SS concept comes now quite clearly to the fore. Again, it

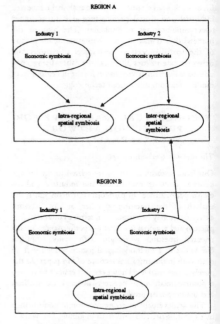

Fig. 2. Economic and spatial symbiosis

is reasonable to claim that, although the local economic effects are the same, the nature of these phenomena is quite different. In Boudeville's theory, local economic growth is explained essentially by the geographical agglomeration of innovative firms. In the SS approach, it is not only the presence of a set of networked firms which is the reason for the generation of local economic growth. In this approach, a regional economy may also very well benefit from the input obtained by inter-regional networked firms. In fact, it is likely that the physical connectivity between two firms located in two different regions may generate exchanges of local know-how and information which increase productivity, and consequently regional performance. In other words, when the connectivity takes place at an inter-regional level, the effects it produces may also have import and export implications.

Thus, in summary, the positive effects at a firm's level are expected to reflect their beneficial influence at the level of the environment in which they perform. Thus, in economic terms, we expect a region to have the possibility to gain from network externalities, by exploiting advantages stemming from its participation in the network. At a macro-level these advantages may be described as the achievement of: (1) spatially dispersed information; (2) new geographic market areas; (3) complementary know-how from different specialized economic areas; and (4) additional specialized input factors from other regions.

METHODOLOGY OF ANALYSING PRODUCTION NETWORK EXTERNALITIES

Up to now in the present study the concept of network externalities has been explained in terms of the positive and increasingly intensive relation between the number of subscribers and the performance of firms. The higher the number of subscribers, the higher the interest for a firm to join a network, and thus the better the effects on its performance. In reality, this definition is far too broad to explain the concept of network externality. In a *static perspective* the interest of a firm is not to join the highest possible number of other firms connected via the network, but only the highest number of these firms that are directly or indirectly related to its own business activities. Thus, the decision to join the network is not simply related to the total number of firms already networked, but to the number of *business-linked firms* already present in the network. The most obvious reason for entering a network is, in reality, the possibility of contacting relevant groups such as suppliers, customers or horizontally related firms in a more efficient and quicker way.

Connectivity is in fact a measure of a linkage between two or more firms in a network. The economic connectivity measures the economic relationships among firms. When these relationships are pursued via a telecommunications network, we can also speak of physical connectivity. What we argue here is that there is a strong relationship between these two kinds of connectivity; in particular *physical connectivity has no reason to exist if economic connectivity does not exist.*

Fig. 3 is a schematic representation of physical connectivity with the use of graph theory. If, according to this theory, we represent firms as 'nodes' or 'vertices', and the physical linkage among them as 'arches' or 'edges', the outcome is an (undirected) graph of vertices and edges representing all potential physical communication (or contact) lines that firms can entertain among themselves.

As we have just mentioned, the real interest of a particular firm, in a static world, is not to be linked to all other possible subscribers, but to achieve full connectivity among only those firms related to its

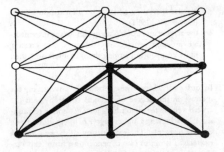

Legend:

○ Firms

● Business-linked firms

— Possible physical connections among firms

━ Physical and economic connections among specific "business-linked" firms

Fig. 3. Undirected graph representing connectivity among firms

specific business. If we represent such firms in our graph with a bold vertex, and their economic relationships with other firms with bold edges, the real matrix of first-order relationships will emerge. With this matrix it is possible to measure the proportion of real physical connectivity of a certain firm with regard to potential economic connectivity.

The physical connectivity is what generates network externalities. *If the benefit a firm receives from physical connectivity is an increasing function of connectivity itself, then positive network externalities exist*, a situation represented by the positive derivative of the benefit function. Thus, so far we have described a way of measuring network externalities under the assumption of a static world.

If we remove the assumption of a static situation, the potential linkages that firms are offered via a telecommunication network become of crucial importance. In fact, in *a dynamic perspective*, the interest of firms is not only to achieve static efficiency by developing better and quicker economic relationships with already existing suppliers and customers. The purpose and aims of networking are also related to the exploitation of other economic advantages, namely:

● the achievement of new markets (ANTONELLI, 1992)

● the development of product and process innovations, with the achievement of new and complementary technical, managerial and organizational know-how (FORNENGO, 1988; RULLANI and ZANFEI, 1988; CAPELLO and WILLIAMS, 1990)

● the control of the development trajectories of the strategic complementary know-how, by maintaining and increasing all strategic information sources (CAMAGNI, 1991)

- the achievement of higher quality in the intermediate products provided by suppliers, and creating more competition among them by increasing their number (CAPELLO and WILLIAMS, 1990).

In order to achieve these economic advantages, the increase in the degree of physical connectivity is the crucial vehicle for establishing new economic relationships, by achieving a higher degree of integration among economic agents. The exploitation of *dynamic network externalities* is in this case dependent on firms' expectations about the degree of 'co-operation' or complementarity of other firms. If they expect that other firms will be willing to co-operate, then the degree of physical connectivity will increase, and, consequently, also the benefits that firms receive from their connectivity.

With the use of this method, various important analytical questions remain from a methodological point of view. The *first open question* is related to the measurement of network externalities via a connectivity index which measures only direct connections. In other words, only *first order connectivity is measured via our method*, while second and higher order connectivity linkages are not taken into account. The choice of measuring a first order connectivity index requires in reality a careful choice. Second and third order connectivity loses the straightforward impact first order connectivity has on the production function, because the most strategic relationships which matter for the productivity of a firm are the direct relationships with suppliers and customers (PORTER, 1990). Relationships among suppliers or customers of the same firm, representing what we call second and higher order connectivity for that firm, do not have the same direct relation with the performance of that firm.

A *second open question* which arises from the method we have presented to measure network externalities is that a connectivity index does not take into account the *intensity* of information flows. While for the first question above we might disregard the importance of indirect connections of a firm on its performance, in the second case it is more difficult to avoid the problem. The intensity of use of a network, and not only its access, has inevitably an impact on corporate performance. Thus, any kind of connectivity index has to be adjusted in order to include a measure of the intensity of use. This problem will be taken into account in our empirical analysis. This point is also related to the problem of distinguishing the effects of simple adoption and of intensity of use of adopted technology. The same approach can be applied to the regional level, by identifying a linkage between a connectivity index (measuring the relationships that firms located in that region have with other firms within and outside the region) and a regional performance index. Using the same logic as in the case of the firm level, the connectivity among firms located in that

region can be measured with the use of graph theory. A positive derivative between these two indices would explain the existence of network externality effects.

A *third open question* of this method is that *the same weight in terms of economic importance is given to each link*, although one can easily readily anticipate that each first order connection is certainly bound to be of strategic importance for the firm, which could otherwise easily refuse the contact.

The same three limitations, as presented in the open questions above for the firm level, are also true for the regional level; again in this case, only first order relationships are taken into consideration, but the intensity of use of these technologies is missing in this approach. As already discussed above, the first and third open questions are not so crucial, since it can very well be that the most important connections influencing the performance of firms are direct connections and that all of them play a role in the performance of firms. The second open question is the most crucial, since the intensity of use is extremely important for our analysis.

The intensity of flows between regions may in principle be measured with the use of spatial interaction models, such as gravity models, designed with two principal nodes, and a factor measuring the obstacles raised by the distance between the two locations:

$$T_{ij} = K \cdot W_i \cdot W_j \cdot f(c_{ij})$$

where:

T_{ij} = the measure of the interaction between i and j
W_i = potential size of node i
W_j = potential size of node j
$f(c_{ij})$ = cost of interaction between i and j.

This model is normally defined at a meso/macro level. In the case of physical connectivity via a telecommunication network between two regions, the cost of interaction is represented by both entry costs and use costs of the network. These costs explain why, although by definition network externalities generate greater performance, there still might be a low intensity of use of a network. A logical explanation of this behaviour is represented by *transaction costs* to be borne, being measured in terms of both entry costs and users' costs (psychological, financial, etc.). Shadow costs of the transaction, i.e. all costs which have to be borne in a transaction process towards the adoption and use of these technologies, can in this case be measured and used as a measure of costs of interaction between regions. This model might be helpful especially at the spatial network level, but it cannot be used for individual behaviour. In most cases, the decision of a firm to join and to use a network is of a discrete nature, so that – if there is a sufficient micro-database of firm behaviour – only discrete choice models can be used. Such models are compatible with spatial interaction models at a meso/macro level (see NIJKAMP and REGGIANI, 1992). Thus the gravity model approach offers a global framework of analysis, which can be empirically validated by using micro-based behavioural choice approaches. A very simple *connectivity index* may be constructed, representing the ratio between the number of real connections to the total number of potential connections.[4] Although very simple in its formulation, it gives a measure of connection for each firm. The first open question mentioned before, querying whether it was the right approach to build a connectivity index only on first order connectivity, is not overcome by the way we build our index. However, we may be confident that second and third order connectivity has not the same effect that first order connectivity has on the production function.

The second open question regarding the lack of a measure of intensity of flows is rather important, since it also reflects at an empirical level the extremely important distinctions between the effects that a rare or an intense use of these technologies has on the production function of firms. We will also run the empirical analysis for a connectivity index weighted with the use of these technologies, thus taking into account their intensity of use. As we will see in the next sections, this index leads to different empirical results. The third open question concerns the same weight given to all connections, or links. This limitation is not overcome by our connectivity index, although for our analysis it is not a strong limitation.

Despite the relatively simple connectivity index used in the empirical analysis, the results obtained are rather satisfactory and provide evidence of what has been conceptually argued in our ES and SS framework. The effects on regional performance are measured in our empirical analysis as the sum of the positive effects that all firms located in the regions receive. Thus, we postulate that the higher the number of firms enjoying network externalities in a region, the higher the regional performance.

The research methodology followed in order to test the existence of production network externalities is based on a correlation analysis between the connectivity index and the performance index. The analysis contains an initial estimation of the correlation coefficient between the 'row' connectivity index,[5] which measures the simple adoption of these technologies by firms, and the performance index, at the national level. Subsequently, the extent to which the inclusion of the regional dimension leads to better correlation coefficients will be analysed. In this respect, *we may expect stronger regional variations in the results for the two different areas.*

The second step of the empirical analysis is devoted to the introduction of the 'frequency of use' variable into our framework. Thus, instead of measuring the correlation between the degree of adoption of these technologies and the performance of firms, the analysis is run between the use of these technologies and the performance of firms. In light of the theoretical reflections expressed in our conceptual framework, *we may expect a stronger correlation in this case* than in the case of the simple

adoption. It goes without saying that in this case also the regional dimension is introduced in the analysis, since significant regional variations are expected.

The second index for the empirical analysis is the *performance index.* A very simple performance index was chosen, which represents the labour productivity of each firm, defined as the ratio between the turnover of firms in 1991 and the number of employees in the same year. This measure may vary according to specific features of firms, namely:

- the sectors firms belong to; in fact, there may be capital-intensive and labour-intensive sectors
- the regions where firms are located; it might very well be that a sector is more productive in one region than in another because of the different regional penetration of innovation in capital and the different skill of the labour force.

To avoid any biased result with the use of our connectivity index, an analysis was undertaken on the database to see whether there was any consistent relationship between some firms' features and their productivity. In particular, an analysis was carried out to see whether the most 'labour-intensive' firms belonged to a particular sector, or were located in a specific region; whether the largest firms were located in the same regions and in the same sector. The results of this analysis showed a completely random relationship among these variables. For this reason we have some confidence that the simple performance index measured as 'labour productivity' may be used in our analysis. The next sections are devoted to the empirical results regarding the existence of production network externalities.

EMPIRICAL RESULTS AT THE REGIONAL LEVEL

The database

The database was collected via a questionnaire to 70 SMEs located in both the North and the South of Italy. Firms belong to different sectors of the economy and are all users of advanced telecommunications technologies. As far as firms in the South of Italy are concerned, the sample of firms has been chosen among those firms which had been involved in the STAR programme, an EC programme on the development of advanced telecommunication networks and services in Objective 1 regions of the Community. Launched in 1987 and completed in 1992, the programme had the specific aim to enhance regional development through the development of these advanced technologies. The choice of the firms related to the STAR programme was mainly due to the policy implications that would have emerged from the analysis. Our analysis serves in fact as a kind of evaluation of what the STAR programme has been able to do in the South of Italy.

The choice to develop the same analysis in the North of Italy was mainly due to two aspects:

- the interest in running the analysis in two regions having two completely different penetration rates of these technologies; the North of Italy has already an advanced adoption rate, while the South of Italy is at a very low penetration level
- the interest in a comparative analysis in different economically developed regions, so that the different socio-economic conditions could be measured in the analysis.

The questionnaire has allowed the realization of a database on the reasons for adoption and non-adoption, on the intensity of use of these technologies and on the effects of the performance of firms.

Relationship between the adoption of telecommunication networks and the performance of firms and regions

In this section we present empirical evidence for our important research issue, i.e. *whether network externalities play a role in the performance of firms and regions*. In particular, in this section the main focus of the analysis is the identification of a possible correlation between the performance index and the connectivity index.

In light of our conceptual framework, we expect to find a correlation between the simple adoption of networks and services and the performance of firms. However, as we said in the introductory section, the simple adoption of a connection does not lead to higher benefits or a better performance of the connected firm. The firm must intensively use these technologies in order to achieve advantages from production network externalities to the networked firms. For this reason, we do not expect to find a high degree of correlation between the performance index and the connectivity index measuring the simple adoption, if no measure of intensity of use is considered.

In order to test the first hypothesis deduced from our conceptual framework, the simple connectivity index described in the previous section was constructed, i.e. the ratio between the real number of connections to the number of potential connections for each firm in our sample. A very simple performance index has been chosen, representing the productivity of each firm and defined as the ratio between the turnover of firms in 1991 and the number of employees in the same year, as suggested in the previous section.

In order to be sure that the results are not biased by sector or size effects, the analysis has also been run taking into account the sector firms belong to and the size of firms. The sector variable has been introduced by running a multivariate correlation between the performance and connectivity indices and the sector firms belong to. The size variable has instead been taken into account by running the multivariate correlation in four different groups of firms with different size, in order to

test whether the exploitation of network externalitie was related to the dimension of firms.[6] If the size of firm has an impact, we may expect an increasing (decreasing value of the correlation coefficient when the size of firm increases (decreases). This methodology has been ap plied also at a regional level. Multivariate analyses witl sector and size variables allow us to separate out networl externality effects from more traditional effects o economies of scale and innovative processes. If there i any relationship between the level of connectivity anc the performance of firms and if this turns out to bt independent from sector size effects, variations in th performance of firms can be mainly attributed to th existence of (production) network externalities.

A correlation analysis was run on these two indice from which very interesting results emerged; a very higl dispersion exists in the way that these indices are relatec in our sample and, thus, a very low correlation exist between them. The Pearson correlation coefficient *F* confirms the first impression, having a value of only 0·069 (see Table 1). With this value we can go a ste; further by claiming that almost no correlation exist between these indices. *Our first hypothesis is thus confirmed since the empirical analysis allows us to conclude that only th simple adoption of these technologies as such has no significan effects on the performance of firms*.

This conclusion is similar to what other empirica studies have pointed out in the case of other advancec technologies. In particular, we refer to the studies of the diffusion of computer aided design (CAD) and com puter aided manufacturing (CAM) technologies during the 1980s.[7] The results of these studies have pointed ou that the simple adoption of these technologies as such di not lead to any increase in the performance of adopting firms. Also in the case of adoption processes o CAD/CAM technologies, the results at the empirica level have not fulfilled the expectations based on the higl technological potentialities of these technologies. Th impact of these technologies on the performance of firm: has in fact been limited by economic and organizationa elements, which have profoundly changed both th speed of adoption and the effects of the adoption on the performance of adopting firms.

Results do not appear to change when the size and the sector variables are introduced in the analysis. The multivariate correlation analysis run introducing the sectoral variable leads to a similar result for the correlation coefficient, which assumes a value of 0·08! When the analysis is repeated in the four groups of firm: with different size (in terms of both employment anc

Table 1. *Correlation matrix*

	National	North of Italy	South of Italy
Row connectivity	0·069	0·398	− 0·058
Weighted connectivity	0·11	0·473	0·085

ze), the correlation coefficient changes randomly, and
oes not demonstrate any relation with the size of the
rms. Before focusing our attention on what happens
vhen the frequency of use is introduced in the analysis,
rather provoking question is to see whether this result
aanges once the regional dimension is taken into
onsideration.

At the regional level our expectations appear to be
erified. A higher degree of correlation appears then in
omparison to the South (see Table 1), where the
tuation does not represent a clear trajectory. These
npressions are sustained by the results of the Pearson
orrelation coefficients, changing to 0·398 for the North
f Italy, and − 0·058 for the South of Italy. The regional
imension is once again important in explaining the
esults of the empirical analysis. The national result is an
verage value of the two regional analyses, which
eparately show a different pattern. For the South the
orrelation is absent, with a value near zero and a
egative sign. For the North of Italy, it is undoubtedly
ue that the situation improves achieving 0·39 as a
orrelation value and thus showing a weak correlation
etween the two indices. This result confirms our
ypothesis of limited effect of adoption on the perform-
nce of firms. Results do not vary in the two regions,
vhere the analysis is run taking into account the sector
o which firms belong. In fact, the multivariate corre-
ation analysis shows a similar correlation coefficient
alue: 0·4 in the North and 0·03 in the South. Moreover,
ne correlation run separately for the four groups of firms
vith different size does not show any clear relation
etween the dimension of firms and the correlation
oefficient values.

These results show that a regional variation exists in
he correlation between the simple adoption of telecom-
nunications technologies and the performance of firms.
This result stimulates the following reflections:

   higher stages of diffusion of these technologies may
   explain: (1) higher levels of know-how guaranteeing
   the exploitation of network externalities; (2) greater
   experience in innovation exploitation; (3) greater
   experience in organizational and managerial changes
   required to introduce these technologies

• a more advanced economic environment allows: (1)
   a larger specialized labour market: (2) a more
   efficient 'imitation effect' from successful adoptions
   of pioneering firms; (3) a higher level of service
   sector for technical, organizational and managerial
   support; (4) a higher degree of entrepreneurship able
   to deal with the risks which accompany all innovative processes; (5) a higher presence of flexible
   industrial structures able to accept the radical
   organizational changes required to exploit network
   externalities.

The next logical step is to see whether our second
ypothesis is correct, i.e. whether an intense use of these

technologies has an impact on the performance of firms.
This is the subject matter of the next section.

*Relationship between the use of telecommunication networks
and the performance of firms and regions*

This section draws attention to the relationship between
the use of advanced telecommunications technologies[8]
and the performance of firms. The performance index
remains the one constructed in the previous section. The
connectivity index is instead adjusted to the frequency
of use of these services.

In this case we expect a strong correlation to exist
between the performance and the connectivity index,
since production network externalities can be exploited
only if these technologies are used by adopters. In fact,
more information and know-how are achieved via the
network only when a systematic and strategic use of these
technologies is put in place. As we have claimed several
times before, the simple adoption is only a necessary but
not a sufficient condition to achieve economic advantages. Moreover, we expect an even stronger regional
variation in the way production network externalities
are exploited, compared with the previous case of
correlation between the simple adoption and the
performance of firms. In fact, an intense and strategic use
of telecommunications technologies depends highly on
the characteristics distinguishing the two areas, i.e. the
different stages of diffusion processes and the different
economic development of the two areas. Entrepreneurship especially, which is a strategic resource assuring
organizational, financial and managerial flexibility to
cope with innovation processes, is of strategic importance in order to exploit production network externalities. This resource is by definition a scarce resource in
backward regions, and thus adoption processes are
expected to produce lower economic advantages.

The results of the correlation analysis at the *national
level* of Italy are presented in Table 1. The results do not
yet show a correlation between connectivity and the
performance of firms. In fact, one group of four firms
shows a high performance level, despite a very low
connectivity level. Moreover, at least three firms are in
an opposite situation, showing a high connectivity level
despite a very low performance level. A very high
percentage of firms is clustered around low–medium
levels of performance and connectivity. The Pearson
correlation coefficient *R* still shows a very low value, viz.
0·11 (Table 1). Also in this case, the sectoral and the size
variables turn out to be insignificant in the analysis.

In light of the previous remarks, the regional analysis
is expected to add much to our interpretative analysis.
The results are satisfactory in this respect; it appears
immediately that there is a better fit for a linear
correlation in the case of the North than for the South.
This impression is confirmed by large differences in the
Pearson correlation coefficients, whose value varies from

0·085 for the South, to 0·473 for the North (see Table 1). These results show that:

- the regional variation in correlation analyses is even higher in the case of the correlation between the simple adoption and the firm's performance; the national correlation value is nevertheless still very low, because it averages an even lower *R* in the case of the South and a higher value for the North
- as expected, the most developed regions are also the ones which gain most from network externality effects, while backward regions are not yet able to achieve economic advantages from their adoption
- the use of these technologies is strategic for the exploitation of production network externalities; in Northern Italy, where these technologies are used more frequently, the economic advantages from their adoption is certainly higher than in Southern Italy.

Even in this case, results are not affected by sector or size effects. The multivariate correlation analysis run between the connectivity and performance indices and the sectoral variables do not vary. In the case of the North of Italy, *R* assumes a value of 0·44 (instead of 0·47), while in the South of Italy it assumes a value of 0·01 (instead of 0·08). When the same correlation analysis is run in the four different classes according to the size of the firms, correlation coefficients change randomly.

In reality some outliers exist, i.e. there are a small number of cases with observed values that fail to confirm the model. In the presence of outliers, the well-known statistical method is the exclusion of the cases that do not belong to the average behaviour (WEISBERG, 1980).[9] Following this strategy, the plot of the sample in the North shows a much clearer correlation pattern, witnessed by a Pearson correlation coefficient achieving a value of 0·57. A similar strategy applied to the sample in the South does not lead to a significant Pearson correlation coefficient, which even decreases to −0·068. Thus, it is impossible to argue that in the South production network externalities are exploited.

The results obtained in this part of the analysis are interesting. *Our hypothesis that firms and regions gain from network externalities was proved to be true in the case of advanced regions. Backward regions, on the contrary, seem to be quite unable to achieve economic advantages from the use of these technologies.* This conclusion confirms what the vast body of literature on the spatial development of technologies claims. The general idea of this literature is that the diffusion processes of new technologies are governed by centripetal forces,[10] i.e. tend to start in the centre, and develop towards the periphery. Our analysis reinforces these results and indicates also that the effects of new technological development take place in the centre and subsequently appear also in the periphery. This phenomenon may be explained by two reasons: (1) the more advanced economic environment in which firms operate in more advanced regions, and which

contains the capacities and know-how to exploit thes technologies; and (2) the more advanced technologica diffusion process in advanced regions which guarantee that the learning mechanisms take place.

CONCLUSIONS

In this paper we have presented a conceptual framework on production network externalities. An approach to the measurement of network externalities has been formulated in order to test our conceptual framework

The results are satisfactory and hence our prior expectations are fulfilled. In fact, our empirical analysis has quite clearly demonstrated that a *simple adoption*, with very low use of these technologies, does not lead to much improvement in firms' performance, and consequently very low positive effects at the regional level are generated. Already at this stage of the analysis, regional variations emerge from the analysis, where a clear dichotomy in the behavioural patterns are manifested between backward and more advanced regions.

This regional discrepancy becomes quite evident once the analysis is run taking into consideration the *frequency of use* of these technologies. In this respect, our hypothesis is that a positive relationship exists between the use of these technologies and the performance of firms. If this correlation is confirmed, production network externalities are demonstrated at an empirical level. The results are positive only for advanced regions. The Pearson correlation coefficient shows in fact a positive correlation only in the case of advanced regions, while backward regions seem to manifest an incapability to exploit production network externalities.

The impact of telecommunications technologies on regional development is not a straightforward mechanism. One of the greatest mistakes would be to expect a direct linkage between the supply of new technologies and economic and regional development. The link between these two elements, technology on one side and economic and regional development on the other, is a rather complex phenomenon. Its successful results stem mainly from a collection of essential elements which have to be present and have to be exploited in the right way.

The next step of analysis is to highlight, from a conceptual and empirical viewpoint, the micro and macro conditions explaining the different capacities of firms and regions to exploit these technologies. The definition of the conditions which have to be present in an area in order to exploit these technologies has important normative consequences for EC programmes like the STAR programme. In fact, what our analysis has pointed out is that the simple diffusion of these technologies does not immediately lead to better economic performance. Some other aspects, at both the supply and the demand side, have to be taken into account in order to exploit these great technological potentialities. These 'accompanying measures' in telecommunications policy oriented programme play critical role. Such aspects have to be investigated more ally in the near future.

Acknowledgement – the first author greatly acknowledges talian CNR funds (project no. 94.00560.CT11, directed by Roberto Camagni).

NOTES

1. The paper is the result of a joint work by the two authors: Capello wrote sections 2, 3, 4 and 5, whilst the introduction and conclusion have been jointly written.
2. In this study the word 'network' refers to a telecommunication network, i.e. a telephone, telex or any advanced digital network transmitting text, data, voice and images. The concept of network externalities is here thus related to telecommunications technologies.
3. In the economic literature, consumption externalities arise when the behaviour of one individual affects (positively or negatively) the consumption of another individual. These externality mechanisms have to be kept separate from the so-called 'production externalities'; by this term a situation is meant where the behaviour of an agent affects (positively or negatively) the production (or related indicators) of another agent.
4. The potential connection of a firm is defined as the total number of existing telecommunication services offered to firms by the national public operator, and it is thus the same for all firms.
5. In this study 'row' connectivity index means the connectivity index constructed taking into account only the adoption data. This index is different from the so-called 'weighted' connectivity index which is derived taking into consideration the 'frequency of use' of adopted telecommunication services. This index was in fact constructed by multiplying the adoption data with a weight derived by the data on the frequency of use: a weight of 1 was given to services used every day, 0·7 to services used weekly, 0·3 for services used monthly and, finally, 0·1 for services used annually.
6. Four groups of firms were chosen: firms having a number of employees between 1 and 10 belonged to the first class; between 11 and 20 to the second class; between 21–50 to the third class; and over 51 to the fourth class. The exercise has also been run measuring size of firms on the basis of their turnover: 0–500 million lire the first; 501 and 5,000 million lire the second, between 5,000 and 10,000 million lire the third and over 10,000 million lire the fourth.
7. For studies on the adoption of CAD/CAM technologies see, among others, CORIAT, 1981; JELINEK and GOLHAR, 1983; AYRES and MILLER, 1983; CAMAGNI, 1984, 1985; COLOMBO and MARIOTTI, 1985.
8. Data on the intensity of use of advanced telecommunication services are available in our database.
9. For a detailed description of the outliers analysis, see Annex 2 of this book.
10. See, among others, BUSHWELL and LEWIS, 1970; EWERS and WETTMAN, 1980; OAKEY *et al.*, 1980; BOITANI and CICIOTTI, 1990; EWERS and ALLESCH, 1990.

REFERENCES

AMIEL M. and ROCHET J. (1987) Concurrence entre réseaux de télécommunications: les conséquences des externalités négatives, *Annales des Télécommunications* **42**(11–12), 642–9.
ANTONELLI C. (1990) Induced adoption and externalities in the regional diffusion of information technology, *Reg. Studies* **24**, 31–40.
ANTONELLI C. (1991) The international diffusion of advanced telecommunications: opportunities for developing countries, OECD Publication, OECD, Paris.
ANTONELLI C. (Ed) (1992) *The Economics of Information Networks*. Elsevier, Amsterdam.
AYRES R. U. and MILLER S. M. (1983) *Robotics: Applications and Social Implications*. Ballinger, Cambridge, MA.
BOITANI M. and CICIOTTI E. (1990) Patents as indicators of innovative performances at the regional level, in CAPPELLIN R. and NIJKAMP P. (Eds) *The Spatial Context of Technological Development*, pp. 139–66. Avebury, Aldershot.
BOUDEVILLE, J. R. (1968) *L'Espace et le Pôle de Croissance*. Presses Universitaires de France, Paris.
BROSIO G. (1986) *Economia e Finanza Pubblica*. La Nuova Italia Scientifica, Rome.
BUSHWELL R. and LEWIS E. (1970) The geographic distribution of industrial research activity in the UK, *Reg. Studies* **4**, 297–306.
CAMAGNI R. (Ed) *Il Robot Italiano*. Il Sole 24Ore, Milan.
CAMAGNI R. (1985) Spatial diffusion of pervasive innovation, *Pap. Reg. Sci. Ass.* **58**, 83–95.
CAMAGNI R. (Ed) (1991) *Innovation Networks: Spatial Perspectives*. Belhaven Pinter, London.
CAMAGNI R. and DE BLASIO G. (Ed) (1993) *Le Reti di Città*. Franco Angeli Editore, Milan.
CAPELLO R. (1994) *Spatial Economic Analysis of Telecommunications Network Externalities*. Avebury, Aldershot.
CAPELLO R. and WILLIAMS H. (1990) Nuove strategie d'impresa, nuovi sistemi spaziali e nuove tecnologie dell'informazione come strumenti di riduzione dell'incertezza, *Economia e Politica Industriale* **67**, 43–72.
COLOMBO M. and MARIOTTI S. (1985) Note economiche sull'automazione flessibile, *Economia e Politica Industriale* **48**, 61–96.
CORIAT B. (1981) Robots et automates dans l'industrie de serie: esquisse d'une 'economie' de la robotique d'atelier, in ADELFI A. (Ed) *Les Mutations Technologiques*. Economica, Paris.
EWERS H. and ALLESCH J. (Eds) (1990) *Innovation and Regional Development*. De Gruyter, Berlin.
EWERS H. and WETTMAN R. (1980) Innovation oriented regional policy, *Reg. Studies* **14**, 161–79.
FORNENGO G. (1988) Manufacturing networks: telematics in the automobile industry, in ANTONELLI C. *New Information Technology and Industrial Change: The Italian Case*, pp. 33–56. Kluwer Academic, New York.
HAYASHI K. (1992) From network externalities to interconnection: the changing nature of networks and economy, in ANTONELLI C. (Ed) *The Economics of Information Networks*, pp. 195–216. North-Holland, Amsterdam.

JELINEK M. and GOLHAR, J. D. (1983) The interface between strategy and manufacturing technology, *Columbia J. World Business*, Spring, 26–36.

MYRDAL G. (1959) *Teoria Economica e Paesi Sottosviluppati*. Feltrinelli, Milan.

NAMBU T. (1986) *Telecommunications Economics*. Nihon Keizai Schimbun, Yokyo.

NIJKAMP P. (1977) *Theory and Application of Environmental Economics*. North-Holland, Amsterdam.

NIJKAMP P. and REGGIANI A. (1992) *Interaction, Evolution and Chaos in Space*. Springer Verlag, Berlin.

OAKEY R., THWAITES A. and NASH, P. (1980) The regional distribution of innovative manufacturing establishments in Britain, *Reg. Studies* 14, 235–53.

PERROUX F. (1955) Notes sur la notion de pôle de croissance, *Economie Appliquée* 7, 307–20.

PORTER M. (1990) *Competitive Advantage of Nations*. Macmillan, London.

RULLANI E. and ZANFEI A. (1988) Networks between manufacturing and demand: cases from textile and clothing industry, in ANTONELLI C. (Ed) *New Information Technology and Industrial Changes: the Italian Case*, pp. 57–96. Kluwer Academic, New York.

SAUNDER R., WARFORD J. and WELLENIUS B. (1983) *Telecommunications and Economic Development*. The Johns Hopkins University Press, London.

STONEMAN P. (1990) The intertemporal demand for consumer technologies requiring joint hardware and software inputs, Working Paper No. 355, Department of Economics, University of Warwick.

STONEMAN P. (1992) The impact of technology adoption on firm performance: heterogeneity and multi-technology diffusion models, Department of Economics, University of Warwick (mimeo).

WEISBERG S. (1980) *Applied Linear Regression*. Wiley, New York.

WENDERS, J. (1987) *The Economics of Telecommunications*. Ballinger, Cambridge, M A.

[10]

Industrial Dynamics and Rational Expectations in a Spatial Setting[1]

M. A. van der Ende and P. Nijkamp

11.1 Introduction

Technological innovation is one of the vehicles for accelerated regional growth. Unfortunately, the measurement of technological innovation is fraught with difficulties. The main goal of technological progress is to improve the competitive position of firms or regions. Whether or not this strategy has been successful can indirectly be assessed by investigating output indicators such as sales or profits, or related indicators such as investment or employment.

The rise and decline of regions depends on a combination of critical factors relating to success and failure, as illustrated by Porter's diamond model (cf. Porter, 1991). Industrial innovation and regional dynamics are closely interwoven phenomena of crucial importance for the emergence or alleviation of spatial disparities (cf. Scott and Storper, 1987). In regional economic literature much attention has been given to the issue of socio-economic convergence and divergence in spatial-economic systems (cf. Friedmann and Weaver, 1979, Gilbert, 1976, Lipschitz, 1986, 1993, or Mera, 1979). Traditionally, income and employment indicators have been used to assess regional dynamics and spatial inequalities. Far less attention has been given to entrepreneurially-oriented indicators such as investment. This is surprising, as new investment – a result of innovative behaviour – may be seen as the driving force behind industrial dynamics in an area. Literature on the investment behaviour of firms in a spatial setting is however, rather scanty. Although in recent years the interest in innovative behaviour of the firm in relation to space has significantly increased (cf. Davelaar, 1991, Freeman *et al.*, 1982, Kleinknecht, 1987, Nijkamp, 1987, 1990), micro-based analyses are hard to find.

The explanation of the dynamics of the investment behaviour of entrepreneurs in relation to innovation may be based on different theoretical frameworks, e.g. accelerator theory, multiplier theory, rational expectations theory and adaptive

---

[1] The authors wish to acknowledge constructive comments on an earlier version given by Professor Daniel Shefer (Technion, Haifa).

expectations theory (cf. Nijkamp *et al.*, 1993, Spear, 1989). However, the uncertainty faced by many entrepreneurs appears to be so great that reliable models explaining the micro investment behaviour of firms are not yet abundant.

In the case of perfect prediction, the firm's expectation in year t-1 on an output variable in year t (denoted as Exp, t-1) should be equal to the realization of the variable concerned in year t (denoted as Real, t). This leads to the following figure (Fig. 11.1).

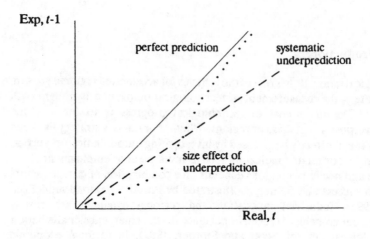

Fig. 11.1   Expectation and realization of a firm's output

In case of a structural (e.g. strategic) misprediction the dashed line may emerge. However, it is often hypothesized that size effects may lead smaller firms to make more biased predictions (see dotted line). These hypotheses are tested in the present study, with particular attention to whether specific regional dynamic effects may also play a role. This requires of course empirical research on firms' behaviour.

Interesting examples of micro-based *empirical* research on spatial aspects of investment behaviour can be found in Meyer-Krahmer (1985) and Begg and McDowall (1987). Meyer-Krahmer (1985) analyzed the influence of innovative behaviour on various entrepreneurial variables associated with industrial dynamics in Germany. It turned out that there was a correlation between the innovation orientation investments and outward orientations of firms. Begg and McDowall (1987) have investigated and evaluated studies on investments from the angle of regional investment incentives in Assisted Areas in the UK. Their results showed a correlation between investment appraisal, investment incentives and successful investment assistance applications. They found, for example, that small firms invest less frequently because they are less well informed.

In our paper we will address in particular the issue of investment planning of individual firms in relation to the expected market development. This means that expected sales growth is assumed to play a critical role. After a survey of some relevant literature (Section 11.2) and a description of the data base (Section 11.3), we will outline the specification of our probit model that aims to predict investment behaviour at a micro level (Section 11.4). Various empirical results are presented in Section 11.5, after which we draw the conclusion in Section 11.6.

11.2 Spatial Investment Behaviour of Firms

As indicated in Section 11.1, one of the main reasons for the insufficient empirical attention given to the entrepreneur's investment behaviour lies in the scarcity of statistical data on realizations and expectations of investment behaviour at a micro level. Thus, detailed studies of spatial industrial dynamics based on actual and expected performance levels of firms have not yet been made. These would require comprehensive data on expected and realized entrepreneurial performance in relation to investment observed at the level of individual firms. Fortunately, such a data set does exist in the Netherlands (cf. for details Section 11.3), where a successful attempt has been made by the Chambers of Commerce to organize a common regionally-based longitudinal survey among Dutch firms regarding their sales, exports, investments and employment. This survey, called ERBO (Enquête Régionale Bedrijfsontwikkeling), is conducted every year in order to gather strategic insight into past and future trends in Dutch business life. It is both retrospective and prospective (i.e. covering both actual and expected output) and regards individual performance indicators of firms. Before presenting the results of our own analysis, we first offer a concise overview of other attempts at investigating or modelling the investment behaviour of individual firms, with a particular focus on links between investment and entrepreneurial expectations.

A general approach to financial investment analysis is represented by the standard *capital asset pricing model*, but this model does not explicitly include a connection between business investments, a firm's expectations and industrial dynamics. In the early history of economics we see some reference to industrial dynamics based on relationships between *investments, profit maximization* and *capital accumulation* (witness the works of Adam Smith, Malthus and Karl Marx). In the post-war period the *acceleration* theory has gained much popularity (cf. for a review, Gabisch and Lorenz, 1989). Following previous work undertaken by Samuelson, Kalecki and Kaldor, a major contribution in this field was offered by Koyck (1954), who tested the lag between output and capacity in various industrial firms (with an exponentially declining importance of past output for predicting capacity adjustments).

In past decades much attention has been given to the *rational expectations* approach (cf. Lucas and Sargent, 1981). The foundation was laid by Muth (1960) who showed that exponential forecast weights of past realizations are optimal for a de-trended time series following a random walk with the superimposition of white noise (as generalized in particular via the Box-Jenkins approach). Muth then concluded that a one-period lagged forecast is the best for all future periods and hence also independent of the forecasted time horizon. In a subsequent article, Muth (1961) argued that reported expectations generally underestimate the extent of changes which will take place, and argued that the rational expectations approach tends to reduce the variance of the actor's expectations much more than the variance of actual realizations. In general, rational expectations lead to *restrictions on lag parameters*. It is noteworthy in this context that Sargent (1971) argued that in many cases the accelerator parameter is underestimated from a rational expectations point of view.

Another issue concerns the link between individual *predictions and decisions*, where usually a quadratic return function and a linear technology functions are assumed (cf., for instance, Hansen and Sargent, 1987). Accounting for these individual links is also necessary to test the validity of the rational expectations model at an aggregate level. Next to accelerator and rational expectations models, we may also distinguish *behavioural* investment theories with particular emphasis on *organizational and bargaining* issues inside the firm. Recent books on finance (cf. Rappaport, 1986 and Schlosser, 1990) look into intra-firm behaviour and illustrate how financial appraisal should guide the bargaining process of strategic acceptance and financial approval of new investments in large firms.

Only a few empirical models have explicitly included *reported* expectations. A first application can be found in Figlewsky and Wachtel (1981) who concluded that the inclusion of inflation expectations tends to lead to a downward bias and that in general the effect of changes appears to be underestimated. They also found that adaptive models perform better than regression models, while in general macro (aggregate) models are not very satisfactory due to heterogeneity in expectations.

Another empirical model was presented by Brown and Maital (1981) who investigated the following relationship for several level variables:

$$\text{Realization } (t) = \alpha + \beta \text{ Prediction } (t\text{-}1) + \widehat{\rho} \ MA(1) + \text{white noise} \quad (11.1)$$

where MA stands for moving (monthly) average. If there is no bias, it is clear that $\alpha = 0$ and $\beta = 1$. However with 12-monthly forecasts, $\widehat{\rho}$ is likely to be large.

Given the estimated impacts of the moving averages, an estimated value of $\widehat{\beta}$ less than 1 does not necessarily imply that predicted changes are more volatile than their realizations.

A related approach can be found in Nijkamp *et al.* (1993) who developed an *adaptive* model for the formation of firm's expectations. An ordered multi-response probit model was used to estimate the existence of a relationship between expectations and realizations. They concluded that, irrespective of sectoral and regional divisions and distribution assumptions, firms are in general not very reliable predictors of their own future.

Finally, we mention the *micro investment* model developed by Broer and Van Leeuwen (1992). On the basis of a putty-clay production structure, they formulated and estimated a qualitative response model. They concluded that firms are profit maximizers rather than cost minimizers and that investments are significantly firm-specific. Furthermore, they found that size is a major independent explanatory variable for investment levels of firms.

In general, we conclude that lack of micro-data on investments and expectations have hampered the development of appropriate behavioural investment models that may explain industrial dynamics in a regional setting. Consequently, most investment models are macro-economic in nature, and their substance is rather weak from a micro-economic perspective. The knowledge of the influence of expectations on investment (or, in general, activity) plans of firms is very anecdotal, so that rigorous tests on rationality in investment behaviour cannot be performed. In general, the findings so far point out that expectations seem to be dynamic and heterogeneous, tending to underestimate future changes. The previous findings will also be used as a background in the models presented in Section 11.5. First however, we will discuss our data base.

11.3 The Data Base

In our study we make use of the above mentioned ERBO survey. This survey is conducted annually by all Chambers of Commerce in the Netherlands in the period September to November. This means that most firms are able to assess their performance in the current year, as well as to provide realistic expectations for the following year. Apart from one free question, which is at the discretion of each individual Chamber, all other questions are standardized over the whole country.

Each firm with 50 employees and over is requested to fill out the ERBO-survey. Smaller firms are surveyed in a stratified sample (organised in such a way that the larger the firm the higher the probability of being drawn). In practice, firms with more than 10 employees have a probability of 90 percent of being selected. In general, the average response rate is fairly high (over 70%), as it is in the interest of entrepreneurs to cooperate in this nation-wide survey.

The ERBO survey has many binary 'yes/no' choice questions (e.g. on investment plans). Sometimes questions are slightly more refined. In the case of sales for instance, firms have to report whether they expect a moderate (lower than 2%) or significant (more than 2%) rise in sales in the next year. This type of qualitative information requires the use of qualitative response models for explanatory purposes.

Since firm size will play an important role, the following stratification is used:

stratum 1 (S1)	1	employee
stratum 2 (S2)	2-9	employees
stratum 3 (S3)	10-49	employees
stratum 4 (S4)	≥50	employees

These size classes correspond to the standard ERBO strata of the Dutch Chambers of Commerce. In our analysis of entrepreneurial expectations we restricted ourselves to four selected Chamber of Commerce areas in the Netherlands, namely Amsterdam, Zaanstad, Utrecht and 's Hertogenbosch. This set contains two large cities (Amsterdam and Utrecht) and two smaller areas with a clear urban core (Zaanstad and 's Hertogenbosch). The two large cities are centrally located in the Netherlands, while the two remaining areas are positioned at the edge of the Dutch Randstad. This allows us to identify the existence of discriminating regional factors, although in a small country like the Netherlands such factors are not likely to be very significant.

The time period for which the ERBO data were analyzed covered the years 1986-1989. This was a deliberate choice, as it is a period in which – after the economic recession at the beginning of the eighties – the Dutch economy showed a stable growth pattern accompanied by a low inflation rate. The previous data have been used in a recent modelling experiment to test the correspondence between expectations and realizations of sales growth at the firm level in each of the four above mentioned regions by means of an adaptive expectations model experiment (cf. Nijkamp *et al.*, 1993).

All ERBO information was put together in a data file which could readily be used for empirical estimation in our dynamic investment model. The structure of this model will be described in Section 11.4 (cf., for details, Van der Ende, 1992).

11.4   Specification of a Probit Model

In our analysis of ERBO data a qualitative response model will be used (cf. Amemiya, 1981, Maddala, 1983). The qualitatively observed variable which we aim to explain is assumed to be normally distributed, so that it is implicitly plausible to use a probit model. Compared to a logit analysis, the main advantage of a probit analysis in multi-response and multi-variate models is the possibility of including correlations between choices without restrictions.

In a qualitative response context, we define expected investments as follows:

$$Y_{it} = \begin{cases} 1, & \text{if firm } i \text{ has investment plans for year } t \\ 0, & \text{if firm } i \text{ has no investment plans for year } t \end{cases} \quad (11.2)$$

We assume that $Y_{it} = 1$ with probability $P_{it} = \phi\,(X_{it}^T \beta_t)$, and $Y_{it} = 0$ with probability $1 - P_{it}$; ϕ denotes the standard normal cumulative distribution. Amemiya (1981) calls this a probit model. Because we cannot identify both location and scale parameters, the scale parameter is normalized to unity. The interpretation of our probit model is that, if some explanatory variable has a positive (zero, or negative) coefficient, its correlation with the probability that firm i has investment plans is positive (zero, or negative). The exact relationship in the probit model runs via the probability distribution ϕ.

In contrast to the scoring method proposed by Maddala, we use here a *Newton-Raphson* process to estimate the probit model. The latter approach is more suitable in case of outliers in the observations on some explanatory variables (which may especially occur at the micro level of analysis).

The standard probit model can be dealt with in two different ways:

a. to estimate a regression function in which the observations are given in terms of values that are larger or smaller than a given threshold value that subdivides the outcome of the regression function into two distinct intervals;
b. to model binary (yes/no) choices and to introduce an imaginary threshold value that has to be exceeded before the choice for 'yes' is made. If the regression model contains an intercept, no loss is incurred if we normalize the threshold value to zero.

If a regression function has to be estimated with more than one threshold (so that the outcome falls in one interval out of many), an *ordered* probit can be specified in which the thresholds should be ordered in value. Becker and Kennedy (1992) have argued that with a priori unknown thresholds: "the direction of the impact of a change in a slope coefficient on the estimated probabilities of only the highest and lowest ordered classifications is unequivocal". An unordered probit model is sometimes also called a multi-nomial probit model (Maddala, 1983).

Finally, we speak of a multi-variate probit model if a k-tuple of choices exist that are not mutually exclusive and can be explained by a k-variate normal distribution. If all correlations of the k-variate normal distribution are zero, the probit model explains independent choices by the individual.

After this brief introduction to probit analysis, we describe in the next section various results reached on the basis of the above mentioned ERBO data. See Van der Ende (1992, 1993) for more extensive treatment.

11.5   Regional Investment Dynamics and Expectation of Enterprises

Insight into the determinants of investment behaviour of firms and their expectations is necessary in the context of both regional policy and general economic policy.

It is a plausible assumption that investments and sales growth (expectations) are closely linked variables, so it makes sense to model investment behaviour of firms (in the form of a qualitative 'yes/no' response variable) with a view to expected and realized sales growth. A distinction will be made here between different *size classes* of firms, as other discriminating features (such as sectoral and regional differences in realizations and expectations of sales growth are not very significant (cf. also Nijkamp *et al.*, 1993).

In reporting expected sales for the future, there is of course the danger of 'strategic' response behaviour of firms leading to biased responses. Oster (1982) studied the behaviour of pharmaceutical manufacturers when in 1979 all but thirteen states of the USA permitted pharmacists to substitute generic drugs for prescribed brand-name drugs. Large manufacturers specializing in brand-name drugs advised prescribing tested, innovative drugs. Smaller firms producing generic drugs promoted competition. Both groups predicted sales increases in 1979 in generic houses at the cost of brand-name manufacturers. The large firms tried to change two provisions in the new act and were partially successful. The reported predictions of the large manufacturers were thus a threat because the large firms may well have taken into account their success before appraising the innovation of drugs.

In general however, we have found in our data base that large firms tend to provide better (i.e. more reliable) estimates of future developments than small firms. We will first present some empirical data on expected sales growth of firms and the existence of investment plans per stratum and per region. We then continue with an explanatory (probit) analysis of investment behaviour.

In our statistical analysis we have mainly looked into the data on sales growth. Firms were requested to report whether the expected change in the sales volume is lower than 0% (i.e. a sales decline), between 0% and 2% (i.e. no change or only a marginal change), or exceeds 2% (i.e. a sales rise). The data and results are recorded according to the four strata of size classes discussed above. The results from the ERBO data base show clearly that large firms in general expect a sales rise more often than small firms (see the year 1986, Table 11.1).

Table 11.1 Expected sales growth in percentages of total number of firms per region per stratum (1986)

Amsterdam	–	0	+	?	Zaandam	–	0	+	?
S1	16	58	26	0	S1	17	60	23	0
S2	13	43	44	0	S2	15	56	29	0
S3	9	46	45	0	S3	11	52	37	0
S4	9	34	57	0	S4	11	35	54	0
Den Bosch	**–**	**0**	**+**	**?**	**Utrecht**	**–**	**0**	**+**	**?**
S1	14	48	36	2	S1	8	61	26	5
S2	10	53	35	2	S2	9	53	34	4
S3	8	41	49	2	S3	8	44	45	3
S4	6	34	57	3	S4	12	34	53	1

Legend: – decline; 0 no change; + rise; ? no information

The usual explanation for the results in Table 11.1 is that large firms plan further ahead than small firms (cf. also Vosselman, 1989). Investment decisions in small firms appear to be made shortly before their implementation. This is confirmed by Table 11.2 which demonstrates that large firms are more likely to plan investments than small firms. For example, in the first stratum, some 25 to 30 percent of firms mention having investment plans, while this percentage for the fourth stratum of large firms increases to 90 percent.

Table 11.2 Investment plans in percentages of total number of firms per region per stratum (1986)

Amsterdam	+	–	?	Zaandam	+	–	?
S1	28	72	0	S1	43	57	0
S2	49	51	0	S2	52	48	0
S3	73	27	0	S3	77	23	0
S4	90	10	0	S4	92	8	0
Den Bosch	**+**	**–**	**?**	**Utrecht**	**+**	**–**	**?**
S1	29	67	4	S1	26	66	8
S2	47	49	4	S2	47	46	7
S3	76	22	2	S3	79	18	3
S4	89	8	3	S4	92	7	1

Legend: + expressed investment plans; – no investment plans; ? no information

It should be added that it is interesting to see that not only is there a clear dichotomy in our sample in terms of investment plans by size class, but also that firms with investment plans are in general more optimistic about their sales expectations (see Table 11.3).

Table 11.3   Expected sales growth of firms with/without (Y/N) investment plans as percentage of total firms per region and per stratum (1986)

Amsterdam	– Y/N	0 Y/N	+ Y/N	? Y/N	Zaandam	– Y/N	0 Y/N	+ Y/N	? Y/N
S1	8/19	45/63	47/18	0/0	S1	15/18	54/64	31/18	0/0
S2	8/17	44/63	48/20	0/0	S2	11/19	51/62	38/19	0/0
S3	7/16	44/51	49/33	0/0	S3	7/23	51/57	42/20	0/0
S4	8/17	36/21	56/62	0/0	S4	10/20	37/20	53/60	0/0

Den Bosch	– Y/N	0 Y/N	+ Y/N	? Y/N	Utrecht	– Y/N	0 Y/N	+ Y/N	? Y/N
S1	8/18	36/53	56/28	0/1	S1	2/9	50/68	48/20	0/3
S2	7/12	46/61	46/26	1/1	S2	5/13	47/62	47/22	1/3
S3	7/11	41/47	52/39	0/3	S3	7/16	42/54	49/30	2/0
S4	6/7	35/33	58/53	1/7	S4	12/24	33/41	54/35	1/0

Legend: – decline; 0 no change; + rise; ? no information

The percentage change realizations of firms with investment plans in a previous year vary significantly, but are in general positive (the lower the stratum, the larger the average rise), whereas those of firms without investment plans are around zero. Comparing estimated sales change expectations with next year's realizations, Van der Ende (1992) concludes that quantitative sales expectations are indeed less biased to zero for firms with investment plans. One hypothesis may be that firms without investment plans do not feel the need to collect complete information concerning sales growth and can therefore only imperfectly forecast sales growth. On the other hand, less well informed firms seem to be less inclined to invest (cf. Meyer-Krahmer, 1985, Begg and McDowall, 1987).

Next, we will try to offer a more complete picture by *explaining the existence of investment plans* on the basis of those multiple variables available in the data set. Using model (11.1) as our starting point, we use a probit analysis to estimate the relative importance of these variables. The dependent variable $P_{i,t}$ is defined here as the probability that a firm i in a given region has investment plans in year t. We will start by relating $P_{i,t}$ to :

248

$$X_{i,t,1} = \Delta_t \text{ sales } (i, t)/\text{sales } (i, t-1) \qquad \text{coefficient } \beta 1, t$$
$$X_{i,t,2} = \Delta_t \text{ employment } (i, t)/\text{employment } (i, t-1) \qquad \text{coefficient } \beta 2, t$$
$$X_{i,t,3} = \Delta_t \text{ export } (i, t)/\text{sales } (i, t-1) \qquad \text{coefficient } \beta 3, t$$
$$X_{i,t,4} = \text{inv } (i, t-1)/\text{sales } (i, t-1) \qquad \text{coefficient } \beta 4, t$$
$$X_{i,t,5} = \text{inv}1(i, t)/\text{sales } (i, t) \qquad \text{coefficient } \beta 5, t$$
$$X_{i,t,6} = \text{inv}2(i, t)/\text{sales } (i, t) \qquad \text{coefficient } \beta 6, t$$

where Δ_t sales (i, t) equals: sales (i, t)-sales $(i, t-1)$. The variables $X_{i,t,1} ... X_{i,t,3}$ are growth-related variables and the variables $X_{i,t,4} ... X_{i,t,6}$ are investment-related variables. The variable inv1 represents replacement investments, while inv2 represents expansion investments. As an investment may be interpreted as growth of capital, we relate the investment likelihood to growth variables only.

The scaling (or standardization) of the growth and investment related variables is both practically convenient (it reduces outliers) and theoretically preferable (because the relative, rather than the absolute, variables indicate the extent to which capacity is utilized). The results of the probit estimations are given in Table 11.4.

Table 11.4 Results of probit analysis for growth variables per stratum and per region (1986) (*t*-values in brackets)

	$\widehat{\beta}_0$	$\widehat{\beta}_1$	$\widehat{\beta}_2$	$\widehat{\beta}_3$	$\widehat{\beta}_4$	$\widehat{\beta}_5$	$\widehat{\beta}_6$
Amsterdam							
S1	-.78(6.9)	1.36(2.0)	-.34(.40)	-.75(.94)	.66(1.2)	1.74(1.4)	2.37(2.1)
S2	-.23(4.2)	1.51(4.5)	.05(.24)	-2.45(1.7)	1.98(3.7)	.17(.36)	2.21(2.5)
S3	.42(5.2)	.70(1.6)	.86(1.9)	-.33(.23)	1.47(1.2)	8.84(3.1)	-.34(.18)
S4	1.13(7.4)	-1.94(2.4)	2.81(2.5)	1.72(1.2)	1.16(.21)	6.35(.65)	33.53(2.3)
Den Bosch							
S1	-.66(6.5)	.55(2.1)	.15(.20)	4.94(1.5)	-.00(.03)	.37(.81)	-.13(.50)
S2	-.22(4.2)	-.09(.55)	.57(3.1)	2.62(2.0)	1.06(3.6)	1.38(2.5)	.77(1.6)
S3	.56(6.8)	-.05(.12)	.42(1.5)	1.24(.98)	1.09(1.5)	1.96(1.4)	1.22(1.1)
S4	1.05(5.2)	-1.12(1.4)	-.36(51)	-.17(.13)	-7.15(2.8)	12.39(1.7)	65.07(2.5)
Utrecht							
S1	-.93(8.1)	2.74(3.5)	-1.83(2.1)	36.0(1.3)	.62(1.0)	3.94(2.5)	2.21(2.0)
S2	-.20(3.9)	.84(2.6)	.61(2.7)	.03(.03)	.96(3.2)	.72(2.0)	1.80(3.3)
S3	.70(8.8)	.91(1.6)	.66(1.4)	.84(.77)	1.18(1.3)	2.17(1.2)	.36(.45)
S4	1.09(5.4)	-.76(.68)	.07(.06)	6.28(2.4)	-2.72(1.2)	59.06(2.3)	26.57(1.3)

Table 11.4 shows that most parameters are significant, although a few very insignificant estimates do exist. All intercepts are in any case significant and the statistical significance increases with the size stratum, i.e. larger firms are more likely to have investment plans. The remaining parts of Table 11.4 can be interpreted in the following way. Small firms (stratum 1) are more likely to have investment plans if sales rise, while firms with more than 50 employees (stratum 4) are less likely to have investment plans if the sales rise. Firms investing in the current year are more likely to invest in the following year. There is apparently no difference between impacts of replacement and expansion investments. If the impact of export growth is significant, it has a positive sign. But, generally, export growth influences only the willingness to invest in so far as it is part of sales growth.

The increase of the intercept per employment size stratum suggests that the number of employees (or possibly another size indicator) is important as well. Hence, we will complement the above estimates with specifications that include a size indicator, i.e. employment, as well (see Table 11.5). Regressing on sales, export and employment levels as well as on the same growth variables as above (i.e., $X_{i,t,1} \cdots X_{i,t,6}$), sales and export levels turn out to be insignificant everywhere, even for one-man firms where employment is not a size indicator. The results from Table 11.5 appear not to differ much from those of Table 11.4.

Another element worth mentioning is that investments may have an irregular pattern of time caused by external constraints (e.g. public regulations, weather conditions, etc.) which explain why expected investments are not always achieved in the following year (cf. Begg and McDowall, 1987, Blundell and Meghir, 1987).

Thus there may be a serious bias in the information on investment plans provided by entrepreneurs. The same holds true for sales expectations data. Are the reported results on expected sales, for example, related to the situation before or after new investments? A straightforward econometric link is therefore not always plausible. Applying bivariate probit to the investment likelihood and sales growth expectations, we found correlations ranging from -0.16 to -0.38 for firms in the two lowest strata. When the estimates of sales growth expectations are assumed to refer to the alternative situation (including the firm's investment plans), the interpretation is that investments will be partly financed out of the sales budget. But since the negative correlations contrast with the data in Table 11.3, the depression trigger hypothesis (see concluding remarks below) is more likely. In this context, a sequential probit approach might then be used (cf. Van der Ende, 1992). Once a firm has planned its actions, it is able to formulate its expectations from the alternative situation. The investment decision does not depend only on expectations with respect to the status quo, but also on expectations from the new situation (a case not taken into account by a sequential probit model). Van der Ende (1992) has derived a probit model that is less restrictive and has a Bayesian interpretation.

Table 11.5   Results of probit analysis for investment probability on the basis of growth variables and (employment) size class per stratum and per region (1986) (t-values in brackets)

	$\hat{\beta}_0$	$\hat{\beta}_1$	$\hat{\beta}_2$	$\hat{\beta}_3$	$\hat{\beta}_4$	$\hat{\beta}_5$	$\hat{\beta}_6$	$\hat{\beta}_7$
Amsterdam								
S1	-.78(7.0)	.96(1.8)	-.39(.47)	-	.71(1.3)	1.81(1.5)	2.48(2.2)	-
S2	-.69(6.7)	1.53(4.6)	.01(.03)	-2.2(1.5)	2.07(3.8)	.27(.58)	2.06(2.4)	1.18(5.3)
S3	.06(.40)	.62(1.3)	.84(1.8)	-.52(.36)	1.65(1.3)	8.75(3.0)	-.46(.25(	.18(2.6)
S4	.99(4.6)	-1.94(2.4)	2.78(2.5)	1.45(.97)	1.50(.27)	5.55(.57)	31.4(2.1)	.01(.85)
Den Bosch								
S1	-.66(6.5)	.56(2.1)	.17(.22)	-	-.01(.05)	.37(.81)	-.13(.49)	-
S2	-.83(8.1)	-.05(.31)	.39(2.0)	2.68(2.1)	1.18(4.0)	1.33(2.4)	.70(1.4)	1.64(7.0)
S3	.37(2.4)	-.05(.14)	.40(1.5)	1.25(.99)	1.13(1.6)	2.03(1.4)	1.06(.96)	.10(1.4)
S4	.47(1.2)	-1.06(1.3)	-.30(.42)	-.16(.12)	-7.0(2.7)	13.2(1.7)	62.3(2.4)	.06(1.6)
Utrecht								
S1	-.92(8.0)	2.98(3.9)	-1.90(2.2)	-	.60(.99)	3.89(2.5)	2.14(2.0)	-
S2	-.66(6.5)	.77(2.3)	.47(2.0)	.07(.06)	.83(2.8)	.87(2.4)	1.80(3.2)	1.17(5.3)
S3	.39(2.4)	.97(1.7)	.67(1.5)	.60(.55)	1.03(1.2)	2.43(1.4)	.49(.61)	.15(2.2)
S4	.84(2.7)	-.76(.68)	.04(.03)	6.60(2.5)	-2.9(1.1)	59.8(2.3)	26.4(1.3)	.02(1.0)

11.6   Concluding Remarks

An important conclusion is that surprisingly little empirical work has been published on revealed expectations and/or realizations of investments of individual firms. One difficulty is obtaining data, another one providing adequate interpretations of such data.

In our study we have used data on revealed expectations on sales growth and investments of individual firms gathered by the Dutch Chamber of Commerce. Our analysis gives some important indications on the quality of the responses. It is also possible to investigate the data by industry. Estimations of the sales growth expectations for specific industries were reported in Nijkamp *et al.* (1993). The observed differences were disappointingly small. One reason may be the heterogeneity in firm size *within* industries and *between* industries. A two-way analysis of variance is important here to identify clear patterns. Theoretically, the principal agent theory might also play a role. Therefore, it is interesting to study the industry data within a common size stratum.

Our study has clearly demonstrated the importance of *size strata* for firms in explaining their investment behaviour and sales growth expectations. These size aspects appeared to be much more relevant than sectoral or regional ones. It appears that small firms are more uncertain than bigger firms. Another observation is that revealed expectations tend to *underestimate* the extent of the changes actually observed. This holds true for all dimensions of the relevant variables (firm size, region, year, industry, expectation indicator etc.).

An interesting point is that the correlation between estimated sales growth expectations and investment plans is by no means always positive. Here the *depression trigger hypothesis* may perhaps offer some explanation for this 'perverse' result, where an expected sales decline may be the reason to invest more. After the investments are carried out, sales growth become then again positive. Thus the definition of the status quo or reference situation (before or after investments) is of critical importance for the interpretation of results. If estimated expectations take the status quo as a reference framework, then it seems likely that the model produces status quo predictions. In any case, our estimation results suggest the existence of a strong relationship between the existence of investment plans and sales growth expectations. This also suggests that Bayesian statistical approaches in relation to decision theory may offer useful insights. It may be worthwhile looking into the way expectations are formed by *learning by doing* mechanisms, in order to test the robustness of the formation of firms' expectations and realizations under varying conditions, e.g. technology trajectories, recession periods, etc.

The link with *regional background variables* does not seem to be very explicit. Firm size dominates in all explanatory statistical analyses. This suggests that firm size creates more investments, which implies that regional dynamics are strongly influenced by the size class composition of firms. It may also explain the rather robust economic rank order position of regions in a country. Nevertheless, the presence of different regions may be caused by intervening regional structure factors (e.g. specific spatial seedbed conditions or a skewed distribution of regional firm size), so that indirectly regional effects may emerge under changing structural conditions, both economic and technological. This issue clearly needs further investigation.

References

Amemiya T. (1981) Qualitative Response Models: A Survey, *Journal of Economic Literature, 29*, 2, 1483-536.

Becker W.E., Kennedy P.E. (1992) A Graphical Exposition of the Ordered Probit, *Econometric Theory, 8,* 1, 127-31.

Begg H., McDowall S. (1987) The Effect of Regional Investment Incentives on Company Decisions, *Regional Studies, 21,* 5, 459-70.

Blundell R., Meghir C. (1987) Bivariate Alternatives to the Tobit Model, *Journal of Econometrics, 15,* 2, 179-200.

Broer D.P., van Leeuwen G. (1992) Investment Behaviour of Dutch Industrial Firms, discussion paper 9105, Ministry of Economic Affairs, The Hague.

Brown B.W., Maital S. (1981) What do Economists Know? An Empirical Study of Experts' Expectations, *Econometrica, 49,* 2, 491-504.

Davelaar E.J. (1991) *Regional Economic Analysis of Innovation and Incubation*, Avebury, Aldershot.

Ende M.A. van der (1992) *Revealed Investment Plans and Expectations in ERBO with Applications of Choice Models*, M.A. Thesis, Dept. of Economics, Free University, Amsterdam.

Ende M.A. van der (1993) Probit with Regression Outliers, research paper, Free University, Amsterdam (mimeo).

Figlewski S., Wachtel P. (1981) The Formation of Inflationary Expectations, *Review of Economics and Statistics, 63,* 1, 1-11.

Freeman C., Clark J., Soete L. (1982) *Unemployment and Technical Innovation*, Frances Pinter, London.

Friedmann J., Weaver C. (1979) *Territory and Function*, University of California Press, Berkeley.

Gabisch G., Lorenz H.W. (1989) *Business Cycle Theory*, Springer-Verlag, Berlin, New York.

Gilbert A. (ed.) (1976) *Development Planning and Spatial Structure*, Wiley, London.

Hansen L.P., Sargent T.J. (1987) Formulating and Estimating Dynamic Linear Rational Expectations Models, *Journal of Economic Dynamics and Control, 2,* 1, 7-46.

Kiefer N.M. (1978) Discrete Parameter Variation: Efficient Estimation of a Switching Regression Model, *Econometrica, 46,* 2, 427-33.

Kleinknecht A.H. (1987) *Innovation Patterns in Crisis and Prosperity*, MacMillan, London.

Koyck L.M. (1954) *An Econometric Study on the Time-Shape of Economic Reactions*, North-Holland, Amsterdam.

Lipschitz G. (1986) The Stability of the Spatial Pattern of Welfare: The Israeli Case, *Geoforum, 15,* 4, 353-66.

Lipschitz G. (1993) Dispersal of High-tech Localities as a Strategy for Regional Development: The Israeli Case, *Tijdschrift voor Economische en Sociale Geografie, 84,* 1, 40-50.

Lucas R.E., Sargent T.J. (eds.) (1981) *Rational Expectations and Expectations and Econometric Practice*, Allen and Unwin, London.

Maddala G.S. (1983) *Limited Dependent and Qualitative Variables in Econometrics,* Cambridge University Press, Cambridge.

Mera K. (1979) Basic Human Needs versus Economic Growth Approach for Coping with Urban-Rural Imbalances, *Environment and Planning A, 11,* 1129-45.

Meyer-Krahmer F. (1985) Innovation Behaviour and Regional Indigenous Potential, *Regional Studies, 19,* 6, 523-34.

Muth J.F. (1960) Optimal Properties of Exponentially Weighted Forecasts, *Journal of the American Statistical Association, 55,* 290, 123-32.

Muth J.F. (1961) Rational Expectations and the Theory of Price Movements, *Econometrica, 29,* 6, 401-13.

Nijkamp P. (1987) *Technological Change, Employment and Spatial Dynamics*, Springer-Verlag, Berlin, New York.

Nijkamp P. (ed.) (1990) *Sustainability of Urban Systems*, Avebury, Aldershot.

Nijkamp P., Rouwendal J., Van der Ende M.A. (1993) Space-Time Patterns of Entrepreneurial Expectations and Performance, *Regional Studies, 27,* 1, 1-11.

Oster S. (1982) The Strategic Use of Regulatory Investment by Industry Subgroups, *Economic Inquiry, 20,* 3/4, 604-18.

Porter M. (1991) *The Competitive Advantage of Nations*, MacMillan, London.

Rappaport A. (1986) *Creating Shareholder Value*, The Free Press, New York.

Sargent T.J. (1971) A Note on the 'Accelerationist Controversy', *Journal of Money, Credit and Banking, 8,* 1, 91-108.

Schlosser M. (1990) *Corporate Finance*, Prentice-Hall, Englewood Cliffs.

Scott A.J., Storper M. (1987) High Technology Industry and Regional Development: A Theoretical Critique and Reconstruction, *International Social Science Journal, 39,* 1, 215-32.

Spear S.E. (1989) Learning Rational Expectations under Computability Constraints, *Econometrica, 57,* 2, 889-909.

Vosselman W.H. (1989) Verwachte en gerealiseerde investeringen, *Maand-statistieken Industrie, 9,* Central Bureau of Statistics, The Hague, 35-45.

PART III

MICRO STUDIES

[11]

BUTTERWORTH
HEINEMANN

0969-6989(95)00029-1

Journal of Retailing and Consumer Services Vol 2, No 4, pp. 229–240, 1995
Copyright © 1995 Elsevier Science Ltd
Printed in Great Britain. All rights reserved
0969-6989/95/$10.00 + .00

Information use and company performance

An application to the retail electrical appliances sector

Hans Ouwersloot, Peter Nijkamp and Piet Rietveld

Department of Spatial Economics, Faculty of Economics and Econometrics, Free University Amsterdam, de Boelelaan 1105, 1081 HV Amsterdam, The Netherlands

While there is no doubt that we are living in an information age, the question as to whether information is really beneficial to its users has not often been addressed empirically. This paper aims to address this issue by analysing information use by retail electrical appliance companies in order to explain differences in company performance. The results suggest that some companies spend too many resources on information, so that information use becomes counterproductive.

Keywords: information use. Porter's model. cluster analysis

he information age has arrived': this is the essage that was convincingly proclaimed by aisbitt (1982), and has been repeated ever since. deed. information technology has made the idespread and cheap use of information possible, ducing numerous new applications. The question at has not been addressed, however, is whether conomic agents are actually better off because of is overwhelming volume of attainable information.

The present paper aims to discuss this important sue. It does so by concentrating on information use companies. Standard microeconomic analysis aggests that an optimal level of information emand exists, but in this paper we assume that not l companies succeed in optimizing their information needs. Hence we expect to find differences in erformance that can be attributed to deviations om optimal use of information. After a conceptual nd formal analysis, this topic is also studied empirically.

The next section of this paper presents a general amework – inspired by the works of Porter 1979,1980) – to model the competing company in s (economic) environment. It is concluded that an mpirical analysis should ideally be directed to a ector that shows distinct characteristics: in particular. sensitivity to information use because of tough ompetition with many identical companies in a ashionable market. The following section then describes the sector that was chosen in view of these considerations: the retail electrical appliances sector. A survey was conducted among Dutch companies to analyse the information behaviour of this sector and to relate this to the performance of the companies. The resulting data are described in the subsequent section, and then analysed in detail. The most remarkable result of this analysis is that at least some companies in the sample seem to use too much information: the more information is used, the lower the relative performance of the company.

A conceptual framework: the Porter model

Our starting point – influenced by Porter (1979, 1980) – is the company competing with its competitors (or rivals) within the industry (or sector). All companies in the industry are facing the same competitive forces from their environment. The company that succeeds in taking the best position with respect to these forces, in comparison with the other companies, will yield the best results, which will be revealed by its performing above the industry's average. In this section we first discuss the competitive forces in a general setting.

Basically, four competitive forces can be identified: *new entrants, buyers, sellers,* and *substitute products*. Porter (1979) provides an elaborate discussion of what determines the strength of the competitors in each of these four areas, which will

229

H Ouwersloot et al

be summarized in discussing the electrical appliances sector in the next section.

These four forces may be further aggregated into two categories: forces in the fields of *price* and *volume*. In addition to these free-market forces, regulators (such as the government) play a significant role in defining the rules of the competition. We explicitly assume that the optimal use of information in any of these areas, including regulators, has an effect on the performance of the company.

Where companies produce qualitatively identical products, using qualitatively identical inputs, competition with suppliers of the input and consumers will concentrate on prices. On the other hand, assuming a fixed demand for the products of the company in its sector, new entrants will fight for some share of this demand (a piece of the cake), while substitute products will compete for some part of the demand (the size of the cake). Thus we may assume that new entrants do not change the total demand for the product of the sector, while substitutes try to reduce the size of that demand.

Figures 1 and *2* illustrate this model. *Figure 1* shows the field of price competition. The bottom end of the line (P_1) indicates the absolute minimum production cost because of input factors that have to be paid for. The upper end of the line (P_4) indicates the absolute maximum price that the consumer is willing to pay for the product. The middle part of the line is the minimum profit margin (MPM) that the company wants to make on the production of the product. The exact use of this margin is of no interest; the usefulness of this interval is found in the existence of a maximum input price P_2 and a minimum selling price P_3. Under certain circumstances they can even coincide. P_2, the lower end of the MPM interval, indicates the maximum amount that the company is willing to pay for the input factors. P_3, at the upper end of the MPM interval, is the minimum selling price of the company. Competition with suppliers is on the interval P_1 to P_2, and with consumers on the interval P_3 to P_4. Note that this latter interval resembles the maximum consumer surplus. The trading prices – P_b for the inputs, and P_s for the output – will by definition be somewhere on these intervals, and the company obviously tries to maximize the selling price P_s, and to minimize its factor inputs buying price P_b. Thus, on the consumer's side, we assume that the company tries to make optimal use of the consumer demand, and tries to sell to each consumer for the maximum price possible. An implicit assumption in the context of price competition is that the volume of traded products to each (group of) consumer(s) is not influenced by P_s, as long as it is below P_4.

Figure 2 depicts the competition that a company faces. In the inner circle the price line of *Figure 1*

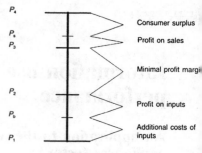

Figure 1 Representation of price competition

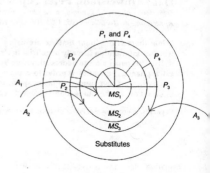

Figure 2 Competitive forces for the industry. MS_i = market share of i

has become a closed circle (P_1 and P_4 are connected here). Within the industry segment companies are indicated with their share of demand. The outer circle indicates the entire market for the products of the companies, and the substitute products. The threat posed by substitute products is that their share of this total market increases, which means that the inner circle is pushed further inwards. Of course, the industry as such can also increase its market share at the cost of the substitute products: the inner circle expands. Even the complete market can grow: the complete circle inflates, and all parts of the market grow, for example, proportionally.

The threat of new entrants is represented by arrows landing in the industry's market share. A the market does not (necessarily) expand when there are new entrants, the latter's activities lead to

decrease of the market share of companies already
in the market. Notice that, in general, this decrease
will take place in the industry itself, as suggested by
arrows A_1 and A_2, but that new entrants can also
enter at the border of the industry, contesting also
the substitutes market (see arrow A_3).

What is basically illustrated by *Figure 2* is the
above-mentioned distinction between price competition and volume competition. An underlying
assumption is that volume is independent of price:
the company's market share is in the first instance a
matter of reaching potential customers. Given that
these customers are identified and bound to the
company – that is, the company has reached some
market share – the company tries to make them pay
their maximum price, P_4. The identification and
finding of customers is achieved by using qualitative aspects such as service levels and image building. The costs that are associated with these efforts
are assumed to be recovered from the minimal
profit margin. Thus these costs may affect the level
of P_3 (the minimal selling price), but it is implicitly
assumed that this level does not have a real effect
on P_v.

The main purpose of the model is to make clear
what factors and actors are important for the
competing company: consumers of the output,
suppliers of the input factors, the government and
rivals, this last including competitors, new entrants,
and producers of substitutes. The competition is
played by taking actions and making decisions, and
these decisions are made on the basis of information. So companies need information about
customers, suppliers, the government, and rivals.

This leads to the hypothesis that is central in this
paper: companies that collect more information
about the competitive forces will *ceteris paribus*
yield better results with respect to these fields. For
example, companies that collect more information
about labour markets will be able to hire labour on
more profitable terms and specifically will pay lower
prices for the same quality of labour than their
competitors. In other words, the marginal productivity of information is positive. Assuming that this
marginal productivity is decreasing, and making the
assumption that the costs of acquiring and using
information are linearly increasing, leads to the
existence of an optimal level of information use.

In real-world situations not all companies will
succeed in optimizing their information demand,
which may then be reflected in lower performance.
Reasons may for example be found in differences in
management, or differences in adjustment time to
changing market conditions. This leads to the
following research issues addressed in this paper:

(1) Can differences in company performance be
     attributed to differences in information use?
(2) If so, can we determine the optimal informa-
     tion use level? Alternatively, can we determine

and typify companies that use too much or too
little information?

These general issues can also be formulated in a
more specific way:

(3) Suppose we have determined which competi-
     tive forces are important, and which are
     relatively unimportant. We then may ask: do
     those companies more actively collecting infor-
     mation on the important forces perform better
     than those who do not focus on the important
     forces?

Note, however, that we shall only be able to
attribute differences in performance to suboptimal
information use when we compare companies that
are otherwise equal; or, alternatively, when we have
full information on all other characteristics of the
company. Another point that is consequential for
empirical research is that information is a production factor, but only in a derived, second-order
sense. Information is useful in making decisions
about everything concerning the company, but is not
directly involved in the production process. We
therefore conjecture that the effect of information is
visible only when the relative performance (ie
compared with that of competitors) is sensitive to
differences in information use.

The implications for empirical research are
manifest. We assume that the effect of information
is most likely to be measurable when two conditions
are met:

(1) competition is tough, with many rivals in the
     same segment of the market; and
(2) the market is persistently in a state of rapid
     change, preferably on both the consumers' and
     the suppliers' side, and also with regard to
     governmental regulations.

Consequently, it is most promising to study companies from an industry that is characterized by many
small companies in a fashionable international
market of consumer products with many suppliers.

The retail electrical appliances sector – sellers of
audio sets, TV sets etc – is considered to be an
industry that meets most features of the ideal typical
industry sketched above, except that there is not
much government regulation in this area. In the
next section, we take a closer look at this industry,
at the same time studying its most important
competitive forces as identified above.

The retail electrical appliances sector

In this section we first give a general, introductory
description of the retail electrical appliances sector
in the Netherlands. Then its competitive forces are
analysed, following the model of the previous

H Ouwersloot et al

Table 1 Expenditures on consumer electrical goods for 1985, 1990 (projection) and 1995 (expected), including VAT (in billions of guilders)

	1985	1990	1995
Vision	1.77	2.25	2.50
Televisions		0.90	1.20
VCR and camcorders		0.87	1.05
Sound	0.915	1.45	1.90
Hi-fi		0.64	1.20
Personal audio		0.275	0.25
Other	0.45	0.60	0.75
Car radios		0.125	0.25
General supplies		0.325	0.35
Total sound and vision	3.135	4.30	5.15
White goods	1.765	2.45	2.85
Total consumer electronics	4.9	6.75	8.00

Source: Pleijster (1991)

Table 2 Some characteristics of the retail electrical appliances sector in 1989

	Total turnover*	Number of firms	Turnover per firm*	Turnover in apparatuses*	Turnover in apparatuses by firm*
Chains	1660 (33%)	420 (12%)	3.95	1920 (30%)	3.80
Organized	1350 (28%)	770 (23%)	1.75	1340 (21%)	1.31
Independent	1990 (39%)	2210 (65%)	0.90	1600 (25%)	0.63
Others				1540 (24%)	
Total	5010	3400	1.65	6400	

Notes:
*Millions of guilders, excluding VAT
*Millions of guilders, including VAT
Source: Pleijster (1991)

section. This section draws heavily on Pleijster (1991): unless stated otherwise, data are from this report.

Table 1 shows total expenditures for the industry in 1985, 1990 (projection) and 1995 (expectation). It also reports expenditures on so-called *white goods* (refrigerators, ovens etc). Although our intention was to keep the study strictly to the electrical appliances sector, in practice it turned out that this restriction was impossible to maintain because of the mixed structure of many companies. Therefore, the white goods sector is mentioned whenever relevant. The union of the two sectors is referred to as the *consumer electrical goods sector*.

For a detailed discussion of *Table 1* we refer to its source. For our purpose the important thing to note is that although many consumer electrical products are in the saturation stage of their product life-cycle, by constant upgrading, introducing 'new' products, miniaturizing etc the sector succeeds in creating a replacement demand that is large enough for it to remain a growth market. This mechanism makes the market a fashionable one.

In 1990 the retail electrical appliances sector consisted of about 2700 enterprises with approximately 3400 stores. For convenience we shall call the stores *firms*. About 420 firms (12%) belong to commercial chains; about 770 firms (23%) cooperate in a less formal way; while the remaining 2210 firms (65%) are independent. (According to the definition in Pleijster (1991) a chain consists minimally of seven firms belonging to the same enterprise.) *Table 2* gives some data on the organization and economic performance of the sector.

Noteworthy from this table is the difference between the categories in terms of turnover per firm, which is much larger for organized and chain firms. In general, entrance to a cooperative is excluded for firms with less than Dfl 1 million turnover. A second interesting result is the much larger share of goods in terms of turnover for chains than for independent firms. The remainder of the turnover is generated by service activities such as repair and installation. We now turn to the discussion of the competitive forces in the sector.

Buyers

Electrical appliances retailers sell their products to households. Porter (1979) mentions a number of factors that determine the strength of the competition by buyers (and sellers, which are more or less opposites). Stated briefly, a buyer (or group of buyers) is powerful if it purchases in large volumes, if the products are standardized or undifferentiated, if the products are relatively expensive, or if there are no significant switching costs.

Applying these criteria to the retail electrical appliances industry it appears that consumers may possess quite a powerful position, as the products that they buy are relatively expensive, and the products are highly standardized and undifferentiated. In addition, there are no switching costs, as there are many retailers with low thresholds. The counterpoint is the weak organization of consumers (only approximately 11% of Dutch households are members of a consumers' association), which means that effectively the goods are bought in small numbers only. Thus firms have to deal only with individual purchases, which are not significant for the performance of the firm as a whole. However, the fact that 65% of the firms are independent shows that they themselves are not particularly well organized either.

Suppliers of input

Table 2 shows that by far the largest part of input consists of supplies of tradables, which is typical for the retail sector. Therefore, we concentrate on the suppliers of these goods in the discussion of the input factors.

As there are only a few Dutch manufacturers of appliances – Philips being the most notable among them – the greater part of supply comes from abroad. These imports are predominantly distributed by approximately 120 so-called *sales houses* (which may belong to foreign companies). In 1989, 83% of supply was directly delivered to retailers, and thus only 17% by wholesale, and this latter percentage has been steadily decreasing for years. Thus on the supply side retailers are dealing with a large number of suppliers, almost all from abroad. Although there are many more firms than suppliers, the number of the latter still seems to be too large to speak of concentrated supply.

A second consideration is that the amount of money involved in transactions between a supplier and a firm represents a relatively large part of the firm's expenditure, whereas it is only a relatively small part of the earnings of the supplier. In other words, each individual supplier is important to the retailer, but an individual retailer is less important to the supplier (compare the analogous argument when discussing the buyer's position). Overall, we may conclude that the competitive forces in this area seem to balance.

Recall that the market for electrical appliances is persistently in a state of rapid change as a result of technical progress, and the need to create replacement demand. The success of retailers can be assumed to depend on their ability to respond to these developments. Thus it is important for retailers to be fully informed about the developments on the suppliers' side, and this offers competitive opportunities. However, these opportunities do not determine the strength of retailers as opposed to their suppliers; but they illustrate the importance of keeping well informed about what is happening on the producer's side.

Substitutes

Loosely speaking, two goods are substitutes if they satisfy comparable needs. In this sense we can think of no true substitutes for electrical appliances. Goods that compete for the same part of the consumer's budget are luxury goods in general, like holidays, but clearly they serve different purposes. It is perhaps interesting to observe, however, that the substitutability of luxury goods, in particular by holidays abroad, was occasionally mentioned in the preliminary interviews that we had with some retailers.

New entrants

The threat of new entrants is by and large determined by the ease with which new businesses can be started. A number of factors that may hinder this start can be identified: economies of scale, product differentiation, capital requirements, cost disadvantages independent of size, and access to distribution channels. The common factor in this list is the (in)ability to start business on a sufficient scale for sufficiently low cost. If initial investments are low, in particular insofar as sunk costs are concerned, there are practically no barriers to entry. Indeed, the retail electrical appliances sector typically has low initial investments.

Another point is that total demand is growing only modestly, leaving little room for new entrants. This aspect, in combination with the low attractiveness of the market due to the high level of price competition, appears to have a significant effect, as the number of firms showed a net decrease from about 3650 in 1985 to 3100 in 1989.

Thus, on theoretical grounds, a strong threat from new entrants can be expected, as there are no real barriers to entry. However, the data show a net decrease in the number of firms, probably due to strong competition. It may thus be the case here that though there are many new entrants, they are nevertheless outnumbered by those leaving the market. This, however, leaves the threat of entrants unchanged.

Government

The government's role as a regulator is of significant importance to the functioning of many industries.

H Ouwersloot et al

For the retail electrical appliances sector, however, governmental actions at the national, regional, or local level are of practically no significance. Yet producers are located all over the world – predominantly in Japan and the USA – and therefore international affairs may be of some concern to Dutch retailers. Examples concern dumping and protectionist policies. Therefore, governmental action on an international level may be of some relevance to the electrical appliances retailers.

Rivals

The above-mentioned fields constitute the domain of competition. This competition is fought with a firm's rivals. Therefore, outperforming competitors requires knowledge not only about these fields, but even more so about the actions of rivals on these fields. Clearly, information about the rivals is of fundamental importance for the firm.

The interesting point about this is who are to be considered a firm's rivals. This largely depends on the consumers that a firm wants to reach, and this again is strongly related to the choice of spatial scale and marketing concepts. These topics deserve some further attention.

Pleijster (1991) indicates that six marketing concepts can be distinguished in the sector. Three of these concepts rely predominantly on the service aspect: a first concept connects this with a broad assortment (*service–choice*), a second one with a medium assortment (*service–normal*), and a third one with a highly specialized assortment (*service–special*). A fourth concept that Pleijster identifies is the *non-concept*: no single aspect of marketing receives special attention. Retailers using this concept typically perform below the sector's average. A fifth concept primarily concerns price competition and only secondarily service competition (*price–service*). This concept is typical for chain stores, who combine this concept with a broad assortment. The final concept is relatively new, and called the *superstore* concept. This makes use of large stores and a very broad assortment, from low-end to high-end products (high-end refers to superior quality products and significantly higher prices, partly due to snob appeal). Moreover, these stores sell derived products in such fields as photography and computers. This last concept is of no practical importance for our current analysis, as there are very few superstores.

Non-concept stores are typically most concerned with survival. They have a defensive strategy in reacting to moves of competitors. Thus, although they may compete with all other types of marketing concept, they are relatively harmless because of a lack of vision.

Tough competition may be expected among firms with the same concept. In addition, the service–choice and price–service concepts concentrate on similar groups of consumers: only the instruments they use differ. Further, service–choice stores have a local or regional basis, while chains (as an entity) perform on a higher spatial level. A chain stores usually have low prices, stores with the service–choice concept also have to be cheap. The resulting low margins necessitate a relatively large (spatial) market. At the other end of the service spectrum, service–special shops are quite distinct, as their prime interest is the sale of high-end products and comparative standards for service. However, this makes the market much thinner, also requiring a spatially large market. Thus both service–choice and service–special stores operate on a relatively large spatial scale, yet address different segments of the market. Therefore, they are considered to be each other's competitors to a minor extent only. Finally, the service–normal concept takes an intermediate position. Its strong points are the local attraction, and concentration on brands that are not obliged to be low-priced. Obviously, this is a vulnerable position, as these stores are threatened from two sides. Nevertheless, a considerable number of stores use this concept.

To conclude: strong competition exists at the low end of the market. At this end, the spatial orientation is relatively wide. High-end stores opt for the same spatial market, yet their target population is different. At this high end, competition is significantly less. In between are vulnerable stores, which address both market segments. They concentrate on a smaller spatial scale, leading to a comparative advantage on the local market.

Summary

The sector's position with respect to buyers is quite weak, implying a potentially strong competitive force. Its position towards sellers is more or less in balance. New entrants and especially substitutes seem relatively unimportant. Rivals are especially important at the low end of the market. Finally national government policy and regulation are unimportant, though international affairs may be of some concern.

Having identified the main competitive forces we now are ready for an empirical analysis. The data that were collected concentrate on company performance on the one hand, and on information use on the other. As it is not immediately clear which variable(s) should be used as a measure of company performance (this also depends on the objectives of the company), data on a number of indicators (turnover growth, profits etc) are collected. A similar measurement problem is encountered on the information side. Therefore data are collected on a number of input sources related to the fields identified above. The next section describes the data and collection procedure in some detail, while the subsequent section presents the statistical analysis.

Information use and company performance

The data

The data used in the empirical analysis are the result of a survey that was held among electrical appliances retailers in November/December 1991. The survey was sent to stores and addressed to the store manager. If questionnaires had been sent to *firms* – many of them with more than one store or department – it was feared that because of the aggregation of departmental data, valuable information on the behaviour of individual actors at the store level would be lost. An implicit assumption in this approach is that store managers can operate independently.

Questions were structured under five headings: general data about the firm. economic data. availability and use of telecommunications media. use of other media. and use of other sources of information. Other media' included electronic media such as videotext. but also newspapers and all kinds of periodicals. 'Other sources' dealt with face-to-face contacts with sales representatives. follow-up education etc.

A total of 893 questionnaires were sent by post, including a stamped return envelope. and followed by a telephone reminder. A gross response of 11.6% and a net response of 8.4% (that is, 75 usable forms) was the result. Possible reasons for this somewhat low response are:

● The questionnaires were distributed shortly before the busiest period for retailers: the month of December.
● Retailers are overwhelmed with all kind of questionnaires, which clearly erodes their willingness to participate.
● There was no accompanying letter of recommendation: for example. from the Chamber of Commerce.
● Apparently. respondents were not convinced of the personal benefits of participating.

In spite of the low response rate. a number of 75 observations is. in general. sufficient for data analysis. Similarly. the quality of the data was modest. but good enough for the tentative analysis of the next sections. Moreover. the sample appeared to be representative with respect to the main characteristics (see below).

Electrical appliances retailers who received a questionnaire had been stratified by location. Eight Chamber of Commerce districts were chosen. according to *Table 3*. Four of these districts are in the highly developed Randstad (the region in the western part of the country. where the four major cities are located: Amsterdam. Rotterdam, the Hague and Utrecht) and the other four are from the (slightly) less developed rest of the country. Similarly. both within the Randstad and from the rest of the country, four urbanized districts versus four semi-urbanized regions were selected.

Table 3 Selection of Chambers of Commerce districts

	Randstad	Outside Randstad
Urban	Amsterdam	Groningen
	Utrecht	Nijmegen
Semi-urban	Haarlem	Roermond
	Gouda	Deventer

Table 4 Representativeness of response (in percentages)

	Randstad	Outside Randstad	Totals
Urban			
Sample	47.0	23.2	70.2
Response	37.5	29.2	66.7
Semi-urban			
Sample	18.0	11.8	29.8
Response	23.6	9.7	33.3
Totals			
Sample	65.0	35.0	100.0
Response	61.1	38.9	100.0

Notes: Sample $n = 893$; response $n = 72$

Table 4 shows the distributions of firms in the sample and the response by location. The column and row totals are comparable, but the cells show a significant deviation, most notably for the urbanized region in the Randstad. With respect to the size of the firms – measured by full-time-equivalent jobs they offer – there appeared to be a reasonable similarity between sample (3.6 jobs) and response (3.4 jobs).

Analysis of the data

Preliminaries

In this subsection we first present and discuss the raw data about economic performance and the data concerning the use of information. We study the representativeness of the response and consider whether differences in performance are related to the characteristics of the firms. We also show how the large number of information-use variables are summarized in a few compound variables.

Tables 5 and *6* consider whether differences in performance can be attributed to a firm's characteristics. Three performance indicators are summarized in these tables: profits as a percentage of turnover. market share, and turnover growth. Market share is reported as a subjective perception of this variable. as it is practically impossible to define it exactly (see the discussion above). Similarly. turnover growth refers to expectations for the next two years.

H Ouwersloot et al

Table 5 Competition indicators by location

	Randstad	Outside Randstad	Totals
Urban			
Mean profit	72	129	98
Market share	90	79	85
Turnover growth	71	81	75
Semi-urban			
Mean profit	104	107	105
Market share	118	119	119
Turnover growth	170	100	154
Totals			
Mean profit	85	124	100
Market share	101	88	100
Turnover growth	108	86	100

Table 6 Economic indicators by company characteristics

	Market share	Turnover growth	Profits
Firm size			
Small	27.3	7.9	15.9
Medium	28.3	13.7	16.3
Large	26.2	11.3	8.5
Chain member			
Yes	33.3	6.0	12.3
No	25.0	11.2	14.3
Purchase organization			
Yes	33.2	14.9	11.0
No	22.2	6.7	15.8
White goods			
Yes	29.7	6.2	13.2
No	26.1	12.3	14.5

Table 5 shows that firms in the urbanized part of the Randstad have lower profits compared with those from the urban regions outside the Randstad. Similarly, firms from semi-urban regions have typically larger market shares. Finally, firms in the semi-urban regions in the Randstad have the highest expectations about turnover growth. From this table we conclude that deviations from the average show no consistent patterns, except that firms in the urbanized part of the Randstad perform typically below average.

Table 6 shows that reported market share is independent of market size. Apparently, larger firms serve larger markets, leading to comparable market shares. However, firms that are organized – by joining a chain, or a purchase organization – report larger market shares than unorganized firms. Concerning growth expectations, it appears that small firms have slightly worse prospects than medium-sized and large firms. Also, those organized in a purchase organization are optimistic about their

growth potential, while chain members expect less growth. Quite interesting is the result that firms who also sell white goods have notably lower expectations about turnover growth than 'appliances only' firms. Finally, the data on profits reveal that large firms have notably lower profits than other firms. Again, we conclude that observed deviations from the averages show no consistent patterns.

Next we discuss the construction of the variable describing the use of information. A number of questions in the survey addressed this topic, and our goal here is to aggregate these data.

Ouwersloot (1994, Chapter 2) discusses the problems involved in information measurement. For the present discussion, the important points are that it is fairly easy to measure the volume of messages (the units in which information is exchanged), but that the informational content of messages is also related to a number of other characteristics of the message, as well as to the semantic model of the receiver. Moreover, a semantic model is strongly personal and difficult to observe. So we conclude that in the present setting direct measurement of information use is practically impossible.

Consequently, we have to stick to indirect measurement of information use. In the present analysis we use volume as a proxy for information use. Obviously, many important aspects of information are neglected in this way. In particular, the characteristics of quality and timeliness of information have to be mentioned in this respect. However two arguments may be mentioned as to why volume is a reasonable proxy in empirical analysis. First, the volume of information used can be considered as an indicator of the importance that the firm attaches to information. If a firm attaches much weight to information use it is reasonable to assume that it will also attach weight to the quality of information. In that case, volume and quality will be positively correlated and volume can be used as a proxy for quality. Second, if a firm uses more information, it will have a higher probability of getting the important facts in time. It will also have more opportunities to verify the information it receives (the positive aspect of redundancy). Thus again we find that volume can be assumed to be strongly correlated with the qualitative aspects of information (in particular its timeliness).

An important category of information source reported in the data concerns the use of a large number of written sources. This ranges from the use of newspapers to professional journals and information provided by local or national government. A second category of information sources covers data on the number of representatives that the respondent receives, as well as the number of suppliers with whom the firm had a self-initiated contact. A third category tells how many public or private exhibitions the respondent visited.

The Porter-style model described earlier is used to organize the data as follows. The number of written

Table 7 Basic statistics of information variables

Variable	Mean	St dev	Maximum
Pinf	2.79	1.47	6
Cinf	2.52	1.08	4
Yinf	1.73	1.50	5
Exhibits	3.59	3.29	22
Repres	12.85	13.08	70

Correlation matrix

	Pinf	Cinf	Yinf	Exhibits	Repres
Pinf	1.00	0.82	0.53	0.32	0.14
Cinf		1.00	0.47	0.26	0.07
Yinf			1.00	0.18	0.08
Exhibits				1.00	0.43
Repres					1.00

sources that the respondent uses, relating to customers, suppliers and regulatory organizations, was used as a variable representing the use of information on prices, costs and volume respectively. In addition, the arithmetic averages were taken of the number of visiting representatives, and contacts with suppliers, and also of the number of private and public exhibitions visited. Thus, five variables resulted: *Pinf, Cinf, Yinf, Exhibits* and *Repres*, representing the use of information in the field of prices, costs, volume, the numbers of exhibitions and visits and contacts with representatives respectively. *Exhibits* and *Repres* also relate to the use of information on suppliers, but as they are quite different in character from the use of written sources they are treated separately. The Appendix shows how the sources are assigned to the information variables.

Table 7 contains the descriptive statistics of the resulting variables. Note that the variables are measured on different scales. Also, all constructed variables are positively correlated – which is not very surprising – but these correlations are relatively weak (with the exception of the correlation between *Pinf* and *Cinf*).

Analysis of information use

In this subsection we analyse the information use as revealed in the dataset, and try to combine this with

the firm's characteristics and performance. Our first goal is to identify information use profiles, and classify the respondents according to these profiles. Then we consider whether these categories correspond to other characteristics and – in particular – to performance measures.

For the classification of the firms in the sample we use a clustering technique. We cluster the respondents on the basis of the five aggregated information variables constructed above: *Pinf, Cinf, Yinf, Exhibits* and *Repres*. These variables were first rescaled to have zero mean and unit variance each. Next, a standard clustering algorithm was applied, using the PC software package SPSS (Norusis, 1990). The algorithm makes use of squared Euclidean distances and the 'average linkage between groups' method. Inspection of the resulting dendrogram and agglomeration schedule leads to the detection of four clusters. In fact, three of them were real clusters in the sense that all points were close together, while the fourth cluster consisted of a kind of residual group. This last group contained only five firms.

Table 8 shows the average scores for each group on the five clustering variables. This table shows that the first cluster scores low on all information variables: therefore this cluster is labelled 'low'. The second cluster shows approximately average scores on all variables (with a minor exception for *Repres*), thus giving rise to the label 'average'. The third and fourth cluster score above average for all variables, and so deserve a 'high' label. A distinction between these two clusters results as the third cluster scores significantly higher for the *Pinf, Cinf,* and *Yinf* variables, which are based on written sources in particular, whereas the fourth cluster scores higher for the other two variables *Repres* and *Exhibits*, which are face-to-face contacts. Therefore the third cluster is labelled 'high-formal' and the fourth 'high-informal'. The last two clusters consist of 12 and five observations only and share a high level of information use: so for practical purposes they are occasionally combined as a 'high' cluster.

In *Table 9* we study whether the suggestive labels given to the clusters are supported by evidence in the data on the availability of communication media. The table shows the average number of

Table 8 Information use per cluster (mean values of information variables per cluster)

	All (n = 75)	Low (n = 19)	Average (n = 39)	High–formal (n = 12)	High–informal (n = 5)	High (n = 17)
Pinf	2.79	1.00	2.95	4.75	3.60	4.41
Cinf	2.52	1.11	2.74	3.92	2.80	3.59
Yinf	1.73	0.58	1.57	4.00	2.00	3.41
Exhibits	3.59	2.38	3.06	4.69	9.70	6.16
Repres	12.85	9.67	9.35	12.75	52.50	24.44

H Ouwersloot et al

Table 9 Availability of communication media per cluster

	All (n = 75)	Low (n = 19)	Average (n = 39)	High–formal (n = 12)	High–informal (n = 5)	High (n = 17)
Telephone						
Number of lines/job	0.73	0.69	0.69	0.86	0.72	0.82
Number of apparatuses/job	1.20	1.13	1.15	1.47	1.06	1.37
Fax						
Percentage ownership	68	47	69	83	100	88

Table 10 Company characteristics per cluster

	All	Low	Average	High–formal	High–informal	High
Member of chain (%)	22.7	26.3	12.8	33.3	60.0	41.2
Member of purchase organization (%)	39.1	35.3	34.3	41.7	80.0	52.9
Member of branch organization (%)	40.0	14.3	51.7	28.6	66.7	40.0
Appliances only (%)	37.3	47.4	38.5	33.3	20.0	23.5
Urbanized (%)	66.7	64.7	71.1	66.7	40.0	58.8
Randstad (%)	61.1	70.6	50.0	75.0	80.0	76.5
Firm size						
Small (%)	38.7	52.6	35.9	33.3	20.0	29.4
Medium (%)	32.0	26.3	41.0	16.7	20.0	17.6
Large (%)	29.3	21.1	23.1	50.0	60.0	53.0
Number of jobs	3.41	3.01	3.15	4.58	4.25	4.50
Sales floorspace (m²)	181	155	133	379	255	337

telephone lines and apparatuses available in each cluster, and the percentage of fax owners. The number of lines and apparatuses are divided by the number of jobs in the companies, to correct for a potential scale effect (the subsequent analysis indeed reveals such a scale effect). Nevertheless, the results show that all three variables more or less confirm the expectation that the availability of telecommunication facilities grows with information use, as reflected in the clusters.

Next we investigate whether relations exist between cluster membership and a number of other variables. *Table 10* considers this point with respect to company characteristics. For example, 26.3% of the firms in the 'low' cluster are members of a chain, 38.5% of the firms in the 'average' cluster sell appliances only, and so on. Some interesting observations emerge:

- Respondents from the 'high' clusters are more often organized in a chain, sector organization, or purchase organization. This higher organization rate is especially found in the 'high–informal' cluster.
- Mixed firms – selling both appliances and white goods – are relatively more represented in the 'high' clusters. This may be due to the fact that

mixed firms have to keep informed about two markets: appliances and white goods.
- Information use typically increases with the size of the firm. This is revealed by all three variables that relate to company size: turnover, employees, and sales floorspace.

The first observation suggests that joining some organization is inspired by considerations of streamlining information flows rather than reducing the information needs. The third observation can be due to two mechanisms. Either these firms are larger because they have more interest in information, leading to better performance and subsequently growth – which is factually the premise of this paper – or large firms have more possibilities to pay attention to information (a simple scale effect). Our static and, moreover, small dataset can give no clues about which mechanism is the relevant one.

Finally, *Table 11* presents the mean scores for the indicated economic performance variables for the clusters. As far as the turnover variables are concerned, no clear patterns emerge. The profit variables, however, show that firms with a 'high' profile perform relatively badly, and also expect to perform below average in the future. The outcome for the market share variable shows a similar

238

Table 11 Economic indicators per cluster

	All	Low	Average	High–formal	High–informal	High
Turnover growth (%)						
1991	4.10	2.07	5.70	0.86	7.00	2.78
1992	6.00	7.00	6.06	4.44	5.75	4.85
Turnover speed	5.75	5.50	6.08	5.65	4.13	5.21
Profits (%)						
1990	14.0	20.3	14.4	12.1	4.0	10.1
1991	14.0	24.4	14.0	11.7	4.2	9.8
1992	13.1	19.0	13.3	12.2	3.8	10.7
Market share (%)	27.5	42.4	25.6	19.0	18.0	18.7

pattern. The opposite holds for firms with a 'low' profile. Thus an inverse dependence emerges between information profile and these economic indicators. According to our theory, this suggests that 'high' profile firms attach too much weight to using information, which consequently becomes counterproductive. In other words, the marginal benefits of information for 'high' profile firms are lower than the marginal costs of the information. We immediately add that this is just a suggestion, as our dataset prohibits firmer analysis and conclusions.

In terms of the research issues as formulated earlier, we have found that:

1) There indeed exists a relation between information use and company performance.
2) Unorganized firms (as they are typically using less information) are the ones that are most likely to show an optimal information demand. Other characteristics are less clear cut.

This latter result allows an interesting explanation. Entry to some organization streamlines information supply, but the only result seems to be that the firm becomes uncritical, and just consumes (or only receives) all information that is handed over to it. Unorganized firms, by contrast, simply have to be critical on the information streams as each piece of information has to be decided upon. This may explain why unorganized firms are much more critical on their information use, leading to the use of less information and better performance.

Finally, it should be clear that our dataset does not permit the investigation of the third issue.

Concluding remarks

For analysing the effect of information on company performance in a competitive environment a model was developed based on Porter's seminal works that suggested the consideration of information use in the areas of costs, prices and volume. The model

was applied to retail electrical appliances firms in the Netherlands, and tested empirically using a self-administered survey. The results from the analysis suggest that firms in this sector might very well be using too much information or (more modestly) might be on the decreasing part of the curve describing the net benefit of information.

Obviously this remarkable result needs confirmation, both on the basis of better datasets, and by exploiting more powerful statistical techniques, and preferably across other sectors as well. Moreover, according to the structure of the theoretical model the distinction between various information areas (suppliers, customers, government regulatory measures etc) should be maintained more strictly. Measurement issues also deserve attention. Both the measurement of information use, and the general issue of measuring company performance, need to be investigated more thoroughly. This latter analysis should also take into account the firm's objectives.

Meanwhile, it may be advisable for management to consider the use of information sources carefully. Apparently, the danger of overconsumption of information is real, in particular when a company is part of a larger organization facilitating information use. Finally, information should be related to those fields where competition is toughest. Although we could not investigate this issue empirically, the theoretical model leading to this point is quite convincing.

References

Naisbitt, J (1982) *Megatrends – Ten New Directions Transforming Our Lives* Warner, New York
Norusis, M J (1990) *SPSS/PC+ Statistics 4.0* Manual for the SPSS statistical package, SPSS Inc, Chicago
Ouwersloot, J (1994) 'Information and communication from an economic perspective' PhD Thesis, Free University Amsterdam
Pleijster, F (1991) *De electrotechnische detailhandel* (The retail electrical appliances sector) Economisch Instituut voor het Midden- en Kleinbedrijf, Zoetermeer

H Ouwersloot et al

Porter. M E (1979) 'The structure within industries and companies' performance' *Review of Economics and Statistics* 61 214–227

Porter, M E (1980) *Competitive Strategy: Techniques f Analysing Industries and Competitors* The Free Press, Ne York

Appendix 1

The construction of the compound information variables

The variables *Pinf, Cinf, Yinf* summarize the number of written publications to which the respondents have access in the field of prices, cost and volume, respectively. The possible sources for each category are listed here.

- *Pinf:* journal on consumer affairs; publications from the sector organization; publications from the employers' organization; publications from the Central Bureau of Statistics (CBS); Publications by GFK Nederland; local newspaper.

- *Cinf:* journal on consumer electronics; public tions from the sector organization; publication from the employers' organization; publication from the CBS.
- *Yinf:* regional newspaper; national newspaper publications from local government; public tions from national government; publication from CBS.

GFK Nederland is a commercial organization tha collects and distributes data on sales of consume electronics products.

[12]

Entrepreneurship and Innovation in the SME Sector[1]

Enno Masurel, Kees van Montfort and Peter Nijkamp

Faculty of Economics and Business Administration, Free University, Amsterdam

3.1 Setting the Scene

Entrepreneurship has become a topical research issue in recent years. In particular, the role of the entrepreneur in innovation processes has received much attention, as is witnessed in the seminal review of Malecki (1997). Many studies in this field appear to refer to Schumpeter (1934) as an important stepping stone. Schumpeter views the entrepreneur as the key actor in the innovation process. In his view, the entrepreneur is a change actor who is permanently seeking new opportunities (see for a review also Nijkamp 2002). The wealth of empirical research in the past decades has clearly demonstrated that the 'entrepreneurial attitude' as an 'animal spirit' is a complex and ambiguous concept that can only properly be studied by thorough empirical research.

Many findings in recent decades have revealed a multitude of drivers for the innovation process. Several authors have suggested that small and medium-sized enterprises (SMEs) play a central role in the innovation process (both product and process innovations). The question whether SMEs exhibit a high degree of innovativeness has recently extensively been studied in the literature. The findings are not always conclusive, and future research is no doubt warranted. In the present paper we will examine the innovation perceptions and attitudes of entrepreneurs and managers in SMEs from the following perspective: which factors do they perceive as critical for success in the innovation process? This exploratory research question can only be answered by solid empirical research on the drivers of innovation behaviour. In this paper, innovations refer to entirely new products (or services), to improved versions of an existing product (or service) or to a new market for an existing product (or service).

The research approach in our study is as follows. Based on an extensive literature survey, we will identify a systematic classification of 14 possible important drivers of innovative behaviour in the SME sector. These factors will act as a test frame for our empirical research on entrepreneurial attitudes regarding innovation.

The authors thank Pascal van der Hart for his role in the data collection process and Ramon Lentink for his statistical assistance.

227

Then the design and findings of an extensive survey questionnaire among SMEs in the Netherlands will be discussed. The empirical results will be derived from multivariate statistical analysis (i.e., factor analysis) of the empirical data. The paper will be concluded with some retrospective conclusions on innovative behaviour of SMEs.

3.2 An Exploratory Literature Review

There is an avalanche of literature on the motives and socioeconomic implication of entrepreneurship in the SME sector (see for recent contributions inter alia Marsili 2000; Peneder 2000).

Although SMEs provide an engine of innovative activity (Thurik 1996), there is only sparse empirical knowledge on the specific success factors of SME innovation, in contrast to innovative behaviour in large corporate organisations. Nooteboom (1994) speaks of dynamic complementarity in innovation between SMES and large firms. SMES are usually strong in applications of basic technologies, in generating inventions, in implementing promising results, and in conquering market niches and residual markets. Their talents and qualities are clearly related to their core characteristics: independence and flexibility, inevitably associated with the personality of the entrepreneur ('entrepreneurial spirit'). Yap and Souder (1994) argue that the small entrepreneurial high-technology firms have to adopt competitive strategies that are very different from the ones used by large corporate organisations, in order to maximise their chances of success with the introduction of new products or services. Large firms are more skilled in exploiting findings from fundamental research and in adopting efficient production methods, thereby benefiting from scale economies. Thus, the performance of small and large firms may differ. We will raise here the question which specific factors can be identified that provide a significant explanation as critical success conditions for innovative behaviour in the SME sector.

In the economic literature seeking to explain the competitive benefits of innovative behaviour a great variety of economic, social, institutional, geographic and technological drivers is normally mentioned (see, e.g., Kleinknecht 1986; Davelaar 1992; Bertuglia et al. 1997). The identification of a systematic list of drivers of innovative attitudes and behaviour in the SME sector – in terms of technogenesis and adoption of new findings – is not easy, as the SME sector is extremely diverse. Economic research has not yet been able to design a generally applicable framework for SME innovation. Consequently, in our analysis we will deploy a rich variety of scientific studies as a source for the selection of indicators that may potentially explain innovation in the SME sector. The validity of this exploratory approach has to be tested by means of empirical fieldwork on SME firms. On the basis of an extensive literature search we were able to extract by way of a systematic classification 14 drivers of SME innovations. And these will successively now be described. This classification was inferred from reading the

xtensive literature by way of an inductive approach and was not based on a prior
efined and specified theoretical construct.

.2.1 Unique Product Advantages

In the literature on SME innovation, a prominent place is assumed by unique
roduct advantages, in terms of product quality, product functions, quality/price
atio and product design. So the specificity of a product is not only related to its
iternal features, but also to its position in the market. The customer should be
rovided with real value, that is superior to competitive products, so that his needs
re optimally satisfied. We refer inter alia to Song and Parry (1997), Atuahene-
iima (1996), Montoya-Weiss and Calantone (1994), Edgett, Shipley and Forbes
1992), Zirger and Maidique (1990), Cooper (1990), Cooper and Kleinschmidt
1987) and Rothwell et al. (1974) for further exposition on the importance of this
ictor for innovative entrepreneurial attitudes.

.2.2 Human Resources Management

second important success factor for the innovation process in the SME sector is
uman resources management, in terms of technological knowledge, marketing
nowledge, customer orientation, and training and development of skills. Invest-
ient in human resources and in labour quality is essential here. All these elements
'ay a key role in the innovation process, as people are one of the major success
ictors. These findings are substantiated in many studies, amongst others by Hera-
eous (1998), Huiban and Bouhsina (1998), Hatch and Mowery (1998), Coopey
al. (1998), Atuahene-Gima (1996), Craig and Hart (1992), Dwyer and Mellor
991) and Cooper (1990).

2.3 Marketing Activities

he proficiency of marketing activities comes at the third place. Many authors, for
stance, Song and Parry (1997), Calantone et al. (1996), Montoya-Weiss and
alantone (1994), Song and Parry (1994), Edgett et al. (1992), Maidique and Zir-
:r (1984) and Rothwell et al. (1974) have stressed the importance of the right
arket entrance, inter alia with the help of communication and efficient market
telligence. Based on this literature survey, marketing activities can be operation-
ised and distinguished into testing of prototypes, provision of additional serves, strength of distribution channels, advertising and promotion, and the pres-
ce of a sales department. This requires of course detailed information on the
m's marketing strategy.

3.2.4 Project Definition

Innovative behaviour is not generic in nature, but addresses specific opportunitie Thus, before the implementation of an innovation, a sharp project definition needed. Consequently, an important critical success factor for the innovation pro ess concerns the specification of the target group, the positioning of the produc the development of the product functions and the technical product specification for details we refer to Song and Parry (1994), Craig and Hart (1992), Coope (1990), Cooper and Kleinschmidt (1987), Maidique and Zirger (1984) and Rotl well et al. (1974). A project definition can also be described in terms of a protoco consisting of a clear definition of the target market prior to the product develop ment stage. Clearly, this factor cannot be seen in isolation from the above de scribed success factors comprising product advantages, human resources mar agement and marketing activities.

3.2.5 Market

Effective demand is a sine qua non for a successful innovation. This holds in par ticular for the SME sector which has only limited possibilities to influence c control the market or to cope with unexpected failures. And therefore, the pres ence of a sufficient market (in terms of size and growth potential) is a succes factor in the innovation process of SME firms. According to Calantone et a (1996), Song and Parry (1994), Yap and Souder (1994), and Zirger and Maidiqu (1990), the market as such contributes significantly to the success of new prod ucts. It goes without saying that this factor is not independent of the above men tioned success factor of marketing activities.

3.2.6 Product-Company Fit

The product identity of a firm is essential for its position in a competitive market Consequently, the importance of a proper product-company fit (i.e., complemen tarity) has often been emphasised in the literature, amongst others by Song an Parry (1994), Yap and Souder (1994), Zirger and Maidique (1990), and Maidiqu and Zirger (1984). In operational terms, the product-company fit refers in particu lar to the integration with the current product assortment (portfolio), with th group of current clients and with the current technological knowledge of the firm.

3.2.7 Pre-Development

The introduction of a new product or service on the market incorporates a high risk for the firm concerned. Since 'forewarned is forearmed', an important key success condition is the execution of feasibility studies in the form of pre development research, in particular in terms of assessment of client wishes and

:mands, analysis of the competition, and technical and financial feasibility in an
rly stage. This early orientation is mentioned in several studies, e.g., by Cooper
d Kleinschmidt (1987), Dwyer and Mellor (1991) and Cooper (1990). Such a
o-active strategy may also be necessary to acquire venture capital.

2.8 Technological Activities

ew technologies are not 'manna from heaven', but require dedicated actions and
a entrepreneurial profile seeking new technological opportunities. In the litera-
re we find several authors who emphasise the importance of a technological ori-
tation, for instance Calantone, Schmidt and Song (1996) and Montoya-Weiss
d Calantone (1994). These authors indicate that greater proficiency in techno-
gical activities increases the likelihood of success for new products. Such tech-
ological activities can be translated into assembling technological knowledge,
exible development, internal testing of a prototype, and organisation of the pro-
ction process.

2.9 Competition

ntrepreneurship in the SME sector is normally characterised by many potential
mpetitors. The development of a competitive course requires insight into the
otives and actions of other competitors, so as to position a new product properly,
terms of degree of market appeal, novelty of the new product and the possibility
r patents. Calantone, Schmidt and Song (1996), for instance, mention the strate-
c importance of collecting and assessing information on the competition in the
arket. Competitive product advantage is also mentioned as a key determinant for
:w product success (see Song and Parry 1997).

2.10 Entrepreneur

he entrepreneur is characterised by a series of creative qualifications (see, e.g.,
ijkamp 2002). It is striking that the entrepreneur as such is hardly mentioned as a
iccess factor in the innovation process. Heunks (1998) shows that a certain com-
nation of order, flexibility and creativity fosters innovation; these are typical en-
epreneurial aspects. It is noteworthy that Quinn (1985) mentions that large firms
ay innovative by behaving like small entrepreneurial ventures. The entrepreneu-
al style may be interpreted in terms of commitment and determination, persis-
nce in problem solving, creativity and team spirit, and motivational capacities.

3.2.11 Project Approach

The introduction of a new product requires a broad range of activities; careful planning prior to the production is a prerequisite for success. Zirger and Maidiqu (1990) have revealed that new product development tends to be more successful the process is professionally planned and well implemented (i.e., project definition). In operational terms, this factor depends on the project leader's strength thorough planning and organisation, careful monitoring of progress, and multidisciplinary composition of the project team.

3.2.12 Innovation Culture

It is well known that innovative behaviour needs proper seedbeds through which creativity can flourish. This is well documented in the incubation theory (see Davelaar 1992, for a review). Pickard (1996) has shown the importance of an innovative culture and open environment in which people feel empowered to take risks. In this situation freedom, support for ideas, time for experimentation, flexibility, trust, and dynamism are very important. In reality, such factors can be assessed in terms of opportunity to air innovative opinions, space to elaborate innovative ideas and support for these innovative ideas as operationalisations.

3.2.13 Financial Means

Each new product or production process requires investment in human resource and in physical equipment. Sometimes this can be very costly for a small firm And therefore, a balance between costs and revenues in the short term is necessary. In this context, Maidique and Zirger (1984) mention the contribution margin of the new product as being important for a new product's success. In operational terms, we may interpret this success condition by means of the internal and external availability of financial means.

3.2.14 Collaboration

Innovative firms tend to operate in industrial networks (including knowledge networks). Exchange of information but also outsourcing may be a strategic move. In general, inter-firm collaboration may be seen as a critical success factor in the innovation process. Many recent studies have highlighted the importance of collaboration for business success of SMEs from various perspectives. We refer here inter alia to Stern et al. (1996) and Galbraith (1980).

After this broad exposition on the various performance conditions for creative SME entrepreneurship, it is necessary to substantiate the above designed multi dimensional framework for innovative behaviour by means of real-world facts And therefore the remainder of this paper is devoted to a statistical application.

3 Data Collection

ised on the above literature review, we were able to identify systematically 14
itical success factors for the (SME) innovation process. This taxonomy of 14
iccess conditions has to be operationalised for further empirical research; they
iay essentially be conceived of as latent variables which have to be measured by
iservable indicators. In our fieldwork we were able to translate these 14 factors
to 50 variables (see Table 3.1). Clearly, such a classification is never unambigu-
is, since most items are not mutually exclusive. In fact, many factors in this
ilti-dimensional table are interrelated. The information on these 50 operational
dications was obtained from survey questionnaires sent to SME respondents. To
it the meaning of the 50 items, the respondents were also asked whether they
reed that this operationalisation was crucial in the innovation process as per-
ived by the respondent. All the fieldwork was done in postal form.

Apart from the direct questions on the 50 items, some other background ques-
ins were formulated concerning, e.g., the involvement in either the manufactur-
g sector or the service sector, the person filling out the questionnaire (entrepre-
ur or manager), the number of innovations in a given year, and the size of the
m.

The field survey was held among Dutch firms in the SME sector. In total, 960
ms were asked to fill out a postal questionnaire. 638 of them were randomly
lected from the Dutch MarktSelect CD-Rom (which comprises over 800,000 or-
misations). The sole selection criterion applied by us was being a SME (i.e., ac-
irding to the official Dutch standard: fewer than 100 employees). The selection
insisted of 388 service firms and 250 manufacturing firms. To increase this sam-
e, in a later stage, 322 more firms were selected from other databases (maga-
nes and personal networks). These latter firms were already known for their in-
ilvement in innovations, although no information was available on their size or
e sector they belonged to. Clearly, the selection procedure as a whole exhibits
ime potential bias as a consequence of random and selective sampling, but as a
hole the dispersion of returned questionnaires was rather balanced, so that some
infidence in the representativeness is warranted.

The response rate for the postal questionnaire was more or less normal for
utch standards. 167 firms (17.4%) returned the completed questionnaire on time.
.3% of the respondents belonged to the manufacturing sector, 27.5% to the
rvice sector, and 25.2% to other sectors. 68.3% of the questionnaires were filled
it by the entrepreneurs themselves; the rest were filled out by others (usually
anagers). It is noteworthy that 26.8% of the SMEs considered had ten or more
iccessful innovations; they may be seen as the real successful innovators in our
mple. It is also interesting that 43.8% of the responding firms did not employ
ore than seven employees (6.9% of the firms appeared to employ in the mean-
ne more than 100 people). The number of seven employees was chosen here be-
iuse this is, according to the standard management literature, the virtual maxi-
um number that an individual superior can usually manage (in terms of span of
introl).

54 Masurel, van Montfort and Nijkamp

Table 3.1. Critical Success Factors in the Innovation Process: Operationalisation

1	Unique Product Advantages	Product Quality
		Product Functions
		Quality/Price Relation
		Design
2	Human Resource Management	Technological Knowledge
		Marketing
		Knowledge
		Customer Orientation
		Training and Development
3	Marketing Activities	Testing Prototype
		Provision of Additional Services
		Strength of Distribution Channels
		Advertising and Promotion
		Sales Department
4	Project Definition	Specification of Target Group
		Positioning Product
		Product Functions
		Technical Product Specifications
5	Market	Size
		Growth Potential
6	Product-Company Fit	Relation with Current Assortment
		Relation with Current Clients
		Relation with Current Technological Knowledge
7	Pre-Development	Determination Client Wishes and Demands
		Competition Analysis
		Technical Feasibility
		Financial Feasibility
8	Technological Activities	Assembling Technological Knowledge
		Development Prototype
		Internal Testing Prototype
		Organization Production Process
9	Competition	Degree
		Novelty of the New Product
		Possibility for Patents
10	Entrepreneur	Commitment and Determination
		Persistence in Problem Solving
		Creativity
		Team Spirit and Motivational Capacities
11	Project Approach	Strength of Project Leader
		Planning and Organisation
		Progress Checking
		Multidisciplinary Composition of Project Team
12	Innovation Culture	Opportunity to Air Innovative Opinions
		Space to Elaborate Innovative Ideas
		Support for Innovative Ideas
13	Financial Means	Internal Disposability
		External Disposability
14	Collaboration	With Other Companies
		With Knowledge Centres
		Involvement of Consultants

Regarding the statistical information collected, it should be mentioned that the opinions of the respondents on the 50 critical success factors were all measured or a five-point Lickert scale. This seems to be meaningful, as the reliability of answers to the question on backgrounds of the success of a new product or service appears to depend strongly on simple operational exercises. The choice of options for the answers was: fully disagree, disagree, no opinion, agree, and fully agree. In next sections we will describe and interpret the results of our empirical analy-

4 Data Analysis

mentioned above, all 14 critical success factors described in Sect. 3.2 were op-
ationalised by means of 50 observable indicators. In order to compare the rela-
e importance of the different critical success factors, we decided to summarise
each critical success factor the corresponding measurable attributes into a few
gregate indicators (preferably one), by using multivariate statistical methods.
erefore, for each success factor a separate factor analysis model was deployed
order to obtain a summary measure for the observable attributes (see Lewis-
ck, 1994). Such a model assumes that the measured operational attributes can
represented by just one unobserved common variable known as a factor (or a
nited number of factors). As is well known, such a data transformation may
ntain a margin of error. Thus, the factor model is basically a measurement
odel for the unobserved common factors (i.e., the newly defined critical success
ctors).

In our numerical exercise, standard SPSS software was used to obtain Maxi-
um Likelihood estimates of the unknown coefficients in the factor analysis
odel. The percentage variances (R^2 values) of the operational features, explained
the unobserved common factors, provided a good indication of the quality of
e factor analysis model used here. Apparently, the model gives a good fit, as all
values fall between 60% and 100%, as is witnessed in Table 3.2. This means
at each unobserved common factor (i.e., critical success factor) is a reasonable
presentation of the corresponding group of operational attributes.

ble 3.2. Results of the Factor Analysis Models

Critical success factor	R^2 value of the Factor Analysis Model of the critical success factors
Unique Product Advantages	0.681
Human Resource Management	0.732
Marketing Activities	0.628
Project Definition	0.816
Market	0.948
Product-Company Fit	0.906
Pre-Development	0.806
Technological Activities	0.948
Competition	0.965
Entrepreneur	0.755
Project Approach	0.771
Innovation Culture	0.887
Financial Means	0.910
Collaboration	0.940

In the second step of our analysis, the estimates for the unknown coefficients of the 14 factor analysis model and the factor scores of all operational features enabled us to estimate the individual firm's scores for each of the unobserved common factors of the 14 separate factor analysis model (see Lewis-Beck 1994). These estimates of the unobserved common factors appear to be all satisfactory indicators of the values of the underlying latent critical success factors.

Next, we used the values of the different critical success factors for each firm, in order to compute the means of the various critical success factors and to compare these means. Of course, it is also possible to compute the correlations between the different critical success factors. From Table 3.3 it follows that all pairs of critical success factors are positively correlated (between 0.07 and 0.56). This means that if a firm has a high (low) value for one specific critical factor, the firm also tends to have high (low) values for the other critical factors.

Table 3.3. Correlations Between Critical Success Factors

	V1	V2	V3	V4	V5	V6	V7	V8	V9	V10	V11	V12	V13	V14
V1	1													
V2	0.12	1												
V3	0.55	0.33	1											
V4	0.48	0.20	0.43	1										
V5	0.17	0.37	0.33	0.07	1									
V6	0.40	0.18	0.48	0.38	0.13	1								
V7	0.46	0.27	0.56	0.48	0.17	0.40	1							
V8	0.39	0.28	0.17	0.29	0.39	0.18	0.22	1						
V9	0.12	0.30	0.22	0.42	0.25	0.20	0.18	0.30	1					
V10	0.38	0.16	0.49	0.39	0.19	0.42	0.33	0.17	0.21	1				
V11	0.21	0.27	0.36	0.50	0.38	0.17	0.21	0.28	0.26	0.30	1			
V12	0.49	0.18	0.47	0.36	0.17	0.46	0.36	0.13	0.20	0.44	0.18	1		
V13	0.18	0.13	0.13	0.26	0.30	0.28	0.19	0.22	0.15	0.18	0.30	0.19	1	
V14	0.29	0.16	0.27	0.18	0.16	0.41	0.47	0.14	0.29	0.31	0.14	0.40	0.21	1

Note: V1=Unique Product Advantages; V2=Human Resource Management; V3=Marketing Activities; V4=Project Definition; V5=Market; V6=Product-Company Fit; V7=Pre Development; V8=Technological Activities; V9=Competition; V10=Entrepreneur V11=Project approach; V12=Innovation Culture; V13=Financial Means V14=Collaboration

Now the main interest of this paper is to compare the means of the different success factors. Table 3.4 depicts these mean values. The critical factors were ranked in decreasing order of importance, from the highest mean to the lowest mean. To show intersectoral differences, Table 3.5 presents the separate mean scores for the manufacturing sector and the service sector, respectively. Table 3.6 contains analogous mean scores for personal qualifications, viz. entrepreneurs and managers. Furthermore, Table 3.7 presents the mean scores for the real innovative firms (ten or more innovations) and the less innovative firms. Finally, Table 3.8 quotes the mean scores for different firm sizes.

Table 3.4. Determinants of Innovation Success

Critical Success Factor	mean score	t-value for difference between current and next mean in row	probability level for difference between current and next mean in row
Entrepreneur	4.34	4.59	0.000*
Unique Product Advantages	4.11	0.36	0.722
Innovation Culture	4.09	0.89	0.375
Project Approach	4.05	1.48	0.140
Technological Activities	3.99	0.12	0.907
Human Resource Management	3.99	0.80	0.424
Marketing Activities	3.95	0.25	0.800
Project Definition	3.94	0.05	0.962
Pre-Development	3.93	1.68	0.096**
Market	3.82	1.43	0.153
Financial Means	3.71	3.53	0.001*
Competition	3.46	0.87	0.386
Product-Company Fit	3.38	1.30	0.197
Collaboration	3.30	–	–

Note: * significant at a 0.05 level; ** significant at a 0.10 level

Table 3.5. Determinants of Innovation Success: Manufacturing Sector vs. Service Sector

Critical Success Factor	mean score manufacturing sector	mean score service sector	t-value for difference between sectors	probability level for difference between sectors
Entrepreneur	4.33	4.35	−0.20	0.839
Unique Product Advantages	4.19	4.00	2.26	0.025*
Innovation Culture	4.13	4.01	1.05	0.296
Project Approach	4.05	4.05	0.03	0.980
Technological Activities	4.04	3.88	1.39	0.167
Human Resource Management	3.99	3.98	0.11	0.917
Marketing Activities	4.05	3.53	2.21	0.029*
Project Definition	3.99	3.84	1.51	0.134
Pre-Development	4.02	3.72	3.16	0.002*
Market	3.84	3.77	0.53	0.594
Financial Means	3.74	3.60	1.10	0.274
Competition	3.54	3.25	2.15	0.033*
Product-Company Fit	3.41	3.38	0.26	0.794
Collaboration	3.38	3.08	2.22	0.028*

Note: * significant at a 0.05 level

58 Masurel, van Montfort and Nijkamp

Table 3.6. Determinants of Innovation Success: Entrepreneurs vs. Managers

Critical Success Factor	mean score entrepreneurs	mean score managers	t-value for difference between respondents	probability level for difference between respondents
Entrepreneur	4.35	4.30	0.56	0.577
Unique Product Advantages	4.12	4.13	−0.99	0.922
Innovation Culture	4.11	4.13	−0.24	0.812
Project Approach	4.01	4.01	−0.28	0.777
Technological Activities	4.05	3.94	0.93	0.355
Human Resource Management	4.00	4.00	−0.05	0.963
Marketing Activities	3.93	4.07	−1.73	0.086*
Project Definition	3.97	3.95	0.20	0.841
Pre-Development	3.91	4.02	−1.18	0.241
Market	3.84	3.75	0.68	0.499
Financial Means	3.73	3.62	0.90	0.369
Competition	3.43	3.57	−1.05	0.294
Product-Company Fit	3.46	3.27	1.50	0.137
Collaboration	3.29	3.33	−0.321	0.749

Note: * significant at a 0.05 level

Table 3.7. Determinants of Innovation Success: Real Innovative vs. Less Innovative Firms

Critical Success Factor	mean score real innovative companies	mean score less innovative companies	t-value for difference between real and less companies	probability level for difference
Entrepreneur	4.34	4.34	0.10	0.493
Unique Product Advantages	4.14	4.08	1.20	0.186
Innovation Culture	4.08	4.10	−0.44	0.563
Project Approach	4.06	4.04	1.00	0.210
Technological Activities	3.99	4.00	−0.25	0.537
Human Resource Management	3.99	3.99	0.07	0.497
Marketing Activities	4.10	3.91	2.30	0.039*
Project Definition	3.94	3.95	−0.87	0.593
Pre-Development	4.08	3.88	2.80	0.027*
Market	3.84	3.80	0.93	0.364
Financial Means	3.71	3.72	−0.55	0.584
Competition	3.46	3.46	0.27	0.463
Product-Company Fit	3.37	3.39	−0.97	0.693
Collaboration	3.30	3.30	−0.12	0.505

Note: * significant at a 0.05 level

Table 3.8. Determinants of Innovation Success: Large vs. Small Firms

Critical Success Factor	mean score large companies	mean score small companies	t-value for difference between large and small companies	probability level for difference
Entrepreneur	4.31	4.38	−0.83	0.407
Unique Product Advantages	4.07	4.10	−0.37	0.711
Innovation Culture	3.99	4.24	−2.58	0.011*
Project Approach	4.04	4.00	0.48	0.631
Technological Activities	3.99	4.02	−0.25	0.803
Human Resource Management	4.02	3.91	1.32	0.189
Marketing Activities	3.85	4.14	−3.31	0.001*
Project Definition	3.99	3.89	1.11	0.269
Pre-Development	3.91	3.91	0.02	0.983
Market	3.81	3.75	0.43	0.665
Financial Means	3.75	3.68	0.55	0.582
Competition	3.48	3.41	0.52	0.602
Product-Company Fit	3.52	3.24	2.03	0.021*
Collaboration	3.23	3.37	−1.12	0.266

Note: * significant at a 0.05 level

5 Interpretation and Results

In this section we will first take a look at the results for the complete set of data (Table 3.4). Using a t-test for paired samples (see Moore and McCabe 1993), we investigated whether the mean scores for any two critical success factors differed significantly. The last column of the table shows which different critical success factors do statistically indeed have different mean scores at a 10 or even 5 percent significance level.

It is noteworthy that our findings differ considerably from the general views expressed in the literature, where for example, entrepreneurship is not so frequently mentioned as a key driver. But from the perspective of the respondents, the entrepreneur is the most essential factor in the innovation process in the SME sector. Next, a closely interwoven cluster of mainly internal factors follows the entrepreneurial factor (viz. unique product advantages, innovation culture, project approach, technological activities, human resource management, marketing activities, project definition and pre-development). The next clusters of explanatory factors comprise mainly external aspects such as market, financial means, competition, product/company match and collaboration. It should be noted however that financial means entail both internal and external aspects. Thus a main finding is that a Schumpeterian type of entrepreneurship – in the sense of a change manager – is an essential success condition for innovative behaviour in the SME sector.

In the next step of our empirical analysis we compared the results for the manufacturing sector and service sector (Table 3.5). Running the t-test for independent samples reveals that unique product advantages, marketing activities, predevelopment strategy, competition and collaboration offer statistically higher scores in the manufacturing sector than in the service sector, while nowhere in the service sector was a critical success factor score higher than those in the manufacturing sector found. The question of intangibility of services might be crucial in this respect. A new service must be considered more carefully and communicated more thoroughly to the potential client than a new product. In the latter case a more objective factor like unique product advantages or visibility might play a more prominent role. The internal factors related to pre-development strategy and marketing activities, and the external factors related to competition and collaboration, underline once more the importance of these advantages.

An interesting finding is also that perceptions and views of entrepreneurs and managers hardly differ, as can be seen from Table 3.6. This phenomenon may be explained by the fact that the management in SMEs is in general very close to the entrepreneur. In both subgroups (i.e., entrepreneurs and managers) the entrepreneur is mentioned as the most critical success factor. The only significant difference is that the managers depend less on marketing activities than entrepreneurs do. As mentioned, several SMEs are very innovative. Table 3.7 presents the results for the real innovators and the less innovative firms. It appears that marketing activities and pre-development strategies are more important for the real innovative firms than for the other firms. These factors appear to offer ultimately the real explanations for successful innovation in the SME field. This seems to be plausible, as both a market coverage and professional preparation are of eminent importance for firm behaviour in the SME sector.

Finally, the data set was subdivided into small and large firms (Table 3.8), in order to test for firm size effects. Innovation culture and marketing activities appear to be more crucial for small firms than for large ones. The lesser importance of marketing for the entrepreneurs might be attributable to self-confidence or firm blindness (myopic behaviour). Economies of scale and bureaucracy might be explanatory factors for the differences between large and small firms. Positioning the innovation culture opposite the product-company fit as a driving force to success brings us back to the earlier mentioned difference between SMEs and large firms: SMEs tend to be strong in applications, whereas large firms tend to profit more from scale economies. Marketing activities might be a specific obstacle for the successful commercialisation of research projects in SMEs.

3.6 Conclusions

The entrepreneur is the crucial success factor in the SME innovation process, according to the opinion of the respondents in our Dutch survey questionnaire. This is an interesting result, as in many cases either institutional impediment or geo

phical/infrastructural factors are mentioned as critical success conditions for
cessful business. Apparently, the human factor prevails.

Although hardly mentioned in the literature, the entrepreneur is also mentioned
a number one factor by the various subgroups: manufacturing and service firms,
repreneurs and managers, real and less innovative firms, small and large firms.
ter entrepreneurship, a cluster of controllable internal success factors appear to
low: unique product advantages, innovation culture, project approach, techno-
ical activities, human resource management, marketing activities, project defi-
ion and pre-development. External aspects (by definition non-controllable) such
market, financial means, competition, product/company match and collabora-
n appear to show up only in subsequent low-order clusters. So the SMEs in-
lved in our research appear to place entrepreneurship and internal factors –
trollable by themselves – on top. This attitude obviously entails a considerable
k of over-estimation of their own role and competence.

Although all subgroups discussed here regard the entrepreneur as the number
factor in the innovation process, some differences appear to occur in the per-
ved importance of other success factors. Unique product advantages, marketing
ivities, pre-development, competition and collaboration are more important for
manufacturing sector than for the service sector. Tangibility of products (as
posed to intangibility of services) might be the explanation for these differ-
es. The expressed opinions of entrepreneurs and managers do hardly differ,
bably due to the fact that the management in SMEs is in general very close to
entrepreneurial tasks. Marketing activities and pre-development strategies are
re important for the real innovative firms than for the less innovative firms.
d finally, innovation culture and marketing activities are more crucial for small
ns than for large ones.

This study has aimed to shed new light on the innovation process of SMEs, es-
ially on the way the SMEs themselves perceive the innovation process. It is
king that non-controllable factors only end up in the rear of explanatory fac-
s. These findings deserve to be investigated more thoroughly by means of other
dies. If a verification based on a larger study and in other countries would lead
similar results, such new aspects would have to be incorporated in public and
vate policy towards SME innovation.

ferences

ahene-Gima K (1996) Differential potency of factors affecting innovation performance
in manufacturing and services firms in Australia. Journal of Product Innovation Management 13: 35–52

tuglia C, Lombardo S, Nijkamp P (eds) (1997) Innovative behavior in space and time.
Springer-Verlag, Berlin

antone RJ, Schmidt JB, Song XM (1996) Controllable factors of new product success:
A cross-national comparison. Marketing Science 15: 341–358

per RG, Kleinschmidt EJ (1987) New products: What separates winners from losers.
Journal of Product Innovation Management 4: 169–184

Cooper RG (1990) New products: What distinguishes the winners? Research and Technology Management 33: 27–31

Coopey J, Keegan O, Emler N (1998) Managers' innovations and the structuration of organization. Journal of Management Studies 35: 263–284

Craig A, Hart S (1992) Where to now in new product development research. European Journal of Marketing 26: 1–47

Davelaar EJ (1992) Regional economic analysis of innovation and incubation. Ashgate, Aldershot

Dwyer L, Mellor R (1991) Organizational environment, new product process activities, and project outcomes. Journal of Product Innovation Management 8: 39–48

Edgett S, Shipley D, Forbes G (1992) Japanese and British companies compared: Contributing factors to success and failure in NPD. Journal of Product Innovation Management 9: 3–10

Galbraith JK (1980) American capitalism. M.E. Sharpe, White Plains

Hatch NW, Mowery DC (1998) Process innovation and learning by doing in semiconductor manufacturing. Management Science 44: 1461–1477

Heracleous L (1998) Better than the rest: Making Europe the leader in the next wave of innovation and performance. Long Range Planning 31: 154–158

Heunks FJ (1998) Innovation, creativity and success. Small Business Economics 10: 263–272

Huiban JP, Bouhsina Z (1998) Innovation and the quality of labour factor: An empirical investigation in the French food industry. Small Business Economics 10: 389–400

Kleinknecht A (1986) Crisis and prosperity in Schumpeterian innovation patterns. MacMillan, London

Lewis-Beck MS (ed) (1994) Factor analysis and related techniques. SAGE Publications, London

Maidique MA, Zirger BJ (1984) A study of success and failure in product innovation: The case of the U.S. electronics industry. IEEE Transaction Engineering Management 3: 192–203

Malecki EJ (1997) Entrepreneurs, networks, and economic development. Advances in Entrepreneurship, Firm Emerge and Growth 3: 57–118

Marsili O (2000) The anatomy and evaluation of industries. Edward Elgar, Cheltenham

Montoya MM, Calantone R (1994) Determinants of new product performance. Journal of Product Innovation Management 11: 397–417

Moore DS, McCabe GP (1993) Introduction to the practice of statistics (second edition). Freeman and Company, New York

Nijkamp P (2002) Entrepreneurship in a modern network economy. Regional Studies (forthcoming)

Nooteboom B (1994) Innovation and diffusion in small firms: Theory and evidence. Small Business Economics 6: 327–347

Peneder M (2001) Entrepreneurial competition and industrial organization. Edward Elgar, Cheltenham

Pickard J (1996) A Fertile Grounding. People Management 24: 28–35

Rothwell R, Freeman C, Horlsey A, Jervis VTP, Robertson AB, Townsend J (1974) SAPHO updated – project SAPHO phase II. Research Policy 3: 259–291

Quinn JB (1985) Managing innovation: Controlled chaos. Harvard Business Review May-June: 73–84 umpeter JA (1912) Theorie der wirtschaftlichen Entwicklung. Duncker und Humbolt, Leipzig

umpeter J (1934) The theory of economic development. Harvard University Press, Cambridge, MA

g XM, Parry ME (1994) The dimensions of industrial new product success and failure in state enterprises in the People's Republic of China. Journal of Product Innovation Management 11: 105–118

g XM, Parry ME (1997) The determinants of Japanese new product successes. Journal of Marketing Research 34: 64–76

n LW, El-Ansary AI, Coughlan AT (1996) Marketing channels. Prentice Hall International, Englewood Cliffs

rik AR (1996) Introduction: Innovation and small business. Small Business Economics 8: 175–176

CM, Souder WE (1994) Factors influencing new product success and failure in small entrepreneurial high-technology electronic firm. Journal of Product Innovation Management 11: 418–432

ger BJ, Maidique MA (1990) A model of new product development: An empirical test. Management Science 36: 867–883

[13]

INVESTMENT EXPECTATIONS OF ENTREPRENEURS

An empirical analysis at the firm level

Cees Gorter
Peter Nijkamp
Eric Pels

August 1996

Department of Regional Economics
Free University
De Boelelaan 1105
1081 HV Amsterdam
The Netherlands

Email: cgorter@econ.vu.nl

Abstract

This paper analyses entrepreneurial investment expectations at the firm level to determine whether or not the expectations for the current period are systematically biased. The empirical findings reveal that the expectations on investments are clearly biased and therefore we conclude that entrepreneurs do not show that they behave rationally. Outliers, identified via two different approaches, appear to play an important role in our estimation results but do not influence the overall conclusion that the investment predictions of entrepreneurs are biased.

Acknowledgments

The authors wish to thank Jos van Ommeren and two anonymous referees for helpful comments.

8

1. Introduction.

Understanding the way entrepreneurs form their expectations will offer better insight into the dynamics of a firm and, at a more aggregate level, into the economic development in a sector, region or economy (see also Van den Ende and Nijkamp, 1995). In this paper we will analyze entrepreneurial investment expectations at a micro-level. The aim is to determine whether or not the performance prediction for the current period (i.e. the prediction for a given period t formed before the end of the period) has a systematic bias. We will do so by using a statistical test developed by Brown and Matial (1981). We find in our analysis that the results are severely affected by outliers. Therefore, in the sequel of the paper we will pay special attention to the effect of outliers and we will also compare two different techniques to identify such outliers.

2. The Test.

When comparing predicted with realized values of a given variable we say an expectation is rational in Muth's sense if "they are equal to the true mathematical expectation conditioned on all relevant information known at the time forecasts were made" (Evans and Gulamani, 1984, p. 3). This means that "rational" expectations have to satisfy certain conditions. The version of the rational expectations hypothesis becomes weaker as more conditions are violated.

The first of these conditions is orthogonality (Anderson and Goldsmith, 1994, p. 383). This means that all available (relevant) information has been used in an optimal manner. Since it is impossible to know *all* available information, there is no test available to test for orthogonality or "full rationality" (see, Brown and Matial, 1981, p.493). The assumption of full rationality can be weakened to partional rationality. This means that the information used, though not complete, is efficiently used; this is the second, efficiency condition. Partial rationality implies under certain conditions full rationality (Brown and Matial, 1981, p. 494). It is however very difficult, not to say impossible, to determine which information has actually been used by entrepreneurs. Again we can weaken the assumption. The third condition is that of noncorrelation of forecast errors (Anderson and Goldsmith, 1994, p. 383). This means that the previous error is information that should be used when the next forecast is made. If we would regress the forecast error on its past values, the coefficients should not differ significantly from zero. The final condition is that of unbiasedness; the weakest form of the rational expectations hypothesis (Anderson and Goldsmith, 1994, p. 383). Following Theil (1966) we can test for unbiasedness of the prediction (i.e., absence of systematic errors) by estimating the following equation

(1) $Y_t = a + \beta \cdot Y^p_{t-k} + u_t$, $(k = 1, 2, ..., n)$

where Y_t is the realization of a variable at period t, Y^p_{t-k} is the prediction for period t formed at time period t-k and u_t is a disturbance term. If we reject the joint hypothesis $a = 0$, $\beta = 1$, the prediction is said to be biased, and as a result the hypothesis of partial (and full) rationality has to be rejected. This means that systematical errors are made in the predictions[1].

Brown and Matial (1994, p. 495) discuss a problem that is inherent in equation (1); the u_t's are likely to be serially correlated because we cannot rule out the possibility that the unknown future forecast errors are correlated. They show that a disturbance which is serially correlated of an Moving Average-type is quite consistent with both partial and full rationality (they also show that the disturbance term u_t is serially correlated of an MA-type).

In this paper we will try to determine whether or not the investment predictions for the current period (made in the current period) are biased. We will base our estimation on equation (1), but now Y^p_{t-k} is the prediction for period t formed before the end of period t (and hence $k = 0$). Therefore, we obtain (adding subscript i to identify firms)

(2) $Y_{i,t} = a + \beta \cdot Y^p_{i,t} + u_{i,t}$

The last "prediction" which we can investigate is the "prediction" made in the preceding period (we need to know the "true" investments). We do not have serially correlated u_t's because we are not confronted with unknown (future) forecast errors in equation (2). So if we find that the u_t's are serially correlated the entrepreneurs did not fully use the information contained in the past forecast errors (see Anderson and Goldsmith, 1994, p. 383). We will test for autocorrelation by means of a Chi-square test.

Blomqvist (1989) tested for a "learning effect". The issue of

---

[1] That is, the prediction is not equal to the mathematical expectation of the realization, conditional on the prediction.

learning is particularly relevant in the case evidence against the rationality hypothesis is found because the test for learning will reveal whether this departure from rationality is temporary or permanent. When the hypothesis of unbiasedness is rejected, we will test whether the bias decreases over time. In case entrepreneurs make systematic errors (a bias), it is interesting to see whether the errors decrease over time. We say the entrepreneurs are "learning" when predictions are biased but the bias decreases over time; that is, improving the forecasts gradually to an outcome consistent with rational expectations.

Given our database (see section 3) we are able to estimate equation (2) for each year from 1986 until 1994. In addition, we can estimate equation (2) using longitudinal data (using the same group of firms over eight years). We notice that the prediction variable in our model is not a "genuine" prediction; it is partly a realization and partly a prediction[2]. Since we have to compare the predictions with the realized investments, we have to construct panel datasets of firms followed over at least two years.

3. Data.

The data used in our analysis originate from a survey held each year (during the months September-November) among Dutch firms by the Chambers of Commerce. The questionnaire contains questions about the past years' realizations and expectations for the current year and the next year. The expectations for next year are qualitative variables. The questions concern employment, output, investment and profit.

All firms with more than 50 employees are interviewed each year. Furthermore, about 70% of the firms with less than 50 employees are interviewed. Detailed micro data on three regions are available: Amsterdam and Utrecht (two central regions) and Den Bosch (in the intermediate zone), for the years 1986-1994.

To be able to confront the expectations for the current year with the realizations (which are not known until some time in next year), we

---

[2] As a result, we could also argue that it is (partly) investigated whether the reported values have a systematic bias. In this interpretation, the finding of a bias would point at systematic misjudgements of enterpreneurs when reporting investment levels. For example, in large firms this failure may be due to the malfunctioning of information flows through the firm. Alternatively, firms may deliberately under- or overestimate investments for strategic reasons.

need to match two successive surveys. It turns out that a firm has a chance of about 50% to be present in two successive surveys (there is a response rate of about 70%; new firms emerge and other firms quit). A group of 470 firms are present in all surveys from 1986 until 1994. Since these 470 firms need not be representative for the sample in every year, we need to estimate also equation (2) for each year separately.

Table 1 shows the average value (in thousands Dutch guilders) and the standard deviation for the prediction error of the firm investments (expectation minus realization). It turns out that (apart from 1993) the realization is always higher than the expectation, indicating an underestimation of the current investments (see also Gorter, Nijkamp and Rienstra, 1995). On the other hand, the standard deviation is of such a scale that we cannot speak of significant differences between the averages. There are however some outliers, extremely high expectations (realizations) with low realizations (expectations). We will return to this issue later on. In 1993 the mean prediction error is positive; the entrepreneurs were apparently rather optimistic as a group. Maybe as a result of this phenomenon, the prediction error is negative again in 1994 and the difference between realization and expectation has never been as large as in 1994 (in absolute value). The 470 companies which can be observed over all eight years have an average expectation (the mean over all companies and years) which is higher than the realization. Notice also that this number is considerably higher than the mean in each year due to the overrepresentation of large firms in the longitudinal dataset.

4. Estimation Results.

In our statistical analysis, we first estimated equation (2) for *all* companies (see Table A1, Appendix 1). We tested for heteroscedasticity (and in the case of the longitudinal data also for autocorrelation). It turns out that the size of the company (measured by the number of employees) causes certainly heteroscedasticity. In most cases there are no specific regional or sectoral influences. We therefore estimated equation (2) for small and large (more than 50 employees) firms separately (It is noteworthy that Van den Ende and Nijkamp (1995) and Gorter, Nijkamp and Rienstra (1995) also found the size of the firm to be influential).

In tables 2 and 3 the results of the statistical experiment are presented. Both the separate hypotheses ($a = 0$ and $ß = 1$) and the joint hypotheses ($a = 0$, $ß = 1$) are rejected in all cases. In most cases a is significantly larger than 0, while ß is significantly smaller than 1. In the longitudinal analysis heteroscedasticity appears to remain for large firms[3], and for small companies the disturbances are serially correlated. The latter finding implies that enterpreneurs in small companies - included in the longitudinal dataset - did not fully use the information in the past forecast errors. In other words, information exists which, if used, could have reduced the forecast error. Using the longitudinal datasets, we tested whether there was a "learning effect". If such an effect were to be found, we would expect it with the larger companies, since we found autocorrelation in the disturbance term with the smaller companies (indicating that not all information from past forecast errors was (fully) used). In table 4 we see that small firms clearly do not learn over time whereas for large firms a weak tendency towards learning is observed (the effect is negative, but not significant at the 5%-level).

So on the basis of the t- and F-tests presented in the above tables (and the LM(H) test in table 3) we may conclude that the expectations on investments are biased. Furthermore, with the longitudinal datasets we do not find any indication that the bias reduces over time. Hence, we do not find evidence of a "learning effect". One can wonder what causes this bias. There are several possibilities. First, the persons responsible for the answers given in the survey might simply not be able to produce accurate predictions due to malfunctioning of information flows through the firm. The systematic bias and absence of a learning effect would be the result of permanent malfunctioning[4]. Second, they may give "false" predictions as a form of strategy, but then one can wonder what would be the gain to the entrepreneurs. On the other hand, the absence of a learning effect and the systematic bias would support this idea to some extent.

---

[3] We tested for heteroscedasticity using sectoral differences as a possible cause. we observe six sectors: agriculture, industrial, construction, wholesale, retail and services. We also tested for heteroscedasticity using regional differences as a possible cause. These did not prove to be significant. the latter test is not reported in tables 2 and 3.

[4] It is questionable whether this explanation is applicable for small firms since the person filling the questionnaire might also be the owner of the firm.

Table 1, Mean and standard deviation of the prediction error of investments[a].

	1987	1988	1989	1990	1991	1992	1993	1994	87-94
prediction error	-2.60 (2016)	-32.88 (1776)	-5.30 (2397)	-28.65 (2663)	-8.35 (1733)	-5.53 (1351)	10.72 (1700)	-82.03 (8382)	87.64 (3152)
observations	2564	3341	3403	3685	4217	4792	3962	3667	3760[b]

a) Standard deviation between parentheses. The average values are influenced by economic development, sample size and the composition of the sample (with respect to sectors), so they cannot be seen as longitudinal series.
b) There are 470 companies which can be followed for eight years, so there are 3760 observations.

Table 2, Estimation results, small companies[a].

	86	87	88	89	90	91	92	93	86-93
a	117.83* (15.85)*	53.14* (6.42)*	154.71* (39.79)*	120.14* (30.14)*	19.59 (12.36)	52.92* (12.95)*	10.22 (8.62)	50.42* (9.83)*	95.64* (14.75)*
β	0.29* (0.01)*	0.84* (0.01)*	0.23* (0.05)*	0.47* (0.05)*	1.03* (0.01)*	0.72* (0.01)*	0.95* (0.01)*	0.62* (0.01)*	0.60* (0.02)*
R^2	0.19	0.70	0.01	0.03	0.82	0.42	0.83	0.73	0.21
n	2032	2784	2826	3042	3546	4130	3383	3072	2480
LM(H)	15.64**	14.74	3.70	5.39	4.87	8.54	9.36	18.68**	8.12
LM(SC)									9.86*
F	1426.24*	137.20*	102.78*	49.71*	10.29*	230.64*	20.79*	1639.98*	151.46*

a) standard error in parentheses. * significant at 5%, we test $a = 0$ and $\beta = 1$. LM(H) is a test for heteroscedasticity with sectoral differences as a possible cause. There are 5 degrees of freedom, chi-square$_5^{0.05} = 11.07$. LM(SC) is a test for (first order) autocorrelation with one degree of freedom, chi-square$_1^{0.05} = 3.84$. F is a test with the joint hypothesis $a = 0$, $\beta = 1$.

Table 3, Estimation results, large companies[a].

	86	87	88	89	90	91	92	93	86-93
a	627.62* (131.24)*	271.33 (187.98)	333.29* (105.20)*	389.98 (204.46)	397.83* (148.45)*	195.08 (117.29)	247.17 (175.20)	966.23 (866.83)	530.05* (127.23)*
β	0.74* (0.01)*	0.90* (0.03)*	0.81* (0.01)*	0.85* (0.02)*	0.81* (0.02)*	0.93* (0.01)*	0.91* (0.01)*	0.90* (0.05)*	0.80* (0.01)*
R^2	0.86	0.70	0.94	0.79	0.76	0.87	0.90	0.38	0.87
n	532	557	577	643	671	662	579	595	1280
LM(H)	6.44	5.34	10.32	10.32	8.54	6.62	3.68	6.38	19.71*
LM(SC)									0.05
F	197.12*	7.88*	248.84	36.15	62.39*	13.82*	29.59*	2.64**	289.68*

a) standard error in parentheses. * significant at 5%, we test $a = 0$ and $\beta = 1$. LM(H) is a test for heteroscedasticity with 5 degrees of freedom, chi-square$_5^{0.05} = 11.07$; LM(SC) is a test for (first order) autocorrelation with one degree of freedom, chi-square$_1^{0.05} = 3.84$. F is a test with the joint hypothesis $a = 0$, $\beta = 1$.

14

Table 4, Test for a "learning effect"[a) b)].

	small	large
constant	452.99	11189.90
	(566.80)	(5685.19)
trend	-3.62	-110.54
	(6.33)	(63.44)
n	310	160

a) dependent variable : forecast error;
   explanatory variables : constant and a linear trend term (t).
b) standard error between parentheses.

Third, the entrepreneurs may simply give a wild guess due to a lack of interest or cooperation. We do observe some cases where expected investments worth hundreds of millions are reported, while realized investments are virtually zero. In the next section we will discuss these (and less extreme) cases or outliers and their impact on the estimation results in more detail.

5. The Impact of Outliers.

Gorter, Nijkamp and Rienstra (1995) who analyzed investment data on a aggregate level found that outliers had a strong influence. The outliers can be identified by using one of the following two methods, which will be described briefly.

The first method identifies outliers on the basis of the explanatory variables in the model (the so-called hat matrix, see for more details, Krasker et al., 1983). We know, before we perform our analysis, that some of the data are flawed; for example typing errors or information that is deliberately held back will (almost certainly) affect the outcomes in our dataset. There are, for example, firms who report to invest several hundreds of millions, while in the end no investment appears to be made (or vice versa). To check for the influence of these (extreme) data points (expectations of several hundreds of millions versus zero realizations or vice versa), we identify these leverage points (or influential X-data) on the basis of the diagonal of the hat matrix $H = X(X'X)^{-1}X'$, where X is the data matrix with n observations and p explanatory variables. Data points are said to be influential if the diagonal element $h_i > 2 \cdot p/n$, where i is the number of the row of X under consideration (see Krasker et al., 1983). Note that in our application, we have only one X-variable namely Y^p.

A second method of identifying outliers is on the basis of (standardized) residuals. The advantage is that we do not, like in the previous method, identify the really large values of the explanatory variables as outliers. For example, a firm which reports to invest a hundred million might be identified as an outlier (no matter the realization), while a firm which reports fifty thousand but invests a hundred million might not be identified as an outlier (on the basis of the hat matrix). On the basis of the (standardized) residuals those firms are identified as outliers which have substantial differences between the expectation and realization. The drawback is that we estimate the model and identify those firms which have the poorest fit as outliers, even though they might contain valuable information.

We estimated equation (2) with the identified outliers excluded[5]. The outliers identified by the first method proved to have a considerable effect; only a few outliers were detected each year, but the estimates changed considerably; a moved closer towards 0 and β moved closer towards 1. But still, in most cases both the separate and joint hypothesis did apparently not hold.

When we estimated the model without the outliers identified by the second method, the results did also change somewhat, but not as much as in the previous case. The estimated a moves closer towards 0, the estimated β does not change substantially.

The two different methods of identification lead to totally different estimation results. The first method of identifying outliers labels an observation as an outlier, if $h_i > 2 \cdot p/n$. The (really) large values of Y^p_t are identified as outliers (see Table A2, Appendix 1). In some cases this can be true; there are firms that report to invest hundreds of millions but invest (almost) nothing. Perhaps these firms may deliberately give wrong information or have no insight into their investments in the current period. On the other hand, there are companies that report to invest on a large scale and do so. These are (wrongly) identified as outliers because this identification method only looks at Y^p_t and therefore cannot distinguish between "false" (with both extreme predictions and realizations) and "true" (with only extreme predictions or observations) outliers. So this method identifies firms as outliers when the

---

[5] Detailed results are available from the authors on request.

reported investments are large and largely exceed the realized investments, but occasionally also firms with large reported investments and zero forecast error.

The second method of identification first estimates equation (2) and then uses the residuals to identify the outliers. It turns out that both small and large values of Y^p_t are identified as outliers. In most cases, the difference between Y_t and Y^p_t is quite substantial (see also Table A2, Appendix 1).

In Figure 1 we show (in a simplified way) what happens with our estimation results when we use either method I (forward identification) or method II (backward identification). Line A is an estimation using a full data set for a particular year. If we use method I to identify outliers (forward identification), values of Y^p_t that exceed the dotted line I are identified. If we re-estimate with the exclusion of these outliers the estimated slope will go up and the constant will drop[6]. The second method identifies those companies as outliers that have Y_t above the upper dotted line II or beneath the lower dotted line II. As a result, only the constant changes significantly. The forecast error of the firms identified by the second method as an outlier is in most cases negative (points in the upper part of the cloud, indicating an under-estimation) and as a result the estimated line moves down.

---

[6] In Table A2, appendix 1, we see that the value of Y^p_t of the outliers identified by the first method is on average higher (as the values of Y_t and the average value of Y^p_t identified by the second method).

Figure 1, Graphic interpretation of the identification methods[a].

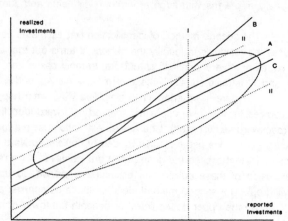

a) Line A is an estimation using the full data set. The dotted lines I and II show the selection made by the two identification methods. Line B is the estimation using identification method I, line C is the estimation using identification method II.

6. Conclusion.

In this paper we have tried to determine whether or not the entrepreneurial expectations for current investments are biased. The overall conclusion is that the expectations are clearly biased and that this bias exhibits a permanent nature. Outliers do affect the estimation results to a large extent, but the conclusion does not fundamentally change when we estimate our regression model with the outliers excluded. Two methods were used to identify the outliers. Both methods have their advantages and their drawbacks. The first method tries to identifies firms with extreme values of Y^p_t as outliers. This seems to be appealing, but in our case only the high extreme values are identified, and these predictions do not always appear to be that poor. The second method selects both small and large values of Y^p_t as outliers. The disadvantage is that we first estimate equation (2) and identify those firms as outliers which give the poorest fit. Both methods however do not affect our conclusion: predicted (or reported) investments are systematically biased and hence the results for the entrepreneurs do not show that they behave rational-

18

ly in the way described above.

The bias is not affected by a learning effect, or in other words, entrepreneurs do not improve on their predictive capabilities. This poses another question: is the bias the result of the entrepreneurs' failure to come up with "good" predictions (in the sense that the overall prediction error is not significantly different from zero) or do entrepreneurs deliberately give false predictions ? For the entrepreneurs' sake (and maybe for the national economy's sake) we hope it is not their inability to provide accurate figures; otherwise expectations and investments on both the firm and sectoral level would be based on biased expectations and false information flows. Anyway, using these investment expectations as an indication of "entrepreneurial confidence" and the well-being of, for example, a sector would be risky, to say the least. Consequently, we recommend the use of other indicators such as expectations on output or employment to signal the firm's future performance. These variables are expected to behave more smoothly and therefore are less likely to exhibit a systematic bias. Further research however should reveal whether this appears to be a fruitful approach.

References

Anderson, M.A. and A.H. Goldsmith (1994), Rationality in the mind's eye: An alternative test of rational expectations using subjective forecast and evaluation data, *Journal of Economic Psychology*, 15, 379-403

Blomqvist, H.C. (1989), The "rationality" of expectations: An experimental approach, *Journal of Economic Psychology*, 10, 275-299

Brown, B.W. and S. Maital (1981), What do economists know ? An empirical study of experts' expectations, *Econometrica*, 49, 491-504

Ende, M van der, and P. Nijkamp (1995), Industrial Dynamics and Rational Expectations in a Spatial Setting, in: Bertuglia, C.S., M.M. Fisher and G. Petro (eds.), *Technological Change, Economic Development and Space*, Springer Verlag, Berlin/Heidelberg, 238-253

Evans, G. and R. Gulamani (1984), Tests for rationality of the Carlson-Parkin inflation expectations data, *Oxford Bulletin of Economics and Statistics*, 46, 1-19.

Gorter, C., P. Nijkamp and S.A. Rienstra (1995), Space-Time Dynamics of Investments, mimeo, Department of Regional Economics, Free University Amsterdam

Krasker, W.S., E. Kuh and R.E. Welsch (1983), Estimation for Dirty Data and Flawed Models, in: *Handbook of Econometrics* (eds. Z. Griliches and M.D. Intriligator), I, 651-698.

Theil, H. (1966), *Applied economic forecasting*, Amsterdam: North-Holland.

Appendix 1.

Table A1, estimation results, all companies[a].

	86	87	88	89	90	91	92	93	86-93
a	174.65	79.57	117.78	117.71	91.40	48.65	48.25	161.02	209.70
	(24.52)*	(30.71*)	(37.60*)	(42.58*)	(25.54*)	(19.35*)	(26.04)	(138.54)	(43.71)^8
β	0.73	0.91	0.80	0.85	0.84	0.91	0.91	0.90	0.80
	(0.01)*	(0.01)*	(0.01)*	(0.01)*	(0.01)*	(0.01)*	(0.00)*	(0.02)*	(0.00)*
R^2	0.83	0.72	0.77	0.73	0.78	0.83	0.90	0.40	0.87
n	2564	3341	3403	3685	4217	4792	3962	3667	3760
LM(H)	28.84*	25.99*	4.59	22.60*	33.54*	35.58*	51.42*	16.76*	48.62*
LM(SC)									2.54
F	836.34*	46.33*	356.60*	144.86*	244.80	102.69*	181.99*	16.11*	800.39*

a) standard error between parentheses.   significant at 5%, we test $a = 0$ and $\beta = 1$. LM(H) is a test for heteroscedasticity with 5 degrees of freedom, chi-square$_5^{0.05} = 11.07$. LM(SC) is a test for (first order) autocorrelation. F is a test with the joint hypothesis $a = 0$, $\beta = 1$.

Table A2, *Average values of identified outliers, small companies[a]*.

	method	86	87	88	89	90	91	92	93
Y^p_t	I	7710	2733	3934	2984	8087	5451	8857	15936
Y_t		3951	2361	1690	1872	6620	4336	7170	9247
Y^p_t-Y_t		3759	372	2245	1112	2067	1115	1687	6689
cases		14	45	35	57	21	45	24	11
Y^p_t	II	6425	1180	464	4403	5811	7473	6447	9183
Y_t		6409	2835	34677	19075	7371	9143	6006	7133
Y^p_t-Y_t		16	-1655	-34213	-14673	-1560	-1670	441	2049
cases		13	31	4	7	27	21	24	18

a) method I: forward identification, method II: backward identification.

Average values of identified outliers, large companies[a]

	method	86	87	88	89	90	91	92	93
Y^p_t	I	70000	38649	90002	80686	36364	33611	84813	112051
Y_t		54641	32222	75749	59735	28251	33997	74053	96588
Y^p_t-Y_t		15359	6427	14253	20952	8103	-387	10760	15463
cases		6	12	6	8	17	21	12	12
Y^p_t	II	15029	36964	48873	37652	35983	32314	61789	4000
Y_t		22048	41010	46660	43962	36724	37085	56651	500000
Y^p_t-Y_t		-7018	-4047	2212	-6310	-741	-4771	5138	-496000
cases		13	6	9	9	9	11	14	1

a) method I: forward identification, method II: backward identification.

Ontvangen: 05-06-1996
Geaccepteerd: 02-10-1996

[14]

A FLOW APPROACH TO INDUSTRIAL SITES, FIRM DYNAMICS AND REGIONAL EMPLOYMENT GROWTH: A CASE STUDY OF AMSTERDAM-NORTH

CEES GORTER, FRANK BRUINSMA & PETER NIJKAMP

Department of Regional Economics, Free University Amsterdam, Boelelaan 1105, 1081 HV Amsterdam, The Netherlands. E-mail: cgorter@econ.vu.nl

Received: October 1998; revised June 2000

ABSTRACT
This paper analyses the relationship between spatial dynamics of firms and employment growth in the region. Moreover, it addresses the facilitating or impeding role of (new) industrial sites in the geographical process of firm and job dynamics, while recognising that the spatial dynamics of firms reflect socio-economic developments at both the regional and national level. To this end, a novel conceptual theoretical framework based on the so-called flow approach, is developed, through which the relationship between spatial dynamics of firms (entries, exits and relocations) and changes in regional employment (job creation and job destruction) can be systematically analysed. Moreover, it also allows us to assess the generative employment effects of firm moves from and to (newly created) industrial sites in the region. To demonstrate in practice the usefulness of this new approach for the regional employment effects of spatial firm dynamics (facilitated or hindered by industrial site developments) an empirical application to the area of Amsterdam-North (the Netherlands) will be presented.

Key words: Industrial sites, regional dynamics, flow approach

INTRODUCTION

In recent years we have witnessed an increasing interest in new theories of regional economic growth which seek to explain regional development from an endogenous efficiency growth in factor inputs (see for a survey Nijkamp & Poot 1998). The competitive economic opportunities of an area are increasingly investigated from the perspective of active 'learning regions' (Morgan 1997), which offer appropriate land inputs in order to stimulate new business. To enhance economic development at the regional (local) level, it is of utmost importance to recognise, identify and utilise the regional (local) resources (Blakely 1994). A prominent archetype of this kind of resource is the local availability of industrial land, since without the control of

industrial land (and premises) it is impossible for local governments to stimulate local business development (Blakely 1994). This implies that the public acquisition of land and the development of land for businesses may possibly be an effective instrument for local economic development (and local job growth). Evaluation studies of local economic initiatives have – as far as we know – given scarce attention to the effectiveness of newly developed industrial sites (Foley 1990; Bartik 1991; Storey 1990). Therefore, the main research question of this paper is how to evaluate local job creation due to the public provision of industrial sites in an appropriate and systematic way.

To this end, this paper focuses on the intricate spatial-economic relationship between the dynamics of firms and of regional

Tijdschrift voor Economische en Sociale Geografie – 2001, Vol. 92, No. 2, pp. 119–138.
© 2001 by the Royal Dutch Geographical Society KNAG
Published by Blackwell Publishers, 108 Cowley Road, Oxford OX4 1JF, UK and 350 Main Street, Malden MA 02148, USA

employment. In particular, the role of (newly created) industrial sites in spatial firm dynamics and their employment implications for the region will be addressed. We will first analyse the interaction between firm and job dynamics from a theoretical perspective by using the so-called flow approach. Next, an empirical application is presented in which the relevant firm and job flows and their correlation are assessed for a particular area of the Amsterdam agglomeration (Amsterdam-North) and the market opportunities for industrial land use are also analysed for this area.

It goes without saying that spatial movements (relocations) of firms have consequences for the spatial dynamics in employment. A crucial element in this relationship, which will be elaborated at length in this paper, is the distinction between *gross* and *net* flows, for both firms and workers (see, for example, Hamermesh 1993, who surveys recent developments in the labour market literature on this topic). Moreover, it is relevant to consider flows of firms and workers into and out of the region of interest (at the meso level) and to highlight the underlying (behavioural) decisions made by the actors inside and outside the regional arena (Armstrong & Taylor 1993). In the case of (re)location patterns of firms, the decisions to move depend heavily on the attractiveness of the current and alternative regions of location. In addition, other factors play a role as well (at the meso level), such as the regional composition of firm size, the sectoral composition (to which differences in mobility behaviour are related), the ease of enlarging the regional supply of industrial sites, and the willingness of firms to stay in the present region. The order of magnitude of these – and other – factors will determine both the spatial dynamics of firms and the corresponding flows into and out of the regional employment stock. To study this phenomenon, we introduce in our paper a conceptual-theoretical framework, through which the spatial dynamics of firms (entries, exits and relocations) and dynamics in regional employment (job creation and job destruction) are mutually connected in a systematic way. This focus will also make it possible to distinguish the generative and distributive components of flows of firms and jobs from and to the region considered.

The structure of the paper is as follows. In the next section a 'playing field of spatial interaction' is introduced to focus on the interplay between the key elements of interest: spatial dynamics of firms and jobs, spatial planning of industrial sites, and spatial economic development. This is followed by an elaboration of the analytical framework for analysing firm and job dynamics in depth. An empirical application of this framework to data on firm and job flows in the region of Amsterdam-North is then presented, in which attention is also paid to the (future) use of industrial sites in this region. And finally, some concluding remarks are offered.

SOME THEORETICAL CONSIDERATIONS ON THE SPATIAL PLANNING OF INDUSTRIAL SITES

A PLAYING FIELD OF SPATIAL INTERACTION

Regional economic dynamics are the result of a complex force field (Suarez-Villa 1989). To analyse the role of industrial site development and the evolution of regions in regional employment growth, it is meaningful to discuss first three major spatial-economic themes that are mutually related and together form a 'playing field of spatial interaction' which encompasses the above mentioned focal points of interest. In general, the spatial dynamics of firms and jobs have to be regarded simultaneously with the spatial planning of industrial sites, and the general patterns of spatial-economic development (Figure 1). Spatial patterns of economic development at the national level mirror the spatial movements of economic activities (firms and households), and are thereby able to show which regions can be considered as economic core regions in a particular country and which ones play a secondary role. The actual assignment of regions into core, intermediate and peripheral areas is usually not constant over time; new spatial patterns of industrial and residential concentration and deconcentration influence the hierarchical position of regions in the course of time. For example, in the Dutch case one observes that at present the spatial spread of economic activities is gradually shifting towards the South East of the country, whereas traditionally the West has formed the economic core (Ministry of Economic Affairs 1997). This phenomenon is sometimes also referred to as large-scale 'urban sprawl' (Lambooy & Manshanden 1992).

Changes in the spatial-economic landscape are related to changes in the demands of firms (and households) for land and real estate in various regions. This new 'demand for land' may then lead to the development of industrial sites at these particular locations. In this case, the role of spatial planning policies is restricted to accommodate the regional/local demand for industrial locations. The planning authorities are then confronted with the question at which particular location(s) in the municipality the site should be built and whether or not this leads to the conversion of greenfield(s). This approach also implies that when opportunities to develop industrial sites in particular places are scarce, spatial-economic development will be impeded (at least in the short term) (Ministry of Economic Affairs 1994). In contrast, the planning of industrial sites may generate new activities in the region at hand. In this case, we see a pro-active and inter-active function of spatial planning (Blakely 1994) in which the Government aims to stimulate certain areas by offering industrial sites (possibly targeted at particular sectors) and encourages proper

responses of firms. In both cases (planning as a leading or following device of spatial development; see (a) in Figure 1) it is inevitable that demand and supply are in a permanent adjustment process, since it takes considerable time to make areas suitable for industrial location (Olden 1995). Moreover, balanced spatial planning is not just a matter of a quantitative balance between demand and supply for industrial areas, but also qualitative aspects become more and more important (e.g. due to globalisation and internationalisation, locational demands of firms vary across regions and among markets). Industrial sites can be seen as locational assets of a region that are increasingly judged by firms on the quality of the local physical environment (Blakely 1994).

So it follows that the spatial planning of industrial land influences and is influenced by regional economic dynamics (Figure 1, (a)). As regards the mutual dependence of firm migration and the planning of sites (Figure 1, (c)), it is illustrative to consider the location decision process of firms. First, potential moving firms make a choice of the region of destination. Second, they make a choice of a specific place within the region, and here premise availability in quantity and quality may come in as a relevant location factor. Therefore, new industrial estates may attract firms by offering suitable buildings/sites for

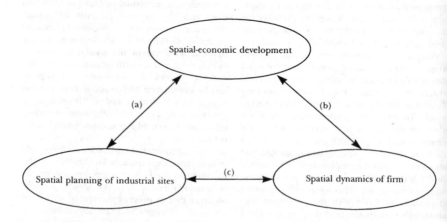

Figure 1. *A playing field of spatial interaction.*

the purposes of these firms. However, it should be emphasised that the availability of sites is a necessary condition (to avoid bottlenecks at the supply side of real estate), but not a sufficient condition to foster local economic development. Other factors like image, firm linkages, living conditions, labour market aspects, and accessibility are also crucial factors (see the section 'The migration of firms and their locational preferences', below). Nevertheless, the demands of firms for specific areas may lead to a wide array of responses in planning and development activities of local or regional authorities. This may occur in particular when certain areas become so attractive that an excess demand for land is taking place.

At the same time, regional development patterns and spatial dynamics of firms are also mutually related phenomena (Figure 1, (b)). On the one hand the location and relocation behaviour of individual firms influences the spatial configuration of economic activities at the regional level (Pellenbarg 1996). On the other the differences in regional growth lead to the attraction of new firms towards booming regions and the movements of existing firms from depressed to high-growth regions.

To further enhance the understanding of these interrelations, it is important to address each of the three core factors in detail. To start with, we focus extensively on the planning process of industrial land and its potential consequences for local economic development. Next, a concise overview is given of the movements of firms (and their locational preferences) and the contemporary regional economic developments in North Western Europe in general and in the Netherlands in particular.

THE SPATIAL PLANNING PROCESS OF INDUSTRIAL SITES: WHAT ARE THE CONSEQUENCES FOR (LOCAL) ECONOMIC DEVELOPMENT?

As outlined in the previous section, we first concentrate on the role of spatial planning of properties (sites) for industrial development. To facilitate the production in industrial sectors, land and buildings are necessary inputs, similar to conventional input factors as labour and capital. From the firm's point of

view, the optimal amount of land is difficult to determine. A choice has to be made between using more land than strictly needed, to have room for future expansion, or to keep the use of land to just a sufficient level to minimise costs of land (Van Haveren *et al.* 1999). But in principle does each industrial firm need space, so that there will be no industrial jobs without industrial floorspace? (Fothergill *et al.* 1987). What about causality in this relation? Do jobs lead to demand for floorspace or does the availability of floorspace lead to industrial jobs in that particular place? In the case of an unregulated land market, this issue is easily resolved. The law of supply and demand through which the price goes up in case of shortage of factory space (excess demand for space) guarantees in principle an efficient allocation of industrial land.

However, industrial firms face high transaction costs to alter their current (possible non-optimal) location, and consequently land markets may not function as smoothly as neoclassical economic theory predicts. Moreover, the market for industrial land (sites) is heavily regulated in many European countries (including the Netherlands). In general, industrial areas are planned at different spatial (national and local) levels. In the Netherlands, the municipalities primarily control the development of industrial sites. This is different to, for example, the UK (and also the USA), where private property provision of industrial estates is not marginal, but dominant (Fothergill *et al.* 1987; Wood & Williams 1992). Nevertheless, there are quite a few recent initiatives in the Netherlands to develop Public Private Partnership (PPP) constructions, particularly in the case of restructuring areas. The dominance of public provision also implies that Dutch firms are mostly located in the planned business areas (BCI 1997).

Spatial plans of industrial sites developed at a particular local (municipality) level are legally binding, whereas the plans made on higher spatial levels (provincial and national level) serve as strict guidelines. This institutional structure means that the province is placed in a position of (planning) control for the municipalities (Groenendijk 1990). To sum up, three governmental institutions at different spatial levels are involved in spatial planning in the Netherlands (as in most North Western European countries, with the exception of Ireland, where industrial sites are provided by regional authorities) (Bruinsma *et al.* 2000). In contrast to other countries, planned segmentation may take place at individual sites in the Netherlands (i.e. industrial estates are heterogeneous business concentrations with mixtures of different industries). The planning procedure is, however, much longer in the Netherlands than in other countries (it may take up to 15–20 years in total) (Bruinsma *et al.* 2000). The plans to designate land can have a time-span of four to six years (including the time for preparation and design). Local governments do have the opportunity to shorten this lengthy decision-making process by using the so-called Article 19 procedure. The designated use of industrial land can then be changed in nine months, but is required to stay in line with the guidelines set at the provincial and national level.

In general, the local government has several reasons to plan the development of industrial estates (CPB 1998; Van Bork 2000):

• avoid negative externalities of industrial activities on other firms, on households, on nature and agricultural activities (due to pollution, noise, emissions etc);
• achieve socio-economic objectives (employment, economic growth);
• offer good connections with existing and planned infrastructure (roads, railways);
• obtain a balanced economic structure (mixture of activities).

Given these considerations, how does the planning take place in practice? The development of Dutch industrial sites consists of two components (Needham 1997):

1. The land development process in which land is converted into space for future, industrial use (with precise and detailed planning rules of the municipality for what will be located where).
2. The building development process in which the new space is used for actual building (done by private or public building developers).

The municipality fully controls the first stage in this process (land development) to have strict public control over physical development, whereas it is much less involved in the second stage of actual building (this is referred to as 'active municipal land policy') (Needham 1997). In principle, local governments offer industrial land for disposal prices such that construction costs are fully covered (with the inclusion of infrastructure facilities). However, the co-ordination of the public actor in the allocation of land is not entirely exercised without market forces for three reasons (Needham 1997; Needham & Verhage 1998). First, the land is bought from previous land owners for 'market value' prices to avoid unnecessary delays in the conversion of land. Second, each municipality faces competition from other municipalities that may also offer space for industrial activities. Third, the land for marketable use (such as industrial estate) is disposed of at a market value, since otherwise it would not be bought if the price is too high.

Needham (1997) also argued that despite market constraints, private developers have hardly been involved in land development because the municipalities have pursued a land policy in which they created sufficient supply of sites to fill the predicted needs of businesses. Moreover, industrial sites have to be provided with infrastructure facilities, which lowers the profitability. As a consequence, local governments often set prices below market values to attract new firms to the area (Van Haveren *et al.* 1999; Van Bork 2000). This underpricing can be further stimulated by instruments that subsidise the development of sites (such as StiRea, a measure financed by the Ministry of Economic Affairs in the Netherlands). On the whole, it implies for the Dutch case that regulatory forces by local government are stronger than market forces in the land market for industrial (business) areas. Hence, the availability of land (quantity) has been more important in the Netherlands than the price for the allocation of industrial land.

In the provision of land (by local governments), one can think of two extreme cases (Fothergill *et al.* 1987). In the first case, we consider the supply of land to be fixed. This creates a barrier to the expansion of existing firms and the relocating of new firms. And

nce, the availability of current premises
asically determines the number of jobs that
ight go down only if employment density
lls. In the second case, we may assume that
dustrial space can be easily extended. Then
ere would be no barrier to growth of incum-
nt firms, the creation of new firms, and the
location of firms. Hence, the location profile
an area and (local) economic growth pros-
ects will fix the number of local jobs.

Since supply is enlarged by public provision
industrial property in the Netherlands, it is
interest to know the benefits in terms of
area's level of economic activity. Fothergill
al. (1987) mention the following main effects.
rst, the improvement in the availability of
dustrial property (premises) leads to a faster
xpansion of existing firms and the attraction
new firms. Second, industrial rents are
duced for firms. Third, vacancy chains of
emises are generated due to the through-
ow of incumbent firms to new places, thereby
aving their old locations vacant. This chain-
fect produces a job gain in the construction
new factories that is the sum of job gains at
ch stage in the chain. Fourth, the quality of
e industrial building stock is improved. This
aper elaborates on the first factor by using
newly developed methodological concept to
aluate firm and job movements, the so-
alled flow approach (see the section 'Spatial
ynamics of firms and regional employment
owth', below).

As regards the generation of new jobs, two
tal issues are at stake to evaluate the effect of
te provision. Jobs can either be new to the
gion or displaced from other industrial sites
the region (due to relocation of firms).
ncumbent firms that move into the new site
ay employ more workers because of this re-
ocation or might have employed more workers
nyway (that is, if they had not moved). The
et result of genuine new jobs is, of course, an
mpirical matter, but to make an adequate
ssessment, one needs a systematic and crystal-
lear approach. This paper aims to provide
ich a methodological tool (see also the
ction 'Spatial dynamics of firms and regional
mployment growth', below).

Public provision of industrial premises is a
pecific form of local employment initiatives
i.e. policies and measures to create local

employment) that can be used. In the evaluation, the focus is usually on the creation of
jobs and the costs associated with that (Willis
1985; Storey 1990; Foley 1992). Willis (1985),
for example, has stated that 'the primary
objective of spatially differentiated aid to
industry is to increase employment above
and over what it would otherwise have been'.
In this respect, it is also of interest to note
that the ability to create jobs by launching
specific local initiatives will depend on the
state and development of the economy at the
national level (Morrison 1987; Doeringer et al.
1987)

Storey (1990) presented a general methodology to evaluate Local Employment Initiatives
(LEI). He showed that – based on micro-
economic theory – the marginal costs of each
potential LEI instrument should be equal to
achieve economic efficiency. He also discussed
the difficulties of evaluation in practice: how
to measure the net effect of an initiative (such
as site/premises provision) on job creation in
the local economy. Furthermore, he looked at
the outcome for the local economy in terms of
unemployment reduction due to the newly
created jobs. In other words, do disadvantaged
groups in the end benefit from an initiative or
not? However, this particular issue is beyond
the scope of this paper. Storey ended up with
a systematic scheme in which employment
criteria are applied to estimate this effect for
the *local* economy.

For our purpose, it is relevant to examine
the consequences of an initiative that provides
industrial land (premises). According to Storey
(1990), this kind of initiative leads to a number
of projected jobs that may feed into actual jobs
in the course of time because the effect may
be estimated before all the units of the new
premises are occupied. The actual jobs measured include 'dead weight' and other policy
jobs, the jobs that would have also been
created if the new site were not built (in the
absence of facilitating the new premises). So
the new jobs are just those jobs that are
actually a result of offering the new facilities. It
is of course not realistic to assume that each
new job that occurs as an initiative is actually
a result of that initiative (Willis 1985). In
the case of the provision of new industrial
premises, it is relevant to ask whether the firms

did really need to settle in the new site or whether they could have found alternative locations as well. This attrition problem can be overcome by using several techniques (Storey 1990), such as asking firms what they thought about the impact of the initiatives on the number of jobs created. One could also apply a treatment/control group approach in which companies assisted by the initiative are compared with similar firms not assisted. But not all new jobs are jobs new to the local economy: new jobs may be transferred from elsewhere (outside the local economy): this is a gain for the local economy, but not for the national economy (with the exception of international companies that come into this area). Economic activities (and the associated jobs) that are new to the local economy may 'crowd out' activities of other firms, either located in the region or elsewhere in the national economy (so-called displacements jobs). An extreme case of displacement happens when firms relocate, thereby transferring businesses and jobs from one place to another. Here we see the emergence of a crucial element in the relationship between the spatial dynamics of firms and the dynamics in local employment (and this will be worked out in full in the section 'Spatial dynamics of firms and regional employment growth', below).

In short, Storey (1990) has pointed out that the net number of new jobs due to a local initiative is equal to the number of projected (actual) jobs minus the 'dead weight' jobs minus the transferred jobs minus the displacement jobs. As mentioned before, the role of transferred jobs will be an important ingredient of our analytical framework of firm and job dynamics to be introduced in the section 'Spatial dynamics of firms and regional employment growth', below.

THE MIGRATION OF FIRMS AND THEIR LOCATIONAL PREFERENCES

Why do firms move from one site to another? It is well known that locational choices are brought forward by a combination of push factors (conditions required are not satisfied) and pull factors (attractiveness of alternative places) (Pellenbarg 1996). For example, some regions are favourable places to settle for firms

due to their geographical accessibility, the avail ability of high quality labour, etc. (Porter 1990) Locational demand of firms will be differen across regions and be dependent on the kin of economic activities (Kleyn & de Vet 1994) The most important location factors for Dutcl industrial firms to move are the following (Kemper & Pellenbarg 1997; B&A-groep 1997 BCI 1997; Rietveld & Bruinsma 1998):

- a lack of space to accommodate economi activities at the present place, due to, fo example, congestion/accessibility problems and related to that, the parking facilities;
- strict environmental regulations;
- a deteriorated landscape of the site (out look of buildings and the environment) high prices for industrial land.

This short list of key factors, based on actua location behaviour, can be supplemented with the locational preferences of Dutch firms What kind of location do firms ideally desire Following Meester (1999) we see that firm attribute high values to:

- their own environment (locational self preference);
- market accessibility (from a national or an international perspective);
- living conditions (to ease the hiring and maintaining of personnel).

The expectation for future requirements o business location for firms is in line with the above mentioned factors (Ministry of Economic Affairs 1997). Key factors for firms will be:

- personnel (quantity and quality), and re lated to this, living conditions in the region;
- local availability of suppliers and knowl edge centres;
- suitable business premises with a potentia to expand;
- accessibility;
- relative geographical position to economic centres (urban areas, corridors and main ports).

A spatial trend that can be observed in many industrialised countries is that firms move from inner urban areas to locations at the urban edge or suburban areas (see, among other studies, Fothergill *et al.* 1987; Chapman & Walker 1991; Hessels 1994). The main easons for this outward shift are found in both push (congestion, high land prices) and pull (cheaper suitable personnel, more space to expand) factors. For industrial relocations in the Netherlands, we observe that firms move from isolated locations to grouped business areas (BCI 1997). Therefore, industrial firm migration patterns cause extra land claims for industrial sites (greenfields) outside the urban field in the Netherlands. In addition, Dutch firms relocate over relatively short distances. In other words, the firms wish to stay in the same region, and apparently have a strong attachment to their current region (Pellenbarg 1985; Meester 1999). Of course, larger and/or (inter)nationally oriented firms have a broader search radius and may move to other regions or countries (Bruinsma *et al.* 1998). The selection of suitable locations is also influenced by factors such as the access to national and international markets, multimodal accessibility, and availability of transport facilities (e.g. mainports for waterway transport or international hubs). Firms also base their relocation decision on the current spatial pattern of known industrial sites, and select their favourable site normally from that given choice set (for example, the site that performs best in terms of accessibility or expected cost-effectiveness).

REGIONAL ECONOMIC DEVELOPMENT

In North Western Europe economic growth tends to take place at the edges of urban agglomerations and along national (international) corridors that connect the main economic centres (MEA 1997). In fact, the spatial pattern of firm settlement is a mixture of concentration and deconcentration at different spatial levels. Concentration is basically caused by agglomeration economics (spillovers), whereas the main underlying forces for deconcentration are a lack of space and congestion at the urban level. In the Dutch case, it can be observed that the core area (Randstad) becomes larger and spreads out to adjacent regions along main corridor (provinces of Noord-Brabant, Gelderland). In this respect, it is interesting to note that Elhorst *et al.* (1999) have recently argued that spatial deconcentration policy may, in fact, improve

national welfare. At the same time. the Dutch urban field becomes internally more concentrated, in particular in the North-Wing of the Randstad (Amsterdam-Schiphol agglomeration).

For industrial sectors, we observe a tendency to move eastwards in Central and Capital Cities (CCC) regions in North Western Europe (Van der Knaap & Sleegers 1995). The spatial picture for Dutch industrial sectors (NEI 1997) generally shows a diffusion of industrial activities with concentric circles and a less prominent impact of urban agglomerations and the transport network system. One of the important factors to sprawl industrial activities is the low price of land found in less central or peripheral areas (NEI 1997). As mentioned in the previous section, the Dutch industrial sector experiences an outward shift from the urban agglomerations which can be explained (TNO/Inro 1997) by the favourable geographical position in a European market perspective, and the closeness of firms to mainports (Airport Schiphol-Amsterdam and Harbour Rotterdam).

CONCLUSIONS

We have argued that the locational preferences of firms for specific areas (see the section 'The migration of firms and their locational preferences', above) may lead to a wide array of responses in planning and development activities of the local or regional authorities. This may occur in particular when certain areas become so attractive that an excess demand for land is taking place. With this observation we come back to the spatial patterns of economic development (see the section 'Regional economic development', above) which reflect – at the aggregate level – the movements of firms across space. However, at the same time these movements are based on individual decisions on firm location and relocation. These changing spatial configurations of firms have to be matched in the 'market' of industrial sites and this adjustment process is not only influenced by market forces (land prices), but also to a large extent by spatial planning of the (local) government (either of a following or a leading nature). The consequences of this planning process for local firm and job gains will be the topic of the next section.

SPATIAL DYNAMICS OF FIRMS AND REGIONAL EMPLOYMENT GROWTH

THE SPATIAL FLOW APPROACH

In this section, the spatial-economic inter-action between the dynamics of firms and changes in employment is analysed by identi-fying the relevant flows of jobs and firms. The dynamics in regional economic activities is reflected by firms moving in, out and within the region of interest. This migration compo-nent of firm relocation has to be comple-mented with the demography of firms, in particular the start of firms ('birth') and firms going bankrupt or leaving the market ('death') in order to arrive at a full description of firm flows (Gordijn & Van Wissen 1994). Changes in firm flows will lead – together with the growth and decline patterns of existing firms in the region – to changes in job flows.

To analyse properly the relationships be-tween the (spatial) dynamics in firms and jobs in general, and to investigate the role of (newly created) industrial sites in the dynamics of regional employment in particular, it is necessary to set out more precisely the anatomy of the regional development process at stake. In particular, an important distinc-tion that has to be made is between gross and net flows, for both firm and job flows. Figure 2 shows concisely the composition of firm and job flows (i.e. the anatomy of the dynamics) from a regional-economic perspective, and the way these flows are mutually related.

The stock of firms in a region changes over time due to firms moving in and out of that region, and to firm 'creation' and 'destruc-tion' in that region. Total regional firm inflow (i.e. the sum of moving in and creation) is

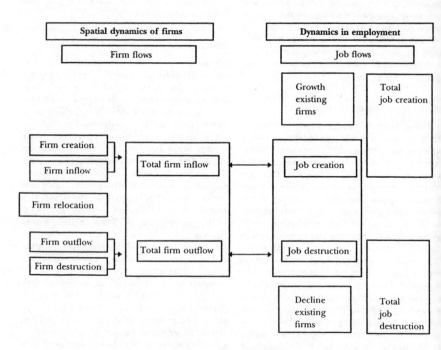

Figure 2. *Spatial dynamics of firms and employment growth: an analytical framework for the flow approach.*

CEES GORTER, FRANK BRUINSMA & PETER NIJKAMP

rectly connected to job creation (by the new
rms) in that region, and the same applies to
tal regional firm outflow and its correspond-
g regional job destruction. Taken together,
e connection becomes clear (Figure 2) be-
veen the gross firm flow (i.e. the sum of total
rm inflow and total firm outflow) and the
ross job flow (i.e. the sum of job creation and
b destruction). Two crucial points need to
e emphasised here (and will be further elab-
rated in the next section, 'The relationship
etween firm and job flows'):

The gross regional firm flow does *not*
include relocations of firms inside the
region (note that it would only be useful
to include these flows in our framework
if, and only if, firms simultaneously move
within the region and expand or reduce
their workforce).
The gross job flow can be defined in two
ways: either with or without the growth and
decline of employment in existing firms in
the region.

different terminology with respect to the
patial dynamics of firms, which is often used
the literature on regional economic devel-
pment, may in fact be misleading when
pplied to the analysis of the link between
rm and job flows in a regional context. This
ay happen when gross regional firm flows
re seen to consist of two parts, the sum of
egional firm creation and firm destruction
turbulence flows) and the so-called mobility
ows which are formed by firms moving in,
ut and within the region of interest. Of course,
egional turbulence (creation and destruc-
on) and regional mobility flows may perfectly
ndicate the extent to which firm movements
ccur in a region, but these concepts are not
seful in analysing the causal economic (em-
loyment) effects of firm flows. For example,
high figure for the sum of mobility flows
nd turbulence flows does not have to be
ssociated with clear growth patterns for the
egional stock of firms, nor will it necessarily
oincide with a positive net change in the
umber of firms. From the above discussion, it
clear that when analysing the role of indus-
ial sites in regional employment dynamics
ttention should be paid to the following two
ey questions:

1. For the choice of the spatial *level* of analysis:
   what is the size of the region of interest?
   This may vary from a particular (newly
   created) industrial site, the neighbourhood, the city or municipality, the district
   or province up to the level of the nation.
   Empirical research is usually based on
   administrative areas (cities or provinces)
   due to reasons of data availability.
2. For the impact of *incumbent firms*: how to deal
   with the effect of existing firms on employment dynamics in the region of interest?
   Obviously, this component of firm expansion
   (or contraction) does not contribute to the
   spatial dynamics of firms, but the growth or
   decline of employment will in practice be
   substantially affected by the development
   patterns of existing firms in the region.
   However, it is somewhat difficult to find out
   whether these changes in employment are
   fully autonomously determined or to some
   extent influenced by the fact that some
   firms enter or leave the region (e.g., giving
   rise to agglomeration economics).

It seems therefore appropriate for the analysis
of the interaction between regional firm
dynamics and regional employment growth
to introduce an explicit distinction between
regional dynamics in either a broad or a
narrow sense (Table 1). Regional firm dynamics in a narrow sense include firm creation
and destruction flows, and flows related to
firms moving in and out of the region. If
we add the relocation firm flows (within the
region) to this concept, we arrive at the regional
firm dynamics in a broad sense (which also
equals the sum of turbulence and mobility
flows). In the case of regional employment
changes, the 'narrow-based' concept includes
job creation and job destruction (as directly
related to firms coming in or out of the region),
whereas the 'broad-based' concept consists of
total job creation and total job destruction
(thus including the jobs created or destroyed
in existing firms). In Table 1, we summarise
the above mentioned concepts of flows.

THE RELATIONSHIP BETWEEN FIRM AND JOB FLOWS

The next step in the analysis of the consequences of available (partly newly created)

Table 1. *Concepts of firm and job flows in a spatial perspective.*

Variable of interest concept	Regional dynamics of firms	Regional dynamics in employment
Narrow-based	Firm flow = inflow and outflow	Job flow = job creation and job destruction related to inflow and outflow of firms
Broad-based	Firm flow-plus = inflow, outflow and relocation-flow	Job flow-plus = total job creation and total job destruction

industrial sites in the region for employment dynamics in that region is to put forward and discuss four potential options to consider the relationship between spatial dynamics of firms (entries, exits and relocations) and in regional employment growth (job creation and job destruction) in general, and between gross/net firm flows and gross/net job flows in particular. In Option 1, the area of interest is purely concerned with the newly created industrial sites in the region, whereas in the other three options the focus is on the region in which the industrial sites are located. So we subsequently consider the following options:

Option 1: Firm inflow <=> job inflow
Option 2: Firm flow <=> job flow
Option 3: Firm flow <=> job flow-plus
Option 4: Firm flow-plus <=> job flow-plus

Option 1 *The newly created industrial sites: firm inflow related to job inflow*

In this case, our general scheme of flows (Figure 2) simplifies greatly. Obviously, firms locating at the newly created industrial sites are new firms; the outflow of firms and firms moving within the area are non-existent. This also implies that the gross firm flow equals the net firm flow. Jobs related to the new firms form the gross – and also the net – job flow. Clearly, a positive relationship emerges between the gross (net) firm flow and the gross (net) job flow.

Option 2 *The industrial sites in a regional context: firm flow related to job flow*

When considered in a regional context, (new) industrial sites offer (additional) space for economic activities within the region. The firm flows emerging in this new situation can be directed both into and out of the region

(flows within the region, i.e. the relocation flows, are excluded from the analysis in this option). The net firm flow can be positive or negative, dependent on the magnitude of the four underlying components, namely firm creation, firm inflow, firm destruction and firm outflow (Figure 2). A positive result for the net firm flow reflects the fact that sufficient land for industrial sites is offered in that region to accommodate this net growth in the stock of firms. For the outcome of the net job flow, a similar uncertainty (like for firms) arises regarding its sign, especially since the average size of the firms moving in and out of the region may also differ. So, it becomes clear that the correlation between the net firm flow and the net job flow is not necessarily positive, whereas the gross firm flow and the gross job flow will be positively related by definition.

Option 3 *The industrial sites in a regional context: firm flow related to job flow-plus*

The difference with Option 2 is that now job creation and job destruction of existing firms in the region are also taken into account to determine gross and net job flows. Most likely, the absolute value of both the gross and the net job flow will be higher, because the 'growth/decline' – components usually outnumber the 'creation/destruction' – components related to firms moving in/out of the region. The important issue in this option is how to interpret a positive correlation between the net firm flow and the net job flowplus. On the one hand, it is unclear to what extent this positive correlation is due to the net growth in jobs of those firms that actually moved from and to the industrial sites. It might just as well be caused by the net growth of jobs in existing firms. So it is now more ficult to consider the direct function of dustrial sites in the observed dynamics of gional employment (job-flow plus). On the her hand, existing firms might benefit (in e long-run) from the moving patterns of ew) firms to the (newly created) industrial es, and then their employment growth tern would be partly due to the economic pulse put forward by the additional supply space for industrial activities. So, in a way, tion 3 shows the maximum effect of spatial namics of firms (facilitated by industrial e development) on regional employment namics (e.g. measured via the number of ditional jobs per firm), whereas Option 2 es the minimum value of this effect.

ption 4 *The industrial sites in a regional context: firm flow-plus related to job flow-plus*

sically, this option is discussed here to argue at it of *no use* for analysing the employment ects of spatial firm dynamics in response to dustrial site development (however, this tion appears to be applied frequently in actice). As we stated before, the relocation w of firms should be excluded from the alysis, because it will overestimate the relant spatial dynamics on the firm-side. A vere flaw in the analysis is made when in this tion the job flows stemming from relocation ws would erroneously be counted as new os, and hence included in the job flow-plus mponent. In practise it often happens that licy-makers make use of the popular slogan at 'new space for industrial activities benefits gional employment substantially'. However, their 'back of the envelope' calculation they croneously) include the job gains related to m relocation flows within the region (Van rk 2000). To sum up, Option 4 is either uivalent to Option 3 (when looking at net ws) or not useful at all when employing the m flow-plus concept.

MPLOYMENT POTENTIAL

discussed in the section 'Some theoretical nsiderations on the spatial planning of indusal sites', above, the availability of industrial eas in a region will affect the economic owth of that region. Excess supply of indus-

trial sites is not likely to lead to higher regional-economic growth rates, but an unmatched demand for land by firms will frustrate the exploitation of the economic potential of that region. Hence, regional growth depends on spatial planning policies that influence the pace and composition of industrial site development. So the question is: what determines the employment potential of industrial sites in a region? We note in passing here that employment potential is defined as the regional potential to attract new firms offering new jobs. Most importantly, the prosperity of the regional economy plays a role in this context. If the current employment density is high from a spatial perspective and the regional economy is booming, the demand for land by (new) firms will be high, and consequently the employment potential of (new) industrial sites is also high. Besides quantitative shortages of land for industrial activities, qualitative discrepancies in this land market might be essential too. For example, the employment potential of an industrial site is likely to be higher in regions with a good *image* as perceived by firms (Pellenbarg 1985). Another determinant worth mentioning concerns the particular geographical location of the site in the region. This factor influences the site's attractiveness, since locations differ in aspects like (road) accessibility, facilities, settlement of other firms in this area, etc. (Bruinsma 1994). In particular, the sectoral composition and the average size of firms that are already settled in the area are important in this respect. It is a well-known fact that new industrial sites are to a large extent filled by firms located in the vicinity of the site and which have grown rapidly in recent years and hence have a need for more space. This observation takes us back to the core question of this paper, that is how to determine properly the *net* employment effect of firms moving from and to (new) industrial sites in a regional context. We concluded that such movements within the region that lead to the settlement at other sites should not be counted as employment gains. The firm's relocation movements just give rise to *redistributive* employment effects and do not yield any *generative* employment effects (note that relocations of firms may actually lead to a loss in national employment if the movements coincide with (labour rationalisation). Obviously, the decomposition of employment gains into generative and redistributive parts depends on the spatial level of analysis chosen: the lower the spatial level the higher the generative employment gains of firms moving from and to (newly created) industrial sites will be. We now offer an empirical study to illustrate the above observations.

THE CASE OF AMSTERDAM-NORTH: AN EMPIRICAL ILLUSTRATION

INTRODUCTION

In this section we test empirically the analytical framework given in Figure 2 by analysing firm flows and related job developments in Amsterdam-North, defined as the part of the municipality of Amsterdam located north of the river IJ (Figure 3). This part of the agglomeration has in past decades not been able to gain its share in the overall economic development of the Amsterdam region. Besides, in the city centre the main economic

activities of the Amsterdam agglomeration shifted increasingly towards the southern an south-western part of the region. This region is well connected to the other major Randsta cities (Rotterdam, the Hague and Utrecht and close to the national airport, Schiphol.

Nevertheless, since the mid 1980s econ omic developments are more favourable i Amsterdam-North. Small firms, which ar over-represented in the North perform eve better in this area than in the Amsterdar agglomeration. Figures based on the 'Surve Regional Firm Development' (held yearly b the Chamber of Commerce) show that th employment (sales) growth rate in the Nort region is about 6.0% (4.7%) per year o average for the period 1985–92, whereas th corresponding employment (sales) figure fo the agglomeration is 4.4% (2.5%). On th whole, Amsterdam-North does not nowaday perform less economically than the averag of the Amsterdam agglomeration.

As regards the spatial planning of indus trial sites, the municipality of Amsterdam ca cope with economic expansion until 2005 even in a high growth scenario when the 'sof

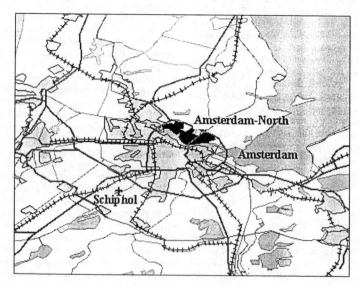

Figure 3. *The Amsterdam region.*

stock' – the capacity of sites that does not yet exist but is planned to be developed in the near future – is used (DRO 1995). The local spatial development plans show that over 50% of the sites for development in the near future (the 'soft' stock) are located in Amsterdam-North (45 hectares to be developed in the Northern IJ Lake). This lake will be reclaimed by sand dredged from a new harbour development on the opposite site of the river IJ (the so-called 'Afrika-haven'). The average pace at which industrial sites are put into use in Amsterdam-North during the last ten years is about 1.3 hectares per year. It can then be shown that the 'hard' stock (stock of unused lots at existing sites to be put into use immediately or within the period of five years) can supply the requirements for 15.6 years, while still keeping an 'iron' stock (the size of the average demand in five years) in reserve. Keeping in mind the large reserve of soft stock, we can conclude that the supply of industrial sites in Amsterdam-North will impose no restrictions on the spatial economic development of the region in general, and the spatial movements of firms into the area in particular.

THE SPATIAL DYNAMICS OF FIRMS AND JOBS

The inflow and outflow and relocation of firms reflect the spatial dynamics of economic activities within a region. Together with the increase and decrease of employment of existing firms, and firm creation and firm destruction, the regional dynamics in employment can be analysed (Figure 2).

In this section the flows of firms and employment are analysed for Amsterdam-North following the structure of Figure 2. Moreover, attention is paid to the generative and distributive effects of spatial firm dynamics. In this case study, movements of firms within the Amsterdam agglomeration (origin or destination, Amsterdam-North) are seen as distributive, whereas all other firm movements, national and international, are considered generative.

Spatial firm dynamics in Amsterdam-North for the period 1989–93

For an analysis of the firm and job dynamics we make extensive use of a report of the Statistical Office of the Municipality of Amsterdam (O+S 1997). In this analysis the annual firm registers are compared for the period 1989–93. By comparing the registers of two successive years, all new and firms no longer trading in the register could be detected as well as firm movements within the Amsterdam agglomeration. However, a major consequence is that it is not possible to make a distinction between the inflow of firms and firm creation, nor between the outflow of firms and firm destruction. This problem is dealt with in an artificial manner. In another report of the Statistical Office of the Municipality of Amsterdam the distinction between new firms' 'starters' and the inflow is made as well as the distinction between firm destruction and the outflow of firms for the period 1989–91 (O+S 1994). In Table 2 the shares of inflow versus creation and outflow versus destruction are given for the period 1989–91 in Amsterdam-North. We assume that the share for the years 1992 and 1993 are equal to the shares given in Table 2.

In Table 3 the spatial firm and employment dynamics are given for Amsterdam-North in the period 1989–93. There is one inconsistency in the table which is not clear from reading the report. The stock of firms increases by 497 firms in the period 1989–93, whereas the balance between total firm inflow and total firm outflow is only 237 firms. This

Table 2. *Shares (percentages) of inflow versus creation and outflow versus destruction in Amsterdam-North (1989–91).*

	Inflow	Creation	Outflow	Destruction
Firms	8.3	91.7	21.7	78.3
Jobs	15.8	84.2	23.2	76.8

Table 3. *Firm and employment flows in Amsterdam-North (1989–93, in absolute numbers).*

Stock of firms 1989	2.584		
Stock of jobs 1989	18.491		
Creation 1989–93			
Firms	1.290*		
Jobs	5.609*	Total inflow	
Inflow 1989–93		Firms	1.728
Firms	438**	Jobs	8.188
Jobs	2.579**		
Relocation 1989–93			
Firms	557	Net flow	
Jobs	3.050	Firms	237
		Jobs	1.417
Outflow 1989–93			
Firms	519**		
Jobs	2.830**	Total outflow	
Destruction 1989–93		Firms	1.491
Firms	972*	Jobs	6.771
Jobs	3.933*		
Net growth jobs new firms after location (inflow 1989–93)			262
Net growth jobs firms existing 1989–93			134
Stock of firms 1993	3.081	Net growth jobs	1.813
Stock of Jobs 1993	20.352	Net growth firms	237

* Estimated, see Table 2. Based on O+S (1994).
** Generative inflow/outflow estimated by percentages given, see Table 2. Based on O+S (1994); distributive inflow/outflow given by O+S (1997).

Source: O+S (1997).

difference can be explained by the huge number of firms created in this period for fiscal purposes (for instance, by pensioners). These firms are not economically productive, so they are not dealt with as firm creations in this study.

When we consider the spatial firm movements, over one-third of the movements (firms and jobs) concern relocations within Amsterdam-North. The outflow of firms and jobs is larger than the inflow in the period 1989–93, so there is a negative balance of 81 firms and 251 jobs lost by Amsterdam-North. In the period 1989–93, 52.9% of the average number of firms and 43.4% of the average number of jobs are involved in a firm movement (10.6% and 8.7% annually, respectively).

The negative balance of the migration flows of jobs (251) and firms (81) is overcompensated by the balance of firm creation

versus firm destruction (1.676 jobs and 318 firms). As a result, there is a positive net flow of 237 firms and 1.417 jobs in Amsterdam-North over the period 1989–93. The net growth in jobs at firms already existing in the period 1989–93 and the growth in jobs of firms moving into Amsterdam-North in the period 1989–93 should be added to the net flow of jobs to reach to the level of the net growth of jobs.

Table 3 gives a complete overview of the absolute flows of firms and jobs. Another way to analyse the flows is to study the relative size of the flows. In other words, what is the size of the flows compared to the stock of firms and jobs? And, what is the average number of jobs per firm in each flow? The picture emerging from the first question is naturally reproducing the signals obtained from the absolute volumes: first, the outflow is larger than the nflow of firms, but the net flow is positive due to the positive difference between job creation and job destruction, and second, the relocation flow is more than twice as large as the net flow of firms into the Amsterdam-North region. The importance of the second question is that many small firms might offer as many jobs as one large firm. This information is given in Table 4.

On average, relatively small firms are involved in firm movements, firm creation and firm destruction: the share in the stock of firms is larger than the share in the stock of jobs (the number of jobs per firm is below the overall average). Only the inflow of firms from outside the agglomeration contributes less to the stock of firms than they contribute to the stock of jobs. However, the absolute number of firms moving from outside the agglomeration towards Amsterdam-North is relatively small.

This pattern of small firms being largely responsible for regional dynamics is quite usual. Starting firms often offer employment to only a few people. If the firm is a success in the initial years, it will grow relatively fast (also in terms of employment). Fast growth often means that these young firms need space to expand, but this is often unavailable at their present locations and requires that they move.

This explains the high mobility of relatively small firms. On the other hand, many young firms fail to succeed, and disappear in the first three years of their existence. This explains the relatively high share of firm destruction, in particular of relatively small firms.

The figures presented in Table 4 can be used to estimate empirically the relationship between firm flows and jobs flows in the Amsterdam-North region. As has been indicated in the section 'Spatial dynamics of firms and regional employment growth', above, different options are available to perform this task. It has also been argued in this respect that the appropriate way to do so is to relate the gross/net firm flow to either gross/net job flow (Option 2 approach) or to the gross/net job flow-plus, which is based on total job creation and destruction in the region (Option 3 approach). Unfortunately, we cannot present the figures on Option 1 due to lack of information on the firm and job flows into new industrial sites in Amsterdam-North.

Let us first summarise the average annual values of the gross and net flows for the period 1989–93, both for firms and jobs in percentages of the average stock of firms and jobs, respectively. In general, one sees that the region shows relatively many moving firms (the annual percentage is 10.6% on average,

Table 4. *Annual shares (percentages) in average number of firms and jobs.*

	Average annual share of firms (2.872)	Average annual share of jobs (19.486)	Average number of jobs per firm (6.8)
Creation	9.0	5.8	4.3
Inflow	3.1	2.6	5.9
Distributive	2.2	1.6	4.8
Generative	0.8	1.1	9.0
Total inflow	12.0	8.4	4.7
Relocation	3.9	3.1	5.5
Destruction	6.8	4.0	4.0
Outflow	3.6	2.9	5.5
Distributive	1.9	1.7	6.6
Generative	1.7	1.2	4.4
Total outflow	10.4	6.9	4.5
Net flow	1.6	1.5	6.0
Net growth jobs existing firms	–	0.4	

whereas the national average is 7%–8% during this period (Kemper & Pellenbarg 1995). So, the figures in Table 5 show that the gross flows are fairly high, especially for firms (more than 20% annually). We also see positive net flows in all cases, which also implies that – independent of the option chosen – net firm and net job flows are positively correlated in the Amsterdam-North region (1989–93). Obviously, the gross flows are also positively related in Option 2. Note also that, as was conjectured before, the net flow of jobs becomes higher when the creation and destruction in existing firms is taken into account. The warning given in the section 'The spatial flow approach', above, that it would be a severe flaw in the analysis when the jobs flows stemming from relocation flows are counted as new jobs can be illustrated by this example. The adding of the relocation flow would result in a significant overestimation of net flow (5% instead of the actual job flow of 1.9%).

As regards the difference between Options 2 and 3, this is most clearly revealed when we compute on the basis of the net numbers the average number of jobs per firm. It then becomes apparent that Option 2 leads to an average net creation of six jobs per firm, whereas Option 3 gives 7.6 jobs per firm on average. In other words, using the broad job-concept of Option 3 (including creation and destruction of existing firms) leads, in the case of Amsterdam-North, to an average result that is 27% higher than that of Option 2 (in which the creation-destruction component is

excluded). Recall that this level of 7.6 job per firm forms an upper bound of the effec that can be attributed to the availability c industrial sites in this region, whereas the leve of six jobs per firm can be seen as a lowe bound.

There is no information about the numbe of jobs created in existing growing firms an the number of jobs lost in existing shrinkin firms. This means that we have no gross flow of job creation and job destruction for th existing firms in Amsterdam-North.

Distributive versus generative firm and job flows

In our theoretical framework we distinguisl relocations, and distributive and generativ firm movements. The relocations withi Amsterdam-North are already shown i Tables 3 and 4 (one-third of the movement are relocations within Amsterdam-North) In Table 6 the inflow and outflow of firm and jobs are specified in movements betwee Amsterdam-North and the Amsterdam ag glomeration and between Amsterdam-Nortl and areas outside the Amsterdam agglom eration.

Table 6 shows that there is a positiv migration balance of firms for Amsterdam North in relation to the Amsterdam agglom eration. However, the outflow of firms t areas outside the agglomeration exceeds th generative inflow of firms. So, the overal negative outflow of firms is caused by th

Table 5. *Empirical results for firm and jobs flows in the Amsterdam-North region (in percentages per year, 1989–93,*

Variable of interest concept	Regional dynamics of firms	Regional dynamics in employment
Narrow-based	Firm flow = inflow and outflow	Job flow = job creation and job destruction related to in- and outflow of firms
	gross: 22.4	
	net: 1.6	
	Option 2 →	*gross:* 15.3
	Option 3 ↘	*net:* 1.5
Broad-based	Firm flow-plus = inflow, outflow and relocation-flow	Job flow-plus = total job creatio and total job destruction
	gross: 26.3	*gross:* >15.3
	net: 1.6	*net:* 1.9

Table 6. *Origin of inflow and destination of outflow of the firms (1989–93).*

	Amsterdam agglomeration (*distributive*)			Out of Amsterdam (*generative**)		
	Firms	Jobs	Jobs/firms	Firms	Jobs	Jobs/firms
Inflow	321 (73%)	1.527 (62%)	4.8	117 (27%)	1.052 (38%)	9.0
Outflow	249 (48%)	1.650 (58%)	6.6	270 (52%)	1.180 (42%)	4.4
Net flow	72	−123		−153	−128	

* estimated by Table 2. Based on O+S (1994).
Source: O+S 1997.

huge number of firms leaving the Amsterdam agglomeration. This result is in line with the findings of Kemper and Pellenbarg (1997), who show a negative migration balance of firm relocation for all Randstad cities in favour of locations in the intermediate zone of the Netherlands.

Although there is a positive balance in distributive movements of firms, the distributive balance of job movements is negative. Relatively small companies move towards Amsterdam-North, whereas relatively large companies move towards the remainder of the Amsterdam agglomeration. The net distributive job loss is of the same magnitude as the net job loss caused by the negative generative firm balance. From outside the Amsterdam agglomeration relatively large firms move towards Amsterdam-North compared to the average firm size of firms moving in the opposite direction.

Another finding is also noteworthy: for firms that had chosen for a relocation out of Amsterdam-North, in most cases there were suitable sites available within Amsterdam-North. However, for the parent companies of those firms strategic motives to locate the firm outside Amsterdam-North appeared to be decisive.

CONCLUDING REMARKS

This paper has concentrated on the intricate relationship between spatial (regional) dynamics of firms and regional employment growth, with a particular focus on the role of spatial planning of industrial sites in this

adjustment process. To analyse this issue consistently, we have introduced a conceptual theoretical framework in which spatial firm flows and related job flows are systematically connected to assess the strength of the link between firms and jobs and the net employment effects of spatial firm movements from and to industrial sites in a region. One of the main elements in this assessment procedure has dealt with the role of the relocation flow of firms (firms moving within the region of interest), and its implication for the nature of the employment effects (generative versus distributive). Moreover, we have put forward that special attention in the assessment is warranted for the choice of the spatial level of analysis and the impact of incumbent firms on regional employment dynamics.

To investigate this topic empirically, an application to the region of Amsterdam has been presented. First, an analysis of the demand-supply conditions on the market for industrial land has put forward that – given the estimated pace at which sites are brought into use and the strategic stock the municipality of Amsterdam prefers – there is enough supply to accommodate the expected demand for industrial land in the Amsterdam agglomeration. For Amsterdam-North in particular, the already developed, or spatially planned, sites appear to offer sufficient supply to cope for many years with the demand as revealed in the past years. It has therefore been concluded that firms that aim to move their plant to the Amsterdam-North area will not be hindered by a shortage of industrial sites.

Next, we considered the extent to which the developments in industrial sites allowed for firm growth (and potentially also job growth) in the Amsterdam-North region. We have used the flow-approach to estimate empirically the precise relationship between firm and job flows in the Amsterdam-North region (for the period 1989–93). By doing so we obtained the following insights. First, industrial site development in Amsterdam-North permitted an annual net growth of about 50 firms. Notably, this growth of firms occurred despite the fact that more firms moved out of the region than entered it. The relocation flow of firms appeared to be about twice as large as the net inflow of firms and about one-third of the mobility flow (during 1989–93). So, there was no lack of opportunities to relocate within the area and moreover, the location profile of the region was favourable for these firms. The net inflow of firms happened to be positively correlated with the net inflow of jobs: measured in a narrow sense (i.e. excluding the net growth of jobs in existing firms) we found an average net creation of six jobs per firm; measured in a broad sense (including this aforementioned component), this figure was 27% higher (7.6 jobs per firm on average). Further inspection of the firm movements (from and to Amsterdam-North) appeared to shed light on the generative and distributive components of the flows. When regarding flows within the Amsterdam agglomeration as distributive, it is found that 27% of the firm inflow and 38% of the job inflow is generative. About half of the outflow of firms moved out of the Amsterdam agglomeration (and took with it 42% of the job outflow). However, for the companies that left the Amsterdam-North region, there were other reasons than the supply of industrial sites that were decisive for their relocation decision. So, in summary, it seems that industrial sites in Amsterdam-North have not hindered spatial movements of firms and jobs within or into this region.

Acknowledgements

The authors wish to thank two anonymous referees for helpful comments on a previous version of this paper.

REFERENCES

ARMSTRONG. H. & J. TAYLOR (1993), *Region Economics and Policy*. Oxford: Allen.

B&A-GROEP (1997), *Vestigingsplaatsfactoren: Belar waardering en knelpunten*. The Hague: B&A-groe

BARTIK. T. (1991), *Who Benefits from State and Lo Economic Development Policies?* Kalamazoo: Upjoh Institute.

BCI (1997), *Locatiegedrag en ruimtegebruik van rece verhuisde bedrijven*. Nijmegen: Buck Consultan International (BCI).

BLAKELY. E.J. (1994), *Planning Local Economic Devel ment, Theory and Practice*. London: Sage Publication

BRUINSMA. F.R. (1994), *De invloed van transportinfr tructuur op ruimtelijke patronen van economische tiviteiten*. PhD thesis. Vrije Universiteit, Amsterdar

BRUINSMA. F.R., C. GORTER & P. NIJKAMP (1998 Nomadic Firms in a Globalizing Economy: Comparative Study. Tinbergen Institute Discu sion Paper. Tinbergen Institute, Amsterdam.

BRUINSMA. F., P. NIJKAMP & R. VREEKER (2000 *Spatial Planning of Industrial Sites in Europe: Benchmark Approach to Competitiveness Analys* Conference proceedings (CD-ROM), Region Science Association International, Port Elizabeth

CHAPMAN. K. & D.F. WALKER (1991), *Industri Location*. Oxford: Blackwell.

CPB (1998), *Een gebrekkige markt en een onvolmaak overheid*. The Hague: Sdu.

DOERINGER. P.B., D.G. TERKLA & G.C. TOPAKIA (1987), *Invisible Factors in Local Economic Develo ment*. Oxford: Oxford University Press.

DRO (1995), *Programma Ruimtelijke investeringe Amsterdam*. Amsterdam: DRO.

ELHORST. P., J. OOSTERHAVEN. F. SIJTSMA & D. STELDE (1999), Welfare Effects of Spatial Deconcer tration: A Scenario for the Netherlands. *Tijdschri voor Economische en Sociale Geografie* 90(2), pp. 17–31

FOLEY. P. (1990), Local Economic Policy and Jo Creation: A Review of Evaluation Studies. *Urba Studies* 29(3/4), pp. 557–598.

FOTHERGILL. S., S. MONK & M. PERRY (1987), *Proper and Industrial Development*. London: Hutchinson.

GORDIJN. H. & L. VAN WISSEN (1994), Demografi van bedrijven. *Planning* 43, pp. 31–43.

GROENENDIJK. J.G. (1990), Coordination of Urba Economic Development Policies in the Netherlands *Tijdschrift voor Economische en Sociale Geografi* 81(4), pp. 289–298.

HAMERMESH. D.S. (1993). *Labor Demand*. Princeton Princeton University Press.

ESSELS. M. (1994), Business Services in the Randstad Holland: Decentralization and Policy Implications. *Tijdschrift voor Economische en Sociale Geografie* 85(4), pp. 371–378.

MPER. N.J. & P.H. PELLENBARG (1995), Een vlucht uit de Randstad? *Economische Statistische Berichten* 80, pp. 465–469.

MPER. N.J. & P.H. PELLENBARG (1997), De Randstad een hogedrukpan. *Economisch Statistische Berichten* 82, pp. 508–512.

EYN. W.H. & J.M. DE VET (1994), Omgaan met schaarse ruimte: tussen plan en markt. *Economische Statistische Berichten* 79, pp. 1080–1084.

VK AMSTERDAM (1985–92), *Enquete Regionale bedrijfsontwikkeling*. Amsterdam: KvK Amsterdam.

AMBOOY. J.G. & W.J.J. MANSHANDEN (1992), De mythe van de grote stad als motor van de economie. *Economische Statistische Berichten* 77, pp. 1045–1049.

EESTER. W.J. (1999), *Subjectieve waardering van vestigingsplaatsen door ondernemers*. PhD thesis. Rijksuniversiteit Groningen, Groningen.

INISTRY OF ECONOMIC AFFAIRS (1994), *Ruimte voor Economische Activiteit*. The Hague: Ministry of Economic Affairs.

INISTRY OF ECONOMIC AFFAIRS (1997), *Ruimte voor Economische Dynamiek*. The Hague: Ministry of Economic Affairs.

ORGAN. K. (1997), The Learning Region: Institutions, Innovation and Regional Renewal. *Regional Studies* 31(5), pp. 491–503.

ORRISON. H. (1987), *The Regeneration of Local Economies*. Oxford: Clarendon Press.

EEDHAM. B. (1997), Land Policy in the Netherlands. *Tijdschrift voor Economische en Sociale Geografie* 88(3), pp. 291–296.

EEDHAM. B. & R. VERHAGE (1998), The Effects of Land Policy, Quantity and Quality is Important. *Urban Studies* 37(1), pp. 25–44.

EI (1997), *Ruimtelijke vestigingspatroon van stuwende bedrijven in Noordwest-Europa: trends en dynamiek*. Rotterdam: NEI.

IJKAMP. P. & J. POOT (1998), Spatial Perspectives on New Theories of Economic Growth. *Annals of Regional Science* 32(1), pp. 7–37.

O+S (1994), *Verschijnen. verschuiven en verdwijnen van werkgelegenheid in Amsterdam in de jaren 1989 t/m 1991*. Amsterdam: O+S.

O+S (1997), *Werkgelegenheidsmutaties in Amsterdam tussen 1989 en 1994*. Amsterdam: O+S.

OLDEN. H. (1995), Just in Time Productie van bedrijventerreinen. *In:* J. VAN DIJK & D.-J. KAMANN, eds., *Ruimte voor Regio's: Beleid en Werkelijkheid*. Groningen: Geo Pers.

PELLENBARG. P.H. (1985). *Bedrijfsrelokatie en ruimtelijke kognitie*. PhD thesis. Rijksuniversiteit Groningen, Groningen.

PELLENBARG. P.H. (1996). Structuur en ontwikkeling van bedrijfsmigratie in Nederland. *Planning* 48, pp. 22–32.

PORTER. M. (1990), *The Competitive Advantage of Nations*. New York: The Free Press.

RIETVELD. P. & F.R. BRUINSMA (1998), *Is Transport Infrastructure Effective? Transport Infrastructure, and Accessibility: Impacts on the Space Economy*. Berlin: Springer-Verlag.

STOREY. D.J. (1990), Evaluation of Policies and Measures to Create Local Employment. *Urban Studies* 27(5), pp. 669–684.

SUAREZ-VILLA. L. (1989), *The Evolution of Regional Economies*. New York: Preager.

TNO INRO (1997), *Economische Netwerken, determinanten van de ruimtelijk-economische dynamiek*. Delft: TNO Inro.

VAN BORK. G. (2000), De Grondmarkt: waar is de overheid niet aanwezig? *Rooilijn* 2, pp. 94–98.

VAN DER KNAAP. B. & W. SLEEGERS (1995), Regional Economic Development and Cohesion in North-West Europe. *Tijdschrift voor Economische en Sociale Geografie* 86(3), pp. 296-302.

VAN HAVEREN. E., D.B. NEEDHAM & F.W.M. BOEKEMA (1999), Ruimtegebruik door bedrijven. *Economische Statistische Berichten* 84, pp. 879–881.

WILLIS. K.G. (1985), Estimating the Benefits of Job Creation from Local Investment Subsidies. *Urban Studies* 22, pp. 163–177.

WOOD. B. & R. WILLIAMS (1992), The United Kingdom. *In: Industrial Property Markets in Western Europe*. London: E&F Spon.

PART IV

POLICY

RGAMON

Telecommunications Policy 26 (2002) 31–52

www.elsevier.com/locate/telpol

Information–communications technologies (ICT) and transport: does knowledge underpin policy?

Galit Cohen[a], Ilan Salomon[b,*], Peter Nijkamp[a]

[a] *Department of Spatial Economics, Free University of Amsterdam, The Netherlands*
[b] *Department of Geography, The Hebrew University of Jerusalem, 91905 Jerusalem, Israel*

Abstract

Cities around the world attempt to imitate the Silicon Valley model by adopting public policies aimed at attracting new high-tech industries and Research and Development activities. The adoption of Information and Communications Technologies (ICT) as elements in a public policy is based on the expectations of policy-makers regarding the potential to harness technology to ameliorate key urban problems such as a deteriorating environment, congestion or lack of communications between citizens and institutions. More specifically, policy-makers are exposed to knowledge about ICT, which is supplied by a variety of sources like scientists, popular media and their own experience. This paper argues that two gaps typify the flow of knowledge consumed by urban decision-makers: the knowledge gap, namely the uncertainty about the actual impacts of ICT on urban issues, and the communication gap which relates to the biases and noise emanating from the process of communicating knowledge between different actors on potential ICT impacts. The communications gap can, to a large extent, be explained by language and cultural differences between scientists and policy-makers. To illustrate and emphasise the gaps and their role in the ICT policy-making process, in this paper a comparison is made with the more familiar case of transportation policy making. © 2002 Elsevier Science Ltd. All rights reserved.

Keywords: ICT policy; Urban policy; Knowledge gap; Transport substitution

Introduction

Urban areas have historically evolved as activity centres which were initially based on physical locational advantages, such as proximity to natural resources or transportation nodes. Among other factors, the costs of distance played a major role in determining a city's position vis-à-vis its

*Corresponding author. Tel.: +972-2-882111; fax: +972-2-322545.

E-mail addresses: gcohen@econ.vu.nl (G. Cohen). msilans@mscc.huji.ac.il (I. Salomon). pnijkamp@econ.vu.nl (P. Nijkamp).

0308-5961/02/$ - see front matter © 2002 Elsevier Science Ltd. All rights reserved.
PII: S 0 3 0 8 - 5 9 6 1 (0 1) 0 0 0 5 2 - 0

surroundings, as well as its internal structure. The size of a city's hinterland was mainly defined b the quality of the transportation infrastructure and technology. Following the Industri Revolution in the 19th century, cities started an unprecedented growth phase as a result of sca economies, alongside accessibility and agglomeration economies.

Distance played a major role in the formation of cities and their internal structur Consequently, geographers and planners have paid much attention to technologies which affe the costs of traversing distance. The costs of distance include energy, time and money, as well a externalities, such as air pollution and noise. Transportation and telecommunications are th prominent 'friction reducing technologies', as both can reduce the costs of distance.

Transportation will continue to play a major role in the future, moving both people and good It is therefore no surprise that local, regional and national decision-makers, have recognised th importance of transportation, along with its costs, and have devised a range of transportatio policies in order to improve the position of their localities.

The dynamics of technological innovations in Information and Communications Technologie (ICT) over the last two or three decades and the consequent popularisation of these technologie have given rise to a growing body of research on the wide range of expected and desired impacts c ICT. Accompanying the rapid technological advances in ICT was an on-going transition into th 'information economy' in which information resources involve a growing share of the labour forc The combination of the two trends was moderated by an institutional change which has favoure competition in lieu of government ownership and operation of telecommunications systems.

Growing attention has been directed since the 1970s to the relationships between transport an ICT. As both technologies facilitate remote activities, there was much interest in the potenti substitution of tele-activities for physical travel (Boghani, Kimble, & Spencer, 1991; Garrison & Deakin, 1988). But, there are many more similarities and differences in these phenomena whic draw the attention not only of the scientific community. Just as the car has affected the shape o urban areas, there is an expectation that ICT will change cities. Horan and Jordan (1998) an Couclelis (2000), for example, have suggested integrating and incorporating transport plannin and ICT policy in urban policy, both being tools to enhance accessibility.

This paper focuses on the emerging public policy regarding transport and ICT. As transpo policy is used to improve the spatial-economic position of particular locations, similar attempts t exploit ICT are widely evident. Of the various aspects of public policy that should be addresse (e.g., agenda setting, problem definition, implementation etc.), we raise in the present paper som questions about the utilisation of scientific knowledge in the process.

We will argue that the public policy process, which is enacted in the discourse of bot transportation and ICT, 'suffers' from similar but not identical problems. Specifically, we wi claim that the knowledge upon which public policy decisions are (or should be) based, differ i two main aspects: a 'knowledge gap' and a 'communication gap'.

The motivation for this study is twofold. On the one hand, with the development of ICT there i a growing belief among officials that technology will remedy many urban problems. This is based to a great extent, on unchallenged assumptions. This paper takes a critical view of the proces through which (urban) decision-makers obtain and use knowledge about the potentia contribution of ICT to ameliorate urban problems. Beyond this rather practical goal lies a second objective that addresses a more general issue, namely how scientific knowledge, produce mostly by public funds, serves the decision-making process in society.

G. Cohen et al. / Telecommunications Policy 26 (2002) 31–52

The paper is organised as follows. Section 2 provides some background on ICT in general and ICT public policy in particular. Section 3 presents a conceptual model of the relationship between knowledge and policy-making, illustrating the process by which available knowledge in both transport and ICT is utilised in a policy-making structure. Section 4 dwells on the communications gap and the knowledge gap, while the conclusions and some tentative policy implications are discussed in Section 5.

Background

With the introduction of the 'knowledge' or 'information economy' during the second half of the 20th century, one is obliged to question whether this new era, with information and knowledge as important resources and with the world-wide introduction of ICT, will alter the 'old' rules of the 'transportation age'. If transport was the "maker and breaker of cities" (Clark, 1957), will ICTs inherit or share this role?

Several authors have labelled the current or forthcoming ICT-dependent developments as the "Information Revolution" or the "Information Age" (see e.g., Castells, 1996; Friedrichs, 1989). ICT has been identified (prematurely) as the cause for the 'Death of Distance' (The Economist, 1995). If the costs of distance are nullified, the whole notion of urban entities is likely to change. This view stands at the basis of many claims for radical changes expected in urban areas, at two different scales. On the one hand, the emergence of 'global cities', which serve a non-contiguous interlands scattered around the world (Castells and Hall, 1994), and on the other hand, the dispersion of the urban area due to the growth in the phenomenon of urbanites living and working in exurban settings (Lehman-Wilzig, 1981).

Clearly, the now completed transition into a service economy and further into an information economy[1] in the presence of ICT, has brought about a new pattern of competition between cities for positive growth (Alles & Esparaza, 1994; Graham, 1999). Such growth is defined in terms of rising economic performance (i.e. rising income or wealth per capita). In recent years, cities have also been competing in providing clean environments and high quality amenities, which are part of the welfare expected by their residents and by business life. In this respect, ICT may play a prominent role as a potential substitute for environmentally non-benign activities.

The inter-city competition is also evident through many statements and documents produced by urban governments and Non-Governmental Organisations (NGOs), which suggest that ICT can and will be an important policy tool to attract activities at a world-wide scale (Goddard, 1995; Graham 1992). Cities are increasingly operating as part of global networks attempting to gain from the competition with other cities in remote, worldwide markets.

The economic success of Silicon Valley in California during the 1980s is still a source of envy to many local decision-makers in the industrialised world.[2] Many have designed policies to replicate the success, but only a few have accomplished such objectives (e.g., Route 128 in the Boston area and route M4 in the UK). Analyses of some of the success and failure stories (see e.g., Saxenian,

---

[1] The Information Economy is one in which information assets play a major role in the economy, and a large share of the labor force is employed by ICT-based occupations. Usually, no quantitative figures are given.
[2] The "Siliconia" fashion is well represented in a web-site that has collected addresses of web-sites that are using the term Silicon outside the original Silicon Valley (http://www.tbtf.com/siliconia.html).

1983) have revealed that the outcome is only in part a result of the policy directed at implemented. Several other factors, including chance, appear to have a crucial effect as well. If s then one is obliged to question what makes some policies more successful than others, and wh other conditions must be met in order to improve the likelihood of success.

Public policies (and even more so, urban public polices) do not operate in a vacuum. Mc actions in complex systems like cities and accessibility, require a balanced approach which tak into consideration the common and the conflicting views of many stakeholders, each with his ov agenda. This is true for both transportation and ICT. In addition to various public agencies, t private sector accounts for important, yet different, developments in transport and IC Therefore, one should bear in mind the limited power of public policy and the crowded poli environment in which it is formed and implemented.

Transport and ICT, as noted above, display many similarities. One major difference, though, the fact that given the time gap in their respective introduction, they are being implemented in very dissimilar backgrounds. The century of motorised transport has had a prominent role in shaping the horse-drawn city into the metropolis of the present. ICT, on the other hand, introduced into an entrenched automobile-dependent city. The substitution of the horse by th automobile presents a clear case of technological substitution. ICT is far from being a perfe substitute for the car, and consequently, its effects on cities cannot be expected to mirror th change brought by the automobile.

Transportation is a mature technology and service system. Even though the uncertain involved in policy-making is still of significant magnitude, there is a sizeable body of knowledg addressing the issues of policy-making (e.g., Meyer & Miller, 1984; Altshuler, 1979; Dunn, 1994 Conversely, ICT is a young concept, and ICT policy-making is still in its infancy. Given th interactions between the two systems, a comparative perspective promises to explain some of th issues surrounding ICT and its emerging impacts.

The main hypotheses put forward in this paper are related to the process that leads to th formulation of public policy regarding ICT and transportation. It is suggested that there is *knowledge gap* in our current understanding of what impacts ICT and transportation have o urban areas. In addition, there is a *communications gap* between the actors involved in the proce that may result in unmet expectations. Such gaps generate and maintain uncertainty vis-à-vis th relationship between technology, society and urban systems. In view of the uncertainty involve it is important to question whether and how the gaps can be reduced to increase the likelihood successful accomplishments.

2.1. Defining ICT

In order to examine the role of (scientific) knowledge in ICT policy-making, there is a need t define ICT and ICT policies. Thus far, no clear and unambiguous agreement on the definition an measurement of the ICT sector has been generally accepted (for different definitions of ICT, se for example, Schwartz, 1990; Graham & Marvin, 1996; Malecki, 1991). At face value, ICT[3] is collection of technologies and applications which enable electronic processing, storing an transfer of information to a wide variety of users or clients. The ICT sector has become a popula

---

[3] Also labelled IT (Information Technology), NIT (New Information Technology) or telematics.

focal point of public policy because of its expected high economic benefits in an information age. However, the concept of ICT is somewhat dubious. Does an information technology that does not include a communications element still count as ICT? And does the information sector include also a broad array of "software" constituents such as research and development? We suggest therefore to adopt a flexible approach and to view all information or (tele) communications technologies as elements of the ICT sector.

Furthermore, we suggest that 'technologies should be interpreted in a broad sense. Technology, in general, and information technology in particular, is not merely a collection of hardware. Technology is a social construct (Salomon, 1998). This means that the use of the hardware is regulated, on the one hand, by the value it provides to the potential user and, on the other hand, by various rules and norms. Against this background it may be meaningful to offer some more characteristic features of ICT.

ICT is currently characterised by:

* very dynamic technological changes, with rapid penetration[4] and adoption rates;
* decreasing costs for new equipment and features;
* a rapidly increasing range of applications and penetration in many realms of professional and personal life;
* an intertwined institutional market place, with the private sector acting in a decreasingly regulated environment; and
* a production and services package dependent on a range of qualities of skilled human resources.

Against the background of the previous section and for the purpose of the current discussion, we define ICT as: *A family of electronic technologies and services used to process, store and disseminate information, facilitating the performance of information-related human activities, provided by, and serving the institutional and business sectors as well as the public-at-large.*

2.2. *ICT policy*

Defining the scope and nature of ICT-related policy is complicated by two factors. First, as seen in the definition above, ICT is a varied entity of both technologies and services. The perception of ICT by different actors is affecting the way that they perceive the role of policy intervention. Second, the general nature of public policy is quite ambiguous. Is policy the collection of activities of a government, or is it a statement of intention? Given that the definition of public policy is also open to discussion, it is evident that addressing the concept of public policy in the ICT area requires some clarification.

A policy can be regarded as a consolidated set of actions aimed at defined target achievement. The term "policy" relates to both processes and actions. While often viewed as an action of an institution, policy can also be manifested in a set of changes within the policy-making structure or merely as a declaration (Dror, 1989). The variety of public policy forms suggests that even in a specific field, there is more than one way to examine public policy, its implications and achievements.

---

[4] Penetration refers to the introduction of a technology into the household, office or factory. Adoption refers to the usage of that technology.

We define an ICT public policy as any public-sector action taken to advance the development of ICT or to promote their use by constituents for the benefit of society. An ICT policy may have one of two basic forms. In one form, ICT is identified as a policy objective or an end for itself. In this case, various policies can be devised to enhance the implementation of ICT through incentives such as tax breaks and even government support for infrastructure implementation or the provision of other incentives (e.g., fiscal policy, land use policy or educational policy) as instruments to achieve ICT development. The second form of policy views ICT as a vehicle to achieve higher-order goals for the city (such as a strong international profile). These two forms can be seen as a hierarchical system of goals and instruments.

Such policies may be focussed on *technical* aspects (e.g., upgrading the telephone system to a digital one). They may also be focussed on non-technical (e.g., instrumental) aspects such as the regulation of ICT to promote universal service or to enhance competition among suppliers; they may include indirect long-term actions as well, such as investments in vocational education in order to improve the quality of future human capital.

The wide diversity of activities which comprise an ICT policy calls for a systematic classification which, in turn, provides a possible explanation for the variety of ICT policies that can be observed in different places and times. The way decision-makers interpret and define ICT policies may affect their policies in this field. It is noteworthy that a European survey (in progress) is aimed at testing this hypothesis. Initial analysis suggests that actors (at the urban level) attach different importance or weights to varied ICT related policies and their potential consequences for urban goals.[5]

ICT-related public policies can be classified into three groups, on the basis of their strategic approach.

2.2.1. Direct policies

Direct policies are intended to promote the availability and use of ICT. Here, ICT development is considered to be the target of the policy. Although the policy aims to achieve broader goals (like economic growth or environmental protection), these goals are often vaguely defined and there are no acceptable sets of indicators to measure the effectiveness of the suggested policy in relation to such broad goals. The direct policies can be evaluated on the basis of measured levels of ICT infrastructure, usage and observed consequences (although the latter are difficult to measure in most cases). Direct policies also include measures taken to restructure (generally, deregulate) the ICT market, and supporting research on ICT. The case of developing ICT-based services, such as municipal Internet sites can also be considered as a direct policy. Yet another type of direct policies is the preparation and implementation of strategic ICT plans which aim at the development of a comprehensive ICT program for a city (see, for example, the proposal for strategic plan for Chicago discussed in Widmayer & Greenberg, 1999).

Another direct policy relates to the goal of equal access to information. Since information itself is an important resource, access (or lack of it) to information may create social gaps and may feed a circular process in which lack of access to ICT widens the income gap and creates additional

---

[5] The survey is conducted by the partners of the European project "TeleCityVision". It aims at comparing ICT policies in cities, their perceptions and background. Detailed findings of the project will be presented in a forthcoming paper.

rriers to the acquisition of ICT (Servon & Horrigan. 1997). Since access to ICT requires
th access to the technology and the ability to use it. such a policy can include both
ments.

The type of information needed to formulate and process direct ICT policies involves in most of
e cases ICT indicators such as those collected and disseminated by international agencies such
International Telecommunication Union (ITU), OECD or Eurostat. These are mostly at the
tional level and not at the local or regional levels. The relevant indicators include such details as
twork parameters, availability and use of ICT-based services and quality of services, tariffs,
venues and estimation of Internet subscribers and computers availability. etc. Unfortunately,
ese may be scattered among many different sources and often based on inconsistent definitions.
ypically. access to such data sources is held by certain agencies which employ professionals of
fferent backgrounds. The data may sometimes be legible and accessible only to particular
ofessionals like engineers, while in other cases it may be legible and accessible to economists,
anners or lawyers.

2.2. Indirect policies

Indirect policies are intended to attain non-ICT goals via the use of ICT. Examples of this type
policy are the use of ICT to disseminate information to the public via the Internet, the
omotion of desired behavioural changes, such as public transport patronage, the use of ICT in
e planning process to enhance public involvement, or adding computer classes to the curriculum
schools. Here, ICT is an instrument (in many cases, one of several) intended to accomplish pre-
efined. mostly social goals in an indirect manner. In such cases. the indicators to evaluate the
blicy are non-ICT impacts, and ICT is considered the "treatment" or part of it.

As ICT is, in this case, a tool to accomplish objectives in the social or economic arenas,
fferent information is expected to be used by policy-makers. Alongside technical knowledge
bout the available ICT tools, policy makers should have a sound basis for their expectations
garding the relationship between ICTs' impacts on the defined policy goals. This is in contrast to
e case of direct policies, which require only a vague picture of these relationships. On the other
and, given that in the case of indirect policies ICT is often one of a few measures being
nplemented to achieve such societal goals, it may be less important to identify the role
f individual policy components. For instance, an urban master plan for education may
clude. among other tools, tele-education program for disabled people. but it would need co-
peration among different experts and decision-makers as well as different types of data and
nowledge.

In many cases, there is no clear distinction between direct and indirect policies, and the division
epends on the context, the framing of the question or the researcher's views. When the discourse
more ICT-oriented and the emphasis is on ICT tools. a policy can be regarded more as a direct
olicy. Nevertheless, the same policy can be evaluated with non-ICT indicators when the viewer is
terested in the broader context. For example. one can investigate the performance of higher
ducation and also include ICT implications within this framework. where the ICT policy here is
direct and the policy evaluation should include both ICT and non-ICT indicators. On the other
and, one may investigate utilisation of ICT to facilitate education and to concentrate on. for
xample. remote education via ICT.

2.2.3. By the way policies

By the way policies (Dery, 1999) are unintended or incidental policy situations that typify t modern state in which there are a multitude of un-coordinated policies. Such "policy-ri environments' deserve attention because they constitute a familiar pattern of public poli processes. The concept of 'by the way' policy offers an important explanation for gaps betwe policy and reality, or in other words, for the failure of many policies.

ICT 'by the way' policies are products or residual effects of policies that are completely remc to ICT policy, and have diverse and unrelated objectives. Still, they are affecting both direct a indirect policies to an extent that justifies the definition of 'by the way' policy as such. F example, the defence industry in the USA was one of the main contributors to the development ICT, although its goals are not related to the civilian use of these technologies (Markusen, 198

In a 'policy rich' environment, the interaction between individual policy measures tends either cancel each other, or mutually support each other. Policy-makers in such environments m become 'policy takers' rather than makers (Dery, 1999).

The identification of the three types of policies, in which ICT is decreasingly a direct poli objective, is instrumental for the analysis of past and future policy analysis. More specifically, can help to distinguish among different policy-making (or -taking) processes regarding ICT, a to recognise varied data and information needs and types of experts needed.

2.3. Transport and ICT: a comparative context

The relationships between transport and telecommunications have drawn much attention ov the last two decades (Hepworth & Ducatel. 1992; Salomon 1986; Mokhtarian & Salomon, 200 There are several obvious reasons for this: both belong to a class of 'friction reduciu technologies', both have a network structure, and in some cases, there is a (much overstate potential for substitution between physical travel and virtual travel.

There are also several differences that should draw attention. The nature of virtual access vers physical access is the most prominent difference from the users' perspective. A number technical characteristics differ in important attributes. For example, the ability to conduct bo synchronic and a-synchronic communications, or the ability to convey different types information, has implications for the interactions between the two systems. Yet anoth important difference is the organizational structure and the role of private and public interests each of these systems.

The characteristics of transportation systems are better known to decision-makers, given tl exposure and visibility of rail and automobility over the last century. The process through whic knowledge is integrated in policy-making in the case of transport is reviewed in a previous pap (Salomon & Cohen, 1999; in other policy arena see Robinson, 1992). It suggested that electe decision-makers often abuse, misuse or ignore information, along with legitimate utilisation information. The use of information is influenced by the degree of uncertainty in the availab knowledge and by the communication flows between knowledge producers and users. The: knowledge and communication gaps are described in Section 4 below, emphasizing the differenc between transport and ICT.

G. Cohen et al. / Telecommunications Policy 26 (2002) 31–52

Incorporating knowledge in public policy: a communications model

Knowledge is here defined as the accumulation and synergy of information. which facilitates
oice or improves decisions. Knowledge which is required for a specific decision is not necessarily
.sed upon dedicated information related to it. It is also based on tacit knowledge, the use of
tuition and the experience of the decision-maker (Nonaka & Takechi, 1995). In our conceptual
odel, knowledge that is not a result of communicating with "knowledge suppliers", is defined as
e personal background of the decision-maker.

It is a widely accepted assumption that policies are designed with the expectation that they will
troduce change. This. in turn, is based on the assumption that policy-making is a rational
ocess based on knowledge accumulated in the policy-maker's cognition.

In an attempt to understand how policies evolve, we will focus on the communications process
rough which reality is transformed to information and then to knowledge, which in turn is part
' the input to decision-making.

Figs. 1 and 2 illustrate a schematic framework of this process. Decision-makers are exposed to
formation which is a partial and possibly biased representation of reality. This distinction is
.sed on the assumption that 'real world attributes' or 'facts' are always viewed through the eye of
e beholder. Hence. 'data' is a representation of 'facts' (and reality) but generally, cannot be
sumed to be identical to facts.

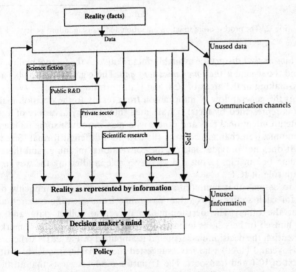

Fig. 1. From reality to policy: a communications process.

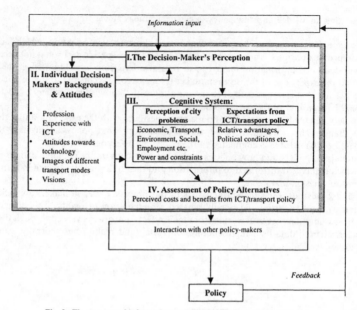

Fig. 2. The process of information utilisation and translation into policy.

There are two factors that distort the available data relative to the factual reality. The first is t̶ *knowledge gap* and the second is the *communications gap*. These gaps seem to play a major role explaining policy-making in the areas of ICT and transportation.

Fig. 1 illustrates the general flow of information from reality to the decision-makers cogniti̶ system. Reality (as represented by facts) is translated into data by a variety of agents. many whom incorporate an intentional bias and others who may introduce some unintentional erro̶ Each of the communication channels conveys the data in a different format. Science fiction is̶ unique channel. It does not provide 'data' in the conventional meaning (and therefore does n̶ originate in the data box in Fig. 1). but it does play a role in affecting the way in which peop̶ perceive the future role of ICT.

It is plausible to assume that users (information recipients) assign, implicitly or explicitly.̶ reliability value for each source. This value may range from scientific research at one end, science fiction at the other. The decision-maker may also collect data and process it 'information' by himself or herself, as indicated by the thick arrow in Fig. 1. marked as "self̶

The box representing the decision-makers mind is amplified in Fig. 2. Its structure builds up̶ Rosenberg and Hoveland (1960) who have suggested the Tripartite model of attitudes. appli̶ here to the context of ICT and transport. The Tripartite model suggests that attitudes which a̶ formed on the basis of stimuli, can be subdivided into three groups: Affective, Cognitive a̶

G. Cohen et al. / Telecommunications Policy 26 (2002) 31–52 41

ehavioural, corresponding to Blocks II, III and IV in Fig. 2. The emphasis on the individual ecision-maker should not imply that he or she is single-handedly formulating policy processes. he box 'Interactions with other policy-makers' in Fig. 2 refers to the other elements of the policy-aking process.

Information, actively sought or passively observed, penetrates through some filters (Block I in ig. 2) into the human mind and is integrated in a mental map[6] that includes numerous templates f sorted data that jointly constitute existing knowledge in a particular topic. Block II in Fig. 2 epresents the attitudes and accumulated background knowledge that the individual decision-aker holds. It is based on experience, previous studies and, to some extent, the beliefs he or she olds with respect to technology and 'vision'. These affect the screening by the filters and the ognitive system (Block I and III, respectively).

Two relevant templates of information can be assumed to exist in the policy-maker's mind: the erception of the city's problems and characteristics and the perception of expectations from ICT nd transport applications. Block IV represents the actions (assessment and decision on policy), /hich feed back as shown in Fig. 1.

Both the perception and the cognitive process are moderated by the individual decision-maker's ackground, depicted in Block II and III. More specifically, a number of elements are at play. The rofessional background serves as a filter which may screen out, or inversely, allow the inclusion f information which is pertinent to the person.

When a decision-maker is committed to a certain agenda or subject to political constraints, the ackground and cognitive components may affect the way he or she is open and willing to accept iformation and utilise it. Decision-makers tend to reject data which contradicts policy that they re unwilling to change (Dery, 1989). Past experience with ICT will also affect both the perception nd the tendency to adopt ICT policies. A more general view of (or attitude towards) technology hat may reside within a person will likewise affect his or her perception of the choice set. The ame can be applied to the image of different transport modes and the way the decision-maker erceives its effects and benefits. The extent to which the decision-maker holds a 'visionary view' f the city and the world may be relevant too, but very difficult to identify and measure.

However, we should keep in mind the limited role of science in the policy-making process. As Veiss puts it, science can serve as *"...a background of data, empirical generalizations and ideas that ffect the way that policy-makers think about problems. It influences their conceptualization of the ssues with which they deal...Often it helps them to make sense of what they have been doing after he fact...sometimes it makes them aware of the over-optimistic grandiosity of their objectives in ght of the meagerness of program resources. At timse it helps them reconsider the entire strategies f action for achieving wanted ends..."(Weiss, quoted in* Lindblom, 1990, p. 270*).*

The information input reaches the decision-maker through one or more channels of ommunications. These different channels are responsible for producing the communication nd knowledge gaps discussed in the next section. The quality of the information that the ecision-makers face depends on these two gaps. As we hypothesised that these gaps differ etween transportation and ICT, we suggest that consequently there are also differences in the uality and accuracy of the knowledge that serves as input in these policy-making processes.

---

[6] A mental map is representation of the real world, as it is registered, and possibly distorted, in a person's cognitive ystem.

4. The knowledge gap and the communications gap

The knowledge gap is defined as the mismatch between our ability to fully understand the entit that is labelled Reality and the box labelled Data in Fig. 1. The latter is a partial representation the real world complexity or reality. Reality consists of 'facts'. However, due to various factor we are confronted with data, which resemble facts, but are not full and accurate representatives facts.

As knowledge accumulates through the communication of tentative explanations about realit the communications gap relates to that part of the knowledge gap, which can be attributed miscommunications between the parties involved. The rational model of policy-making assume that decision-makers base their actions on knowledge (Simon, 1957; Dror, 1989). However, th notion of what constitutes knowledge is dubious. Certainly it is not just what the scientif community regards as legitimate knowledge. Knowledge is, as noted earlier, the accumulation information that facilitates decision-making or choice, marked as Box III in Fig. 2.

But knowledge is not a monolithic entity. The objective of identifying the rules which explai "reality", is often characterised by competing explanations for complex situations, whic emphasise the presence of uncertainty. This is particularly evident in the discourse about th relationship between technology and society at large, as well as between technology and variou interfaces with the individual's daily life.

4.1. The knowledge gap

When different and incongruent bodies of knowledge are presented to decision-makers, the may lose interest. As non-scientists they may be foreign to the mode of research, an consequently, they may fail to understand the differences in the relationship between researc assumptions and conclusions. Thus, they may judge research results as irrelevant. Keynes (cited i Sharpe, 1975) suggested that governments "hate to be well informed", as it complicates decisior making. Obviously, when the scientific community suggests more than one answer or predictio to a socio-economic problem, it leaves more space for accepting other views or other (perhar equally important) considerations. Hence, the concept of the "knowledge gap" involves th uncertainty and fragmented nature of our current knowledge of ICT's and transport's broa social and economic impacts.

4.1.1. Sources of uncertainty

We argue that at present, we still have a collection of fragmented elements of knowledge o both ICT and transport systems, although experience with and exposure to the latter has resulte in a better understanding of what can be accomplished with policy tools. Even less is known abou the interactions between the two systems. Our ability to forecast ICT impacts for urban areas, precondition for devising public policies, suffers from a knowledge gap. Whether ICT promote dispersal or centripetal forces is still a debated question. Various aspects of the relationship between ICT and its impacts still, and for some time to come, involve high levels of uncertainty

Uncertainty is an inherent attribute of forecasts. But, we argue that in the case of ICT, th knowledge gap belongs to a class of technology-society interactions that are more complex tha many other fields, or even other technologies. There are a number of reasons for this complexity rst, the *dynamic* technological developments of ICT curtail much of the forecasting ability. We il to know what tomorrow's IC technologies will be like in terms of their features, their costs or en their usefulness for different potential users (Crandall, 1997). This is further complicated by e fact that social and institutional processes, which are involved in the adoption and similation of ICT, operate at a very different pace compared to the pace of technological lvances. Furthermore, there are synergistic effects between social and technological developents which constrain the ability to explain and forecast cause and effect.

Second, with all the research aimed at understanding (and forecasting) the process of hnological penetration and adoption, *behavioural modelling* is still limited in its ability to oduce sound forecasts. ICT may be involved in many different facets of human life, like sidential patterns, work patterns, learning, leisure and shopping activities. At best, we can esently accomplish some partial forecasts for simple, single applications. However, the mplexity of the possible interactions is far from being understood. Methods developed to alyse Stated Preference[7] are promising but these too are still in their infancy and require further velopment to become practical tools.

There is another characteristic of ICT which makes it difficult to study in comparison to nsportation. While queues of congested traffic, accidents and even some pollution are very sible, ICT is largely *invisible* (Batty, 1990; Graham & Marvin, 1996). Neither the technological ments, nor the traffic upon them can be seen.[8] The lack of visibility is not just a result of the ysical nature of these systems. It also stems from the fact that much of the information nstituting the traffic on ICT is private in nature and not subject to measurement and public cess. Urban and transport planners have a long tradition of dedicated data gathering struments which facilitate the identification of present and future trends. This invisibility may ve a number of policy implications. The data needed for ICT policy-making does not lend itself similar collection instruments and there is no similar tradition of public access as in the case of nsport. Conversely, the absence of visual data can be seen, by the decision-makers, as an vantage, as it will enable them to make decisions without the "burden" of data and analysis at would be required when visible data is available. A lacuna of data enables decision-makers to ly more heavily on their "gut" feeling and "visions" when no other data are available.

The paucity of empirical research in this field, (as one possible consequence of the invisible ture of ICT) is another obstacle to the reduction of uncertainty. As a relatively young field, ICT search is often inductive in nature. There is still a lack of theoretical and conceptual work, giving e to speculations and anecdotes as suggestive theory. The field of ICT and its spatial impacts uld benefit much from contributions to the empirical testing of a wide diversity of hypotheses kinson, 1998).

Yet another factor that contributes to the relatively high level of uncertainty in ICT, as mpared to transport, is the lack of *institutional* data and knowledge. Much of the data is in the nds of the private sector, and as noted, is neither visible nor accessible. But, there is an ditional implication. It enables analyses which are based on inconsistent definitions, sumptions and measurement methods. The differences in the translation of reality into data

---

[7] Stated Preferences is an experimental technique used to model hypothetical choice behaviour when some alternative tions (e.g., new ICT) are not familiar to the respondent (Salomon, 2000).

[8] Some new techniques allow a visualisation of flow on ICT networks.

(see Fig. 2) is to a large extent a result of inconsistent assumptions adopted by the 'channel' translating the facts. Consider, for example, data about tele-workers (or telecommuters, in t American language). Entirely different estimates of the number (or share) of tele-workers featu in the literature, depending among others on the interest of the data supplier (Salomon, 199 Mokhtarian, 1991). One can estimate the number of tele-workers, based on a wide definitic which includes all those not working in a traditional workplace. This approach will include individuals whose work involves much travel, such as travelling agents and may use advanc mobile ICTs. Others, who define tele-workers as those using ICT and work at home, often do n distinguish between occasional tele-work and regular tele-work. Each approach, usir inconsistent definitions, leads to different conclusions about the extent of tele-work. In t present context, it implies that "Reality" (the real number of telecommuters on any particul day) is represented in the Data box by very diverse figures. Network statistics are anoth example. Even presumably simple estimation of the number of American people who surf on t Internet at a given point in time varies by as much as 58 million people, depending on t definition of Internet users and the methods employed (see http: www.thestandard.com/researc metrics). Since the private sector is very interested in the on-line behaviour of households ar firms, there are many private attempts to build data bases and offer (mostly not free of charge) variety of surveys and market research.

Two types of 'knowledge gaps' may be in effect. The first is the obvious case in which phenomenon is only partially understood, due to its complexity or novelty. As such, it is diffict for policy-makers to justify a policy regarding such a phenomenon. There is only one way reduce this type of gap: more research. The awareness of this gap exists mainly among members the research community, who naturally, aspire to reduce it. The second gap occurs when differe parts of the scientific knowledge are not integrated into a comprehensive body of knowledg When the available knowledge is spread among different disciplines, fragmented and eclectic, it of limited value, as it is primarily exposed to members of narrowly defined fields of knowledg

In summary, the current scientific knowledge of ICT's social, economic and spatial impacts still scarce and much of it is anecdotal. We still fail to explain, within an empirically support(theoretical framework, such issues as penetration pace, future costs, patterns of adoption, tl interactions with other technologies and with other socio-demographic, economic and cultur trends. An often cited and valid critique of forecasts is that present day forecasters tend to app incumbent norms and values, which may well be altered when today's children mature wi computer literacy as a second language (Warren, Warren, Nunn, & Warren, 1999).

The scientific community, of course, is not the only source of legitimate knowledge, especially the ICT field, in which the competitive environment encourages the private sector to play a maj(role in technological progress and promotion. Other sources of knowledge (e.g., promotion drive literary and journalistic stories) are substituting and complementing for science, as decisior makers adopt views that are presented to them by various types of experts. The scientif community does not have a monopoly on knowledge. At best, its 'monopoly' is limit(to the scientific method and the transparency of assumptions and models, and consequently it less likely to generate or support myths (Graham, 1997; Salomon, 1998). However, in tl case of ICT research, we suggest that the scientific community itself contributed to number myths, especially those which belong to the utopianism–futurism approaches (Graham & Marvi 1996).

Although roughly a century older, knowledge about transportation systems is also far from
ng comprehensive. The wide range of externalities, both positive and negative, still challenges
transport planning profession. The relationships between transport infrastructure investment,
nomic growth, advanced technologies and urban development are still puzzling researchers.
ile history provides us with evidence that relates transportation investments with urban (or
ional) growth, the policy implications are not straightforward. The impacts of an added
rastructure facility in an already developed system, may be of marginal importance for further
wth (Banister & Berechman, 2000). Much more needs to be understood before a
nprehensive transport policy can be devised and successfully implemented (Meyer & Miller,
4).

.2. Who are the "experts"?

Information intended for policy-makers is supplied by a variety of sources. It is noteworthy to
ntify and compare the type of expertise required to produce knowledge in the fields of ICT and
nsport, respectively. ICT carries a range of different meanings for both users and non-users.
r some, it is a set of technologies. For others, it may mean a set of services and still others may
w it as a tool for enhancing social cohesion of a community (or vice versa). The view one holds
ends very much on the discipline practised or acquired by the individual and the degree of
osure to other competing perspectives. It also depends very much on the basic perception of
d attitudes toward technology.
A variety of disciplines address ICT issues. Engineers and computer experts play a major role in
technological development and are generally less aware of the social and economic facets of
technologies they develop. On the other hand, social scientists in various fields (economics,
iology, geography, law, psychology, etc.) naturally tend to focus on those aspects in which
ir discipline reigns. Clearly, ICT-related interdisciplinary or multidisciplinary studies are still
atively rare. In many cases, the aspiration to engage in cross-disciplinary research falls short of
egration and synthesis and tends to remain at a point at which 'the other' perspective is
ognised at a very rudimentary level. Those who are concerned about urban and regional
velopment, find that telecommunications policy research usually contains very specialised
ups with just a few links to the implications of ICT on urban development (Goddard, 1995;
aham & Marvin, 1996). It is not clear yet (especially in the light of our definition of ICT policy)
o are the relevant experts to develop ICT policy and what is the appropriate balance between
different disciplines. As will be shown in the next section, communication problems play a
jor role in slowing multidisciplinary collaboration.
Transportation systems also embrace more than one discipline. As in the case of ICT, there are
erts on infrastructure, traffic and technology (mostly engineers) as well as economists,
graphers and urban planners who investigate the social effects of transport systems. However,
contrast to ICT planning, there is a considerable level of mutual recognition and growing co-
eration among the different groups, probably a result of the fact that transport systems are
ture.
Historically, three phases of transport policy can be discerned, and with each, a broadening of
scope of analyses and knowledge were introduced. Until the 1960s transportation policy
ant almost exclusively investment in infrastructure. It was devised through a mutual
derstanding of highway engineers and economists, who were captives of the belief that more

infrastructures will lead to less congestion and more development. During the 197
transportation systems management (TSM) emerged as a policy goal. During the 198
transportation demand management (TDM) surfaced as the new approach to address the ills
transport systems. This transition reflects the growing adjustments among the different facets
transportation systems and the necessity to combine different aspects of transport measures
order to achieve desired goals. Transport planning and policy-making are commonly associa
with certain professional backgrounds, which are established and institutionalized as such. I(
professionals, on the other hand, still lack the "professional label" that associates them with iss
of urban planning and public policy.[9] Their education and knowledge is considerably differ
from those dealing with transport. With ICT infrastructure being much less obtrusive to
environment and urban cohesion than the case of transport, there is less of a need to contain
engineers' actions.

4.2. The communications gap

The communications gap relates to situations where the transmission of information betwe
two agents involves a distortion of the content, due to problems stemming from the transmissi
process itself. Two factors seem to explain much of the communications gap: Language a
culture. Before explaining these, we briefly describe the existing channels which are used
communicate data to policy makers.

4.2.1. Who are the decision-makers?

Although it is easy (from a methodological point of view) to distinguish between politicia
who are the decision-makers, and bureaucrats, in charge of policy implementation, in reality b
are making decisions and formulating policies (Lipsky 1978; Lindblom & Woodhouse 199
Thus, we are considering both elected politicians and administrative staff as decision-make
However, it is clear that these two groups of decision-makers are not identical. Elected politici
tend to deal with broader policy issues than most of the administrative professionals. Thus, t
need more "external" input than the professionals in charge. Naturally, the type and level
information would vary in those cases, as well as the choice of communication channe
Moreover, it is more likely that the administrative decision-makers would have a relev
education or professional background than the politician. But again here the problem of "who
the experts?" (Section 4.1.2) holds also here and suggests that professional decision-makers hav
fragmented knowledge and expertise regarding ICT.

4.2.2. Channels of communication

Much of the knowledge gap that falls between "reality" and "information" in Fig. 1, is a res
of the limited understanding of the complex phenomenon of introducing a new technology i
society. The complexity, as noted earlier, is due to the diverse interactions between technologi
elements, human adoption and regulation patterns. The rapid technological developments le
the research and analyses well behind. This is true for the new ICT, but also partly true for so
mature elements of transportation systems.

---

[9] One area of ICT public policy, which did receive much attention, is the industry structure and issues of regulat

Communications channels are characterised by certain inherent noise levels, which lead to loss accuracy in transmission. This is particularly true when the channels are human beings that are ble to introduce different types of bias. The scientist, on the one extreme, tends to use nfriendly" data through scientific reports and articles. On the other extreme, we can find vertisement material, which often excels in the use of visual demonstrations, buzzwords and an sy-to-grasp logic. Between these extremes lie scientific policy-oriented reports, executive nmaries, journalistic writings, reports by interest groups (for profit and non-profit) and popular dia. In the case of ICT, contrasting the more mature case of transport, science fiction literature y also be regarded as an information channel.

Scientific knowledge is not the only data source for decision-makers. Hence, a priori its tential to affect them is limited. It is one of a series of sources, to each of which the user assigns ne subjective evaluation in terms of validity and reliability. However, even when the scientific annel is dominant, we argue that the immanent differences between the scientific world and the licy-making arena add more difficulties to the communications among the different groups. We ggest that the communications gaps arise from two main intertwined factors: language and lture. The basic argument is that decision-makers, in particular elected politicians, act in an vironment which is quite divorced from that used by scientists, in particular those who serve in ademic (as opposed to Research & Development) institutions.

.3. Language differences

Different groups in society adopt languages or jargon which best serve their needs, but will en result in communication problems in inter-groups context. Nowhere is this more evident an in the case of scientists and politicians. The 'language' barrier can be attributed to the lowing issues: Dealing with *uncertainty* is the bread and butter of scientific forecasting, and as ch is embedded in a series of *assumptions* which are integral qualifiers of any forecast. recasting future passenger kilometres, the demand for rail service or the number of tele-work casions, are all provided with a set of assumptions and they are subject to corrections when the sumptions are violated. Some of the assumptions that are integrated in any forecast may be ntroversial, and the forecast users should be aware of them. While scientific practice questions ese assumptions as part of the scientific process, decision-makers are often foreign to the notion limiting assumptions and tend to ignore them. Politicians expect science to deliver unqualified recasts and often they have a problem dealing with qualifying assumptions.

Technical terms often create a communications gap. Decision-makers are not always sufficiently owledgeable in the technical concepts and jargon. Consequently, they may perceive a concept in ry different ways from the meaning intended by the scientist or the professional. In the case of T, the technical terms and variety of technologies are still not widely adopted. Consider the ms used by transportation professionals, many of which have become part of the common guage, like congestion, travel time or delay. The parallel terms of ICT have yet to be recognised d adopted. 'Ehrlangs', 'noise-to-signal ratio', ' broadband broadcast' serve as some examples. The use of *metaphors* is another problematic issue. The language which describes new hnologies is often relying on concepts with which the audience is more familiar. The ICT arena blessed with an exceptional amount of metaphors. We find that the more the subject under cussion is hidden and invisible, the more we need metaphors as a bridge to understand concepts. Hence, we are talking about 'information superhighways' that are connecting

48 G. Cohen et al. / Telecommunications Policy 26 (2002) 31-52

'tele-cottages' in 'wireless neighbourhoods and 'intelligent environments'. The gateways to su 'virtual cities' are the 'teleports'. Such metaphors are useful for introducing new concepts with requiring a deep understanding of them. Still, some caution should be exercised in an uncriti use of metaphors, since they can be misleading. The case of teleports illustrates the point. If size and centrality of an airport or a seaport earned the relative positioning of a city in industrial age, it follows, according to some viewers, that a teleport is a necessity in information age, as the information age port. Some cities adopted this concept, promoted amc others, by the World Teleport Association. We speculate that the adoption of a teleport conc made sense to decision-makers, who had unknowingly, suffered from a knowledge gap. ICTs h evolved in directions which relied on technologies that have rendered teleport no advantage t Nevertheless, for a while at least, some cities could market their position as information-age cit given the availability of a teleport.

The *time gap* between a scientific innovation and its introduction and dissemination are als contributing factor to the knowledge and communication gaps. It is often the case that years by between the innovation, which may even make some headlines, and the time its offspri technology is introduced to the market place. Policy-makers often operate with an election-te clock, and expect solutions to be implemented within an election term. By contrast, progress science and consequent innovations are made available in the marketplace on a very differe temporal pattern. Policy questions which generate research may produce answers long after politicians are gone or have lost interest. This time gap between the production of knowledge a the urgency of obtaining answers results in making non-scientific channels more attractive policy-makers. The private sector is indeed a major supplier of optimistic information in su contexts.

4.2.4. Cultural differences

The organisational culture of institutions or academic disciplines provides further explanat for the disparity between scientists (professionals) and policy-makers. Perhaps the most evid underlying cultural factor is the fact that academics generally are educated to take a *scepti perspective* on knowledge, whereas policy-makers are educated to think in an *action-orien* mode. This explains why scientists tend to emphasise limiting assumptions, while politicians pre an assumption-free statement about *facts*.

Another related cultural factor is the degree of social commitment that each part carries. In ideal world, scientists are committed to increasing knowledge and are motivated by curiosity, a not by a commitment to solve social problems. Political decision-makers, on the other hand, h a social commitment, and scientific understanding is not their prime objective. The so commitment emphasises the need to act even when the uncertainty is high. Scientists would pre to continue the investigation to reduce the uncertainty thereby delaying the action.

Assuming that both scientists and decision-makers are rational players, the rationale may be identical, as it may be guided by different criteria.[10] Scientists often tend to be quite naive w regard to how knowledge and rational arguments should affect the way in which the real wo

---

[10] Rational choice, according to Manski (1995) is one in which "each member of the population orders alternative terms of preference and chooses the most preferred alternative among those available"(p. 88). As preference may d among politicians and scientists, they may still be rational.

erates, while politicians gain a completely different understanding of what makes the real
rld. Hence, criteria that are highly important to the scientist can be irrelevant to the decision-
ker and vice versa. This gap often rests in an emphasis of the seemingly irrelevance of the ivory
vers. Occasionally, this gap gives rise to a legitimisation of ignorance and a de-legitimisation of
demic research.

Vision, in contrast to *rational thinking*, is another cultural difference. Scientists are often
med, by politicians and others, for a lack of vision. Vision is a view of a desired future, which is
t a product of a rational analysis-planning procedure. By contrast, it is a product of a
alitative synthesis, driven more by intuition (and wishful thinking) than by scientific tools.
litical elected officials are sometimes able to define and advance certain visions, which may be
ful in the political domain. This does not mean that the politicians are wrong or the scientists
right, but it is certainly a source of cultural tension.

The discourses of both transport and ICT policies suffer from the same problems regarding
tural differences. These differences are inherent in the relationships of science and policy and
d to characterise most (if not all) policy areas. Cultural differences are, of course, not divorced
m language gaps. Languages tend to be affected by culture.

Policy implications

The future impacts of ICT on the city depend on a variety of background social and economic
nds, actions and technological developments. One of them is ICT urban policy. In order to
derstand different ICT policies employed in different cities and among different public actors,
s paper examined the role of scientific knowledge in the process of decision-making and offered
conceptual framework explaining the process. Although the knowledge and communications
ps are not unique to the ICT case, we claim that the ICT discourse suffers from relatively wide
owledge and communication gaps.

The wide definition of ICT policies used in this paper supplies one possible explanation
the variations in ICT-related policies. It seems that there is no unified agreement
out the contents of ICT policies and their operational definitions. Since the formulation
policies depends, among others, on the perception of the possible action/policies in
field, different perceptions of the nature of ICT policies (and, in particular, urban
licies) would lead to widely diverging policies. While one decision-maker limits his or her
tions to ICT infrastructure-related policies or tele-services to the community, another
n expand the declared ICT policy aimed at high-tech education and programs for
xible offices. Even though two cities can have the similar policies, each may frame it in a
ferent context. Hence, when we want to compare different cities with regards to their ICT
licy, much attention should be given to the development of a set of definitions and
easurement tools.

There is wide agreement among scientists that ICT will have important implications for society
large, and for the city in particular. However, the tools to accomplish desired goals or to
derstand the possible impacts are less clear, i.e., the 'knowledge gap'. When science cannot
liver concrete useable knowledge, it is not surprising to find decision-makers who resort to

50   *G. Cohen et al. / Telecommunications Policy 26 (2002) 31–52*

alternative channels of knowledge acquisition and who may be misusing available scien[t] knowledge.

The comparison between ICT and transport can shed some light on the nature of the I discourse. In contrast to transport policies, ICT policies do not (yet) play an important role public debate. While transport-related political comments (and criticism) are frequently hea[r] ICT related commentary appears to be less critical in nature. ICT policy, at present, faces [l] scrutiny and criticism. but also entertains less public support. Moreover, in many cases responsibility for ICT is perceived to rest with the private sector. implying a less activist pu[b] policy.

Both transport and ICT systems are potentially space-shaping systems. While transport system leaves physical footprints (roads, airports or rail lines). the spatial impacts ICT are more anticipated than observed. However, the popular hypothesis that sugge[st] substitution of travel by ICT assumes that the geographical impacts are in fact occurri[ng] but are not quite as visible as those of transport. The "invisible" ICT-based activities are pected to substitute for travel with all its negative externalities. Consequently, it is a[s] assumed that in the absence of direct environmental externalities. ICT can be develo[ped] and promoted without government intervention, and be properly managed by the private sec[tor] That, of course, results in a very different public and professional discourse in transport and ICT.

Vision has an important role in ICT policy. Alongside the accumulated knowledge (transfer via the different channels), the image of the future city and the connotations one has of "information society" influence the formulation of policies. Where the "vision" is dominat[e] there is less room for "dry" knowledge. As Melody puts it, *"so far. the preparation of informa[tion] society statements has not been a costly proposition. However, if and when these 'visions' l[ead] countries to make major commitments of resources and/or adopt fundamental changes in pu[blic] policies, they will become extremely important"* (Melody, 1996, p. 244).

The growing penetration and popular adoption of ICT give rise to wide and dive[rse] expectations and policies geared to affect economic and social systems. A clear example is popular belief in the substitution of travel. which at present, cannot be supported by hard d[ata] (Salomon, 1998). The knowledge gap and the communications gap stand at the basis of s[uch] expectations. The knowledge gap exists since the research community has yet to identify conditions which lead to substitution or complementary relationships between transport a[nd] telecommunications technology. Yet, much of the discourse on the subject is nurtured by vari[ous] parties which generate the communication gap by building hopes on the basis of anecdotal a[nd] wishful thinking, ambiguity with regard to concise definitions and concluding generalisati[ons] without testing basic (but doubtful) assumptions.

One important conclusion with regard to the practical implication of this paper, is desirability of educating professionals and decision-makers in communication. While this sou[nds] like a very simple and trivial conclusion, this paper has shed light on the specific importance of 'cross-cultural' discourse and on the importance of reducing the knowledge gap. Although communication and knowledge gaps exists in many (if not all) policy areas. the emerging field ICT and its social and spatial implications tends to amplify these gaps. As a relatively young fie[ld] the need to develop communications tools sit alongside the necessity to develop research a[nd] policy tools.

ferences

es, P., & Esparaza, A. (1994). Telecommunications and large city-small city divide: Evidence from Indiana cities. *Professional Geographer*, 46(3). 307–316.
shuler, A. (1979). *The urban transportation system: Politics and policy innovation.* Cambridge. MA: The MIT press.
kinson, R. D. (1998). Technological changes and cities. *Cityscape: A Journal of Policy Development and Research.* 3(3), 129–170. http://www.huduser.org/publications/periodicals/cityscpe/index.html).
nister, D., & Berechman, Y. (2000). *Transport investments and economic development,* London: UCL press.
ity, M. (1990). Invisible cities. *Environment and Planning B*, 17(1). 127–130.
ghani, A., Kimble, E., & Spencer. E. (1991). *Can telecommunications help solve america's transportation problems?.* Cambridge, MA: Arthur D. Little.
stells, M. (1996). *The rise of the network society.* Oxford: Blackwell Publishers.
stells, M., & Hall, P. (1994). *Technopolies of the world: The making of 21st century industrial complex.* London: Routledge.
rk, C. (1957). Transport: Maker and breaker of cities. *Town Planning Review*, 28, 237–00250.
uclelis, H. (2000). From sustainable transportation to sustainable accessibility: Can we avoid a new 'tragedy of the commons'? In D. Janelle, & D. Hodge (Eds.), *Information, place and cyberspace: Issues in accessibility.* Berlin: Springer.
ndall, R. W. (1997). Are telecommunications facilities infrastructure? If they are, so what? *Regional Science and Urban Economics*, 27(2). 161–179.
ry, D. (1989). *Data and policy change.* Dordrecht: Kluwer Academic Publishers.
ry, D. (1999). Policy by the way: When policy is incidental to making other policies. *Journal of Public Policy. 18*(2). 163–176.
or, Y. (1989). *Public policymaking re-examined* (2nd edition). New Brunswick, NJ: Transaction Publishers.
nn, J. A. (1994). Transportation policy. In S. Nagel (Ed.), *Encyclopedia of policy studies.* Illinois: Marcel Dekker.
edrichs, J. (1993). The information revolution and urban life. *Journal of Urban affairs, 11*(4). 327–337.
rrison, W., & Deakin, E. (1988). Travel, work, and telecommunications: A long view of the electronic revolution and its potential impacts. *Transportation Research, 22A*(4), 2246–2390.
ddard, J. B. (1995). Information and communications technologies. corporate hierarchies and urban hierarchies in the new Europe. In J. Broychie. M. Batty, E. Blakely, P. Hall, & P. Newton (Eds.). *Cities in competition: Productive and sustainable cities for The 21st century* (pp. 127–138). Australia: Longman.
aham, S. D. (1992). Electronic infrastructures in the city: Some emerging municipal policy roles in the UK. *Urban Studies, 29*. 755–781.
aham, S. (1997). Telecommunications and the future of cities: Debunking the myths. *Cities. 14*(1). 21–29.
aham, S. (1999). Global grids of glass-on global cities, telecommunications and planetary networks. *Urban Studies. 36*(5-6), 929–949.
aham, S., & Marvin, S. (1996). *Telecommunications and the city. Electronic spaces, urban places.* London: Routledge.
oworth, M., & Ducatel, K. (1992). *Transport in the information age: Wheels and wires.* London: Belhaven.
ran, T. A., & Jordan, D. R. (1998). Integrating transportation and telecommunications planning in Santa Monica. *Journal of Urban Technology. 5*(2). 1–20.
aman-Wilzig, S. (1981). Will cities become obsolete? *Telecommunications Policy, 5.* 326–328.
dblom, C. H. (1990). *Inquiry and change: The troubled attempt to understand and shape society.* New Haven. Conn: Yale University Press.
dblom, C. E., & Woodhouse. E. J. (1993). *The policy making process.* Englewood Cliffs, New-Jersey: Prentice Hall.
sky, M. (1978). Standing the study of public policy implementation on its head. In W. D. Burnham. & M. W. Weinberg (Eds.), *American policy and public policy.* Cambridge, MA: MIT press.
lecki, E. J. (1991). *Technology and economic development.* New York: Longman Scientific and Technical.
nski, C. (1995). *Identification problems in the social sciences.* Cambridge, MA: Harvard University Press.
rkusen, A. (1988). *Regions: The economics and politics of territory.* Totawa, NJ: Rowman & Littlefield.
lody, W. H. (1996). Towards a framework for designing information society policies. *Telecommunication Policy. 20*(4). 243–259.

Meyer, M. D., & Miller, G. J. (1984). *Urban transportation planning. A decision-oriented approach*. New York: McG Hill Book Company.

Mokhtarian, P. (1991). Telecommuting and travel: State of the practice, state of the art. *Transportation, 18*(4), 319–

Mokhtarian, P., & Salomon, I., (2001). How derived is the demand for travel some conceptual and measuren consideration. *Transportation Research A, 35*(8), 695–719.

Nonaka, I., & Takechi, H. (1995). *The knowledge-creating company*. Oxford: Oxford University press.

Robinson, J. B. (1992). Of Maps and territories: The use and abuse of socioeconomic modeling in support of decis making. *Technological Forecasting and Social Change, 42*, 147–164.

Rosenberg, M. J., & Hoveland, C. I. (1960). Cognitive, affective and behavioural components of attitude. *Organisation and change: An analysis of consistency among attitude components* (pp. 1–14). New Haven: University Press.

Salomon, I. (1986). Telecommunications and travel relationships: A review. *Transportation Research A, 20A*(3), 2 238.

Salomon, I. (1998). Technological change and social forecasting: The case of telecommuting as a travel substit *Transportation Research Part C, 6*, 17–45.

Salomon, I. (2000). Can telecommunications help solve transportation problems? In D. Hensher, & K. Button (E *Handbook of transportation modelling*. Amsterdam: Pergamon Press.

Salomon, I., & Cohen, G. (1999). The use. abuse, misuse and disuse of scientific knowledge in transportation plann *Presented at the fifth NECTAR Meeting*. Delft, October.

Saxenian. A. (1983). The urban contradictions of Silicon Valley. *International Journal of Urban and Regional Resea 7*(2). 237–261.

Schwartz. G. G. (1990). Telecommunications and economic development policy. *Economic Development Quarterl* 83–91.

Servon. L. J., & Horrigan, J. B. (1997). Urban poverty and access to information technology: A role for l government. *Journal of Urban Technology, 4*(3), 61–81.

Sharpe. L. J. (1975). Social scientists and policy making. *Policy and Politics, 4*(4), 3–27.

Simon. H. A. (1957). *Models of man: Social and rational*. New York: John Wiley.

The Economist, 1995. The death of distance. September 24, 1995.

Warren. R., Warren. S., Nunn, S., & Warren, C. (1999). The future of the future in planning: Appropriating cyberp visions of the city. *Journal of Planning Education and Research, 18*(1), 49–60.

Widmayer, P., & Greenberg. G. 1999. The digital network infrastructure and metropolitan Chicago. Putting our m together. Notrhwestern University (http://www.metropolanning.org).

[16]

OUTLOOK ON EUROPE

A COMPARATIVE INDUSTRIAL PROFILE ANALYSIS OF URBAN REGIONS IN WESTERN EUROPE: AN APPLICATION OF ROUGH SET CLASSIFICATION

FRANK BRUINSMA, PETER NIJKAMP & RON VREEKER

Department of Spatial Economics, Vrije Universiteit, De Boelelaan 1105, 1081 HV Amsterdam, The Netherlands. E-mail: fbruinsma@feweb.vu.nl

Received: January 2002

ABSTRACT

This paper analyses the locational suitability of industrial sites in five urban regions in Western Europe for five classes of economic activity. In the selected regions a total of 46 industrial sites and office locations were visited and judged on their suitability for each of the five classes of economic activity. Given the small sample size and the qualitative nature of the information collected, conventional statistical tools could not be applied, and rough set analysis was used. This proved to be a useful tool in identifying the major driving forces in the relative competitive position of the European regions. The study shows that the regions are not competitors in all aspects, but have their own individual geographic-economic specialisations.

Key words: Urban industrial profiles, rough set analysis, Western Europe

THE NEED FOR INDUSTRIAL PROFILE ANALYSIS

It has been rather fashionable in the post-war period to adopt a linear evolutionary view on economic development, characterised by a structural transition from a rural economy to an industrial economy, followed by a shift to a service economy and next an information and knowledge economy. The so-called deindustrialisation hypothesis (Bluestone & Harrison 1982) has highlighted these trends and suggested that in a modern economy the most profitable economic activities are to be found in the service sectors. But it has often been neglected that in a world with rising GNP and material welfare, physical products have to be made in even larger volumes. They can be outsourced to remote production locations, but the consumption of material goods is still on a rising scale. Trade in physical goods is still rising, but may also cause high transport and environmental costs (Van Veen-Groot & Nijkamp 2001). Furthermore, countries with advanced service and information economies may be able to use the competitive advantages of these sectors to build a new industrial edifice that is efficient and also environmentally friendly. As a consequence, in recent years we have witnessed a renewed interest in so-called reindustrialisation strategies, through which regions and cities aim to reinforce their industrial-economic base with the help of the modern ICT sector. Regions and cities seem to start a new wave of industrial policy.

Several industrial regions in Europe are competing with each other in order to attract

Tijdschrift voor Economische en Sociale Geografie – 2002, Vol. 93, No. 4, pp. 454–463.
© 2002 by the Royal Dutch Geographical Society KNAG
Published by Blackwell Publishers, 108 Cowley Road, Oxford OX4 1JF, UK and 350 Main Street, Malden MA 02148, USA

the most favourable international firms. A major determining factor is of course the attractiveness of the site, which is not only contingent on the geographical location, but also on a broad spectrum of additional factors, such as links to knowledge centres, accessibility, efficiency in planning procedures, attributes of local policy-makers, availability of public amenities and subsidies. For any regional government it is of paramount importance to have proper insight into the competitive profile of its own region relative to that of other regions. A systematic profile analysis can identify the weak and strong elements of the area under consideration. Seen from this perspective, a taxonomy of competitive profiles of different regions may bring to light the most pronounced factors for policy support.

This paper aims to offer a methodology and empirical results on industrial profile analysis applied to a set of potentially mutually competing regions in Western Europe. This study was initiated by the Dutch Ministry of Economic Affairs, and served to create a framework for mapping out the strong and weak elements of various important regions in this area relative to the Dutch industrial profile. This task required intensive fieldwork based on available statistics, expert opinion and site visits. The indicators used were often not measured in quantitative terms, so that a major part of the study comprises a qualitative industrial profile analysis with the aim of positioning the Dutch Randstad against possible important competitors in the relevant Western-European region.

The paper is organised as follows. In the next section the study design and the data collection process is concisely described. Given the small sample size of the regions considered and the qualitative nature of the information collected, conventional statistical tools cannot be applied, and as a consequence the authors used recent analysis tools developed in the field of artificial intelligence, in particular rough set analysis. This method is briefly introduced in the third section. The next section is devoted to a description of the data base and of the results of the rough set analysis. The final section offers some policy conclusions.

AIMS AND SCOPE OF THE COMPARATIVE INDUSTRIAL PROFILE ANALYSIS

In recent years we have seen an increased interest in the new role of regions in a dynamic and often globalising business environment. Regions have become multi-faceted economic, social, cultural and environmental systems making up an organic assembly of multiple interacting subsystems and they exhibit complex evolutionary patterns in which growth and decline are in turn present (Kohno *et al.* 2000).

There is also a tendency to emphasise the new role of the region as the creator of a portfolio of locational opportunities. The main question is, of course, whether sufficient and effective governance strategies – in both the public and the private sector – can be developed that guarantee a solid and sustainable regional development. European regions are increasingly losing the protection provided by national borders. Vanishing borders mean the opening of regional economies to new networks and new social and economic influences, introducing particularly an increased competition between regions. The emphasis in this study will be on a strategic comparison – by way of a benchmark – of the potential performances of industrial and office sites and of spatial planning procedures in European regions. Regions are in fierce competition in attracting foreign – European, US and Asian – investors. The supply of infrastructure, including industrial sites and office locations, is one of the remaining opportunities in the common European market through which countries can compete. Differences in spatial planning procedures and in strategies in the countries concerned may strongly affect the supply – both quantitatively and qualitatively – of industrial sites and office locations.

The paper aims to offer a systematic, comparative inventory of industrial sites and office locations in various European regions in terms of their locational suitability for one or more of the following five classes of economic activities:

1. Chemical industry.
2. Distribution and value added logistics (VAL)

ble 1. *Inspected sites and their suitability for the selected economic activities.*

egion	Number of sites inspected	Suitable for the following economic activities:				
		Chemical industry	Distribution & VAL	Assembly & production	High-tech industry	European headquarters
ussels-Antwerp-Ghent	14	6	10	4	6	2
reater Copenhagen	5	3	3	2	1	1
orthrhine Westfalia	7	2	5	1	1	0
e-de-France	11	6	6	3	8	4
andstad	9	2	4	3	2	2

Assembly and production requiring a multi-modal terminal.
High-tech industry.
European headquarters of corporate companies.

learly, more and different activity sectors uld have been distinguished, but from the erspective of Dutch economic policy and ainport strategies these five sectors may be garded as the most relevant.

In our comparison five major core regions ith a promising potential on the Northwestern European mainland have been selected or further study: Brussels-Antwerp-Ghent Belgium), Greater Copenhagen (Denmark), e-de-France (France), Northrhine Westfalia Germany), and Randstad (The Netherlands).

In the selected regions a total of 46 idustrial sites and office locations have been ispected (Table 1). All sites were judged on heir suitability for each of the above listed five conomic activities. On the basis of extensive eldwork, among others the following information for each site was collected:

Size of the site, percentage of directly available land for grants, and planned site extensions.
Price (minimum/maximum) and rent.
Accessibility by road, rail, waterways and public traffic, and the presence of an intermodal terminal.
Representativeness (image) of the site and the buildings.
Availability of governmental subsidies.
Greenfield or brownfield development.

A number of remarks are in order here before presenting the results of the fieldwork. First, since we are interested in the suitability of individual sites for specific economic activities, it is important to note that here the price of land is assumed to act as a supply attractiveness factor: in the case of individual sites, the lower the land price the easier it is to attract (foreign) companies. Clearly, the selection of inspected sites is too limited to guarantee an entire representativeness for all sites in each region and for all selected economic activities. Nevertheless, this approach is warranted as this particular choice has been supported and validated by using regional expert panels.

A first – qualitative – analysis based on the information collected in the exploratory stage of the research led to some initial general conclusions. All sites in all regions are easily accessible by car. In Randstad the sites are also relatively accessible by waterways, while the sites in Brussels-Antwerp-Ghent are relatively well connected to multi-modal terminals. The representativeness of sites and buildings hardly differs between the regions considered. Between the types of activities, notable differences are observed: obviously the sites and buildings for office activities are most representative. By investigating the size of the sites, the percentage of land directly available for grants and the planned extensions for the five economic activities, some interesting regional differences were found during the empirical research. Overall, Ile-de-France appears to perform very well, Northrhine Westfalia scores near average, and Brussels-Antwerp-Ghent scores slightly below average on most aspects for most activities. The scores of Randstad are most diverse and Greater Copenhagen is a negatively scoring out-layer. Given these

2002 by the Royal Dutch Geographical Society KNAG

results, Greater Copenhagen does not seem to be an important player in the Northwestern European economic force field. The strong and weak location factors are in a qualitative sense concisely summarised in Table 2.

The information on the strong and weak competitive elements in each of the regions under consideration is qualitative in nature, and by no means crisp. Consequently, standard

parametric statistical tools cannot be deploye to analyse these data. In order to avoid ; intuitive or subjective interpretation of tl data base on industrial profiles in Europ a suitable technique appropriate for sm; sample qualitative data is necessary. Rece advances in artificial intelligence have prove that such – deterministic – methods do exi through which taxonomic statements on sc

Table 2. *Relative strong and weak location factors for economic activities of European regions (average scores are r presented).*

	Brussels-Antwerp-Ghent	Northrhine Westfalia	Ile-de-France	Randstad	Greater Copenhage
Chemical industry	*Strong* Access by car *Weak* % granted*	*Strong* Subsidy Land price	*Strong* Access by car % planned**	*Strong* Access by water Size sites *Weak* Representative-ness	Strong % granted* *Weak* Size sites
Distribution & VAL	*Strong* Multi-modal Land price *Weak* % granted*	*Strong* % planned** Subsidy *Weak* Access by rail Multi-modal	*Strong* Access by car Land price	*Strong* Access by rail Size sites *Weak* Land price	*Strong* % granted* *Weak* Access by ca Multi-modal
Assembly & production	*Strong* Multi-modal *Weak* Access by water % granted*	*Strong* Multi-modal % planned** Subsidy	*Strong* Access by car Access by rail Representative-ness	*Strong* Access by rail Size sites *Weak* Multi-modal	*Strong* % granted* *Weak* Land price
High-tech industry	*Weak* % granted*	*Strong* Representative-ness Subsidy *Weak* Access by car	*Strong* Size sites % planned** *Weak* % granted*	*Weak* Size sites Land price	*Strong* % granted* *Weak* Access by ca Size sites
European headquarters	*Strong* Representative-ness	*Weak* Access by car & public transport % granted*	*Strong* Rental price % planned** Size buildings	*Strong* % granted* *Weak* Rental price	*Weak* Access by ca & public transport Size buildings

* % granted is the percentage of the sites directly available for grants.
** % planned are the planned site extensions.
Source: BCI/VU 1999.

FRANK BRUINSMA, PETER NIJKAMP & RON VREEKER

rmation can be inferred. Rough set
lysis is able to cope with these problems,
ong as the information of each variable is
ernally consistently classified. Before pre-
ting the results of the rough set analysis
he details of the rough set approach are
en in the next section.

E OF QUALITATIVE ANALYTICAL
THODS: ROUGH SET THEORY

e results in Table 2 and their interpretation
based on a qualitative judgement of the
dings of the authors' field work. There is,
wever, a need to provide more solid, robust
dings on which regional policy can be
veloped. As mentioned before, it is necess-
to apply less intuitive and more rigorous
thods that are able to deal with hard –
antitative – and soft – qualitative – infor-
tion.
There is a variety of explanatory methods
qualitative or categorically defined phen-
ena, such as dummy variable methods,
it analysis, fuzzy set analysis and so forth.
r the present problem of comparing quali-
ive case study results, rough set analysis is a
rticularly appropriate method.
Rough set analysis is essentially a decision
pport tool from operations research, which
es to formulate decision rules of an 'if-then'
ture (Pawlak 1991; Slowinski 1995). Here
offered a concise introduction to rough set
eory (for further details see Van den Bergh
al. 1997; Matarazzo & Nijkamp 1997;
aijens & Nijkamp 2000; Button & Nijkamp
97).
A rough set is a set for which it is uncertain
advance which objects belong precisely to
at set, although it is in principle possible to
entify all objects that belong to the set at
nd. Rough set theory takes for granted the
istence of a finite set of objects for which
me information is known in terms of factual
ualitative or numerical) knowledge on a class
attributes (features, characteristics). These
tributes may be used to define *equivalence*
lationships for these objects, so that an ob-
rver can classify objects into distinct equiva-
nce classes. Objects in the same equivalence
ass are, on the basis of these features
ncerned, *indiscernible*. In case of multiple

attributes, each attribute is associated with a
different equivalence relationship. The intersection of multiple equivalence relationships
is called the indiscernibility relationship with
respect to the attributes concerned. This
intersection generates a family of equivalence
classes that is a more precise classification of
the objects than that based on a single equivalence relationship. The family of equivalence
classes generated by the intersection of all
equivalence relationships is called the family
of elementary sets. The classification of objects
as given by the elementary sets is the most
precise classification possible, on the basis of
the available information.
Next, is introduced the concept of a *reduct.*
A reduct is a subset of the set of all attributes
with the following characteristic: adding another attribute to a reduct does not lead to
a more accurate classification of objects (i.e.
more granules), while elimination of an
attribute from a reduct does lead to a less
accurate classification of objects (i.e. less
granules).
Finally, the *core* of a set is the class of all
indispensable equivalence relationships. An
attribute is indispensable if the classification
of the objects becomes less precise when that
attribute is not taken into account (given the
fact that all attributes have been considered
until then). The core may be an empty set and
is, in general, not a reduct. An indispensable
element occurs in all reducts. The core is
essentially the intersection of all reducts.
Based on the previous concepts, rough set
theory is now able to specify various decision
rules of an 'if-then' nature. For specifying
decision rules, it is useful to represent our
prior knowledge on reality by means of an
information table. An information table is a
matrix that contains the values of the attributes of all objects. In an information table
the attributes may be partitioned into *condition*
(background) and *decision* (response) attributes. A *decision rule* is then an implication
relationship between the description of the
condition attributes and that of a decision
attribute. Such a rule may be exact or approximate. A rule is exact if the combination of the
values of the condition attributes in that rule
implies only one single combination of the
values of the decision attributes, while an

INDUSTRIAL PROFILE ANALYSIS OF URBAN REGIONS IN WESTERN EUROPE

approximate rule only states that more than one combination of values of the decision attributes corresponds to the same values of the condition attributes. Decision rules may thus be expressed as conditional statements ('if-then').

In practice, it is possible to use both decision rules implied by the data contained in the information table and, if necessary, in further rules supplied and suggested by experts. The former may be accompanied by an indicator of their 'strength', for example the frequency (absolute or relative) of events in agreement with each decision rule. Moreover, both the former and the latter rules may be based on suitable and different sets of condition attributes, containing a larger or smaller number of attributes (even a single attribute). This latter case implies that the value assumed by an attribute is sufficient to guarantee that the decision attribute (or attributes) will assume certain values whatever the values of the other condition attributes.

Decision rules, which constitute the most relevant aspects of rough set analysis, may be directly applied to problems of *multi-attribute sorting*, that is, in the assignment of each potential object (action, project, alternative, etc.) to an appropriate predefined category according to a particular selection criterion. In this case, the classification of a new object may be usefully undertaken by a comparison between its description (reflected in the values of the condition attributes) and the values contained in the decision rules. These are more general than the information contained in the original information table and also permit a classification of new objects more easily than would be possible by using a direct comparison between the new and the original

objects. In general, decision rules in rou set analysis allow the creation of conditio transferable inferences, as the 'if' conditi specify the initial conditions, while the 'th inference statements highlight the logical v conclusions for cases outside of the initial of objects. In this way, rough set analysis also be used as a tool for conditional trans ability of results from a case study to a r situation.

In this paper's case study, the central qu tion is the identification of the strong – even decisive – elements that contribute t major extent to the competitive position of European regions considered. Given the s information base, the above described meth is suitable *par excellence* for the identification the relative position of these regions by way a qualitative benchmark approach.

RESULTS OF ROUGH SET ANALYSIS

Application of rough set analysis – In c comparative industrial profile study the pendent variable is the suitability of a site the selected economic activities. In Table the suitability of the inspected 46 sites for combinations of – economic activities described and classified, based on field formation. The rough set analysis then tr to explain the suitability of the sites by independent variables, as classified in Table

The rough set analysis generates decisi rules that show how combinations of values independent variables lead to a unique val of the dependent variable. For instance, i site has a surface of 0–50 ha and has a mu modal terminal connection, then it is alway site suitable for distribution and VAL activiti None of the other classified dependent varia

Table 3. *Classification of sites by their suitability for economic activities.*

1	At least three economic activities (excluding European headquarters)	9
2	Chemical industry; distribution & VAL	5
3	Distribution & VAL: assembly & production	6
4	Chemical industry; high-tech activities	3
5	Chemical industry	3
6	Distribution & VAL	5
7	High-tech activities	5
8	European headquarters	10

FRANK BRUINSMA, PETER NIJKAMP & RON VREEKER

ble 4. *Classification of the independent variables.*

riable	Class 1	Class 2	Class 3	Class 4	Class 5
e site	<50 ha	50–100 ha	100–200 ha	>200 ha	
granted	<25%	25–50%	50–75%	>75%	
planned	0	1–100%	>100%		
nd price	<50 Dfl	50–100 Dfl	100–200 Dfl	>200 Dfl	
ccessibility by car	<=8	8 < x <=9	>9		
ccessibility by public transport	<=8	8 < x <=9	>9		
ılti-modal terminal	Yes	No			
presentativeness	<=8	8 < x <=9	>9		
bsidy	Yes	No			
eenfield/brownfield	Greenfield	Brownfield			
gion	Brussels-Antwerp-Ghent	Ile-de-France	Northrhine Westfalia	Randstad	Copenhagen

lues can be explained by those two values of e independent variables. Of course, there ay be more decision rules that explain why edicated sites are suitable for distribution ad VAL activities. Although only eight types site are classified, the model appears to enerate 34 decision rules.

Based on these 34 decision rules (which will ot be reproduced here), rough set analysis eks to identify the minimal set of decision iles that explains all variation in the depen-ent variable (the classification of sites). From iese minimal sets, the importance of the idependent variables can be distilled. If an idependent variable shows up in all minimal its, it means that the classification of sites

cannot be explained without this variable. Such a variable is – as mentioned above – called a core variable. Table 5 shows that in the data set considered there are 12 minimal sets, while Table 6 shows that variables 1 (size of the site) and 7 (multi-modal terminal connection) are the only two core variables in the empirical application. The finding that the variable 'multi-modal terminal connection' is a core variable, comes as no surprise: only a few economic activities (distribution & VAL and assembly & production) will use multi-modal terminals.

A European benchmark – Since the analysis aims to develop a European benchmark of

Table 5. *Minimal sets.*

{1,4,6,7,9,10,11}	{1,4,5,7,8,11}	{1,3,4,6,7,10,11}	{1,2,4,5,7,8}
{1,2,5,7,8,9,11}	{1,3,4,7,8,9,10,11}	{1,2,4,6,7,8,9,10}	{1,2,3,4,7,8,10}
{1,2,3,7,8,9,10,11}	{1,4,5,6,7,11}	{1,2,3,5,7,8,9}	{1,2,4,5,6,7}

able 6. *Frequency of the independent variable in the minimal sets.*

Size site	12	7	Multi-modal terminal	12
% granted	7	8	Representativeness	8
% planned	5	9	Subsidy	5
Land price	9	10	Greenfield/brownfield	6
Accessibility by car	6	11	Region	7
Accessibility by public transport	5			

Table 7. *Frequency of the regional variable in the decision rules.*

1	At least three economic activities (excluding European headquarters)	0
2	Chemical industry; distribution & VAL	3
3	Distribution & VAL; assembly & production	5
4	Chemical industry; high-tech activities	0
5	Chemical industry	0
6	Distribution & VAL	0
7	High-tech activities	4
8	European headquarters	0

industrial sites and office locations, the role of the region as one of the explanatory variables is crucial. Therefore, the individual decision rules need to be analysed. In 12 of the 34 decision rules, the region plays a role. Table 7 shows the relation between the classification of sites and the region as an explanatory variable. The region where the site is located is important for three types of sites: chemical industry/distribution & VAL; distribution & VAL/assembly & production; and high-tech. It is important to note that apparently for the region where the sites are located there is not much difference between the selected regions for the other five classes of economic activities. This implies, for instance, that the suitability of a site to locate European headquarters is not specifically dependent on the region where the site is located.

This study – using a benchmark approach – is most interested in the classes of sites suitable for combinations of economic activities where the region is a differentiating factor. These classes are discussed below.

Chemical industry, and distribution & VAL
Sites suitable for chemical industry in combination with distribution & VAL activities are different in three regions: Brussels-Antwerp-Ghent, Greater Copenhagen and Northrhine Westfalia. In all three regions these sites lack planned extensions and the price of land is relatively low (50–100 Dfl). The differences between the three regions are explained by the different sizes of the sites. The smallest sites are located in Greater Copenhagen (0–50 ha), the sites in Brussels-Antwerp-Ghent are one category larger (50–100 ha) and the sites in Northrhine Westfalia are the largest (100–200 ha). Furthermore, the sites in Northrhine

Westfalia are suitable for chemical industry i combination with distribution & VAL activitie are relatively poorly accessible by car.

Distribution & VAL, and assembly & production
The rough set model appears to generate fiv decision rules with a regional factor tha differentiate for sites suitable for distributio & VAL, and assembly & production activitie All five decision rules have a poor accessibili by public transport and a location near multi-modal terminal in common. These tw factors are enough to select sites suitable fo distribution & VAL and assembly & produc tion activities in Ile-de-France and Greate Copenhagen. For Northrhine Westfalia an Brussels-Antwerp-Ghent an additional facto concerns the size of the sites: the sites shoul be larger then 200 ha. However, the fina decision rule also concerns Brussels-Antwerp Ghent, and in this rule the site should b relatively small (50–100 ha), but some exten sions are planned. In other words: in Brussels Antwerp-Ghent sites suitable for distributio & VAL and assembly & production activitie are either large or small (with some planne extensions); however, they have a poor accessi bility by public transport and a location near multi-modal terminal in common.

High-tech
Three out of four of the decision rules gen erated for sites suitable for high-tech activities have in common a small site (0–50 ha) and a lack of planned extensions. This concerns sites in the regions: Randstad, Northrhine Westfalia and Greater Copenhagen. North rhine Westfalia and Greater Copenhagen have an additional characteristic: over 50% of the sites are available for grants.

Brussels-Antwerp-Ghent is the subject of the fourth decision rule. In this region sites suitable for high-tech activities are relatively large (100–200 ha), between 25% and 50% is not yet occupied, nevertheless extensions are planned. Finally, the sites are relatively accessible by car.

METHODOLOGICAL AND POLICY PERSPECTIVES

The specific classification method used in this paper – rough set analysis, appears to be a fruitful tool for identifying the major driving forces in the relative competitive position of European regions. Its strength is the ability to use soft information in small sample contexts. Having identified the relative importance of attributes of industrial sites in Europe, a next step might be to use the results as an input for a subsequent multi-criteria evaluation approach. This would be a possibility for future research.

The results obtained from the comparative industrial profile analysis are illuminating. There is a great diversity in terms of competitive potential among all Northwestern European regions investigated. From a global perspective, these regions may be regarded as mutual competitors. A closer look shows that although the regions have overlapping competitive domains, they are not competitors in all aspects. Apparently, some geographic-economic specialisation – in terms of the supply of different facilities by the industrial sites under investigation – has taken place.

Are the above findings of importance for policy development, in particular for Dutch national and regional governments? Only for one economic activity – the high-tech industry – the Randstad area has a different stock of sites: their surface is small and they lack planned extensions. Compared with direct neighbouring areas, i.e. Northrhine Westfalia and Brussels-Antwerp-Ghent, the situation in Northrhine Westfalia is identical; however, those sites are more attractive for foreign investors due to the available grants. The supply of sites in Randstad seriously lags behind the supply of sites in Brussels-Antwerp-Ghent, where there is still a large share of easily accessible sites available for direct occupancy by foreign investors.

In principle, it is a political rather than scientific choice to decide whether it pays off to make huge efforts to invest in the development of sites suitable for the high-tech industry in Randstad. Complementary and supporting economic tools such as cost-benefit analysis might support such a decision.

In general, the total supply of industrial sites and office locations does show significant differences in the selected regions on the Northwestern European mainland. Only Greater Copenhagen – as a minor player in the European economic field – structurally lags behind in the supply. All regions compete on global markets and are able to attract investors from the same pool. But in the course of history, each of these regions has specialised in different portfolios of economic activities.

Acknowledgements

This paper is partly based on a study funded by the Dutch Ministry of Economic Affairs. As part of the Competitiveness Report 2000 (Ministry of Economic Affairs, 1999), Buck Consultants International and the Department of Spatial Economics of the Free University examined spatial planning procedures and the supply of industrial sites and office locations in a European benchmark study (BCI/VU 1999). In addition to the benchmark of core regions as presented here, the study also included a benchmark of corridor regions. The authors wish to thank Wim Pijpers, Paul Volleman and Dion Sluijsmans for their contributions to the study, and the Ministry of Economic Affairs for its financial support of the project.

REFERENCES

BAAIJENS, S. & P. NIJKAMP (2000), Meta-Analytic Methods for Exploratory and Explanatory Research. *Journal of Policy Modeling*, 22, pp. 821–858.

BCI/VU (1999), *Internationale Benchmark Bedrijventerreinen, Kantorenlocaties en Ruimtelijke Ordening.* Nijmegen: Buck Consultants International.

BLUESTONE, B. & B. HARRISON (1982), *The Deindustrialization of America: Plant Closings.* New York: Basic books.

BUTTON, K. & P. Nijkamp (1997), Environmental Policy Assessment and the Usefulness of Meta-Analysis. *Socio-Economic Planning Sciences* 31, pp. 231–240.

INDUSTRIAL PROFILE ANALYSIS OF URBAN REGIONS IN WESTERN EUROPE

KOHNO, H., P. NIJKAMP & J. POOT. eds., (2000), *Regional Development in a Globalizing World.* Cheltenham: Edward Elgar.

MATARAZZO, B. & P. NIJKAMP (1997), Methodological Complexity in the Use of Meta-Analysis for Empirical Environmental Case Studies. *Journal of Social Economics* 34, pp. 799–811.

MINISTRY OF ECONOMIC AFFAIRS (1999), *Toets op het Concurrentievermogen 2000.* The Hague: Ministry of Economic Affairs.

PAWLAK, Z. (1991), *Rough Sets.* Dordrecht: Kluwer

SLOWINSKI, R. (1995), *Intelligent Decision Supp* Dordrecht: Kluwer.

VAN DEN BERGH, J.C.J.M., K. BUTTON, P. NIJKAMP G. PEPPING (1997), *Meta-Analysis in Environme Economics.* Dordrecht Kluwer.

VAN VEEN-GROOT, D. & P. NIJKAMP (2001), Glo ization, International Transport and the Glo Environment. *International Journal of Sustain Transport.* 3, pp. 344–357.

[17]

Urban Studies, Vol. 35, No. 9, 1481–1500, 1998

A Meta-analytical Evaluation of Sustainable City Initiatives

Peter Nijkamp and Gerard Pepping

Paper first received, May 1997; in final form, October 1997]

Summary. The role of the city in environmental management is increasingly coming to the fore. A central element in creating urban environmental sustainability is the adoption of appropriate energy policies, since most environmental externalities in cities are directly or indirectly related to energy use. The current practice demonstrates an overwhelming variety of initiatives and policies, so that the actual success of such strategies in a cross-sectional comparative perspective is hard to evaluate. In this context, this paper offers an application of meta-analysis, as this approach is an interesting analytical contribution towards a better understanding of the critical success factors of urban energy policies. The paper starts with a general overview of the issue of urban sustainability and sets out the importance of energy policies at the urban level. It continues by offering a methodological framework for the assessment of critical factors related to the performance of sustainable energy strategies. Using a database containing information on experiences and expert expectations regarding renewable energy initiatives in 12 European cities spread over 3 countries (Italy, The Netherlands and Greece), we offer a cross-European comparative analysis of the performance of urban renewable energy technologies. This comparative analysis consists of a statistical explanation based on a probit analysis of urban sustainability data and the application of a specific meta-analytical method, called rough set analysis. The paper ends with a concluding section on policy lessons.

1. Introduction

Sustainable development has become one of the touchstones of urban policy in recent years. Consequently, the notion of the 'sustainable city' has gained much popularity in many countries (see, for example, Nijkamp and Perrels, 1994; Haughton and Hunter, 1994; Selman, 1996). There is at present considerable analytical and political interest in the conditions needed for a successful sustainable city. The urban focus of the sustainability debate is largely caused by the

fact that (large) cities are the major consumers of natural resources and the major producers of pollution and waste (see Girardet, 1992). Furthermore, the sphere of influence of a city extends far beyond its own territory, so that cities are sometimes regarded as islands of opportunities in seas of decay (see van Geenhuizen and Nijkamp, 1995). A currently vogue term in this context is that of the 'ecological footprint', which refers to the fact that the environmental bur-

Peter Nijkamp and Gerard Pepping are in the Department of Regional Economics, The Free University, De Boelelaan 1105, 1081 HV Amsterdam, The Netherlands. Fax: 31-20-4446004. E-mail: pnijkamp@econ.vu.nl (Peter Nijkamp) gpepping@econ.vu.nl (Gerard Pepping).

den of a city—through use of scarce inputs and through pollution emissions—may have a formidable geographical coverage. Thus, the environmental carrying capacity of a city would have to be placed in a much wider setting (see Rees, 1992; Wackernagel and Rees, 1996).

A central element in creating urban environmental sustainability is the adoption of appropriate energy policies, since most environmental externalities in cities are directly or indirectly related to energy use. Many cities have in recent years developed sustainable city strategies. Current practices demonstrate an overwhelming variety of initiatives and policies, so that the actual success of such strategies in a cross-sectional comparative perspective is hard to evaluate. In this context, meta-analysis may offer a contribution towards a better understanding of the critical success factors of urban sustainability policies (see van den Bergh *et al.*, 1997). Meta-analysis serves to synthesise research findings from previous studies or to formulate transferable policy conclusions from previous policy experiences.

The focus of this paper is on energy use, with particular emphasis on the role played by renewable energy in cities as a key element in achieving sustainable urban development. Renewable energy policies comprise a wide spectrum of options ranging from solar, thermal or wind energy to photovoltaic (PV) energy systems and combined heat and power (CHP) applications. Renewable energy provision may offer a significant contribution to the improvement of local or regional environmental quality conditions. As a result, new policy initiatives focusing on the intricate relationship between renewable energy alternatives and local sustainability conditions are no doubt warranted.

Clearly, the role of renewable energy differs for different cities in different geographical locations. Several cities have been remarkably successful in some respects (for example, Odense, Mannheim), but others are lagging behind (see for an overview Nijkamp and Perrels, 1994). This paper offers an explorative research effort that aims to identify

the factors that are important with regard to the development of sustainable energy policies in cities. In this context, it provides methodology for evaluating energy policies at the urban level, based on a set of critical success factors derived from the so-called Pentagon model. This methodology is used in an explanatory statistical analysis, followed by a qualitative rough set analysis for categorical data, to examine whether there are significant factors contributing to the rate of success of sustainable energy technologies in a range of European cities. The empirical part will focus in particular on Dutch, Italian and Greek urban sustainability initiatives.

The paper is organised as follows. Section 2 starts with a general overview of the issue of urban sustainability. Subsequently, section 3 sets out the importance of energy policies at the urban level, followed by a concise sketch of sustainable energy policies. In section 4, a methodological framework is provided for the assessment of critical factors related to the performance of sustainable energy strategies. In section 5, we offer the empirical context for a cross-European comparative analysis of the performance of renewable energy technologies, while we make a plea for meta-analysis as a proper tool for drawing policy-relevant lessons from various sustainability experiences. Then we proceed with a statistical explanation based on a probit analysis of urban sustainability data (section 6). Section 7 contains a short introduction to the specific meta-analytical method used, called rough set analysis, and offers also the results of the application of the rough set analysis. Finally, the paper ends with a concluding section on policy lessons.

In our empirical study, we will be facing the problem that cities have only recently recognised the need to monitor energy use and related environmental consequences. In addition, impact studies of renewable energy policies hardly exist and there is no common methodological approach for assessing these impacts. The meta-analysis presented in this paper has therefore an exploratory character. We will, *inter alia*, make use of expert opinions on the performance of various energy

d environmental technologies in several
European cities. This forms a contrast with
conventional meta-analytical studies that
make use of different empirically based im-
act studies of the same phenomenon. Nevertheless, the results may be of great interest
for sustainable city initiatives.

**Sustainability as a Trade Mark of Euro-
ean Cities**

The role of the locality in environmental
management is increasingly coming to the
fore. And in recent years, the interest in
urban environmental issues has risen to an
unprecedented degree. This awareness has
also been induced by various policy initiatives. For example, the Commission of the
European Communities (CEC) launched its
Greenbook on the Urban Environment
1990), the Organization for Economic Co-
operation and Development (OECD) published its report on *Environmental Policies
for Cities in the 1990s* (1990), while many
other institutions (international, national, regional and local) followed this new wave of
interest in urban environmental research
projects, preparing urban quality of life programmes and the like. Various new concepts
were advocated, such as the 'green city', the
'eco-city', the 'eco-polis', the 'zero-emission
city', the 'liveable city', the 'resourceful
city' and the 'environmental city'. Nowadays, there is apparently a broad concern
about the sustainable future of our cities. In
the spirit of the Rio Conference, a broad
array of local initiatives on environmental
quality has emerged, known as the Local
Agenda 21 (see Selman, 1996; and Whittaker, 1995).

Especially in the European context, the
reinforced focus on the city seems warranted,
as the European countries (especially those
in the EU) are facing a stage of dramatic
restructuring and transition as a consequence
of the move towards the completion of the
internal market. However, the aim to make
Europe—and its cities—internationally more
competitive in economic terms may be at
odds with its environmental sustainability. In

the long history of Europe, numerous cities
with an extremely valuable and vulnerable
socio-cultural heritage have emerged which
deserve strict protection in the interest of
current and future generations. Therefore,
what Europe is facing nowadays is a problem
of ecologically sustainable urban development.

Sustainable development has of course a
global dimension, but it is also increasingly
recognised that there is close mutual interaction between local and global processes: cities are open systems impacting on all other
areas and on the earth as a whole, and *vice
versa*. Therefore, the urban focus for
analysing sustainability is certainly warranted. Sustainability in an urban setting describes the potential of a city to reach a new
level of socioeconomic, demographic, environmental and technological performance
which in the long run reinforces the foundations of the urban system itself. Thus urban
sustainability ensures a long-term continuity
of the urban system. It has to be added that in
an open spatial system cross-boundary flows
and external development stimuli may play
an important role: non-sustainability may
even be imported or exported (as witnessed
in the notion of 'ecological footprint' alluded
to above). In any case, the emphasis on the
environmental potential of the city may enhance our insight into the feasibility of sustainability objectives formulated at a given
institutional policy level. In summary, sustainable cities are cities where socioeconomic interests are brought together in
harmony (co-evolution) with environmental
and energy concerns in order to ensure continuity in change.

A situation of non-sustainability of a city
would imply a structural decline of the economic base of a city (reflected, *inter alia*, in
population decline, environmental degra-
dation, inefficient energy systems, loss of employment, emigration of industries and
services, and unbalanced socio-demographic
composition). Environmental decay is usually
one of the first signs of non-sustainability.

Cities certainly qualify as focal points for
sustainability research and planning, as they

play a decisive role as nodal points for people and their activities. In many cases, they also face the most severe environmental problems, such as air and water pollution, noise, waste, declining quality of urban life and destruction of urban landscapes and architecture. This also explains the current heightened public awareness and concern about the quality of the urban environment (including concern for public health). The broad nature of urban sustainability suggests also that urban policies aiming to achieve sustainable development should be strategic in nature, integrative, visionary regarding the role of the private sector, focused on the provision of market incentives, and more oriented towards the needs of citizens.

The question whether a given urban development is sustainable or not is co-determined by the targets set by policy-makers. There is not a single unambiguous urban sustainability measure, but a multitude of quantifiable criteria which may be used in an empirical test. Measurable indicators, including minimum performance levels and critical threshold levels, will then have to be estimated, defined and used in forecasting tools so as to improve awareness of sustainable development issues in modern cities. Local authorities will have to share their tasks with all other players in the urban space (including the private sector). Nevertheless, it goes without saying that urban sustainable development is a process riddled with conflicts and incompatibilities. Key commitment to a strict environmentally sustainable urban development in a city is necessary for the successful implementation of sustainability policies. Clearly, also economic (market-based) incentives are necessary in order to cope effectively and efficiently with the negative externalities of modern city life. Failure to develop a balanced urban development policy will reinforce urban sprawl and will spread inner-city problems to a much larger area. Environmentally benign urban policies may, on the other hand, attract new investments, favour urban employment, and hence contribute to an increase in quality of life.

3. Energy Policies at an Urban Lev[e] Benefits and Options

Sustainable city strategies have a 'Mid[a] character with many faces. After the abo[ve] sketch of various urban sustainability po[li]cies, we will now spell out important adva[n]tages of the potential of energy policies in[a] sustainable city context. Urban areas are [by] definition centres of economic activity cha[r]acterised by economies of scale and densi[ty] Given that a spatial clustering of activiti[es] implies a concentration of energy use, [it] seems plausible that urban areas are a su[it]able geographical entity as a focal point [for] energy policy. Admittedly, large energ[y] consuming industries have usually relocat[ed] themselves from the core areas to the urb[an] fringe, but that leaves the notion of urb[an] areas as large concentrations of (direct a[nd] indirect) energy users, both for producti[on] and consumption, essentially unaffected (s[ee] Owens and Rickaby, 1992). It is certain[ly] true that the majority of the world populati[on] lives in urban areas, and that makes the[se] areas suitable as focal points of energ[y] environmental policies. Such areas offer al[so] scale advantages in the production and dist[ri] bution of energy (see Camagni *et al.*, 199[?] In the light of these observations, one m[ay] list several reasons why a well focused e[n] ergy-environmental planning strategy at t[he] urban level is a promising activity in t[he] framework of sustainable urban develo[p] ment.

First, there is the obvious reason that m[ost] production, consumption and transport acti[v] ities in a country take place in urban areas. [It] is noteworthy that in most countries the lev[el] of urbanisation is still increasing, not only [in] prosperous regions but also in less favour[ed] regions. Thus, a clear focus on urban energ[y] planning may enhance the effectiveness [of] energy and environmental strategies in ma[ny] countries.

Next, decentralisation of energy and r[e] lated environmental policy has become a m[a] jor device in current policy-making in mo[st] Western countries. The city is of course [a] natural institutional decision-making unit this context, as it covers a well-focused study area without running the risk of a heterogeneous policy structure with many horizontally organised planning agencies (and related competence questions). Thus the involvement of one identifiable decision-making agency at the urban level is of major importance and may enhance the institutional effectiveness of energy and environmental planning.

A related obvious advantage may be the direct involvement of the locality, based on a bottom-up strategy for new energy-saving programmes and related environmental management programmes (for instance, in the case of district heating). This may increase the support of the general public for changes in, amongst other things, energy production, distribution and/or consumption and in lifestyles.

Finally, in terms of efficiency of data gathering and/or data availability as a support system for balanced sustainability policies, the city is usually a more suitable statistical entry providing systematic data sets on environmental, energy and socioeconomic indicators.

There is thus a variety of benefits involved in sustainability policies at the urban level. Nevertheless, there is not a single strategy for enhancing the environmental and energy sustainability of cities. In practice, a variety of options exist for a sustainable urban energy policy. Household activities and consumption, industrial and commercial activities and transport are—in addition to electricity production—the main sources of energy use. Many European experiences have shown that considerable savings are still possible in all these sectors.

In industry, new technologies and a better insulation of industrial and office buildings may lead to a considerable rise of energy efficiency, although this clearly has a long lead-time in normal circumstances. In the residential sector, housing insulation programmes may also lead to drastic energy savings in both space heating and air conditioning (for example, by means of better insulation, heat pumps, solar energy installa-

tions, wind turbines and economisers for central heating systems). And also in the transport sector considerable savings are, in principle, possible (for example, through more energy-efficient engines, vehicle weight reduction or—in the long run—through more energy-efficient physical planning aimed at a reduction of commuting distance and/or a shift of the modal split in favour of public transport).

At a more integrated and intermediate level of urban energy planning, various possibilities are offered by central heat distribution, by recycling of energy from heat, by combined heat and power either in district heating or in co-generation, or by using urban/industrial waste as a fuel for generating plants. Especially at a local level, these energy-saving options are likely to be more efficient than at a broader regional level, as generally such options require fairly high energy demand densities.

In general, urban energy planning may comprise a whole set of different and complementary energy policy strategies ('packaging' of policy measures), such as industrial co-generation, district heating, combined heat and power (CHP) generation (using steam turbines, internal combustion engines, gas turbines or combined cycle gas turbines), PV systems, combined urban waste management and energy production, load management and institutional reforms in the structure of utilities. In the sequel of our study, we will address in particular renewable energy systems, as these systems are underresearched and too often neglected.

4. Framework for Assessing Critical Success Factors of Renewable Energy Policies

The selection of various desirable renewable energy strategies for a sustainable city is partly an analytical and partly an empirical question, which may in principle be solved by using various assessment techniques and sophisticated (and nowadays computerised) evaluation methods. However, the choice in favour of a certain sustainability strategy does not necessarily mean that this particular

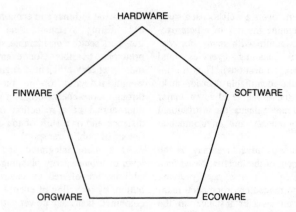

Figure 1. The 'pentagon prism' of critical success factors for the introduction of renewable energy technologies.

option can easily be implemented, since there may be many obstacles (i.e. high transaction costs) preventing an efficient implementation of an environmentally benign renewable energy system in a city. Several renewable energy policies may have a 'double dividend' character—i.e. they may favour environmental quality and may also reduce the costs of energy consumption. The advantages of the 'double-edged sword' of such a policy may be offset by significant transformation costs (both financially and institutionally). In this regard, a trade-off between all benefits and costs involved is necessary. While advantages of an urban renewable energy system are amongst others an improvement of local environmental quality, a reduction in (global) greenhouse gases and a cost saving in energy use, the costs of the installation of such a new energy system consist of direct investment costs in technical equipment and network adjustments and transaction costs due to inertia in institutions and among citizens. A basic aspect of investments in renewable energies is the lumpiness of the related capital stock, causing irreversibilities and thus high capital investment costs, which causes a tendency towards risk avoidance among urban governments.

It should be added that the assessment of urban renewable energy strategies should not only take place on the basis of direct technical (engineering) criteria, but also on the basis of their overall contribution to urban welfare, income and employment. Thus, what is needed is a socioeconomic evaluation.

In this context, the use of the 'pentagon prism' (see Figure 1) is meaningful, as this approach highlights the critical success factors (or failure factors) which act as necessary conditions—though not sufficient conditions—for a successful introduction of a new technology. This approach has demonstrated its validity in various European infrastructure policy analyses (for a detailed exposition, see Nijkamp *et al.*, 1994). Here only a concise explanation will be given.

The pentagon prism takes for granted that in general the success conditions of most large-scale projects in urban, transport and environmental planning are contingent upon a set of five decisive factors. These factors appear to be: technological (hardware) factors, information (software) factors, decision-making and institutional (orgware) factors, efficiency and financial (finware) factors, and environmental and safety (eco ware) factors. We will now interpret these factors in more detail for the urban sustainability initiatives discussed in the present paper.

Hardware factors refer to the level of technological sophistication of the renewable energy system used; for instance, a waste incineration plant with a high degree of heat recovery to be fed back into the public electricity network. Clearly, such investments require many resources and hence may face many barriers, which can only be overcome if one adopts a long-term viewpoint on urban sustainability as a *sine qua non* for long-range continuity.

Software factors refer to information provision and communication to citizens in order to induce environmentally-benign behaviour; for instance, an advertisement campaign to use energy-saving bulbs for household and office lighting. This requires pro-active and anticipatory policy strategies, since otherwise short-term policy and socio-political barriers will be too strong.

Next, orgware concerns the institutional and managerial efficiency in the urban energy-environmental sector; for instance, the introduction of market-oriented regulations or competition in the energy sector (for example, third-party access to the electricity network infrastructure). It also requires a sufficient integration of various urban policies, such as land use and transport.

The next success factor is finware, which is concerned with the cost-saving and financing aspects of new energy initiatives; for instance, a financing scheme to stimulate the use of PV systems in urban energy provision. This factor is especially important for investments with a long pay-back period.

And finally, we have ecoware, which deals with the urban social and quality-of-life conditions for the implementation of new energy initiatives in a sustainable city context.

All these five critical areas may influence the implementation process and potential success rate of renewable energy technologies. They may act as potential driving factors to eliminating bottlenecks for the attainment of environmental benefits for the city. Our empirical analysis will take the pentagon prism as its frame of reference.

It is clear that most urban renewable energy initiatives are of an incremental nature and mean mostly only a marginal improvement in urban sustainability. In this respect, it is meaningful to refer to the pentagon prism, as its use may allow us to identify for each of the above-mentioned five success factors a set of appropriate indicators or scores which may be quantified by experts or planners as a proxy for the degree of success of a new renewable energy technology. In this way, alternative energy options can be compared from different perspectives and for different cities.

The strategic remarks presented above may serve as guidelines for empirical research for evaluating urban sustainable energy policies. On the basis of this framework, we will provide in the next sections a quantitative empirical analysis which aims to identify which factors are important in regard to the potential success rate of implemented sustainable energy technologies in European cities. We will then adopt the principles of the pentagon approach described in the previous section as a framework for identifying and assessing the critical success conditions for these urban energy policies. In addition to the factors embedded in the pentagon prism, we will also investigate whether there are differences among various European countries in the success rates of the implemented technologies.

In our applied approach, two complementary methods will be used. A standard statistical analysis will be carried out based on a probit analysis. And, secondly, we will employ a more recently developed meta-analytical method, rough set analysis. We will start, however, with a description of the information source for our policy evaluation and its use in a meta-analytical framework.

5. The Information Base for the Meta-analysis of Urban Sustainability Initiatives

In our comparative analysis of urban sustainability initiatives, we will use a meta-analyti-

Table 1. Case-study cities in the three countries investigated

Country	Large cities	Medium-sized cities
The Netherlands	Amsterdam	Almere
	Rotterdam	Gouda
Italy	Milan	Pavia
	Turin	Brescia
Greece	Thessaloniki	Mytilini
	Chania	Ptolemaïda

cal approach for identifying key factors influencing the success rate of individual energy-saving technologies in cities. Meta-analysis was originally a statistical procedure for combining and comparing research findings from different studies focusing on similar phenomena (see Hedges and Olkin, 1985; Light and Pillemer, 1984; and Wolf, 1986). Meta-analysis is particularly suitable in cases where research outcomes are to be judged or compared (or even transferred to other situations), especially when there are no controlled conditions. Given the comparative purposes of meta-analytical methods, it is clear that the information basis for carrying out a meta-analysis has to be designed with a maximum of uniformity with respect to the case to be compared. In the past decade, a variety of meta-analytical methods have been developed (see, for example, Hunter *et al.*, 1982; and Rosenthal, 1991). Most meta-analytical techniques are designed for sufficiently large numbers of case studies, so that statistical probability statements can be inferred. In this context, standard regression methods or—in case of categorical data—discrete choice methods are often employed (see also section 6). And in this respect, meta-analysis has clearly demonstrated its validity and usefulness as a methodological tool for comparative study in the social sciences. Recent applications in the field of transport science and environmental science can be found in Button and van den Bergh (1997), Button and Kerr (1996) and Button and Nijkamp (1997), while a broad overview can be found in van den Bergh *et al.* (1997).

Meta-analysis is essentially a mode of thinking and may comprise a multiplicity of different methods and techniques, which are often statistical in nature. Especially in the case of quasi-controlled or non-controlled comparative experimentation, the level of information is often not cardinal, but imprecise (for example, nominal, qualitative, fuzzy). In recent years, rough set theory has emerged as a powerful analytical tool for dealing with 'soft' data. Rough set theory aims to offer classification of data (measured on any information level) by manipulating these data in such a way that a range of consistent and feasible cause–effect relationships can be identified, while it is also able to eliminate redundant information. This method will be used in section 7, where we will also give a concise introduction to rough set theory (for more details, see also Pawlak, 1991; Slowinski and Stefanowski, 1994; Greco *et al.*, 1995; and Matarazzo and Nijkamp, 1997).

Our comparative policy study concerns Dutch, Italian and Greek urban sustainability initiatives. These three countries were selected in the framework of an exploratory study commissioned by the European Commission. The choice of the particular case cities was determined by the aim to compare cities that were different with regard to their size, their political-organisational arrangements and their urban environmental initiatives carried out (for example, different levels of adoption). The participating cities, which certainly form a contrast from the above-mentioned viewpoints, are presented in Table 1.

The Dutch cities chosen are Amsterdam, the capital city of the Netherlands which is

ɔw experimenting with a large-scale appli-
ɪtion of photovoltaic roof panels in one of
s newly built areas; Rotterdam, a large port,
ɛing the first city in the Netherlands with a
ɪrge-scale district heating system developed
ɪst after the Second World War; Almere, a
ɪedium-sized new town with a recent appli-
ɪtion of district heating, which has the
ɪghest population growth rate in the Nether-
ɪnds, so that this dynamic city may be an
ɪteresting test case for new urban spatial
ɛvelopment and integrated urban energy
ɪlanning; and, finally Gouda, the city playing
ɪe pioneering role in the Netherlands in the
ɪrea of solar water heating applications.

The Italian case cities are Milan, one of
ɪe most attractive large business centres in
ɪe Mediterranean, with its recent methanisa-
ɪon (which is apparently only to the detri-
ɪent of a district heating system), its
ɪdvanced differentiated waste collection sys-
ɛm and its new urban traffic plan; the city of
'urin, the first city that developed an urban
ɪnergy plan and a large district heating sys-
ɛm already deeply rooted in its territory;
ɪrescia, an interesting and successful exam-
ɪle of large district heating plants and inte-
ɪrated systems to supply energy; and, finally,
'avia, a small provincial city that is in the
ɪentre of heavy and numerous transport
ɪnovements that are far beyond its natural
ɪapacity, and for this reason needs a general
ɪrban mobility plan focused on a reduction in
ɪnergy use and environmental decay.

The Greek case studies are Chania, a rela-
ɪvely large city on Crete where recently
ɪome initiatives have been started up by the
ɔrganisation for the Development of West-
ɛrn Crete (wind energy and photovoltaic ap-
ɪlications, both in an early project phase);
Thessaloniki, the second-largest city of
ɔreece, where some small-scale applications
ɔf solar space and water heating exist;
Mytilini, the medium-sized capital city of the
ɪsland of Lesvos with a windmill park; and
finally Ptolemaïda (and its neighbour town
Kozani), that play a pioneering role in
ɔreece in the area of district heating.

The information source for our comparative study of sustainable city initiatives was
provided by various qualified experts involved with the energy initiatives in the
above case-study cities. They comprised
amongst others policy-makers, engineers and
representatives from energy companies.
These experts were interviewed by means of
structured interview lists, which aimed to
assess the relevance and successes/failures of
the various city initiatives by using the pentagon prism as an analytical framework.
They were also asked to give quantitative
scores for both the perceived rate of success
of the respective technologies, and the experienced (in case of existing applications)
and expected (in cases of non-existing implementations) extent to which the five pentagon factors act as bottleneck factors to the
introduction or the viability of these technologies. This information has been systematically collected by means of a common
checklist in all three countries (see Table 2).

The level of success of a certain technology in a given city was measured by asking
respondents as to the probability that an existing technology will be implemented at a
larger scale in their city, or that new investments will be made in an as-yet-not-imple-
mented energy technology. The rate of
success is assumed to depend on how the
technologies score with regard to the critical
factors from the pentagon model which have
been distinguished in the former analysis.
For instance, it seems plausible that the probability that an already-implemented technology in a city will be expanded, is larger when
there exist no severe bottlenecks on the
financing of the expansion of these investments. The perceived success rates are assessed on a categorical scale from 1 to 5
(from a very low to a very high probability to
enlarge the technology implementation or to
start new investments in it).

For the scores on the critical key aspects
judged by the various local experts the following rank-order scale is used:

5 The aspect concerned is not a barrier at all;
   on the contrary, the way in which the
   condition is met is regarded as a reason for

Table 2. Taxonomy of critical success factors for the adoption process of renewable urban ene~
technologies

Pentagon factors		Critical success conditions
Technological (hardware)	R&D activities Technological know-how Technical information on other relevant technologies Climatic conditions	Role of technology Minimum efficient size Compatibility with existing technologies
User-related (software)	Public awareness Adaptation of households Adaptation of large users Reliability for end-users	Co-operation in use Participation of large users Critical mass of users
Financial (finware)	Initial governmental subsidies Incomplete depreciation of old technologies Sunk costs	Profitability for supply actors Financial participation of users Profitability for households Profitability for large users
Organisational (orgware)	Organisational co-operation of supply actors Division of responsibilities Adjustment costs of management	Market conditions Timing of introduction Managerial learning processes Requalification of existing staff
Ecological and social (ecoware)	Visual disturbance Harmony with public space functions	Harmony with building functions Environmental awareness Non-tangible social benefits

the success of the application of the technology.

4 The aspect is a condition that is sufficiently met by the application of the technology.

3 The aspect is neither a clear positive nor a clear negative critical factor, or it is irrelevant.

2 The aspect is a barrier which with some effort may be overcome in the near future.

1 The aspect acts as a major bottleneck.

By interviewing systematically a large group of experts, it was possible to collect information on a representative set of 60 situations, each of which concerns a (real or hypothesised) use or implementation of a particular technology in one of the 12 cities investigated. In the next two sections, we will present the empirical results from these expert experiments, by applying a probit analysis (section 6) and a rough set analysis (section 7).

6. A Probit Analysis for the Explanati~ of the Pentagon Factors

The database on the sustainable city init~ tives in our sample is rich. From a method~ logical perspective, it is now interesting ~ test the relevance of the five key fact~ incorporated in our pentagon prism. T~ number of observations (60) allows a statis~ cal regression analysis with the (perceive~ rate of success of the technologies as a d~ pendent variable, and the critical pentag~ factors as independent variables. As all o~ data are of an ordinal nature, we will utili~ the ordered probit model in our appli~ analysis.

The analysis will be carried out in tw~ steps: at the overall level of the pentag~ factors; and, at the level of individual co~ ponents of the pentagon factors. First, ~ will carry out the analysis for the ma~ groups of pentagon factors. In this case, ~ have five independent factors. Each of the~

Table 3. Probit results for sustainability success rates with main pentagon groups as independent variables

Variable (means)	Probit estimate	Standard error	*t*-value	p > |*t*|
Hardware	0.47524	0.2661	1.79	0.080
Software	− 0.44192	0.2459	− 1.80	0.078
Finware	0.41688	0.2338	1.78	0.081
Orgware	0.26103	0.2788	0.94	0.354
Ecoware	0.00865	0.1955	0.04	0.965
Constant				
Alpha_1	0.78893	0.8861	0.89	0.377
Alpha_2	1.23062	0.8963	1.37	0.176
Alpha_3	2.13628	0.9540	2.24	0.030
Alpha_4	3.03258	0.9882	3.07	0.003

Measures of fit

Likelihood ratio chi-squared with 5 d.f., prob = 0.0113	14.7923
− 2 log likelihood for full model	162.0846
− 2 log likelihood for restricted model	176.8769
Percentage correctly predicted	36.6667

s quantified by taking the average score of the critical factors belonging to the respective main group of pentagon factors (where we implicitly assume that the intervals between the score values 1–5 are equal). We have chosen this pragmatic approach of aggregating the values of the elements of these factor groups in order to obtain a tentative insight into the relative influence of the main Pentagon factors (for instance, the influence of financial factors compared to hardware factors). Furthermore, in our analysis we use the original measurement scale of the dependent variable—i.e. the perceived success rate, which is a categorical (ordered) scale ranging from 1 to 5.

In Table 3, the results are shown of the ordered probit analysis that compares the influences of the five groups of pentagon factors on the perceived success rate of renewable energy technologies. The majority of the five factors appear to have a positive coefficient. This positive influence was to be expected for the reason that the less stringent the bottleneck factors are, the higher the probability of a successful implementation. Two positive coefficients appear to be significant: these concern hardware and finware. This tentative investigation thus indicates that—in addition to the technological impact of renewable energy options—financial aspects appear to be, in a general sense, decisive for the potential success of the renewable energy technologies in cities.

In a second stage, we have undertaken a more rigorous analysis by carrying out the analysis for each of the constituents of the main groups of pentagon factors. For each of these groups, we have run a separate ordered probit analysis. In these cases, we can take full account of the ordinal character of the data by creating dummy variables for relevant categories of the score values. For this purpose, we have created three classes of score values. The reference class is the category of score values 1 and 2 (reflecting respectively major bottlenecks and modest obstacles). Two dummy variables (D1 and D2) are next created, reflecting respectively that the aspect is neutral/not relevant and that the aspect is sufficiently met or even a driving force for the implementation of the technology at hand. Table 2 will be used as the overall framework for our test.

We will now concisely evaluate the results of our ordered probit analysis, as given in

Table 4. Probit results for hardware factors

Variable		Probit estimate	Standard error	t-value	$p > |t|$
R&D activities	D1	− 0.39272	0.7765	− 0.51	0.616
	D2	− 0.51650	0.7974	− 0.65	0.521
Technological know-how	D1	0.14737	1.2155	0.12	0.904
	D2	0.84383	0.9964	0.85	0.402
Technical information on other technologies	D1	0.23373	0.7743	0.30	0.764
	D2	0.80192	0.7385	1.09	0.284
Climatic conditions	D1	0.91308	1.0024	0.91	0.368
	D2	1.15468	0.9317	1.24	0.222
Role of technology	D1	0.47341	0.5261	0.90	0.373
	D2	0.43474	0.6331	0.69	0.496
Minimum efficient size	D1	− 0.48104	0.5816	− 0.83	0.413
	D2	− 0.74503	0.5632	− 1.32	0.193
Compatibility with existing technologies	D1	− 0.26638	0.7124	− 0.37	0.710
	D2	− 0.41625	0.6283	− 0.66	0.511
Constant					
Alpha_1		− 0.44330	0.9789	− 0.45	0.653
Alpha_2		− 0.04165	1.0108	− 0.04	0.967
Alpha_3		0.87348	1.0368	0.84	0.404
Alpha_4		1.86949	1.0475	1.78	0.082
Measures of fit					
Likelihood ratio chi-squared with 14 d.f., prob = 0.4883		13.4913			
− 2 log likelihood for full model		160.8517			
− 2 log likelihood for restricted model		174.3430			
Percentage correctly predicted		50.0000			

Tables 4–8. When we focus only on the hardware factors in order to explain the success of renewable energy systems, it appears that not much can be said on the individual influence of each of these factors when they are compared with one another (see Table 4). Roughly half of the independent variables turn out to have a positive coefficient compared with the base. In this particular case, none of the separate factors can be qualified as really significant, but from the factors with positive coefficients compared with the base, it appears that the relatively highest significance is offered by the climatic situation of the site. This suggests that the locational climatic conditions that affect the efficiency of the energy technologies in the city, have a larger beneficial impact on the success of the technologies than the technological state of these technologies alone. However, it has to be admitted that the significance of this factor is not impressive.

For the software factors, the results conform more closely to our expectations. In this case, the majority of the variables have a positive coefficient compared with the base (see Table 5), while these are in most cases higher for the second dummy variable. The participation of large users appears to have the largest significance, which seems to be an interesting and plausible result.

In the case of finware factors, the picture is again less clear, although there is one variable with a positive and significant contribution, and this is the profitability of the suppliers (Table 6).

Looking at organisational factors (Table 7), it appears that one variable has a clearly significant (positive) contribution and this is offered by the market conditions (second dummy variable). This finding indicates that

Table 5. Probit results for software factors

Variable		Probit estimate	Standard error	*t*-value	p > |*t*|
Public awareness	D1	− 0.65019	0.6652	− 0.98	0.334
	D2	0.23284	0.7584	0.31	0.760
Adaptation of households	D1	0.00629	0.9030	0.01	0.994
	D2	0.31797	0.8791	0.36	0.719
Adaptation of large users	D1	0.11229	1.0584	0.11	0.916
	D2	− 0.94098	1.0567	− 0.89	0.378
Reliability for end-users	D1	0.63280	0.8940	0.71	0.483
	D2	0.57865	0.9305	0.62	0.537
Co-operation in use	D1	0.41753	0.6869	0.61	0.547
	D2	0.56519	0.7093	0.80	0.430
Participation of large users	D1	0.20003	0.5559	0.36	0.721
	D2	1.13786	0.6863	1.66	0.105
Critical mass of users	D1	− 0.14372	0.4429	− 0.32	0.747
	D2	0.15026	0.5843	0.26	0.798
Constant					
Alpha_1		− 0.78051	1.3241	− 0.59	0.559
Alpha_2		− 0.32819	1.2211	− 0.27	0.789
Alpha_3		0.63814	1.1729	0.54	0.589
Alpha_4		1.62452	1.2071	1.35	0.186
Measures of fit					
Likelihood ratio chi-squared with 4 d.f., prob = 0.3330		15.6847			
− 2 log likelihood for full model		158.6582			
− 2 log likelihood for restricted model		174.3430			
Percentage correctly predicted		41.6667			

importance of external conditions created by other actors for the success of renewable energy projects, which appears to be more critical than organisational matters that are internal to local sustainability projects.

Finally, we take a look at social/environmental factors in the ecoware component of the pentagon model (Table 8). Analysing these factors separately, it appears that the harmony with public functions of a specific site for the renewable energy technology has a significant, positive coefficient for the first dummy variable. Also, this result seems to offer a plausible explanation.

A check on the robustness of the above results was next carried out by focusing on all explanatory variables with significant coefficients from the partial analyses, and carrying out the ordered probit analysis for these variables separately. By starting with all these variables simultaneously and elimi-

nating these one by one on the basis of their degree of insignificance (the sequential elimination procedure advocated by Theil, 1971), it appeared that the hardware-related factor of climatic conditions remained significant in all these model runs, while the other factors tended to become statistically insignificant.

In order to have a further check on the robustness of the results of the ordered probit analyses, we have also applied for the respective cases a binomial logit model on the data. The dependent variable was then classified into a category for negative and neutral scores, and a category for positive scores, respectively (the robustness of the assignment of the neutral score was checked by shifting the neutral category to the category with positive scores). These logit models did not provide additional or more interesting results. A plausible reason is that relevant information in these models is lost

Table 6. Probit results for finware factors

Variable		Probit estimate	Standard error	t-value	$p > |t|$
Initial governmental subsidies	D1	0.45417	0.7741	0.59	0.561
	D2	0.38871	0.6868	0.57	0.574
Incomplete depreciation of old technologies	D1	−0.28883	0.6227	−0.46	0.645
	D2	−0.27169	0.9899	−0.27	0.785
Sunk costs	D1	0.00797	0.5157	0.02	0.988
	D2	0.02262	0.7041	0.03	0.975
Financial participation of users	D1	−0.26673	0.4111	−0.65	0.520
	D2	0.43133	0.4970	0.87	0.390
Profitability for supply actors	D1	0.84936	0.5065	1.68	0.101
	D2	0.78931	0.5882	1.34	0.187
Profitability for households	D1	0.36331	0.5032	0.72	0.474
	D2	0.93466	0.9308	1.00	0.321
Profitability for large users	D1	−0.51745	0.7217	−0.72	0.477
	D2	−1.03956	0.8230	−1.26	0.213
Constant					
Alpha_1		−1.23662	0.7634	−1.62	0.113
Alpha_2		−0.82362	0.6700	−1.23	0.226
Alpha_3		0.15686	0.6786	0.23	0.818
Alpha_4		1.16081	0.7081	1.64	0.109
Measures of fit					
Likelihood ratio chi-squared with 14 d.f., prob = 0.4074		14.5803			
−2 log likelihood for full model		159.7627			
−2 log likelihood for restricted model		174.3430			
Percentage correctly predicted		31.6667			

due to the ordering of the dependent variable. A major problem inherent in the use of the discrete data models is apparently the low level of measurement of the success rates of the introduction of new energy technologies in cities. Seen from this perspective, it seems plausible to resort to non-parametric statistical approaches (dealing with categorical data), as embedded in rough set analysis. This will be set out in the next section.

7. A Rough Set Analysis for Identifying Success Conditions for Urban Sustainability

Rough set analysis is an exploratory, non-parametric statistical method that is able to handle a rather diverse and less directly tangible set of factors in a decision-theoretical context, normally in the form of 'if ... then' statements. Rough set analysis, proposed in the early 1980s by Pawlak (1982, 1991) provides a formal tool for transforming qualitative data set, such as a collection of past examples or a record of experience, into structured knowledge, in the sense that it has the ability to classify objects in distinct classes of attributes (van den Bergh et al. 1997). In such an approach, it is not always possible to distinguish objects precisely on the basis of given numerical information (descriptors) about them. This imperfect information causes indiscernibility of objects through the values of the attributes describing them and prevents them from being unambiguously assigned to a given single class or category. In this case, the only sets which can be precisely characterised in terms of values of ranges of such attributes are lower and upper approximations of the set of objects. Rough set theory has proven to be a useful tool for a large class of such quality

Table 7. Probit results for orgware factors

Variable		Probit estimate	Standard error	t-value	p > |t|
Organisational co-operation of supply actors	D1	− 0.45356	0.7391	− 0.61	0.543
	D2	0.04093	0.7697	0.05	0.958
Division of responsibilities	D1	0.11932	0.7181	0.17	0.869
	D2	0.38687	0.7880	0.49	0.626
Adjustment costs of management	D1	0.13576	0.8202	0.17	0.869
	D2	− 0.71071	0.9057	− 0.78	0.437
Market conditions	D1	0.14155	0.4768	0.30	0.768
	D2	0.85581	0.4509	1.90	0.065
Timing of introduction	D1	0.77852	0.5788	1.35	0.186
	D2	0.27013	0.4810	0.56	0.577
Managerial learning processes	D1	− 0.06616	0.7044	− 0.09	0.926
	D2	0.67038	0.7170	0.94	0.355
Requalification of existing staff	D1	− 0.62773	0.4469	− 1.40	0.167
	D2	− 0.30131	0.6956	− 0.43	0.667
Constant					
Alpha_1		− 0.95391	0.8755	− 1.09	0.282
Alpha_2		− 0.50157	0.6990	− 0.72	0.477
Alpha_3		0.43585	0.7175	0.61	0.547
Alpha_4		1.46882	0.7742	1.90	0.065
Measures of fit					
Likelihood ratio chi-squared with 14 d.f., prob = 0.1743		18.7604			
− 2 Log likelihood for full model		155.5826			
− 2 Log likelihood for restricted model		174.3430			
Percentage correctly predicted		35.0000			

Table 8. Probit results for ecoware factors

Variable		Probit estimate	Standard error	t-value	p > |t|
Visual disturbance	D1	0.45248	0.5544	0.82	0.419
	D2	0.28094	0.5128	0.55	0.586
Harmony with public space functions	D1	0.93288	0.5594	1.67	0.102
	D2	− 0.14986	0.5491	− 0.27	0.786
Harmony with building functions	D1	− 0.35565	0.5035	− 0.71	0.484
	D2	0.26922	0.5275	0.51	0.612
Environmental awareness	D1	− 0.10440	0.4729	− 0.22	0.826
	D2	0.42067	0.5533	0.76	0.451
Non-tangible social benefits	D1	1.31168	5.5725	0.24	0.815
	D2	1.39684	5.5688	0.25	0.803
Constant					
Alpha_1		0.18545	5.5705	0.03	0.974
Alpha_2		0.63554	5.5674	0.11	0.910
Alpha_3		1.63911	5.5812	0.29	0.770
Alpha_4		2.59579	5.5865	0.46	0.644
Measures of fit					
Likelihood ratio chi-squared with 10 d.f., prob = 0.1943		13.5554			
− 2 log likelihood for full model		160.7876			
− 2 log likelihood for restricted model		174.3430			
Percentage correctly predicted		43.3333			

Table 9. Independent variable classes

Class number	Range in which mean score value falls
1	[0; 3]
2	< 3; 3.5]
3	< 3.5; 4]
4	< 4; 5]

tive or fuzzy multi-attribute decision problems. It can effectively deal with problems of explanation and prescription of a decision situation where knowledge is imperfect. It is helpful in evaluating the importance of particular attributes and eliminating redundant ones from a decision table, and it may generate sorting and choice rules using only the remaining attributes so as to identify new choice options in policy problems and next to rank them. An extensive empirical application of rough set theory to a comparative study on regional tourist multipliers can be found in Baayens and Nijkamp (1998).

It is clear from the various recent applications of rough set theory, that it is essentially a classification method, devised for non-stochastic information. This also means that ordinal or categorical information can easily be taken into consideration. This makes rough set analysis particularly useful as a meta-analytical tool in case of incomplete, imprecise or fuzzy information on phenomena to be compared. In the context of our evaluation of sustainable city initiatives, a rough set analysis applied to our data set may be useful for the following purposes:

—assessment of the significance of particular condition attributes;
—construction of a minimal subset of variables ensuring the same quality of description as the whole set—i.e. the reducts of the set of attributes;
—intersection of those reducts giving a core of attributes that cannot be eliminated without disturbing the quality of description of the set of attributes; and
—elimination of irrelevant attributes.

The use of rough set analysis for the sea of explanatory factors for the success rate urban energy policy options in our st employs two successive steps:

Information survey. In our case, the inf mation survey is derived from the ordi score data discussed previously. In our proach we distinguish six dependent tributes, namely the main pentagon gro (five in total) and a variable characteris the country in which the particular techn ogy is applied. For each group of pentag factors, an average value is calculated fr the scores of the elements belonging to group. For the rough set analysis we use— contrast to the statistical analysis—a s sample of the expert interview data namely, only data on the expert opini regarding existing applications of renewa energies. This concerns useful informat on 19 cases, each of which represents a implementation of a particular technology a given city.

Classification of information. Next, all obs vations are classified into various categor for each attribute separately. This applies both categorical and ratio information. general, some sensitivity analysis on classification used is meaningful, as a b ance has to be found between homogene and class size. This classification exerc leads then to a so-called decision table, which all observations on urban sustainab ity initiatives are sub-divided into disti classes for each relevant attribute.

In our case, only the independent variab have to be classified (as these are continu variables given the averaging procedu As indicated above, the dependent varia is already of a discrete nature, w values ranging from 1 to 5. Any furt classification of the dependent varia would lead to a loss of information. classes created here for the independent v ables are shown in Table 9. Applying classification of the original data, a set coded variables results (Table 10). From coded information table, four main sets levant performance indicators and outputs an be calculated: the reducts, the core, the wer and upper approximations and the accuracy and quality of the classification. These will now be described and interpreted.

We will first pay attention to the reducts— e. all combinations of explanatory or independent variables which can completely determine (or explain) the variation in the dependent variable, without needing other explanatory variables. For all sub-samples, the reducts are given in Table 10. A first conclusion to be drawn from Table 10 is that there are three competitive sets of explanatory factors (consisting of subsets of the predefined factors), on the basis of which the levels of success of the technologies are fully discernible and hence can be explained. The first explanation is that technological factors, user-related factors and socio/locational factors are decisive factors for this success rate. The second, equally valid, possibility is that the success rate of the technologies is fully determined by the countries in which they are applied (Netherlands, Italy or Greece), together with technological factors and socio/locational factors. Finally, there is a reduct consisting of all distinguished factors except socio/locational factors. This latter gives obviously only little information on the contribution of the distinguished factors to the success rate of the sustainability strategy used and is hence less relevant.

Next, we discuss the core—i.e. the set of variables that are present in all reducts, or that are part of all competitive explanations. There appears to be only one variable belonging to this core, namely technological factors. This is apparently a crucial factor in urban sustainability policy, a result also obtained with the probit analysis.

Finally, we will take a look at the third and fourth factors. We have to assess then the lower and upper approximations and derived accuracy of relationships for each value class of the decisional variable. The latter is the lower divided by the upper approximation of each class. From this information, we can calculate the accuracy and quality of the classification—i.e. in relation to the choice of

thresholds. In our application, both the accuracy of the classification and the quality of the classification appear to have the highest possible value, 1, so that the robustness and reliability of the results from the rough set analysis leave nothing to be desired.

The overall conclusion which we can draw from the application of this meta-analytical approach is the following. We can distinguish three groups of factors with a decreasing rate of influence on the success rate of urban sustainable energy policies, based on the frequencies of their occurrences in the reducts (Table 11). First, there are prominent technological factors which make up the only variable belonging to the core. This means that technological factors may be regarded as the dominant factors influencing the success rate of sustainable city initiatives. A second group of key variables consists of the country where the implementation takes place, besides user-related factors and social/environmental factors. These variables occur twice in the reducts. We may therefore conclude that the geographical circumstances, at both national and local scales, are rather strong explanatory factors compared to the third group of factors, which consists of financial and organisational forces.

8. Conclusion

In this paper, we have tried to develop a methodology for a systematic evaluation of innovative energy policies at the city level in the context of urban sustainability. In our empirical application, we have taken into account the influence of a variety of factors reflected by the pentagon prism (technological, user-related, financial, organisational and ecological/social aspects), and also the country in which these urban policies are conducted.

A statistical analysis of potentially influencing factors on the success rate of renewable energy technologies, applied to both existing and future (hypothetical) situations, resulted in two key forces with a significant influence—technological aspects and financial aspects. More detailed aspects

Table 10. Coded information table of expert score data on existing applications of urban renewable energy technologies

Country	City	Technology	Class in which mean score value falls					Score of success rate
			Hardware	Software	Finware	Orgware	Ecoware	
Greece	Mytilini	Wind energy	2	1	2	1	1	4
Greece	Ptolemaïda	CHP/DH	4	4	3	4	4	4
Greece	Ptolemaïda	CHP/DH	4	3	3	2	2	5
Greece	Mytilini	Wind energy	1	1	2	1	1	5
Greece	Ptolemaïda	CHP/DH	4	4	4	4	3	5
Italy	Turin	CHP/DH	1	4	4	3	4	4
Italy	Turin	CHP/DH	1	3	3	1	3	4
Italy	Brescia	CHP/DH	4	4	3	4	3	5
Italy	Milan	CHP/DH	3	4	4	4	4	4
Italy	Brescia	PV system	3	3	1	1	3	1
Netherlands	Rotterdam	Refuse incineration	4	1	2	1	3	5
Netherlands	Rotterdam	Wind energy	3	1	1	1	1	4
Netherlands	Rotterdam	Wind energy	3	1	1	2	1	5
Netherlands	Almere	CHP/DH	3	2	3	1	4	4
Netherlands	Amsterdam	PV system	1	1	1	1	3	3
Netherlands	Gouda	Solar water heating	1	1	1	3	1	5
Netherlands	Gouda	Solar water heating	3	3	1	3	3	4
Netherlands	Almere	CHP/DH	3	3	3	3	3	4
Netherlands	Amsterdam	PV system	3	2	1	3	2	2

Note: The two Greek cities of Chania and Thessaloniki and the Italian city of Pavia have not been included in this analysis run, because in these cases we had no information for all of the distinguished factors of the pentagon prism. The creation of an extra class for missing information would lead to a decline of the usefulness of the results.

Table 11. Results of the rough set analysis

Minimal sets
1. {hardware, software, ecoware}
2. {country, hardware, ecoware}
3. {country, hardware, software, finware, orgware}

Core
{hardware}

Accuracy of classification 1
Quality of classification 1

at seemed to have some influence were: cal climatic conditions (affecting the ficiency of a given technology), the partici- tion of large-scale users, the profitability of ppliers, external energy market conditions d the harmony or compatibility of the tech- •logy with the locality.

The rough set analysis, applied to existing plementations of renewable energy tech- •logies, also provided some interesting con- usions. In this analysis, technological ctors also appeared to have the strongest ative influence on the success rate of the levant technologies. In addition, this analy- s suggested that the geographical circum- ances, at both national and local scales, are latively strong explanatory factors, and at ast stronger than financial or organisational ctors. Thus, the rough set analysis confirms e main result of the statistical analysis on e influence of hardware factors, but in ad- tion puts more emphasis on the role of te-specific conditions. It is also interesting see that financial aspects seem to be envis- ;ed as more important when not-yet-exist- g cases are included in the sample. This dicates that—especially with regard to in- ?stment decisions—the financial aspects ay play an important role, and that in later 1ases (after the financing of the project) the iccess of the technologies is—in the eyes of e experts—more dependent on other fac- rs.

Given the result that, in addition to techno- •gical factors, the spatial differences are early important for the success of sustain- •le city policies, it is worthwhile to carry

out further research on this issue. The tech- nique of meta-analysis can be used for as- sessing the question of which cities are likely to be successful in their energy policies, and whether and why such cities are more sus- tainable than others. For the purpose of com- parative policy evaluation, it would of course be most important if we identify which form of renewable energy is best suited in which type of city. Therefore, not only factors re- lated to the application of the particular tech- nologies should be taken into consideration, but also socioeconomic and morphological characteristics of cities. It would be interest- ing to carry out more meta-analytical re- search which concentrates on such characteristics of localities in the context of urban ecology.

References

BAAYENS, S. and NIJKAMP, P. (1998) Meta-analytic methods for explanatory and exploratory policy research, *Journal of Policy Modelling*. (forth- coming).

BERGH, J. C. J. M. VAN DEN, BUTTON, K., NIJKAMP, P. and PEPPING, G. (1997) *Meta-analysis of En- vironmental Policies*. Dordrecht: Kluwer.

BREHENY, M. J. (Ed.) (1992) *Sustainable Develop- ment and Urban Form*. London: Pion.

BUTTON, K. and KERR, J. (1996) The effectiveness of traffic restraint policies: a simple meta- regression analysis, *International Journal of Transport Economics*, 23, pp. 213–225.

BUTTON, K. and NIJKAMP, P. (1997) Environmental policy analysis and the usefulness of meta- analysis, *Socio-economic Planning Sciences*, 5, pp. 215–219.

BUTTON, K. and VAN DEN BERGH, J. C. J. M. (1997) Meta-analysis of environmental issues in re- gional, urban and transport Economics, *Urban Studies*, 34, pp. 927–944.

CAMAGNI, R. and CAPELLO, R. (1996) *The role of indivisibilities and irreversibilities in renew- able energy adoption processes, an evolution- ary approach*. Paper presented to the 36th European Congress of the Regional Science Association, Zurich, 26–30 August.

CAMAGNI, R., CAPELLO, R. and NIJKAMP, P. (1997) Towards sustainable city policy, *Ecological Economics*, pp. 32–46.

CEC (COMMISSION OF THE EUROPEAN COMMUNI- TIES) (1990) *Greenbook on the Urban Environ- ment*. Brussels: CEC.

GEENHUIZEN, M. S. VAN and NIJKAMP, P. (1995) *Sustainable cities: challenges of an integrated planning approach.* Research Memorandum 1995-18, Faculty of Economics, Free University, Amsterdam.

GIRARDET, H. (1992) *The Gaia Atlas of Cities.* London: Gaia Books.

GRECO, S., MATARAZZO, B. and SLOWINSKI, R. (1995) *Rough set approach to multi-attribute choice and ranking problems.* ICS Research Report 38/95, Warsaw University of Technology.

HAUGHTON, G. and HUNTER, C. (1994) *Sustainable Cities.* London: Jessica Kingsley.

HEDGES, L. V. and OLKIN, I. (1985) *Statistical Methods for Meta-analysis.* New York: Academic Press.

HUNTER, J. E., SCHMIDT, F. L. and JACKSON, G. (1982) *Advanced Meta-analysis: Quantitative Methods for Cumulating Research Findings Across Studies.* Beverly Hills: Sage.

LIGHT, R. J. and PILLEMER, D. B. (1984) *Summing Up: The Science of Reviewing Research.* Cambridge, MA: Harvard University Press.

MATARAZZO, B. and NIJKAMP, P. (1997) Meta-analysis for comparative environmental case studies, *Journal of Social Economics,* 34, pp. 799–811.

NIJKAMP, P. and PERRELS, A. H. (1994) *Sustainable Cities in Europe.* London: Earthscan.

NIJKAMP, P., VLEUGEL, J., MAGGI, R. and MASSER, I. (1994) *Missing Transport Networks in Europe.* Aldershot: Avebury.

OECD (ORGANISATION FOR EUROPEAN CO-OPERATION AND DEVELOPMENT) (1990) *Environmen-

tal Policies for Cities in the 1990s.* Pari OECD.

OWENS, S. and RICKABY, P. (1992) Settlements a energy revisited, *Built Environment,* 18, p 247–252.

PAWLAK, Z. (1982) Rough sets, *Internation Journal of Information and Computer Science* 11, pp. 341–356.

PAWLAK, Z. (1991) *Rough Sets: Theoretical A pects of Reasoning About Data.* Dordrech Kluwer.

REES, W. E. (1992) Ecological footprints and a propriated carrying capacity, *Environment ar Urbanisation,* 4, pp. 121–130.

ROSENTHAL, R. (1991) *Meta-analytic Procedur for Social Research.* Beverly Hills: Sage.

SELMAN, P. (1996) *Local Sustainability.* Londo Paul Chapman.

SLOWINSKI, R. and STEFANOWSKI, J. (1994) Han ling various types of uncertainty in the roug set approach, in: W. P. ZIARKO (Ed.) *Roug Sets, Fuzzy Sets and Knowledge Discovery,* p 174–192. Berlin: Springer.

THEIL, H. (1971) *Principles of Econometrics.* Ne York: John Wiley.

WACKERNAGEL, S. and REES, W. E. (1996) *O Ecological Footprint.* Gabriola Island, B(New Society Publications).

WHITTAKER, S. (1995) *An International Guide Local Agenda 21.* London: HMSO.

WOLF, F. (1986) *Meta-analysis: Quantitati Methods for Research Synthesis.* Beverly Hil Sage.

[18]

JOURNAL OF REGIONAL SCIENCE, VOL. 35, NO. 4, 1995, pp. 579–597

COMPARATIVE REGIONAL POLICY IMPACT ANALYSIS: EX POST EVALUATION OF THE PERFORMANCE OF THE EUROPEAN REGIONAL DEVELOPMENT FUND*

Peter Nijkamp and Eddy Blaas

Dept of Economics, Free University, De Boelelaan 1105, 1081 HV Amsterdam,
The Netherlands

ABSTRACT. This paper addresses the issue of ex post impact analysis of regional policies in the European Community. The analysis is both methodological and applied in nature. After a concise overview of existing impact assessment methods, a two-step approach by means of an exploratory frequency method and an explanatory rational expectations-based model is proposed in order to provide an empirical framework for cross-regional comparative evaluation of the performance of the European Regional Development Fund (ERDF). The scope and applicability of the method is illustrated by means of a case study for Dutch regions.

EUROPEAN REGIONAL POLICY: INTRODUCTION

The completion of the internal market in Europe serves to improve the competitive position of European countries (including their sectors and regions) on both internal and global markets. At the same time it is increasingly recognized that socioeconomic discrepancies between E.C. nations—and in particular between regions in the E.C.—do not show clear signs of convergence (Armstrong and Taylor, 1993). If it is true that Europe becomes the "home of regions" rather than the "home of nations," then the regional problem deserves to be treated with priority (Nijkamp, 1990, 1992, 1993). This also explains the renewed policy interest for regional development from a European perspective, reflected inter alia in drastic increases of E.C. budgets for regional development policy in all member states. The recent expansion of the "European space" with Austria, Finland and Sweden reinforces this interest. However, the financial expenditures for achieving equity objectives are looked at with much scrutiny by the European Commission. In light of the current budgetary problems, it is understandable that the need for a critical judgement of all public expenditures by national and supranational governments has arisen (see also Bohm and Lind, 1993).

One of the prominent areas with significant financial support from governmental bodies (regional, national, and European) is *infrastructure,* with particular emphasis on enhancing regional development. Infrastructure support has become

---

*The authors wish to acknowledge constructive comments made by two anonymous referees on a previous version of the paper.

Received December 1992; revised December 1993 and March 1994; accepted April 1994.

580   JOURNAL OF REGIONAL SCIENCE, VOL. 35, NO. 4, 1

one of the main vehicles of regional policy in Europe.   When critically review
regional policy performance, one needs to make an assessment of the effe
generated solely by a particular measure of regional policy intervention. Clearly,
using public investments in infrastructure as a policy instrument for regio
development, we are implicitly referring to an *active strategy* for opening n
opportunities for the business sector: a strategy where infrastructure is favor
and generating private investments (Rietveld, 1989; Townroe, 1979; Vickerm
1991).

The ERDF (European Regional Development Fund) is the major source
E.C. initiatives for regional restructuring in the Community. It commits the m
part of its available funds to infrastructure projects (see Table 1). This table sho
that, for both the amounts committed and the number of programs, projects a
studies undertaken, until recently more than 75 percent falls under the heading
infrastructure. Recently, it has become common to request also co-financing
infrastructure projects by regional or national governments. Given the h
amounts of money involved, the European Commission has—in response
concerns voiced by the European Parliament—expressed the need for a criti
evaluation of the past performance of regional development policy by the E.C.

This development in policy evaluation runs parallel to the current gene
trend towards a more critical assessment of the efficiency of the public sect
where increasingly "value for money" is set as a prominent goal. Recent studies
program and project evaluation in public policy and administration call incre
ingly for attention to straightforward, unambiguous and widely applicable anal
cal tools for assessing the socioeconomic performance of public bodies in vari
fields of policymaking (see for a recent overview, Williams and Giardina, 1993; a
Van Pelt, 1993).

It should furthermore be noted that E.C. transfers are special types of fis
redistribution among member countries or regions, as they aim at restoring eq
competitive conditions among countries or regions without favoring any particu
industry.   ERDF Commitments concern essentially overhead investments
regions with particular emphasis on the elimination of locational impediments
growth.

TABLE 1:   Percentages of Amounts Committed, and Number of Programs,
Projects and Studies Undertaken, by Type of Investment, 1975–1988

	Amounts Committed (%)	Number of Programs, Projects and Studies (%)
Community Program	0.8	0.01
National Programs of Community Interest	5.8	0.2
Industry, Services and Craft	13.6	23.5
Infrastructure	79.6	75.5
Internally Generated Development	0.1	0.3
Studies	0.2	0.5

Source: CEC (1988).

In this paper we will outline a new method which has been developed to assess post the impact of ERDF Commitments on different regions inside a national onomy over a longer period (i.e., the past fifteen years).   This approach may also nction as a basic framework and an operational tool for monitoring and assessing ie mesoeconomic (regional-sectoral) effects of the ERDF in the future.

We have named this new method the PARADISE Approach (Policy Assessent of Regional Achievements and Developments Induced by Stimuli of ERDF). his analytical framework has been designed in such a way that in principle—ven the common statistical data base for European regions—a cross-sectional alysis of all E.C. regions is possible. This use of common types of data means viously that the model contents and structure have to be based on the E.C. untries with the poorest data availability. This has of course meant major nitations for the specification of the model for the PARADISE approach. But if ie wants to have an analytical instrument that can be used for comparative irposes in different countries and regions, then a minimum commonality is cessary. And even in that case it may be difficult to have such data for *all* relevant riods under consideration and for *all* relevant geographical scales. The PARAISE framework consists of two steps. The first (exploratory) step used here is sed on a performance assessment by means of a so-called *frequency analysis* sed on simple statistical (descriptive) counting. This idea is in the next step tended with a *simple explanatory model* to test the existence of a causal antitative relationship between the economic development of a region and ssible explanatory background variables for this development. The ERDF ommitments in this model are then regarded as one such explanatory variable.

The key issue of the PARADISE approach is to identify the significance of gional economic impacts of ERDF transfers to less favored areas of the ommunity by using directly *available* indicators for regional performance. Given ie data limitations, it seems plausible to select new private investments in the gion—being the immediate measurable response of the business sector—as a easure of success of ERDF Commitments. The analytical problem is then to ickage such indicators into a general operational analysis for evaluating in a oss-regional sense the effects of ERDF money.

The paper is organized as follows. In Section 2 we will give a concise scription of various impact methods for policy analysis. Next, in Section 3 we will itline in detail the impact assessment method developed and applied here (i.e., the equency table method and the causal explanatory model). This method will be sted for a case study focussed on regions in the Netherlands. The results of these npirical tests are shown and discussed in Sections 4 and 5. In the last section we ill offer some retrospective and prospective conclusions.

IMPACT ASSESSMENT METHODS: A CONCISE OVERVIEW

Impact assessment methods deal with the estimation of expected conseiences of policy measures aimed at (socio-) economic development. Regional ipact assessment methods may focus on all impacts which are relevant for roups or sectors in) a region, or on regional goals to be achieved by implementing

582   JOURNAL OF REGIONAL SCIENCE, VOL. 35, NO. 4, 19

a specific policy (e.g., by means of cost-effectiveness analysis). Whether impacts a
judged from a particular policy angle or from a broader regional perspective, it
clear that in all cases a reliable estimation of expected policy consequences has to I
made. This holds for both ex ante and ex post impact assessment; ex ante impac
refer then to foreseeable relevant consequences for regions prior to the impleme
tation of a given policy (or development), whereas ex post impacts refer to realiz
consequences after implementation (Diamond and Spence, 1983).

In the practice of regional policy evaluation a wide variety of impact asses
ment techniques has been developed, which might broadly be subdivided into *a
hoc* impact assessment methods and *structured* impact assessment metho
(Folmer, 1985). Both classes will concisely be discussed here, with a particular vie
on their relevance for regional and infrastructure planning.

Ad hoc Impact Assessment

Ad hoc impact analyses refer to a measurement problem for which r
possibility exists to develop a formal operational model, due to time constraint
nonrepetitive situations, or lack of data (for example, the impact of a ne
bioscience park on the regional economy). Two approaches may then be adopted.

(a) An *informal analysis* by using expert views (e.g., Delphi techniques) or I
taking a global expert look at some available data elsewhere (for instance, tl
effects of science parks in other regions).

(b) A *comparative analysis* based on cross-regional or cross-national exper
ences with more or less similar regional policy problems and policy measures (fe
instance, the regional effects of the creation of new bioscience parks in differel
countries).

Despite low costs and easy use of ad hoc impact analyses, they usually do n
offer the same rate of precision, controllability and transferability as structure
impact analyses do. In practice, however, such ad hoc methods may be helpful, a
they are able to generate within a limited time horizon relevant insights into tl
expected consequences of policy. This requires that sufficient expertise ar
experience be available so as to make realistic estimates of impacts of changes o
relevant regional welfare or performance indicators.

Structured Impact Assessment

Through structured impact analyses the effect of (a set of) policy measures o
(a set of) relevant policy variables can be systematically traced under varyin
conditions.   A first pathfinding influential contribution to structured (economi
impact analysis can be found in Tinbergen (1956). When we deal with structure
spatial impact analyses based on formal—usually quantitative (econometric c
statistical)—techniques and models, it is also meaningful to make a distinctio
between micro and macro approaches.

Micro Studies. At the micro level one deals with individual observations o
actors who are (supposed to be) exposed to and affected by policy measures. Micr
studies are normally related to survey methods (e.g., interviewing, sel

lministration). The information is extracted from surveys explicitly referring to
.licy issues. On the basis of such micro-based methods, it is possible to collect very
tailed insights into behavioral responses at a disaggregate level.

On the other hand, gathering this kind of information is costly and time
nsuming. Also there is a chance of biased information due to the survey
chniques used. For example, there might be measurement errors caused by the
terviewer or errors because of communication barriers and misperceptions of the
spondent. For the information on attitudes of individual actors one has to rely on
e perception of people responding to the survey concerned. They may be tempted
use a survey for manipulating future policy decisions in order to reach a desirable
rection of policy measures (see Nijkamp et al., 1993). In some types of surveys
strument bias can arise—an inadequately specified type of policy measure may
ad to a biased response.

Finally, it is noteworthy that micro studies can be further classified into
ntrolled experimentation, quasi-experimentation and nonexperimentation (Camp-
·ll and Standley, 1966; Forkenbrock et al., 1990; and Isserman, 1990). This has
·en further discussed in Blaas and Nijkamp (1993).

In the case of infrastructure impact assessment, it would for instance be
·ssible to interview land owners, investors, local municipalities, etc. to find out
.anges in behavior, attitudes or perceptions after the implementation of a new
·ad link. The same could be undertaken on the user side, such as taxpayers,
·mmuters, residents, tourists and visitors, etc. In various cases, this is a
·eaningful way of gathering necessary insights into the impacts of new infrastruc-
.re.

Macro Studies. The class of macro approaches is not entirely separated from
icro analyses, as macro studies are often based on aggregated results of surveys
·ld by bureaus of statistics. These aggregate surveys, however, usually do not
·plicitly refer to policy issues and related impacts and therefore do not involve the
·sk of biased information as in the case of the micro studies mentioned above.
·oreover, macro studies are sometimes less costly and less time consuming than
icro approaches.

Macro studies can be subdivided into studies *without an explicit formal model*
·d those incorporating *a mathematical model.* Examples of the first class are

(a) a qualitative impact systems model (see for instance Nijkamp and Van Pelt,
1990, for strategic policy evaluation in a city in India),

(b) with/without impact methods, sometimes refined in the form of shift-share
methods for regional growth (see, e.g., Moore and Rhodes, 1973), and

(c) contingency table analysis and log-linear analysis (as developed, e.g., by
Brouwer, 1988, for a statistical analysis of spatial behavior).

hus there are various non-formal modeling approaches which might be help-
·l—in particular as complementary methods—in regional policy analysis.

Examples of the second class (impact approaches with a formal model) are

(a) *single equation* models (mainly apropriate for a partial impact assessment,
but easier to pursue), and

The Regional Science Research Corporation 1995.

584   JOURNAL OF REGIONAL SCIENCE, VOL. 35, NO. 4, 19

(b) *multiequation* models (in particular suitable for getting a coherent pictu of all relevant interwoven impacts, but more difficult to estimate in a statistica proper way).

In general, the use of a formal model would be preferable in regional impa analysis, but data requirements are often prohibitive. Nevertheless, in vario cases a simple input-output model may be helpful in identifying all direct ar indirect economic impacts (via an impact chain) of regional policies. As a compr mise, the use of simulation models has gained a great deal of popularity in rece years. Such models may be used in a structured causal impact chain, even thoug some (or all) coefficients may not be based on hard empirical facts but on plausib "guestimates" (see Giaoutzi and Nijkamp, 1993, for an application).

The use of structured macro models may thus in principle offer mu assistance in estimating the various impacts caused by public policy. Unfort nately, most impact models suffer from severe lack of data, so that broad applicable, multiequation models for assessing the impacts of policy are n abundant. At best, simulation models seem to offer a compromise alternative.

In the next section we will present a new approach for assessing ex post t impacts of regional policy in Europe, based on ERDF Commitments in the pa fifteen years.

3.   AN ERDF IMPACT ASSESSMENT METHOD:
THE PARADISE APPROACH

Before discussing details of the available ERDF data, we will present t methodology of our approach. The ERDF impact assessment framework used our analysis will be presented here—as already pointed out in Section 1—as two-step approach, on the basis of an exploratory frequency and a statistic explanatory analysis.

Frequency Analysis

As mentioned already in the introduction to this paper, the first component the impact assessment tool designed here is a performance assessment by means a so-called exploratory frequency analysis. This approach is based on a cros sectional comparison of the relative performance of various regions in a country terms of two or more strategic policy-relevant variables in a given year. Th approach will now be sketched in a simple expository form.

Consider a relevant *policy (control) variable B* and a relevant *impact (depe dent) variable A*, observed on a set of relevant regions r ($r = 1, \ldots, R$). All values the variables are standardized and related to population size (or any oth meaningful reference variable) of the regions at hand in order to ensure a unifor and properly weighted comparison of all regions. The average values of the variables across all regions are denoted by A^* and B^*, respectively. Now we make dichotomous classification of these regions according to the question whether not all variables are above the regional average. This is indicated in a cros classified table (see Table 2). Such a table can be constructed for each time peri

TABLE 2:   A Cross-classified Frequency Table
for Regional Policy Evaluation

	$B_r > B^*$	$B_r < B^*$
$A_r > A^*$	I	II
$A_r < A^*$	III	IV

der consideration, while the results in terms of frequency can of course easily be mbined.

As we can see, the frequency table includes four quadrants when we consider o different variables. The meaning of the entries in these quadrants is straight- rward. For example, quadrant I shows the number of regions which have for both riables A and B values above the regional average in a given year. The other adrants can be interpreted analogously.

These tables can now be used to explore the hypothesis that there exists a sitive correlation between the variables A and B. The direction of causality nnot, however, be derived directly from these tables in a static setting. Notice also at no conclusions can be drawn concerning the strength of the correlation tween these variables, as we are only investigating frequencies.

The variable that is supposed to be the dependent variable is represented in e vertical column (i.e., the variable A). We are now most interested in the figures the quadrants I and IV. When the sum of the number of regions in these two adrants is above fifty percent of the total number of regions, there is in general arly a positive correlation between the two variables. This conclusion is of course ore strongly valid as the number of regions in quadrants I and IV is significantly gher than the figures in quadrants II and III.

This impact method is easy to handle and presents a directly interpretable cture of a possible influence of one or more explanatory (or control) variables on a ependent) regional response variable. Clearly, such a hypothesis can be tested ore rigorously by means of chi-square statistics or in more extensive cases by eans of contingency table analysis (e.g., by using log-linear models). The limited tabase in the context of our study on European regions does not allow, however, ch statistically more appropriate tests. In any case, in order to attach sufficient lidity to the results of a frequency analysis, it is in general required to have at ast a total number of 10 to 15 regions, dependent on the availability of rresponding data at a specific regional level (offered by E.C. Eurostat statistics). irthermore, it may sometimes be necessary to group some small interacting gions into one larger region in order to avoid a bias caused by interdependent rder effects between regions. Clearly, this possibility is also limited, because a fficient number of regions has to remain for the sake of statistically valid results. nally, regions which have not yet received any ERDF Commitments in the past ould not be excluded in the frequency analysis because of the need for a no-policy ference framework for evaluating the ERDF Commitments.

The above method can be applied for any combination of policy-relevant variables under study, nor is there a restriction on the number of variabl considered, although too many variables will decrease the transparency of tl frequency tables. Furthermore, by means of this method it is also possible to u time series (in order to examine the stability of correlations over time), time lags the influence of the explanatory variables on the dependent variable has a tin delay) and moving averages (a method to be used if possible outliers in the data s of a specific variable are to be eliminated). Especially in view of the (usual) time la in the impact of infrastructure on regional growth and the frequent irregul: pattern of public expenditures on infrastructure (as a result of public budg management and lumpiness of infrastructure), these aspects are very important our case study (see also Van den Ende and Nijkamp, 1992). The possibility including such elements is obviously dependent on the available time series data. the data set for the variables covers only a limited number of years, a long tin series of frequency tables including time lags and moving averages is of course n possible.

For the assessment of ERDF impacts, our method considers private inves ments as a dependent variable and ERDF Commitments, public investments ar changes in (regional) gross value added as explanatory variables. This can b explained as follows. The private investments as a dependent variable serve as a (indirect) first-order indicator for the economic development in a region. In genera most firms tend to respond to public stimuli by increasing their investments (whic in turn may generate additional employment and hence regional growth). Furthe more, firms may be looking ahead (i.e., they invest more if they expect a highe future value added) or looking back (i.e., they invest more if a rise in value adde has actually taken place). We thus postulate that private investments provide th best first response variables of public policy. Clearly, in our case the development private investments depends not only on ERDF Commitments in a given regio but also on other regional public investments and of course on the change in gros value added in that region (either expected or realized). One might argue that ther will be multicollinearity between the ERDF Commitments and public investment However, in our approach the values of the ERDF Commitments will be subtracte from the level of public investments, so as to allow a separate indentification impacts (one of the goals of this study). Besides, it appears that the levels of ERD Commitments are relatively low in comparison to the public investment values (fc example, in the Dutch regions supported by the ERDF Fund the ERDF Commi ments amount on average to approximately two percent of the total publi investments). In Section 4 we will discuss the results of this method for empiric studies applied to regions in the Netherlands, but first we will present a simpl explanatory model designed for our purposes.

A Simple Explanatory Model

In this section we will present a simple explanatory model for assessing ex pos the impact of the ERDF expenditures. The basic idea is that ERDF Commitment together with (national and regional) public expenditures will attract new entrepre neurial activities which will first manifest themselves as new private investments

Such new investments might next lead to additional employment, which is also often regarded by policy makers as a regional performance indicator and hence will be considered here as well. As pointed out above, for the explanation of entrepreneurial behavior a simple hypothesis based on rational expectations is used, which means that (realized or foreseen) increases in value added will also lead to a rise in private investments.

For the assessment of the impacts of the ERDF Commitments on a region's economic development, we therefore use the following causal model as a frame of reference:

1) $$I_{pr} = \alpha_0 + \alpha_1 I_{cr} + \alpha_2 I_{(o-c)r} + \alpha_3 \Delta GVA_r$$

where

ΔGVA_r = change in gross value added in region r,
I_{cr} = ERDF Commitments for region r,
$I_{(o-c)r}$ = public investments minus ERDF Commitments in region r,
I_{pr} = private investments in region r,
α_0 = intercept, and
α_i = reaction coefficient ($i = 1, 2, 3$).

Equation (1) can be represented in terms of three complementary types of investment equations, based respectively on an active response model, a conventional investment model and a passive response model.

For the first equation, the active response model reads as follows:

2) $$I_{pr} = \alpha_0 + \alpha_1 I_{cr} + \alpha_2 I_{(o-c)r} + \alpha_3 \Delta GVA_r^{(+\sigma)}$$

where it is postulated that private investments depend inter alia on the economic situation entrepreneurs expect to emerge in the near future. This is represented by the change in the gross value added with an expected positive (forward) time lag σ.

For the second equation, the conventional investment behavior, we assume:

3) $$I_{pr} = \beta_0 + \beta_1 I_{cr}^{(-\sigma)} + \beta_2 I_{(o-c)r}^{(-\sigma)}$$

where the investments in the private sector depend only on the (past) investments made by the public sector in the region and on ERDF Commitments.

The third equation

4) $$I_{pr} = \delta_0 + \delta_1 I_{cr} + \delta_2 I_{(o-c)r} + \delta_3 \Delta GVA_r^{(-\sigma)}$$

is based on a passive response model, i.e., the private investments undertaken by the entrepreneurs depend among others on the economic situation in the past few years. This is represented by the change in gross value added with a negative time lag σ.

In addition to these three investment equations, a further analysis of regional employment impacts was made by investigating the labor-investment ratio

5) $$L_r = \mu_0 + \mu_1 I_{pr}^{(-\sigma)}$$

588   JOURNAL OF REGIONAL SCIENCE, VOL. 35, NO. 4, 1995

in order to explore indirectly a possible second-order relationship between the ERDF subsidies and total employment in a region. Clearly, one should carefully interpret the results of this equation because of the intransparent nature of forces active on regional labor markets (see Gorter et al., 1992).

The explanatory model is rather flexible in that it can be based on moving averages of the specific data and/or can be used with different time lags. Again this is dependent on the availability of long time series of data. This model can be applied both for regions which have and which have not (yet) received any ERDF support and allows a cross-regional comparison of impacts of the explanatory variables.

In Section 4 a selection of empirical results for both the frequency tables and the regression analyses applied to the Equations (2)–(5) will be presented and discussed.

4. EMPIRICAL APPLICATION USING FREQUENCY ANALYSIS

The most appropriate data source to be used for the PARADISE approach is Eurostat (the Statistical Office of the European Communities) because of the consistency in definition of all variables needed for our method for all regions in the European Community. In an extensive study (see Blaas and Nijkamp, 1992, 1993) the PARADISE-model was applied to various regions in Europe (in particular, The Netherlands and Italy). In the framework of the present paper we will limit ourselves to a presentation of results from Dutch regions.

Despite the small size of the country, regional policy has always been an important issue in the Netherlands, especially in light of the lagging economic performance of various regions in the eastern and southern part of the country. These regions have in the past years also been supported financially by ERDF transfers. Therefore, it seems relevant to use the Dutch situation as a test case for both the frequency analysis and the explanatory model.

The information at the Dutch Central Bureau of Statistics and Eurostat made it possible to build a complete multiregional data set for all variables under consideration—I_p, I_c, I_o and GVA—for the period 1975–1987 for all regions.

We will now discuss the frequency analysis. It will be based here on the 11 provinces of The Netherlands, which are the main administrative regions in the country. Given the time period considered, it was also possible to include time lags and moving averages in the frequency analysis.

In our numerical analysis we examined six time lags varying from zero to five years, so that private investments (I_p) were dependent on the variables ERDF Commitments (I_c), public investments minus the ERDF Commitments ($I_{(o-c)}$) and the change in Gross Value Added (ΔGVA) with various time lags. Although it appeared that there were some minor changes in the results when varying the time lags, most outcomes were rather robust. Using a time lag of four years appeared to lead to the most satisfactory statistical results (see Table 3). (See Blaas and Nijkamp, 1992, for a comparison of all results when a series of different time lags is used.)

Table 3 reveals various interesting results. It should be noted that frequency

TABLE 3:   Frequency Tables for 11 Dutch Regions, Based on Absolute Data Standardized for Population, with a Time Lag of 4 Years

Year		$I_c > I_c^*$	$I_c < I_c^*$	$I_{(o-c)} > I_{(o-c)}^*$	$I_{(o-c)} > I_{(o-c)}^*$	$\Delta GVA > \Delta GVA^*$	$\Delta GVA < \Delta GVA^*$
1980	$I_p > I_p^*$	2	3	1	4	1	4
	$I_p < I_p^*$	2	4	2	4	1	5
1981	$I_p > I_p^*$	2	2	2	2	2	2
	$I_p < I_p^*$	1	6	2	5	0	7
1982	$I_p > I_p^*$	0	3	0	3	2	1
	$I_p < I_p^*$	1	7	3	5	4	4
1983	$I_p > I_p^*$	1	2	0	3	3	0
	$I_p < I_p^*$	2	6	2	6	4	4
1984	$I_p < I_p^*$	0	4	1	3	1	3
	$I_p > I_p^*$	2	5	0	7	1	6
1985	$I_p < I_p^*$	0	4	1	3	1	3
	$I_p > I_p^*$	1	6	0	8	1	6
1986	$I_p > I_p^*$	1	4	2	3	4	1
	$I_p < I_p^*$	2	4	0	6	2	4
1987	$I_p > I_p^*$	1	4	1	4	1	4
	$I_p < I_p^*$	2	4	0	6	4	2
Total	$I_p > I_p^*$	7	26	8	25	15	18
	$I_p < I_p^*$	13	42	9	46	19	36

Notes: I_c = ERDF Commitments, I_p = Private investments, $I_{(o-c)}$ = Public investments−ERDF Commitments, and ΔGVA = Change in Gross Value Added.

bles are given here for eight years. A time lag of four years means that the private vestments in 1980 are confronted respectively with the ERDF Commitments, iblic investments (minus the ERDF Commitments) and the change in Gross alue Added in 1976. In 1981 the private investments are then compared to the lues of these three variables in 1977, etc. The results can be interpreted in the me way as shown in Table 2.

It appears from Table 3 that regions with below average ERDF Commitments e predominantly regions with below average private investments in The Nether- nds. It is interesting to observe that regions with a fairly good performance (i.e., ove average) do not necessarily exhibit a strong correlation with ERDF transfers. hus weaker regions seem to benefit most. If we next take a look at the correlation tween private investments (the dependent variable) and the public investments d the change in Gross Value Added (as the explanatory variables, from the ntral column and right-hand column of Table 3, respectively), it appears that ere is also in this case a fairly strong positive correlation for each pair of these riables. In each year about 60 percent of the total number of regions is contained quadrants I and IV, which seems to support the hypothesis underlying the equency analysis.

Next, Table 4 summarizes the results in Table 3 for all years under nsideration. Concerning the left-hand column (I_p compared to I_c), the total imber of regions in the first and the fourth quadrants is quite large in the years 80 to 1983, but is decreasing in the following four years. Thus the impact of

he Regional Science Research Corporation 1995.

TABLE 4:   Number of Dutch Regions in
Quadrant I + IV as Percentage of Total Number of Regions

Year	I_p vs. I_c	I_p vs. $I_{(o-c)}$	I_p vs. ΔGVA
1980	55	45	55
1981	73	64	82
1982	64	45	55
1983	64	55	64
1984	45	73	64
1985	55	73	64
1986	45	73	73
1987	45	64	27
Total	56	61	58

ERDF seems to become less evident, a situation which can be explained from tl
stronger position of various Dutch peripheral areas in recent years. The relatio
ship between ERDF Commitments and private investments is thus providir
time-dependent results. However, for a more satisfactory statistical analysis of tl
influence of ERDF Commitments on private investments one should make use
an explanatory model (see Section 5).

In addition to the analysis of frequency tables based on annual data one ma
also construct similar tables for moving averages in order to correct for outliers.
is then also possible to investigate the influence of a varying time lag. In our Dutc
case study, we have compared for seven time periods the results for time la
ranging from zero to two years. Also in this case a longer time lag (i.e., two year
showed relatively the best results. The outcomes are presented in Table 5; the
show largely the same pattern as that depicted in Table 3.

Finally, it is again possible to present the findings of our frequency analysis i
a concise form. Table 6 is based on Table 5 and presents about the same results a
those in Table 4. We may conclude here that the frequency analysis based o
moving averages leads to more conclusive results than the analysis based on lagge
absolute data.

5.   EMPIRICAL ANALYSIS USING AN EXPLANATORY MODEL

Now we will present the results of the explanatory model for assessing tl
regional impact of the ERDF expenditures. This model may be seen as a
indispensable, behaviorally-oriented extension of the frequency analysis as a
impact assessment tool for ERDF Commitments. The frequency table analysis
mainly meant to be an exploratory tool. The explanatory model however, serves t
test the existence of a causal quantitative relationship between the econom
development of a region and various explanatory background variables for thi
development. Clearly, the ERDF Commitments in this model are only one of suc
explanatory variables. In a way analogous to the frequency method, we will in thi
second stage of the PARADISE approach again use absolute values and movin
averages of all relevant variables.

ABLE 5:   Frequency Tables for 11 Dutch Regions, Based on Moving Averages
and Standardized for Population Size with a Time Lag of 2 Years
[Time Periods 1 (1977, . . . , 1981) to 7 (1983, . . . , 1988)]

Time Period		$I_c > I_c^*$	$I_c < I_c^*$	$I_{(o-c)} > I_{(o-c)}^*$	$I_{(o-c)} < I_{(o-c)}^*$	$\Delta GVA > \Delta GVA^*$	$\Delta GVA < \Delta GVA^*$
1	$I_p > I_p^*$	3	2	2	3	3	2
	$I_p < I_p^*$	1	5	1	5	2	4
2	$I_p > I_p^*$	2	1	1	2	2	1
	$I_p < I_p^*$	1	7	1	7	1	7
3	$I_p > I_p^*$	1	2	1	2	2	1
	$I_p < I_p^*$	1	7	1	7	0	8
4	$I_p < I_p^*$	1	4	1	4	2	3
	$I_p > I_p^*$	2	4	0	6	0	6
5	$I_p < I_p^*$	1	3	1	3	1	3
	$I_p > I_p^*$	3	4	0	7	1	6
6	$I_p > I_p^*$	1	3	1	3	1	3
	$I_p < I_p^*$	3	4	0	7	1	6
7	$I_p > I_p^*$	1	3	1	3	1	2
	$I_p < I_p^*$	3	4	0	7	1	6
'otal	$I_p > I_p^*$	10	18	8	20	13	15
	$I_p < I_p^*$	14	35	3	46	6	43

Notes: I_c = ERDF Commitments, I_p = Private investments, $I_{(o-c)}$ = Public investments−ERDF
mmitments, and ΔGVA = Change in Gross Value Added.

Various model experiments with different time lags and moving averages were
plied to Dutch regions. For the sake of brevity and presentation, the results from
r regression analysis will only be presented for four major regions in The
etherland (North-Netherland, East-Netherland, West-Netherland, and South-
etherland) and for the country as a whole. Clearly, various complementary
sults may be achieved according to different combinations of regions, the number
time lags, the time span of moving averages and the specification given in
quations (2)–(4). In order to avoid a lengthy presentation of a great many
atistical regression results, we have chosen to present a qualitative overview of all

TABLE 6:   Number of Regions in Quadrant I + IV as
Percentage of Total Number of Regions

Time Period	I_p vs. I_c	I_p vs. $I_{(o-c)}$	I_p vs. ΔGVA
1	72	64	64
2	82	73	82
3	73	73	91
4	46	64	73
5	46	73	64
6	46	73	64
7	46	73	73
Total	58	70	72

these model results, by looking into the question of how frequently in ea regression model any of the explanatory variables contributes significantly explaining the variance in the dependent variable (based on a 95 percent confider interval).[1]

The results are presented in Table 7.   These results show that our regressi analyses based on moving averages perform much better than do the results bas on absolute data.   The investment equation based on conventional behav [Equation (3)] appeared to show the best results compared to the other t investment equations (active and passive response). This is mainly caused by t fact that the variable Change in Gross Value Added performs poorly in these t investment equations. When we eliminate this variable in the model, the resu appear to be to a large extent similar for the three investment equations.

A look at the separate variables shows that public investments give the b results when the calculations are based on absolute data. The application of movi averages leads to very good results for the variable ERDF Commitments. Furthe more, it appears that the Change in Gross Value Added has hardly a positi significant effect on private investments. A possible explanation is—as indicat before—the indirect nature of the effects of this variable on private investmen Finally, it appears that the employment equation also performs quite well and th there is no relevant difference due to the use of different time lags when t calculations are based on moving averages. The results based on absolute da show that a shorter time lag leads to better results regarding public investments

We may thus conclude that an explanatory model based on a regressi analysis appears to be more powerful than the frequency table analysis, both as hypothesis testing device and as a mechanism for yielding estimates of t consequences of ERDF expenditures. The results of this simple explanatory mo show that there are several regions which (for different time lags) have be positively influenced by ERDF Commitments. Clearly, it is possible to gauge t extent of influence by means of the values of the reaction coefficients of the ERI Commitments on the private investments.

In our experimental study for The Netherlands, it was clear that the ERI expenditures in the past have certainly influenced the private investments in t regions considered. According to the explanatory model there is some statisti evidence that the effects differ between the regions supported by the ERDF. If v compare the regions in terms of the number of positive reaction coefficients f ERDF commitments (for different investment equations and time lags used), appears that investments in some regions are more strongly influenced by tl ERDF Commitments than in other regions. Given the aggregate ERDF figur used, it can not entirely be inferred whether such differences between regions a due to a different nature of projects supported by the ERDF in specific regions.

---

[1]In our case study we have also undertaken a regression analysis in terms of variables express in constant prices. The results were not significantly better compared to the analysis based on variab in current prices.

Absolute Values

Equation	$I_{pr} = \alpha_0 + \alpha_1 \cdot I_{cr} + \alpha_2 \cdot I_{\omega-c'r} + \alpha_3 \cdot \Delta GVA_r^{(+n)}$			$I_{pr} = \beta_0 + \beta_1 \cdot I_{cr}^{(-n)} + \beta^2 \cdot I_{\omega cr}^{(nt)}$			$I_{pr} = \delta_0 + \delta_1 \cdot I_{cr} + \delta_2 \cdot I_{\omega-c'r} + \delta_3 \cdot \Delta GVA_r^{(-n)}$			$L_r = \mu_0 + \mu_1 \cdot I_{pr}^{(nt)}$
Variable	I_{cr}	$I_{\omega-c'r}$	ΔGVA_r	I_{cr}	$I_{\omega-c'r}$	I_{cr}	$I_{\omega-c'r}$	ΔGVA_r	I_{pr}
Time lag	0 1 2 3 4 5	0 1 2 3 4 5	0 1 2 3 4 5	0 1 2 3 4 5	0 1 2 3 4 5	0 1 2 3 4 5	0 1 2 3 4 5	0 1 2 3 4 5	0 1 2 3 4 5
Region:									
North									+
East	▽ +			▽		▽			O
West	▽ + + O	+ + O		▽		▽	+ + O		O O O
South	O	O		O		O	+ O	O	O O
Netherlands	+	+	+	+	+	+			

Moving Averages

Equation	$I_{pr} = \alpha_0 + \alpha_1 \cdot I_{cr} + \alpha_2 \cdot I_{\omega-c'r} + \alpha_3 \cdot \Delta GVA_r^{(+n)}$			$I_{pr(-n)} = \beta_0 + \beta_1 \cdot I_{cr}^{(-n)} + \beta_2 \cdot I_{\omega-c'r}$		$I_{pr} = \delta_0 + \delta_1 \cdot I_{cr} + \delta_2 \cdot I_{\omega-c'r} + \delta_3 \cdot \Delta GVA_r^{(-n)}$			$L_r = \mu_0 + \mu_1 \cdot I_{pr}^{(nt)}$
Variable	I_{cr}	$I_{\omega-c'r}$	ΔGVA_r	I_{cr}	$I_{\omega-c'r}$	I_{cr}	$I_{\omega-c'r}$	ΔGVA_r	I_{pr}
Time lag	0 1 2	0 1 2	0 1 2	0 1 2	0 1 2	0 1 2	0 1 2	0 1 2	0 1 2
Region:									
North	O	O	O			O	+		O
East	+ +	+ +		▽ +		+ +	+		O O +
West	+ ▽	+	+			+ ▽			+
South	+	+	+			+	+		+
Netherlands	+	+	+			+			O

Note: Symbols denote only statistically significant coefficients based on a confidence level > 95%. Legend: I_{cr} = ERDF Commitments in region r; $I_{\omega-c'r}$ = Public investments in region r minus ERDF Commitments in region r; ΔGVA_r = Change in regional Gross Value Added; L_r = Total employment in region r; ∇ = variable I_{cr} is not considered because of absence in the region concerned; + = significant explanation with: $0.5 < $ R-squared adjusted < 1; O = significant explanation with: R-squared adjusted < 0.5.

order to give a conclusive region-specific answer, much more detailed case stu research at the regional project level would be necessary.

4. CONCLUDING REMARKS

The ERDF Commitments are supposed to be a major instrument of region policy that is meant to act as an adequate vehicle for improving the welfare positi of lagging (less favored) regions in the European Community. The Commitmer of the ERDF have a strategic meaning, i.e., these expenditures help and/ encourage the provision of overhead instruments or facilities which are a prereq site for future economic development or remove bottlenecks for existing develc ments. It has always been difficult, however, to demonstrate the effectiveness Community expenditures on investments for the economic development of region. Therefore, the main goal of this study was to develop a strategic impa assessment method for the ERDF that would meet the criteria and conditions uniform applicability in all regions of the E.C., given the available data. This ru out, for instance, quasi-experimental approaches and branch-specific researc although it is evident that in subsequent research such more focussed case stu work will be necessary.

For the ex post assessment approach of ERDF Commitments we ha developed the PARADISE approach consisting of an exploratory frequency tak analysis and a (simple) explanatory model. The frequency table analysis is main meant to be a statistical exploratory tool in the sense of offering evidence on tl average effect of ERDF expenditures from the past. This analysis allows also f some experimentation with impacts of time lags between the ERDF expenditur and mesoeconomic indicators. The explanatory model in combination with regre sion analysis is far more powerful, both as a hypothesis testing device and as mechanism for yielding estimates of the consequences of ERDF expenditures. Bo steps of the PARADISE model proved to be simple and operational when it w: tested for The Netherlands.

A key requirement of the method is that it should be able to identify releva regional economic effects in all E.C. regions resulting from the ERDF. O preliminary conclusion regarding the PARADISE approach (both the frequenc table analysis and the simple explanatory model) is that it has the ability to provi a quantitative assessment of effects due to ERDF expenditures. In the empiric studies, it was shown that the ERDF expenditures in the past have had significant influence on the private investments in the regions considered.

The frequency table analysis revealed some changes over time in the correl tion between private investments and ERDF Commitments. This is possibly due the influence of other factors on this correlation which fluctuate over time. F example, when the public investments in certain regions are extremely low in given time period, it is almost impossible that the (relatively small) size of tl ERDF Commitments has a sufficiently large critical mass to induce privat investments to such an extent that these adopt values above the regional average i the specific regions. This affects of course the strength of the pairwise correlatic between ERDF Commitments and private investments. Here statistical methoc aling with nonlinear correlation and/or regression might be helpful. To catch the namics of such phenomena even nonlinear spatial dynamics models (see e.g., ijkamp and Reggiani, 1995) might be helpful, for instance, with the help of mulation experiments.

National and E.C.-wide economic developments might in principle also have impact on regional outcomes, but various tests demonstrated that adding this ctor to the set of explanatory variables did not in most cases lead to significantly tter results. Probably, fluctuations in the national and the E.C.-wide economy e reflected in the Regional Gross Value Added that was already included in the odel.

The use of different time lags in our explanatory model did not significantly iprove the results in favor of one specific time lag. In the frequency analysis in our se study, time lags of four years appeared to lead to more favorable results.

A quantified comparison of the impacts on the regions throughout the uropean Community is only possible if the model is used with data from the same urce. Fortunately, the statistical office of the European Community (Eurostat) is aking substantial progress in harmonizing the necessary data, although at this age Eurostat is not yet able to provide all detailed data on all past years and/or all gions receiving ERDF support. In particular, Eurostat data are not available on rious public investments in many regions in some past years. In addition, for ivate investments for several regions mainly data for investments in the dustrial sector are available instead of data on investments in the entire business ctor. These data are, however, normally available in the national statistical fices. Clearly, there is always a danger of inconsistency of definitions and riables used in a model for cross-national or cross-regional comparative research, d therefore it is a sine qua non to build up a database as a next step of a broader mparative European analysis. Once such a data base does exist, the PARADISE odel as a general strategic impact method for assessing ERDF Commitments ems to offer a rather promising analytical framework. In principle, the PARA- ISE approach has the potential to act as a regular tool in European regional policy aluation. It may therefore be interesting to give some further thoughts on how to iprove the model (with a specific view on the explanatory part).

First of all, the use of quarterly investment data, if available in central atistical offices, would greatly improve the modeling of time lags. Secondly, a ore dynamic model might be able to capture the impact of changes in ERDF penditures on changes in private investments. This possibility would be worth me more experimentation. Besides, the use of net private investments (instead of oss investment expenditures) and a limitation of public infrastructure to direct frastructure (i.e., excluding "soft" infrastructure like housing, schools, hospitals, c.) and also investments by public industrial companies would improve the basis our explanatory model. And finally, more definite results may be obtained by sing this regression approach for regions from different countries in Europe. One the possibilities is to pool cross-section and time series data to arrive at a more mplete data set which allows for more unambiguous statistical results regarding e impact of ERDF expenditures.

The PARADISE approach finds its strength in its ability to underta comparative regional policy assessments in different countries and regions usi (more or less) the same type of available data. Seen from this perspective, it can used on a regular basis. The struggle for a theoretically more sophisticated mo can only be overcome if—with the expansion of the European space—t European statistical office puts much effort in the development of a compatible a consistent European database.

REFERENCES

Armstrong, Harry and Jim Taylor. 1993. *Regional Economics and Policy.* London: Harvest Wheatsheaf.
Blaas, Eduard W. and Peter Nijkamp. 1992. "Methods of Regional Impact Assessment: A N Approach to the Evaluation of the Performance of the European Development Fund," Rep DGXVI, Brussels: Commission of the European Communities.
——. 1993. *Impact Assessment and Evaluation in Transportation Planning.* Boston: Kluwer.
Bohm, Peter, and Hans Lind. 1993. "Policy Evaluation Quality: A Quasi-experimental Study Regional Employment Subsidies in Sweden," *Regional Science & Urban Economics*, 23, 51–66.
Brouwer Floor, 1978. *Integrated Regional Environmental Modeling.* Dordrecht: Martinus Nijhoff.
Campbell, Ted D. and John C. Standley. 1966. *Experimental and Quasi-Experimental Designs Research.* Chicago: Rand McNally.
CEC (Commission of the European Communities), 1987, "The Regions of the Enlarged Communi Third Periodic Report on the Social and Economic Situation and Development of the Communit Brussels: CEC.
——. "European Regional Development Fund in Figures 1975/1988," Brussels: CEC.
——. 1988, 1989, "European Regional Development Fund; Thirteenth/Fourteenth Annual Rep (1987/1988) from the Commission to the Council, the European Parliament and the Economic a Social Committee," Brussels: CEC.
——. 1990. "Directorate General for Regional Policies; Structural Policies Objectives 1 and Application for Assistance; Confinancing of Operational Programmes," Brussels: CEC.
Diamond, Derek and Neil Spence. 1983. *Regional Policy Evaluation.* London: Gower.
Ende, Martin van den, and Peter Nijkamp. 1993. Industrial Dynamics and Rational Expectations i Space-Time Setting, Research Paper, Dept. of Economics, Free University, Amsterdam (mim graphed).
Folmer, Henk. 1985. *Regional Economic Policy: Measurement of its Effects.* Dordrecht: Martin Nijhoff.
Forkenbrock, D. J., T. F. Pogue, N. S. J. Foster, and D. J. Finnegan, 1990. Road Investment to Fos Local Economic Development, Report Midwest Transportation Center, University of Iowa, Iowa.
Giaoutzi, Maria and Peter Nijkamp. 1993. *Decision Support Methods for Regional Sustainable Pla ning.* Aldershot, U.K.: Avebury.
Gorter, Cees, Peter Nijkamp, and Piet Rietveld. 1992. "The Duration of Unemployment on the Dut Labour Market," *Regional Science and Urban Economics*, 22, 151–174.
Isserman, Andrew. 1990. Research Designs for Quasi-experimental Control Group Analysis in Regio Science, Research Paper, Regional Research Institute, West Virginia University, Morgantown.
Moore, Barry and John Rhodes. 1973. "Evaluating the Effects of British Regional Economic Polic *Economic Journal*, 83, 87–100.
——. 1976. "Regional Economic Policy and the Movement of Manufacturing Firms to Developme Areas," *Economica*, 43, 17–31.
Nijkamp, Peter. 1990. "Spatial Developments in the United States of Europe," *Papers of the Regior Science Association*, 69, 1–11.
——. 1992. Border Regions and Infrastructure Networks in the European Integration Proce Research Memorandum, Dept of Economics, Free University, Amsterdam.

kamp, Peter and Michel van Pelt. 1989. "Spatial Impact Analysis in Developing Countries: Methods nd Application," *International Regional Science Review*, 12, 211–228.

kamp, Peter and Aura Reggiani. 1995. "Non-linear Evaluation of Dynamic Spatial Systems," *Regional Science and Urban Economics*, 25, 183–210.

kamp, Peter, Jan Rouwendal, and Martin van den Ende. 1993. "Space-time Patterns of Entrepreneur-al Expectations and Performance," *Regional Studies*, 27, 1–11.

t, Michel van. 1993. *Project Evaluation and Sustainable Development in Third World Countries*. Aldershot, U.K.: Avebury.

tveld, Piet. 1989. "Infrastructure and Regional Development, a Survey of Multiregional Economic Models," *The Annals of Regional Science*, 23, 255–274.

bergen, Jan. 1956. *Economic Policy: Principles and Design*. Amsterdam: North Holland.

wnroe, Peter M. 1979. "The Design of Local Economic Development Policies," *Town Planning Review*, 50, 148–163.

:kerman, Roger, (ed.). 1991. *Infrastructure and Regional Development*. London: Pion.

lliams, Alan, and Emilio Giardina (eds.). 1993. *Efficiency in the Public Sector*. Aldershot, U.K.: Edward Elgar.

The Learning Capabilities of Regions: Conceptual Policies and Patterns

**Marina van Geenhuizen and
Peter Nijkamp**

3.1 INTRODUCTION

With the increased territorial openness, factor mobility, and the weakening of national protective measures, regions are growing in importance as the spatial framework for economic competition. It is now recognized that knowledge – with learning as the most important process – constitutes one of the few important sources of competitiveness (cf. Camagni, 1991; Knight, 1995; Kuklinski, 1996; Lambooy, 1997; Morgan, 1997). The awareness of the social embeddedness of economic interaction (Grabher, 1993) has given a further impetus to the recognition of the region as a main territorial framework for learning and knowledge-based economic growth. The core argument is that tacit knowledge – with its crucial role in innovation – is highly territorial-specific because of its embodiment in individuals, its social and cultural context and, therefore, its need for proximity.

At the same time, the speed and complexity of knowledge development is higher than ever before. For example, there is a constant shortening of the life cycles of products and time to market and an increase in the integration of products and services, in hybrid technologies, in functionality and in the number of product variants (customizing) (den Hertog and Huizenga, 1997). These developments make it even more urgent to devote attention to learning and knowledge-based growth.

Over the past two decades, research has concentrated overwhelmingly on innovation, with shifts in focus from innovation in its own right to innovation embedded in socio-cultural processes, institutions and networks. At the same time, there has been a move from a static to a dynamic approach to innovation (cf. Amin and Thrift, 1994; Bertuglia *et al.*, 1997; Ratti *et al.*, 1997). The recent 'passion' for learning regions may be seen as a further step in an attempt to uncover the basic processes underlying the dynamics of innovation and regional economic growth.

38

The fact that the study of learning regions is relatively new explains the lack of a proper definition of learning regions as an analytical and testable concept. Associated with this is a shortage of cross-comparative research using a similar analytical framework leading to generic insights into learning regions. This chapter is an attempt to shed light on various underexposed conceptual and empirical issues, paying particular attention to policy and empirical implications.

The chapter is structured as follows. First, there is a brief conceptual exploration of learning regions and the learning involved, as well as of the conditions that facilitate learning (Section 3.2). This section is rather short, as Chapter 1 also partly deals with these issues. In order to avoid too much overlap, the description is only brief. In order to stress diversity in learning, the chapter continues with a discussion of different learning patterns associated with particular product types (Section 3.3). An empirical study conducted in various European cities serves to underline this diversity. This can be found in Appendix 1, at the end of the chapter. Section 3.4 explores the inherent complexity of learning regions in the light of policies to improve their performance. The findings in this section form the input for a discussion of appropriate policy approaches and of the research needed for a problem diagnosis (Section 3.5). The final section of the chapter 3.6 draws some conclusions.

3.2 CONCEPTUAL EXPLORATION

The concept of a learning region has two connotations. First, it refers to areas which have a body of knowledge (incorporated in research institutes and laboratories, higher education facilities) through which they can augment their productivity. Secondly, the concept refers to areas which use this body of knowledge to try to achieve a better performance through active and comprehensive learning. This section explores important notions associated with learning regions, derived from the literature. It focuses first on the purpose of learning, learning actors and learning networks, and the type of knowledge involved. There follows an exploration of the notion of learning capability.

The concept of learning regions is often associated with the need for improved competitiveness in global markets. Thus, learning is not an aim in itself, but serves to improve the actors' performance, although it is not always clear what this improved performance implies. It may refer to innovation and profitability, sustainability, or merely efficiency. The same vagueness holds for competition, where there is vagueness about which regions are being competed with, about the dimensions of competition and the level of ambition (for example, catching up, defeating) and, hence, the amount of learning effort needed. There is no doubt that part of the competitive strength of a region is determined by its natural, physical conditions, but part is contingent on indigenous managerial and learning skills. For example, regions can capitalize on their 'main port' function, and can even outperform others by exploiting their 'brain port' potential.

With regard to the actors involved, learning certainly refers to regional firms, but there are two reasons for including other categories of regional actors. First, learning for innovation is increasingly taking place in different networks. Secondly, part of the learning is rooted in the region, which points to local authorities and supporting organizations as participants in learning. Learning therefore takes place at different levels. When we explore what is being learned, it is necessary to distinguish between two types of knowledge: explicit knowledge, embodied in machines, patents, documents, computer programmes, etc., and implicit knowledge, embodied in human beings. The former is also called formal, codified knowledge and the latter tacit knowledge (Nonaka and Takeuchi, 1995). Tacit knowledge is rooted in practice and experience, and transmitted by apprenticeship and training through 'watching and doing' forms of learning, strongly 'coloured' by the social and cultural setting. It cannot be readily articulated and is therefore not easily communicable or tradable. Because of its wholly personal embodied nature, it can be traded only through the labour market.

An area of tacit knowledge – connected with creativity and intuition – is now widely regarded as making the most important contribution to new combinations and new applications in product innovation. This is also referred to as serendipity (den Hertog and Huizenga, 1997). Unexpected events, failure and chance play an important role here. The awareness of the role of tacit knowledge forms the basis for the articulation of the need for spatial proximity in innovation, and provides the ground for the need to study regions as an important spatial framework for learning (Morgan, 1997).

It should be emphasized that a different area of tacit knowledge produces routines. These are forms of rule-guided behaviour in which incremental adjustments are made to preexisting patterns. There is a danger, however, that routines blind actors to new developments in the external environment, so that decision-making tends to rely on old success stories and well-known solutions, even where the environment is changing rapidly. In evolutionary approaches to the subject, this phenomenon is known as path dependence (Arthur, 1994; Boschma and Lambooy, 1998; van Geenhuizen, 1998). In a situation of path dependence it is difficult to abandon technologies or product-markets, etc. once they have been selected, because of an accumulation of experience, routines, and capital in the past. In other words, the increasing returns from a previously selected behaviour makes a withdrawal from this behaviour less likely. The above observations point to at least two basic types of learning, namely, one leading to tacit knowledge, which produces new combinations and applications, and one leading to the removal of obsolete routines (de-learning).

Regional learning capability may be conceived of as a set of conditions that allow regional actors to learn and improve their performance. Various preconditions can be identified for the adoption of an integrated approach:

1. *Consensus* among the regional actors involved. Learning as a collective action needs to be accepted as a meaningful strategy. In addition, a certain level of trust is necessary, so that the benefits of learning are also contingent on its acceptance (Morgan, 1997; Nooteboom, 1996).
2. *Networking to promote knowledge creation and flow.* Innovation is an interactive process within firms, between firms (suppliers, contractors), and between firms and various institutions. Accordingly, networking is important to enhance serendipity.
3. *Transformation of knowledge.* Because of differences in vocabulary and frameworks, knowledge cannot always flow smoothly (Kamann, 1994; Williams and Gibson, 1990). Thus, transformation is necessary, for example, in flows between basic and applied knowledge, and between different disciplines.
4. *Management of human capital.* This concerns the resident population and the work force in local firms. There needs to be sufficient investment in skills for learning and skills for management, and for learning itself in art and science at different levels, in different combinations, and through formal as well as informal education.
5. *Management of public stocks of knowledge.* This includes the updating of archives, libraries, etc., and providing access to them.
6. *Identification of new learning and knowledge needs.* This precondition is concerned with the monitoring of needs while anticipating new developments. Producing early warning signals is important here.

A key condition at a higher level is the self-organizing power to co-ordinate, preserve and renew the above preconditions (cf. Amin and Thrift, 1994; Camagni, 1991; Ratti *et al.*, 1997; Storper, 1996). This ability can develop only if there is a certain social and cultural coherence in the region and sets of common aims and conventions (routines) directing socio-economic behaviour. The common aims cover a wide range of interrelated fields, reflecting the multi-faceted nature and setting of learning networks, i.e. ranging from culture and education to the labour and housing markets (Knight, 1995). Such circumstances develop spontaneously in certain regions, but in other regions there seems to be a need for system integrators, such as a key person (natural leader) or a public-private agency (Bramanti and Senn, 1997).

Networking has been identified as an important precondition for learning. Networking means here an intentional participation by regional actors in networks, the formation of new networks and the dissolution of old ones. Learning networks can be defined as sets of connected exchange relationships among actors involved in learning (cf. Cook, 1982; Håkansson, 1989). Network behaviour may be both co-operative and competitive. As with many other networks, a structural approach allows a number of components and aspects to be distinguished. Networking is therefore about establishing linkages in order to acquire strategic resources for learning, such as human capital and finance for R&D, and information about the external environment. Active networks undertake activities such as R&D, brainstorming in group sessions, or simply working together and learning-by-doing. Networks can become active learning networks only if there is access to facilities (or channels) to promote learning interaction. Good examples of these are access to the Internet and to data banks. The interaction within and between networks is defined by the type of relationship involved, for example, simple and complex, symmetrical and asymmetrical, horizontal and vertical relationships. Power is an important aspect of networks, in view of steering. Power differs within and between networks in respect of access to resources and information, and the potential to exclude unwanted participants. Power can be seen as asymmetric exchanges, and dependence as the outcome of the exertion of power. There is a continuum of inter-organizational dependence in learning relationships, based on the type of compensation between the partners (Contractor and Lorange, 1988). In the learning of firms, technological training (in return for a fee) seems to be at one end of the spectrum and joint ventures (in return for shares) at the other end.

Like other networks, learning networks are relatively closed. They may be almost entirely closed if the knowledge involved is strategic and property rights are at stake. There are two other important characteristics of learning networks, namely, their spatial range and their socio-economic stability over time. The spatial range is variable and has increased in recent decades through telecommunications. As we have previously indicated, simple learning based on tacit knowledge needs physical proximity. Similarly, stability over time is variable, but seems to be relatively strong for tacit learning.

The above discussion underlines a differentiation in learning networks, but the common concern of network actors is to increase knowledge more efficiently than in the absence of networks. Networks are therefore vehicles for efficient behaviour. Network externalities may be derived from a higher speed, a greater coverage of knowledge, or synergy with other knowledge and so on. An interesting example of externalities can be found in telecommunication networks. Here, positive externalities increase with the number of subscribers to the networks (Capello, 1997). This seems to be equally true of learning networks using telecommunications, such as in a discussion on a web-site, but the situation appears to differ for learning networks based on face-to-face contact. With these, the optimum may be reached very quickly as the number of participants increases, because of diseconomies of density and the limited capacity of human beings to interact intensively with a great many actors.

3.3 DIVERSITY IN PATTERNS OF LEARNING

Several authors point to differences in knowledge development according to the dominant culture and conventions (den Hertog and Huizenga, 1997). Storper (e.g., 1996), for example, highlighted the differences between product types, dependent upon the uncertainty in the markets and technologies involved. Examples of product types are dedicated products and generic products. The critical condition for dedicated products is the existence of a community of specialists working on the redesign of the product within tight time limits, using their tacit and customary knowledge of the product. Such an interpersonal community of knowledge developers is often based on traditionally acquired skills. Constant communication is necessary to carry out the specific technological development, with communication between producers and users being the most essential. This pattern applies not only to certain craft-based European industrial districts, but also to the most specialist parts of high-technology industries, such as non-merchant semiconductor production in Silicon Valley and the medical and scientific instruments industry in Orange County (near Los Angeles) (Storper, 1996).

By contrast, the production of generic products depending upon highly specialized inputs, is based on formal processes of communication and learning. Knowledge development here relies on forms of communication that can be extended over large distances, because the information is codified and the exchange is planned at regular intervals (business meetings, seminars, etc.). At the same time, however, the producers are often tied to the same type of interpersonal communities of knowledge workers for the development of their newest technology inputs as in the previous case. This pattern means that regions dominated by such industries – such as fine chemicals – may include formal learning and tacit learning, but may equally lack substantial knowledge development *in situ* (in a disconnected case). We may therefore conclude that the importance of knowledge development and tacit learning in regional production may differ according to the product composition of firms in the region.

The above discussion refers to different types of learning as relatively stable patterns, but there may be a variation in the type and intensity of learning over time. We may distinguish between high levels of learning for a new product (design) or a new application followed by lower levels of learning for process innovation in order to reduce costs. Such time patterns are associated with the product life cycle and various variations of this cycle (van Duijn, 1984; van Geenhuizen, 1993), or with what Nooteboom (1998) calls the cycle of learning and organization. Needless to say, regional economies may show different compositions in this respect.

A broad discussion is now in progress about learning, knowledge, knowledge infrastructure, learning regions and the role of universities in all this. A very interesting paper has been published by Michael Gibbons *et al.* with the title 'The new production of knowledge'. It calls attention to a new form of knowledge production, the context in which it is pursued, the way it is organized, the reward systems it utilizes and the mechanisms controlling the quality of what is produced. In the authors' view, the social characteristics of knowledge production have been well articulated in the disciplinary sciences, chemistry, biology and physics, for example, which is the main reason why these are taken as paradigmatic of sound knowledge production in the sciences. Where social sciences and the humanities have tried to imitate the physical sciences, similar social systems have been put in place to govern the production of knowledge in these areas, too. In fact, 'the new production of knowledge' places science policy and scientific knowledge in its broader context within contemporary societies. For this reason, this approach to knowledge production is necessary not only for all those concerned with the changing nature of knowledge, but also for those involved in relations between R&D and social, economic and technological development. It is precisely here that we will be confronted with all kinds of problems inherent in the learning capabilities of regions.

The diversity of the patterns of learning has been described in several publications, often with reference to a pilot study. Peter Maskell, for example, describes and analyses the role of localized learning and regional embedded knowledge for the development of the furniture industry in Denmark. The success of this development is closely related to locally and regionally developed learning, in which the historical and social dimensions play an important part. Many case studies have been put forward in publications by John Goddard, who has studied the role of knowledge and the knowledge infrastructure in general and of the universities and higher education institutions, in particular. The OECD has even launched a project in which the role of higher education institutions has been highlighted in relation to regional needs. We might conclude from all these examples and case studies that the patterns of regional and local learning are highly diverse, as are the results.

3.4   COMPLEXITY OF LEARNING NETWORKS IN RELATION TO POLICY MAKING

This section focuses on three characteristics of learning networks, in view of the potentials for steering. Three characteristics have been put forward in recent literature on policy making, i.e., diversity, closeness, and dependence (de Bruijn and ten Heuvelhof, 1995; Koppenjan *et al.*, 1993). The section also discusses uncertainty in framing policy for learning networks arising from erratic moves and unpredictable outcomes.

As indicated in the previous sections, learning networks show a high level of diversity. This diversity is sometimes reinforced by a multi-layered network structure, in which actors at higher spatial levels influence the local level, as where multinationals decide upon the closure or opening of a local laboratory, or national governments lay down university budgets. Diversity often implies a different perception of problems and policy options and – in serious cases – a controversy. This may be true of the policy for learning-based economic growth itself, where it appears to be a time-consuming endeavour without immediate gains in terms of new employment (Morgan, 1997). A policy for learning regions may therefore face opposition from the labour unions or organizations for the unemployed. A situation of limited consensus between the relevant actors may lead to faint support for policy programmes and only a partial implementation of measures, leading to unexpected outcomes.

We stated earlier that learning networks are to some extent closed. This means that they have their own frame of reference and are therefore susceptible only to selected steering signals. The dependence in learning networks may relate to finance, for example, research budgets, or to political support or protection, etc. In the context of steering, a situation of dependence means that a powerful actor or network forms a useful starting point for the implementation of change, because the other actors (networks) tend to follow.

The characteristics described above result in a continuous change in learning networks within certain limits, such as the entry or exit of new actors, the merging or dissolution of networks, and shifts in power. What also happens is that the content of policy problems changes over time. Actors may redefine their problem, for example, because of a discrepancy between the original definition and the emergence of new insights or coalitions with other actors. For purposes of steering this means that there is a need for monitoring and evaluation.

It is important to note that the setting of knowledge creation is becoming increasingly complex. There is a shift from a hierarchical, disciplinary division of labour-based knowledge production to a mode in which research problems overlap disciplinary boundaries and focus strongly on application.

In terms of organization, a larger number of actors is involved (apart from universities, research centres), with an increased emphasis on teams (consortia) working on a temporary basis.

There is little experience of policies for learning regions, but there is experience of policies for innovative milieux, and of policies that similarly involve a multi-actor, multi-level and multi-disciplinary field, i.e. transport. We may accordingly expect policies for learning networks to produce erratic moves and unpredictable outcomes, firstly because decision making is still based on insufficient knowledge of the capability for learning and of learning itself. There is a limited empirical understanding of the conditions under which the localized collaboration of firms facilitates learning, or of the conditions under which localized learning leads to innovation and improved profitability or employment growth (cf. Brouwer *et al.*, 1993; Eskelinen, 1997; Oinas and Virkkala, 1997). It is also difficult to obtain and model reliable data of learning processes and knowledge in the regional economy. There is no standard production function of knowledge, no input–output recipe for assessing the impact of a unit of knowledge on economic performance, etc. This means that problem diagnosis and, therefore, solutions are insufficiently supported by solid quantitative data.

Even less is known about networks, particularly in the context of a relatively long-term dimension. Network dynamics are dominated by non-linear relationships, including chaotic dynamics. With the latter, small changes in the initial conditions or parameters may lead to disproportionately large dynamics, which may cause particular networks or regions to follow a different development path from others, e.g., they may suddenly become highly active in learning, while others may collapse or stagnate (cf. Kamann, 1997; Nijkamp and Reggiani, 1998).

Unpredictability also stems from the nature of policy making itself. The degree of rational and neutral behaviour in policy making is always limited, so that procedures are imperfect. Non-rational behaviour and subjectivity cannot be eliminated from decision making, particularly if the problems are complex (cf. Hofstee, 1996). The potential imperfections include: ill-defined and ill-structured problem definition, problem analysis that is hampered by lack of knowledge in the field concerned and of decisions in related fields, a disregard of potentially relevant alternative solutions, and absence of evaluation of current measures and developments (van Geenhuizen and Nijkamp, 1998b; Hall, 1990; Rietveld, 1993).

While exploiting its creative potential to acquire, digest, and deploy strategic knowledge more efficiently than its competitors, a region needs to become aware of the above imperfections and uncertainties in policy making. As an alternative to reducing uncertainty, a useful strategy is to use uncertainty creatively in order to find new policy solutions.

3.5 POLICY APPROACHES

This section first discusses important policy approaches to match the network and interactive nature of regional learning, i.e., network management and participatory policy making (de Bruijn and ten Heuvelhof, 1995). We then discuss the research needed to underpin policy initiatives.

Network management means influencing the diversity, dependence, and closeness of networks in order to provide opportunities for change. This is therefore a form of meta-steering, leading to changes in the network structure to facilitate an effective use of instruments (the operational level). For example, an important characteristic of learning capability is the fragmentation of intermediary networks (cf. Bartels, 1996). In this context, network management means first letting these networks merge or co-operate in a single 'platform' and then implementing measures by targeting the 'platform' in order to improve performance.

Moreover, in an interactive approach, much attention is paid to participatory policy making. The latter generally aims to achieve consensus between different actors, in order to increase support for policy solutions, although there may be various specific aims (Ester *et al.*, 1997). The aim may be merely to advise and provide information about actors' interests and values, in which case, the method works through citizen consultation, workshops and conferences where actors can disclose their information, opinions and values. An important result of the process is that the actors cross the borders of their own frame (frame reflective learning) and establish new networks and communication, based on a change of attitude. There are also participatory approaches, in which actors actively contribute to the design or redesign of policy solutions. The latter seems to be essential in learning region policies, because learning as a common action cannot work without the full support of all the local actors. A specific form of participatory policy making is 'creative steering', which has been developed in order to find new solutions in traffic infrastructure policy making. Creative steering takes chaos as a starting point and accepts contributions from all the actors who are willing to participate. A major aim is originality, rather than proving an argument right or wrong. The results of creative steering may be elaborated in several rounds in order to create a policy document of sufficiently high quality.

Apart from the policy areas of housing and community development and transport infrastructure, there is little experience with the participatory approach. A preliminary analysis suggests that the following factors influence the success of this approach (van Geenhuizen and Nijkamp, 1998b):

- *Motivation*; a sufficient number of relevant actors need to be convinced of the problem and of co-operation as an appropriate way of finding solutions.

- *Transparency* of aims and procedures, and *trust*, meaning that stakeholders are convinced of a potentially genuine participation (as opposed to symbolic participation).
- *Removal of barriers* between stakeholders, such as those created by 'languages' and types of argumentation.
- An *adequate role* for the process manager as the facilitator of communication and interaction between stakeholders (dependent upon the aim of the participation).
- A *short lapse of time* between participation and the implementation of the results. It seems that changes in actors' attitudes completely disappear after two years.

The above conditions indicate that participatory policy making requires careful preparation in terms of a clarification of the procedures to be followed (including competence and authority). More importantly, the selection of the appropriate actors and networks and a preliminary definition of the problem, including the level of aggregation and spatial scale, require careful preparation. This observation leads to a consideration of the empirical research that needs to be done. Research is needed on the specificity of the regions, so that a policy can be designed that matches the local situation. Various research lines can be mapped out in a (self)diagnosis:

1. To establish a picture of the interrelatedness of the regional economy, using micro-level data on input, output, and origin, destination, etc., in a *filière* or chain-like approach (Kamann, 1997). This analysis also reveals ownership structures, capital flows, knowledge flows, etc., in such a way as to provide indications of the regional embeddedness of firms.
2. To beam in on the relevant learning networks to which regional firms are tied and the key characteristics of these networks, including spatial range.
3. To explore the links between inter-firm collaboration, learning processes and the innovative behaviour of firms, particularly the circumstances under which localized collaboration leads to innovation and better performance by firms. The composition of the regional economy in terms of types and level of learning (related to product types) is relevant here.
4. To identify bottlenecks in learning networks and in the preconditions for their functioning. For example, to uncover the socio-cultural coherence, or lack of it, in the region. Cognitive maps of actors covering both the territorial dimension and the industrial dimension may be used (Kamann, 1997).
5. To analyse recent 'shocks' in the regional economy (such as the closure

of a large firm) and to uncover the composition of responses of key actors, i.e., in terms of wishes to protect an old technology (based on routines) or to restructure the industry with the aim of introducing new key technologies. This type of analysis serves to find out whether the region is tending to a lock-in situation (Grabher, 1993).

6. To identify labour market dynamics which influence localized learning processes, e.g., the match between labour demand and supply, in and out-migration of knowledge-based firms, and the supply of training programmes. To identify housing market dynamics connected with localized learning processes, such as the match between demand and supply of housing for knowledge workers, and the in and out-migration of the latter (Knight, 1995).

7. To design forms of participatory policy making that fit the local problem situation, e.g., taking into account the distribution of power.

The above research can certainly not be done overnight. Given a situation in which various future processes and policy outcomes remain uncertain, significant flexibility is needed in the steering and monitoring of ongoing developments.

3.6 CONCLUDING REMARKS

Learning regions is an attractive concept, because it calls for attention to be paid to the institutional side of regions. The concept suffers from some vagueness, however, particularly in regard to competition between regions. In addition, various cause-and-effect chains have not been very well tested. This presents interesting opportunities for cross-comparative regional research using a common analytical framework.

Learning takes place at different levels, for example, in and between firms, and in local and regional authorities. There is learning for product innovation, the unlearning of old routines, and the acquiring of learning skills. The diversity in the networks involved causes a wide differentiation in the regional composition of learning. Diversity is partly associated with the product types of local firms. An empirical part of this study might demonstrate a differentiation in innovation based on the stage in the life cycle of the products involved. In addition, it could be shown that only selected learning networks contribute to innovation. Within a broad range of networks – covering different activities and different degrees of dependence – training networks appeared to be the most important.

In general, policies for learning regions have to deal with diversity, closeness and dependence in a dynamic setting. According to the nature of the network (interaction) and the need for consensus, policy approaches should preferably follow models of network management, including participatory approaches aimed at increasing support. In this way, policy making itself becomes a specific type of regional learning. One policy line appears to be undisputed, that is, a sufficient investment in human capital. Other policy lines are dependent on the diagnosis of the specific shortcomings of the learning capability of individual regions.

The mission of the region, that is, to improve its learning capability, will yield significant results, mainly in the medium term, although particular measures may accelerate the pace of change. It would meanwhile be sensible to carry out a number of pilot projects in order to produce some short-term results in particular areas, and to test, through a systematic monitoring of current developments, whether the long-term objectives are still valid.

APPENDIX 1:   LEARNING NETWORKS IN EUROPEAN CITY REGIONS

This section presents the empirical results of a study of the relevance of different learning networks and different industrial sub-sectors in the context of innovation. The results are based on a data set derived from the URBINNO study and compiled from extensive structured interviews with manufacturing firms in the United Kingdom (208 firms), the Netherlands (33) and Italy (32) (Nijkamp *et al.*, 1997). The firms were selected to be representative of sectors both in the early stages and in the later stages of the product life cycle. The former include firms in machinery and equipment (SIC 29), electrical machinery and apparatus (SIC 31), medical precision and optical instruments, clocks and watches (SIC 33), and motor vehicles and trailers (SIC 34). In order to have a sufficient number of firms covering the later stages of the product life cycle, the database includes textile, clothing and leather industries (SIC 17–19), and basic metal and metal industries (SIC 27 and 28). The results reported here focus on the type of learning networks involving these firms and the local or regional university and the contribution of these networks to innovation, against the background of the different stages in the product life cycle. In selecting the type of learning networks, attention was paid to activity (such as consultancy and participation in seminars) and to dependence (low in consultancy and short training courses, but high in joint ventures). Labour market links were also included, that is, recruitment networks involving the local university.

Among the networks based on a commercial agreement, those representing low dependence tend to dominate (Table A3.1). Over 30 per cent of the firms

Table A3.1 Learning networks of firms[a] with local or regional universities and colleges

Type of activity	Dependence[b]	Participation (Percentage share of all firms)
Consultancy		
Consultancy	-	32.9
Testing (analysis)	-	31.6
Subcontracting	+	13.9
Joint ventures	++	9.3
Training networks		
Short courses	-	46.0
Courses for technical qualification	-	51.0
Courses for management qualification	-	36.1
Seminars	-	30.9
Recruitment networks		
Technical staff	+	27.0
Management staff	+	14.0

Notes:
a.   N = 273 (non-response of around 8 per cent).
b.   - = low; + = high; ++ = very high.

make use of consultancy and testing (analysis) services at the university, whereas under 10 per cent have established a joint venture with a view to knowledge sharing. Much more important than commercial links are training links with the university. Around 50 per cent of all firms take advantage of short training courses and training for technical qualifications. This means that universities are an essential actor in the learning network in city regions in terms of enhancing the skills and learning abilities of local firms. Training networks result in low dependence, but the impacts may last a long time, because they are embodied in human capital.

The next step was an explanatory investigation of the innovative behaviour of firms by using logit analysis. The independent variables were participation in the three types of learning network distinguished in Table A3.1 and the different manufacturing sectors (Annexe 1). Another learning network was also taken into consideration, that is, training supplied by local or regional public sector institutes or agencies. Because of an incomplete data-set, the logit analysis had to exclude a few indicators which may be expected to affect the propensity to innovate, such as size of firm and its growth rate. The results in Table A3.2 suggest that industries representing earlier stages in the product life cycle contribute significantly to the propensity of a firm to innovate. In addition, training networks are positively related to innovation, but commercial learning networks and recruitment networks are not.

In addition, a rough set analysis was carried out using the same database. Rough set analysis is a fairly recent classification method of an if-then type. The analysis classifies objects into equivalence classes using available attributes which act as equivalence relationships for the objects considered. A class which contains only indispensable equivalence relationships is called a core. An attribute is indispensable if the classification of the objects becomes less precise when that attribute is omitted. In order to carry out the classification, the values of the attributes of all the objects are subdivided into condition (background) attributes and decision (response) attributes. Rough set data analysis basically evaluates the importance of attributes for a classification of objects, reduces all superfluous objects and attributes, discovers the most significant relationships between condition attributes and the assignment of objects to decision classes, and represents these relationships in the form of decision rules (see van den Bergh *et al.*, 1997).

In the present analysis, the decision attribute (dependent variable) is that of whether the firm has introduced an innovation. The condition attributes (explanatory variables) are the same as in the above logit analysis.

It appears that 71.4 per cent of all firms can be classified into either the

Table A3.2   *Results of a logit analysis*[a]

-2Log Likelihood: 367.30157 (restricted model)		
-2Log Likelihood: 323.41300 (full model)		
Variable	Estimated coefficient	Standard error
IND29DUM	1.0613	0.3427
IND31DUM	1.2892	0.4229
IND33DUM	1.2720	0.5115
IND34DUM	2.0964	0.5507
LINKTRAI	0.9321	0.2799
Constant	−1.6011	0.2635

Note: a. Based on Theil's sequential elimination procedure

Table A3.3   Results of rough set analysis[a]

	Innovation	No innovation	Quality of classification
Classification with core attributes	69	126	0.714
Classification with a temporarily reduced condition attribute			
Industry	26	57	0.304
Training links	60	104	0.601
Assistance	56	110	0.608
Commercial links	56	112	0.615
Recruitment links	61	118	0.656

Note: a. Lower approximations for rough set classes.

innovation category or the no innovation category (Table A3.3). All condition attributes belong to the core, meaning that an exclusion of one of them would reduce the accuracy of the classification. In addition, the relative importance of the condition attributes can be investigated by dropping each of them successively from the core (the lower rows in Table A3.3). The results indicate that the quality of the classification is lowest when Industry is excluded (only 30.4 per cent can be classified). Further, of all the learning networks, those concerned with Training make the strongest contribution to the classification. These results confirm the pattern found using logit analysis.

The previous empirical study has demonstrated a specific participation of firms in learning networks with local universities. There is a clear preference for low dependence relationships leading to long-term impacts, that is, training or retraining of employees. The analysis has shown that training networks tend to promote more innovation than commercial learning networks and recruitment links. However, the basic determinant of innovation appeared to be the manufacturing sector, that is, relatively young sectors. The latter result confirms the need to take into account the sectoral composition of the regional economy in relation to the level and type of learning. The empirical research has also shown that rough set analysis is a helpful method for explanatory research into learning networks, because it matches a situation of qualitative research based on interviews using categorical (binary) data and often producing a relatively small number of observations.

54   *The learning region paradigm explained*

Annexe 3.1

Independent variables in the logit analysis (Table A3.2):

Sector

IND29
IND31
IND33
IND34
IND17
IND18
IND19
IND27
IND28

Learning Networks
LINKCOMM
LINKTRAI
LINKRECR
ASSTRAIN

ACKNOWLEDGEMENTS

The authors wish to thank Aki Kangasharju, who undertook the data analysis as a part of a project funded by the Academy of Finland.

REFERENCES

Amin, A. and N. Thrift (eds) (1994), *Globalization, Institutions, and Regional Development in Europe*, Oxford: Oxford University Press.
Arthur, W.B. (1994), *Increasing Returns and Path Dependence in the Economy*, Ann Arbor: University of Michigan Press.
Bartels (Bureau Bartels) (1996), *Establishing Trust. A Knowledge and Innovation Strategy for the Region of Rotterdam*, Utrecht: Bureau Bartels.
Bergh, J.C.J.M van den, K. Button, P. Nijkamp and G. Pepping (1997), *Meta-Analysis for Meso Environmental Policy*, Dordrecht: Kluwer.
Bertuglia, C.S., S. Lombardo and P. Nijkamp (eds) (1997), *Innovative Behaviour in Time and Space*, Berlin: Springer.
Boschma, R. and J. Lambooy (1998), 'Economic evolution and the adjustment of the spatial matrix of regions', in J. van Dijk and F. Boekema (eds), *Innovation in Firms and Regions*, Assen: Van Gorcum, pp. 121-37.

Bramanti, A. and L. Senn (1997), 'Understanding structural changes and laws of motion of milieux: A study on NorthWestern Lombardy', in R. Ratti, A. Bramanti and R. Gordon (eds), *The Dynamics of Innovative Regions: The GREMI Approach*, Aldershot: Ashgate, pp. 47–73.

Brouwer, E., A. Kleinknecht and J.O. Reijnen (1993), 'Employment growth and innovation at the firm level. An empirical study', *Evolutionary Economics* 1993 (3), pp. 153–9.

Bruijn, J.A. de and E.F. ten Heuvelhof (1995), *Network Management. Strategies, Instruments and Norms* (in Dutch), Utrecht: Lemma.

Camagni, R. (ed.) (1991), *Innovation Networks: Spatial Perspectives*, London: Belhaven.

Capello, R. (1997), 'Telecommunication network externalities and regional development: policy implications', in P. Rietveld and C. Capineri (eds), *Networks in Transport and Communications: A Policy Approach*, Aldershot: Ashgate, pp. 13–36.

Contractor, F. and P. Lorange (1988), *Cooperative strategies in international business*, Lexington, MA: Lexington Press.

Cook, K. (1982), 'Network structures from exchange perspective', in P. Marsden and N. Lin (eds), *Social Structure and Network Analysis*, New York: Free Press, pp. 177–99.

Duijn, J.J. van (1984), 'Fluctuations in innovations over time', in C. Freeman (ed.), *Long Waves in the World Economy*, London: Frances Pinter, pp. 19–30.

Eskelinen, H. (1997), *Regional Specialisation and Local Environment. Learning and Competitiveness*, Stockholm: NordREFO.

Ester, P., J. Geurts and M. Vermeulen (eds) (1997), *Designers of the Future* (in Dutch), Tilburg: Tilburg University Press.

Geenhuizen, M. van (1993), '*A Longitudinal Analysis of the Growth of Firms. The Case of the Netherlands*', Rotterdam: Erasmus University (Ph.D. thesis).

Geenhuizen, M. van (1998), 'An evolutionary approach to firm dynamics: adaptation and path dependence', in G. Lipshitz, P. Rietveld, P. and D. Shefer (eds), *Regional Development in an Age of Structural Economic Change* (forthcoming).

Geenhuizen, M. van and P. Nijkamp (1998a), 'Improving the knowledge capability of cities: the case of mainport Rotterdam', *International Journal of Technology Management*, 15 (6/7), pp. 691–709.

Geenhuizen, M. van and P. Nijkamp (1998b), *Regional and Urban Policy Beyond 2000: New Approaches with Learning as Device*, Research Memoranda, Amsterdam: Free University.

Grabher, G. (ed.) (1993), *The Embedded Firm. On the Socioeconomics of Industrial Networks*, London: Routledge.

Håkansson, H. (1989), *Corporate Technological Behaviour: Co-operation and Networks*, London: Routledge.

Hall, P. (1990), *Great Planning Disasters Revisited*, London: UCL Department of Geography.

Hertog, F. den and E. Huizenga (1997), *The Knowledge Factor. Competition as a Knowledge-Based Firm* (in Dutch), Deventer: Kluwer.

Hofstee, W.K.B. (1996), 'Psychological factors in decision making' (in Dutch), in P. Nijkamp, W. Begeer and J. Berting (eds), *Considering Complexity in Decision Making: A Panoramic View*, The Hague: SDU Uitgevers, pp. 49–58.

Kamann, D.J.F. (1994), 'Spatial barriers and differentiation of culture in Europe', in P. Nijkamp (ed.), *New Borders and Old Barriers in Spatial Development*, Aldershot: Avebury, pp. 35–63.

Kamann, D.J.F. (1997), 'Policies for dynamic innovative networks in innovative milieux', in R. Ratti, A. Bramanti and R. Gordon (eds), *The Dynamics of Innovative Regions: The GREMI Approach*, Aldershot: Ashgate, pp. 367–91.

Knight, R.V. (1995), 'Knowledge-based development: policy and planning implications for cities', *Urban Studies*, (2), pp. 225–60.

Koppenjan, J.F.M., J.A. de Bruijn and W.J.M. Kickert (1993), *Network Management in Public Administration. Potentials for public steering in policy networks* (in Dutch), The Hague.

Kuklinski, A. (ed.) (1996), *Production of Knowledge and the Dignity of Science*, Warsaw: EUROREG.

Lambooy, I. (1997), 'Knowledge production, organisation and agglomeration economies', *Geojournal*, **41** (4), pp. 293–300.

Maillat, D., G. Lechot, B. Lelocq and M. Pfister (1997), 'Comparative analysis of the structural development of milieus: the watch industry in the Swiss and French Jura arc', in R. Ratti, A. Bramanti and R. Gordon (eds), *The Dynamics of Innovative Regions*, Aldershot: Ashgate, pp. 109–37.

Morgan, K. (1997), 'The Learning Region: Institutions, Innovation and Regional Renewal', *Regional Studies*, **31** (5), pp. 491–503.

Nijkamp, P. (1996), 'Policy and policy analysis: narrow margins versus broad missions' (in Dutch), in P. Nijkamp, W. Begeer and J. Berting (eds), *Considering Complexity in Decision Making: A Panoramic View*, The Hague: SDU Uitgevers, pp. 129–46.

Nijkamp, P. and A. Reggiani (1995), *Interaction, Evolution and Chaos in Space*, Amsterdam: Elsevier.

Nijkamp, P. and A. Reggiani (1998), *The Economics of Complex Systems*, Amsterdam: Elsevier.

Nijkamp, P., A. Kangasharju and M. van Geenhuizen (1997), 'Local and innovative behaviour: A meta-analytic study on European cities', in G. Lipshitz, P. Rietveld and D. Shefer (eds), *Regional Development in an Age of Structural Economic Change* (forthcoming).

Nonaka, I. and H. Takeuchi (1995), *The Knowledge-Creating Company. How Japanese Companies Create the Dynamics of Innovation*, Oxford: Oxford University Press.

Nooteboom, B. (1996), 'Trust, opportunism and governance: a process and control model', *Organizational Studies*, (17), pp. 985–1010.

Nooteboom (1998), 'Innovation, location and firm size', in J. van Dijk and F. Boekema (eds), *Innovation in Firms and Regions*, Assen: Van Gorcum, pp. 75–9.

Oinas, P. and S. Virkkala (1997), 'Learning, competitiveness and development', in H. Eskelinen (ed.), *Regional Specialisation and Local Environment. Learning and Competitiveness*, Stockholm: NordREFO, pp. 263–77.

Ratti, R., A. Bramanti and R. Gordon (eds) (1997), *The Dynamics of Innovative Regions. The GREMI Approach*, Aldershot: Ashgate.

Rietveld, P. (1993), 'Policy analysis in traffic, transport and spatial planning; improving the quality of decision making?' (in Dutch), in P. Rietveld and H. Boerenbach (eds), *Policy analysis and decision making in traffic and spatial planning*, The Hague: Platform Beleidsanalyse.

Simmie, J. (ed.) (1997), *Innovation, Networks and Learning Regions?*, London: Jessica Kingsley.

Storper, M. (1996), 'Innovation as collective action: conventions, products and technologies', *Industrial and Corporate Change*, **5** (3), pp. 761–90.

Williams, F. and D.V. Gibson (eds) (1990), *Technology Transfer. A Communication Perspective*, Newbury Park, London: Sage.